Pine to Prairie
Cookbook

Telephone Pioneers of America
C.P. Wainman - Chapter #18

Expression
of
Appreciation

We want to thank all of those who so graciously shared their secret recipes. To those presidents, past, and present, who contributed their expertise. To our dedicated chapter president for his wonderful ideas. To the chapter administrator for his support in this venture. And last, but not least, the wonderful crew who typed, sorted, and put together the recipes as you see them now.

Published By
Cookbook Publishers, Inc.
P.O. Box 12918
Lenexa, Kansas 66212

B

OFFICERS

A.T. Ike Isakson .... Chapter President

George Rehschuh .... Pioneer Administrator

Roy Bergstrom .... Chapter Life Member Rep.

Charles Fellman .... Chapter Life Member Rep.

Gertrude (Gertie) Helm .... Bismarck Council President

Phil Imholte.................. Detroit Lakes Council President

Robert (Bob) Broas .... Duluth Council President

George R. Walker..................... Range Club President

M.J. (Mary) Hennessy.......... Lake Agassiz Council President

Chet Way..................... Minneapolis Council President

Harriett Haggard .... Anoka Club President

Tom Curran............... Red River Valley Council President

Ronald Schwartz .... Rochester Council President

Don Billadeau.................... St. Cloud Council President

F.W. (Frank) Woodford .... Western Plaines Club President

James J. (Jim) Tuft .... St. Paul Council President

Norma McKnight................ Life Member Club President

John R. Berglund .... Life Member Club President

Norma Bougie.................... Life Member Club President

Robert F. Trombley............... Life Member Club President

Donald McArthur .... Life Member Club President

William Harwood................. Life Member Club President

Winnifred Johnson............... Life Member Club President

C.R. (Pete) Peterson .... Life Member Club President

COOKBOOK COMMITTEE

Gerri Ruprecht .... Typist

Judy Ayer .... Typist

Sue Burgess .... Typist

Jane Murpny.............................Artist

Judy Ayer .... Sorter

Don Billadeau............................ Sorter

Joan Buttweiler.......................... Sorter

Elsa Ditty............................... Sorter

Sue Loehrer.............................. Sorter

Eileen Rekowski .... Sorter

Lois Sandberg............................ Sorter

Lorraine Solberg......................... Sorter

TABLE OF CONTENTS

Appetizers, Pickles, Relishes - - - -   3

Soups, Salads, Vegetables - - - - - 43

Main Dishes - - - - - - - - - - - 129

Bread, Rolls, Pastry - - - - - - - 315

Cakes, Cookies, Desserts - - - - - - 373

Candy, Jelly, Preserves - - - - - - 575

Beverages and Miscellaneous - - - - 587

1748-81

APPETIZERS
PICKLES
RELISHES

A HANDY SPICE GUIDE
TO MAKE YOU BECOME A SEASONED SEASONER

ALLSPICE....a pea-sized fruit that grows in Mexico, Jamaica, Central and South America. Its delicate flavor resembles a blend of cloves, cinnamon and nutmeg. USES: (Whole) Pickles, meats, boiled fish, gravies. (Ground) Puddings, relishes, fruit preserves, baking.

BASIL....the dried leaves and stems of an herb grown in the United States and North Mediterranean area. Has an aromatic, leafy flavor. USES: For flavoring tomato dishes and tomato paste, turtle soup; also use in cooked peas, squash, snap beans; sprinkle chopped over lamb chops and poultry.

BAY LEAVES....the dried leaves of an evergreen grown in the eastern Mediterranean countries. Has a sweet, herbaceous floral spice note. USES: For pickling, stews, for spicing sauces and soup. Also use with a variety of meats and fish.

CARAWAY....the seed of a plant grown in the Netherlands. Flavor that combines the tastes of Anise and Dill. USES: For the cordial Kummel, baking breads; often added to sauerkraut, noodles, cheese spreads. Also adds zest to French fried potatoes, liver, canned asparagus.

CURRY POWDER....a ground blend of ginger, turmeric, fenugreek seed, as many as 16 to 20 spices. USES: For all Indian curry recipes such as lamb, chicken, and rice, eggs, vegetables, and curry puffs.

DILL....the small, dark seed of the dill plant grown in India, having a clean, aromatic taste. USES: Dill is a predominant seasoning in pickling recipes; also adds pleasing flavor to sauerkraut, potato salad, cooked macaroni, and green apple pie.

MACE....the dried covering around the nutmeg seed. Its flavor is similar to nutmeg, but with a fragrant, delicate difference. USES: (Whole) For pickling, fish, fish sauce, stewed fruit. (Ground) Delicious in baked goods, pastries and doughnuts, adds unusual flavor to chocolate desserts.

MARJORAM....an herb of the mint family, grown in France and Chile. Has a minty-sweet flavor. USES: In beverages, jellies and to flavor soups, stews, fish, sauces. Also excellent to sprinkle on lamb while roasting.

MSG (MONOSODIUM GLUTAMATE)....is a vegetable protein derivative for raising the effectiveness of natural food flavors. USES: Small amounts, adjusted to individual taste, can be added to steaks, roasts, chops, seafoods, stews, soups, chowder, chop suey and cooked vegetables.

OREGANO....the leaf of a safe bush growing in Italy, Greece and Mexico. USES: An excellent flavoring for any tomato dish, especially Pizza, chili con carne, and Italian specialties.

PAPRIKA....a mild, sweet red pepper growing in Spain, Central Europe and the United States. Slightly aromatic and prized for brilliant red color. USES: A colorful garnish for pale foods, and for seasoning Chicken Paprika, Hungarian Goulash, salad dressings.

POPPY....the seed of a flower grown in Holland. Has a rich fragrance and crunchy, nut-like flavor. USES: Excellent as a topping for breads, rolls and cookies. Also delicious in buttered noodles.

ROSEMARY....an herb (like a curved pine needle) grown in France, Spain, and Portugal and having a sweet, fresh taste. USES: In lamb dishes, in soups, stews and to sprinkle on beef before roasting.

SAGE....the leaf of a shrub grown in Greece, Yugoslavia and Albania. Flavor is camphoraceous and minty. USES: For meat and poultry stuffing, sausages, meat loaf, hamburgers, stews and salads.

THYME....the leaves and stems of a shrub grown in France and Spain. Has a strong, distinctive flavor. USES: For poultry seasoning, in croquettes, fricassees and fish dishes. Also tasty on fresh sliced tomatoes.

TURMERIC....a root of the ginger family, grown in India, Haiti, Jamaica and Peru, having a mild, ginger-pepper flavor. USES: As a flavoring and coloring in prepared mustard and in combination with mustard as a flavoring for meats, dressings, salads.

BRAUNSCHWEIGER BALL

1 lb. Braunschweiger
1/4 c. mayonnaise
1/3 c. chopped dill
  pickles
1/4 c. chopped onion

2 Tbsp. dill pickle juice
1 tsp garlic salt
1 tsp. Worcestershire sauce
3 drops Tabasco sauce
4 oz. cream cheese

Outside Coating:

4 oz. cream cheese
2 Tbsp. milk

2 Tbsp. mayonnaise

Mix in a blender, mold into ball and chill. Top with 4 ounces cream cheese mixed with 2 tablespoons milk and 2 tablespoons mayonnaise.

Jean Lucier, St. Cloud, Mn.

BRAUNSCHWEIGER LOAF

1 lb. Braunschweiger
1/4 c. mayonnaise
1/3 c. chopped dill pickles
1/4 c. chopped onions
2 Tbsp. pickle juice

1 tsp. garlic salt
1 tsp. Worcestershire sauce
3 drops Tabasco sauce
4 oz. Philadelphia cream
  cheese

Mix mayonnaise, dill pickles, onions and pickle juice first in blender. Add remaining ingredients. Place in mold and let set in refrigerator until firm.

Topping:

4 oz. Philadelphia cream
  cheese
2 Tbsp. milk

Mayonnaise
Garlic salt

Mix till creamy.

Diane Schmitz, St. Cloud, Mn.

BRAUNSCHWEIGER SPREAD

1/2 lb. Braunschweiger	1 pkg. dry onion soup mix
1 c. sour cream	Dash of Worcestershire sauce

Mix all ingredients thoroughly and refrigerate.
Kathy Bischof, St. Cloud, Mn.

CARAMEL CORN

2 c. brown sugar	1 tsp. salt
2 sticks margarine	1 tsp. soda
1/2 c. syrup	1 1/2 c. unpopped corn

Boil 5 minutes, remove from heat, add 1 teaspoon soda. Pour over popped corn that has been placed in a greased roaster. Bake 1 hour at 200° - stir every 15 minutes. Cool on foil. Use 1 1/2 cups popped corn.
Gina Michels, Willmar, Mn.

CARAMEL CORN

2 c. brown sugar, packed	1/2 tsp. salt
1/2 c. white Karo syrup	7 qt. popped corn, spread
1 1/2 sticks margarine	on cookie sheets
Generous 1/2 tsp. cream of tartar	

Bring brown sugar, Karo syrup and margarine to a full boil, cook for 5 minutes. Add cream of tartar and salt. Pour over popcorn and stir. Bake at 200° for 1 hour, stirring every 15 minutes. Store in sealed containers.
Rosie Schudar, Fargo, N. D.

CARAMEL POPCORN

6 qt. popped corn	1 c. butter
2 c. brown sugar	Pinch of cream of tartar
1/2 c. dark corn syrup	

Mix all ingredients and boil for 6 minutes. Pour over popped corn. Bake in shallow pan at 250° for 1 hour. Stir every 15 minutes. Keeps in a covered container for a long time. Add peanuts if desired.
Jeanette Ploof, St. Cloud, Mn.

4

CARAMEL CORN

Have ready, 1 cup unpopped popcorn (no salt). Pop corn and put into large roaster. Set aside and make **syrup.**

1/2 c. white Karo syrup   2 sticks margarine
2 c. brown sugar

Bring to a boil. Boil for 5 minutes. Take off heat, add 1/2 teaspoon baking soda, mix until foamy. Pour over popcorn and stir well. Bake at 250° for 1 hour. Stir every 15 minutes. Cool and pat.

Ginnie Andersen, St. Paul, Mn.

BAKED CARAMEL CORN

1 c. margarine   1/2 tsp. soda
2 c. packed brown sugar   1 tsp. vanilla
1/2 c. corn syrup   6 qt. popped popcorn
1 tsp. salt

Melt butter. Stir in brown sugar, corn syrup and salt. Bring to boil, stirring constantly. Boil without stirring for about 5 minutes. Remove from heat and stir in vanilla and soda. Gradually pour over popcorn, mixing well. Put into 2 large cookie sheets. Bake at 250° for 1 hour, stirring every 15 minutes. Remove from oven and cool completely. Break apart and store in tightly covered container. Makes about 6 quarts.

Georgia Berg, Fargo, N. D.

BAKED CARAMEL POPCORN

Have ready, 5 quarts popped corn. Mix together:

1/2 c. dark syrup   1 c. butter
1/2 tsp. salt   2 c. brown sugar

Boil together 5 minutes. Then mix in 1/2 teaspoon soda. Pour over popcorn, place in oven at 250° for 1 hour. Stir every 15 minutes. Spread on waxed paper to cool.

Pat Anderson, Minneapolis, Mn.

MICROWAVE CARAMEL FOR POPCORN

1/2 c. brown sugar
8 large marshmallows

1 stick (1/2 c.) margarine
or butter

Microwave brown sugar and margarine for about 1 minute, then add marshmallows for about 30 - 40 seconds. High setting for microwave.

"Swede" Fellman, Brainerd, Mn.

OLD FASHION CARAMEL CORN

1 c. sugar
1/2 c. water
1 1/2 Tbsp. vinegar
3 Tbsp. butter

2 Tbsp. molasses
1/2 tsp. salt
2 qt. corn, popped

Combine sugar, water and vinegar. Boil to soft ball. Add remaining ingredients and boil to hard-crack stage. Remove from heat and pour immediately over popped, unsalted popcorn.

Joan Billadeau, St. Cloud, Mn.

OVEN CARAMEL CORN

1 c. peanuts

20 c. popcorn*

Combine and boil for 5 minutes:

2 c. brown sugar
1 c. butter or margarine

1/2 c. white corn syrup
1 tsp. salt

After 5 minutes, add:
1/2 tsp. soda

1 tsp. vanilla

Stir and pour over popcorn and peanuts immediately. Spread in a large baking pan (15x11 inches). Bake 1 hour at 250°, stirring every 15 minutes. This delight stores and freezes well, if you can keep it around that long.
*One cup of Orville Redenbacher's Gourmet Popping Corn will make the 20 cups needed for this recipe.

Carolyn Brudevold, Fargo, N. D.

RAINBOW GELATIN POPCORN BALLS

1 c. corn syrup
1/2 c. sugar
1 small box gelatin (any
  flavor)

1/2 lb. salted peanuts
9 c. popped corn

Combine sugar and syrup and bring to a boil. Remove from heat. Add gelatin. Stir till dissolved and add peanuts. Pour over popcorn, mixing well. Shape into 1 1/2 inch balls. Makes 4 dozen. Wrap in waxed paper or plastic wrap. Store in airtight container.

CHEESE PUFFS

Melt 1 stick oleo, add 1 cup water, bring to a full boil. Take off heat. Add 1 cup flour, stir vigorously. Will form a ball. Add 3 eggs, stir vigorously, add 2/3 cup shredded Cheddar cheese. Drop by spoonfuls onto cookie sheet. Bake at 400° for 40 - 45 minutes. When cooled, these are really good filled with chicken, turkey or ham salad, or plain with lasagna.

Karen Rupert, St. Cloud, Mn.

HOT SAUSAGE AND CHEESE PUFFS

1 lb. hot or sweet
  Italian sausage
3 c. Bisquick

1 lb. shredded sharp Cheddar
  cheese
3/4 c. water

Remove sausage from casing and cook in large skillet until browned, breaking up meat with fork (cook 8 - 10 minutes). Spoon into large bowl and cool completely. Add cheese, Bisquick and water and mix with fork until blended. Roll into 1 inch balls and place on cookie sheet 2 inches apart. Bake at 400° for 10 - 15 minutes. Cool on racks.

To freeze: Freeze in single layer on cooky sheets. Place in plastic bag when frozen.

To reheat: Remove desired number and arrange in single layer on cooky sheet and bake at 375° for 10 minutes.

Ruth Rehschuh, Minneapolis, Mn.

OLIVE CHEESE PUFFS

1 lb. Cheddar cheese
3 1/2 c. flour
1 3/4 sticks margarine,
    softened

2 drops Tabasco sauce
1 tsp. Worcestershire
    sauce

Grate cheese and mash well with margarine. Add Tabasco sauce and Worcestershire sauce. Stir in flour and mix well. Drain olives and pat dry. Using about 1 teaspoon ful of dough for each olive, wrap the olive with dough. Freeze on cookie sheet and store in plastic bag in freezer until ready to serve. Bake 15 minutes in preheated 400° oven.

Mary Jo Olson, Detroit Lakes, Mn.

CREAM CHEESE BALL

2 (8 oz.) pkg. cream
    cheese
1 small (6 oz.) can
    crushed pineapple,
    drained

1/4 c. chopped green pepper
2 Tbsp. chopped onions
1 Tbsp. Lawry's salt
2 c. chopped pecans

Mix all ingredients well except 1 cup nuts. Place 1 cup nuts on foil and roll cheese ball in it. Chill.

Mickey Parks, Minneapolis, Mn.

CRAB BALL

1 lb. can red salmon
    or Snow crabmeat
8 oz. Philadelphia
    cream cheese
1 Tbsp. lemon juice

2 tsp. grated onions
1 tsp. horseradish
1/4 tsp salt
1/4 tsp. liquid smoke
1/2 c. chopped pecans

Drain and flake salmon - remove skin and bone. Combine and mix thoroughly. Roll into ball and chill a couple of hours. Roll ball in pecans and parsley flakes.

George McGinn, Minneapolis, Mn.

HAM BALL

8 oz. Philadelphia cream
   cheese
1/4 c. Miracle Whip
2 c. ground ham
2 Tbsp. chopped parsley
   or flakes

2 tsp. grated onion
1/4 tsp. mustard
1/4 tsp. Worcestershire
   sauce
1/2 c. ground nuts

    Combine all ingredients. Mix thoroughly. Roll into ball. Chill.

            George McGinn, Minneapolis, Mn.

HOT CRABMEAT APPETIZER

1 (8 oz.) pkg. cream
   cheese
1 (6 oz.) can crabmeat
2 Tbsp. chopped onion
1 Tbsp. cream

1/2 tsp. horseradish
1/4 tsp. salt
Dash of pepper
1/3 c. chopped almonds

    Mix all ingredients except almonds and spread in an 8 inch pie plate. Sprinkle with almonds. Bake at 375° for 15 minutes. Serve hot with crackers.

            Ruth Rehschuh, St. Cloud, Mn.

DON'S WIFE'S YUMMY CHEESE BALL

Cream together:
2 (8 oz.) pkg. cream
   cheese
3 Tbsp. salad dressing
   (mayonnaise)
1 (8 oz.) pkg. sharp
   Cheddar cheese,
   grated

1/4 green pepper
1 Tbsp. chopped onion
1 Tbsp. Worcestershire
   sauce
2 tsp. chopped pimento

Add to taste:
Garlic salt
Tabasco sauce

Salt

    Form into balls (2 large or 4 small). Chill for 2 days. Before serving, roll in parsley or nuts. (Jake's a good parsley chopper if you need help or advice!) Cheese Balls may be frozen.

            Don Billadeau, St. Cloud, Mn.

1748-81

THE BEST CHEESE BALL

2 (8 oz.) pkg. cream
  cheese, softened
1 (8 oz.) jar Cheddar
  cheese spread, softened
1 - 2 tsp. chopped onion

1 Tbsp. chopped green olive
  with pimento
1 tsp. Worcestershire sauce
1 small bag sliced almonds

Beat cheeses together until creamy. Mix in olive, onion and Worcestershire sauce. Chill until firm. Chop almonds until fine. Shape mixture in ball and roll in almonds. Serve with crackers.

Meredith Mueller, Anoka, Mn.

CHEESE BALL

1 jar Roka Blue cheese
2 jars Old English sharp
  cheese
1 (3 oz.) pkg. cream
  cheese

1 tsp. Worcestershire sauce
1/4 c. dried parsley
1 c. ground pecans
1/4 c. ground parsley
2 Tbsp. minced onion or juice

The day before serving, let cheese soften at room temperature. Stir in 1/4 cup parsley and 1/2 cup pecans and shape into ball. Place in bowl lined with waxed paper. Before serving, roll in remaining pecans and 1/4 cup ground parsley.

CHEESE BALL

1 pkg. cream cheese
  (large), softened
1 pkg. (small) shredded
  Cheddar cheese

2 tsp. chopped green pepper
2 tsp. crumbled, cooked
  bacon
2 tsp. pimento

Sprinkle in according to taste:

Lemon juice
Worcestershire sauce

Onion salt
Garlic salt

Mix together with your hands. Shape into 1 large ball or 2 small balls. Refrigerate until sets, then roll in sunflower seeds, nuts.

Mary Hocking, Fargo, N. D.

CREAM BALL

2 large pkg. cream
 cheese, softened
1/2 c. chopped green
 pepper

1 c. well drained crushed
 pineapple
2 Tbsp. chopped onion
1 Tbsp. Lawry's seasoned salt
1 1/4 c. walnuts

Mix all together, reserve some nuts to roll ball in.
Chill well before forming into ball. Roll in nuts.
Myrtle Daml, Anoka, Mn.

PINEAPPLE CHEESE BALL

2 (8 oz.) pkg. cream
 cheese
1/2 c. chopped green
 pepper

1 c. drained, crushed
 pineapple
2 Tbsp. chopped onion
1 Tbsp. seasoned salt
1 1/2 c. chopped walnuts

Reserve 1/2 cup nuts. Mix all other ingredients well
and roll in a ball. Chill well and roll in reserved nuts before
serving.
L. Richards

SNOW BALL CHEESE BALL

2 (8 oz.) pkg. cream
 cheese
4 tsp lemon juice

4 Tbsp. crushed pineapple
4 Tbsp. chopped green
 pepper
5 Tbsp. chopped walnuts

Roll in coconut.
Mrs. Art Larson (Toni), Minneapolis, Mn.

CARAMELIZED CHICKEN WINGS

1/2 c. water or more
1/3 c. sugar
1/3 c. soy sauce

6 minced green onions or
 1 Tbsp. dry onion flakes
6 chicken wings, disjointed

Simmer covered for 30 minutes, uncover and simmer till
tender and caramelized (watch carefully, can burn easy).
Delicious cold and served with potato salad.
Karen Rupert, St. Cloud, Mn.

1748-81

36 CHICKEN WINGS

1/2 c. soy sauce
1 c. pineapple juice
1 clove garlic, mashed
2 Tbsp. minced onion

1 tsp. ground ginger
1/4 c. packed brown sugar
1 c. beer
1/4 c. butter

Marinate 36 chicken wings 3 - 4 hours in refrigerator. When ready to cook, drain and save juice. Brown chicken wings in butter, add 1/4 cup juice. Simmer 35 to 40 minutes. Add more juice as needed.

Ron Ness, St. Cloud, Mn.

MARINATED CHICKEN WINGS

1 c. water
1 c. soy sauce
1/4 c. sugar
1/4 c. pineapple juice

1/4 c. oil
1/4 c. garlic salt
1 tsp. ground ginger
4 - 5 lb. chicken wings

Cut the "flipper" off the end of the wing and discard. Mix all other ingredients well. Add wings and marinate overnight. Lay wings on baking sheet with some of the marinade and bake at 350° for 45 minutes, turning occasionally.

L. Richards

CHOPPED BEEF SPREAD

1 small onion, chopped
1 (8 oz.) pkg. Philadelphia
   cream cheese
1 (3 oz.) pkg. Philadelphia
   cream cheese

2 pkg. "Buddig Brand"
   chopped beef, cut up
1/4 c. chopped olives (green)
2 Tbsp. real mayonnaise

Cream room temperature cheese with mayonnaise. Add olives, onions and beef. Mix. Refrigerate overnight. Serve with crackers.

Carol Erickson, Minneapolis, Mn.

12

COCKTAIL MEAT BALLS

1 lb. ground beef
1/4 c. dry bread crumbs
1 tsp. salt

1 egg, slightly beaten
1 onion (small), chopped
1/4 tsp. pepper

Sauce:

1 (12 oz.) bottle chile
   sauce
2 tsp. brown sugar

1 Tbsp. Worcestershire sauce
1 (10 oz.) jar grape jelly
1 Tbsp. lemon juice

Combine meat ball ingredients and form into balls the size of walnuts or smaller. Place on cookie sheet and brown them in oven (400°) for 10 minutes. Place sauce ingredients in saucepan that won't stick, and bring to boil, stirring constantly. Add meat balls to sauce. Cover and simmer 30 minutes. Serve warm from chafing dish.
Lydia Skaret, Austin, Mn.

WHIPPED HAMBURGER BALLS

1 lb. hamburger
2 Tbsp. flour
1/4 tsp salt
1/8 tsp. black pepper

1 small onion, minced
1/8 tsp. poultry seasoning
1 (10 1/2 oz.) can consomme

Put meat into large bowl. Add remaining ingredients except consomme and fat. Beat with spoon or electric mixer. Add consomme slowly, beating constantly. When consomme is entirely absorbed, chill mixture for several hours, then drop into 16 small mounds on broiler pan covered with aluminum foil. Broil quickly on both sides. Makes 4 servings.
Marge Johnson, Minneapolis, Mn.

FRUTA DE COMPOTA

Cut into serving pieces:
1 fresh pineapple or
   1 can pineapple
   chunks

2 apples
2 oranges
2 bananas

(You may also add any other fresh fruits.) Pour into crystal ball. Add 1/2 cup dry white table wine. Mix well. Let stand for 2 hours, stirring occasionally. Serve in

1748-81

champagne glasses or China cups. Eat the fruit with a
fork, then drink the juice.

Mrs. Frank Van Gorp, Alexandria, Mn.

AUTHENTIC SWISS FONDUE

A fondue eaten correctly is as digestable as any other
dish. Generally one drinks a good bottle of Swiss white
wine, or a little glass of Kirsch, or any other white spirit,
during or after the fondue.

Rub an earthenware casserole with a clove of garlic,
which should then be crushed and left in the bottom of the
casserole. Count per person 150 to 200 grammes (6 to 7
ounces) of rich Gruyere or Emmental cheese, grated (or
half Gruyere, half Emmental can be used). Add a knob of
butter and pour over the whole mixture 1 to 1 1/2 deciliters
(1/4 pint) of dry white wine per person. Place the casserole over a moderate flame and stir with a wooden spoon. If
the cheese forms into a thick mass, continue to stir and it
will be re-absorbed. As soon as the mixture commences to
cook, stir in a liqueur glass of good Kirsch in which you
you have dissolved a teaspoon (for 4 persons) of potato
flour or corn flour and a little grated nutmeg. Salt and pepper to taste. A knifepoint of bicarbonate of soda at the
last moment will make the fondue lighter. Place the casserole on a spirit lamp which can be regulated, with the flame
just high enough to keep the fondue cooking gently during
the meal. Serve with bread diced in large pieces with plenty
of crust. Spear a piece of bread with your fork, dip it into
the fondue, stir and ... good appetite!

I use an electric, Teflon coated fondue pot for this on
the setting for cheese and it works very well. We had
this fondue in Switzerland and thought it was excellent.

Ione Brown, Past President, St. Cloud
Council

CHICKEN LIVER PATE

1/4 lb. butter
1/2 lb. chicken livers
1 apple, pared and
    chopped
1 medium onion, chopped
1/4 c. + 2 Tbsp. chicken broth

1/4 c. brandy
1 tsp. gelatin
Salt and pepper
1/4 tsp. marjoram
2 hard-boiled eggs

14

Saute livers, onion and apple in butter for 10 minutes over very low heat, until livers are cooked, but not brown and add salt and pepper, marjoram, brandy and half of chicken broth. Simmer briefly. Dissolve gelatin in remaining broth and add to livers. Place in blender with eggs. Blend till smooth. Chill 12 hours. Serve with crackers or Melba toast.

Betty Ladd, St. Paul, Mn.

CHICKEN LIVER PATE

8 oz. raw chicken livers
2 eggs, boiled
2 Tbsp. celery

2 Tbsp. diced onion
Seasonings

Boil liver until tender. Drain, reserve juice. Drop liver pieces, one at a time to chop in blender. Add to blender the eggs, celery, onions and seasonings; blend until smooth. Add reserved juice to make mixture moist.

Colleen Knaus, Grand Forks, N. D.

LIVERWURST BALL

1 lb. liverwurst
2 pkg. green onion dip
   mix

1 Tbsp. milk
1 tsp. sugar

Mash up all together (use hands). Form into ball and chill. Frost with:

2 (3 oz.) pkg. cream
   cheese

1/8 tsp. Tabasco sauce
1 Tbsp. milk

Beat together with electric mixer until smooth. Spread over ball and garnish.

Rosie Schudar, Fargo, N. D.

LIVER SPREAD

8 oz. chicken liver
1/2 c. water
1 c. chicken bouillon
1/4 c. chopped onion
1/4 tsp. thyme

3 slices crisp bacon, crumbled
1/2 c. butter or margarine
1/4 tsp. dry mustard
1/8 tsp. garlic salt
Dash of pepper

1748-81

Simmer together liver, water, bouillon, onion and thyme 15 minutes. Save 1/4 cup of the broth and drain the rest. Add bacon, margarine, mustard, salt and pepper to meat mixture. Blend in blender or electric mixer with saved broth and chill at least 3 hours.

Kathy Bischof, St. Cloud, Mn.

NUTS AND BOLTS

6 oz. pkg. pretzels	1 pkg. Cheerios
1 pkg. Wheat Chex	Salted peanuts
1 pkg. Rice Chex	Cashews

Mix above ingredients together in a large roasting pan. Melt together in a saucepan:

1 c. salad oil	2 tsp. celery salt
1/2 c. margarine	1/4 tsp. garlic salt
2 Tbsp. Worcestershire sauce	

Pour over cereal mixture and stir in. Bake at 200° for 1 1/2 hours. Can be stored in freezer.

Rita Aaker, Marshall, Mn.

OLIVE LIVER PATE

1 env. unflavored gelatin	1 Tbsp. chopped parsley or chopped green onion
1 (10 1/2 oz.) can beef broth or bouillon	2 tsp. lemon juice
1 1/2 c. liver sausage	1/2 tsp. salt
1 c. dairy sour cream best (or 2 pkg. cream cheese)	1/8 tsp. pepper
	1 (4 1/2 oz.) can chopped ripe olives
	Worcestershire sauce
	Dry mustard

Soften gelatin in 1/2 cup cold broth, heat rest of broth. Add gelatin mixture and stir to dissolve. Stir sausage until soft and creamy. Stir in gelatin, add sour cream, rest of ingredients. Turn into 3 1/2 cup mold.

PECAN SPREAD

1 (8 oz.) pkg. cream
   cheese
2 Tbsp. milk

2 1/2 oz. dry chipped beef,
   chopped
1/4 c. green pepper
1/2 c. sour cream

Combine above in shallow baking dish. Heat and crisp on stove:

1/2 c. pecans
2 tsp. butter

1/4 Tbsp. salt

Sprinkle over other mixture. Bake at 350° for 20 minutes. May serve warm or cooled on sliced black rye.
Mary Hopman, Grand Forks, N. D.

PICKLED GIZZARDS

1/2 box pickling spice
Gizzards

Onions
Bottle French dressing

Boil gizzards until tender, about 3 1/2 hours. Cool, cut into chunks. Add onions. Put a bottle of French dressing over the gizzards. Put into jar.
Avis Paulsen, Verndale, Mn.

SALMON PARTY BALL

1 (16 oz.) can salmon
1 (8 oz.) pkg. cream
   cheese, softened
1 Tbsp. lemon juice

2 tsp. grated onion
1 tsp. prepared horseradish
1/4 tsp. liquid smoke
1/2 c. chopped pecans

Drain and flake salmon, removing bones and skin. Combine salmon, cheese, lemon juice, onion, horseradish, 1/4 teaspoon salt and liquid smoke. Mix well. Chill several hours. Shape salmon mixture into ball; roll in nut mixture. Chill.

Jean Lucier, St. Cloud, Mn.

SAUCY FRUIT CUP

1/4 c. honey
3 peeled, crushed
  cardamon seeds
6 mint leaves, crushed
1 Tbsp. lemon juice
1 (7 oz.) bottle 7-Up

2 c. plums
2 c. pineapple chunks
1 c. Mandarin oranges
2 bananas, sliced
1/2 c. maraschino cherries

Simmer honey, cardamon seeds and salt for 5 minutes. Add mint. Cool. Add lemon juice. Strain, cover and keep cold. Before serving, add 7-Up and pour over fruit. Canned fruits are chilled and drained. Serves 6.

GERMAN SAUERKRAUT BALLS

1 medium onion, finely
  chopped
1/4 c. butter or margarine
1/2 c. flour
1/2 c. water

1 lb. sauerkraut, chopped
  and drained
1 egg, beaten
1/2 c. milk
1 c. bread crumbs
Shortening for deep frying

In a saucepan, saute onion in butter until soft. Blend 1/4 cup of the flour with water and stir into onion. Add sauerkraut and mix well. Cook over low heat, stirring until thick. Cool and shape into 1 inch balls. Roll in 1/4 cup flour. Mix egg and milk and dip balls into mixture, then roll in bread crumbs. Let stand 15 minutes. Deep fat fry until golden brown in fat preheated to 365°. Drain on paper towels and serve with wooden picks. You can add 1/2 pound ground ham or corned beef to sauerkraut mixture. These can be reheated in the oven and they freeze well. Makes 3 dozen.

Kathy Bishof, St. Cloud, Mn.

SHRIMP PU-PU HAWAIIAN

Blend 1 (8 ounce) package cream cheese (room temperature) with 2 tablespoons mayonnaise, about 1/2 teaspoon curry powder. Make a circle of the cheese mixture, about 3 inches deep on a bread and butter size plate. Pat out. Pat on 1 can broken shrimp. Sprinkle on 3 finely chopped green onions. Sprinkle over all, 1 grated, hard-boiled egg

seasoned with a little salt. Garnish with paprika or parsley.
Chill. To serve, place a knife beside the plate and have a
plate of mixed crackers near by, or cocktail rye bread.
Marion Baihly

SUPER, SUPER BOWL SUNDAY SNACK

1 lb. Jimmy Dean's hot
   sausage
1 lb. hamburger
1/2 c. finely chopped onion

2 lb. Velveeta cheese
1 pkg. cocktail rye or
   pumpernickel breads

Brown and drain meats and onion, melt cheese (cut into
chunks) into meat mixture (will make very thick mixture).
Spread on breads. Place on cookie sheet. Top each with
sliced green or black olives (optional). Bake at 350° to 345°
until hot (bubbly).
Jeanne Segebarth, Minneapolis, Mn.

WOODCHUCK

2 1/2 c. grated sharp
   Cheddar cheese
2 c. tomato juice
2 eggs
1 (5 or 7 oz.) jar stuffed
   olives

2 Tbsp. flour
Salt
Paprika
Crackers

Melt grated cheese in tomato juice in a double boiler.
Slightly beat eggs and add, stirring constantly. Add flour
to juice from olives and slowly add to mixture. Add salt and
paprika. Cook until thick. Slice olives and add to above.
Serve on crackers.
Marge Johnson, Minneapolis, Mn.

BEAN DIP

1 lb. ground beef
1 small onion
1 can jalapeno bean dip

1 bottle taco sauce
1 lb. Cheddar cheese,
   shredded

On bottom of oblong cake pan, spread jalapeno bean
dip - on top of this put ground beef that has been browned
and drained. Add chopped onion. Pour taco sauce over

mixture evenly. Top with shredded Cheddar cheese. Bake at 350° for 30 minutes. Serve hot with Tostidos or Dorito corn chips (plain). (Quantities are subject to taste.)
Carol Erickson, Minneapolis, Mn.

BEAN DIP

1 lb. hamburger, browned and drained
1 lb. Velveeta cheese
1 small diced onion

1/2 can tomato paste
1 can green chillies
2 cans Campbell's chili beef soup
1/2 Tbsp. Worcestershire sauce

Heat through and serve warm with taco chips.
Gina Michels, Willmar, Mn.

CHEESE DIP

Blend in blender:
8 oz. cream cheese

1/2 c. beer

Add:
1/4 c. beer
8 oz. Cheddar cheese

1 clove garlic

Blend until well mixed. This makes a very good vegetable dip.
Rita Aaker, Marshall, Mn.

HOT CREAM CHEESE DIP

1 (8 oz.) pkg. cream cheese, softened
1 Tbsp. milk
1 pkg. finely snipped, dried chipped beef (about 3/4 c.)
1/8 tsp. pepper

2 Tbsp. instant minced onions
2 Tbsp. finely chopped green peppers
1/2 c. sour cream
1/4 c. chopped walnuts

Blend cream cheese and milk. Stir in beef, onion, green pepper and pepper. Mix well. Add sour cream. Spoon into baking dish - sprinkle with walnuts. Bake at 350° for 15 minutes.
R. W. Neale, St. Cloud, Mn.

CHILI TOMATO SAUCE DIP

1 small onion, minced
2 - 3 cloves garlic, minced
2 Tbsp. vegetable oil
1 (16 oz.) can whole
   tomatoes, chopped fine

1/2 tsp. ground cumin
1/2 tsp. oregano
1 tsp. salt
8 - 10 pieces dried chili
   peppers

    Saute onion and garlic in oil. Add chopped tomatoes and juice, then rest of ingredients. Simmer over low heat 20 to 30 minutes, stirring occasionally.
    Evelyn Walls, St. Paul, Mn.

CRAB DIP

Cream cheese
Onion

Shrimp cocktail sauce
Crabmeat

    Mix cream cheese and onion together. Spread on plate and top with layer of shrimp cocktail sauce. On top of that, place crabmeat. Serve with crackers. Especially good with pumpernickel crackers.
    Gina Michels, Willmar, Mn.

CURRY DIP

2 tsp. curry powder
1 c. mayonnaise
1/2 tsp. horseradish

1 tsp. vinegar or lemon juice
1 Tbsp. dry onion flakes
1/2 tsp. garlic powder

    Sue Hick, Detroit Lakes, Mn.

HOT CHIPPED BEEF DIP

11 oz. cream cheese,
   softened
2 Tbsp. milk
1 (2 1/2 oz.) jar dried
   beef, cut into pieces

1/4 c. chopped green pepper
   (optional)
1 small onion
1 c. sour cream

    Mix cream cheese, milk, beef, green pepper and onion in baking dish. Bake for 20 minutes. Serve with Melba rounds, can sprinkle toasted pecans on top.
    Lois Ceynar, Sauk Centre, Mn.

DILL DIP

2/3 c. Miracle Whip
2/3 c. sour cream
1 Tbsp. dehydrated green
onion flakes or instant
minced onions

1 tsp. dill weed or celery
seed
1 tsp. Beau Monde seasoning
1 Tbsp. parsley flakes

Mix together and refrigerate before eating.
Shirley Peterson, Willmar, Mn.; Lu Boyer,
Grand Forks, N. D.: Sue Hick, Detroit Lakes, Mn.; Marge
Johnson, Minneapolis, Mn.; Colette Moger, St. Cloud, Mn.

ROSE NORD'S DILLY DIP

1 c. sour cream
1 c. mayonnaise
1 Tbsp. minced onion

1 Tbsp. parsley flakes
1 Tbsp. dill weed
1 Tbsp. garlic salt

Mix together and let set overnight. Excellent dip for
raw vegetables.
Harriet Maselie, Minneapolis, Mn.

HOT DIP

1 (8 oz.) pkg. cream
cheese
1 c. sour cream
1 pkg. dried beef, cut
into small pieces

2 Tbsp. milk
2 Tbsp. chopped onions
2 Tbsp. green peppers
Pepper to taste

Combine and put into baking casserole. Bake 15 minutes at 350°. Top with chopped walnuts. Serve with
crackers.
A. T. Isakson, Fargo, N. D.

HOT MEXICAN DIP

1 can chili (no beans)
3/4 - 1 lb. Velveeta cheese

1 can chopped green chilies

Cube cheese and mix in an oven baking dish. Heat in
350° oven until cheese melts. Serve with tortilla chips.
Georgine Isakson, Fargo, N. D.

HOT MEXICAN DIP

2 (1 lb.) cans chili without
  beans
1 lb. Velveeta cheese,
  diced

1 (4 oz.) can diced green
  chilies, drained
1 bunch green onions,
  chopped, tops included

    Mix in 2 quart casserole. Bake 1 hour at 350° until
cheese is melted. Can also be put into electric fondue pot -
heat on medium until hot and cheese is melted. Stir occasionally. Serve hot with Doritos or corn chips.
        Mrs. William Meyer, St. Paul, Mn.

PARTY DIP

8 oz. sour cream
2 Tbsp. French dressing
1/3 c. ketchup

1 Tbsp. onion, minced
1/4 tsp. salt

    Mix together until smooth. Serve with chips.
        Arlene Byrne, Rochester, Mn.

HOT PECAN DIP

1/2 c. chopped pecans
2 tsp. butter
1/4 tsp. salt
1 (3 oz.) pkg. smoked
  beef, chopped fine
1/4 c. chopped green
  pepper

1 (8 oz.) pkg. cream cheese,
  softened
2 tsp. milk
1 small onion, grated
1/2 tsp. garlic salt
1/4 tsp. black pepper
1/2 c. dairy sour cream

    Toast pecans in butter and salt. Whip remaining in-
gredients together and place in a buttered 8 inch glass
pie plate. Sprinkle with pecans on top and bake 20 minutes
at 350°. Serve hot.
        Hellen Bartels

PIQUANT DIP

1 1/2 c. sour cream
1/2 c. mayonnaise
1/2 c. bottled chile sauce
2 tsp. prepared mustard

Few drops Tabasco sauce
1 tsp. Worcestershire sauce
1 Tbsp. horseradish
1 Tbsp. cut chives

1748-81

1 tsp. sugar   2 Tbsp. dry white wine

Mix all together and chill. Dip fresh vegetables in it. Makes 2 1/2 cups.

SHEILA'S HOT CHEESE DIP

Combine:

1 small onion, chopped
2 lb. hamburger, browned
  and crumbled

1 bunch green onions,
  chopped
1 can Old El Paso tamalies
  and chilies

Combine these ingredients in a crock pot set on low temperature. Add:

3 lb. Velveeta cheese   3 lb. hot pepper cheese

Ready when all cheese is melted. Stir often so cheese doesn't scorch. Leave in crock pot to serve warm. Serve with taco chips for a dip or over rice for a casserole. This recipe makes a full crock pot. Keep leftovers in refrigerator, or you may freeze it.
                 Sheila Christensen, Fargo, N. D.

SHRIMP DIP

1 (8 oz.) pkg. cream
  cheese
1/2 c. mayonnaise or
  salad dressing
2 tsp. lemon juice

3 tsp. chili sauce
1 tsp. horseradish
1/4 tsp. Worcestershire sauce
5 oz. can shrimp pieces

Soften cream cheese to room temperature. Add all of the ingredients except the shrimp and whip up. Fold in shrimp before serving.
                 Sharon Christian

SHRIMP DIP

8 oz. Philadelphia cream
  cheese
1 1/2 sticks butter
2 cans small shrimp

Juice of 1 lemon
4 Tbsp. mayonnaise
1 Tbsp. onions, minced

Mix all preceding ingredients except shrimp with mixer or blender. After well mixed, fold in small shrimp and salt to taste. Very good with crackers!

Pamela J. Syverson, Minneapolis, Mn.

SHRIMP DIP

1 can broken shrimp, rinse in cold water
3/4 stick butter
2 Tbsp. lemon

2 Tbsp. onion, grated or chopped very fine
1/4 c. salad dressing

Mix with fork till well blended. Very good spread on Hi-Ho crackers.

Phyliss Brossart, Rugby, N. D.

POM POM'S SHRIMP DIP

8 oz. cream cheese
Frozen shrimp, thawed

4 hard-boiled eggs
1 or 2 Tbsp. mayonnaise

Put cream cheese in mixer with mayonnaise and shrimp. Add one shake of curry powder. Spread into a flat dish and cover with chopped eggs. Sprinkle with parsley if desired.

Personnel Dept., Minneapolis, Mn.

RAW VEGETABLE DIP

8 oz. sour cream
2 Tbsp. dry onions
2 tsp. dill weed

1 1/3 c. Hellmann's mayonnaise
2 Tbsp. parsley flakes
2 tsp. Beau Monde seasoning

Mix all above ingredients in a bowl and refrigerate for 24 hours before serving. Optional: Use colored dry salad onions to add some color. Very good anytime!

Pamela J. Syverson, Minneapolis, Mn.

SHRIMP DIP
(Good)

2 (3 oz.) pkg. cream
   cheese
3 Tbsp. chili sauce
1/2 tsp. onion juice

1 (5 oz.) can shrimp
1/4 c. salad dressing
2 tsp. lemon juice
1/4 tsp. Worcestershire sauce

Mix in order. Makes 1 pint.
Colleen Kraus

SOURDOUGH DIP

1 c. mayonnaise
1 c. sour cream
1 can water chestnuts,
   chopped

1 pkg. frozen spinach,
   chopped (thaw and wring
   out liquid)
1 pkg. Knorrs onion soup
   (serving of 6)

Mix together and let set overnight. Place in spooned
out sourdough bread. Place bread cubes around loaf.
Betty Bosquez, Minneapolis, Mn.

SPINACH DIP

Mix together and chill for at least 6 hours:

1 pkg. frozen spinach,
   squeeze out all liquid
   after thawed

1 box Knorr vegetable soup
   mix
1 c. mayonnaise
1 c. sour cream

Good served in hollowed out round sourdough bread,
using broken bread to dip in spinach dip.
Linda Johnson, Anoka, Mn.

SPINACH DIP

1 box frozen chopped
   spinach, thawed and
   drained (squeeze dry)
   use raw
1 c. sour cream
1 c. Hellmann's mayonnaise

1 env. Knorr vegetable soup
   mix (dry)
1 small can water chestnuts,
   drained and diced
2 Tbsp. chopped fresh onion

   Mix well and refrigerate overnight.
26   Kayce Waterbury, St. Paul, Mn.

TACO DIP

2 lb. hamburger   1 green pepper
2 - 3 onions

Simmer 10 minutes. Add 2 tablespoons chili powder.
Add:

1 can tomato soup   1 (8 oz.) can tomato sauce
1 (6 oz.) can tomato paste

Simmer 10 minutes in crock pot; then add 1 pound Velveeta cheese and all the hot sauce you want.
Ruth Berge, Windom, Mn.

GINNY'S TACO DIP

Bottom layer:

1 can refried beans   1 pkg. taco seasonings

Next layer:

1 pkg. frozen avocado dip   2 Tbsp. sour cream

Next layer: Mixture of cut up -

Onions   Black olives
Green olives   1 can green chilies

Top layer: Shredded Cheddar cheese

Use Doritos to dip into this. When you're done, this dip looks like a pie.
Ginny Posthumus, St. Cloud, Mn.

TACO DIP

1 (8 oz.) ctn. sour cream   1 pkg. taco seasoning
1 (8 oz.) pkg. cream cheese

Combine and spread on plate. Top with chopped lettuce, onions, cheese, etc. Scoop with taco chips.
Gina Michels, Willmar, Mn.

TACO DIP

3/4 c. sour cream
8 oz. cream cheese,
  softened
Pinch of garlic powder

1 pkg. Kraft jalapeno pepper
  dip
2 tsp. lemon juice

    Mix together and spread on center of plate. Layer with 1/2 head lettuce (shredded), Cheddar cheese (grated), tomato, green pepper, onion, olives, mushrooms. (Last 4 items to own taste.) Top with more cheese. Place round chips (tostados) around plate.
           Mrs. Lu Boyer, Grand Forks, N. D.

TACO MEXICAN DIP

3 medium ripe avocados
2 Tbsp. lemon juice
1/2 tsp. salt
1/4 tsp. pepper
1 c. (8 oz.) dairy sour
  cream
1/2 c. mayonnaise or salad
  dressing
1 (1/4 to 1 1/2 oz.) pkg.
  taco seasoning mix
2 (10 1/2 oz.) cans plain or
  jalapeno flavored bean dip

1 large bunch green onions
  with tops, chopped (1 c.)
3 medium sized tomatoes,
  cored, halved and chopped
  (2 c.)
2 (3 1/2 oz.) cans pitted ripe
  olives, drained and
  chopped
1 (8 oz.) pkg. sharp Cheddar
  cheese, shredded
Large round tortilla chips

    1. Peel, pit and mash avocados in a medium sized bowl with lemon juice, salt and pepper. Combine sour cream, mayonnaise and taco seasoning mix in bowl. 2. To assemble, spread bean dip on a large shallow serving platter (8x13 inches). Top with seasoned avocado mixture. Sprinkle with chopped onions, tomatoes, olives. Cover with shredded cheese. Serve chilled with round tortilla chips.
           Bev Larson, Bismarck Council

TUCSON DIP

1 jar Old English cheese
  spread
1 jar Roka cheese spread
2 tsp. Worcestershire sauce

1 jar Smokey or Bacon
  Pieces spread
2 (3 oz.) pkg. cream cheese
3/4 Tbsp. garlic salt

Mix well until blended. Serve with potato chips or corn chips.

Ruth Rehschuh, Minneapolis, Mn.

VEGETABLE DILL DIP

1 c. sour cream
1 c. mayonnaise (not Miracle Whip)

3 tsp. each dill weed, Lawry's salt, minced onion, parsley flakes

Make night before.
Elsie Ekblad, St. Paul, Mn.

VEGETABLE DIP

1 large pkg. Philadelphia cream cheese
2 chicken bouillon cubes, dissolved in 1/2 c. boiling water

Onion (fresh or dried)
A little celery salt

Blend in blender or whip with egg beater. Then fold in 1 small carton sour cream. Serve with radishes, carrots, celery, cucumbers, etc.

Gloria Smith, Windom, Mn.

VEGETABLE DIP

1 c. sour cream
1 c. mayonnaise
1 1/2 tsp. dill weed
1 1/2 tsp. minced celery

1 1/2 tsp. minced dry onions
1 1/2 tsp. Beau Monde seasoning

Char Niemann, Frazee, Mn.

VEGETABLE DIP

1 pt. Hellmann's mayonnaise
1 pt. cottage cheese
1/2 c. onion, chopped
1/2 tsp. salt

1/4 tsp. Tabasco sauce
1/2 Tbsp. Worcestershire sauce
1/2 Tbsp. celery seed
1 Tbsp. dry mustard
1 tsp. pepper

Mix well and chill (mixes well in a blender).

1748-81 Ron Ness, St. Cloud, Mn.

WEBSTER'S WACKY WOMBERO DIP

Mix 1 can of Hormel chili (without beans) to 1 jar of Cheez Whiz. Put into crock pot or fondue pot and serve warm with taco chips.

Kathy, Minneapolis, Mn.

YVONNE'S "HOT" CHEESE DIP

Saute 2 - 3 large chopped onions in 1/4 pound of butter. In crock pot, cook slowly:

2 lb. Velveeta cheese
10 oz. Colby cheese
1 large can of whole
  tomatoes, chopped and
  drained

1 small can El Paso green
  chili peppers, chopped
1/2 can jalapeno peppers,
  chopped
1 small can Carnation milk

Add onions and butter. Serve warm with Tostito or taco chips. Can be frozen.

Donna Moy, Detroit Lakes, Mn.

DILLED PICKLED BEANS

1 lb. green beans *
6 c. boiling water
3 1/2 tsp. pickling salt

1 c. white vinegar
1 garlic clove
Dill

*Save liquid from beans.

Wash, string and drain beans. Put beans into kettle with boiling water and 1 teaspoon pickling salt. Boil until almost tender. Drain, saving 1 cup liquid. Put vinegar, bean liquid and rest of pickling salt into kettle and boil. Pack beans, bunch of dill, 1 clove garlic into hot sterilized jars. Top with hot vinegar mixture and seal. Yield: 2 pints.

BEET PICKLES

Cook beets and peel. Then cook 10 minutes in:

1 c. sugar
1 c. vinegar

1 c. water
Few mixed spices

Seal.

Kathy Bischof, St. Cloud, Mn.

PICKLED BEETS

Syrup:

2 c. sugar　　　　　　　3 c. vinegar
2 c. water　　　　　　　3 1/2 tsp. pickling spice

Boil 5 to 8 minutes. Pour over sliced, cooked beets in jars and seal tight.

Recipe from Minneapolis, Mn.

BEET PICKLES

Cook beets (with 1 - 1 1/2 inches green) until tender and put in cold water. Rub off skins. Cut into good size for pickles.

Brine:

1 pt. vinegar　　　　　　3 1/2 c. sugar
1 qt. water　　　　　　　1/2 can pickling spice

Double until enough to cover beets. Boil and pour on beets and heat to simmer (about 1/2 hour). Seal and process in boiling water bath 10 - 15 minutes.

Robin Knutson, Willmar, Mn.

BREAD AND BUTTER PICKLES

1. Slice 1 gallon cucumbers (unpeeled) and 8 large onions; add 2 green peppers (shredded) and 1/2 cup salt. Place in a large bowl and cover with ice cubes and a clean, dry towel. Set bowl aside to stand for 3 hours. 2. Drain water off and add:

5 c. sugar　　　　　　　2 Tbsp. mustard seed
1 1/2 tsp. turmeric　　　1 tsp. celery seed
1/2 tsp. cloves　　　　　5 c. vinegar

3. Place over low flame until scalding. Do not boil, but keep over low flame until cucumbers are transparent. Use a wooden spoon for mixing. Put into sterilized jars and seal.

BREAD AND BUTTER PICKLES

Slice thin:

4 qt. cucumbers	1 red pepper
6 onions	1 green pepper

Put into large pan (roaster). Sprinkle with 1/3 cup salt. Put about 3 or 4 trays ice cubes on top. Leave set for 3 hours. Mix:

3 c. vinegar	2 Tbsp. mustard seed
5 c. sugar	1 1/2 tsp. turmeric
1 1/2 tsp. celery seed	

Add squeezed out cucumbers, onion, pepper. Heat to boiling with vinegar mixture. Put hot into jars and seal.

Recipe from Minneapolis, Mn.

BREAD AND BUTTER PICKLES

5 medium onions, sliced	1 tsp. celery seed
8 medium cucumbers, sliced	2 c. sugar
1/2 c. salt	3/4 tsp. turmeric
1 c. water	1/2 tsp. mustard seed
1 1/2 c. vinegar	

Wash and slice cucumbers. Mix onions and cukes and arrange in layers. Sprinkle with salt. Let stand 2 hours. Heat other ingredients to boiling. Add cukes and onions, draining accumulated liquor. Boil slowly until tender. Pack into sterilized jars. Seal. Yield: 4 pints.

Mary Ann Hanson, Detroit Lakes, Mn.

BREAD AND BUTTER PICKLES

To 1 gallon sliced and peeled cucumbers, add 1/2 cup salt, 8 onions, sliced and ice water to cover. Soak 3 hours. Drain. Add:

5 c. vinegar	1 tsp. celery seed
5 c. sugar	1 1/2 tsp. turmeric
2 Tbsp. mustard seed	1/2 tsp. ground cloves

Cook 5 minutes. Makes 9 pints per batch, but 1 1/2 batches of brine will make 2 batches of pickles.

Linnea Pajari, Detroit Lakes, Mn.

CUCUMBER SLICES (Pickles)

Slice thin, enough unpeeled cukes to fill 2 (1 quart) jars. Slice 1 onion and 1 green pepper and add to the cukes. Mix:

2 c. sugar	1 tsp. salt
1 c. vinegar (more if preferred)	1 tsp. celery salt

Pour into jars filled with sliced cukes and peppers. Can be kept for 3 months in refrigerator - very good with fried Sunnies, Crappies and Northerns. I use 5 quart ice cream pail.

Georgine Isakson, Fargo, N. D.

ESPECIALLY GOOD DILL PICKLES

Wash fresh cukes (small) and let stand at least 2 hours in cold water. Then pack in clean quart jars with 2 - 3 stems dill in middle of jar.

Brine:

12 c. (3 qt.) water	1 c. pickling salt
4 c. vinegar	1/2 tsp. alum

Let come to good boil and pour over cukes. Seal at once and process 5 - 10 minutes in boiling water bath.

Robin Knutson, Willmar, Mn.

DILL PICKLES

This was given to a bride in 1923. Dill pickles for a 2 quart jar:

Dill	Cucumbers
1/4 c. salt	1/4 c. vinegar (dark or
Cold water	white)

Place a head of dill in the bottom of jar. Fill the jar with medium sized cucumbers, add salt (not iodized) and vinegar. Fill jar with cold water. May add 1 bay leaf and clove of garlic. Add alum the size of a pea. Seal jar. If you prefer sweet dill pickles, turn off the brine after pickles are seasoned. Cut into desired pieces and make a hot sweet pickle brine seasoned with cinnamon stick.

Ruth Brown, Owatonna, Mn.

DILL PICKLES

Cucumbers, washed and soaked in cold water overnight	13 c. water 1 c. salt (pickling) 1 1/2 c. vinegar

Boil and pour over pickles and put 2 slices of onion on top in jar. Put 2 pieces of dill in jar. Cut pickles as desired.

Kathy Bischof, St. Cloud, Mn.

24 HOUR DILL PICKLES

Refrigerate dill in bottom of gallon crock jar. Cut onions on top, 3 buds of garlic. Fill jar with pickles, cut lengthwise. Boil and pour over pickles hot:

1 qt. water	3/4 c. sugar
1 pt. vinegar	1/4 c. salt

Put on more dill. Eat in 24 hours.

Mary Ann Hanson, Detroit Lakes, Mn.

PICKLED EGGS

1 c. brown vinegar	4 cloves
2 c. water	Few peppercorns
2 Tbsp. salt	Few whole allspice
Bay leaf	Few banana peppers
1/2 tsp. mustard seed	

Heat and pour over boiled, peeled eggs. Let stand for about 24 hours.

Bev Larson, Bismarck Council

PICKLED FISH RECIPE

Fillet fish and cut into small pieces. Add 5/8 cup of salt to each quart of fish, cover with white vinegar. Let stand 4 to 6 days. Stir with hands occasionally and keep at 40°. Take out of salt solution and rinse with cold water thoroughly. Use wide mouth jar and place layer of fish and layer of onion alternately. Cover with solution of:

1 qt. white vinegar	1 1/2 c. sugar
1 qt. white Port	5/8 oz. pickling spices

Refrigerate and let stand for week before using.
John Hortel, Fargo, N. D.

HERRING (PICKLED FISH)

Skin fish, clean and cut into small pieces like herring. Put into jar. Make brine of cold salt water strong enough to hold an egg. Pour over fish and put into refrigerator for 50 hours. Drain well and cover with vinegar. Put back into refrigerator for 50 hours. Drain well. Use fresh vinegar and cook:

2 c. vinegar	1 tsp. whole allspice
1 1/2 c. sugar	1 tsp. whole cloves
1 tsp. whole mustard seed	1 tsp. whole black pepper

Boil 5 minutes. Cool before pouring over fish. Slice onions between. Maybe slice of lemon. Let stand for a week.
Stan and Phylis Patyk, Sauk Centre, Mn.

PICKLED FISH
(Northerns, Sunfish, Crappie)

Soak 1 gallon cleaned fish in salt water (strong enough to float an egg) for 24 hours. It is approximately 1/2 cup salt to 1 quart of water. Do not use iodized salt. Then drain well. Then soak in white vinegar for 24 hours. Be sure to use enough vinegar to cover fish entirely, then drain well. Then boil 4 cups of white vinegar and 2 1/2 cups sugar till sugar is dissolved. Then cool well. To this mixture, add 1 cup of white Port wine. Then take scant 1/4 cup of pickling spice and tie in cheesecloth bag. Slice 2 raw

1748-81

onions. Pack fish and onions alternately and add bag of pickling spice somewhere in middle. Pour solution over packed fish and onions. You may have to make more solution to cover fish. Let set 4 to 7 days before eating.

PICKLED FISH

Cut into small strips. Soak in salt brine (float a potato) for 28 hours. Wash thoroughly. Soak in white vinegar for 12 hours. Pour off vinegar. Pack into jar, not too hard (tight). Mixture until covered:

1/2 c. white vinegar
1/2 c. water

1/4 c. sugar
1/2 c. Muscatel wine

Add onions and pickling spice to each jar. We use Italian Swiss Colony Muscatel or homemade white grape wine.
Joan Buttweiler, St. Cloud, Mn.

PICKLED NORTHERN

Fish
Pickling salt
White vinegar
3 c. sugar

1 c. white wine
Pickling spices
Onion

Fillet fish and cut into 1 inch or smaller pieces. Soak in a salt brine that will float an egg. (Use pickling salt.) Soak for 48 hours. Drain well and cover with white vinegar for 24 hours. (Don't use metal container.) An ice cream pail works fine. Put 4 cups vinegar on stove and bring to boil, remove and stir in 3 cups sugar and 1 cup white wine. Add 1/2 box or 1 ounce of pickling spices. Pack alternate layers of fish and sliced onions into jars or plastic containers. Cover with marinade. Store in refrigerator - ready in a couple of days.
Chuck Haggard, Anoka, Mn.; Margaret Miller, St. Cloud, Mn.

KOSHER PICKLES

Pack cucumbers into sterile jars, add to each quart jar:

1 large head dill
1 clove garlic
1 slice onion

1/2 tsp. alum
1 chillie tephines (red pepper)
1 stick carrot and celery

Boil:
1 qt. vinegar
1 c. pickling salt

3 qt. water

Pour in each jar to 1/4 inch of top. Seal. Let set at least 6 weeks.

Karen Rupert, St. Cloud, Mn.

KOSHER SWEET PICKLES

Have ready, one quart boughten Kosher dill pickles, sliced thin. Boil for 2 minutes:

3 c. sugar
1 c. cider vinegar

2 sticks cinnamon

Pour over pickles. Cool and refrigerate. Good to the last bite. Best after 2 days.

Aster Paulsrud, Willmar, Mn.

REFRIGERATOR CUCUMBERS

1 c. vinegar
2 c. sugar

1 rounded tsp. salt
1 tsp. celery seed

Stir above together and add:

6 c. thinly sliced
  cucumbers

1 c. thinly sliced onion

Mix together and put into a covered jar in refrigerator. Ready to eat in about 24 hours. Will keep well a couple of months.

Louis Rodecker, St. Paul, Mn.; Karen Rupert, St. Cloud, Mn.

REFRIGERATOR PICKLES

8 c. sliced cucumbers
1 c. diced onion

1 c. diced celery
1 c. green pepper, diced

Cover with 1 1/2 tablespoons salt (no water) for 1/2 hour and drain (do not rinse).

Syrup: Bring to boil and when cool, pour over drained cucumbers. Put into jars and keep in refrigerator - keeps all winter -

2 c. sugar
1 c. vinegar

1 tsp. celery
1 tsp. mustard seed

Garlic or pimento can be added.
Gerri Ruprecht, St. Cloud, Mn.

REFRIGERATOR PICKLES
(No Cooking)

1/4 c. pickling salt
2 c. sugar
2 c. dark cider vinegar

3/4 tsp. celery seed
3/4 tsp. whole mustard seed
3/4 tsp. turmeric

Mix in jar until salt and sugar dissolve. Cut up onions and slice cucumbers as desired. Pack real hard into jars - put in above brine - cover to let stand 4 days in refrigerator - ready to eat!! Makes 6 pints brine recipe. Double it, and should make a gallon. You may also peel the slices for a different flavor.
Thomas E. Broman, Pine City, Mn.

APPLE RELISH

1/2 c. water
1/4 c. lemon juice
1/2 c. raisins
4 1/2 c. tart red apples
 (about 3 lb.)

1 pkg. powdered pectin
5 1/2 c. sugar
1/2 c. broken walnuts or
 pecans
3 or 4 drops red food coloring

Wash, stem, core and chop apples fine. Do not peel. Combine in large kettle with 1/2 cup water, 1/4 cup lemon juice and 1/2 cup raisins. Stir in pectin. Bring to boil over high heat, stirring constantly. Add sugar; beat again, stirring to full bubbling boil. Boil hard 1 minute. Add 1/2 cup nuts. Remove from heat; add food coloring if desired. Alternately skim and stir for 5 minutes. Ladle into scalded containers. Seal with 1/8 inch of melted paraffin. Makes 9 (6 ounce) glasses.

BEET RELISH

Cook beets until done. Peel and put through chopper, then measure:

6 c. beets	1 tsp. cinnamon
4 c. sugar	1/2 tsp. cloves
2 c. vinegar	

Combine all together. Boil until thick. Then put into jars and seal.

Karen Rupert, St. Cloud, Mn.

CARROT RELISH

6 c. grated carrots	4 c. grated cucumbers
6 large finely ground onions	

Sprinkle above with a scant 1/3 cup of salt. Let stand overnight. Drain, then add:

4 peppers (2 red and 2 green), finely chopped	3 1/2 c. white sugar
	1 tsp. celery seed
4 c. vinegar	1 tsp. mustard seed

Boil together 15 minutes. Place in hot, sterilized pint canning jars. Seal. Makes 5 or 6 pints.

GREEN TOMATO RELISH

24 large green tomatoes	4 c. vinegar
4 sweet red peppers	2 Tbsp. salt
3 green peppers	2 tsp. celery seed
8 large onions	2 tsp. mustard seed
3 1/2 c. sugar	

Grind first 4 ingredients in food chopper. Combine with remaining ingredients and bring to a boil. Boil for 15

1748-81

minutes, pour into sterilized jars and seal.   Makes about 8
quarts.

QUICK CORN RELISH

1/3 c. sugar
1 Tbsp. cornstarch
1 tsp. instant minced
   onion
1 tsp. turmeric
1/2 tsp. celery seed
1/4 c. vinegar

1/4 c. water
1 (12 oz.) can vacuum packed
   kernel corn
2 Tbsp. finely chopped green
   pepper
1 Tbsp. finely chopped
   pimiento

Combine first 8 ingredients in a saucepan. Cook and
stir over medium heat until mixture thickens and boils. Stir
in green pepper and pimiento. Chill. Makes 1 3/4 cups.

SHERRIES RELISH

1/2 small head cauliflower,
   cut into flowerets
2 carrots, cut into 2 inch
   strips
2 stalks celery, cut into
   1 inch strips

1 green pepper, cut into 1
   inch strips
1 (4 oz.) jar pimentos,
   drained and cut
1 small jar olives, black and
   green
1 can mushrooms (optional)

In large skillet, bring to a boil 1/4 cup water, 3/4 cup
apple cider vinegar or wine vinegar, 1/2 cup safflower oil,
1 tablespoon honey, 1 teaspoon salt, 1/2 teaspoon oregano,
1/4 teaspoon pepper and 1 clove garlic (optional). Add vegetables and simmer. Cover for 5 minutes. Refrigerate 24
hours in a quart jar, covered.
Mary Paul, Minneapolis, Mn.

SWEET TOMATO RELISH

12 green tomatoes
6 green peppers

3 red peppers
4 onions

Put through food grinder. Pour boiling water over,
let stand 10 minutes. Drain for 1 1/2 hours. Combine

drained vegetables with:

1 1/2 c. vinegar   1 tsp. celery seed
2 c. sugar   1 tsp. salt
1 tsp. mustard seed

Boil about 3 minutes. Makes 8 (1/2 pint) jars. I don't use all the juice left over.

Recipe from Minneapolis, Mn.

** NOTES **

** NOTES **

SOUPS
SALADS
VEGETABLES

TO QUICK–FREEZE VEGETABLES

Vegetables for freezing are prepared as for cooking, then blanched (scalded) and packed dry, or with the brine. The dry pack is less trouble and is satisfactory for all vegetables except green peppers.

Blanching vegetables is important because it minimizes loss of flavor and color. To blanch in boiling water, put about one pound of vegetables in a fine-mesh wire basket with a wire cover to hold food under the water and lower into rapidly boiling water, enough to cover food. Cover the kettle and then COUNT THE TIME RECOMMENDED FOR EACH vegetable. After blanching, chill quickly and thoroughly, plunge the vegetables into ice water, or hold under cold running water. When completely chilled, remove and drain, and PACK AT ONCE.

VEGETABLE	HOW PREPARED	BLANCHING
ASPARAGUS	Wash, cut, sort into groups according to thickness of stalk. Blanch, chill, pack.	3 to 4 minutes in boiling water, depending on size.
BEANS, GREEN AND WAX	Wash, stem, slice, cut or leave whole. Blanch, chill, pack.	Cut: 2 minutes in boiling water. Whole: 2 1/2 minutes in boiling water.
BEANS, LIMA	Shell, wash, blanch, chill. Remove white beans, which may be used for cooking. Pack.	1 to 2 minutes in boiling water, depending on size.
CARROTS	Remove tops, wash, scrape. Slice lengthwise or cross-wise as preferred, or leave small carrots whole.	Whole: 4 1/2 minutes in boiling water. Sliced: 3 minutes in boiling water.
CAULIFLOWER	Break heads into flowerets about 1 inch across. Wash, blanch, chill, pack.	3 to 4 minutes in boiling water.
CORN, ON COB	Husk, trim away silk and spots. Wash, blanch, chill, pack.	7 minutes in boiling water for slender ears. 9 for medium, 11 for large.
CORN, KERNELS	Same as corn on cob. After chilling, cut off kernels and pack.	
GREENS Beet, Chard, Kale, Mustard, Spinach, Collards, etc.	Wash, discard bad leaves, tough stems. Blanch, chill, pack.	2 minutes in boiling water.
PEAS	Shell, sort, blanch, chill, pack.	1 to 2 minutes in boiling water, depending on size.
PEPPERS, GREEN	Wash, cut away seeds, slice. Blanch, pack in brine of 1 tsp. salt to 1 c. cold water.	3 minutes in boiling water.

BORSCH

1 medium head cabbage,
  chopped up
1 lb. carrots, diced
1/4 stalk celery, cut up
10 potatoes, diced

2 cans shoestring beets
  (juice and all)
3/4 green pepper
2 large onions
Salt and pepper

Cook a roast (cheap cut) with onions, salt and pepper. Cook till meat falls off bone, remove meat, bone and onions. Add all other vegetables plus 1 small can tomato paste.

1 large can whole
  tomatoes, mashed up

1 Tbsp. sugar
Salt and pepper

Cook up vegetables, then cut up meat and put into soup. Let simmer till done. Best the next day.
Tim Croner, St. Paul, Mn.

BOUJA
(Makes 4 gallons)

7 lb. potatoes
1 1/2 lb. onions
2 lb. carrots
2 lb. cabbage
1 small bunch celery
38 oz. green beans
46 oz. tomatoes
1/2 lb. barley (scant)

1/2 c. + 2 Tbsp. salt
4 tsp. pepper
1 heaping Tbsp. pickling
  spices (tied in cloth)
1 1/2 lb. beef
1 1/2 lb. pork
1 (3 lb.) chicken

Joan Billadeau, St. Cloud, Mn.

CAULIFLOWER SOUP

1 medium head cauliflower
1/4 c. butter
2 Tbsp. grated onion
2 Tbsp. grated celery
2 Tbsp. all-purpose flour
4 c. hot chicken bouillon

2 c. hot milk or light cream
Salt and white pepper
1 egg yolk
1/4 c. heavy cream
2 Tbsp. Madeira
Parsley
Paprika

1748-81

Trim cauliflower. Cook in boiling water till tender. Drain, divide into flowerets. Reserve about 1/4 of flowerets. Force remaining cauliflower through a strainer or food mill, or puree in blender. Melt butter and cook onion and celery in it for 2 minutes. Stir in flour. Do not brown. Gradually stir in hot bouillon. Add strained cauliflower. Stir in hot milk or cream. Season with salt and pepper to taste. Cook over medium heat, stirring constantly, until sauce coats spoon. Beat egg yolk with heavy cream. Remove soup from heat and gradually stir into egg yolk. Stir in Madeira. Add cauliflowerets and garnish with parsley and paprika. Serve very hot. Makes about 2 quarts.

Marge VanGorp, Alexandria, Mn.

CHRISTMAS EVE OYSTER STEW

2 c. milk
1/2 c. cream
1/4 lb. butter, cut into
   small chunks
1 pt. fresh oysters

1 tsp. salt
Dash of freshly ground black
   pepper
1 Tbsp. chopped parsley
   (optional)

Pour the milk and cream into a heavy kettle on low heat. Use wooden spoon for stirring. Add oysters and their liquor at the same time, while milk and cream are still cold. Stir gently, as mixture is heating to keep oysters moving. Do not allow broth to boil. When oysters are done, they will rise to the top and be curled around the edges (takes about 15 minutes). Last, add butter, salt, pepper and parsley. Stir until steamy and butter is melted. Serve in coffee mugs with garlic toast or oyster crackers. Serves 4. (To serve 12, this can be multiplied by 3.)

Ione Brown, Past President St. Cloud
Council

CLAM CHOWDER

1 1/2 pt. clams, chopped
3 c. potatoes, diced
1 1/2 c. kernel corn,
   drained
Salt and pepper to taste

1 tsp. thyme
1 can evaporated milk (large
   can)
1 medium onion
1/2 lb. butter

Cook potatoes, onions and seasoning until tender. (Cover the potato mixture with about 1 inch over the mixture with water. When done, add milk, clams and corn. Bring to a boil slowly. Add butter and serve. Serves 6.

Mary Ann Ohman, Fargo, N. D.

EASY CLAM CHOWDER

1 can "Doxee" or "Snow's"
  brand clam chowder
1 can cream of celery soup

1 can milk
1 can minced clams, drained

Combine clam chowder, cream of celery soup and milk in the top of a double boiler. Gently stir in drained clams. Allow to heat to a near boil. Add a dash of freshly ground black pepper. Add 1 pat of butter and allow it to melt. Enjoy!

I learned to make this while visiting a relative in San Francisco. It is very simple to prepare and I think as good as a clam chowder made from scratch.

Ione Brown, Past President, St. Cloud Council

CREAM OF CAULIFLOWER SOUP

1 medium head cauliflower
3 qt. water
3 tsp. salt
4 chicken bouillon cubes

5 oz. (10 Tbsp.) butter
5 oz. (1 c.) flour
2 pt. half & half cream
1/4 tsp. white pepper

Place cauliflower in pot. Cover with water and add salt. Simmer until cauliflower is tender (do not overcook). Take cauliflower out of pot and let cool. Then dice. Add bouillon cubes to water and let dissolve, keeping broth warm. Melt butter in saucepan. Add flour, mixing well. Add to broth, stirring rapidly until smooth. Heat cream and add to broth. Add white pepper, cauliflower and more salt if needed. Simmer for about 10 minutes. Add chopped parsley before serving. Serves 20.

Norma Lee, Wadena, Mn.

CREAM OF POTATO SOUP

1 1/2 c. sliced onions	1/8 tsp. white pepper
4 Tbsp. butter or margarine	1 bay leaf
4 c. diced potatoes	1 stalk celery
4 c. chicken broth	1 egg yolk
1 tsp. salt	1 c. half & half

Saute the onions in the butter 5 minutes. Add the potatoes. Cover and cook over low heat 5 minutes. Add the broth, salt, pepper, bay leaf and celery. Cover, bring to a boil and cook over low heat 30 minutes. Discard the bay leaf and celery. Puree the soup in a blender or force through a sieve. Beat the egg yolk and cream in a bowl and gradually add the hot soup, stirring steadily to prevent curdling. Return to the saucepan. Heat, but do not boil. Taste for seasonings. Serves 6 to 8.

Mary C. Vander Laan, Andover, Mn.

CZECH CABBAGE SOUP

Simmer 1 1/4 heads green cut cabbage in 1 1/2 quarts of salted water for 45 to 60 minutes. Keep covered. While this is cooking, prepare an herb mixture. To 1/2 pint of water, add:

2 cloves garlic	1 bay leaf
1/2 tsp. caraway seed	1 tsp. oregano
1/2 tsp. whole black pepper	

Let simmer 10 - 15 minutes. Then let stand another 10 minutes to cool and absorb more flavors before stirring into cabbage mixture. For thickening, blend 1 cup flour into 1/4 pound (1 stick) melted butter or margarine. Slowly add to cabbage mixture whipping with wire whip until blended well. Simmer 10 minutes, stirring. Then add 1/2 quart scalded milk, 2 ounces of American cheese slices. Add nutmeg, mace, salt, white pepper and ground oregano to taste before serving.

Cecilia Bulera, St. Paul, Mn.

DIET CABBAGE SOUP

3 c. tomato juice
2 c. chopped cabbage
1/2 medium green pepper
1 tsp. onion flakes
    or 1 onion, chopped
1 chicken and 1 beef bouillon

1 c. water
2 ribs celery, chopped
1 can mushrooms
1 bay leaf (optional)
4 or 5 carrots, cut up

Simmer until vegetables are tender. You can add cooked chicken or beef, if desired.

Karen Rupert, St. Cloud, Mn.

EASTER SOUP
(Zurek Wielkanocny)

2 c. rolled oats
2 c. warm water
Crust of sour rye bread
1 1/2 lb. Polish sausage
1 1/2 qt. water

1 Tbsp. prepared horseradish
1 tsp. brown sugar
1 tsp. salt
1/4 tsp. pepper

1. Mix oats and warm water. Add bread crust, let stand until mixture sours, at least 24 hours. Strain; reserve liquid. 2. Cook sausage in 1 1/2 quarts water, 1 hour. Remove sausage, skim off fat. Combine skimmed broth and oatmeal liquid. 3. Add horseradish, brown sugar, salt and pepper. Slice sausage, add to broth. Bring to boil. 4. Serve hot with boiled potatoes and hard-cooked eggs (sliced) (important). About 4 servings.

Pat Bruchert, Minneapolis, Mn.

FINN SOUP

Have ready, 1 pound side pork, cut into about 1 1/2 inch pieces and fried brown. In a kettle put in potatoes, carrots, onions, cover with water and boil. Add the fried side pork, cook till vegetables are done. I add dumplings to mine.

Karen Rupert, St. Cloud, Mn.

GERMAN POTATO-BEAN SOUP

6 large potatoes, cubed
1 large onion, diced
Ham, cubed

2 chicken bouillon cubes
3 c. water

Combine all ingredients and cook on low in crock pot 8 hours. Before serving, add 2 cans pork 'n beans and 1/2 pint cream. Turn to high to heat through completely. Leftovers can be frozen.

Pat Wentz, Grand Forks, N. D.

HAMBURGER SOUP

Brown and drain well, 2 pounds ground beef. Combine remaining ingredients and simmer 1 hour:

1 qt. tomatoes, run
  through blender just a
  bit
8 c. water
1 1/2 c. diced celery
2 c. cut carrots

1 c. diced potatoes
1/3 c. rice
1 small onion, diced
1 c. shredded cabbage
Salt and pepper to taste

Mike and Vonnie Bakke, Willmar, Mn.

MINESTRONE SOUP

1 lb. stew meat (don't
  brown)
1/2 c. navy beans

Garlic powder to taste
Oregano to taste

Add water to more than cover. Simmer 4 hours. Add any amount of carrots, tomatoes, potatoes. Cook until carrots are tender. Near end of cooking time, add:

1/4 c. raw rice

1/2 c. elbow macaroni

Mrs. Clayone Carlson (Roy), Fargo, N. D.

OX-TAIL SOUP
(Russian)

Approx. 1 lb. beef tail sections
1 medium onion (whole)
1/2 c. quick barley

1 c. dry baby lima beans
2 carrots, chopped
Salt and pepper to taste

Cover the beef with cold salted water. Bring to a boil, then reduce heat and simmer about 1 1/2 hours. Skim some of the fat. Add onion, barley, beans and carrots. Return to a boil, then simmer about 1 more hour. Meat should be very tender and beans and carrots done to taste.
*Serve with slices of heavy dark bread and butter. Serves 4.

Deborah Wiss, Minneapolis, Mn.

SPLIT PEA SOUP

2 c. green split peas
1 ham bone with some meat on it
1/2 c. chopped onion
2 c. chopped celery with leaves
2 carrots, sliced

1 c. milk
2 c. beef bouillon
6 kosher-style garlic frankfurters, sliced
Salt
10 peppercorns, cracked

Soak peas in 2 quarts water overnight. Bring to a boil in the same water, reduce heat, add ham bone and peppercorns, cover and simmer for 1 hour. Add vegetables and simmer for 1 hour. Remove ham bone, cut meat from it, discard bone and chop meat fine. Press the rest of the soup through coarse sieve or food mill. Add chopped ham, milk, bouillon and sliced frankfurters and simmer for 20 minutes. Add salt if necessary. Serves 6.

Marge Johnson, Minneapolis, Mn.

TOMATO SOUP

Melt 3 tablespoons butter or margarine. Add:

2 Tbsp. flour

2 c. tomatoes

Cook for a few minutes. Add 1/4 teaspoon soda, 1 teaspoon salt, 1/8 teaspoon pepper. Add 3 cups milk. Heat, but do not boil.

1748-81   Mrs. Clayone Carlson (Roy), Fargo, N.D.   49

APPLE CHEESE SALAD

1 c. hot water
2/3 c. red cinnamon candies
1 small pkg. lemon jello
1 1/2 c. sweetened
   applesauce

1/8 pkg. cream cheese
1/2 c. chopped nuts
1/2 c. finely chopped celery
1/2 c. mayonnaise

Pour hot water over cinnamon candy. Stir until dissolved. When still hot, add lemon jello. Stir until dissolved. Add applesauce, pour half of mixture into an 8x8x2 inch pan. Chill. Blend cream cheese, mayonnaise, nuts and celery. Chill jello and apple mixture. Pour remainder of apple and jello on top and chill till firm.

           Elaine Asher, Minneapolis, Mn.

APRICOT JELLO SALAD

1 (20 oz.) can crushed
   pineapple and juice

1/2 c. sugar

Bring to boil. Take off heat, add 1 (3 ounce) box of apricot jello. Stir to dissolve. Cool and add 1 (8 ounce) package cream cheese and 5 tablespoons milk creamed in blender. Fold in 8 ounces Cool Whip.

           Sharon Brogren, Willmar, Mn.

APRICOT SALAD

1 box orange jello (regular
   size)
1 can crushed pineapple
   (#202 can)
3/4 c. sugar

1 medium sized ctn. Cool Whip
2 small jars apricot baby
   food with tapioca
1 (8 oz.) pkg. cream
   cheese, softened

Put jello and pineapple in pan and heat until mixture simmers. Add sugar, baby food and cut up cream cheese. Dissolve and mix well. Do not beat. Chill real well. Add Cool Whip slowly. Do not beat. Put into bowl, garnish with chopped nuts.

           Mary Ann Ohman, Fargo, N. D.

AVOCADO SHRIMP BOAT

2 large avocados
Lemon juice
2 medium tomatoes
1 tsp. sugar
1/2 tsp. salt
Black pepper
1/8 tsp. turmeric
1 tsp. chopped parsley
2 green onions, minced

Sprig fresh mint, chopped
  fine
1/2 Tbsp. vinegar
1/2 Tbsp. water
Dash of cayenne pepper
2 Tbsp. French dressing
1 c. cooked shrimp
Watercress

Halve the avocados, scoop out pulp, dice. Rub shells
with lemon juice and set aside. Peel and chop up the tomatoes. Mix all remaining ingredients except shrimp and
watercress. Pour over the tomatoes and avocado pieces.
Mix carefully. Add shrimp last. Pile in shells of the avocado
and top with watercress sprigs; chill. Makes 4 servings.

BEAN SALAD

1 can yellow beans,
  drained
1 can green beans,
  drained

1 can kidney beans, drained
1 large onion or 5 small
  onions
2 small or 1 large green
  pepper

Dressing:

1/2 c. apple cider vinegar
  or white
1/2 c. brown sugar

2 1/2 c. salad oil
Pinch of salt

Mix cold and pour over vegetables. Let stand at least
2 hours. Best to set overnight. (6 to 8 servings)
Marie Miller, St. Paul, Mn.

3 BEAN SALAD

1 (#2) can green beans
1 (#2) can yellow beans
1 (#2) can kidney beans
1 small jar pimento
3/4 c. French cut onion
  rings

3/4 c. sugar
1/3 c. salad oil
2/3 c. vinegar
1 tsp. salt
1 tsp. pepper

1748-81

Drain beans. Mix with onion and pepper. Combine remaining ingredients for dressing and pour over vegetables - marinate several hours or overnight.
Kay Buzzel, Marshall, Mn.

BLUEBERRY JELLO MOLD

1 (3 oz.) pkg. black
  raspberry jello
1 (3 oz.) pkg. orange
  jello
3 c. water

3 Tbsp. lemon juice
3 Tbsp. sugar
1 can Wilderness blueberry
  pie filling

Make jello, add juice, sugar and blueberry mix. Fill large Tupperware mold.
Mary Paul, Minneapolis, Mn.

IT'S THE BERRIES - BLUEBERRY SALAD

Dissolve 1 large package jello (grape) in half the amount of water called for. Add 1 can blueberry pie filling mix. Chill. Serve with Dream Whip if desired.
Kathaleen Bischof, St. Cloud, Mn.

BROCCOLI AND CAULIFLOWER SALAD

1 bunch broccoli flowerets
1 head of cauliflower
1 c. celery

1 onion or 8 green onions
1 c. sour cream
1 c. salad dressing

Make at least 24 hours ahead.
Diane Schmitz, St. Cloud, Mn.

BUTTER PECAN'S SALAD

1 (9 oz.) ctn. Cool Whip
1 pkg. instant butter
  pecan pudding mix
1 large can crushed
  pineapple, undrained

1 c. miniature marshmallows
1/2 c. pecans
1/2 c. Bitso Brickle (Heath
  Brand)
Small amount of Cool Whip to
  top salad with

Put the can of crushed pineapple (juice and all), the

cup of miniature marshmallows, 1/4 cup Bitso Brickle and the 1/2 cup pecans in a bowl. Then add the softened Cool Whip and butter pecan pudding mix. Mix thoroughly. Top bowl with a ring of Cool Whip and sprinkle 1/4 cup Bitso Brickle on top of salad and Cool Whip. Refrigerate.

Gloria Smith, Windom, Mn.

CABBAGE SALAD

1 small onion, cut fine
1 green pepper, chopped
  (optional)

1 head cabbage, shredded
Salt to taste

Mix and let stand for 3 hours. Boil for 3 minutes the following:

1/2 c. vinegar
1/2 c. sugar

1/2 tsp. dry mustard
1/2 tsp. celery seed

Cool and pour over cabbage - let stand until next day.

Bonnie Steffens, St. Cloud, Mn.

CAULIFLOWER-BROCCOLI SALAD

1 head cauliflower (buds
  only)

1 broccoli (buds only)
1 bunch green onions

Chop very fine.

1 large (10 oz.) pkg.
  frozen peas
1 c. mayonnaise

1 c. sour cream
1 1/2 tsp. garlic salt

Mix all together - let marinate overnight.

Peni Lundeen, St. Cloud, Mn.

CAULIFLOWER - BROCCOLI SALAD

1 medium onion, chopped
1 large or 2 small bunches
  broccoli

1 medium head cauliflower
1 lb. carrots, sliced

All vegetables should be bite size.

Salad Dressing: Mix together -

1 c. mayonnaise
1 c. salad dressing

1 Tbsp. Worcestershire sauce
2 Tbsp. milk

Stir together vegetables and dressing. Refrigerate overnight before serving.

Mary Erickson, Detroit Lakes, Mn.

CHEESE PINEAPPLE SALAD

1 pkg. lime jello
1 pkg. lemon jello

2 c. hot water

Mix and let get cold. Add 1 (No. 2) can crushed and drained pineapple. Let set slightly. Add:

1 c. canned milk (I
  whip this)
2 Tbsp. horseradish

1/2 c. chopped nuts
10 oz. cottage cheese
1 c. thick mayonnaise

Mix and chill in mold. Makes 20 small molds.

Harriett Haggard, Anoka, Mn.

IT'S THE BERRIES - CHERRY SALAD

Dissolve 1 large package jello (cherry or lemon) in half the amount of water called for. Add 1 can blueberry pie filling mix. Chill. Serve with Dream Whip if desired.

Kathaleen Bischof, St. Cloud, Mn.

CHERRY SALAD

1 can condensed milk
1 can cherry pie filling
1 large can crushed
  pineapple (do not drain)

1/2 c. chopped nuts
1 large ctn. Cool Whip
1/2 bag miniature
  marshmallows

Mix in same order as above. Garnish with chopped nuts.

Mary Ann Ohman, Fargo, N. D.; Mary Jo Conneran

CHICKEN SALAD

3 c. diced chicken
1 c. shredded carrots
2 hard-cooked eggs

1 c. diced celery
3 Tbsp. minced onion
1 c. salad dressing

Mix and refrigerate overnight. Just before serving, add 1 (No. 2 1/2) can shoestring potatoes.

Elsa Ditty, St. Cloud, Mn.

54

CITRUS SALAD

2 c. boiling water
1 small can crushed
   pineapple, not drained

2 (3 oz.) pkg. jello
   (2 lemon or 1 lemon and
   1 orange)

Mix together in a serving bowl and let it thicken a little. Add 1 can instant lemon pie filling and 1 (9 ounce) carton Cool Whip. Mix together until creamy. Pour into a 9x12 inch glass pan. Place in the refrigerator until it is set.
                Jean Taylor, Grand Forks, N. D.

COLE SLAW

In large bowl, mix:
1 c. mayonnaise
2 Tbsp. milk
2 Tbsp. cider vinegar

1 1/2 tsp. sugar
1/2 tsp. salt
1/8 tsp. pepper

Add 1 medium head cabbage (finely shredded) and 1 large carrot. Toss gently until well coated. Cover and refrigerate about 1 hour.
                June Neal, Sauk Centre, Mn.

FAVORITE SLAW
(Recipe used 55 years)

2 1/2 c. finely shredded
   cabbage, salted
1/3 c. water

1/3 c. sugar
1/3 c. vinegar
1/8 tsp. ground black pepper

Boil together last 4 ingredients for 5 minutes. Pour over cabbage. Let stand about 30 minutes. Cover with saucer to hold cabbage in mixture.
                Ruth Braun

HOT SLAW

Cabbage
Eggs
Butter
Milk

Salt
Paprika
Pepper

Shred cabbage - place in ice water. Heat 1 cup milk in double boiler. Add 3 or 4 egg yolks, well beaten. Stir and

1748-81

cook. When cool, add a little vinegar. Mix with drained
cabbage. Add seasoning.
Darlene Lee

CRANBERRY SALAD

Put 1 small can crushed pineapple in 2 cup measure.
Fill with boiling water. Pour over a package of lemon jello
and stir to dissolve. Chop 2 cups raw cranberries, add
1 chopped orange- no rind. Add 1 cup sugar, let stand
until jello mixture starts to thicken. Mix the two together
and mold.
Thelma Olson, St. Cloud, Mn.

CRANBERRY MARSHMALLOW SALAD

1 qt. cranberries	2 Tbsp. lemon juice
1 c. water	1/2 c. celery, cut fine
1 c. sugar	1/4 c. walnut meats, broken
1/4 lb. pkg. marshmallows, cut into halves	

Wash and pick over cranberries. Add water and cook
until berries burst. Remove from flame and with a wooden
spoon, press through sieve. To the cranberry puree, add
the sugar and then cook for 2 minutes. Remove from flame
and add the marshmallows, folding over and over until
marshmallows are partially melted. Set aside to cool; then
add lemon juice, chopped celery and nutmeats. Pour into
individual molds and place in refrigerator. Chill until
firm. Unmold on crisp lettuce and serve with mayonnaise.
Serves 7 to 8. Wouldn't this salad be grand served with
roast turkey, oyster dressing, candied sweet potatoes,
buttered broccoli and hot rolls. I have used this recipe
served with whipped cream for a dessert.
Erma P. Swanson, Minneapolis, Mn.

FROZEN CRANBERRY SALAD

1 c. cranberry jello	3 Tbsp. lemon juice

Fork cranberries to a mush and add juice. Spoon into
paper baking cups in muffin tins. Whip 1 cup cream, add
1/4 cup mayonnaise, 1/2 cup powdered sugar and 1 cup

chopped nuts. Spoon over cranberry mixture in cups and freeze.

Char Bailey, St. Paul, Mn.

CREAMY FRUIT SALAD

1 (16 oz.) can fruit
cocktail, undrained
1 (16 oz.) can pineapple
tidbits, undrained

1 pkg. instant vanilla or
coconut pudding mix
2 c. miniature marshmallows
3/4 c. whipped topping

Combine fruits with pudding and stir well to blend. Add marshmallows and topping. Bananas can be added if desired. Keeps well 2 to 3 days in refrigerator.

CRISP MACARONI SALAD

3/4 c. macaroni
1 c. ripe olives
1 (6 1/2 or 7 oz.) can
tuna
2 hard-cooked eggs

2 c. finely shredded cabbage
1/2 c. mayonnaise
2 tsp. prepared mustard
2 Tbsp. vinegar
1 tsp. salt

Cook macaroni in boiling salted water until tender. Drain and rinse thoroughly with cold water. Cut olives from pits into large pieces. Drain oil from tuna and flake coarsely. Dice eggs. Combine macaroni, olives, tuna, eggs and cabbage. Blend in mayonnaise, mustard, vinegar and salt and toss lightly with salad mixture. Serves 4 to 6 generously.

CHRISTMAS CRANBERRY SALAD

2 boxes cherry jello
dissolved in 1 1/2 c.
hot water, let partially
set
1 1/2 c. cranberries,
chopped

1 1/2 c. apples, chopped
1 1/2 c. crushed pineapple
1 c. sugar poured over the
fruit and left for 2 hours

When jello is partially set, whip until foamy. Fold in 1 cup cream, whipped. Fold in fruit. Pour into mold and let set.

Mary Ann Ohman, Fargo, N. D.

CHRISTMAS RIBBON SALAD

Dissolve 2 packages lime jello according to package directions and pour into large cake pan (9x13 inches) and chill until set. Pour 1 package lemon jello into top of double boiler and dissolve in 1 cup boiling water. Add 1/2 cup marshmallows (7) and stir into jello until melted. Remove from heat and add 1 cup pineapple juice and 1 (8 ounce) package cream cheese. Beat with rotary beater until blended. Add 1 (No. 2) can crushed pineapple which has been drained, to above mixture and fold in 1 cup mayonnaise and 1 cup whipped cream. Chill until thickened and pour over lime layer. Chill. Dissolve 2 packages of cherry jello according to package directions and chill in bowl until partially set. Then pour over chilled salad. Chill. Serve on lettuce leaf. Very pretty.

CUCUMBER ONION JELLO MOLD

1/2 c. cucumber, diced	1 1/2 tsp. vinegar
3/4 c. cottage cheese	3/4 tsp. salt
1 pkg. lemon-lime jello	1/2 c. Miracle Whip
4 green onions, chopped	1/4 tsp. paprika
1 1/2 c. hot water	

Shirley Peterson, Willmar, Mn.

DAYTON'S HOT TURKEY SALAD
(Doubled)

4 c. cooked diced turkey (or chicken)	4 Tbsp. lemon juice
4 c. diced celery	1 c. grated Cheddar cheese
1 c. toasted slivered almonds	2 c. mayonnaise
2 tsp. diced onion	1 tsp. salt
	2 c. crushed potato chips

Mix all ingredients except potato chips together and place in baking dish. Top with crushed potato chips and place in preheated oven at 400° for 15 minutes. Makes 12 servings - serve with fruit cups or salad and roll.

Betty Carlson

DELICIOUS SALAD

2 boxes shell macaroni,
   cook as directed, drain,
   rinse
1 can French style green
   beans, drained
1 can diced carrots,
   drained

1 can red kidney beans,
   drained and rinsed off
1 box frozen peas, cooked,
   drained and cooled
1/2 c. onion, chopped
1/2 c. celery, chopped
3/4 c. green pepper, chopped

Mix 1 pint Miracle Whip, 1 big teaspoon prepared mustard, 1 cup half & half, 1/2 cup sugar. Mix this and then toss gently with salad ingredients. Add 2 cups chopped ham, chicken or beef. Refrigerate, covered. You can make this 2 - 4 days ahead. Keeps a long time in refrigerator.
Margaret Hulst, Waltham, Mn.

EASY SUMMER SALAD

25 watermelon balls
25 cantaloupe balls

25 green grapes

Mix with 1 can Wilderness peach pie filling. Chill.
Darlene Lee

FLUFFY GELATIN SALAD

1 (1 lb. 4 oz.) can crushed
   pineapple, drained
1 c. small curd creamed
   cottage cheese

2 c. miniature marshmallows
1 1/2 c. frozen whipped
   topping, thawed
1 (3 oz.) pkg. lime flavored
   gelatin

Combine pineapple, cottage cheese and marshmallows. Fold in whipped topping. Sprinkle dry gelatin over mixture and blend well. Refrigerate. Serves 5 to 6. Salad may be varied by use of different fruits and other flavors of gelatin.
Erma P. Swanson, Minneapolis, Mn.

FRUIT SALAD

1 c. buttermilk   1 pkg. instant vanilla pudding

Mix together. Add 8 or 9 ounces Cool Whip. Add:

2 (16 oz.) cans mixed   1 small can pineapple tidbits
   fruits for salads,   or chunks, drained
   drained

Fresh fruit can be added, such as cantaloupe and green grapes. Just before serving, add 15 chocolate covered graham crackers. Serves 8.

Sue Peterson, Grand Forks, N. D.

FRUITED CHEESE SALAD

1 qt. frozen whipped   3 c. cottage cheese
   cream, thawed

Blend together, then blend in 2 (3 ounce) packages orange-pineapple jello (dry). Then stir in:

1 (11 oz.) can Mandarin   1 (13 1/2 oz.) can pineapple
   oranges   tidbits

Kathy Neels, St. Cloud, Mn.

FRUIT SALAD

1 c. cocoanut   1 c. Mandarin oranges,
1 c. miniature marshmallows   drained
1 c. pineapple tidbits,   1 c. sour cream
   drained

Mix well drained fruits together. Add 2 tablespoons sugar to sour cream if desired. Pour over fruit and mix lightly. Chill for several hours before serving. Serves 4 - 6.

Darlene Schlottman, St. Cloud, Mn.

FROZEN CABBAGE

Shred 1 medium head cabbage, sprinkle with 2 teaspoons salt. Let stand 1 hour. Grind together:

1 green pepper   6 carrots

Add to cabbage. Boil:

1 c. water   1 c. vinegar
2 c. sugar   1 tsp. mustard seed

Cool and pour over cabbage. Put into containers and freeze.

Darlene Lee

FROZEN CRANAPPLE SALAD

In blender chop raw cranberries to make 1 cup.

2 small red apples with   1 c. whipping cream
  peelings, shredded   1/2 c. chopped walnuts or
1 c. miniature marshmallows   pecans
3/4 c. sugar

Combine cranberries, apples, marshmallows and sugar. Allow to stand overnight in refrigerator. Whip cream until stiff. Fold in nuts. Combine with cranberry apple mixture and spoon into a Bundt pan or large mold. Freeze 10 to 12 hours.

Ginnie Andersen, St. Paul, Mn.

FROZEN FRUIT CUP

1 large can concentrated   1 (#2) can crushed pineapple
  orange juice   3 bananas, crushed
1 small can concentrated   1/2 c. sugar or more accord-
  frozen lemonade   ing to taste
2 c. ginger ale or 7-Up   Fruits added: Bing cherries,
                                    grapes, peaches, canta-
                                    loupe (not watermelon)

Spoon into Dixie Solo Cups and freeze. Can be used for breakfast or dessert for a dinner, or whatever.

Lila M. Nelson, Windom, Mn.

1748-81

FROZEN CHERRY SALAD

1 can cherry pie filling
1 (14 oz.) can Borden's
   sweetened condensed milk

1 (13 oz.) can crushed
   pineapple, drained
1/2 tsp. banana flavoring
1/2 tsp. cherry flavoring

Mix all together and fold in 1 quart (large size) Cool Whip. Pour into 9x13 inch pan and freeze.
Dolly Nokes, Willmar, Mn.

FROZEN GRAPE SALAD

2 (3 oz.) pkg. cream
   cheese
2 Tbsp. mayonnaise
2 Tbsp. pineapple juice
   or syrup from pineapple
2 c. Tokay grapes, halved
   and seeded

24 marshmallows, quartered,
   or 2 c. miniature
1 (#2) can (2 1/2 c.) pineapple bits, drained
1 c. heavy cream, whipped

Soften the cream cheese; blend with mayonnaise. Beat in the pineapple syrup. Add marshmallows and drained pineapple bits. Fold in whipped cream and grapes. Pour into a 1 quart refrigerator tray. Freeze until firm. Cut into squares. Makes 8 servings.
Mrs. W. E. Gollehon, Fargo, N. D.

GREEN SALAD MOLD

1 env. unflavored gelatin
1 Tbsp. sugar
1 tsp. salt
1/8 tsp. pepper
1 3/4 c. water
1/4 c. vinegar

1 Tbsp. lemon juice
1/4 c. chopped scallions
1 c. shredded raw spinach
1 c. chopped celery
1/4 c. shredded raw carrots

Mix gelatin, sugar, salt and pepper thoroughly in a saucepan. Add 1/2 cup of the water. Place over low heat, stirring constantly until gelatin is dissolved. Remove from heat and stir in remaining 1 1/4 cups water, vinegar and lemon juice. Chill mixture to unbeaten egg white consistency. Fold in scallions, spinach, celery and carrots. Turn into a 3 cup mold or individual molds and chill until firm. Unmold by dipping mold into warm water to depth of the

gelatin. Loosen around edge with tip of a paring knife. **Place**
serving dish on top of mold; turn upside down. Shake,
holding dish tightly to mold. Garnish with tomatoes and
olives. Serves 6 (29 calories per serving).

GREEN VEGETABLE SALAD MOLD

1 pkg. lime gelatin
1/2 c. water
1 can cream of asparagus
  soup
1/2 c. salad dressing or
  mayonnaise

1 Tbsp. vinegar
1 tsp. grated onion
Dash of pepper
1/2 c. shredded cucumber,
  unpared
1/4 c. diced celery
1 Tbsp. snipped parsley

Mix gelatin and water in saucepan. Gradually blend in
soup. Heat and stir to dissolve gelatin. Add salad dressing,
vinegar, onion and pepper. Beat smooth with electric or
rotary beater. Chill until partially set. Turn into large
chilled bowl and beat until thick and frothy. Fold in the
vegetables: Spoon into 5 cup ring mold or 6 to 8 individual
molds. Chill until firm.

ICE CREAM FRUIT SALAD

1 (3 oz.) pkg. lemon
  jello
1 pt. vanilla ice cream
1 can fruit cocktail, chopped

1 c. juice from fruit
  cocktail, boiled
1/2 c. chopped nuts

Dissolve jello in hot juice, let cool very few minutes.
Add ice cream - stir till smooth. Add fruit cocktail and
chopped nuts. Turn into mold and chill until firm.
Shirley Way, Minneapolis, Mn.

LAYERED DELIGHT SALAD

1 head lettuce, shredded
3 - 4 stalks celery
3 - 4 green onions, cut
  up
1 can water chestnuts,
  sliced

1 pkg. frozen peas
2 c. mayonnaise
2 Tbsp. sugar
Cheese, grated
Bacon, crumbled
Egg (hard-boiled), sliced

In large bowl layer first 4 items. Frozen peas should be rinsed in cold water and drained. Over the peas spread mayonnaise. Sprinkle sugar and then cheese. Let stand in refrigerator 8 hours or overnight. Garnish with crumbled bacon and sliced, hard-boiled egg. Do not toss.

Carol Arndt, Windom, Mn.

LAYERED LETTUCE SALAD

Chopped lettuce
Chopped onion
Chopped celery
1 pkg. frozen peas,
   thawed, drained well

1 can sliced water
   chestnuts
1/2 lb. Mozzarella cheese

Layer above mentioned ingredients in salad bowl. Mix together 1 cup salad dressing with 1 teaspoon sugar. Frost salad with dressing, cover with foil and leave in refrigerator overnight. Serves 8.

Rosa Gerrels, Minneapolis, Mn.

LAYERED LETTUCE SALAD

1 head lettuce
1 c. celery, diced
4 eggs, hard-cooked and
   sliced
1 (10 oz.) pkg. frozen
   peas
1/2 c. diced green pepper

1 sweet onion (medium size),
   chopped
8 slices bacon, fried and
   diced
2 c. mayonnaise
2 Tbsp. sugar
4 oz. grated Cheddar cheese

Tear the cleaned crisp lettuce into small bite sized pieces and place in a 9x12 inch dish. Layer rest of ingredients in the order given, do not cook peas. Add the sugar to mayonnaise and spread over top as you would frosting. Top with grated cheese. Cover and refrigerate for 8 to 10 hours. Bacon bits can be used for bacon.

Rita Aaker, Marshall, Mn.

24-HOUR SALAD

Place in a 13x9x2 inch dish:

1 head shredded lettuce
4 stalks celery, sliced thin
1 small red onion, sliced
 thin

1 pkg. frozen peas, uncooked,
 rinsed and drained
1 can water chestnuts,
 drained and sliced
1 green pepper, chopped

Cover with 2 cups mayonnaise mixed with 2 tablespoons sugar. Sprinkle Parmesan cheese liberally. Cover with Saran Wrap - refrigerate overnight. Before serving, fry 1/3 pound bacon until crisp, drain. Break into bits and sprinkle over top. Slice 4 hard-boiled eggs over top for garnish.
Dena Stoddard, Minneapolis, Mn.

24 HOUR LAYER SALAD

In 9x13 inch Pyrex cake pan, put: First layer - 1 head lettuce (shredded). Second layer - 1/4 cup celery (chopped fine). Third layer - 1/4 - 1/2 cup diced sweet onion. Fourth layer - 1 (10 ounce) package frozen peas (raw). Fifth layer - 1 pint mayonnaise (spread around over all ingredients above). Then sprinkle on 2 tablespoons sugar. Sixth layer - 4 - 6 ounces shredded cheese. Seventh layer - 8 strips crisp fried bacon, crumbled. Cover with plastic or foil and refrigerate at least 5 to 8 hours. Lettuce stays crisp and delicious. This salad keeps several days. May use 1/2 cup chopped green pepper between celery and onions. Bac-O's also work very well in place of bacon.
Mike and Vonnie Bakke, Willmar, Mn.

7 LAYER SALAD

In a 9x13 inch Tupperware pan, layer the following:

1/2 head of lettuce,
 chopped
1/2 head of cauliflower,
 broken up
1/4 c. onion, chopped

1/3 c. celery, chopped
1/3 c. carrots, shredded
1/4 c. sugar
1/4 c. Parmesan cheese

Spread 1 cup salad dressing completely over the top. Refrigerate at least 2 hours. May top with bacon bits, croutons or hard-boiled egg slices. May also use grated sharp cheese or desired cheese instead of Parmesan cheese.

Fern Groskreutz, Service Representative, Litchfield, Mn.

MAKE AHEAD LETTUCE SALAD

In 9x13 inch pan:

Layer of cut up lettuce (thick layer - more than a head)

Layer of celery, diced (about 2 c.)

Layer of green pepper, diced (2 small or 1 large)

Layer of green onions (1/2 doz. whole, green as well as white)

Layer of water chestnuts, sliced

1 (10 oz.) pkg. frozen peas, uncooked, sprinkled over

Dressing:

2 c. Mayonnaise or Miracle Whip

3 Tbsp. sugar

Spread over top of salad. Sprinkle with 2 - 3 ounces Parmesan cheese. Let stand 24 hours or overnight. When ready to serve, sprinkle with crumbled bacon.

Diane Schmitz, St. Cloud, Mn.

LEMON FILLING SALAD

1 can Wilderness lemon pie filling

1 can Mandarin oranges, drained

1 can fruit cocktail, drained

1 can pineapple tidbits, drained

2 c. miniature marshmallows

1 (9 oz.) ctn. Cool Whip

Add Cool Whip to pie filling and blend well. Fold the well drained fruit and marshmallows in. This salad can be made the night before you want to serve it. Serves about 20.

Marilyn Helgeson, Fargo, N. D.

LEMON JELLO SALAD

Set 1 package of lemon jello with 2 cups boiling water. Set until thick.

Top for salad: Take juice of an 8 ounce can of pineapple and enough water to make 1 cup. Add -

2 Tbsp. flour
1/2 c. sugar

1 egg, beaten
2 Tbsp. butter

Boil until thick - cool. While cooling, mix into the lemon jello, the following:

2 bananas, diced
1 c. miniature marshmallows

1 (8 oz.) can pineapple, drained

Whip 1 cup cream and add with "top" over jello.
Mrs. W. A. Carlson

MACARONI SALAD

Dice:
4 carrots
4 celery sticks

1 large onion
4 dill pickles

Add:
2 cans tuna

1 can peas

Boil about 2 small boxes shell noodles until soft.

Dressing:

2 1/2 c. mayonnaise
1 1/2 Tbsp. mustard

1/4 c. milk
1 Tbsp. Worcestershire sauce

Mix over all ingredients and chill.
C. Landwehr, Minneapolis, Mn.

HEARTY MACARONI SALAD

1 (7 oz.) box shell
   macaroni, cooked in
   salted water, rinse in
   cold water, drain, cool

1 (10 oz.) box frozen mixed
   vegetables, cook in salted
   water, drain, cool

1748-81

4 hard-boiled eggs, cooled, cut into pieces
1/2 c. celery, cut into small pieces
1/2 c. sweet gherkin pickles, cut into small pieces
1/4 c. chopped red onion (or other onion)
1 rounded c. ham, cut into pieces
1/2 c. mayonnaise
1/2 c. Miracle Whip salad dressing
1/4 c. sweet pickle liquid
1/2 tsp. salt
1/8 tsp. pepper
2 tsp. prepared mustard

Put macaroni in large bowl and add vegetables, celery, pickles, onion and meat. Mix together the mayonnaise, Miracle Whip, pickle liquid, salt, pepper, mustard. Stir into macaroni mixture. Fold in eggs gently. Chill well.
Norma Haugland, Fargo, N. D.

MANDARIN DUET SALAD

Orange Jello Ring:

6 oz. orange flavored gelatin
2 c. boiling water
1 pt. orange sherbet
1 can Mandarin oranges, drained

Dissolve gelatin in water. Immediately add orange sherbet and stir until melted. Add oranges and pour into mold.

Ambroisa Fruit Salad (center):

1 can Mandarin oranges, drained
1 (13 oz.) can pineapple chunks, drained
1 c. flaked coconut
1 c. miniature marshmallows
1 c. commercial sour cream or 1/2 c. whipped cream

Rosa Gerrels, Minneapolis, Mn.

MARINATED VEGETABLE SALAD

2 qt. cherry tomatoes
2 lb. mushrooms
1 (12 oz.) can black olives, drained
1 (10 oz.) can green olives, drained
2 (8 oz.) cans water chestnuts, drained
2 (8 1/2 oz.) cans artichoke hearts, drained
2 heads cauliflower, cut up

1 large head fresh broccoli, cut up

2 (8 oz.) jars mild peppers, drained

Marinade:

1 1/2 c. red wine vinegar with garlic

Salt and pepper to taste
1 c. sugar

Place vegetables in plastic container with lid. Pour marinade over. Chill for several days before serving.
Kathy Bischof, St. Cloud, Mn.

MOCK CHICKEN SALAD

7 lb. pork shoulder, cooked and cut into small cubes
7 lb. veal shoulder, cooked and cut into small cubes
1 c. French dressing

8 c. apples, cored, cut into cubes
8 c. chopped celery
1 1/2 c. ripe olives, chopped
3 c. salad dressing
1/4 c. (2 lemons) lemon juice
1/2 tsp. thyme
2 Tbsp. salt

Pour French dressing over meat. Mix thoroughly until each piece is coated. Let stand in refrigerator at least 2 hours to blend flavors. Add apples, celery and olives to meat. Combine salad dressing, lemon juice, thyme and salt. Pour over mixture. Stir lightly to blend. Keep salad in refrigerator until ready to serve. Serve on crisp lettuce or other salad greens. Yield: 50 servings (3/4 cup per serving).

MOLDED CHICKEN SALAD (OR TUNA)

2 env. Knox unflavored gelatine
1 c. cold water
1 (10 1/2 oz.) can condensed cream of celery soup
1/2 tsp. salt

2 Tbsp. lemon juice
1 tsp. instant minced onion
1 c. salad dressing
2 Tbsp. diced pimento
1 c. diced celery
2 c. diced cooked chicken

Sprinkle gelatine over water in medium saucepan. Place over low heat; stir constantly until gelatine dissolves, about 4 minutes. Remove from heat; stir in undiluted cream of

celery soup, salt, lemon juice, instant minced onion and salad dressing; beat with rotary beater until smooth, chill, stirring occasionally until mixture mounds when dropped from a spoon. Add celery and chicken. Turn into a 6 cup loaf pan or mold. Chill until firm. (6 servings)
Marie Doty, Austin, Mn.

MOM'S WILTED LETTUCE

Lettuce (leaf)
6 - 8 green onions, sliced
3/4 c. sugar

3/4 c. vinegar
1/4 c. water
6 - 8 slices bacon

Cut lettuce, add sliced onion and sugar - toss. Fry bacon till crisp - remove from pan. Crumble. Add vinegar and water to bacon grease - let come to boil. Pour over lettuce, onion and bacon, mix well. Serve at once.
Chet Way, Minneapolis, Mn.

ORIENTAL SALAD

1/2 lb. medium sized shrimp
3/4 c. corn oil
1/4 c. vinegar
1 tsp. salt
1/4 tsp. pepper
2 hard-cooked eggs, chopped fine

1 (3 1/4 oz.) can sardines, drained
2 c. cold, cooked rice
1/2 c. cashew nuts, chopped
1/4 c. finely chopped onion
2 Tbsp. chopped parsley
2 Tbsp. chili sauce

Cook and clean shrimp. Shake corn oil, vinegar, salt and pepper in tightly covered jar; pour 1/2 cup over shrimp. Chill. Chill eggs and sardines. Drain shrimp. Mix rice, cashews and mound on lettuce leaves on plate. Sprinkle with egg. Arrange shrimp and sardines around rice. Mix chili sauce, onion and parsley into remaining dressing. Serve over salad. Serves 6.

OVERNIGHT FRUIT SALAD

1 (#2) can crushed
  pineapple, undrained
1 (3 3/4 oz.) pkg. instant
  pudding, lemon,
  coconut cream or pistachio

1 large can fruit cocktail,
  well drained
2 c. miniature marshmallows
1 (8 oz.) ctn. frozen
  whipped topping, thawed

Mix dry instant pudding into undrained pineapple. Stir until thick. Add drained fruit cocktail and marshmallows. Stir in whipped topping. Put into refrigerator overnight or several hours until well chilled. This is pretty made with pistachio pudding. Extra maraschino cherries, cut and drained, can be added for color.
>
> Liz Tuft, St. Paul, Mn.

OVERNIGHT SALAD

1 lb. grapes
1 lb. marshmallows

1 small can crushed pineapple

Cook until thick:
4 egg yolks, beaten
1/4 c. cream

1/4 tsp. salt
Juice of 1 lemon

Mix with fruit. When cool, add 1/2 pint whipped cream and let stand overnight. Add 1 cup chopped nuts when ready to serve.
>
> Stan and Phylis Patyk, Sauk Centre, Mn.

OVERNIGHT FRUIT SALAD

1 pkg. tiny macaroni
  rings
Red coloring
1 can pineapple chunks
  (save juice)
1 can fruit cocktail

1 small bottle maraschino
  cherries
1 c. sugar
2 Tbsp. flour
2 tsp. lemon juice
2 eggs, beaten

Cook macaroni rings in salted water. When almost done, add food coloring to desired shade. Drain pineapple chunks, fruit cocktail, cherries. Cook until thick pineapple juice, sugar, flour, lemon juice and eggs. Cool. Pour over fruit and macaroni and let stand overnight. Before serving, add 1/2 pint whipped cream with little sugar and vanilla.
>
> Marie Miller, St. Paul, Mn.

OVERNIGHT FRUIT SALAD

1 (#2) can undrained, crushed pineapple
1 (3 3/4 oz.) pkg. instant pudding (lemon, coconut cream or pistachio)
1 large can fruit cocktail, well drained
2 c. miniature marshmallows
1 (8 oz.) ctn. frozen whipped topping

Mix pudding into undrained pineapple. Mix until thick. Add drained fruit cocktail and marshmallows. Fold in whipped topping. Put into refrigerator overnight. This is pretty made with pistachio pudding. Maraschino cherries added on top for color.
Florence Peine, St. Paul, Mn.

EASY ORANGE SALAD

8 inch pan or mold
2 small pkg. orange jello or 1 large pkg.
1 1/2 c. hot water
1 pt. orange sherbet
1 or 2 cans Mandarin oranges, drained

Dissolve jello in hot water and then add the sherbet. Add drained Mandarin oranges and mold.
Marilyn Helgeson, Fargo, N. D.

FROZEN PEA SALAD

Cook frozen peas. Gently toss with equal amounts of chopped celery, green onions, chopped. Add mayonnaise, black olives, sliced. Just before serving, add shoestring potatoes. (Can also add leftover chicken, turkey, ham.)
Karen Rupert, St. Cloud, Mn.

PEA SALAD

6 c. torn iceberg lettuce
1 c. chopped celery
4 hard-cooked eggs, sliced
1 (16 oz.) can Green Giant Brand Kitchen Sliced green beans
1 c. chopped green pepper
1/3 c. sliced onion rings
1 (17 oz.) can LeSeuer Brand small early peas
2 c. real mayonnaise
1 c. Cheddar cheese, coarsely grated

In a large salad bowl, layer the lettuce, celery, green beans, eggs, green pepper, onion and peas in order given. Spread mayonnaise over the top of the salad; sprinkle with grated cheese. Cover well and let stand for 8 hours or overnight.

Marge Johnson, Minneapolis, Mn.

PINEAPPLE GLOW SALAD

2 (8 oz.) cans crushed
  pineapple in juice
1 (6 oz.) pkg. jello
  (orange, lemon or lime)
1/2 tsp. salt
2 c. boiling water
2 Tbsp. lemon juice
1 c. finely shredded carrot

Drain pineapple, measuring juice. Add water to juice to make 1 1/2 cups. Dissolve gelatin and salt in boiling water. Add measured liquid and lemon juice. Chill until thickened. Fold in pineapple and carrot. Spoon into 6 cup mold or individual molds. Chill until firm, about 3 hours. Unmold. Serve with salad greens and mayonnaise if desired. Makes 5 cups or 10 servings.

Bev Larson, Bismarck, N. D.

PISTACHIO SALAD

Mix:
18 oz. ctn. Cool Whip   1 pkg. pistachio pudding

Add:
1 (16 oz.) can crushed   3 c. miniature marshmallows
  pineapple, drained

Cool 1 hour or longer before serving.
Diane Schmitz

PISTACHIO SALAD

1 (3 oz.) pkg. pistachio
  pudding mix (use dry)
1 (#2) can crushed
  pineapple and juice
1/2 c. chopped walnuts
1 c. miniature marshmallows
1 (4 oz.) ctn. Cool Whip

Mix gently. Refrigerate 8 hours.
Elsie Ekblad, St. Paul, Mn.

1748-81

CHARLIES CAFE POTATO SALAD

5 c. cooked, diced
  potatoes (7 medium or
  large)
2 tsp. vinegar
2 tsp. sugar
1/4 c. chopped green
  onions or chives
2 - 3 tsp. salt

1/4 c. chopped celery
4 hard-boiled eggs, sliced or
  chopped
*1 c. Hellmann's mayonnaise
1/2 c. sour cream
2 Tbsp. chopped pimento
Black ripe olives, diced
  (optional)

Mix sugar and vinegar. Sprinkle over potatoes and allow to set about 30 minutes. Mix mayonnaise and sour cream. Fold into ingredients. Add salt to taste. Refrigerate overnight for best flavor.

*Hellmann's mayonnaise is crucial to the taste of this potato salad. Use their regular mayonnaise, not the Spin Blend.

GERMAN POTATO SALAD

1 c. diced bacon
1 c. chopped onion
1/2 tsp. pepper
2/3 c. sugar
1 1/3 c. water
1 c. diced celery (optional)

3 Tbsp. flour
3 tsp. salt
2/3 c. vinegar
8 c. sliced potatoes,
  cooked in skins

Fry bacon, drain. Use 4 tablespoons fat in skillet. Add celery, onions, salt and flour. Cook gently, add sugar and vinegar, pepper and water. Bring to a boil, pour over potatoes and bacon. Cover and bake in 3 quart casserole 30 minutes at 350°. Serves 15.

Carol Watnemo, St. Paul, Mn.

HOT GERMAN POTATO SALAD

6 medium sized (2 lb.)
  potatoes
1/4 lb. bacon, diced
2 Tbsp. finely chopped
  onion
1/4 c. water
1 Tbsp. flour

1/4 c. vinegar
1 tsp. salt
2 tsp. sugar
1/4 tsp. ground black pepper
1 Tbsp. finely chopped
  parsley (optional)

1. Boil potatoes in skins until fork tender. Peel and slice while hot. Keep warm. 2. Fry bacon until golden; add onion and cook, stirring 3 minutes. Do not drain. Add flour-water, vinegar, salt, sugar and pepper to bacon mixture - heat to boiling. Pour over hot sliced potatoes, toss gently. Serve warm or hot. (4 - 6 servings)

Ruth Braun, Owatonna, Mn.

POTATO SALAD

2 c. Miracle Whip
1 c. sour cream
1/2 c. half & half
1/4 c. sweet pickle juice
1/2 c. chopped celery
1/4 c. chopped onion
8 - 10 cooked, chopped
  eggs

3 Tbsp. prepared mustard
3 Tbsp. sugar
1 Tbsp. vinegar
8 - 10 lb. cooked potatoes
  in salt
1/4 c. chopped sweet pickle
  relish

Mix dressing, add to warm cut up potatoes, celery, onion, relish, eggs. Toss lightly with spatula. Cool for 1 day.

Alice Carrigan, Windom, Mn.

POTATO SALAD WESTERN STYLE

6 cooked, sliced potatoes
2 raw onions, sliced very
  thin

6 slices bacon (fry crisp and
  crumble)

Dressing:

1/4 c. olive oil
1/2 c. salad oil
1/4 c. tarragon vinegar
1 Tbsp. lemon juice
1 garlic clove, split
1/4 tsp. Tabasco sauce

1 1/2 tsp. salt
1/4 tsp. dry mustard
1 tsp. sugar
1 tsp. paprika
1/2 tsp. pepper
1/3 c. beer

Place all ingredients in jar. Seal tightly and shake well. Refrigerate at least 24 hours. Shake again before using. Pour over potatoes and onions. Refrigerate 2 to 3 hours, stirring several times. Serves 6. This dressing is also good on any salad.

SOUR CREAM POTATO SALAD

7 medium potatoes	1 c. mayonnaise
1/2 c. salad oil	1 c. sour cream
2 Tbsp. vinegar	2 tsp. dill weed
1 tsp. salt	3/4 c. diced celery
4 hard-cooked eggs	Garlic salt, onion, salt
1/3 c. green onions	and pepper to taste

Cook the potatoes in jackets. Peel while warm and slice. Mix together oil, vinegar, salt, garlic salt, onion salt and pepper. Pour mixture over potatoes and let stand for 2 hours (or overnight in refrigerator), covered. Add eggs, onions, mayonnaise, sour cream, celery and dill weed. Mix well and chill.

R. W. Neale, St. Cloud, Mn.

PRETZEL JELLO SALAD

Mix and press into 9x13 inch pan:

1 1/2 to 2 c. crushed pretzels	1 stick oleo
	3 Tbsp. sugar

Bake at 350° for 7 minutes. Blend and spread over crust:

8 oz. Philadelphia cream cheese	1 medium bowl Cool Whip
	1 c. sugar

Dissolve 2 packages strawberry jello in 2 cups boiling water. When cool, add 2 (10 ounce) boxes frozen strawberries. Let set and then pour over cream cheese mixture. Refrigerate.

Sue Hick, Detroit Lakes, Mn.

PRUNE SALAD

24 unsweetened cooked prunes, cut up	1 c. hot water
Rind of 1 orange, grated	3/4 c. prune juice (in bottle)
Juice of 1 orange	Walnuts
1 pkg. lemon jello	

Melt jello in hot water, add orange and prune juice and

rind. Add rest of mixture. Makes 8 small molds.

Topping: Whip 1/4 cup cream. Mash 1/2 banana, 1/4 cup celery, cut fine. Mix together, put on top of mold.
Aster Paulsrud, Willmar, Mn.

PURPLE PASSION SALAD
(Large Recipe)

1 lb. dark cherries,
  pitted and halved
1 can chunk pineapple
1 c. miniature marshmallows

1 c. chopped nuts
1 (8 oz.) pkg. cream cheese
1 large ctn. Cool Whip

Reserve 1/4 cup cherry juice. Blend with cream cheese. Drain cherries and pineapple and fold into cream cheese mixture. Fold in nuts and marshmallows. Let stand several hours (or overnight). Add Cool Whip 1 hour before serving.
Mrs. Ronald Schwartz, Owatonna, Mn.

QUICK APRICOT FRUIT SALAD

1 c. cottage cheese
1 can fruit cocktail,
  drained

8 oz. Dream Whip
1/2 of a 3 oz. pkg. apricot
  jello

Add in order above - no liquid - sprinkle jello over all. Mix well. Marshmallows and/or nuts may be added. Any flavor jello may be used.
Shirley Way, Minneapolis, Mn.

EASY QUICK SALAD

4 oz. cottage cheese
5 oz. Ready Whip

1 (3 oz.) pkg. jello (any
  flavor)

Fold together. Add 3 cups fruit (grapes, pineapple, bananas, apples, etc.).
Darlene Lee

QUICK FRUIT SALAD

1 can fruit cocktail, do
   not drain
1 can pineapple tidbits,
   do not drain

1 can Mandarin oranges,
   drained

Mix all 3 fruits. Sprinkle 1 box lemon instant pudding over the fruit. Let this stand overnight in refrigerator. Before serving next day, add 1 cup small marshmallows, 2 or 3 bananas, depending on size. If you prefer - red apples (leave peeling on), may be added for color. Grapes if you prefer.

Mildred Sjostrom, St. Peter, Mn.

QUICK TOMATO ASPIC SALAD

2 c. tomato juice
1/2 Tbsp. instant onion
1/2 tsp. salt
Dash of pepper

1 1/2 Tbsp. lemon juice or
   vinegar
1 (3 oz.) pkg. jello (lemon
   or fruit)

Bring tomato juice and onion to a boil. Add jello and salt, pepper and lemon juice. Stir well. Set aside to cool. Pour into mold. Makes 4 - 6 servings. Good salad with cottage cheese balls or dab of salad dressing.

Mrs. E. F. Braun, Owatonna, Mn.

RASPBERRY SALAD

Bottom layer: In 9x13 inch pan -

1 pkg. raspberry jello
1 c. boiling water

1 pkg. frozen raspberries

Set. Spoon 1 cup sour cream over it.

Second layer:

1 pkg. raspberry jello
1 c. boiling water
1 c. small marshmallows

1 can small pineapple tidbits
   and juice
1 large banana, sliced

Madaline Danich, St. Paul, Mn.

RASPBERRY-APPLESAUCE MOLD

2 c. thick, smooth
applesauce or 1
(1 lb. 1 oz.) can
applesauce
1 (3 oz.) pkg. raspberry
flavored gelatin

1 tsp. grated orange rind
3 Tbsp. orange juice
1 (7 oz.) bottle lemon-lime
carbonated beverage

Heat applesauce to boiling. Dissolve gelatin in hot applesauce. Add remaining ingredients. Chill until firm. Makes 6 servings.

Mrs. Don Bredenberg, Bemidji, Mn.

RAW VEGETABLE SALAD

1 head cauliflower
1 bunch broccoli
1 (10 oz.) pkg. frozen
peas, thawed

1 bunch green onions
1 c. sour cream
1 c. salad dressing
(Miracle Whip)

Cut up cauliflower and broccoli flowers and onions (greens included) in small pieces. Add thawed pieces. Combine sour cream and salad dressing and pour over vegetables. Mix well and let marinate overnight. Garlic powder and other desired seasonings may also be added to dressing.

Mavis Ann Hjielberg, St. Paul, Mn.

RHUBARB SALAD

3 c. diced rhubarb
1/2 c. sugar

1/4 tsp. salt

Cover and cook on low till tender, then bring to a boil and add:

2 pkg. strawberry jello
2 c. cold water

1/4 c. lemon juice
2 c. finely chopped celery

Pour into a mold and let set.

Elsa Ditty, St. Cloud, Mn.

1748-81

SEAFOAM SALAD

1 c. pear juice, heated   1 small pkg. lime jello
  to dissolve jello

    Let set until partially set. Whip 2 small packages of cream cheese, add in mixer, 1 (No. 2 1/2) can pears until in quite small pieces. Whip 1/2 pint of whipping cream - fold into jello. Put into mold.
               Bonnie Steffens, St. Cloud, Mn.

SEAFOOD SALAD

1 loaf sandwich bread   5 eggs, hard-boiled,
2 Tbsp. chopped onion   chopped

    Remove crusts from bread. Butter slices on one side and cut into cubes. Mix with onion and eggs and refrigerate overnight. Next day, add:

2 cans shrimp, drained   1 c. chopped celery
1 can crabmeat, drained   2 c. mayonnaise

    Mix all together and serve.
               Dee Olson, St. Paul, Mn.

SAN FRANCISCO SALAD

    Toss 2 quarts of bite sized mixed salad greens, 1 cup sliced mushrooms and 1 (11 ounce) can drained and chilled Mandarin oranges. Just before serving, pour on 1 (3 ounce) can French fried onions and 1/2 cup Italian dressing. Toss gently. Makes 6 to 8 crunchy, delicious servings.
               Mary Kozel, Grand Forks, N. D.

SHRIMP CAULIFLOWER SALAD

1 1/4 c. cauliflower (raw)   1 Tbsp. lemon juice
10 oz. shrimp, cooked   3/4 tsp. salt
  (frozen)   Dash of pepper
2 Tbsp. French dressing   1 Tbsp. minced onion
1 c. cooked rice   1 Tbsp. chipped olives
1/4 c. slivered green pepper   1/3 c. mayonnaise

Pour French dressing over shrimp and chill overnight if possible - toss the rest together lightly.

Bonnie Steffens, St. Cloud, Mn.

SHRIMP SALAD

Cook 1 box shell macaroni according to directions (add 1 teaspoon shortening, margarine or oil and macaroni won't stick). Do not overcook.

1/2 pkg. frozen small
  shrimp
4 hard-cooked eggs,
  chopped

1 c. chopped celery
1/2 carrot, grated for color
  or about 1 Tbsp. chopped
  pimento

Add Gedney salad dressing, or your favorite.

Cecilia Leverson, Fargo, N. D.

SHOESTRING SALAD

Mix:
1 c. carrots, shredded
1 c. celery, diced
1 very small onion,
  chopped fine

2 cans tuna or 1 can tuna
  and 1 can chicken
1 - 1 1/2 c. salad dressing

Blend together. Just before serving, add 1 medium sized can of shoestring potatoes.

Helen Martin, Fargo, N. D.

SPINACH SALAD WITH HOT BACON DRESSING

1 lb. fresh spinach,
  washed, dried and
  chilled
4 slices bacon, diced
2 tsp. brown sugar

1/4 c. sliced green onions
1/4 tsp. salt
1 1/2 Tbsp. vinegar
1/8 tsp. dry mustard
Dash of paprika

With scissors, snip spinach coarsely into a salad bowl. Cook diced bacon in a skillet over low heat until crisp. Add sugar, green onions, salt, vinegar, mustard and paprika. Bring to the boiling point and remove from heat. Just before serving, pour the hot dressing over the spinach and toss lightly until leaves are coated. Serves 4.

SPRING SALAD

1 (3 oz.) pkg. orange
   jello

1 1/2 c. boiling water
1/4 c. sugar

Dissolve and add:
1 (8 oz.) pkg. cream
   cheese
2 Tbsp. lemon juice

1 c. celery, chopped
1/2 c. orange juice
1 c. shredded carrots

Refrigerate.
         Linda Seidel, Audubon, Mn.

SUNSHINE SALAD

1 small ctn. cottage
   cheese
1 pkg. orange jello, sprinkle
   over cheese
1 c. crushed pineapple,
   drained

1 small can Mandarin oranges,
   drained
Cherries or grapes for color
1 c. whipped nondairy
   topping

Mix, refrigerate until set.
         Kathy Bischof, St. Cloud, Mn.

TACO SALAD

Brown 1 to 1 1/2 pounds ground beef. Add 1 package
taco seasoning mix and 1/2 the amount of water shown on
package. Simmer until moisture is absorbed. Mix with:

1 head shredded lettuce
1 to 2 c. shredded
   cheese
1 bottle French dressing

1 pkg. crushed Doritos
   Nacho cheese and/or taco
   flavor

Top with hot sauce or sour cream.
         Fran Jenniges, Detroit Lakes, Mn.

TACO SALAD
(With Doritos Regular Chips)

1 (8 oz.) pkg. softened   3 - 4 Tbsp. mild taco sauce
   Philadelphia cream
   cheese

Beat together until well mixed. Spread on plates. Top with:

Chopped lettuce   Onions
Tomato   Cheddar cheese

Serve above with Dorito chips.
Carole Wells, St. Paul, Mn.

TACO SALAD

1 head lettuce   1/2 of an 8 oz. bottle mild
1 c. cheese (I use   taco sauce or 1 pkg. taco
   Velveeta), cut up   seasoning and 1 can tomato
1 can whole tomatoes   sauce
1 lb. hamburger   1 pkg. corn chips

Brown hamburger, salt and pepper. Add taco sauce. Break up lettuce into salad bowl. Add cheese. Drain juice from tomatoes into hamburger mixture. Stir and let simmer. Cut tomatoes into lettuce mixture. When ready to serve, add hamburger mixture to lettuce, toss; add about 1/2 of the corn chips and toss again. Serve the rest of the corn chips on the side.
Cecilia Leverson, Fargo, N. D.

TACO SALAD

1 lb. ground beef   1 can kidney beans (optional)
1 Tbsp. chili powder   1/2 lb. grated Cheddar cheese
2 large tomatoes   1 pkg. taco chips
1/8 tsp. pepper   1 small bottle French or
1 large onion   Thousand Island dressing
1 head lettuce   1 bottle taco sauce

Brown meat, add chili powder and pepper, drain. Let cool. Cut lettuce, add cheese, tomatoes, onion and meat.

At serving time, mix salad, chips and dressing and taco sauce together.

Dolly Nokes, Willmar, Mn.; Joanne Kunz, Jamestown, N.D.: Becky Neal, Sauk Centre, Mn.; Kathy Bishof, St. Cloud, Mn.; Gretchen Marquart, Fargo, N.D.: Avis Paulsen, Verndale, Mn.

TAPIOCA JELLO SALAD

1 pkg. tapioca pudding
1 small pkg. fruit jello
  (orange)

1 pkg. Dream Whip,
  whipped

Cook tapioca pudding as directed, put into an 8x11 inch pan. Cool. Chill jello until slightly thick. Whip Dream Whip, beat 1/2 of Dream Whip with the jello. Pour on top of tapioca. Top with rest of Dream Whip. Can be all mixed together and add Mandarin oranges.

Kathy Neels, St. Cloud, Mn.

TBULA SALAD

1 c. bulgar wheat
1 bunch parsley
2 tomatoes
1 bunch mint leaves
  (optional)

1 large onion
2 cukes
1/4 c. oil (olive)
Salt and pepper
6 Tbsp. lemon juice

Wash wheat, chop all ingredients fine and mix.

Noreen Topel

24 HOUR SALAD
(Serves 6)

2 large green peppers,
  cut into rings
2 large fresh tomatoes,
  slice unpeeled

2 large mild onions, separate
  into rings

Put into large crockery or glass bowl. Mix:

1 1/2 c. vinegar
2 tsp. salt
1 tsp. celery seed

1 1/2 c. vegetable oil
1/2 c. sugar
1/2 tsp. garlic salt

84

Pour over vegetables. Cover and refrigerate for 24 hours.

Lorine Kelly, Minneapolis, Mn.

TUNA FISH SALAD

3 c. Creamettes, cooked
1 1/2 c. celery, chopped
Sweet pickle relish
Seasoning

1 large can tuna (I use
   Kraft's Light N Lively
   low calorie)

Mary R. Jones, Spirit Lake, Ia.

VEGETABLE SALAD

Break up or chop:
1 large cauliflower
1 bunch broccoli
Carrots

2 bunches green onion
1 c. celery

Marinate overnight or 24 hours in a small bottle of Wish-Bone Italian dressing. Drain. Add dressing:

1 1/2 c. Miracle Whip
1 tsp. salt

4 Tbsp. Heinz chili sauce
2 Tbsp. lemon juice

Refrigerate 3 or 4 hours. Radishes may be added just before serving.

Avis Paulsen, Verndale, Mn.

VEGETABLE SALAD

1 can white corn
1 can French style
   green beans
1 can (small) peas

1 green pepper
1 small jar pimento
Onion and celery to taste

Bring to boil:
1/2 c. oil, sugar and
   vinegar
1 tsp. salt

1/2 tsp. dry mustard
1 tsp. seasoned salt
1/2 tsp. celery salt

Pour over vegetables. Cool.
Madaline Danich, St. Paul, Mn.

24 HOUR VEGETABLE SALAD

1 head lettuce, broken
   into large bowl
1/2 c. diced celery
1/2 c. diced green pepper
1 (10 oz.) pkg. frozen
   peas (don't cook)

1 medium onion, chopped
1 3/4 - 2 c. Miracle Whip
2 Tbsp. grated Cheddar
   cheese
Bacon bits

Layer these ingredients and chill (covered) for 24 hours.

    Kathy Neels, St. Cloud, Mn.

MOLDED WALDORF SALAD

2 c. cranberry juice
1 (3 oz.) pkg. lemon
   flavored gelatin
1/4 tsp. salt

1 c. chopped apples
1/2 c. cut celery
1/4 c. cut up walnuts

Heat 1 cup of cranberry juice to boiling. Dissolve gelatin in it, add rest of juice and salt. Chill until almost set. Stir in apples, celery and nuts. Chill until set.

    Evelyn Fellows, Austin, Mn.

WATERGATE SALAD

Mix together:
1 pkg. pistachio (instant)
   pudding mix
1 (9 oz.) ctn. Cool Whip

1 can crushed pineapple, do
   not drain
1/2 - 1 c. miniature
   marshmallows

    Marilyn Helgeson, Fargo, N. D.

WATERGATE SALAD
(Pistachio Pudding)

With the weather getting warmer, here is a recipe for a refreshing salad that is easy to make and just takes a few minutes to prepare.

1 box Jell-O pistachio
   pudding mix (unmade)
1 medium ctn. Cool Whip
1 c. small marshmallows

1 large can crushed pineapple
   with juice
1/2 c. walnuts (cut up or
   whole)

Mix the pudding, crushed pineapple with juice, Cool Whip and marshmallows together and pour into a large size cake pan. Garnish with the walnuts on top and refrigerate for 2 hours.

Note: The walnuts can be mixed right in with the other ingredients.

YUM YUM SALAD

1 (20 oz.) can crushed
   pineapple, drained
1 can cherry pie filling
   (Wilderness)
1 (8 oz.) ctn. frozen Cool
   Whip, thawed

1 can sweetened condensed
   milk (Eagle Brand)
2/3 c. chopped pecans or
   walnuts

Mix all ingredients in bowl and refrigerate overnight.
Olga Pederson, Minneapolis, Mn.

ANYDAY DRESSING

1 medium onion   1/2 c. celery

Chop fine and saute in 4 tablespoons butter or oleo. Add:

10 slices dried bread,
   cubed
1 1/2 tsp. salt
1/4 tsp. pepper

1 tsp. sage or poultry
   seasoning
1 can chicken rice soup
1/2 soup can of water

Mix well. Bake 1 hour at 325°.
Mary Benson, Windom, Mn.

BANANA CREAM DRESSING
(For Fruit Salads)

3 very ripe bananas
2 Tbsp. brown sugar

2 Tbsp. honey
1 c. heavy cream, whipped

Place banana chunks, sugar and honey in blender and blend till smooth. Fold into the whipped cream. Pour over fruit salad and mix. Makes 3 cups.
Dee Olson, St. Paul, Mn.

1748-81

COLE SLAW DRESSING

3/4 c. vinegar   1 tsp. salt
1 c. powdered sugar

Bring to a boil and simmer a few minutes. Put into a pint jar:

1/2 c. salad oil   1 small onion, grated
1 tsp. celery seed

Add simmered ingredients and shake well.
Arlen Freichels, Sauk Centre, Mn.

COLE SLAW DRESSING

1/2 c. salad oil   3/4 c. sugar
1/2 c. vinegar   Diced onion and green pepper

Mix in a glass jar until sugar dissolves.
Ruth Braun, Owatonna, Mn.

COTTAGE CHEESE SALAD DRESSING

1 clove garlic   6 Tbsp. cottage cheese
1/2 green pepper, chopped 1 tsp. salt
2 radishes, chopped   1/4 tsp. paprika
2 hard-cooked egg yolks, 3 Tbsp. lemon juice
  mashed   1/2 c. buttermilk

Rub inside of bowl with garlic. Combine green pepper, radishes and egg yolks in bowl, add remaining ingredients. Mix thoroughly. Pour over hearts of lettuce or any green salad.

FRENCH DRESSING

1 can tomato soup   1 tsp. salt (not needed)
2/3 can Mazola oil   2 cloves garlic, do not cut
1/3 can vinegar   1/2 strong onion (cut groove)
1/2 to 1 c. sugar

Beat well until mixture is blended. (One quart.)
Bonnie Steffens, St. Cloud, Mn.

FRENCH DRESSING

1 c. salad oil
1/2 c. sugar
1 tsp. salt

1/4 c. vinegar
1/3 c. catsup
1 small onion, minced

Mix in blender and chill immediately. Makes about 1 pint.

Pat Langfitt, Fargo, N. D.

FRENCH DRESSING

3/4 c. sugar
1 c. catsup
1/2 c. vinegar

1 c. oil
1 tsp. salt
1 tsp. paprika (optional)

Beat well with beater or blender. Add a medium sized onion, grated. Keep in refrigerator.

Georgine Isakson, Fargo, N. D.

FRENCH DRESSING

1 c. Crisco oil
2/3 c. ketchup
1/2 c. sugar
1 small onion, diced up
1/4 c. vinegar

1/4 c. lemon juice
1/2 tsp. paprika
1 tsp. salt
1/2 tsp. pepper

Shake well and keep in refrigerator.

C. Landwehr, Minneapolis, Mn.

FRENCH DRESSING

1 c. sugar
1 c. vinegar or lemon
  juice or half & half
2 tsp. celery seed
Dash of pepper
1 can tomato soup

2/3 c. catsup
1 c. oil
2 tsp. salt
2 tsp. paprika
1 medium onion, very finely
  chopped

Combine all ingredients thoroughly and store in refrigerator.

Karen Rupert, St. Cloud, Mn.

1748-81

FRUIT SALAD DRESSING

1 c. fruit juice (pineapple preferred)*
2 Tbsp. flour

1/4 c. sugar
Pinch of salt

*If short, add either lemon or orange juice to equal 1 cup.

Heat juice. Add all dry ingredients. Cook until thick. Cool. Add to whipped cream when serving.

Ruth Braun, Owatonna, Mn.

GLAZE FOR HAM

Six minutes in microwave:

1 c. brown sugar
2 1/2 Tbsp. cornstarch

Touch of ginger
2 c. orange juice

Clara Lisko, Bismarck, N. D.

HUBBLE HOUSE DRESSING

1 pt. Miracle Whip
1 can tomato soup
8 oz. tartar sauce
3 grated sweet pickles
2 tsp. pickle juice

1/3 c. vinegar
3 Tbsp. chili sauce
1 Tbsp. grated onion
4 Tbsp. sugar

Mrs. E. F. Braun, Owatonna, Mn.

MARINATED VEGETABLES

1/3 c. salad oil
2/3 c. vinegar
1 c. sugar

2 tsp. salt
1/8 tsp. pepper

Bring to boil, cool; pour over raw vegetables.

Mary Perron, Owatonna, Mn.

MOCK SOUR CREAM

Mix equal parts cottage cheese and buttermilk in blender. Add 2 teaspoons lemon juice.
Darlene Lee

ORANGE CREAM CHEESE SALAD

1 pkg. orange gelatin, dissolved in 1 c. boiling water

1 (3 oz.) pkg. cream cheese (room temperature)
1 c. miniature marshmallows

Dissolve gelatin in water in a saucepan. Add cream cheese and miniature marshmallows. Stir over low heat until melted. Cool. Add:

1 c. crushed pineapple
1 c. shredded carrots

1 c. Dream Whip

Edith Weber, Fargo, N. D.

PAPAYA SEED DRESSING

1 c. sugar
1 tsp. salt
1 tsp. dry mustard
1 c. wine or tarragon vinegar

2 c. salad oil
1 small onion, chopped
3 Tbsp. fresh papaya seed

Place all dry ingredients and vinegar in blender. Turn on blender and gradually add salad oil and onion. When thoroughly blended, add papaya seeds. Blend only until seeds are the size of coarse ground pepper.
Note: The piquant flavor this dressing has, is excellent on either fruit or tossed green salads. Taken from a Hawaiian Cook Book.
Betty Carlson

POTATO SALAD DRESSING

4 eggs
1/2 c. sugar
1/3 c. vinegar

1/3 c. milk
Salt and pepper
1 tsp. dry mustard

Cook just to boil. Use about half & half with Miracle Whip in potato salad. Keeps in refrigerator.
1748-81   Linnea Pajari (Dick), Detroit Lakes, Mn.   91

DRESSING FOR POTATO SALAD

Beat 4 - 5 eggs, add:

1 c. sugar
1 c. vinegar (use a little less)

1 tsp. mustard
Dash of salt

Cook in double boiler until thick.
Elsa Ditty, St. Cloud, Mn.

LEM'N LIME SEAFOOD DRESSING

1/2 tsp. salt
1/2 tsp. celery seed
1/2 tsp. dry mustard
1/4 c. lem'n lime juice

1/4 c. mayonnaise
1/2 c. chili sauce
1/2 tsp. hot pepper sauce
1/2 c. salad oil

Mix salt, celery seed and mustard. Add remaining ingredients and beat well. Use on seafood salads. Yield: 1 1/2 cups dressing.
Kathy Bishof, St. Cloud, Mn.

DELICIOUS SALAD DRESSING

1 c. Miracle Whip
1 Tbsp. chili sauce
1 tsp. mustard
1 Tbsp. vinegar

Pinch of sugar
1 hard-boiled egg, chopped
1 ctn. sour cream

Combine all ingredients.
Mary Perron, Rochester Council

ZIPPY SALAD DRESSING

1/2 c. lem'n lime juice
1/3 c. olive or corn oil
1/3 c. olive juice (from jar of olives)

1/3 c. bottled liquid pectin
1 Tbsp. Mexican or Greek seasoning mix (below)
Salt, pepper to taste

Combine ingredients in a jar and shake well before pouring over salad. Less than 30 calories per tablespoon.

Mexican Seasoning Mix:

2 Tbsp. oregano

1 tsp. marjoram

2 Tbsp. cumin seed
2 tsp. instant minced garlic
1 tsp. mixed pumpkin spice

2 to 4 tsp. dried red pepper
flakes, or to taste

Greek Seasoning Mix:

4 Tbsp. dried mint leaves
2 Tbsp. dried tarragon
2 Tbsp. dried parsley flakes
2 tsp. ground nutmeg

1 tsp. ground cinnamon
2 tsp. instant minced garlic
2 tsp. dried lemon peel

Kathy Bischof, St. Cloud, Mn.

DRESSING FOR SLAW

1 1/4 c. sugar
2 tsp. salt
2 tsp. dry mustard
1/2 medium onion, grated

1 c. + 3 Tbsp. vinegar
1 pt. salad oil
1/8 c. celery seed (optional)

Combine sugar, salt, onion, mustard and half of vinegar; beat. Gradually add oil and beat in remaining vinegar gradually. Add celery salt and beat until thick. Store in refrigerator and shake before using.

Clara Lisko, Bismarck, N. D.

THOUSAND ISLAND DRESSING

1 qt. salad dressing
1 can tomato soup
1/2 c. (scant) chopped
onion
5/8 c. pickle relish (no
juice - squeeze out all
juice)

2 1/2 Tbsp. sweet pickle
juice
2 1/2 Tbsp. chili sauce
2 1/2 Tbsp. sugar
2 1/2 Tbsp. vinegar
1/4 tsp. prepared mustard

Stir.

Carol Brand, Windom, Mn.

THOUSAND ISLAND DRESSING

1 1/2 c. mayonnaise
1/4 c. chili sauce

3 Tbsp. sweet pickle relish
2 hard-boiled eggs

Spin in blender till well chopped and mixed. Makes about 1 pint.

THOUSAND ISLAND DRESSING

Place into blender:

1 1/2 c. chili sauce
1/2 c. drained sweet
  pickle relish

1 large chopped onion
1 cut up green pepper
1 (3 oz.) bottle stuffed green
  olives

Cover and blend until well chopped and mixed. Stir this into 1 quart Miracle Whip. Store in refrigerator. (About 6 cups.) Also real good on any fish for a tartar sauce.

Karen Rupert, St. Cloud, Mn.

WESTERN DRESSING

1 c. sugar
1 c. ketchup
1 Tbsp. minced onion

1 can tomato soup
1 c. vinegar
1 c. salad oil

Boil 10 minutes.
Darlene Lee

BAKED CORN

2 eggs, slightly beaten
1 pt. corn (whole kernel
  or cream style)
1 c. coarsely crumbled
  soda crackers

1/2 tsp. celery salt
1 c. milk
6 Tbsp. melted butter
1/2 tsp. salt
1/8 tsp. pepper

In a bowl, slightly beat the 2 eggs, all remaining ingredients and blend well. Bake in a 2 quart baking dish at 350° for 1 hour or until knife inserted in center comes out clean.

C. Landwehr, Minneapolis, Mn.

BAKED VEGETABLE DISH

1 pkg. frozen broccoli
1 pkg. frozen Brussels
   sprouts

1 pkg. frozen cauliflower

Cook each according to directions on package. Put into 9x13 inch pan. Pour 1 can mushroom soup over vegetables, also grated cheese over this. Bake 1/2 hour at 350°.
      Mike and Vonnie Bakke, Willmar, Mn.

BARBEQUED BEANS

1 lb. hamburger
1 onion, diced
1 large can pork & beans
1/2 c. catsup
1 Tbsp. Worcestershire sauce

2 Tbsp. brown sugar
2 Tbsp. vinegar
1/2 tsp. salt
1/2 tsp. pepper

Brown hamburger and onions. Add salt and pepper. Add remaining ingredients. Bake 35 minutes at 350°.
      Ruth Smith, ⌐t. Paul, Mn.

BAR-B-Q BEANS IN CROCK POT

1 lb. Jimmy Dean's
   sausage, brown and
   drain
1 small jar Uncle Ken's
   B-B-Q sauce
1/2 c. chopped onion

1 large can pork and beans
1 medium can lima or butter
   beans
1 medium can red kidney
   beans

Mix together in crock pot or slow cooker and cook on low all day (6 hours).
      Jeanne Segebarth, Minneapolis, Mn.

BEAN BAKE

1/2 lb. bacon
2 onions

1 1/2 lb. ground beef

Cut up bacon, brown to crisp - drain grease from pan set bacon aside. Brown meat and onions and drain grease. Salt and pepper to taste. Mix 2 regular size cans pork and beans with:

1 large can lima or butter beans	5/8 c. brown sugar
	1 1/2 Tbsp. vinegar
1 large can kidney beans	1/2 green pepper, chopped
1/2 c. catsup	1 tsp. prepared mustard

Add to meat and bacon. Bake at 350° for 1 hour. Serves 12.

Helen Evenson, Litchfield, Mn.

"BEANS"

1 chopped onion	1/2 c. molasses
1/2 c. brown sugar	1/2 c. vinegar

Cook 15 minutes. Add 1 can of the following, drained:

Lima beans	Green beans
Butter beans	1 can pork and beans
Kidney beans	(with juice)

Fry 1/2 pound bacon real crisp and crumble on top. Bake 1 hour at 350°.

Irma Holmstrom, Bismarck, N. D.

BAKED BEANS

Pick over, wash and soak overnight, 1 quart white beans. Boil up in some water, add 1/2 teaspoon soda, boil a few minutes longer or until when you blow on a few beans the skins will crack. Drain. Into pan, place:

1/2 c. chopped onions	2 c. tomato sauce
1 1/2 c. bacon or ham, cubed	1 Tbsp. salt
	1/2 tsp. pepper
1/2 c. white sugar	1/2 tsp. dry mustard

Add beans and enough water to cover. Stir and bake in slow oven until tender, for 3 or 4 hours (300° - 325°). If you prefer, cook in pressure cooker for 40 minutes.

Georgine Isakson, Fargo, N. D.

BAKED BEANS

Cook 5 - 6 strips bacon, cut into fourths; drain. Crumble and cook 1 pound hamburger. Add:

1 onion, sliced
2 Tbsp. dark molasses
  (Brer Rabbit)

1/2 c. catsup
1/4 c. brown sugar
1/2 tsp. dry mustard

Stir above all together and heat through. I freeze this mixture and add to 2 (3 pound) cans B & M beans for large amount. Or, I divide it and freeze smaller amounts and add to B & M beans as needed. I sometimes bake my own beans and add this to it, but B & M's are just as good and easier. I keep cover on to bake until the last few minutes. Stir before serving if too moist. Takes about 1 hour at 325° or until piping hot.

Marge Johnson, Minneapolis, Mn.

BAKED BEANS

Soak 1 pound navy beans overnight. Rinse, add water to cover and bring to a boil. Take off heat and add:

1/4 c. molasses
2/3 c. brown sugar
1/2 tsp. dry mustard
1 medium onion, chopped

1/3 lb. chopped, uncooked
  bacon
1 chopped ham, including
  fat

Bake for 4 - 6 hours or until soft. Check often in case water needs to be added. Stir. Bake at 350°.

Mary Hocking, Fargo, N. D.

BAKED BEANS

Cut up and fry 1/4 pound bacon. Add 3 small onions, cut up into rings. Add:

3/4 c. brown sugar
1/4 c. vinegar

1/2 tsp. dry mustard

Simmer 10 - 15 minutes. Put into slow cooker and add:

1 can butter beans,
  drained

1 can navy beans,
  drained

| 1 can kidney beans, drained | 1 large can Bush's beans |

Bake at 350° for 2 hours.

Vivian McMonigle, Detroit Lakes, Mn.

BAKED BEANS SUPREME

| 1 chopped onion
1 lb. chopped bacon, fried lightly and drained | 1 medium size can of each:
Kidney beans, lima beans, butter beans, pork & beans |

Mix together, add:

| 1/2 c. vinegar | 1/2 tsp. garlic salt |
| 1 c. brown sugar | 1 Tbsp. mustard |

Bake at 350° for 4 hours (if too juicy, remove cover last 1/2 hour).

Marilyn Helgeson, Fargo, N. D.

BEAN BAKE

| 1/2 lb. bacon
2 onions | 1 1/2 lb. ground beef |

Cut up bacon, brown to crisp - drain grease from pan, set bacon aside. Brown meat and onions and drain grease. Salt and pepper to taste. Mix:

2 regular size cans pork & beans	1/2 c. catsup
	5/8 c. brown sugar
1 large can lima or butter beans	1 1/2 Tbsp. vinegar
	1/2 green pepper, chopped
1 large can kidney beans	1 tsp. prepared mustard

Add to meat and bacon. Bake at 350° for 1 hour. Serves 12.

Helen Evenson, Litchfield, Mn.

98

EASY BAKED BEANS

2 cans white beans
5 or 6 strips bacon
4 Tbsp. brown sugar
2 Tbsp. molasses

Onion, chopped
1/2 c. catsup
1 tsp. mustard

Bake at 350° about 30 minutes or 1 hour.
Bev Larson, Bismarck, N. D.

CALICO BEANS

1 to 2 lb. hamburger
1/2 c. onion, chopped

1/2 lb. bacon, cook, brown
   and cut into pieces

Add:
1/2 c. catsup
1 tsp. salt
3/4 c. brown sugar
1 tsp. mustard

2 tsp. vinegar
1 (#2) can pork & beans
1 (#2) can kidney beans
1 (#2) can lima beans

Bake 40 minutes at 350°. Can use 1 large can of Bush
beans in place of kidney and lima beans.
Mary Jane Schmitz, Wadena, Mn.

CALICO BEANS

Brown:
1/4 lb. bacon
1 lb. ground beef

1/2 c. chopped onion

Drain and add:
1/2 c. brown sugar
1/2 c. catsup
2 Tbsp. vinegar
1 (#2) can drained lima
   or butter beans

1 (#2) can kidney beans
1 (#2) can pork & beans
1 Tbsp. mustard
1 tsp. salt

Bake in crock pot slowly or bake in 350° oven for 1
hour.
Linda Johnson, Anoka, Mn.

CALICO BEANS

4 - 8 slices bacon, cut
  into strips
1 lb. ground beef
1/2 c. chopped onions
1/2 c. brown sugar
1/2 c. ketchup
2 Tbsp. vinegar

1 Tbsp. mustard
1 tsp. salt
1/4 tsp. garlic salt
1 can kidney beans
1 can pork & beans
1 can beans & franks

Brown bacon, ground beef and onions. Add remaining ingredients and mix. Bake at 300° for 1 1/2 hours or at 350° for 1 hour.

Betty Michon, Detroit Lakes, Mn.

CAMPERS BEANS

In large skillet brown 1 pound hamburger, drain off grease. Add:

1 env onion soup mix
  (dry)
1 can kidney beans
1 large can pork and beans

1 c. water
1 c. catsup
1 Tbsp. vinegar

Simmer for 45 minutes. Very good heated over next day.

Bernita Engel, Minneapolis, Mn.

DIFFERENT CALICO BEANS

1/2 lb. hamburger
1/2 lb. bacon

1 large chopped onion

Brown hamburger. Dice bacon and saute with onion. Drain partially:

1 can kidney beans
1 can butter beans

1 can lima beans
1 can white corn

Combine:
3/4 c. brown sugar
2 tsp. vinegar
1 tsp. prepared mustard

1/2 c. catsup
1/2 tsp. salt
Pepper to taste

Combine all ingredients, pour over meat mixture and bake for 1 hour at 350°.

Fran Toler, Minneapolis, Mn.

MARGE PYE'S BAKED BEANS

Soak 1 pound Northern navy beans overnight. (Cover with water.) Parboil in soak water with 1/2 teaspoon baking soda for 1/2 hour. Put beans into baking dish, cover with water. Save water that's left to add if necessary. Add:

1 tsp. mustard (dry)   2 Tbsp. dark molasses
1/2 small onion, cut up

Mix and add 1/2 pound salt pork (rinse off pork). Put some pork slices on top. Bake at 350° for 3 hours. Add water if necessary.

Marge Pye, St. Paul, Mn.

OLD SETTLERS BEANS

1/2 lb. hamburger,   1 large can B & M beans
  browned   1 can butter beans, drained
1/2 lb. bacon, cubed   1 can kidney beans, drained
  and fried   1 can lima beans, drained
1 onion, fry with meat

Combine everything in large roaster and pour over:

1/3 c. catsup   1/2 tsp. dry mustard
1/4 c. vinegar   3/4 c. brown sugar
2 Tbsp. molasses

Stir up gently and bake at 350° for about an hour.

Karen Rupert, St. Cloud, Mn.

BAKED BEAN AND SAUSAGE CASSEROLE

1 (10 oz.) pkg. frozen   1 lb. Italian link sausage or
  lima beans   pork link sausage
3 (1 lb.) cans baked   1/2 lb. smoked ham, cut
  beans   into 1/2 inch cubes
2 (1 lb. 4 oz.) cans kidney 1 tsp. salt
  beans, drained   1/2 tsp. pepper

1/2 tsp. mustard

1/4 c. brown sugar, packed

1 (8 oz.) can tomato sauce

1 medium onion, chopped

1/2 c. catsup

Cook lima beans 10 minutes. Drain, mix with the beans. Place sausage in skillet, add small amount of water. Cover and simmer 5 minutes. Drain. Then pan fry for a few minutes until brown. Don't prick. Cut each sausage into 4 to 5 pieces. Heat oven to 400°. Mix sausage, ham and beans and add rest of ingredients and pour over the beans. Bake, uncovered, 1 hour in a 3 quart dish.

Elsa Ditty, St. Cloud, Mn.

BEETS IN ORANGE SAUCE

1 (#2) can sliced beets

1 Tbsp. sugar

1 c. orange juice

3/4 tsp. salt

1 tsp. grated orange rind

2 Tbsp. butter

1 Tbsp. cornstarch

Mix cornstarch, sugar and salt. Blend in orange juice. Cook over low heat until it thickens. Stir in butter and orange rind. Drain beets and add to thickened mixture. Heat thoroughly. Yield: 4 servings.

HARVARD BEETS

3 c. cooked, diced beets

2 Tbsp. sugar

1 c. liquid (beet juice
   with water)

1 tsp. salt

Pepper

3 Tbsp. flour

1/3 c. vinegar

Shirley Peterson, Willmar, Mn.

CHEESE-BROCCOLI SIDE DISH

1 pkg. frozen broccoli

1 (4 oz.) jar Cheez Whiz

1 can whole kernel corn

Cook broccoli. Drain, then place in casserole with un-drained corn and cheese. Top with dry bread crumbs or croutons. Bake at 350° for 40 minutes.

Kathaleen Bischof, St. Cloud, Mn.

BROCCOLI-CORN

1 (16 oz.) can cream corn
1 (10 oz.) broccoli, cooked and drained
1 egg, beaten

1/2 c. saltine cracker crumbs (12)
1 Tbsp. instant onion
2 Tbsp. melted butter
Dash of pepper

Topping:

1 Tbsp. melted butter

1/4 c. cracker crumbs (6)

Bake in 350° oven for 35 - 40 minutes.
Elsie Ekblad

BROCCOLI RICE

1 small pkg. broccoli (frozen)
1 c. Minute Rice (raw)

1 can cream of mushroom soup

Cook broccoli and drain. Put into buttered casserole dish with cream of mushroom soup. Fix the can of soup with milk (1 can) and add. Put in 1 cup of Minute Rice and drained broccoli. Bake at 350° for about 30 minutes. Can put cheese on top (optional).
Ruth Berge, Windom, Mn.

BAKED CABBAGE PUFF

3 c. finely shredded cabbage
2 c. coarse dry bread crumbs (French bread is excellent for this)
1 1/4 c. grated Cheddar cheese

2 eggs
1 tsp. salt
1 tsp. prepared mustard
1/8 tsp. pepper
2 c. milk
1 Tbsp. chopped pimento

Cover cabbage with cold water and heat to boiling, remove and drain well. In a buttered, shallow 2 quart baking dish, arrange cabbage, crumbs and cheese in layers, making 2 layers of each. Beat eggs with salt, mustard and pepper. Add milk and chopped pimento and mix well. Pour over the cabbage mixture. Press down with fork or spoon so liquid is absorbed. Let stand 20 minutes. Bake in 350°

oven until puffed and set in center of dish, about 45 - 50 minutes. Serve from dish. Makes 6 - 8 servings.

Kathy Bischof, St. Cloud, Mn.

CABBAGE ROLLS

1 medium cabbage	1 Tbsp. minced onion
1 lb. ground round steak	1/8 tsp. poultry seasoning
1 clove garlic, minced	1 (20 oz.) can tomatoes
Salt and pepper	1 lb. fresh sauerkraut
1/4 c. cold water	

Cut out core of cabbage and put cabbage into kettle of boiling water. Boil, and with tongs, remove 8 outside leaves as they wilt. Remove head of cabbage, drain and chop. Put half in kettle. Cut out and discard coarsest part of ribs from the 8 leaves. Mix beef, garlic, 1 teaspoon salt, 1/8 teaspoon pepper and the next 3 ingredients. Divide into 8 portions and put each on a cabbage leaf. Roll up, tucking in ends. Put on cabbage in kettle. Top with remaining chopped cabbage, tomatoes and sauerkraut. Season; add 1/2 cup boiling water. Cover; simmer 45 minutes. Makes 4 servings, about 280 calories each.

FROZEN CABBAGE

Have ready, 1 medium head cabbage (shredded). Sprinkle with 2 teaspoons salt. Let stand 1 hour. Grind together 1 green pepper and 6 carrots. Add to cabbage. Boil:

1 c. water	1 c. vinegar
2 c. sugar	1 tsp. mustard seed

Cool and pour over cabbage. Put into containers and freeze.

Darlene Lee

CABBAGE SLAW

1 c. sugar	1 large head cabbage
1/2 c. vinegar	1 onion
1 tsp. salt	Grated carrots
1 tsp. celery seed	6 stalks celery
1 tsp. mustard seed	Green pepper
104	Kathy Bischof, St. Cloud, Mn.

CARROTS AU GRATIN

Melt 3 tablespoons butter and saute 1/3 cup onion till tender. Stir in:

3 Tbsp. flour   1/8 tsp. pepper
1 tsp. salt

Add 1 1/2 cups milk gradually. Stir till thick and add 1 cup grated American cheese and let the cheese melt. Add:

4 c. cooked, sliced and   1 Tbsp. dry parsley
   well drained carrots

Put into a 10x6 inch greased pan. Top with a little crushed corn flakes that have had a little melted butter added to it. Bake at 350° for 20 minutes.

Elsa Ditty, St. Cloud, Mn.

MARINATED CARROTS

5 c. carrots, sliced,   1 can tomato soup, undiluted
   cooked, cooled   1/2 c. salad oil
1 medium onion, sliced   1 c. sugar (white)
   into rings   3/4 c. vinegar (white cider)
1 green pepper, sliced   1 tsp. prepared mustard
   into rings   1 Tbsp. Worcestershire
1 small jar pimento,   sauce
   chopped   1 tsp. salt
1 or 2 cans mushrooms   1 tsp. pepper
   sliced (optional)

Wash, peel and cut carrots into 1/4 inch pieces. Cook until firm, but tender. Do not overcook. Drain and cool. Combine last 8 ingredients- soup, oil, sugar, vinegar, mustard, Worcestershire sauce, salt and pepper in saucepan. Bring to a boil and stir until sugar is dissolved. In large bowl, combine carrots, onion, green pepper, pimento and mushrooms. Pour hot mixture over the vegetables and marinate overnight in refrigerator. Must marinate at least 12 hours. Stores in covered jar in refrigerator up to 2 weeks. (This is a colorful and appetizing side dish to serve on any occasion.)

Helen-May Johnson, Chanhassen, Mn.

CAULIFLOWER AND GREEN BEANS CURRY

2 c. cottage cheese
1 Tbsp. lemon juice
1 Tbsp. chopped parsley
1 1/2 tsp. curry powder

1 head cauliflower
2 (9 oz.) pkg. frozen
  green beans

In a blender or mixer, combine cottage cheese, lemon juice, parsley and curry. Sauce may be warmed over low heat, stirring constantly; however, sauce is equally good served at room temperature. Place whole cauliflower into boiling, salted water; cover and cook about 15 minutes, or until slightly tender. (The rising steam cooks top part of head.) Cook beans according to package directions; drain. Place drained cauliflower into center of platter and surround with beans. Pour sauce over cauliflower and serve immediately. Makes 6 to 8 servings.

EXOTIC CELERY

4 c. celery, cut into 1 inch
  pieces
1 can water chestnuts,
  chopped

1 can cream of celery soup
1/4 c. diced pimento

Cook celery in salted water 8 minutes, drain. Add water chestnuts, soup and pimento. Place in 1 quart casserole and top with 1/2 cup crushed soda crackers and 1/4 cup slivered almonds (optional). Bake 35 minutes at 350°.
Evelyn Walls, St. Paul, Mn.

CORN SOUFFLE

3 c. cream style corn
  (frozen Green Giant)
6 eggs, beaten
3 Tbsp. grated or chopped
  onion
2/3 c. bread crumbs

2/3 c. grated cheese
2/3 c. heavy cream
About 6 squirts of hot sauce
  8 grinds of pepper
1 tsp. salt
1/2 c. parsley (optional)

Mix, put into buttered mold. Set in a pan of hot water. Bake 1 1/2 hours in 350° oven.
Thelma Olson, St. Cloud, Mn.

CORN STUFFING BALLS

1/2 c. chopped onion
1/2 c. chopped celery
4 Tbsp. margarine
1 (17 oz.) can cream style
  corn
1/2 c. water

Salt and pepper to taste
1 tsp. poultry seasoning*
1 (8 oz.) pkg. herb seasoned
  stuffing mix*
3 eggs, slightly beaten
1/2 c. margarine, melted

Saute onion and celery in 4 tablespoons margarine in saucepan. Add corn, water and seasonings to saucepan and bring to a boil. Place stuffing mix in large bowl. Pour corn mixture over stuffing mix and toss lightly. Stir in eggs. Shape into 7 or 8 balls. Place in baking dish and pour melted margarine over all. Bake at 375° for 25 minutes. Good served with pork or chicken.

*Can substitute 5 cups dry bread cubes and add more poultry seasoning to taste.

Carolyn Brudevold, Fargo, N. D.

BAKED CORN

2 eggs
1 (12 oz.) can cream
  style corn
4 tsp. half & half

2 tsp. flour
Butter, salt and pepper to
  taste

Add eggs and corn and beat, then add other ingredients and beat. Bake at 350° for 45 minutes.

Irene Wall, Little Falls, Mn.

CORN PIE (VEGETABLE)

2 c. whole kernel corn,
  fresh or canned
2 Tbsp. butter or margarine
1 c. milk

1/2 tsp. salt
2 Tbsp. chopped onion
2 eggs, beaten
2 Tbsp. flour

Simmer onion in butter slowly until cooked, but not browned. Add flour, then salt, corn and milk. Add small amount of mixture to beaten eggs, then add balance of cooked mixture. Cook 1/2 minute.

Crust: Blend together -

1/2 c. butter or margarine   1 1/4 c. soda cracker crumbs

Put in 8 inch pie pan, press on bottom and sides, saving 1/3 for top. Pour in corn mixture and top with crumbs. Bake 30 - 35 minutes at 350°.

1748-81   Eleanor Lauer, St. Cloud, Mn.

BAKED CRANBERRIES

1 qt. cranberries	2 c. sugar
2 c. water	

Wash and drain berries. Dissolve sugar and water. Add berries, mix well. Bake in a slow oven until tender. Do not brown. Stir occasionally. Do not break berries.
Darlene Lee

CREAMY CUKES

1/2 c. sour cream	1 tsp. sugar
1/4 c. salad dressing	1 tsp. salt
2 Tbsp. lemon juice	1/4 tsp. pepper

Slice cukes and onions and cover with the above. Keeps well in refrigerator.
Mrs. Jerve, St. Cloud, Mn.

CUCUMBERS

7 c. sliced cucumbers	1 c. green pepper
1 c. onions, sliced	

Soak with salt overnight. Boil:

2 c. sugar	2 Tbsp. salt
1 c. white vinegar	1 tsp. celery seed or salt

Rinse cucumbers and pour juice over them. Let set overnight.
Sue Hick, Detroit Lakes, Mn.

CUCUMBERS IN SOUR CREAM
(Mizeria ze smietana)
(mi-ZEH-ri-a zeh shem-TA-known)

3 large cucumbers	2 1/2 tsp. salt

Pare and slice. Sprinkle salt over and let stand 1 hour. Drain and pat dry. Combine:

1 c. sour cream	2 Tbsp. drained capers
	1 1/2 tsp. dill weed

108

1 tsp. sugar
1/2 tsp. pepper

2 green onions, thinly sliced
(with tops)

Toss cukes with sour cream mixture and refrigerate 1 hour before serving.

DANISH CUCUMBERS

Wash and slice 1 cucumber into thin slices (unpeeled). Put into a bowl and sprinkle with 1 teaspoon salt and 3 tablespoons sugar. Press down with spoon and add 1/2 cup vinegar.

Irene Wall, Little Falls, Mn.

DOMATES YEMISTES
(Stuffed Tomatoes)

10 round, ripe tomatoes
or substitute green
peppers to add color
1 lb. hamburger
1/4 c. raisins (optional)
1 Tbsp. parsley flakes or
fresh parsley (about
1/4 c., chopped)

1 Tbsp. oregano
1 medium sized onion
1 Tbsp. salt or salt to
taste
2 Tbsp. oil (preferably
olive oil)

Grind and saute onion in oil; add hamburger and brown slightly; add rest of seasonings. Slice tomatoes on top, leaving 1/2 inch intact. Cut around inside of each tomato and remove all of the inside without making holes in tomatoes. Cut the insides until fine and drain the juice; throw away seeds. Add this to mixture, all except the juice. Then stuff tomatoes loosely and put into a baking pan upside down. Add a little of the juice (more will be released from the tomatoes), then add some olive oil over the tomatoes (about 1/2 inch thick potato slices may be added all around the pan and in spaces between the tomatoes, salted and peppered to taste). Bake about 2 hours or until tomatoes look wrinkled on top and most of the juice is absorbed.

SUPREME FRENCH STYLE GREEN BEANS

1 can French style
  green beans

1 can cream of mushroom
  soup

Place in 1 quart covered casserole. Sprinkle top with Durkee's canned onion chips. Bake approximately 1 hour at 350°. This was also a prize winning recipe I won on.

Kathey Bischof, St. Cloud, Mn.

HERB BUTTERED GREEN BEANS

2 cans green beans
1/4 c. butter
1 Tbsp. instant minced
  onion

1/4 c. minced celery
3/4 tsp. salt
1/4 tsp. dried basil
1/4 tsp. crushed rosemary

Heat beans. Melt butter and add remaining ingredients. Simmer a few minutes. Toss with beans. Serves 8.

Dee Olson, St. Paul, Mn.

TANGY GREEN BEANS

3 slices bacon
3 Tbsp. bacon drippings
2 Tbsp. chopped onion
3 Tbsp. vinegar

1/4 tsp. salt
1/8 tsp. garlic salt
1 (#2) can green beans

Brown bacon in skillet. Remove and break into small pieces. Brown onion in drippings. Measure 3 tablespoons drippings and blend vinegar and seasonings with bacon, beans and drippings. Heat thoroughly and serve. Serves 4. (If home canned beans are used, they should first be boiled 15 minutes.)

GUACAMOLE

3 ripe avocados
1/2 tomato, diced
1/8 c. onion, diced
Very small amount jalapeno
  pepper, diced

3 oz. sour cream
1/4 tsp. salt
1/4 tsp. lemon juice

Peel and seed avocados. Mash well with fork. Finely

dice tomato, onion and jalapeno pepper. Add all remaining ingredients to avocados and continue mashing until smooth. Refrigerate. Makes 6 servings.

L. Richards

STEWED TOMATO SALAD

1 can stewed tomatoes
1 pkg. lemon jello
1/4 c. green pepper

1 c. celery
1 medium size onion
3/4 c. Miracle Whip

Heat tomatoes to boiling. Stir in jello. Cool. Add chopped pepper, celery and onion. Stir in Miracle Whip. Pour into oiled mold. This is a good salad to serve with ham.

Marge Hewitt

MARINATED CARROTS

2 lb. fresh carrots
1 large onion, sliced into
   thin rings
1 large green pepper,
   cut into thin strips
1 can tomato soup, undiluted

1 c. sugar
1/3 c. salad oil
3/4 c. vinegar
1 tsp. salt
1/2 tsp. pepper
1/2 tsp. dill weed

Wash, peel and cut carrots into slices. Cook until just tender. Do not overcook. Drain and cool. Combine soup, sugar, oil, vinegar, salt, pepper and dill weed. Bring to a boil and stir to dissolve sugar. In 2 quart casserole, combine carrots, onion and green pepper. Pour hot soup mixture over vegetables. Cover and refrigerate overnight.

Evelyn Walls, St. Paul, Mn.

MARINATED TOMATOES

2/3 c. salad oil
1/4 c. vinegar
1/4 c. chopped parsley
1/4 c. chopped green
   onion

1/4 tsp. pepper
1 clove garlic, crushed
2 tsp. thyme or marjoram
9 tomatoes, skin removed
1 tsp. salt

1748-81

Mix all ingredients except tomatoes. Pour over tomatoes and refrigerate overnight. Serves 9.

Dee Olson, St. Paul, Mn.

MARINATED VEGETABLES

1 bunch broccoli, cut into small flowerets
1 cauliflower, cut into small flowerets
1/2 jar sliced, stuffed olives, drain well
1 small can ripe olives, sliced and drained

2 or 3 cans sliced mushrooms, drained
1 small sweet onion, chopped
1 green pepper, chopped
3 stalks celery, chopped
1 large bottle Italian dressing

Mix first 8 ingredients together, add bottle of Italian dressing. Marinate overnight.

Evelyn Walls, St. Paul, Mn.

MUSHROOM DISH

4 Tbsp. butter
1/4 c. finely chopped onion
1 lb. fresh mushrooms

1/4 c. dry bread crumbs (croutons)
1/2 c. sour cream

Melt butter over moderate heat; add onions. Cook 3 to 5 minutes or until soft and transparent, not brown. Add mushroom slices and cook 3 to 5 minutes. Shake pan so they won't stick. When light and delicate brown, sprinkle with bread crumbs and gently toss with wooden spoon. Remove from heat. In small bowl, beat sour cream with wire whip for 2 minutes, stir into skillet. Toss lightly until well coated.

Noreen Topel

MUSHROOMS WITH MADEIRA

1/2 lb. mushrooms
3 Tbsp. bouillon
1/4 c. butter
2 Tbsp. Madeira
8 small white onions

3 tsp. flour
1 Tbsp. minced parsley
1/2 bay leaf
Salt
Cayenne pepper

112

Melt the butter and cook onions in it for 5 minutes. Do not brown. Add the mushrooms that have been washed, but not peeled. When well coated with butter, add the parsley, flour, bouillon and seasoning. Cook until onions are tender. Add the Madeira and cook 1 minute. Serve garnished with croutons and herbs. Serves 6.

POLISH WILD MUSHROOMS WITH ONIONS
(Grzybkami Z Cebuli)

1 qt. mushrooms
1/2 c. butter or margarine
1 large onion, chopped
1 can mushroom soup

1 can Carnation evaporated
   milk
Salt and pepper to taste

Drain mushrooms thoroughly. Saute onion in butter and add mushrooms. Cook for 10 minutes. Add mushroom soup and stir. Slowly add evaporated milk. Simmer for 20 minutes, stirring occasionally. Can be used as a sauce over meat, rice, noodles, etc., or as a main dish. Serves 8.
Gloria A. Kuckowski, St. Paul, Mn.

STUFFED MUSHROOMS

2 c. (16 oz. or 1 pt.)
   whole fresh mushrooms
2 Tbsp. butter or oleo
1/4 c. chopped almonds
2 Tbsp. chopped onion
   or 1 1/2 tsp. instant

1/2 tsp. salt
1 tsp. lemon juice
1/2 c. (1 slice) crumbled
   bread crumbs
1 Tbsp. sherry or water

Wash mushrooms and stems (save). Arrange mushrooms in shallow pan. In small mixing bowl, combine oleo, almonds until golden, about 3 minutes. Add rest of ingredients except mushroom caps. Mix well and spoon into cups - cook covered with waxed paper. Simmer on 1/2 power about 8 - 10 minutes or until hot. If made ahead and refrigerated, time will need to be increased.
Karen Rupert, St. Cloud, Mn.

ONIONS

Have ready, 3 medium onions (sweet Bermuda), slice as for rings. Soak overnight in:

1 c. water   3/4 c. vinegar (dark)
1 c. sugar

(These should be put in glass bowl with a weight on top plate). Drain and stir in Hellmann's salad dressing with a little celery salt. Store in a cool place - not refrigerated.

Jim Bregel, Windom, Mn.

BUTTER SAUTEED ONIONS

1/4 c. butter or margarine,   1 c. onions, chopped
   melted   medium

Saute onions until golden or if you wish with a few brown pieces. Pour over dumplings. Mix gently and serve, or serve in small ceramic pitcher, hot, to be poured over individual servings as desired. Serves 6 to 8.

Gloria A. Kurkowski, St. Paul, Mn.

FESTIVE FILLED ONIONS

4 medium onions   1/2 tsp. salt
1 (10 oz.) pkg. frozen   2 Tbsp. oleo or butter
   chopped spinach   1/2 c. shredded Cheddar
1/4 c. milk   cheese
2 Tbsp. flour   1 Tbsp. oleo
                                3 Tbsp. dry bread crumbs

Peel onions and halve crosswise, place cut side down in an 8 inch round pan. Cover with waxed paper and microwave 7 - 9 minutes or until onions are tender-crisp. Remove centers, keep for other uses. Separate halves into about 2 - 3 layers of onion. Place center side up in baking dish. Stuff as desired.

Spinach Stuffing: Microwave spinach in covered bowl 5 - 6 minutes or until thawed. Drain well. Combine milk, flour and salt. Stir into spinach and butter. Microwave 2 - 2 1/2 minutes or until thick. Stir in cheese, microwave 1

114

tablespoon butter until melted, stir in crumbs. Fill cups with spinach, top with crumbs. Set aside until ready to reheat. Microwave, covered with waxed paper, on 1/2 power, 8 - 10 minutes or longer if cold.

Karen Rupert, St. Cloud, Mn.

ONION PIE

Precook 2 medium onions in 2 tablespoons butter. Melt 1/4 cup butter in a 9 inch pan. Add 1 cup soda cracker crumbs. Press mixture on bottom and sides of pan. Arrange precooked onion slices in shell. Sprinkle with 1 cup shredded Mozzarella cheese. Beat together:

1 c. milk	2 tsp. dried parsley flakes
2 eggs	1 tsp. salt

Pour over onions. Bake at 350° for 45 minutes till top starts to brown.

Karen Rupert, St. Cloud, Mn.

EASY AU GRATINS

Butter cake pan and add:

1/4 c. melted or cubed margarine or butter	2 c. sour cream
	Salt and pepper
1 large pkg. frozen hash browns	1/3 c. chopped onion
	2 c. grated cheese

Bake 1 hour at 350°.

Mary Hocking, Fargo, N.D.

CHEESE POTATOES

2 lb. frozen hash browns	2 c. shredded Cheddar cheese
1 tsp. salt	1 c. milk
1/4 c. chopped onion	1/2 c. melted butter
1 can cream of chicken soup	1/4 tsp. butter
	1 c. sour cream

Combine butter, cream, soup and milk. Mix cheese and thawed hash browns, salt, pepper and onion and mix all together. Pour into buttered 9x12 inch pan. Top with

crushed potato chips. Cover with foil and bake at 350° for
45 - 60 minutes.

Ruth Rehschuh, Minneapolis, Mn.

HASH BROWNS

1 (2 lb.) pkg. frozen hash   1 pt. whipping cream (ctn.)*
  browns   1/2 c. melted butter
2 c. shredded Swiss cheese   Salt and pepper to taste

Add in that order in 9x13 inch pan. Bake at 325° for
1 1/2 hours.
*Do not whip cream - pour on.

Mary Klaers, Willmar, Mn.

HASH BROWN POTATOES

Have ready 1 package frozen hash browns (Ore-Ida).
Pour into bowl and chop up.

1 can cream of chicken   1 can cream of mushorom
  soup   soup
2 c. sour cream   1 medium onion

Mix together. Put into buttered baking dish, 8x11
inches. Sprinkle top with paprika. Bake 1 1/2 hours at
350°, uncovered.

Lenora Buck, Fargo, N. D.

DELUXE HASH BROWNS

1 (32 oz.) pkg. frozen   1 green pepper
  hash browns   Chopped onions to taste
1 can cream of potato   1 (12 oz.) ctn. sour cream
  soup   Salt, pepper, parsley
1 can cream of celery   flakes, paprika
  soup

Put frozen potatoes, soups, onions, green peppers,
sour cream, salt, pepper in large mixing bowl. Let stand
until you can mix it. Place in slightly greased 9x13 inch
pan. Sprinkle parsley flakes and paprika on top. Bake
uncovered, in 300° oven for 1 1/2 to 2 hours.

Elsie Ekblad

DELUXE HASH BROWNS

1 (32 oz.) pkg. frozen
   hash browns
1 can cream of potato soup

1 can cream of onion soup
1 pt. sour cream

Combine all ingredients and put into a lightly greased 9x13 inch pan. Bake at 300° for 1 1/2 - 2 hours. Do not cover.

Karen Rupert, St. Cloud, Mn.

ONION AND BUTTER POTATOES

Melt 1 stick margarine. Stir in 1 envelope onion soup mix. Have ready, 6 large peeled and sliced potatoes. In large casserole, put about 1/4 cup water. Layer potatoes and soup and butter mix. Cover and bake at 350° for 1 hour.

Ginnie Andersen, St. Paul, Mn.

OOOH-LA-LA POTATOES

6 medium potatoes
1 c. shredded Cheddar
   cheese
6 Tbsp. butter

3/4 c. sour cream
3 chopped green onions
1 tsp. salt
1/4 tsp. pepper

Cook potatoes in skin, cool. Peel and crumble with fork. Combine cheese and 4 tablespoons butter in a large saucepan; heat and stir until cheese is almost melted. Remove from heat; blend in sour cream, onions, salt and pepper. Fold in potatoes. Spoon into greased 2 quart casserole dish. Dot with 2 tablespoons butter. Cover and bake for 25 minutes at 350°. Serves 6 - 8.

Jean Shirley, Fargo, N. D.

ORIENTAL PICK-UP STICKS

4 - 6 potatoes, unpeeled
1/2 c. melted butter
1/4 c. soy sauce

Crushed cereal flakes
Sesame seeds

Scrub potatoes. Cut each into 6 or 8 wedges - lengthwise. Arrange in a 9x13 inch pan. Combine melted butter

1748-81

and soy sauce. Pour over potatoes, stir to coat each wedge. Spread in pan. Sprinkle with cereal flakes and sesame seeds. Bake in 400° oven for 35 minutes or till lightly browned. Serves 4 - 6.

BAKED HASH BROWN POTATOES

1 (32 oz.) pkg. frozen
   hash brown potatoes
1 can cream of potato
   soup
1 can cream of celery
   soup

1 large onion, chopped
1 green pepper, chopped
1 (8 oz.) ctn. sour cream
1/2 tsp. salt
Dash of pepper

Mix soups, sour cream and seasonings together. In 9x13 inch pan, put potatoes, onions and green pepper. Pour soup mixture over potatoes. Bake, uncovered, 1 1/2 to 2 hours at 300°.
   Evelyn Walls, St. Paul, Mn.

VEGETABLES - CZECH POTATOES AND BARLEY

2/3 c. barley
1 c. water or milk
2 Tbsp. shortening
1 tsp. salt

2 lb. potatoes, peeled
1 medium onion
1/4 c. chopped butter

Cook barley in water or milk, shortening and salt, until tender (45 minutes). Boil potatoes in water too. Cover, drain and mash. Mix barley and potatoes, brown onion in butter and pour it over mixture. Serves 4 to 6.
   Mrs. Cecilia Bulera, St. Paul, Mn.

PARTY POTATOES

1 can cream of celery
   soup
1 can Cheddar cheese
   soup
1 ctn. sour cream
Paprika

2 tsp. salt
1/4 c. chopped green onion
1/2 c. shredded Cheddar
   cheese
1 (2 lb.) bag frozen hash
   brown potatoes

Combine all but potatoes first before mixing thoroughly with potatoes. Transfer into ungreased 9x12 inch baking dish or casserole. Sprinkle generously with paprika; cover and bake at 350° for 1 1/4 hours. Serves 8 generously. (Could easily be doubled to serve 16 - 18 adults. Tasted fine reheated in the microwave the next day, too.)

Mrs. Don Bredenberg, Bemidji, Mn.

PATIO POTATOES

1 c. sour cream
1 can cream of potato
   soup
1 can cream of celery
   soup
1/2 c. half & half

1 (32 oz.) bag frozen hash
   browns
1 medium onion, finely
   chopped
1 tsp. salt
1/2 tsp. pepper
Paprika

Preheat oven to 325°. Lightly butter a 2 quart casserole, set aside. Mix all ingredients except paprika together in a large bowl. Turn into prepared casserole. Sprinkle with paprika to taste. Bake in 325° oven for 1 1/2 hours. Yield: 10 servings.

Dolly Nokes, Willmar, Mn.

PIZZA POTATOES

Fill 3 quart casserole with sliced potatoes.

1 (16 oz.) can tomatoes
1 can cream of potato
   soup
1 can Cheddar cheese
   soup

1 (4 to 6 oz.) pkg. sliced
   pepperoni
About 4 oz. Cheddar cheese
Salt and pepper to taste

Put all together and bake about 1 hour at 350° or till potatoes are tender and it is thickened.

Marion Round, Faribault, Mn.

ROADSIDE POTATOES

3 c. half & half
1/2 c. butter or margarine
1 tsp. salt
1 medium onion (optional)

2 (12 oz.) pkg. frozen hash
   browns, thawed
1/2 c. or more grated
   Parmesan cheese

1748-81

Heat cream and butter together, add salt. Place thawed potatoes in a thin layer in oblong baking dish or pan. Pour cream mixture over potatoes, sprinkle top with cheese. Bake at 325° for 1 hour.

Lynn Mehelich, Sauk Centre, Mn.; Linda Graf, Fargo, N. D.

SCALLOPED POTATOES
(From Jacket Boiled Potatoes)

6 potatoes, peeled and sliced
1 large onion, peeled and sliced

1 can cream of mushroom soup
1/2 can milk
1/2 tsp. salt and pepper
American or Cheddar cheese, grated

Combine all ingredients except cheese and pour into greased casserole. Sprinkle with grated cheese and bake in preheated 350° oven for 35 - 40 minutes.

Shirley Pelzel, St. Paul, Mn.

SCALLOPED POTATOES

Microwave time: 29 1/2 minutes

3 Tbsp. butter
2 Tbsp. flour
1 tsp. salt

1 tsp. pepper
3 c. milk

Place butter in 1 quart measuring cup. Microwave at high 1/2 minute or until melted. Blend flour and seasoning. Gradually stir in milk. Microwave at high 8 - 10 minutes. Stir every 3 minutes.

3 1/2 to 4 c. thinly sliced white potatoes

2 Tbsp. onion, minced

Layer half of potatoes and onions and sauce in greased 2 quart casserole. Repeat layers and cover. Microwave at high 17 - 19 minutes, stirring after 10 minutes. Remove from oven and let stand 5 minutes before serving. Makes 4 - 6 servings.

Arlene Byrne, Rochester, Mn.

SWEET POTATOES

1 (18 oz.) can sweet
  potatoes
1/3 c. sugar

1/2 stick butter
1/2 tsp. salt
1 egg

Beat potatoes until smooth. Then add other ingredients. Mix 1/4 cup butter, 1/4 cup sugar, 1/4 cup flour. Beat. Spoon on top. Top with nuts. Bake at 350° for 1 hour.

Madonna Mueller, Jamestown, N. D.

QUICK QUICHE

1 unbaked pie shell
1 egg white, lightly
  beaten
3 eggs

1 c. shredded combined Swiss
  and Cheddar cheeses
1 c. milk
Dash of nutmeg

Saute onions, green pepper and mushrooms. Add cooked crumbled bacon or chopped ham. Brush pie shell with egg white. Sprinkle cheese evenly over bottom. Beat eggs and milk in medium bowl. Blend in nutmeg and add garnish if desired. Pour into pie shell. Bake until top is golden or tester inserted in center comes out clean, 35 to 45 minutes at 350°. Cool 5 minutes.

Bev Larson, Bismarck Council

CURRIED RICE

Saute 1 cup chopped onion in 3 tablespoons butter for 3 - 4 minutes. Add:

1/2 tsp. salt
1/2 tsp. curry powder

1 c. uncooked rice

Cook for 3 minutes, then add:

1 can consomme

1/2 c. water

Cook on low heat, covered, for 30 minutes.
Joan Billadeau, St. Cloud, Mn.

GREEN RICE

1 small box Minute Rice   2 boxes spear broccoli

Cook broccoli, cut up into small pieces, drain. Cook rice. Put together with:

1 can celery soup or   3/4 lb. Velveeta and
   onion soup if desired   Cheddar cheese

Add a little milk, salt and pepper. Top with potato chips if desired before baking. Bake at 350° for 45 minutes to 1 hour.

Erlene Gallion, St. Cloud, Mn.

ITALIAN RICE

1 c. rice   1 medium onion, diced
3 c. water   1/4 tsp. turmeric
2 chicken bouillon cubes   1/2 c. cheese cubes
2 Tbsp. butter   (Cheddar or American)

In medium saucepan, brown together butter, onion, rice. Be careful not to burn onions. When browned, add water, bouillon cubes and turmeric. Bring to boil. Simmer approximately 20 - 25 minutes. When liquid is absorbed, add cheese. Makes approximately 6 servings.

Sue Dierkhising, St. Cloud, Mn.

PARMESAN RICE

Saute 1 small onion in 2 - 3 tablespoons butter. Add 1 can drained mushrooms and a chicken bouillon cube. Add 1 cup uncooked regular rice and saute until translucent. Add 2 1/2 cups water. After rice is cooked, add 1/2 cup Parmesan cheese and 2 tablespoons parsley flakes. Serves 4.

Faye Matson, Bismarck, N. D.

WILD RICE STUFFING

1 pkg. Uncle Ben's long   1/4 lb. butter or margarine
   grain and wild rice mix   1 c. hot water
1 1/2 c. sliced celery   1 (2 oz.) jar sliced pimentos
1 1/2 c. sliced mushrooms

1/2 c. chopped parsley
  or celery leaves

1 (8 oz.) pkg. herb stuffing
  mix

Cook rice as directed on package. Meanwhile, saute celery and mushrooms in butter or margarine 2 minutes. Add herb stuffing mix with hot water, add pimentos and parsley; mix well. Add hot, cooked rice and mix. Use as stuffing or as side dish. If used as a side dish, can be kept warm in covered dish in oven.

           Phyllis Curran, Red River Valley Council

GERMAN SCALLOPED SAUERKRAUT

3 c. sauerkraut,
  canned or homemade,
  drained

2 red apples, cored and
  sliced
1/4 c. brown sugar

Layer in casserole - sauerkraut, apples and brown sugar. Cover and bake at 350° until apples are tender. Delicious served with pork.

           Kathy Bischof, St. Cloud, Mn.

GERMAN SAUERKRAUT

1 jar sauerkraut
1/2 c. chopped onion
1 tsp. butter or margarine
6 strips bacon, fried
  crisp and crumbled

5 Tbsp. applesauce
Salt and pepper to taste
1 1/2 c. water

Use a skillet that will hold all ingredients. Brown slightly 1/2 cup onion with 1 teaspoon butter. Set aside. Fry bacon crisp. Set aside and save grease. Open and pour out all juice from sauerkraut. Refill jar with tap water and empty this. Put sauerkraut, onions, water, salt and pepper in skillet and cook, uncovered, until water is gone. Then add applesauce, crumbled bacon and grease. Heat to warm. For variation, add 1/4 cup of vinegar to water.

           Don Billadeau, St. Cloud, Mn.

FIESTA ONIONS
(Salad)

Peel and slice thin into rings, 6 large Spanish onions (or white onions). Soak 3 hours in brine made of:

1/2 c. vinegar	3/4 c. sugar
1 1/2 c. water	

Drain. Mix:

1 1/2 c. Miracle Whip salad dressing	3 tsp. celery seed
	Salt and pepper to taste

Pour over onions and mix. Serve in a clear glass bowl.

Norma Haugland, Fargo, N. D., Red River Valley Council

STUFFED PEPPERS FOR TWO

Put 2 large green peppers into pan with 1 cup water and cook about 5 minutes. Cut off stem end. Fill with:

1 lb. ground beef, browned, drained	1/3 c. chopped celery
	1 1/2 c. dry bread crumbs
1/3 c. chopped onion	1 can vegetable beef soup

Bake in pan at 325° for 30 minutes.

Mrs. Ronald Schwartz, Owatonna, Mn.

MARINATED VEGETABLES

1 1/2 c. green beans, cut	1/2 c. pimentos, sliced
1/2 c. mushrooms, stems and pieces	1/2 c. radishes, sliced
	1 c. zucchini, sliced
3 Tbsp. dehydrated onion flakes or minced onion	2 c. cauliflower, cut into small pieces
1 cucumber, sliced	

Marinade:

1/2 c. vinegar	Pepper (optional)
1/2 c. water	1 1/2 tsp. seasoned salt
1 tsp. heaping monosodium glutamate	1/2 tsp. garlic powder
	Artificial sweetener to equal 2 tsp. sugar

Pour over vegetables, marinate overnight.

Karen Rupert, St. Cloud, Mn.

EASY GARDEN VEGETABLE PIE

2 c. chopped fresh
  broccoli or sliced fresh
  cauliflowerets*
1/2 c. chopped onion
1/2 c. chopped green pepper
1 c. shredded Cheddar
  cheese (about 4 oz.)

1 1/2 c. milk
3/4 c. Bisquick* baking
  mix
3 eggs
1 tsp. salt
1/4 tsp. pepper

Heat oven to 400°. Lightly grease pie plate, 10 x 1 1/2 inches. Heat 1 inch salted water (1/2 teaspoon salt to 1 cup water) to boiling. Add broccoli. Cover and heat to boiling. Cook until almost tender, about 5 minutes; drain thoroughly. Mix broccoli, onion, green pepper and cheese in pie plate. Beat remaining ingredients until smooth, 15 seconds in blender on high speed or 1 minute with hand beater. Pour into pie plate. Bake until golden brown and knife inserted halfway between center and edge comes out clean, 35 to 40 minutes. Let stand 5 minutes before cutting. Garnish as desired. Refrigerate any remaining pie. (6 servings)
  *One package (10 ounces) frozen chopped broccoli or cauliflower, thawed and drained, can be substituted for the fresh broccoli or cauliflower. Do not cook.
  High altitude directions (3500 to 6500 feet): Cook fresh broccoli or cauliflower about 7 minutes.

VEGETABLE MEDLEY

1 pkg. frozen onions
  (small)
1 pkg. frozen Brussels
  sprouts
1 pkg. frozen broccoli

1 pkg. frozen cauliflower
1 can mushrooms
1/2 pkg. carrots, preboiled
  5 minutes
1 small jar Cheez Whiz
1 can mushroom soup

Place all vegetables (uncooked) in 3 quart casserole. Spoon cheese and soup over. Bake 1 hour at 350°. Uncover, bake 1/2 hour more.
           Gwen Stall, St. Paul, Mn.

FIRE AND ICE TOMATOES

6 large ripe tomatoes
1 large green pepper
1 large red onion
3/4 c. vinegar
1 1/2 tsp. celery salt
4 1/2 tsp. sugar

1/8 tsp. mustard seed
1/2 tsp. salt
1/8 tsp. cayenne pepper
1/8 tsp. pepper
1/4 c. cold water
1 large cucumber

1. Peel tomatoes; cut into quarters. Halve peppers; seed and slice into strips. Slice onion into thin rings. Arrange vegetables, each separate from the others, in neat sections in a large baking dish (not metal) or serving platter. 2. Combine vinegar, water and all the seasonings in a small saucepan. Bring to boiling and boil 1 minute. Pour over vegetables. Cool slightly. Refrigerate vegetables with sauce until quite cold. 3. Just before serving, pare and slice cucumber; arrange with other vegetables.
Carolyn Brudevold, Fargo, N. D.

SCALLOPED CARROTS

4 c. diced carrots
1 medium onion, chopped
3 Tbsp. butter
3/4 c. diced Velveeta cheese

1 can cream of celery soup
3 c. bread crumbs
1/2 c. melted butter

Cook carrots until not quite done. Saute onions in 3 tablespoons butter. Mix in other ingredients. Top with croutons mixed with melted butter. Bake at 350° for 30 minutes, uncovered.
Lois Thelen, Detroit Lakes, Mn.

TOMATO PIE
(Serves 6)

1 pkg. Pillsbury biscuit
  dough
1/2 onion, chopped

1 green pepper
1 c. Mozzarella cheese,
  grated
1 1/2 c. mayonnaise

Mix cheese and mayonnaise together. Line pan with biscuits (I use a regular size pie pan). Slice about 4 medium tomatoes over biscuits. Saute onion and green pepper, sprinkle over tomatoes, then spread cheese and mayonnaise over top. Bake at 350° for 45 minutes.
126   Midge Daulton, St. Paul, Mn.

TOMATOES VINAIGRETTE

10 tomatoes	2 1/2 tsp. salt
2 1/2 c. vegetable oil	1 1/4 tsp. pepper
3/4 c. wine vinegar	1 1/4 tsp. dry mustard
5 tsp. oregano	5 cloves garlic, crushed

Arrange tomatoes on a glass dish, shake oil, vinegar, oregano, salt, pepper, mustard and garlic. Pour over tomatoes, cover and refrigerate at least 2 hours. Arrange on lettuce with 10 green onions, finely chopped and 5 tablespoons snipped fresh parsley.

Esther Carney, Fargo, N. D.

SKILLET ZUCCHINI

3 Tbsp. butter	1/2 tsp. salt
1 1/2 c. fresh onion rings, thinly sliced and separated	Pepper and garlic powder to taste
2 c. thinly sliced zucchini	1 c. fresh tomatoes, cut up
	1 can (4 oz.) sliced mushrooms, drained

Place butter in frying pan and add onion rings; saute, stirring frequently. Add zucchini, cover and cook 6 minutes, stirring occasionally. Add seasonings, tomato and mushrooms. Cover and cook 4 more minutes. This is super, super!

** NOTES **

MAIN DISHES

HANDY CHART OF KITCHEN MATH WITH METRIC

KITCHEN MATH WITH METRIC TABLES

Measure	Equivalent	Metric (ML)
1 Tbsp.	3 tsp.	14.8 milliliters
2 Tbsp.	1 oz.	29.6 milliliters
1 jigger	1½ oz.	44.4 milliliters
¼ cup	4 Tbsp.	59.2 milliliters
1/3 cup	5 Tbsp. plus 1 tsp.	78.9 milliliters
½ cup	8 Tbsp.	118.4 milliliters
1 cup	16 Tbsp.	236.8 milliliters
1 pint	2 cups	473.6 milliliters
1 quart	4 cups	947.2 milliliters
1 liter	4 cups plus 3½ Tbsp.	1,000.0 milliliters
1 oz. (dry)	2 Tbsp.	28.35 grams
1 pound	16 oz.	453.59 grams
2.21 pounds	35.3 oz.	1.00 kilogram

THE APPROXIMATE CONVERSON FACTORS FOR UNITS OF VOLUME

To Convert from	To	Multiply by
teaspoons (tsp.)	milliliters (ml)	5
tablespoons (Tbsp.)	milliliters (ml)	15
fluid ounces (fl. oz.)	milliliters (ml)	30
cups (c)	liters (l)	0.24
pints (pt)	liters (l)	0.47
quarts (qt)	liters (l)	0.95
gallons (gal)	liters (l)	3.8
cubic feet (ft3)	cubic meters (m3)	0.03
cubic yards (yd3)	cubic meters (m3)	0.76
milliliters (ml)	fluid ounces (fl oz)	0.03
liters (l)	pints (pt)	2.1
liters (l)	quarts (qt)	1.06
liters (l)	gallons (gal)	0.26
cubic meters (m3)	cubic feet (ft3)	35
cubic meters (m3)	cubic yards (yd3)	1.3

DEEP-FAT FRYING TEMPERATURES WITHOUT A THERMOMETER

A 1-inch cube of white bread will turn golden brown:

345° to 355°	65 seconds
355° to 365°	60 seconds
365° to 375°	50 seconds
375° to 385°	40 seconds
385° to 395°	20 seconds

TABLE OF PROPORTIONS

Gelatin (unflavored) - 1 Tbsp. thickens 2 cups liquid

Salt

Soups & Sauces	1 tsp. to 1 qt. sauce
Dough	1 tsp. to 4 cups flour
Cereals	1 tsp. to 2 cups liquid
Meat	1 tsp. to 1 lb. meat
Vegetables	½ tsp. using 1 qt. water

SIMPLIFIED MEASURES

dash = less than 1/8 teaspoon

3 tsp. = 1 Tbsp.
16 Tbsp. = 1 cup
1 cup = ½ pt.
2 cups = 1 pt.

2 pt. (4 c.) = 1 qt.
4 qt. (liquid) = 1 gal.
8 qt. (solid) = 1 peck
4 pecks = 1 bushel
16 oz. = 1 lb.

If you want to measure part-cups by the table-spoon, remember:

4 Tbsp. = ¼ cup
5 1/3 Tbsp. = 1/3 cup
8 Tbsp. = ½ cup

10 2/3 Tbsp. = 2/3 cup
12 Tbsp. = ¾ cup
14 Tbsp. = 7/8 cup

CONTENTS OF CANS

Of the different sizes of cans used by commercial canners, the most common are:

Size	Average Contents
8-oz.	1 cup
picnic	1¼ cups
No. 300	1¾ cups
No. 1 tall	2 cups
No. 303	2 cups
No. 2	2½ cups
No. 2½	3½ cups
No. 3	4 cups
No. 10	12 to 13 cups

I lived in the Azores, Portugal for two years, and as a result, the enclosed menu has become my favorite, particularly for first time guests. I hope that all enjoy them as much as I have in the past years.

MENU:

Caldo Verde (Green Soup)
Alcatra (Roast Beef)
Fruta de Compota (Compote)

CALDO VERDE
(Portugese Green Soup)
(Serves 8)

Combine:
2 1/2 qt. water   4 potatoes, peeled and diced
4 Tbsp. olive oil

Cook over medium heat for 30 minutes. Drain and reserve liquid. Force through a sieve, or mash as fine as possible. Return them to the liquid in the saucepan. Add:

2 tsp. salt   1/2 tsp. pepper

Cook over low heat for 15 minutes. Wash 1 pound spinach and remove tough fibers (may substitute cabbage). Add to potato mixture and cook over medium heat for 15 minutes. Serve hot or cold.

ALCATRA
(Roast Beef - Serves 8)

This recipe was designed for the tougher cuts of meat. In Portugal, it is cooked in a special clay pot, but it can be successfully done in a roaster or casserole. In using the clay pot, the pot absorbs some of the flavors of the meat which are again released into the meat in the next roasting.

6 lb. pot roast or any   2 onions, sliced
  lean meat   3 whole cloves
1 bay leaf   2 Tbsp. tomato paste
1 Tbsp. salt   3 cloves garlic, minced
6 whole peppercorns

2 parts white wine and   1/4 lb. bacon, diced
  1 part water*

    *Enough to cover (it will take about 1 quart of white wine. Use <u>dry</u> wine.

    Place meat in casserole and cover with sliced onions. Add bay leaf, garlic, cloves, pepper, salt and tomato paste mixed with a little water. Place diced bacon on top. Bake in 400° oven for 2 hours. Reduce heat to 325° and continue cooking until tender and brown, about 1 - 1 1/2 hours. About 45 minutes before it is done, add fresh carrots, cut into 1 inch slices. Fifteen minutes before serving, add canned potatoes. (Fresh potatoes may also be cooked with the meat.)

    Serve with tossed salad, preferably with oil and vinegar dressing.

FRUTA DE COMPOTA

    Cut into serving pieces:

1 fresh pineapple or   2 oranges
  1 can pineapple chunks   2 bananas
2 apples

    (You may also add any other fresh fruits.) Pour into crystal bowl. Add 1/2 cup dry white table wine. Mix well. Let stand for 2 hours, stirring occasionally. Serve in champagne glasses or China cups. Eat the fruit with a <u>fork</u>, then drink the juice.

             Mrs. Frank Van Gorp, Alexandria Mn.

BAKED STEAK

2 lb. round steak, about   1 (4 oz.) can mushrooms,
  1 inch thick   not drained
1/4 lb. butter or margarine   1 env. dry onion soup mix

    Cut steak into serving size pieces and place in 9x13 inch pan. Spread butter on meat. Add mushrooms and sprinkle with soup. Cover pan with foil and seal. Bake about 2 hours at 325°. Serves 6 - 8 people.

           Carol Arndt, Windom, Mn.

BEEF BURGUNDY

3 lb. stew beef (I like
   to use sirloin tip roast),
   cut into bite sized
   pieces
1 pkg. onion soup mix

1 c. burgundy (you can use
   part beef broth and less
   burgundy if you wish)
1 can cream of celery soup
1 can cream of mushroom soup

Mix together in small roaster - cook, covered, for 3 hours at 325° to 350°. Serve with the noodles.

Noodles:

12 oz. noodles (egg
   noodles), cooked as
   directed
1/2 c. butter, melted
Salt and pepper to taste

1 c. sour cream
1 c. or pkg. slivered almonds,
   toasted
1/2 c. grated Parmesan
   cheese

Cook noodles till tender - drain and rinse with boiling water. Combine rest of ingredients- put into casserole and cook at 350° about 30 minutes. (Can make ahead and refrigerate till ready for oven.)
        Alice Ann Hanson, Grand Forks, N. D.

BEEF JERKY

1 1/2 lb. flank steak
1 tsp. liquid smoke
1/3 tsp. garlic powder
1/3 tsp. black pepper

1 tsp. Accent
1 tsp. onion powder
1/4 c. Worcestershire sauce
1/4 c. soy sauce

Semi-freeze meat and slice 1/8 inch thick, with grain. Marinate overnight in a glass dish. Lay slices directly on oven grates and place cookie sheet beneath to catch drippings. Open oven door a crack and roast at 125° to 140° F. for 8 to 12 hours. Check for desired dryness.
        Jean Shirley, Fargo, N. D.

BEEF AND OLIVE RAGOUT

1/2 c. minced celery
2 Tbsp. butter
1 medium green pepper,
   sliced

1 clove garlic
1 (10 1/2 oz.) can condensed
   tomato soup
1/4 c. burgundy or other dry
   red wine

1748-81

1/4 tsp. salt
Cooked noodles
1 lb. round steak
1/2 c. sliced onion

1 (4 oz.) can sliced
mushrooms (save liquid)
1/4 c. stuffed olives
1/8 tsp. pepper

In skillet brown meat in butter; add celery, onion, green pepper, mushrooms and garlic. Cook until vegetables are almost tender. Stir in soup, wine, mushroom liquid, olives, salt and pepper. Cover and cook 1 hour or until meat is tender. Serve with noodles. Makes 4 servings.

BEEF ORIENTAL

1 lb. boneless round
steak
1/2 c. each diagonally
sliced carrot, celery
and green onion
1/4 tsp. ground ginger
2 Tbsp. butter or oleo
1 can beefy mushroom
soup

1 1/2 c. water
1 (16 oz.) can Chinese
vegetables, drained
1 Tbsp. cornstarch
1 Tbsp. soy sauce
1 tsp. brown sugar
1/2 tsp. salt

Freeze meat 1 hour to firm (makes slicing easier). Slice into thin strips. In skillet cook carrot, celery, onion and ginger in butter until tender. Push to one side. Add meat and cook just till color changes, about 3 - 4 minutes. Add remaining ingredients. Cook, stirring until thickened. Serve over cooked rice with additional soy sauce. Makes 5 cups.

Jane Bohline, Minneapolis, Mn.

BEEF STROGANOFF

Have ready, 1 pound trimmed beef tenderloin, sliced 1/4 inch strips, 2 inches long. Brown in 1/4 cup butter. Add 6 ounces mushrooms (about 2 cups) and 1/2 cup chopped onion. Add 1 can condensed beef broth. Heat to boiling. Blend 1 cup sour cream with 2 1/2 tablespoons flour. Stir into broth. Cook, stirring constantly until thickened. Add salt and pepper to taste. Serve over noodles or rice. Makes 4 to 5 servings.

Recipe from Minneapolis, Mn.

BEEF STROGANOFF

Have ready, 1 round of steak, cubed. Brown. Add:

Onion   1 can mushrooms

Simmer 3 hours. Add:

1 can cream of celery   1 can cream of mushroom
  soup   soup
1 can cream of chicken   1 (12 oz.) ctn. sour cream
  soup

Add water or milk for gravy. Put on rice, toast or mashed potatoes or noodles.

Bev Barglof, Detroit Lakes, Mn.

CHOPPED BEEF STROGANOFF

1 1/2 lb. ground beef   3 Tbsp. flour
  (or very thin sliced   2 Tbsp. tomato paste
  beef, cut into strips)   2 1/2 c. water
1 env. onion soup mix   3/4 c. sour cream

In skillet stir meat until browned. Blend in onion soup mix, flour, tomato paste. Add water and simmer, covered, 15 minutes. (If too thick, add water.) When ready to serve, stir in sour cream. Serve over noodles or rice.

BEEF TOSTADA PIE

1 1/2 lb. lean ground   1/8 tsp. pepper
  beef   1 c. crushed tortilla chips
1 large onion, chopped   1 c. shredded Cheddar
1 medium green pepper,   cheese
  chopped (1 c.)   Whole tortilla chips
1 1/2 tsp. chili powder   1 (8 oz.) can tomato sauce
3/4 tsp. salt   1 (16 oz.) can tomatoes,
1/4 tsp. garlic salt   drained and cut up

Brown beef and onion, drain excess fat. Stir in green pepper and seasonings, tomato sauce and tomatoes. Sprinkle 1/2 cup crushed chips in lightly greased 8 inch pan. Layer with half meat mixture, 1/2 cup cheese, remaining 1/2 cup crushed chips and remaining meat mixture. Wreath top with whole chip. Bake at 350° for 30 - 35 minutes. Top with remaining cheese.

1748-81   Sue Hick, Detroit Lakes, Mn.

ENCHILADA SAUCE AND ENCHILADAS

Sauce: Heat in heavy saucepan, 1/4 cup salad oil. Add:

1 medium onion, chopped
1 can tomato paste

1 clove garlic, mashed, or
1/2 tsp. garlic salt

Simmer over low flame 3 minutes, then add:

1 1/2 c. water
1 tsp. vinegar
1/2 tsp. oregano
1/2 tsp. salt

1 tsp. sugar
1/8 tsp. cayenne pepper
2 tsp. chili powder

Bring to boil. Reduce flame. Simmer 15 minutes to blend flavor.

Enchiladas: Brown 1 pound ground beef with salt and pepper. Place tortilla shells over beef mixture to soften. Fill tortillas with ground beef, slices of Cheddar cheese and some enchilada sauce. Roll and place with folded edge down in 9x9 inch pan. Pour more sauce and cheese over rolled enchiladas. Bake in 350° oven for 15 minutes or until cheese melts. Makes 4 enchiladas. To serve, top each enchilada with sour cream (optional).
Sue Peterson, Grand Forks, N. D.

FILET DE BOEUF EN CROUTE "EXCELLENCE"
(Beef Wellington - English derived from French Haute Cuisine)
(Serves 4 - 6)

Pastry:

4 c. flour
1 tsp. salt
1/2 c. butter

1/2 c. shortening
1 egg, slightly beaten
1/2 c. ice water

Have ready:
2 - 3 lb. filet of beef
2 Tbsp. cognac
Salt
Freshly ground pepper
6 slices bacon

8 oz. chicken liver pate
3 - 4 truffles (very
difficult to obtain, can be
made without)
1 egg, slightly beaten

Place flour, salt, butter and shortening in bowl, cut

and blend. Add egg, ice water to make dough. Wrap in
waxed paper and chill. Preheat oven to 450°. Rub filet with
cognac and season with salt and pepper. Lay bacon over
top - place meat on rack, 15 minutes - rare; 20 - 25 minutes
for medium. Remove from oven and remove bacon. Cool
to room temperature. Spread pate all over top and sides.
Cut truffles into halves - sink pieces in line across the top.
    Roll out pastry in rectangle, 18 x 12 x 1/4 inch thick.
Place filet - top (truffles) down in middle of pastry. Draw
along side up to overlap filet. Brush with egg to seal. Trim
excess (on ends), make envelope fold, egg to seal. Decorate
with trimmings down center. Bake 30 minutes at 425°.
Serve with:

Sauce Madere:

1/3 c. chopped shallots   1/2 c. + 3 Tbsp. Madiera wine
3 Tbsp. butter   1 1/2 c. brown sauce*

    *Elpagnolef - French nearly as important as the wine,
nothing more French. Closest substitute - beef gravy.*
    Cook shallots and 1 tablespoon butter till brown. Add
1/2 cup wine. Reduce to half, add brown sauce. Cook 10
minutes. Strain through sieve. Bring to boil again. Turn
off, add remaining butter. Stir until butter melts, add rest
of wine.
    *Can substitute with brown gravy mix, adding shallots,
etc. for sauce.
                    Carolyn Smith, Fargo, N. D.

                BEST ROAST BEEF IN THE WORLD

Roast of beef   1 can cream of mushroom soup
1 env. onion gravy mix   Small amount of A.1. Steak
                                     sauce

    Line roaster with aluminum foil. Put roast in roaster
and put ingredients on top of roast. Add small amount of
water in bottom of roaster. Baking time depends on size of
roast, but longer the better. Makes its own gravy.
                    Judith Volkers, Rogers, Mn.

BUTTER BASTED RUMP ROAST

1 (5 lb.) rolled rump roast
1 Tbsp. lemon juice
1 c. melted butter

2 Tbsp. minced onion
1 Tbsp. Worcestershire sauce

Prepare the charcoal briquets for indirect cooking, by stacking them to the sides on the fire grill. Make an aluminum foil drip pan for the area between them. Allow the coals to gray all over before putting on the meat, especially if starter fluid has been used to ignite them. This assures that all fluid has been burned away and will not affect the flavor of the meat. Salt and pepper the roast generously and place it over drip pan on upper grill. Put the cover on the kettle (Weber) and roast for no less than 23 minutes per pound for medium or use a meat thermometer. Mix the remaining ingredients well and baste the roast each 15 minutes during roasting time. Potatoes and onion, sliced; add butter, salt and pepper wrapped in foil and placed alongside of meat 1 hour before the roast is done.

CHILDREN'S PARTY BAR-B CUPS

Depending on how many children:
1 can Pillsbury buttermilk
   or country style biscuits
1 lb. hamburger

1/2 c. chopped onion
Salt and pepper to taste

Brown and drain the hamburger, onion and salt and pepper. Add:

1/2 c. catsup
1/2 c. B-B-Q sauce

1/4 c. honey or 2 Tbsp.
   brown sugar
1 c. shredded Cheddar
   cheese to sprinkle on top

Press biscuits into muffin tins and up the sides to edges. Fill with meat mixture. Sprinkle Cheddar cheese on top. Bake at 400° until crusts are brown (approximately 15 minutes).

Jane Segebarth, Minneapolis, Mn.

DELECTABLE POT ROAST

3/4 c. sour cream
4 thin slices salt pork
1 large onion, sliced
1 scallion, chopped,
  tops and all
1 large carrot, sliced
1 clove garlic, chopped

3 to 4 lb. beef roast (rolled
  rump or bottom round)
Salt and pepper
3/4 c. dry red wine (claret
  or burgundy)
3 Tbsp. flour
1/4 c. water
1 Tbsp. lemon juice

Bring sour cream to room temperature. Put 2 slices of pork in heavy skillet or kettle. Add onion, scallion, carrot and garlic and cook over medium heat 3 to 4 minutes. Rub roast with 1 teaspoon pepper and dash of salt. Brown well. Turn heat off and let pan cool 5 minutes. Heat wine a little; add to meat, stir in sour cream. Put remaining pork on top of roast, cover tightly, simmer 2 1/2 hours. Make gravy with flour, water and lemon juice. (6 servings)

DEVILED SWISS STEAK

Brown round steak dredged in flour in hot fat with onions, salt and pepper. Mix:

1 pt. jar tomatoes
1 c. water
2 Tbsp. Worcestershire
  sauce
1 Tbsp. dry mustard

1 Tbsp. brown sugar
1 1/2 tsp. salt
1 tsp. lemon juice
Dash of pepper and
  paprika

Pour over meat in skillet. Bake at 350° for 1 hour.
Sue Hick, Detroit Lakes, Mn.

DINNER ON A BUN

1 loaf French bread
1 1/2 lb. lean ground
  beef
1 small can Carnation
  milk
1/2 c. crushed soda
  crackers
1 egg
1 Tbsp. mustard

1/2 c. chopped onion
1 1/2 tsp. salt
3/4 tsp. Accent
4 oz. grated American or
  Cheddar cheese (save some
  for sprinkling on after
  baked and return to oven
  till melted)

Cut French bread in half lengthwise. Mix above ingredients and spread on each half. Wrap bread in heavy duty foil (bottom and sides - leave top unwrapped). Bake at 350° for 40 minutes.

Gerri Ruprecht, St. Cloud, Mn.

FLEISHKUHLE
(German Dish)

3 1/2 c. flour	1/2 c. cream
1 1/2 tsp. salt	1/2 c. water

This will make a soft dough. Add additional flour or liquid as needed. Make small dough balls the size of buns and let rest on bread board for 30 minutes or so.

Meat Mixture:

2 lb. hamburger (some pork if preferred)	Salt, pepper, garlic and onion salt to taste

Mix thoroughly. Roll out small balls of dough to size of breakfast plate, spread meat on one side, flap dough over and seal edges. Trim with saucer. Deep fry at 375° until brown on both sides.

Gertie Helm, Bismarck, N. D.

GERMAN MEAT AND SAUERKRAUT
(Serves 6 - 8)

6 bratwurst	3 lb. sauerkraut, rinsed with cold water and drained
6 Polish sausage, cut into 2 inch lengths	2 green apples, peeled and diced
6 medium onions, peeled and cut into halves crosswise	1 red bell pepper, diced
	2 (12 oz.) bottles light beer
1/4 lb. bacon, unsliced	1 Tbsp. caraway seed
6 pork chops (smoked)	1 Tbsp. paprika
	6 whole peppercorns

Brown bratwurst on all sides in skillet. Remove and place in kettle or Dutch oven. Repeat with Polish sausage and onions. Place bacon and pork chops in kettle, add remaining ingredients, cover and simmer gently 1 hour. Remove bacon. Serve steaming hot with German white wine, cooked green beans and large chunks of dark bread.

138   Evelyn Sullivan, St. Paul, Mn.

GIANT BURGER

1 1/2 lb. ground beef
1 (3 oz.) pkg. cream
  cheese, softened

1 Tbsp. drained horseradish
1 1/2 tsp. salt
1 Tbsp. prepared mustard

Mix meat with salt. Divide in half. Put into bottom of an 8 inch pie plate. Mix remaining ingredients, spread within 1 inch of edge of meat. Spread remaining meat over cheese, pinch seal edges. Bake, uncovered, in 350° oven for 40 - 45 minutes.

Wanda Thompson, Minneapolis, Mn.

GREEK BEEF AND NOODLES

1 lb. round steak, cut
  into thin strips
1 clove garlic, minced
1 Tbsp. margarine or
  butter
1 c. onion rings (about
  1 small onion)
3/4 c. mayonnaise (Kraft)

1/3 c. flour
2 c. milk
1 tsp. salt
1 tsp. dill weed
1 (8 oz.) pkg. egg noodles,
  cooked and drained
1 c. ripe olives, halved
1 tomato, cut into wedges

Saute meat and garlic in margarine or butter. Add onion rings, cook until tender. Combine mayonnaise and flour, gradually add milk. Cook over low heat, stirring constantly until thickened. Blend in seasonings. Remove 1 cup sauce. Add remaining sauce and olives to noodles; mix well. Spoon noodle mixture onto serving platter; top with meat mixture. Place reserved sauce on meat mixture; garnish with tomato wedges at both ends of platter.

Don Billadeau, St. Cloud, Mn.

HAMBURGER DELUXE

Brown together:
1 chopped onion

1 1/2 lb. ground beef

Add:
3 c. frozen French fries
1 c. cooked, diced celery

2 c. diced carrots
1 box frozen peas

May add 1 can tomato soup or tomato juice. Bake 45 minutes in 350° oven.

Shirley Pelzel, St. Paul, Mn.

HAMBURGER HEAVEN

1 lb. hamburger
1 medium onion, chopped
3 stalks celery, chopped
1 can mushrooms
1 can black olives

1 pkg. medium noodles
1/2 c. cheese, cubed
  (Cheddar, American)
1 large can tomatoes
1 c. water

    Brown hamburger, onions and celery. Combine the other ingredients except cheese. Bring to boil. Simmer until noodles are tender and liquid is absorbed. Add cheese.
                Sue Dierkhising, St. Cloud, Mn.

HAMBURGER STROGANOFF

    Brown and drain 1 1/2 pounds hamburger. Add:

1/2 pkg. onion soup mix
1 can cream of chicken
  soup

1 can water
2 Tbsp. butter
2 Tbsp. parsley

    Simmer 1/2 hour. Add 8 ounces sour cream just before serving over either rice or chow mein noodles.
              Mrs. Ronald Schwartz, Owatonna, Mn.

HAMBURGER STROGANOFF

    Melt 1/4 cup butter in heavy skillet. Add and cook slowly until soft 1/2 cup minced onion. Add:

1 lb. ground beef

1 clove garlic, peeled (or
    garlic powder)

    Stir until lightly browned. Stir in:

2 Tbsp. flour
1/4 tsp. pepper

1 tsp. salt
1/2 lb. mushrooms, sliced

    Cook 5 minutes. Add 1 can cream of chicken or mushroom soup. Simmer 10 minutes. Stir in 1 cup sour cream. Heat, taste and add more salt if needed. Serve over egg noodles.
              C. Landwehr, Minneapolis, Mn.

HAMBURGER NOODLE STROGANOFF

1 lb. hamburger	2 c. cooked noodles
1/2 c. onion, chopped	1/2 c. water
1 can cream of mushroom	1/2 tsp. paprika
soup	1/2 tsp. salt
1/2 c. sour cream	1/8 tsp. pepper

Brown beef and onion. Add remaining ingredients. Pour into 1 1/2 quart shallow baking dish. Bake 25 minutes at 400° or until hot. Garnish with tomato slices and buttered bread crumbs the last 5 minutes if desired. Makes about 4 1/2 cups.

Kathy Neels, St. Cloud, Mn.

HAMBURGER PIE

Brown 1 pound hamburger with onions. Add 1 (15 ounce) can of tomato sauce and spices (oregano, Italian seasoning). Simmer 15 minutes. Butter sides and bottom of pie pan and line with crescent rolls. Pour hamburger and tomato sauce mixture into pan and sprinkle Mozzarella cheese on top. Bake at 450° for about 30 minutes. Wha-la! Dinner is served.

HARD TACK
(Norwegian)

1 c. rye meal or graham	1/4 tsp soda
flour	2 Tbsp. melted butter
1/2 c. white flour	1 Tbsp. sugar
1/2 tsp. salt	1/2 c. milk

Roll thin on floured board. Cut into squares. Bake 15 minutes on cookie sheet in 350° oven or on lefsa grill.

Alvera Solvie, Glenwood, Mn.

HOT CORNED BEEF BARBECUE

1 tsp. chili powder	3/4 c. catsup
2 Tbsp. cider vinegar	3/4 c. water
2 Tbsp. Worcestershire	2 (12 oz.) cans corned beef
sauce	8 hamburger buns
1/8 tsp. cayenne pepper	8 whole sweet pickles

Put into skillet chili powder, vinegar, Worcestershire sauce and cayenne pepper. Stir catsup into seasoning. Add water to catsup mixture. Break up corned beef and add to mixture. Cook over medium heat, stirring constantly about 20 minutes or until most of the liquid has evaporated and mixture is thick. Place hamburger buns, split side up, on cooky sheet and broil 4 inches from heat, about 2 minutes or until lightly toasted. Spoon mixture on bottom half of bun, put tops on. Garnish each with sweet pickle on a toothpick.

HOUSE OF SCHWARZENBERG POT ROAST

4 lb. top round beef, rolled	1 medium onion, sliced
2 tsp. salt	2 tomatoes, quartered
1/8 tsp. pepper	1 c. bouillon
4 strips bacon	1 c. white or red wine
1 whole carrot	1/4 c. cognac or whiskey
1 stalk celery	2 Tbsp. sherry
2 Tbsp. parsley	1 large head cabbage, quartered
Pinch of marjoram	3 Tbsp. flour
Pinch of sage	3 Tbsp. water
1 bay leaf	1 Tbsp. cream
2 Tbsp. butter	

Wipe meat, sprinkle salt and pepper. Cover with bacon strips. Place in Dutch oven with carrot, celery, parsley and spices. In separate pan, saute onions in butter until tender; add to meat with tomatoes, bouillon, wine, cognac and sherry. Cover, simmer slowly for 3 hours. About 20 minutes before done, remove cover and add quartered cabbage and replace cover. When done, remove meat to warm platter and arrange cabbage around meat. Boil down liquid in Dutch oven, thicken with flour. Add cream, stir well. Serves 8.

Marion Baihly

IMPOSSIBLE HAMBURGER PIE

1 lb. ground beef	1 c. shredded Cheddar cheese
1 1/2 c. chopped onion	1 1/2 c. milk
1/2 tsp. salt	1/4 tsp. pepper
3/4 c. Bisquick	3 eggs

Lightly butter a 10 x 1 1/2 inch Pyrex pie plate. Cook ground beef and onion until meat is browned. Drain. Add salt and pepper and mix well; spread in Pyrex pie plate. Sprinkle with cheese. Beat remaining ingredients in blender for 15 seconds or 1 minute with hand beater. Pour into pie plate. Bake until golden brown and silver knife inserted in center comes out clean. Let stand 5 minutes before cutting. (Refrigerate leftovers.)

Ruth Rehschuh, Minneapolis, Mn.

ITALIAN BEEF ROAST

1 (6 lb.) round or rump roast

3 large onions
1 tsp. salt

Place beef in roaster 1/2 filled with water. Add salt and onions. Cover roast in a 500° oven 1/2 hour. Reduce heat to 325° and continue roasting till tender (about 3 hours). Remove from oven, let stand overnight. Next day, remove fat and slice very thin. Strain liquid and add:

1/2 tsp. garlic salt
1 tsp. oregano
1/4 tsp. basil
1/2 tsp. salt

1 tsp. Accent
1/2 tsp. Italian seasoning
Green pepper slices

Bring all to boiling point. Place sliced beef and liquid in flat pan. Place in oven at 350° for 30 minutes. Stir a couple of times to combine well. Serve on hard rolls, warm or as roast beef dinner.

Linda Seidel, Audubon, Mn.

ITALIAN DELIGHT

1 lb. ground lean beef
1 Tbsp. cooking oil
1 onion, large, chopped fine
1 large can creamed corn

1 can tomato soup
Salt and pepper to taste
1/2 - 3/4 c. grated cheese
1/2 pkg. spaghetti, cooked and drained

Brown beef in oil. Add onion. Add remaining ingredients. Mix well. Top with cheese. Bake.

Doris Schmidt, Willmar, Mn.

IVA BLEHR'S BEEF IN SHERRY

2 lb. stewing beef or
   cut up round steak
1/2 pkg. dried onion
   soup

1 can cream of mushroom soup
1 can water
1/2 c. sherry (or any
   wine)

Put into casserole, cover and bake in oven 3 1/2 hours at 325°.

Karen Rupert, St. Cloud, Mn.

JELLIED CORNED BEEF

1 pkg. lemon jello
1 3/4 c. boiling water
2 Tbsp. vinegar

1/2 tsp. prepared mustard
1 c. drained peas

Dissolve jello, add vinegar, let partially set. Mince beef with mustard. Add peas, mix carefully. Set in bread loaf pan overnight. Serve with potato chips, cake and coffee. A quick luncheon, ready ahead.

Mrs. James R. McQuaid, Anoka, Mn.

KAU KAU BEEF

2 lb. sirloin steak, cut
   into 1 1/2 inch chunks
1/2 c. salad oil
1/2 c. red wine vinegar
1/2 c. sliced onions
1 clove garlic, chopped
1 Tbsp. pickling spices
   (remove red peppers)

Salt
8 to 12 large button
   mushrooms
4 to 6 (1 1/2 inch) squares
   green pepper
4 to 6 small white onions,
   peeled
4 to 6 cherry tomatoes
Wooden handled skewers

Combine oil, vinegar, onions, garlic, spices and salt. Marinate steak in 1/3 of sauce for 4 to 6 hours. To string skewers, first place mushrooms about 6 inches from handle, then piece of steak, a square of pepper, a piece of steak, an onion, a piece of steak, a tomato, a piece of steak and finish with a mushroom. Baste with barbecue sauce; barbecue, turning and basting frequently for 15 to 20 minutes. To serve, loosen meat with fork, then slide contents off skewer onto each plate.

144

KRAUTWICKEL

1 medium head cabbage
1 1/4 c. rice
4 Tbsp. butter or
   shortening
1/2 lb. lean ground beef

2 large onions, chopped
4 - 5 tomatoes, peeled fresh
   or canned
1 1/4 c. beef broth
Salt, pepper, rosemary to
   taste

Scald cabbage and remove leaves. In a pan with a tight fitting lid, saute raw rice and onion in margarine until light and yellow, stirring constantly. All at once, add 3 cups of water and simmer 20 minutes, covered. Fill each leaf of cooked cabbage with cooked rice, roll up and place in a greased glass baking dish. Brown meat with large chopped onions, add tomatoes, broth and spices. Pour over rolls and bake 30 minutes at 350°, covered.
Kathy Bishof, St. Cloud, Mn.

PERFECT STANDING RIB ROAST
(Start your dinner before leaving for the day)

Choose at least a 2 pound rib roast, allowing 3/4 to 1 pound per person. Any time during the day, place the room temperature roast, sprinkled with salt, pepper and seasoned salts, on a rack in an open pan for exactly 45 minutes in a preheated 375° oven. Do not add water. Do not cover. Do not baste. Turn off oven, leave roast in oven with door closed. Turn oven on for another 45 minutes before serving (60 - 70 minutes for a 10 - 12 pound roast).
Marge Johnson, Minneapolis, Mn.

ITALIAN STEAK

2 lb. round steak, cut
   into serving pieces
1 c. chili sauce
1/2 c. water
1/4 c. vinegar
1 Tbsp. Worcestershire
   sauce

1 clove garlic, cut up
1 large onion, sliced
1 green pepper, sliced
4 oz. can mushrooms
1/4 c. stuffed olives, sliced
1/2 tsp. thyme
Salt and pepper to taste

Brown steak in skillet. Combine ingredients. Pour over steak. Cover tightly. Simmer on top of range or bake at 350° for 1 1/2 to 2 hours. Note: Ingredients may be more or less as desired to taste.
1748-81   Mary Kozel, Grand Forks, N. D.   145

LAMB PAPRIKA BLINTZES

2 c. pancake mix
1 egg, well beaten
2 c. milk

2 Tbsp. melted butter
1 Tbsp. brandy, if desired

While griddle is heating, add milk, brandy and melted butter to well beaten egg. Add pancake mix. Stir lightly, do not overmix. Use 1/3 cup measure to make uniform, round 6 inch pancakes. Hold cup close to griddle and pour batter all at once. When top side is full of bubbles, turn pancakes. Brown. Place pancakes in single layer on cooky sheet. If to be served at once, keep pancakes hot by placing in a 325° oven. Yield: 14 (6 inch) pancakes.

Filling (for 14 Blintzes):

1/2 c. minced onion
3 Tbsp. butter
2 lb. lean ground lamb
3 Tbsp. flour
1/2 tsp. Worcestershire
   sauce
1 c. sour cream

2 tsp. paprika
1/4 tsp. garlic salt
1/2 tsp. salt
1/4 tsp. black pepper
1 c. chicken bouillon (made
   from 2 chicken bouillon
   cubes and 1 c. boiling
   water)

Cook onion slowly in melted butter in heavy frying pan until tender, but not brown. Pull to one side of pan. Add lamb. Cook until browned, pulling apart with a fork or pancake turner. Stir in flour and seasonings. Cook a few minutes, then add bouillon and simmer about 15 minutes. Remove from heat. Stir in sour cream. Both filling and pancakes may be made ahead and placed in refrigerator until cool. Then roll the filling in the pancakes and place in heatproof shallow dish. Or, put together for heating in oven just before serving. Just before serving, place a good sized spoonful of the lamb filling in middle of each pancake. Pull pancake edges up over filling, overlap. Hold in place with a toothpick. Place filled pancakes in shallow baking dish or heatproof platter. To bake: Drizzle a little melted butter over pancakes. Sprinkle with grated Parmesan cheese. Bake in a 400° oven for about 8 minutes. Serve piping hot with a choice of toppings - sour cream, Parmesan cheese or a cranberry relish.

146

OPEN-FACED PIZZABURGER

1 (12 oz.) can luncheon
  meat
1/4 lb. American cheese
1/2 small onion

1 (6 oz.) can tomato paste
1/2 tsp. oregano
Hamburger buns
Grated Parmesan cheese

Put luncheon meat, cheese and onion through a meat grinder. Add tomato paste and oregano. Spread on split buns, covering edges. Sprinkle with grated Parmesan cheese. Place under broiler until cheese melts. Serves 10.
Rita Aaker, Marshall, Mn.

PEPPER STEAK

1 1/2 - 2 lb. round steak,
  partially frozen
2 Tbsp. oil
1 small onion, sliced into
  strips
1/4 tsp. garlic salt

2 large green peppers, sliced
  into strips
1 c. celery, sliced
1 Tbsp. soy sauce
3 tsp. cornstarch in 2 Tbsp.
  water
1 can beef consomme

Slice steak into thin strips; sear in hot oil. Add onion, pepper, garlic salt, celery and 1/2 the consomme. Cook 5 minutes. Add the cornstarch mixture and stir vigorously while it thickens. Add more consomme if needed. Add soy sauce and simmer 4 - 5 minutes. Serve over rice. Serves 6.
Dee Olson, St. Paul, Mn.

PEPPER STEAK

1 lb. round or sirloin
  steak, cut into strips
1/4 c. salad oil
1 clove garlic, minced
1 Tbsp. soy sauce
1 tsp. salt
1/4 c. water

1 c. green peppers, cut
  into strips
1 c. chopped onion
1/2 c. chopped celery
2 Tbsp. cornstarch
1 c. water
2 tomatoes, cut into eighths

Brown beef in oil, add garlic and cook until yellow. Add soy sauce, salt and 1/4 cup water. Cook 45 minutes. Add vegetables and cook 10 minutes. Stir in cornstarch blended with 1 cup water. Add tomatoes and cook 5 minutes. Serve over hot fluffy rice.
Mary Perron, Owatonna, Mn.

1748-81

PHEASANT LA CHASSEUR

1 pheasant	4 green onions
Salt	1 oz. brandy
Pepper	1 c. dry white wine
Lemon juice	2 fresh tomatoes, peeled
1 Tbsp. butter	1/2 c. chicken broth
1 Tbsp. olive oil	1/4 c. minced parsley
1 doz. mushrooms	Pinch of tarragon

Cut pheasant into serving pieces, rub the pieces with lemon juice, salt and pepper. In a heavy iron skillet put the butter and olive oil. When hot, brown the pheasant until golden. Then add mushrooms, onions (including the tops), brandy, wine, tomatoes (chopped), chicken broth and parsley. Cover and cook over a gentle fire for 1/2 to 1 hour, depending on the age of the pheasant - or until tender. Before serving, sprinkle with tarragon.

PIZZA ROLL

1 pkg. Chef-Boy-Ar- Dee pizza mix	1/3 c. chopped onion
1 lb. ground beef	1/2 tsp. oregano
Salt and pepper	1/2 c. Cheez Whiz
	1 egg, mix slightly

Brown meat and onion - add oregano. Stir in cheese, egg and grated cheese from pizza mix. Mix pizza dough with 2 tablespoons shortening. Add 1 cup very warm water. Mix to form a smooth dough. Cover and let stand 5 minutes. Knead dough on floured board until no longer sticky. Roll into 12x14 inch rectangle and spread with mixture of ground beef, leaving 1 1/2 inches on each side. Fold and roll like a log. Pinch edges together and put on cookie sheet. Brush with 2 tablespoons melted butter and sprinkle with parsley. Bake at 450° for 15 minutes. Serve with pizza sauce from mix.

Mrs. Ronald Schwartz, Owatonna, Mn.

ROAST BEAR

Tons of bear meat go to waste every year, simply because hunters do not know the value of their game. They make the kill, skin the bear out, keep the hide and leave the carcass to rot in the woods. Jim Blake, an Alaskan friend of mine, labels such waste of good meat a criminal act and gets "blood in his eyes" every time the subject is mentioned. And after enjoying several bear meat dinners with Jim, I am inclined to agree with him, because Jim can do as much with a bear carcass as a chef at the Waldorf can do with a baby beef. He takes a tremendous amount of pride in fixing his bear roasts, and it was with considerable reluctance that he gave me his recipe. Allow the meat to age in a cold place for about 5 days. Then take a 10 or 12 pound cut from high on the ham and trim off all the outside fat, leaving only red meat showing. Prepare a marinade as follows:

1 pt. vinegar	1 small pinch sage leaves
1 pt. water	1/4 tsp. nutmeg
1 tsp. allspice	1 medium sized onion, cut fine
10 whole cloves	2 stalks green celery,
6 bay leaves	chopped fine
	1 flower of dill

Mix all ingredients in an enamel cooking pot and bring to a boil. Remove from the stove and allow to cool. Then pour the mixture into an earthenware jar that is large enough to take the roast. Rub the roast with a mixture of salt and pepper, and then place it in the cool marinade. Allow it to soak for 24 hours, turning it over in the mixture about every 4 hours.

After the soaking, take the meat out of the marinade and wipe it dry. Then roast it as you would a piece of beef. It will be as tender and full of flavor as the finest meat you have ever eaten.

Kathy Bischof, St. Cloud, Mn.

ROAST WILD DUCK PROVENCALE

Soak one dozen pitted ripe olives for 1 hour in a little olive oil flavored with a sliver of garlic. Melt 4 tablespoons butter in a skillet, add 1 onion and 3 stalks of celery, all finely chopped and saute them until soft. Remove the skillet from the fire, add 3/4 cup toasted bread crumbs, the olives, 2 teaspoons cognac and salt and pepper to taste. Divide the stuffing between 2 wild ducks, truss the ducks and butter the breasts generously, sprinkle with salt and pepper. Place the ducks on a rack in a roasting pan, pour over them 1/2 cup red wine and 1/4 cup water. Roast in a 450° oven for about 30 minutes, basting frequently. Lower heat to 300° and cook for 1 hour, covered. Skim off the fat from the pan juices, stir in 1/2 tablespoon cornstarch mixed to a paste with a little water. Stir until the gravy is thickened. Add 2 tablespoons butter, do not boil. Pour the gravy over ducks.

SAUERBRATTEN

Step 1:

1 (3 - 4 lb.) beef roast	3 bay leaves
Vinegar (to soak roast in)	8 whole cloves

Find bowl that will hold the roast. Pour vinegar to cover roast, add bay leaves and whole cloves. Let soak in covered bowl for 7 days, in refrigerator. Remove from bowl, let drain for 2 hours. Save vinegar from bowl.

Step 2:

1/2 c. chopped onions	4 Tbsp. molasses (get this
Vinegar saved from	from bakery; it is thicker
soaking meat	and richer than store
	molasses)

Brown meat on all sides, then add onions, vinegar and molasses and cook slowly, covered, for at least 2 hours or until done.

Step 3: Remove meat, set aside. Add:

1 Tbsp. powdered	Salt and pepper to
beef bouillon (instant,	taste
not cubed)	

Take 4 tablespoons flour, mix with water in separate bowl to make paste (consistency of tomato juice), add 1/2 to liquid meat was cooked in. Heat, stirring constantly until thickened. If not thick enough, add a little more paste. Cut meat and serve with gravy.

Don Billadeau, St. Cloud, Mn.

SHERRIED WILD RICE STUFFING

1 1/2 c. wild rice
3 c. hot turkey or
  chicken stock
1 Tbsp. butter
6 strips bacon, diced
3 c. chopped celery
1 c. chopped onion
1/2 c. dry sherry
1/2 c. filberts, coarsely
  chopped

Wash rice well and soak for 2 hours in water to cover; drain. In a pan, combine the drained rice, hot turkey stock and butter; cover and simmer 25 minutes or until almost tender, and the liquid has been absorbed. Meanwhile, fry bacon until crisp and remove from pan, reserving 1/2 cup drippings. Add celery and onion to the pan and cook until soft. Lightly mix the sauteed vegetables and bacon into the cooked rice; add sherry and mix lightly. Stir in nutmeats. Use to stuff a 12 pound turkey.

SOUPER SKILLET PASTA
(Quick 'n Easy)

1 lb. ground beef
1 (16 oz.) can tomatoes,
  or 2 pt. home canned
3 c. water (2 c. if using
  home canned tomatoes)
1 pkg. Lipton beef flavor
  mushroom mix or onion
  mushroom mix
2 level tsp. oregano (or to
  taste)
1 box medium shell macaroni,
  uncooked
1/3 c. Parmesan cheese
1 medium pkg. Mozzarella
  cheese

Brown ground beef in large kettle, drain. Add tomatoes, water, mushroom mix and oregano. Bring to boil. Add uncooked macaroni and cook on medium heat for 20 minutes or until macaroni is tender. Stir in Parmesan cheese. Top with Mozzarella cheese until melted. Serve with tossed salad and garlic bread.
Dee Dee Olson, Fargo, N. D.

SPANISH RICE WITH GROUND BEEF

1 c. uncooked rice
1/4 c. butter or bacon
  fat
2 Tbsp. chopped green
  pepper
1/4 c. onion, chopped into
  small pieces
1 lb. ground beef
1 1/2 c. water
1 tsp. salt

1 Tbsp. chili powder combined with 1/4 c. cold water

1 small clove garlic, chopped
1 c. canned tomatoes
2 Tbsp. pimiento, cut into 1/2 inch pieces

Melt 2 tablespoons butter and let sizzle. Add 1 cup un-cooked rice; stir about 2 minutes, until brown; mix well. Place in another pot. Combine chili powder with water, mix well. Melt other 2 tablespoons butter to brown meat. Saute till brown, add garlic that has been put through press; add onions and green pepper, saute about 2 minutes. Add chili powder with water, tomatoes, broken up, and pimiento, cut into 1/2 inch pieces. Mix about 1 minute; add salt and rice; blend and cook 1 minute, blending well while it cooks. Place meat mixture in a 1 1/2 quart casserole and add the water. Cover. Bake, covered, in a 350° oven for 45 minutes.

SUPER NACHOS

1 lb. lean ground beef
1 large onion, chopped
1 lb. refried beans
1 (4 oz.) can green chiles, drained and chopped (for milder taste, remove seeds)
1 c. sour cream

2 1/2 c. shredded Monterey Jack or mild Cheddar cheese
3/4 c. taco sauce
1/4 c. chopped green onion*
1 c. pitted ripe olives*
1 medium avocado, mashed*
Tortilla chips

Brown beef and onion. Drain. Season with salt. Spread refried beans in a 10x15 inch ovenproof dish. Top with meat. Sprinkle with chili peppers, then cheese. Drizzle taco sauce over all. If made ahead, cover and chill. Bake at 400° for 20 minutes. Garnish with green onions and olives. Mound avocado in center. Top with sour cream. Tuck tortillas around the outside. Serve immediately.

For a hotter flavor, use 4 diced jalapeno peppers in place of green chiles.
*Optional.
Con Mucho Gusto!!!!

SURPRISE HAMBURGER

1 lb. ground beef
1 large onion, chopped
1 small clove garlic,
  chopped
1/2 green pepper, chopped
2 Tbsp. shortening
2 Tbsp. flour
1/2 c. red table wine

1/4 c. catsup
1/2 c. grated Cheddar cheese
1 c. chopped pimiento-stuffed
  olives
1 tsp. Worcestershire sauce
Salt and pepper to taste
6 hamburger buns

Saute beef, onion, garlic and green pepper in shortening until meat is no longer red, stirring with a fork so that meat is separated into bits. Sprinkle flour over meat and blend well. Add wine and catsup; cook, stirring constantly until mixture boils and thickens. Remove from heat. Add cheese, olives, Worcestershire sauce, salt and pepper. Cut a thin slice from the top of each bun and hollow out insides; fill with meat mixture (about 1/2 cup per bun); replace tops. Place in a baking pan; cover with a lid of aluminum foil and bake at 350° for 30 minutes. Good served with cole slaw and potato chips. These can be prepared ahead of time. Serves 6.

SWEET AND SOUR MEAT

3 lb. stew meat, cut
  into small pieces*
1/2 c. flour
1/4 tsp. pepper
1/4 c. soy sauce
1/2 c. sugar

1/2 tsp. salt
3/4 c. catsup
1/2 c. water
2 tsp. Worcestershire sauce
1 medium onion, chopped fine

Preheat oven to 300° F. Arrange meat in 9x13 inch cake pan. Make sauce of remaining ingredients and pour over meat, covering all pieces. Cover pan tightly with aluminum foil. Bake for 3 hours. Serve with rice. (8 to 10 servings)
  *Can substitute chuck steak, pot roast, round steak, pork ribs, or beef ribs, cut into pieces.
Marie Miller, St. Paul, Mn.

TACO MIX PIE BAKE

1 lb. ground beef
1/4 c. green onions
   including tops

1 env. taco mix

Cook meat and onions, drain off fat. Add 1 can refried beans. Line a 9x13 inch pan (ungreased) with 1 roll (8) crescent rolls. Pinch together like a crust. Spread meat mixture on top. Add:

1 c. sour cream mixed with
   1 egg

1 c. taco cheese

Bake at 375° for 25 - 30 minutes. Serve with:

Chopped lettuce
Tomato, chopped

Onions, chopped
Mild taco sauce

Carole Wells, St. Paul, Mn.

SHISH KABOBS

1 1/2 - 2 lb. round or
   sirloin steak, 1 inch
   thick, cut into 1 inch
   cubes

2 large onions
3 green peppers
Fresh mushrooms
Cherry tomatoes

Marinate beef in marinade sauce for 24 - 48 hours. Cut onions and green peppers into 1 inch strips. Alternate ingredients on skewers ending each with a cherry tomato. Bar-b-que over medium coals for 20 minutes, turning often. Serves 6.

Renee Ulberg, Bismarck, N. D.

TERIYAKI SHISH KABOBS

Marinade:

Juice from 1 lb. can
   pineapple chunks
1/4 c. soy sauce
1/2 c. sherry wine
1 clove garlic, minced

1/4 tsp. pepper
1/2 c. salad oil
3/4 tsp. ginger
1 medium onion, chopped
1 tsp. salt

Kabobs:

1 1/2 lb. sirloin, 1 inch thick, 2 inch squares	Cherry tomatoes
2 onions, quartered	Water chestnuts
Green pepper squares	Fresh mushrooms

Marinate meat and water chestnuts all day in marinade. Alternate meat squares on skewers with onions, green pepper, tomatoes, mushrooms, water chestnuts and pineapple chunks. Brush vegetables with marinade. Broil on charcoal grill or under broiler for 15 minutes. Serves 4.

Elynor Pederson, Minneapolis, Mn.

TERIYAKI STEAK
(Serves 4)

1/4 c. vegetable oil	1/2 tsp. pepper
1/2 tsp. ginger	1/2 c. soya sauce
1/4 c. water	4 cloves garlic, diced
2 Tbsp. brown sugar	2 lb. flank steak

Mix all ingredients together. Marinate steaks for about 8 hours, piercing every hour with a fork. Grill over hot charcoal. Cut into slanted strips when serving.

Arlene Gnoinsky, Fargo, N. D.

VEAL IN WINE WITH MUSHROOMS

2 (4 1/2 oz.) cans mushroom caps	2 cans condensed cream of mushroom soup
1/4 c. cooking oil	1 c. white wine
3 lb. veal, cut into 1 inch cubes	1/2 c. chopped onions
	1 tsp. oregano

Have ready:
1 c. sour cream	5 1/3 c. fluffy rice

Drain mushrooms, measure liquid and add enough water to make 1 cup. Meanwhile, heat oil in saucepan. Add veal and saute until browned. Then stir in mushrooms, liquid, mushroom soup, 1/2 cup of the wine, the onions and oregano. Bring to a boil. Cover and reduce heat. Simmer until veal is tender, about 1 1/4 hours, stirring the mixture occasionally. Just before serving, add the remaining 1/2

1748-81

155

cup wine, the mushrooms and sour cream. Serve over hot rice. Makes 8 to 10 servings.

WILD RICE AND STEAK DISH

1 1/2 lb. steak, cubed	1 medium onion, chopped

Brown and add the following:

1 can chicken rice soup	1/4 c. white rice
1 can cream of mushroom soup	1/2 c. wild rice (washed)
1 can water	1 c. chopped celery
1 can mushrooms and juice	1 Tbsp. soy sauce

Bake at 350° for 1 1/2 hours.
Sue Hick, Detroit Lakes, Mn.

WRAPPED RAOST

Honorable Mention: Leo V. Carlson, Rogers Route, International Falls, Mn.

4 lb. beef roast - blade cut	2 Tbsp. brown sugar
1 pkg. dry onion soup	2 Tbsp. vinegar
Garlic salt (optional)	1 Tbsp. horseradish (bottled)
1 can tomato paste	Heavy aluminum foil

Combine onion soup, salt, tomato paste, sugar, vinegar and horseradish. Place meat in foil; brush generously with sauce and seal in foil. Cook over charcoal for 2 hours.

YUKAMUSH

Brown 1 pound hamburger. Add:

1 c. carrots, sliced	1 c. celery, sliced
1 c. onions, sliced	

Toss and cook 3 minutes. Break 2 eggs and toss. Add:

3 c. cooked Minute Rice	3 Tbsp. soy sauce

156

Add 2 cups shredded cabbage and toss. Vegetables should be crisp.

Diane Schmitz & L. Richards, St. Cloud, Mn.

BACON AND EGGS BREAKFAST

Cut up and fry 1 pound bacon, remove from skillet, pour off grease. Combine:

5 eggs, well beaten   5 rounded tsp. flour

Beat flour into the eggs. Add 5 scant cups of milk and mix up. Salt and pepper. Pour this into skillet and simmer, stirring almost constantly. This will look like it is curdling, but keep cooking. Add browned bacon and keep simmering to evaporate extra juice.

Karen Rupert, St. Cloud, Mn.

BREAKFAST CASSEROLE

1 lb. pork sausage	6 eggs
2 c. milk	2 slices white bread, cubed
1 tsp. dry mustard	1 tsp. salt
Dash of pepper	1 c. grated Cheddar cheese

Brown and drain meat. Beat eggs and add rest of ingredients. Pour into buttered 8x10 inch pan. Let stand in refrigerator overnight. Remove 1/2 hour before baking. Bake at 350° for 45 minutes.

Ruth Rehschuh, Minneapolis, Mn.

BREAKFAST EGG DISH

6 slices bread, remove crusts	1 tsp. dry mustard
6 eggs	2 c. milk
1 tsp. salt	1 lb. Cheddar cheese, grated
	Ham

Butter 9x13 inch dish. Butter one side of the bread, place buttered side down. Cover with the grated cheese. Then top with as much diced ham as you might want, you can omit the meat if you want. Beat the eggs and add the milk, salt and mustard. Pour over the bread and cheese, etc., and refrigerate overnight. Bake for 1 hour at 325°. It can bake a little longer and be O.K.

1748-81   Elsa Ditty, St. Cloud, Mn.

BREAKFAST SOUFFLE

16 slices white bread,
  crusts trimmed off
1 large can Spam, diced
1 pkg. Cracker Barrel extra
  sharp Cheddar cheese,
  grated

6 eggs
3 c. milk
1/2 tsp. dry mustard

In a 9x13 inch baking pan, cover bottom with 8 slices of bread. Cover bread with Spam and cheese. Top this with layer of remaining bread. Mix eggs, milk and dry mustard together and pour over bread mixture. Cover and refrigerate overnight. Remove in morning and let stand about 1 hour. Cover with corn flake crumbs and 1/2 cup melted butter. Bake at 350° for 1 hour. Best when served with fresh fruit bowl.
Jacquie Amacher, Willmar, Mn.

EGGS AND HAM FOR BRUNCH

7x11 inch pan
7 slices bread, cubed
1 lb. can precooked,
  smoked ham, diced
1/2 lb. Old English Kraft
  cheese, cubed

3 eggs, beaten
2 c. milk
1/2 tsp. dry mustard
1/2 tsp. salt
1/4 lb. melted margarine

Grease pan lightly. Mix bread and ham and put in the pan. Add cheese. Mix together beaten eggs, milk, dry mustard and salt; pour over bread, ham and cheese. Pour margarine over mixture in pan. Cube 1 1/2 slices of bread and put on top. Cover with foil and refrigerate overnight. Bake at 325° for 1 hour, uncovered.
Thelma Olson, St. Cloud, Mn.

EGG OMELET

8 slices bread, cubed
1 lb. bacon or sausage,
  fried and crumbled

1 c. grated Cheddar cheese
1/2 green pepper
1 Tbsp. onion

Beat 6 eggs, add 3 cups milk. Grease 9x13 inch pan, sprinkle bacon or sausage, cheese, green pepper and onion over bread crumbs. Pour egg mixture over and place in refrigerator 6 hours or overnight. Bake 55 minutes at 325°.
158   Narda Mae Veile, Fargo, N. D.

EGG AND SAUSAGE CASSEROLE

1 lb. bulk sausage	1/2 - 1 tsp. salt
6 slices bread, cubed	4 or 5 eggs
1/4 c. grated cheese	2 c. milk

Brown sausage and drain. Add bread, cheese and salt. Beat eggs and milk. Mix all ingredients together and pour into a greased casserole (10 x 6 1/2 x 2 inches). Refrigerate overnight. Bake at 350° for 45 minutes, covered. Uncover and bake at 325° for 15 minutes more.

Pat Langfitt, Fargo, N. D.

MARY JANE'S FRENCH TOAST

8 - 10 slices French bread	1 Tbsp. granulated sugar
4 eggs	1/4 tsp. salt
2 Tbsp. Grand Marnier	1/2 tsp. vanilla
wine	4 Tbsp. butter or margarine
1 c. milk	Confectioners sugar

Arrange slices in a shallow pan or container. Beat rest of ingredients except confectioners sugar, with rotary beater. Pour over bread, turn slices till thoroughly coated. Cover and refrigerate overnight. Melt butter in skillet or griddle and cook slices 3 - 4 minutes. Turn, cook 2 minutes. Sprinkle with confectioners sugar.

Mary Jane Schmitz, Wadena, Mn.

FRENCH TOAST DOLLS

1/4 c. flour	1 tsp. sugar
1 egg	6 slices bread
1/2 c. milk	Powdered sugar
1/8 tsp. salt	Cinnamon

Cut bread into dolls or other shapes with cooky cutters. Make a smooth batter of flour, egg, milk, salt and sugar. Dip bread cut-outs into batter and fry in hot fat about 1/4 inch deep in heavy skillet. Fry about 3 minutes on each side or until golden brown. Drain on absorbent paper. Sprinkle toast with cinnamon and powdered sugar and serve at once. If desired, serve with butter and syrup or jam instead of the powdered sugar and cinnamon.

GRANOLA

2 c. rolled oats
2 1/2 c. raw wheat germ
1 c. bran
1 c. rye or wheat flakes
1 Tbsp. cinnamon

1/2 c. chopped walnuts
1/2 c. chopped cashews
1/2 c. sunflower seeds
1/2 c. sesame seeds
1/2 c. raw coconut

Mix together:
1/4 c. molasses
1/4 c. honey

1/2 c. safflower oil

Add to dry ingredients. Mix well till all ingredients are coated. Spread on cookie sheet. Bake 15 - 20 minutes at 350°, stirring frequently. Other ingredients such as pumpkin seeds, raisins, dates or other nuts may also be added.

Evelyn Walls, St. Paul, Mn.

HAM AND EGG BRUNCH

6 - 7 slices bread, cubed
1 lb. precooked ham,
  cubed

1/2 lb. Cheddar cheese,
  cubed

Grease 9x13 inch pan lightly. Pat cubed bread into bottom of pan and then layer of ham, then a layer of cheese. Beat together:

3 eggs
2 c. milk

1/2 tsp. dry mustard
1/2 tsp. salt

Pour over whole pan. Melt 1/4 teaspoon butter and pour on top. Cover and refrigerate overnight. Uncover to bake at 325° for 1 hour.

Note: One-half pound cubed Swiss cheese will also add a distinctive flavor over Cheddar cheese.

Harriett Maselie, Minneapolis, Mn.

MARIA'S EGG DISH

2 lb. link sausages,
  cooked, drained and
  cut up
3/4 lb. Cheddar cheese,
  grated

8 slices bread, trim crusts
  and cube
4 eggs, beaten
1 can mushroom soup
2 1/4 c. milk

Grease dish; put cut up bread on bottom. Add sausage, then cheese. Beat eggs; add milk and soup, pour into casserole. Let set in refrigerator overnight. Bake in morning at 325° for 1 1/2 hours, covered.

Marge Johnson, Minneapolis, Mn.

BEST PANCAKES YOU EVER ATE

1 c. milk	2 Tbsp. baking powder (no
1 egg	joke, 2 Tbsp.)
2 Tbsp. vegetable oil	1 c. flour
2 Tbsp. sugar	1/2 tsp. salt

Mix oil, egg and milk. Add dry ingredients. Add 2 more tablespoons milk. Fry on griddle (350°) until bubbles.

Lois Sandberg, St. Cloud, Mn.

BON APPETIT BLUEBERRY PANCAKES
(Makes about 20 pancakes)

1 c. all-purpose flour	1 egg, beaten
1 c. whole wheat flour	1/4 c. vegetable oil
4 tsp. baking powder	Juice of 1/2 lemon (about
1 Tbsp. sugar	1 1/2 Tbsp.)
1 tsp. salt	1/8 tsp. vanilla
1/4 tsp. cinnamon	1/2 c. drained, canned
2 c. milk	blueberries

Garnish:
Blueberries   Powdered sugar

Combine flours, baking powder, sugar, salt and cinnamon in large bowl and mix well. Stir in milk, egg, oil, lemon juice and vanilla; do not overmix. Gently fold in canned blueberries. Preheat griddle or electric skillet to 400° F.; grease lightly. Stir through batter several times. Using about 1/4 cup of batter for each (pancakes should be 3 to 4 inches in diameter), cook pancakes till done, turning once, about 3 to 4 minutes. Garnish with blueberries, sprinkle with powdered sugar and serve.

Julie Mosman, St. Cloud, Mn.

FLEISKPANKAKA
(Swedish Oven Pancake)

5 eggs, beaten   Salt
4 c. milk   1/4 c. sugar
Cinnamon

Beat well and add 1 1/3 cups flour, gradually. Add 1/2 pound diced salt pork, browned. Pour into a large greased cake pan. (I wouldn't recommend glass). Bake at 400° for about an hour. Watch it carefully and if it gets too brown, turn down the oven. This will puff up nicely and then it will fall. Don't worry -- it's supposed to do this. Done when a toothpick comes out clean. This is really a special tasty treat served with syrup and sausage.
                    Mrs. Don Bredenberg, Bemidji, Mn.

OLD FASHIONED BUCKWHEAT CAKES

1 1/2 c. buckwheat   1/2 tsp. salt
1/2 c. white flour   1 Tbsp. melted shortening
5 tsp. baking powder   2 c. milk
1 Tbsp. molasses

                Ruth Braun, Owatonna, Mn.

UGNSPANKAKA
(Oven Pancakes)

4 eggs   1 c. flour
2 c. milk   2 tsp. sugar
2 Tbsp. butter   1 scant tsp. salt

Melt butter in a 9x13 inch baking pan while preheating oven. In a bowl, beat eggs, add milk, sugar, salt and flour. Grease the baking pan with the melted butter and pour excess into the batter. Mix. Pour batter into the baking pan. Bake 20 minutes (or until puffy and browned) in a 425° oven. Cut into squares and serve immediately with syrup, fruit, etc. Good for brunch or supper with bacon or sausages.
                    Marian Pearson, St. Paul, Mn.

OVEN BAKED PANCAKES

2 eggs
1 c. milk
2 Tbsp. melted butter

1 1/4 c. pancake mix
Brown & Serve sausages **or**
  bacon, cooked

Beat eggs until light and fluffy. Combine with milk; add mix and butter. Beat until smooth. Pour into 2 greased 8 inch round cake pans. Arrange sausage or bacon on batter, spoke fashion. Bake at 450° for 15 minutes. Cut into 5 wedges. Serve hot with butter and syrup.
Helen Schmidt, Fargo, N. D.

PANCAKES

1 egg
1 1/2 c. buttermilk
1 c. flour
1/2 tsp. soda

1 tsp. baking powder
2 Tbsp. oil
1 scant tsp. salt
1 tsp. sugar

Put egg and milk into bowl. Add dry ingredients sifted together and oil. Beat with rotary beater until smooth. Fry on hot griddle. Makes 12 cakes.
Charles L. Anderson, Brainerd, Mn.

PANCAKES

4 eggs
3/4 c. sugar
1/2 tsp. salt
1 qt. buttermilk

4 c. flour
2 tsp. baking soda
2 Tbsp. baking powder
1/2 c. oil

Beat eggs and sugar together till creamy. Add rest of dry ingredients. Last, add the oil. These are very good.
Mrs. William G. Speare, Rugby, N. D.

PLETTS
(Tiny Swedish Pancakes)

2 eggs
3 c. milk
3 tsp. sugar

1 1/2 c. flour
1 tsp. salt
2 Tbsp. butter

Beat eggs, add milk and flour gradually with salt and

sugar. Heat Pletts pan slowly with melted butter. Stir batter well. Bake 3 minutes, flip over and cook until golden brown. Serve with Lingonberry Jam or honey. Yield: 6 servings.

Note: Plett pans can be purchased at Maid of Scandinavia, Minneapolis, Mn.

Clara O. Johnson, Chanhassen, Mn.

SPEEDY POTATO PANCAKES
(Makes 5)

Use blender:

1 medium or small egg	1 medium large raw potato
1 tsp. salt	(about 9 inch circumference)

Toss egg and salt into blender. Peel and cut up potato, add to egg. Blend all on blend or grind for about 15 seconds. Add 1 level tablespoon flour, blend a few seconds. Fry in bacon fat. We like thin and crisp pancakes. To get them crisp, use extra large amount of fat in frying.

Carmen Benshoof (Mrs. Julian), Fargo, N.D.

3 WEEK PANCAKES

Dissolve 1 package yeast in 1/4 cup warm water. Mix together, then add yeast:

6 beaten eggs	1/4 c. vegetable oil
1 qt. buttermilk	

Stir together and add to above mixture:

4 c. flour	3 Tbsp. sugar
2 Tbsp. baking soda	Dash of salt
2 Tbsp. baking powder	

Beat on low with beaters until smooth. Lasts 3 weeks in refrigerator. Stir batter each time before using.

Lorraine Solberg, St. Cloud, Mn.

SAUSAGE SOUFFLE

8 - 10 slices bread,
  cubed without crust
3/4 lb. sharp Cheddar
  cheese
1 1/2 - 2 lb. pork
  sausage, rolled and/or
  linked

1/4 tsp. mustard
4 eggs
2 1/4 c. milk
1 can cream of mushroom
  soup
1/4 c. milk

Put bread into casserole (3 quart square) or 9x13 inch pan. Grate cheese over bread cubes. Fry sausage, drain and arrange on top of cheese. Add fresh mushrooms, salt and pepper. Beat eggs, milk, mustard, salt, pepper and pour over sausage. Let stand overnight in refrigerator. Add soup mixture before baking. Bake at 325° for 1 hour.

Doris Schmidt, Willmar, Mn.

SCOTCH EGGS
(Serves 6)

2/3 lb. ground pork
1 1/3 lb. ground beef
6 eggs, hard-boiled
  with shells removed
1 c. bread crumbs

1/2 c. flour
Garlic salt
Pepper
Cloves (optional)

Mix ground pork and beef together. Season according to taste. Set aside. Roll hard-boiled eggs in flour. Make a meat ball around egg with 4 - 5 ounces of meat. Roll lightly in bread crumbs. Deep fry in vegetable oil for 2 or 3 seconds (until it holds together). Put in pan with 1/4 inch water. Cover with tin foil and cook until meat is done. Scotch eggs are served hot or cold as hors d'oeuvres in pubs throughout Scotland.

Marge Johnson, Minneapolis, Mn.

SUNDAY BREAKFAST CASSEROLE

Brown:
1/2 c. chopped onion

1/2 c. green pepper

Add:
2 c. cubed ham, bacon or
  sausage

1 c. grated Cheddar cheese

Mix together:

1 doz. eggs	1 c. milk

Add:

1 pkg. thawed frozen	1 tsp. salt
hash browns	1/2 tsp. pepper

Mix all together and put into 9x13 inch pan. Top with more grated cheese and parsley flakes if desired. Bake 30 minutes or until set, at 350°. Serves 10 - 12. Good with sliced tomatoes or fresh fruit and toast.

L. Richards

CRANBERRY-NUT WAFFLES

1/2 c. halved cranberries	1 tsp. baking soda
1/4 c. sugar	1 tsp. salt
1/2 tsp. cinnamon	1 tsp. baking powder
2 eggs, separated	1/4 c. melted shortening
2 c. thick sour cream	1/2 c. chopped pecans
2 c. sifted flour	

Combine cranberries, sugar and cinnamon. Set aside. Beat egg yolks thoroughly and add cream. Sift together flour, soda, salt and baking powder. Stir into egg mixture. Add shortening. Beat egg whites until stiff and fold into mixture. Add cranberries and pecans. Bake in hot waffle iron. Makes 8 waffles.

WAFFLES WITH HAM APPLESAUCE

Filling:

2 Tbsp. butter	1/4 tsp. ground cloves
1/4 c. chopped onion	1/3 c. seedless raisins
2 c. canned applesauce	1 1/2 c. diced, cooked ham

Waffles:

2 c. sifted all-purpose	2 eggs, separated
flour	1 1/4 c. milk
1 Tbsp. baking powder	6 Tbsp. melted shortening
1/4 tsp. salt	(or use a waffle mix)
2 Tbsp. sugar	

For filling, melt butter and saute onion in it until light brown; add applesauce, cloves and raisins; simmer 3 minutes. Add ham and simmer 3 minutes longer.

For waffles, sift together flour, baking powder, salt and sugar. Beat egg yolks; add milk. Combine with dry ingredients, mixing until smooth. Add shortening. Beat egg whites stiff; fold in. If waffle mix is used, blend according to package directions. Bake in hot waffle iron. Serve applesauce filling on top or between waffles. Yield: 4 servings.

SOUR CREAM WAFFLES

Honorable mention: Mrs. Carl Sundell, Duluth, Mn.

1 egg yolk	2 tsp. sugar
1 c. dairy sour cream	1 tsp. baking powder
1/2 c. milk	1/4 tsp. soda
3 Tbsp. butter, melted	1/4 tsp. salt
1 c. flour	1 stiffly beaten egg white

In electric mixer bowl, blend egg yolk, sour cream, milk and butter. Stir in dry ingredients; beat until smooth. Fold in egg white. Bake at medium heat on electric waffle baker. Yield: 2 (10 inch) waffles.

CORN FRITTERS

1 c. corn	1/2 tsp. salt
1 egg	1 tsp. baking powder
1/3 c. milk	

Add enough flour to make soft dough. Drop off spoon in hot fat and fry until done.

Phyliss Brossart, Rugby, N. D.

CABBAGE ROLLS

Remove core, parboil cabbage head. Run water over to cool. Separate leaves and cut off thick stem, don't cut so holes appear.

2 lb. hamburger	1/2 c. sour cream
4 eggs	2 handfuls rice

1 diced onion   Salt and pepper

Mix well by hand, roll in cabbage leaves, put into roasting pan. Mix:

2 cans whole tomatoes,   1/2 c. sour cream
   some mashed and juice   1 c. water
1/2 bottle ketchup   Salt and pepper
1 small can tomato paste

Mix well, pour over cabbage rolls. Cover and bake at 350° for 3 hours, or till cabbage is tender (best on second day).
Tim Croner, St. Paul, Mn.

CHINESE-STYLE DINNER WITH CABBAGE AND RICE

1 Tbsp. fat or oil   1 1/2 c. water
3 stalks celery, cut into   1/4 c. soy sauce
   thin 1 inch strips   1/2 small head cabbage,
1 small onion, thinly   chopped
   sliced   About 1 1/2 c. cut up, cooked
2 Tbsp. cornstarch   fresh pork (left from pork
About 2 c. cooked   shoulder roast)
   rice (2/3 c. uncooked)

Heat fat in a large pan. Add celery and onion and cook until lightly browned. Mix cornstarch, water and soy sauce. Pour into pan with celery and onion. Cook and stir until thickened and clear. Stir in cabbage and meat. Cover and cook about 3 minutes, leaving cabbage crisp. Serve on rice. Makes 4 servings; about 3 cups meat mixture and 2 cups rice.
Kathy Bischof, St. Cloud, Mn.

GOLABKI
(Go-WOMB-key)
(Stuffed Cabbage Rolls)

1/3 c. regular rice,   1/2 tsp. salt
   cooked   Dash of pepper
1 large head cabbage   4 slices bacon, cut into 1 inch
1 egg   pieces
1 lb. ground beef   1 (16 oz.) can tomatoes
1/2 c. chopped onion   1 (8 oz.) can tomato sauce

168

1 bay leaf   Dairy sour cream

1. Cut core out of cabbage; run hot water into cored area to help in removing the 8 outer leaves. Set the 8 leaves aside and chop the remaining cabbage (about 6 cups) and place in a 12 x 7 1/2 x 2 inch baking dish; sprinkle lightly with salt. Cut the heavy center vein out of the reserved cabbage leaves. Boil leaves till limp (about 3 minutes); drain and set aside. 2. Beat egg slightly, combine with cooked rice, browned ground beef, 1/4 cup chopped onion, salt and pepper - mix well. Place about 1/4 mixture in center of each leaf - fold in sides and roll ends over rice. Place rolls, seam side down on top of chopped cabbage. 3. In saucepan, cook bacon and remaining 1/2 cup onion till bacon is crisp. Stir in drained tomatoes, tomato sauce and bay leaf. Simmer, covered, 5 minutes. Remove bay leaf and pour over cabbage rolls. Cover and bake at 350° for 1 1/4 to 1 1/2 hours. Serve with sour cream. Serves 4.

Patty Ginter, St. Cloud, Mn.

KALDOMAR
(Cabbage Rolls)

1 large head cabbage
1 c. rice, cooked
1 c. milk
1 lb. beef, ground

1 lb. pork shoulder, ground
2 eggs
1 tsp. sugar
Salt and pepper

Cook cabbage in boiling water for 3 minutes. Drain and cut off heavy stem from each leaf. Mix meat, eggs, rice, milk, salt and pepper and sugar. Put 3 tablespoonfuls of the meat mixture on each cabbage leaf and roll together and fasten with toothpicks. Brown in frying pan. When brown, put into roasting pan. Bake in moderate oven for 2 hours.

Clara O. Johnson, Chanhassen, Mn.

KIELBASA POLSKA AND CABBAGE

1 lb. Hillshire Farm
    Polska Kielbasa
1 medium firm head of
    green cabbage
6 slices bacon
2 Tbsp. sugar

1 tsp. minced garlic
1/2 tsp. crushed red pepper
    (optional)
2 tsp. caraway seed
1 medium onion, chopped
1/4 c. water
1 tsp. seasoned salt

Cut cabbage into small wedges in large skillet. Fry bacon until crisp. Remove. Add following ingredients to drippings. Cabbage, onion, sugar, water and spices. Cook, covered, over medium heat 10 to 15 minutes. Add Polska Kielbasa. Return cover and continue to cook 10 - 15 minutes or until sausage is done. Top with crumbled bacon. Serves 6.

Marie Miller, St. Paul, Mn.

STUFFED CABBAGE

12 to 14 large cabbage leaves	1/2 tsp. dry mustard
2 lb. ground beef	1/4 tsp. pepper
15 wafers, finely rolled (about 1 c. crumbs)	1/2 tsp. basil
	2 eggs, well beaten
1 c. chopped onion	1 tsp. salt
	1/2 tsp. garlic salt

Soak cabbage leaves in boiling water for about 2 minutes. Drain. Combine remaining ingredients and mix well. Spoon about 4 tablespoons of mixture into center of each leaf. Fold over, envelope style. Secure with toothpicks, if necessary. Place in shallow baking dish. Pour sauce over cabbage rolls and bake in moderate oven (325° F.) 45 minutes. Serve from chafing dish. Serves 8.

Sauce: Combine -

2 (8 oz.) cans tomato sauce	1/2 c. chili sauce
1 Tbsp. horseradish	

Heat.

Mrs. Corinne Vevea, Anoka, Mn.

BAKED BEAN AND SAUSAGE CASSEROLE

1 can lima beans or butter beans	1/2 tsp. pepper
	1 tsp. dry mustard
1 large can pork & beans	1 (8 oz.) can tomato sauce
1 can kidney beans	1/2 c. catsup
1 lb. "hot" pork sausage	1/4 c. brown sugar
1 Tbsp. salt	1 medium onion, chopped

Fry sausage and onion until well browned. Add sausage and onions to beans. Combine seasonings, tomato

170

sauce, catsup, brown sugar and add to beans. Pour bean mixture into 3 quart baking dish. Bake, uncovered, 1 hour at 400°.

Mrs. W. A. Carlson

BAKED CABBAGE CASSEROLE

1 medium head cabbage, chopped	1 (10 oz.) box frozen peas 1 medium onion, chopped

Layer vegetables in a 2 quart casserole. Add salt and pepper if desired, then combine 1 can mushroom soup and 1 can milk. Pour over the vegetables. Crumble 4 slices of American cheese, 4 slices Swiss cheese and 6 tablespoons butter over top. Bake at 350° until vegetables are tender.

BEEF STEW CASSEROLE

Cut beef into cubes, brown in Dutch oven. Add water to cover generously. Cook in oven until tender. Thicken gravy with flour and water mixture to thin to medium gravy (if not brown enough, add Kitchen Bouquet). Add potatoes. Cook till potatoes are done.

Bev Barglof, Detroit Lakes, Mn.

BROCCOLI CASSEROLE

Prepare in low dish or casserole (a 9x9x2 inch is perfect):

1 pkg. cut or chopped broccoli	1 slice white bread, cubed small
1 (#2) can cream style corn	3/4 c. margarine, melted
2 eggs, beaten lightly	1 c. corn flakes, crushed 2 Tbsp. margarine, melted

Thaw broccoli or steam enough to thaw. Combine with corn, bread cubes, 3/4 cup margarine and eggs. Cover with corn flakes which have been mixed with the 2 tablespoons margarine. Bake at 350° for 30 - 40 minutes.

Note: Since I never buy creamed corn, I use a can of mushroom soup to make up for moisture and add small can of peas. Also, I use only 1/4 cup margarine instead of 3/4. Real good.

Mrs. E. F. Braun, Owatonna, Mn.

BROCCOLI CASSEROLE
(Make ahead and refrigerate)

2 c. cooked Minute Rice
2 pkg. thawed, chopped
  broccoli
1 (8 oz.) jar Cheez Whiz
1 can cream of chicken
  soup

1 can water chestnuts,
  chopped
3 Tbsp. butter
1/4 c. chopped onion
1/2 c. chopped celery
1/2 c. milk

Saute onions and celery in butter. Add soup and milk and 1/3 of cheese. Add rest of ingredients. Spoon rest of cheese on top. Bake at 350° for 40 minutes.

Gina Michels, Willmar, Mn.

BROCCOLI CASSEROLE

Cook and separate 2 packages chopped frozen broccoli. Do not overcook. Add:

1 c. grated Cheddar cheese
1 can mushroom soup
1 c. chopped celery

2 oz. jar chopped pimento
1 Tbsp. dehydrated onion
Salt and pepper

Mix and add 1 cup sour cream. Bake, uncovered, at 350°.

Diane Schmitz, St. Cloud, Mn.

BROCCOLI CASSEROLE

1 (1 lb.) bag frozen
  broccoli
1 (14 oz.) can bean
  sprouts

1 can sliced water chestnuts
2 cans cream of celery
  soup

Put broccoli in bowl and let thaw. Add drained bean sprouts. Add drained water chestnuts and mix well. Add soup and mix this. Pour into a 3 quart (ungreased) casserole and bake at 350° until bubbly.

Ollie Prestegard, Anoke Telephone Pioneer Club

BROCCOLI CASSEROLE

1/4 c. fine chopped onion
6 Tbsp. butter
2 Tbsp. flour
1/2 c. water
8 oz. Cheddar cheese, shredded

2 (10 oz.) pkg. frozen chopped broccoli, thaw very, very well
3 eggs, beaten well
Cracker crumbs

Saute onion in 4 tablespoons butter until soft. Stir in the flour and then add water, cook until thickened and has come to a boil. Blend in cheese and combine sauce with the broccoli. Add eggs and gently mix until blended. Put into a greased (buttered) casserole (1 1/2 quart). Bake at 325° for 35 to 45 minutes.

Elsa Ditty, St. Cloud, Mn.

BRUNCH CASSEROLE
(Serves 8 - 10)

8 slices white bread, crusts removed and cubed

1 lb. pork sausage, browned and drained
3/4 lb. grated Cheddar cheese

Place bread in 9x13 inch greased baking dish, top with sausage and cheese. Mix and pour over:

4 beaten eggs
3/4 tsp. prepared mustard

2 1/2 c. milk
1/8 tsp. salt

Cover and refrigerate overnight. Before baking, mix and spread over top:

1 c. mushroom soup
3/4 c. milk

1 c. mushrooms, drained, if desired

Bake at 300° for 1 1/2 hours. Allow 10 - 15 minutes to set before serving.

Kay Buzzell, Marshall, Mn.

CABBAGE CASSEROLE

Shred or slice 1 head cabbage, set aside. Saute:

1 lb. ground beef   Seasonings of your choice
1 sliced onion

In 2 quart casserole, layer cabbage, then meat, ending with cabbage. Pour 1 (15 ounce) can tomato sauce over all. Cover and bake 1 hour at 325° or 350°. Uncover and bake 1/2 hour longer.

Evelyn Walls, St. Paul, Mn.

CARROT CASSEROLE

1 to 2 lb. carrots, cooked   8 oz. Cheez Whiz
1 can mushroom soup   1 can French fried onion
1 can water chestnuts, sliced   rings

Mix together (except the onion rings). Put into a 2 quart casserole and bake at 350° for 30 to 45 minutes. Last 5 minutes, put onion rings on top. Serves 8. (Freezes well.)

Helen Schmidt, Fargo, N. D.

CARROT AND ONION CASSEROLE

2 medium onions, sliced   1/4 tsp. pepper
3 Tbsp. butter   1/2 tsp. thyme
3 c. cooked, sliced carrots   2 Tbsp. chopped pimento
1 (16 oz.) jar Cheez Whiz   1 2/3 c. coarse cracker
                              crumbs

Separate onions into rings and saute a few minutes in butter. Heat cheese spread over boiling water until melted. Combine cracker crumbs, pepper and thyme. Layer onions, carrots, cheese and crumbs in greased shallow pan. Sprinkle with pimento. Bake, covered, for 15 minutes at 350°. Uncover and bake 15 minutes longer.

Lois Ceyner, Sauk Centre, Mn.

CASSEROLE MEAT BALLS

1 lb. hamburger
1 egg
3 slices bread, soaked
   in milk

1 onion, diced
Salt and pepper

Beat with electric mixer until fluffy. Form balls and stuff in desired amount of cheese. Brown in skillet. Place in casserole dish. Top with cream of mushroom soup and shredded cheese. Bake at 350° for 40 minutes.
Marilyn Pommier, Willmar, Mn.

CASSEROLE POTATOES

8 - 10 medium potatoes
1 (8 oz.) pkg. cream
   cheese
1 (8 oz.) ctn. sour cream

1 tsp. garlic salt
1/4 c. grated onion
Butter
Paprika

Boil potatoes until done. Mix remaining ingredients. Whip potatoes and beat in mixture, adding milk if necessary. Put into casserole, top with butter and paprika (use plenty of butter). Bake at 350° for 30 to 45 minutes. May be made the day before and refrigerated until baking time.
Lorraine Mero, Minneapolis, Mn.

CELERY CASSEROLE

4 c. celery, cook about
   8 minutes
1 can water chestnuts
1 c. sour cream

1 can cream of chicken or
   cream of celery soup
1/8 tsp. celery salt
1/4 c. slivered almonds

Mix and put into a casserole and top with 1/2 cup bread crumbs and 2 tablespoons butter. Bake at 350° for 35 minutes.
Elsa Ditty, St. Cloud, Mn.

CHEESY TURKEY CASSEROLE

1/3 c. chopped green
   pepper
3 Tbsp. chopped onion
2 Tbsp. butter or margarine
2 Tbsp. flour
1 c. milk
2 c. cut up cooked turkey

1 (2 1/2 oz.) jar sliced
   mushrooms
1 c. (4 oz.) shredded sharp
   cheese
1/2 tsp. salt
1/2 tsp. dry mustard
1/2 tsp. lemon pepper
3 1/2 oz. spaghetti, cooked

Cook and stir green pepper and onion in butter until tender. Stir in flour. Cook and stir over low heat until bubbly. Remove from heat. Stir in milk and mushrooms with liquid. Heat to boiling, stirring constantly. Remove from heat; stir in 1 cup cheese, salt, lemon pepper and mustard. Stir until cheese is melted and sauce is smooth. Stir in spaghetti and turkey. Pour into ungreased, 1 1/2 quart casserole. Cover. Bake 40 minutes in 350° oven. Remove cover and sprinkle 1/2 cup cheese around edge of casserole. Bake 5 minutes more.

Johanna Singewald, St. Paul, Mn.

CHICKEN CASSEROLE

1 frying chicken
1 c. raw rice (regular
   or converted)
1/2 pkg. (dried) onion
   soup
1/2 tsp. salt
Pepper

1 can or 2 c. chicken broth
   or 2 1/4 c. liquid with
   drippings that chicken is
   browned in
1/4 c. flour
1/2 c. fat or Crisco

Cut chicken into serving pieces, flour and brown. Put dried soup and raw rice in the bottom of roaster or baking dish. Arrange chicken on top and pour over the broth. Cover tightly and bake 1 1/4 hours at 375°.

Marion Gugat, Sauk Centre, Mn.

CHICKEN CASSEROLE

1 c. cooked chicken
1 can cream of chicken
   soup
1 can cream of mushroom
   soup

1 small can mushrooms
1 c. whole cashews
2 c. chow mein noodles
2 tsp. pimento or more if
   desired

1 small can evaporated milk 1/2 green pepper
1 c. celery Salt and pepper to taste

Mix all ingredients, reserving 1 cup chow mein noodles for on top. Bake at 275° for 1 1/2 hours.
Mary Perron, Owatonna, Mn.

CHICKEN CASSEROLE

Toast and butter 10 slices of bread. Cube. Cover bottom of 9x13 inch pan. Beat 4 eggs, add:

1 1/2 c. milk
1 1/2 c. chicken broth
1 1/2 c. diced celery
1/2 c. melted margarine

Little salt and pepper
3 c. cooked chicken or
turkey, cut fine

Pour over the layer of croutons, then add the rest of the croutons. Refrigerate overnight. Bake at 325° (if glass) for 1 1/4 hours. Uncover, put on a layer of Velveeta cheese and 1 can of cream of mushroom soup diluted with milk. Bake, uncovered, till it gets bubbly and browns a little, about 20 minutes.
Emily Hoeft, Paynesville, Mn.

CHICKEN CASSEROLE

Chicken chunks
1 pkg. frozen broccoli
1/2 c. sour cream

1 c. Minute Rice
1 can Cheddar cheese soup

Layer chicken and broccoli. Mix remaining ingredients and pour on top. Bake at 350° for 25 minutes.
Dee Fletcher, Pelican Rapids, Mn.

CHICKEN OR CRABMEAT CASSEROLE

Mix:
3 c. chicken or crabmeat
2 c. chopped celery
1 c. cooked rice
3/4 c. mayonnaise
1 can cream of chicken soup

3 Tbsp. chopped onion
1 tsp. lemon juice
1 c. sliced water chestnuts
3 hard-cooked eggs, chopped
Salt, pepper, Accent to taste

Place in large casserole. Saute in 1 stick of butter:

1 c. crushed corn flakes   1/2 c. sliced almonds

Sprinkle on casserole. Bake at 350° for 30 minutes. Can be made the night before and refrigerated.
Irene Moe, Fargo, N. D.

CHICKEN CURRY CASSEROLE

1 whole chicken, cut up
   or 4 good sized breasts
1 large bag of frozen
   broccoli pieces
1 can cream of chicken soup
1 can milk
1 c. mayonnaise

2 Tbsp. lemon juice
1 1/2 tsp. curry powder
1 small pkg. slivered almonds
   (optional)
1 large pkg. (3 c. shredded)
   Cheddar cheese

Boil chicken, debone. Place chopped broccoli on bottom of 9x13 inch pan. Place cut up chicken on top of broccoli. In saucepan mix soup, milk, mayonnaise, lemon juice and curry powder. Heat until thick, pour over chicken and broccoli. Sprinkle shredded Cheddar cheese on top of sauce mixture, then sprinkle slivered almonds on top. Bake at 350° for 45 - 55 minutes. This is great served with wild rice.
Jeanne Segebarth, Minneapolis, Mn.

CHINESE SEAFOOD CASSEROLE

1 can cream of mushroom
   soup
3/4 c. sherry
2 small cans tuna or
   crabmeat, flaked
1/2 c. walnuts, coarsely
   chopped
1 small can water chestnuts

1/2 c. finely chopped onions
1 c. sliced celery
Dash of Worcestershire sauce
1 small can sliced mushrooms
   and liquid
1 (#303) can Chinese noodles
1 c. potato chips, bread or
   cracker crumbs

Mix soup and sherry. Combine other ingredients except noodles and add to soup mixture. Then carefully stir in the noodles. Place in a 2 quart casserole. Sprinkle crumbled potato chips or bread or cracker crumbs on top. Bake in 350° oven for 45 minutes. Serves 10.

COMPANY CASSEROLE

1 1/2 lb. hamburger
1 medium onion

Salt and pepper
2 (8 oz.) cans tomato sauce

Brown hamburger, onion, salt, pepper. Add tomato sauce, stir and set aside. Cook an 8 ounce package of wide noodles and set aside. Combine together:

1/4 c. sour cream
1 c. cottage cheese
8 oz. cream cheese

1/3 c. green onion, sliced thinly

Spread 1/2 of the noodles in a 3 quart casserole dish. Cover with all the cheese mixture, then layer the rest of noodles and pour on the tomato. Bake 35 minutes at 350°. Serves 10.

Linda Borgman, Sauk Centre, Mn.

CRABMEAT CASSEROLE

1 1/2 c. crabmeat (canned)
1 c. skim milk
1/2 c. mushrooms
2 Tbsp. diced green pepper

2 Tbsp. Melba toast crumbs
1 pimiento, diced
1/4 tsp. salt
Pepper to taste

Heat milk and add remaining ingredients. Pour into greased casserole and bake, uncovered, in a 350° oven for 30 to 40 minutes. Makes 4 servings, 88 calories per serving.

CROWN CASSEROLE

Fry 2 slices bacon till crisp, crumble. Put 1/2 cup onions in drippings, cook till tender. Add:

1 c. cooked peas or green beans
3 to 4 c. cooked, chopped potatoes

1 can cream of mushroom soup
1/2 can water

Mix together. Cut about a dozen wieners nearly in half and put around edge of casserole. Pour mixture in - top with bacon. Bake at 375° for 1/2 hour. Salt and pepper to taste.

Marion Round, Faribault, Mn.

1748-81

DOUBLE SHRIMP CASSEROLE

4 oz. (3 c.) medium noodles
1 can cream of shrimp
  soup
3/4 c. milk
1/2 c. mayonnaise or
  salad dressing
1/4 c. diced celery
1 Tbsp. chopped green onion
1/4 tsp. salt
1/3 c. shredded cheese
1 c. cooked shrimp
1/4 c. chow mein noodles

Cook noodles according to package directions. Drain.
Combine soup, milk, mayonnaise, celery, onion and salt,
mix well. Stir in cheese, shrimp and cooked noodles in 1 1/2
quart casserole. Bake uncovered in moderate oven (350°)
for 30 to 35 minutes. Top with chow mein noodles, bake 10
minutes longer.

Becky Neal, Sauk Centre, Mn.

EGG CASSEROLE

3 c. croutons (can use
  prepared dressing cubes)
2 c. sharp cheese, shredded
1 lb. pork (ground) sausage,
  browned
1 lb. links, browned, cut
  into pieces

1. Beat 7 eggs and 3 cups milk. 2. Add 3/4 teaspoon
dry mustard. 3. Line 9x13 inch pan with croutons.
4. Top with cheese and sausage. 5. Pour egg mixture over
and refrigerate overnight. 6. Before baking, add can of
cream of mushroom soup and 1/2 cup milk (combine and pour
over top). 7. Bake at 300° for 1 1/2 hours. 8. May be
baked ahead and reheated.

Carolyn Smith, Fargo, N. D.

EASY SCALLOPED HAM CASSEROLE

1 (10 1/4 oz.) can cream
  of mushroom soup
1 Tbsp. instant minced
  onion
1/2 tsp. salt
Dash of pepper
2 (15 oz.) cans sliced
  potatoes, drained
1 (8 oz.) can sweet peas,
  drained
1 1/2 c. diced, cooked ham

Combine soup, onion and seasonings in a 2 quart casserole. Stir in remaining ingredients. Bake in preheated
350° oven for 45 - 50 minutes or until bubbly. If desired,

sprinkle with French fried onions and bake for an additional
2 - 4 minutes. Makes 6 - 8 servings.
Kathy Bischof, St. Cloud, Mn.

ENCHILADA CASSEROLE

1 1/2 lb. hamburger
1 - 2 Tbsp. flour
1 large onion, chopped
1 clove minced garlic
1 env. chili seasoning
   mix or taco mix
About 1 c. mashed Fritos

1 large can tomato sauce
1 large can water (if needed)
1 pkg. (1 doz.) corn tortillas
1 large can refried beans
10 - 12 oz. grated Colby or
   Longhorn cheese (save
   about 1/2 c. for topping)

In large skillet, brown hamburger and onions. Add
garlic. Stir in flour and seasonings. Add tomato sauce and
water. Stir - simmer while you cut tortillas into bite sized
pieces. In 2 1/2 quart casserole dish, layer alternately -
meat sauce, tortilla pieces. refried beans and cheese. Begin
and end with meat sauce. Bake about 1/2 hour to 45
minutes in 375° oven. Top with Fritos and cheese. Return
to oven and bake until cheese is bubbly. Serve hot with
chopped lettuce, tomatoes and onion.
Kathy Neels, St. Cloud, Mn.

FLUFFY POTATO CASSEROLE

2 c. mashed potatoes
   (hot or cold)
1 (8 oz.) pkg. cream
   cheese (room temperature)
1 small onion, finely
   chopped

2 eggs
2 Tbsp. flour
Salt and pepper to taste
1 can French fried onion
   rings

Put everything but onion rings into large mixer bowl.
Beat until fluffy and well blended. Spoon into a greased 9
inch baking dish. Spread onion rings over top. Bake uncovered at 300° for 35 minutes.
Dee Olson, St. Paul, Mn.

GREEN BEAN CASSEROLE
(With Sour Cream)

1/2 c. sliced onions	1/2 tsp. grated lemon peel
1 Tbsp. minced parsley	1 c. sour cream
2 Tbsp. butter	5 c. green beans (fresh
2 Tbsp. flour	canned or frozen)
1 tsp. salt	1/2 c. grated yellow cheese
1/4 tsp. pepper	2 Tbsp. melted butter
	1/2 c. bread crumbs

Cook onions (sliced thin) and parsley in 2 tablespoons butter until tender, not brown. Add flour, salt, pepper and lemon peel. Add sour cream and mix well. Stir in beans. Put into casserole and top with grated cheese. Combine butter and bread crumbs and sprinkle on top of casserole. Bake at 350° for 30 minutes. If using canned beans, drain. Cook fresh or frozen beans first. Serves 4 to 6.

GROUND BEEF CASSEROLE

1 lb. ground beef	1/2 c. milk
1 can cream of mushroom	1/2 c. diced celery
soup	1/2 c. diced onions
1 can cream of chicken	1/4 c. mayonnaise
soup	3 Tbsp. diced green pepper
1 (4 oz.) pkg. egg	Salt
noodles, cooked	

Brown celery, onions and green pepper in butter until yellow. Add beef and brown. Blend soups and milk and mayonnaise. Add to beef and cooked noodles. Place in large casserole, garnish with cashews. Bake in 350° F. oven for 1 hour.

Harriett Maselie, Minneapolis, Mn.

HERB SPINACH CASSEROLE
(A good vegetable casserole)

Cook and drain 1 (10 ounce) package of frozen spinach. Mix with:

1 c. cooked rice	2 slightly beaten eggs
1 c. shredded sharp	2 Tbsp. butter
Cheddar cheese	1/3 c. milk

182

2 Tbsp. chopped onion
1/2 tsp. Worcestershire
  sauce

1 tsp. salt
1/4 tsp. rosemary or
  thyme

Pour mixture into 10 x 6 x 1 1/2 inch baking dish. Bake at 350° for 20 or 25 minutes or until knife inserted halfway between center comes out clean. Cut in squares to serve.

Dorothy Pierce, St. Paul, Mn.

LOW CAL VEGETABLE CASSEROLE

1 onion, sliced
2 c. celery, cut into
  3 inch strips
2 c. French cut green
  beans

1 1/2 c. carrots, cut into
  3 inch strips
3/4 c. green pepper

Mix together and put into casserole.

Sauce:

2 c. tomatoes
4 Tbsp. butter
1/4 tsp. pepper

2 tsp. salt
3 Tbsp. tapioca
1 Tbsp. sugar

Mix and pour over vegetables. Bake at 375° for 1 1/2 hours, covered. Stir and bake, uncovered, 1/2 hour more.

Lucille Jansen, Sauk Centre, Mn.

MARGE'S VEGETABLE CASSEROLE

Cook as on package until almost done:

1 box French cut
  green beans, frozen,
  drained

1 box chopped or broken
  broccoli, frozen, drained
1 box cut cauliflower, frozen,
  drained

In large bowl combine vegetables with:

1 can mushrooms
Slivered almonds
Pearl onions

1 can sliced water chestnuts
1 can cream of mushroom
  soup

Bake in casserole 50 - 60 minutes at 350° to 400°, covered, or uncovered. Sprinkle top with French fried onion rings.

Marge Johnson, Minneapolis, Mn.

MEAT LOAF CASSEROLE

Mix:

2 lb. hamburger	1 chopped onion
1/2 c. catsup	1 beaten egg
1 tsp. salt	1/2 tsp. pepper

Pat out and spread with mixture of the following, then roll up:

3 c. bread crumbs	1/2 tsp. poultry seasoning
1 c. beans (green)	1/2 c. water
3 stalks celery	1 onion, diced

Bake at 350° for 50 minutes. Remove excess fat. Make up 3 cups mashed potatoes, spread over top and sides of roll. Bake at 350° 10 minutes or until lightly browned.

Florence Brainard, Britton, S. D.

MEXICAN CASSEROLE

1 lb. hamburger	2 c. Bisquick
1/2 c. chopped onion	1/2 c. water
1 can cream of chicken soup	1 1/2 c. crushed corn chips
1 (10 oz.) can enchilada sauce	1 c. shredded Cheddar or Colby cheese
1/2 tsp. garlic salt	1/2 c. milk
1/8 tsp. pepper	Parsley flakes and paprika if desired

Brown hamburger and onion; drain. Stir in soup, enchilada sauce, garlic salt and pepper. Simmer while preparing crust. Mix Bisquick and water until soft dough forms. Pat dough into pan and 1 1/2 inches up sides to form crust. Sprinkle 3/4 cup corn chips over crust. Spoon meat mixture into crust. Sprinkle with cheese and remaining corn chips. Pour milk over casserole; sprinkle with parsley and paprika. Bake 25 to 30 minutes at 350° in 13x9 inch pan, or until crust is golden. For easier serving, let stand 5 minutes before cutting.

Mrs. Glen Sparks, Minneapolis, Mn.

184

OVEN CROQUETTES

2 c. leftover beef, lamb,
   veal, chicken or turkey,
   diced
1 medium onion
1 small green pepper
3/4 c. fine dry bread
   crumbs

1 tsp. salt
1 egg, well beaten
2 cans tomato sauce
1/2 c. leftover gravy
1/2 c. water
1 tsp. horseradish

Grind meat, onion and green pepper. Then add bread, salt, egg and 1 can of tomato sauce. Mix well and form into 8 cakes or croquettes. Then mix tomato sauce, water, gravy and horseradish. Pour this into shallow, greased baking dish. Brush the croquettes with melted fat and set them in the sauce. Bake in hot oven (400°) for 20 to 25 minutes, basting with sauce after 15 minutes. Serves 4.

PARTY CASSEROLE

1 lb. hamburger
8 oz. pkg. noodles
2 (8 oz.) cans tomato
   sauce
3 Tbsp. butter
1/2 pt. cottage cheese

8 oz. cream cheese
1/4 c. thick sour cream
1 Tbsp. green pepper, finely
   chopped
1/3 c. onions, finely chopped

Boil noodles for 10 minutes in salted water; drain and set aside. Brown hamburger in 1 tablespoon butter; stir in the tomato sauce. Remove from heat and set aside. Stir together the cottage cheese, creamed cheese and sour cream in a bowl along with the chopped green pepper and onions. Spread half of the cooked noodles in a buttered casserole and then cover the noodles with all the cheese mixture. Put the remaining noodles on top of cheese mixture and pour a couple of tablespoonfuls of melted butter over them. On this base, put the blend of hamburger and tomato sauce. Bake at 350° for 20 to 30 minutes. Serves 6.

PIZZA CASSEROLE

1 1/2 lb. ground beef
1/2 c. chopped onion
1/4 c. green olives, chopped
1 (4 oz.) can mushrooms,
   sliced

1 tsp. salt
1/8 tsp. oregano
1/4 tsp. pepper
1 (12 oz.) pkg. egg noodles

1748-81

2 (10 oz.) cans or jars
  pizza sauce
1 (8 oz.) can tomato sauce
1 c. milk

1 c. sliced pepperoni
1 (8 oz.) pkg. shredded
  Mozzarella cheese

Brown ground beef with onions, olives, mushrooms and spices. Cook noodles as directed and drain. Combine noodles and beef mixture with all remaining ingredients, except cheese. Turn into 4 quart baking dish. Sprinkle cheese over top. Bake in 350° oven, covered, for 45 minutes, then continue to cook, uncovered for an additional 15 minutes.

Phyl Mathe, St. Paul, Mn.

PORK CHOP CASSEROLE

1 Tbsp. shortening
6 pork chops
1 can cream of mushroom
  soup
1 Tbsp. minced onion
1 tsp. minced parsley
1 1/2 tsp. seasoned salt

1 1/2 c. water
1 (5 oz.) pkg. precooked
  rice (2 1/4 - 2 1/2 c.)
1/2 tsp. garlic powder
1/4 tsp. anise
1/2 tsp. caraway
1/8 tsp. cinnamon

Melt shortening in heavy skillet; add chops and cook over medium heat until lightly browned on both sides. Remove chops and set aside. Combine mushroom soup, onion, parsley, salt and water in saucepan; mix well and bring to boil. Place rice in large greased casserole; pour hot soup mixture over top. Place browned chops on top. Cover; bake at 350° for 1 hour or until chops are tender. Yield: 6 servings.

PORK CHOP AND RICE CASSEROLE

Boil 4 or 6 pork chops for about 5 minutes, remove from water. Lay chops in pan (I use a roaster). Put a slice of onion and a slice of green pepper on each chop. Tear a small bay leaf and spread around the bottom of pan. Put 2 cups of raw rice around the chops. Add 2 cans stewed tomatoes, 3 or 4 scoops of instant beef bouillon. Add enough water so the rice will not dry out. Bake, covered, for 1 hour.

Bettie Mallon, Minneapolis, Mn.

186

POTATO CASSEROLE

6 - 8 medium potatoes,
  cooked and shredded
  (can use 1 lb. frozen
  hash browns)

1 can cream of chicken soup
1 pt. sour cream
1 1/2 c. shredded sharp
  cheese
1/3 c. chopped onion

Mix together and bake in 3 quart casserole at 350° for 1 hour. Can be prepared ahead and kept in refrigerator until baking.

Jo Nell Murack, Fargo, N. D.

POTATO CASSEROLE

1 (24 oz.) bag frozen
  hash browns
2 cans cream of potato
  soup

1 can cream of celery soup
1 (8 oz.) ctn. sour cream
1 small onion, chopped
1 c. grated cheese

Mix all ingredients and top with cheese. Bake at 350° for 1 hour.

Mary Perron, Owatonna, Mn.

REUBEN CASSEROLE

1 lb. 11 oz. can sauerkraut,
  drained
2 medium tomatoes, sliced
2 Tbsp. Thousand Island
  dressing

2 (4 oz.) pkg. corned beef,
  diced
8 oz. shredded Swiss cheese
1 c. rye crackers, crushed
1/4 c. melted butter

In 9x13 inch pan, spread layer of sauerkraut, top with tomatoes, dot with dressing. cover with corned beef and sprinkle cheese on top. Mix crumbs with butter and sprinkle on top. Bake at 425° for 20 - 25 minutes.

Gail Peterson, Frazee, Mn.

RICE-BROCCOLI CASSEROLE

1 c. rice (raw), cooked
  till tender

1/4 c. celery, chopped
1/2 c. onion, chopped

Saute in 3 tablespoons butter and add 1 package frozen

chopped broccoli cuts. Mix together:

1 can mushroom soup	1/2 c. Cheez Whiz (or
3/4 c. milk	grated cheese)

Mix all ingredients together, put into casserole and bake 30 - 40 minutes at 350°. Serves 6.

Linda Seidel, Audubon, Mn.

RICE   CASSEROLE

1 can condensed cream	1 tsp. lemon juice
of mushroom or celery	1 box frozen peas, thawed
soup	1 1/3 c. Minute Rice
1/4 c. chopped celery	1/4 c. cheese crumbs
1 1/4 c. milk	1/4 c. chopped onion
1/4 tsp. salt	1 can tuna

Heat soup, milk and salt in saucepan. Bring to boil over medium heat and stir. Pour half into greased 1 1/2 quart casserole, then in layers: Minute Rice as it is, tuna, peas and celery, etc. Sprinkle with paprika, cover and bake at 375°, 20 - 25 minutes.

Kathy Bischof, St. Cloud, Mn.

RICE   CASSEROLE

1 large bunch fresh broccoli	1 can cream of celery soup,
chopped and partially	undiluted
cooked	2 c. diced celery
2 c. cooked rice	1 c. onion
1 can water chestnuts,	1 large jar Cheez Whiz
sliced	

Add Cheez Whiz to warm rice so it melts in. Add remaining ingredients and bake in greased casserole. Bake at 350° for 50 minutes.

Thank you Harriett, that really sounds good!

Harriett Maselie, Minneapolis, Mn.

188

SALMON CASSEROLE

1 (1 lb.) can salmon
1 c. corn flakes
2 eggs, well beaten

1 c. milk
1/4 tsp. salt

Flake salmon and combine with other ingredients. Pour into buttered casserole. Cover with buttered corn flakes. Bake 45 minutes at 350°.

Mavis Ann Hjulberg, St. Paul, Mn.

SAUERKRAUT CASSEROLE

1 1/2 lb. hamburger
1 small onion, chopped
  (optional)
1/4 tsp. pepper
1 tsp. salt
1 lb. can drained
  sauerkraut #1103

2 c. wide egg noodles
  (Koluski noodles), do not
  cook
1 can creamed mushroom soup
1 can creamed celery soup
1/2 c. grated Cheddar cheese

Brown meat, onion, take 1/2 meat mixture, put into casserole. Then a layer of sauerkraut. Follow with the rest of meat and layer of sauerkraut. Sprinkle noodles on top. Pour on soups. Bake 1/2 hour. Take out of oven. Sprinkle cheese on top and bake 1/2 hour longer.

Note: One-half pound pork, steak ground can be used with 1 pound hamburger.

A. Mayer, St. Paul, Mn.

SAUERKRAUT-MEAT CASSEROLE

Make layers in glass baking dish or casserole:

1 (8 oz.) can sauerkraut
2 c. Minute Rice, sprinkle
  on evenly
1 lb. hamburger, browned
  and drained

1 pkg. Wyler's dry onion
  soup mix
1 can stewed tomatoes or
  1 can tomato soup

Layer the above ingredients, cover with foil and bake 1 hour at 300°. Use no seasonings as onion soup is sufficient.

Karen Rupert, St. Cloud, Mn.

SEAFOOD CASSEROLE

1 can cream of mushroom
  soup
1 can cream of chicken
  soup
1 small can evaporated
  milk
2 c. Chinese noodles (1 can)

1 c. cooked celery
1 c. seafood or chicken (or
  1 can each of tuna or
  shrimp)
1 small can button mushrooms
1/4 pkg. slivered almonds
Green pepper and pimento
  may be added if desired

    Bake in casserole (set in hot water) for 1 1/2 hours at
275° and 1/2 hour at 325°. Do not cover. Serves 6 - 8.
              Del Hadersbeck, St. Cloud, Mn.

SHARON'S HASH BROWN CASSEROLE

2 lb. pkg. frozen Southern
  style hash browns
1 pt. whipping cream
2 c. grated Swiss cheese

Salt
Pepper
Paprika
1/4 lb. melted butter (1
  stick)

    Place hash browns in large 9x13 inch casserole dish.
Add seasonings. Pour whipping cream over potatoes. Top
with grated Swiss cheese. Pour melted butter over all.
Bake uncovered at 325° for 1 1/2 hours.
              Peni Lundeen, St. Cloud, Mn.

SHIPWRECK CASSEROLE
(This is a good winter time casserole)

1 lb. ground beef
3 small onions, chopped
1 c. potatoes, cubed
1 c. carrots, cubed
1 c. celery, cubed

1 can peas, juice and all
1 can kidney beans
1 can tomato soup
1 can tomatoes

    Brown ground beef. Salt and pepper to taste. Add
onions and potatoes. Cook until potatoes are slightly
browned. Add rest of the ingredients and bake at 350° for
1 1/2 hours or until potatoes and carrots are done.
              Dorothy Pierce, St. Paul, Mn.

STUFFED STEAK CASSEROLE

8 slices snipped bacon
3/4 c. minced onion
1/4 c. bread crumbs
3 Tbsp. catsup
2 tsp. salt

6 cube steaks
1 c. beef consomme
1/2 c. burgundy wine
1 1/2 Tbsp. flour

Fry bacon until crisp and remove from pan. Saute onion in same pan until golden and drain off fat. Mix crumbs and catsup with onions and bacon. Rub steaks with salt and spread some of the mixture on each steak. Roll and fasten with toothpicks. Place in baking dish; add consomme and burgundy wine; cover and bake 1 hour in hot oven (400°). Remove meat, stir in remaining liquid and add flour to make gravy. Serve over meat. Serves 6.

SUMMER SQUASH CASSEROLE

2 lb. yellow summer
   squash (6 c.)
1/4 c. chopped onion
1 can cream of chicken
   soup

1 c. sour cream
1 c. shredded carrots
1 (8 oz.) pkg. herb seasoned
   dressing
1/2 c. butter or margarine,
   melted

In saucepan cook sliced squash and onion in boiling, salted water for 5 minutes, drain. Combine soup and sour cream. Stir in shredded carrots. Fold in drained squash and onion - combine stuffing mixture and butter. Spread half of stuffing mixture in bottom of 12x9x2 inch baking dish. Spoon on vegetable mixture - sprinkle remaining stuffing on top. Bake at 350° for 25 to 30 minutes or until heated through. Serves 12.

Georgine Isakson, Fargo, N. D.

SUMMER YELLOW SQUASH CASSEROLE

2 lb. yellow summer
   squash, sliced (6 c.)
1/4 c. chopped onions
1 can cream of chicken
   soup
1 c. dairy sour cream

1 c. shredded carrots
1 small can water chestnuts,
   sliced
1 (8 oz.) pkg. stuffing mix
   (seasoned)
1/2 c. butter or margarine

Cook sliced squash and chopped onion in boiling water 5 minutes and drain. Combine chicken soup and sour cream. Stir in shredded carrots, water chestnuts. Fold in drained squash and onion. Combine stuffing mix and butter. Spread 1/2 of stuffing mix in bottom of baking dish. Spoon vegetable mixture on top. Sprinkle remaining stuffing mix over vegetables. Bake at 350° for 25 to 30 minutes.

SUPER SUPPER CASSEROLE

3 Tbsp. butter
1 can cream of celery soup
2 c. elbow spaghetti, cooked
2 Tbsp. lemon juice
1 c. cream style cottage cheese
1/4 c. dairy sour cream

1/2 c. sliced water chestnuts
1/4 c. finely diced green pepper
1 (1 lb.) can red salmon
1/2 c. buttered crumbs
1 (10 oz.) pkg. frozen beans or peas
1 tsp. salt

Blend butter and soup into hot spaghetti. Arrange half of mixture into a greased 11x7x2 inch baking pan. Combine lemon juice, cheese, sour cream, salt, chestnuts and green pepper. Spoon into casserole. Break salmon into bite sized pieces and combine with remaining spaghetti. Arrange around outer rim of baking dish, leaving slight depression in center. Rim casserole with buttered crumbs. Bake in a 350° oven for 45 minutes. Cook, drain and butter green vegetables. Heap in center of baked casserole and serve hot. Makes 6 to 8 servings.

SWEDISH BAKED RICE CASSEROLE

1 qt. homogenized milk   1/2 c. rice

Boil 1 hour, over low heat, stirring frequently.

3 egg yolks (4 if small eggs)
1/2 c. granulated sugar

1/2 tsp. salt
1 tsp. vanilla

Beat egg yolks, sugar, salt and vanilla, add gradually to hot rice mixture by blending in a little of hot rice mixture first to egg mixture (to avoid curdling). Cook mixture only until egg yolks are cooked. Pour into buttered casserole, top with meringue made from remaining egg whites

beaten stiff and sweetened with 2 or 3 tablespoons sugar.
Brown the meringue. Do not bake longer than to brown
meringue.

Mae Styrlund, Edina, Mn.

SWEET POTATO CASSEROLE

1 large can sweet potatoes, drained	2 eggs
1/2 c. melted butter	1 tsp. vanilla
1/3 c. evaporated milk	3/4 c. sugar

Mix and beat well. Pour into casserole (2 quart).

Topping:

1/4 c. melted butter	1/2 c. brown sugar
1 c. pecans	1 c. flour

Mix dry ingredients. Add butter, mix well. Pour
over potatoes. Cook 40 - 50 minutes at 350°.

Kay Buzzell, Marshall, Mn.

TACO CASSEROLE

10 taco shells, coarsely broken	2 Tbsp. dried minced onion
1 1/2 lb. ground beef	1 (8 oz.) can tomato sauce
1 pkg. taco seasoning mix	2 c. (1/2 lb.) grated Jack cheese
1/2 c. water	1 c. shredded lettuce
	1/2 c. fine chopped raw tomatoes

Place 1/2 taco shells in a lightly greased 1 1/2 quart
casserole. In 10 inch skillet, brown beef until crumbly.
Drain. Add taco mix and water. Simmer 10 minutes. Stir
in onion and tomato sauce. Spoon over taco shells. Sprinkle with 1 1/2 cups cheese, rest of taco shells and remaining
cheese. Bake in 350° oven for 15 - 20 minutes or until hot.
Top with lettuce and tomatoes and serve with taco sauce.
Serves 6.

Phyllis Kerr, St. Cloud, Mn.

TRICKY TURKEY CASSEROLE

2 c. cooked turkey, diced
1 can condensed cream of
   mushroom soup
1 (8 oz.) can cooked peas

6 - 12 small cooked white
   onions
Prepared stuffing mix
1 1/2 c. milk
2 Tbsp. butter

Place diced turkey meat in casserole. Spread the soup over it. Add a layer of peas and then the onions. Sprinkle the prepared stuffing mix over top to about 1 inch depth. Heat the milk and butter together and pour evenly over the top. Bake in a moderately hot oven, 400°, until bubbly and browned, about 25 minutes. Serves 4.

TUNA CASSEROLE

1 (8 oz.) pkg. noodles
2 (7 - 8 oz.) cans tuna fish
2 cans mushroom soup
1 c. milk
2 tsp. salt

1 can asparagus or beans
   (about 3 1/2 c. or #2 1/2
   can)
2 c. grated cheese
Pepper to taste

Cook noodles as per directions on package (about 15 minutes). Place a layer of cooked noodles in bottom of buttered casserole, then layer fish, vegetables and cheese. Season with salt and pepper. Repeat until all ingredients are used. Pour over the mushroom soup and milk. Dot with butter. Bake 45 minutes at 350°.

Chuck Haggard, Anoka, Mn.; Dee Olson, St. Paul, Mn.

TUNA CASHEW CASSEROLE

Combine:
1/2 c. chow mein noodles
1 can mushroom soup
1/2 c. water
1 (6 oz.) can tuna fish
1/2 c. crushed cashew nuts

1/4 c. minced onion
1 c. diced celery
Dash of pepper
1/4 tsp. salt (if unsalted
   nuts are used)

Mix all ingredients well and place in a 1 1/2 quart casserole dish. Sprinkle with 1/2 cup chow mein noodles. Bake, uncovered, at 350° for 30 minutes.

Marie Miller, St. Paul, Mn.

VEGETABLE CASSEROLE

Butter 1 1/2 quart casserole. Heat 1 can mushroom soup and 1 package frozen onions in cream sauce. Add 1 small jar of Cheez Whiz to onions. In bottom of casserole, break apart 1 package of frozen cauliflower, 1 package frozen Brussels sprouts and 1 package frozen broccoli cuts. Pour cream sauce over and bake 45 minutes to 1 hour at 350°.

Arlene Gnoivsky, Fargo, N. D.

WILD RICE AMANDINE EN CASSEROLE

Wash 2 cups wild rice in several changes of cold water and drain. Heat 1/2 cup olive oil or butter, stir in 2 tablespoons each chopped onion and chives, 3 tablespoons chopped green pepper. Stir the mixture into the rice and cook over a very gentle heat, stirring constantly until the rice begins to turn yellowish. Stir in 4 - 4 1/2 cups hot chicken broth or game stock, made with the bones and trimmings. Season to taste with salt and freshly ground pepper and lastly, add 3/4 cup blanched, shredded almonds. Turn the mixture into a casserole and bake, covered, at 300° for 45 minutes until rice is tender.

WILD RICE CASSEROLE

1 c. wild rice	2 Tbsp. butter
1 (10 1/2 oz.) can consomme	1/2 c. celery, finely chopped
1 (10 1/2 oz.) can mushroom soup	1/2 c. onion, finely chopped

Wash wild rice, place in casserole, cover with consomme, add onions and celery and soak for 3 hours, then add mushroom soup and butter. Bake 1 hour at 350°.

Kathy Bischof, St. Cloud, Mn.

WILD-RICE-CHICKEN CASSEROLE

1/2 c. long grain white rice	4 Tbsp. butter
1/2 c. raw wild rice, washed	4 Tbsp. flour
	1 tsp. salt
	1 c. broth

1 1/2 c. evaporated milk
2 c. diced chicken, turkey,
   wild duck or goose
1 (4 oz.) can sliced
   mushrooms

1/4 c. pimiento
1/3 c. chopped green pepper
1/3 c. sliced almonds

Wash and soak rice in hot water for 30 minutes. Melt butter, blend in flour and salt. Add broth and milk, stirring constantly until thick. Mix sauce, chicken, rice, mushrooms, pimiento and green pepper. Pour into a greased 6x10 inch pan. Top with almonds. Bake at 350° F. for 35 to 40 minutes. (6 - 8 servings)

Mrs. W. R. Pagel, Lisbon, N. D.

WILD RICE CASSEROLE

1 lb. hamburger
1 onion, chopped
1 can tomato soup

1 can chicken rice soup
1 can chicken gumbo soup
1 c. wild rice

Brown hamburger and onion; drain. Add soups, rinse out soup cans and add water to get mixture very soupy; then add rice.

Mrs. Glen Sparks, Minneapolis, Mn.

WORLD'S FAIR CASSEROLE

2 Tbsp. butter
2 Tbsp. chopped onion
1 c. cooked ham, cubed
1/8 tsp. tarragon
1 can condensed cream of
   chicken soup
1/2 c. water

1 1/2 c. cooked egg noodles
1/2 c. French style green
   beans, cooked or canned
2 Tbsp. fine dry bread
   crumbs
1 small clove garlic, minced

Melt 1 tablespoon butter, add onion, ham and tarragon; cook until onion is tender and ham is brown. Stir in soup, water, noodles and green beans. Pour into greased casserole. Lightly brown crumbs and garlic in remaining tablespoon of butter; sprinkle over top of casserole. Bake in oven at 350° for 30 minutes. Yield: 4 servings.

ZUCCHINI VEGETABLE CASSEROLE

Layer in casserole:

Zucchini, peeled and
  sliced 1/4 inch thick
Onion

Tomatoes, sliced 1/4 inch
Croutons

Put tomato wedges on top and bake for 1 hour at 375°. Remove from oven, sprinkle with grated cheese and return to oven until cheese melts.

Georgia Berg, Fargo, N. D.

TOASTY CHEESE BAKE

8 slices white bread
1/2 lb. ground beef
1/4 c. chopped onion
2 Tbsp. chopped celery
1 Tbsp. prepared mustard
1/2 tsp. salt

1 c. shredded American cheese
1 egg, slightly beaten
3/4 c. milk
1/2 tsp. salt
1/8 tsp. dry mustard
Dash of pepper

Heat oven to 350°. Toast bread, butter both sides. Cook and stir meat, onion, celery, prepared mustard and 1/2 teaspoon salt until meat is brown and onions tender. Alternate layers of toast, meat mixture and cheese in greased baking pan (9x9x2 inches). Mix remaining ingredients, pour over layers in pan. If you wish, sprinkle with paprika. Bake, uncovered, 30 to 35 minutes. (4 to 6 servings)

Lenora Buck, Fargo, N. D.

TRIPLE CHEESE BAKE

2 - 3 c. ham, diced
10 oz. box frozen broccoli
  cuts
1 c. Cheddar cheese,
  shredded
1 c. Mozzarella cheese,
  shredded

1 c. milk
3 eggs
1 Tbsp. flour
1 tsp. salt
1 c. American cheese,
  shredded

Cook broccoli according to directions on the package. Drain well. Layer a greased 9x13 inch pan with ham, broccoli and cheese. Mix the remaining ingredients and pour over the first. Bake at 350° for 30 to 40 minutes until bubbly and golden brown.

Deb Nordby, Fargo, N. D.

1748-81

BAKED CHICKEN DISH

1 can of each cream of
chicken, onion soup and
celery soup

1 c. uncooked rice

Mix all soups and the rice. Spread in bottom of buttered casserole. Lay pieces of chicken on top and dot with butter. Sprinkle with Parmesan cheese and bake 2 hours at 350°, uncovered.

Louise B. Meyer, Little Falls, Mn.

CHEESY CHICKEN

1 1/2 c. Minute Rice
1 pkg. Lipton dry onion
soup mix
1 can Cheddar cheese soup

1 can milk
1 can water
Chicken breasts

Pour rice into bottom of 9x13 inch pan. Pour onion soup mix over rice. Dilute Cheddar cheese soup with milk and water, pour over rice and onion soup mixture. Place chicken breasts on top of this. Bake at 350° until done.

Claren Kane, Sauk Centre, Mn.

CHICKEN ALLISON

Line 9x13 inch cake pan with 1 package dried beef. Cover bottom. Next, layer 12 halves boned chicken breasts. Cut 6 slices of bacon into halves and put over chicken. Bake 1/2 hour, uncovered, in 350° oven. Next, mix exactly 1 pint sour cream with 1 can cream of mushroom soup, undiluted. Put over chicken and return to oven for 1/2 hour more. Serve.

Mary Paul, Minneapolis, Mn.

CHICKEN BAKED WITH BARBECUE SAUCE

Have ready, 2 broiler fryers, cut up. Arrange chicken pieces in a single layer in a well buttered large, shallow baking pan. Spoon barbecue sauce over chicken so pieces are well coated.

Barbecue Sauce:

2 cans tomato sauce

1 medium onion, chopped

198

| 1 clove garlic, minced | 2 Tbsp. sugar |
| 1/4 c. soy sauce | 1 tsp. dry mustard |

Bake, uncovered, in hot oven (400°) about 1 hour or until chicken is tender.

Linda Seidel, Audubon, Mn.

CHICKEN BREASTS IN SOUR CREAM

6 chicken breasts	1 can mushroom soup
1 can sliced mushroom	1/2 c. dry white wine
1/2 pt. sour cream	Paprika
Salt and pepper	

Remove skins from chicken. Salt and pepper pieces. Arrange in a shallow baking dish. Drain mushrooms and arrange over chicken. Mix soup, sour cream and wine. Pour over chicken, sprinkle with paprika and bake at 350° for 1 1/2 hours. (6 servings)

Dee Olson, St. Paul, Mn.

CHICKEN BREASTS IN WINE

1/4 c. flour	1/4 c. salad oil
1 tsp. seasoned salt	1/4 c. butter
1/4 tsp. pepper	Rosemary
2 lb. chicken breasts	1/4 c. dry sherry
	Water

Combine flour, seasoned salt and pepper. Coat chicken breasts with seasoned flour. Heat salad oil and butter in medium hot skillet and fry chicken slowly until golden brown. Remove from skillet and place single layer in shallow baking pan. Sprinkle a pinch of rosemary over each chicken breast and pour sherry over the chicken. Add a little water to bottom of pan. Cover and bake in moderate oven (350°) for 45 to 50 minutes or until tender.

CHICKEN CANAPES

| 1 (6 oz.) can chopped, broiled mushrooms | 2 (5 to 6 oz.) cans boned chicken, very finely chopped or 2 c. very finely chopped cooked chicken |
| 1/2 c. very finely diced celery | |

2/3 c. dairy sour cream
1 tsp. grated onion
1/2 tsp. salt
1/2 tsp. curry powder

Cherry tomatoes, sliced
Parsley
Canape shells

Make canape shells by using your favorite 2 crust pastry recipe. Divide dough in half. Roll out dough; cut into small rounds with 1 3/4 inch scalloped cutter. (I use my star shaped cookie cutter.) Fit into tiny muffin pans. Prick shells with fork and bake at 425° for 7 minutes, approximately. Cool. Mix all ingredients except tomatoes and parsley and chill. Just before serving, spoon chicken mixture into shells and garnish with slice of tomato and a bit of parsley. Makes 5 dozen.

CHICKEN CANELONI

Chicken breasts, deboned
Mustard
Mozzarella or Swiss cheese
3 tomatoes
Salt and pepper

1 small jar mushrooms, sliced
Parsley
Green onions
Olive oil
White wine

Flatten breasts between waxed paper. Sprinkle salt and pepper, parsley, mustard, slice of cheese. Roll up in flour and saute in olive oil. Remove from pan. Saute green onions in olive oil. Dip tomatoes in boiling water for 10 seconds or until skin can be removed, cut into halves. Squeeze out juice and seeds. Chop and add these, mushrooms and chicken back to pan. Pour in white wine and simmer till warm.
Joan Billadeau, St. Cloud, Mn.

CHICKEN IN THE CHIPS

Have ready 1 fryer, cut up. Dip into 1/4 pound melted oleo or butter. Roll in crushed potato chips. Place on foil on cookie sheet. Bake approximately 1 hour at 350°.
I won a National Prize with this recipe.
Kathy Bischof, St. Cloud, Mn.

CHICKEN DELIGHT

6 boned and halved
   chicken breasts
12 strips bacon
2 (3 oz.) pkg. dried beef

1 c. Swiss cheese, shredded
2 c. sour cream
2 cans cream of chicken soup

Cover bottom of 9x13 inch pan with dried beef. Wrap each breast in a strip of bacon. Place on the dried beef. Mix the sour cream and the soup and spoon over the chicken. Bake, uncovered, at 300° for 2 hours. Sprinkle with cheese and place in oven till cheese melts.

Deb Nordby, Fargo, N. D.

CHICKEN DELIGHT
(Serves 4-6)

Have ready, 1 package chicken breasts or 1 whole chicken. Bake in foil 1 hour at 400°. Cool and bone chicken. Cut into cubes. Barely cook 2 - 3 (10 ounce) boxes frozen broccoli. Make sauce:

2 cans cream of chicken
   soup
3/4 c. mayonnaise

1 tsp. lemon juice
1/4 tsp. curry powder
1/2 c. grated Cheddar cheese

Grease an 11 1/2 x 7 1/2 inch dish - layer with broccoli and chicken. Pour sauce over - top with buttered crumbs (bread). Sprinkle with paprika. Bake at 375° for 30 - 40 minutes.

Carolyn Smith, Fargo, N. D.

CHICKEN DIVINE

1 - 4 c. cooked, cubed
   chicken
2 1/2 c. brown rice (raw)
1 can cream of mushroom
   soup
1 can cream of celery soup
2 soup cans of the chicken
   broth

1/2 - 1 c. minced onion
1/2 - 1 1/2 c. chopped celery
1 can mushrooms, minced
1/2 tsp. sage
1/2 tsp. thyme
1/4 tsp. marjoram
Salt and pepper to taste

Saute onion and celery in butter. Mix all together in casserole. Cover with foil and bake at 350° for 2 hours.

The last 1/2 hour, cover with Chinese noodles or crushed crackers, drizzled with butter. Additions of cut up water chestnuts or bamboo shoots or cashew nuts help to vary the recipe.

Kathy Neels, St. Cloud, Mn.

CHICKEN IN A DISH

1 chicken breast (or other desired pieces) per serving
1 medium raw potato, sliced, per serving
1 carrot, sliced, per serving
1 Tbsp. sour cream, per serving
1 Tbsp. dry onion soup mix per serving

Using the little foil dishes from "frozen pot pies" or a 12 inch square of heavy broiler foil, add the sliced potato, then 1 carrot, next a chicken breast or enough chicken for 1 serving; top with 1 tablespoon sour cream and 1 tablespoon dry onion soup mix. Wrap securely with foil, using a double seam closing. Cook over coals 1 1/2 hours, turning carefully.

CHICKEN GOURMET

1 stick margarine
1 clove garlic, minced
1 1/2 tsp. salt
2 tsp. chili powder
Dash of pepper
4 whole chicken breasts, halved
Juice of 1 lemon
2 tsp. Worcestershire sauce

Melt margarine in small saucepan; blend in garlic, salt, chili powder, pepper, lemon juice and Worcestershire sauce. Place chicken in shallow baking dish; pour mixture over chicken and cover. Bake 40 minutes at 350°. Remove cover; reduce heat to 325°. Cook for about 60 minutes or until tender, basting frequently. Place on heated platter; spoon sauce over chicken. Garnish with broiled cling peaches and mint jelly. Yield: 8 servings.

202

CHICKEN KIEV

4 medium chicken breasts
Salt
8 Tbsp. chopped green
   onion

8 Tbsp. chopped parsley
1/4 lb. stick butter (use
   butter only)
Flour, egg, bread crumbs,
   hot oil

Cut chicken breasts into halves lengthwise and remove skin and cut away from bone. Place each piece, boned side up, between Saran Wrap. Pound until not quite 1/4 inch thick. Salt, then put 1 tablespoon onion and parsley on each piece of meat. Cut butter into 8 equal parts and place on the end of each piece of meat. Roll up like a jelly roll, tucking in sides of meat to seal. Dust with flour, dip in beaten egg, then roll in fine dry bread crumbs. Chill chicken at least 1 hour. Fry in deep hot fat, about 5 minutes. Serves 6.

Dee Olson, St. Paul, Mn.

CHICKEN KIEV

Herb Butter:

1 c. butter, softened
2 Tbsp. chopped parsley
1 1/2 tsp. dried tarragon
   leaves

1 clove garlic, crushed
3/4 tsp. salt
1/8 tsp. pepper

Have ready:

6 boned whole chicken
   breasts (each 1/4 lb.)
3/4 c. unsifted all-purpose
   flour

3 eggs, well beaten
1 1/2 c. packaged dry bread
   crumbs
Salad oil or shortening for
   deep frying

In small bowl, mix with rubber scraper, butter and the rest of the Herb Butter ingredients. On foil, shape into 6 inch square. Freeze until firm (40 minutes). Wash chicken, dry well, remove skin. Cut each breast in half. To flatten chicken, place each half smooth side down on sheet of waxed paper. Cover with second sheet. Using mallet or side of saucer, pound chicken to 1/4 inch thickness. Be careful not to break the meat. Cut frozen pats. Place one pat of Herb Butter in center of each piece. Bring long ends of chicken over butter, making sure no butter is showing. Fasten with toothpick. Roll in flour on waxed paper. Dip in beaten egg, roll in crumbs, shaping each piece in palm of hand. Refrigerate, covered, about 1 hour. Heat oil in large skillet or Dutch oven (360°). Add chicken pieces, 3 at a time for 5 minutes.

Diane Schmitz, St. Cloud, Mn.

CHICKEN CONTINENTAL

1 fryer chicken, cut up	1 tsp. salt and pepper
1/3 c. seasoned flour	1 Tbsp. minced parsley
1/4 c. shortening	1/2 tsp. celery flakes
1 can cream of chicken	1/8 tsp. thyme
soup	1 1/3 c. water
2 Tbsp. onion	1 1/3 c. Minute rice
	1/2 tsp. paprika

Roll chicken in seasoned flour. Saute in shortening until tender. Combine soup, onion and seasonings in saucepan; gradually add water and blend. Bring to a boil, stirring constantly. Reserve 1/3 cup soup mixture; pour remaining soup over rice in 9x13 inch baking pan. Stir just to moisten all rice. Top with chicken and remaining soup. Cover and bake at 375° about 20 minutes. Sprinkle with paprika; garnish with parsley.

Mrs. Roger Esser, Fargo, N.D.

CHICKEN LOAF

1 lb. hamburger	1 can chicken noodle soup
2 c. oatmeal	1/2 tsp. each sage and
1 egg, beaten	poultry seasoning
1 Tbsp. onion, diced	Salt and pepper to taste

Mix ingredients together well. This loaf has a most unusual flavor. It is delicious even for company.

Marge Johnson, Minneapolis, Mn.

CHICKEN AND RICE

In 9x13 inch pan, sprinkle 1 envelope Lipton onion soup mix. Next layer - 1 cup uncooked rice. Next layer - Cut up uncooked chicken in serving pieces and arranged on the rice. Add 1 1/2 cans milk and water to 1 can cream of chicken soup, mix and pour over chicken. Bake 2 hours at 350°. You may have to add more water if it gets too dry.

204   Marilyn Helgeson, Fargo, N. D.

CHICKEN IN SOUR CREAM WITH DUMPLINGS

2 (1 lb.) pkg. frozen
  chicken thighs,
  breasts, drumsticks
  or wings
1/2 c. flour

1 tsp. paprika
2 Tbsp. butter or margarine
1 can condensed cream of
  mushroom soup
1 c. sour cream

Thaw chicken as directed on package. Place flour and paprika in paper bag; add 2 or 3 pieces of chicken at a time and shake well. Brown chicken in butter. Blend in soup and sour cream. Cover; simmer 45 minutes or until chicken is tender.

Dumplings:

1 1/2 c. sifted flour
2 1/2 tsp. baking powder
1 tsp. salt
1/3 c. milk

2 eggs, slightly beaten
Parsley
Caraway

Sift dry ingredients together; add milk and eggs; mix until flour is moistened, but not smooth. Drop dumplings by spoonfuls into simmering chicken and sauce. Cover; cook 15 minutes longer. Do not lift lid during cooking time.
Yield: 6 - 8 servings.

CHICKEN ON SUNDAY

3 c. Minute Rice
1 can milk

1 can cream of celery soup
  (may substitute cream of
  chicken or mushroom)

Mix together and pat into well greased 9x13 inch pan. Lay chicken (cut into serving pieces) on rice, skin side up. Salt and pepper to taste. Sprinkle with 1/2 package dry onion soup mix. Cover. Bake at 275° for 2 hours.
Renee Ulberg, Bismarck, N. D.

CHICKEN SUPREME
(Make Ahead)

2 1/2 c. diced chicken
2 cans cream of mushroom
  soup

1 can milk
1 onion
1 can chicken broth

1/2 stick butter

1 (8 oz.) can mushrooms

1/2 lb. Velveeta cheese, diced

1 (7 oz.) pkg. Creamettes

Mix all ingredients together. Pat into 9x13 inch pan. Refrigerate overnight. Remove from refrigerator 1 hour before baking, cover with buttered bread crumbs. Sprinkle with paprika and bake 1 hour at 350°. Let stand 10 minutes before serving.

Gina Michels, Willmar, Mn.

CHICKEN AND WILD RICE

1/2 c. white rice

1/2 c. wild rice

1 pkg. onion soup mix

2 cans water

1 can cream of chicken soup

1 cut up chicken

Put rice in 9x14 inch baking pan. Mix in onion soup mix. Add water. Arrange chicken on top. Slightly dilute cream of chicken soup and pour over chicken. Bake, uncovered, 2 hours at 350°.

Marge Johnson, Minneapolis, Mn.

CHICKEN AND WILD RICE

Have ready, 4 whole chicken breasts cut into large pieces. Simmer in water with salt and pepper, bay leaf, celery and onion.

1 pkg. long grain and wild
   rice mix, cook as directed

1 medium onion, chopped

1/2 lb. fresh mushrooms,
   sliced

1 c. celery, chopped

1/4 c. butter

1 can water chestnuts, sliced

3/4 c. mayonnaise

1 can each cream of mushroom
   and cream of chicken soup

Saute onion, celery and mushrooms in butter. Combine all ingredients. Season to taste. Place in large casserole. Bake uncovered, for 30 to 45 minutes at 350° or until bubbly.

Betty Ladd, St. Paul, Mn.

CHINESE CHICKEN
(Serves 8 - 12)

6 chicken breasts, cooked
and cut up
2 boxes frozen Italian
green beans
1 box frozen Chinese
green pea pods

2 cans water chestnuts,
sliced
2 jars sliced mushrooms
1 raw onion, sliced thin

Sauce: Melt 3 cans mushroom soup with 1 pound grated Cheddar cheese, 2 teaspoons oregano and salt and pepper to taste.

Mix meat and vegetables in 9x13 inch pan. Pour sauce over and top with French fried onion rings. Bake 1 1/2 hours at 350°. Serve with Celery Seed Bread:

1/2 c. butter
1/4 tsp. salt
1/4 tsp. paprika

1/2 tsp. celery seed
Dash of cayenne pepper
1 lb. loaf (day old) unsliced
bread

Remove crust from bread. Slice loaf in half lengthwise, and then across to make "sticks" Melt ingredients and pour over bread. Refrigerate. Heat in oven wrapped in foil, uncovered.

Carolyn Smith, Fargo, N. D.

CHINESE CHICKEN
(Serves 6)

4 boneless chicken breasts
3 Tbsp. vegetable oil
2 Tbsp. soy sauce
1/2 tsp. salt
1/4 tsp. pepper
2 tsp. cornstarch
1/4 c. cold water
1/4 tsp. sugar

2 red peppers, cut into
1/2 inch strips
2 green peppers, cut into
1/2 inch strips
6 scallions, including green
portion, cut into 1/2 inch
slices

Combine chicken with 1 tablespoon each of the oil and soy sauce, the salt and pepper and cornstarch. Let stand 1 hour, stirring every 15 minutes. Heat remaining oil in a large skillet or wok. Saute peppers 3 minutes. Add chicken mixture and remaining ingredients. Cook over medium heat, stirring 5 minutes or until chicken is tender. Serve with rice.

1748-81　　　　Madelyn Richard, Minneapolis, Mn.

CHOW MEIN

Boil leftover turkey, bones and all, about 1 1/2 hours. Remove skin and bones. Dice meat and return to broth. Add:

1 c. chopped onion
3 c. diced celery
1 can bean sprouts

1 can water chestnuts, sliced
1/4 c. soy sauce

Boil until celery is done. Thicken with cornstarch. Serve on rice or noodles.

Joyce Haugen, Fargo, N. D.

CHOW MEIN

1 1/2 - 2 lb. cubed pork (lean)
2 stalks celery, chopped
2 medium onions, diced
2 cans cream of mushroom soup

2 cans chicken rice soup
5 cans water
1 c. rice (converted)
1/2 bottle soy sauce

Saute celery and onions together. Brown meat - just searing outside. Mix all ingredients in large roaster pan and bake, uncovered, at 325° for 3 - 4 hours. Serve over chow mein noodles. Serves 8 - 10 people. Recipe can easily be divided or multiplied.

Jacquie Amacher, Willmar, Mn.

CHICKEN CHOW MEIN

1 1/2 Tbsp. oil
4 chicken breasts, skinned, boned and cut up
1 level tsp. salt

2 tsp. soya sauce
2/3 c. water
*2 c. fresh Chinese vegetables
1 tsp. cornstarch

Heat oil in pan until very hot. Add chicken and salt. Saute for 2 minutes. Add 1 teaspoon soya sauce. Add vegetables, stir and cook for 3 minutes. Add 1/3 cup of water, cover and cook for 3 minutes. Now make your gravy by mixing 1 teaspoon cornstarch and 1 teaspoon of soya sauce to remainder of water. Add to chow mein and stir until gravy reaches desired consistency. Serve with steaming hot rice. Makes 3 to 4 servings. Entire recipe should be cooked over high flame.

Variations: Pork, beef, shrimp, mushrooms, etc. can be substituted for chicken.

*Prepackaged in produce section of grocery store.
Connie Vivier, Fargo, N. D.

MARTY'S PORK CHOW MEIN

2 lb. pork butt
1 large onion
1 can mushrooms
1 can water chestnuts
    (optional)

1 can bamboo shoots (optional)
6 stalks celery
2 cans bean sprouts
Salt and pepper

Cut meat into 1 inch pieces. Put into covered pan with 1 tablespoon oil and cook until liquid is all gone and meat browns lightly. Pour liquid from bean sprouts and mushrooms over meat, add salt and pepper to taste, cook until tender, about 1/2 hour. Add celery, onions, mushrooms and bean sprouts. Add 1 to 2 teaspoons Kitchen Bouquet (for color - optional). Simmer 15 minutes, thicken with 2 tablespoons cornstarch mixed with a little cold water. Serve over chow mein noodles and rice. Serves 4 to 5.
Marty Eger, St. Paul, Mn.

CREAM BAKED CHICKEN

2 to 3 lb. chicken, cut
    up
1/2 c. flour
1 tsp. salt
1/4 tsp. pepper

1/4 c. shortening
1 c. sour cream
3 Tbsp. Lipton onion soup
1/2 c. milk

Coat chicken with flour, salt and pepper and brown in skillet. In saucepan mix soup mix, sour cream, stir in milk and beat with rotary beater - heat "do not boil". Place chicken in casserole, pour in sauce mix - cover and bake at 350°. Makes 4 - 6 servings.
Irma Holmsten, Bismarck, N. D.

DELUXE BAKED CHICKEN

1 chicken, cut up
Dried beef
Bacon

1 can cream of mushroom
    soup
1/2 pt. sour cream

Put dried beef on bottom of 9x13 inch pan, lay chicken on this and lay 1/2 slices of bacon on each piece. Mix 1 can soup and the sour cream together and pour over top and sprinkle with paprika. Bake 3 hours at 275°. (Can prepare all ahead and keep in refrigerator and bake next day.)

Karen Rupert, St. Cloud, Mn.

FESTIVAL CHICKEN SPAGHETTI

2 large hens
1/2 lb. butter
2 large onions, chopped
2 c. thinly sliced celery
4 cloves garlic, minced
2 lb. ground round steak
3 (#1) cans tomatoes
Salt and pepper to taste

2 tsp. chili powder
1/2 tsp. oregano
1/2 tsp. basil
3 (12 oz.) pkg. spaghetti
Chicken stock
2 lb. American cheese,
    grated

Boil hens in enough salted water to cover. Save stock. Bone chicken and cut into bite sized pieces. Put butter in a large skillet, add onions, celery and garlic and simmer. Add ground round steak, fry slightly; add tomatoes and cook until like hash. Add salt, pepper, chili powder, oregano and basil. Cook spaghetti in the strained chicken stock. Using a very large baking dish, put a layer of cooked spaghetti, a layer of sauce, a layer of chicken and a layer of cheese. Repeat this 3 times, ending with cheese on top. Bake in a 200° oven for 2 hours. Serves 20.

FLUFFY RICE AND CHICKEN

1 can mushroom soup
1 can milk
3/4 c. regular rice

1 env. onion soup mix
1 chicken, cut up

Cover with foil and bake at 350° for 40 minutes. Uncover and bake another 15 - 20 minutes.

Martie Athey, Detroit Lakes, Mn.

OVEN BAKED CHICKEN

Place cut up chicken on pan - brush with melted butter or margarine. Sprinkle with bread crumbs or crushed soda crackers. Salt and pepper. Bake till done.

Darlene Lee

OVEN BAKED CHICKEN

Melt 1/2 cup butter in bottom of baking dish. Mix in bag:

1/3 c. flour	1 tsp. dry mustard
1 tsp. salt	1 tsp. paprika
1/8 tsp. pepper	

Coat chicken in bag. Place skin side down in buttered pan. Bake at 400° for 45 - 60 minutes. Turn chicken over after 30 minutes.

Sue Hick, Detroit Lakes, Mn.

LUAU CHICKEN WITH RICE

1/4 c. diced Spam	2 Tbsp. butter or margarine
1 c. diced celery	1 (19 oz.) can Campbell's
2 Tbsp. sliced green onions	chunky chicken rice soup
1 Tbsp. soy sauce	2 Tbsp. water
1 Tbsp. cornstarch	Chow mein noodles

In saucepan, lightly brown Spam and cook celery in butter till tender. Add soup, onions and soy sauce. Blend cornstarch and water till smooth, then add to soup mixture. Cook, stirring till thickened. Serve over noodles with additional soy sauce. Makes about 3 cups.

Robert McFarlin, Rochester, Mn.

PRESSED CHICKEN LOAF

1 (3 lb.) stewing chicken	1/4 tsp. dry mustard
2 qt. water	1 tsp. salt
2 tsp. salt	1 tsp. unflavored gelatin
1 c. chopped celery	3 Tbsp. cold water
5 hard-cooked eggs, diced	

Simmer chicken in 2 quarts water with salt until the meat falls from the bones. Remove chicken and chill both chicken and stock. Skim fat off stock. Then skin the chicken and chop fine. Add celery, seasonings and hard-cooked eggs to meat; mix thoroughly. Meanwhile, soften gelatin in cold water, then dissolve into 2 cups of heated chicken stock. Let cool until partially gelled. Add to chicken mixture. Pour into small containers; slice when cold.

Kathy Bischof, St. Cloud, Mn.

SWEET AND SOUR CHICKEN

Have about 25 chicken wings, cut at the joints - discard tips. Place wings in dish and pour over mixture of:

1 c. water	1 tsp. ground ginger
1 c. sugar	1 c. soy sauce
1/4 c. pineapple juice	1/4 c. salad oil

Refrigerate overnight. Remove wings from marinade and place in single layer on shallow pan. Bake uncovered in 350° oven for 45 minutes or until brown and tender.

Betty Ladd, St. Paul, Mn.

SWEET 'N SOUR DRUMSTICKS

20 chicken drumsticks	1 tsp. dry mustard
1/4 c. peanut oil	4 green onions, cut diagonally
3/4 c. water	into 1 inch pieces
1/4 c. soy sauce	1 (8 oz.) can water chestnuts,
1/4 c. sherry	drained and sliced
2 Tbsp. brown sugar,	1 Tbsp. cornstarch
packed	

In large frying pan, cook chicken over heat in oil, browning on all sides, 15 minutes; drain oil. Combine 1/2 cup water, soy sauce, sherry, brown sugar and dry mustard; pour over chicken. Simmer, covered, 20 to 30 minutes or until chicken is tender. Remove chicken to warm platter. Combine cornstarch with remaining 1/4 cup water; stir into sauce. Cook, stirring until thickened. Fold in green onions and water chestnuts; heat through. Serve with chicken. Makes 4 to 6 servings.

SWEET-SOUR CHICKEN WINGS

12 chicken wings (or more)
1 (8 oz.) bottle Russian salad dressing
1 pkg. (env.) dried onion soup
1 (10 to 12 oz.) jar apricot preserves

(Makes a lot of sauce.) Crack wings apart and break off tips. Don't use tips. Lay out in casserole or large pan. Sprinkle soup over chicken. Pour salad dressing over that and spread preserves over the top. Bake 2 hours at 300° uncovered.

Joyce Schmalz, Fargo, N. D.

DON'S CHILI

1 1/2 - 2 lb. lean hamburger
1 qt. whole tomatoes
1 can tomato soup refilled with water
1 large or 2 small cans kidney beans
2 onions, large, diced
4 stalks celery, diced
1 pkg. Schilling chili mix or 1 Tbsp. chili powder
4 - 6 garlic cloves, smashed and diced, or 1 tsp. garlic powder
1 tsp. ground cumin
Salt and pepper to taste
1 or 2 Tbsp. sugar to taste

Brown and crumble hamburger to almond size. Drain off any grease. Add all ingredients into a 5 quart pan with cover. Heat slowly to boiling, stirring 3 to 4 times. Reduce heat and simmer 1 hour with cover on. This is a large batch, but freezes well. Check during cooking - may need to add water.

Don Billadeau, St. Cloud, Mn.

CHILI

1 can stewed tomatoes
1 can barbequed beans
1 can kidney beans
1 lb. hamburger, browned
Salt and pepper
Onion (however much you want)
Green pepper (as much as you want)
Brown sugar (to your taste)

I mix all this together and let it simmer for at least 1/2 hour, stirring occasionally. After it's dished up, serve with canned French fried onion rings sprinkled on top. This re-heats or freezes well.

1748-81   Mrs. Don Bredenberg, Bemidji, Mn.   213

CHILI

1 lb. ground beef
1 large onion (1 c.)
1 green pepper (3/4 c.),
   chopped
1 can (2 c.) tomatoes

1 (8 oz.) can tomato sauce
1 can kidney beans
1 tsp. salt
2 Tbsp. chili powder
1 bay leaf

Simmer for 1 hour.

Bev Barglof, Detroit Lakes, Mn.

CINCINNATI CHILI

1 qt. water
2 medium onions, grate
   fine
2 (8 oz.) cans tomato sauce
5 whole allspice
1/2 tsp. red pepper
1 tsp. ground cumin
4 tsp. chili powder
1/2 oz. bitter chocolate

2 lb. ground beef
4 cloves garlic, minced
2 Tbsp. vinegar
1 large bay leaf (whole)
5 whole cloves
2 tsp. Worcestershire sauce
1 1/2 tsp. salt
1 tsp. cinnamon

Add ground beef to water in 4 quart pot. Stir until beef separates to a fine texture. Boil slowly for 1/2 hour. Add all other ingredients. Stir to blend. Bring to boil. Reduce heat and simmer uncovered for about 3 hours. Last hour, pot may be covered. Refrigerate overnight so fat may be skimmed off before eating. Beans may be added during the last hour of simmering, if desired.

Mary Jo Olson, Detroit Lakes, Mn.

TEXAS CHILE
(Serves 8)

3 - 4 lb. chuck blade
   steak, cubed
1/4 c. oil
1 1/2 c. chopped onions
2 medium green peppers,
   chopped
4 garlic cloves, crushed
   or use garlic salt

2 (8 oz.) cans tomatoes
1 (12 oz.) can tomato paste
2 c. water
1/2 c. chile powder
1/4 c. sugar
2 Tbsp. salt
2 tsp. oregano
3/4 tsp. pepper

Brown meat in oil. Remove meat from pan. Put onions

and peppers in pan and add garlic, cook over medium heat. Cook 10 minutes, return meat to pan, add remaining ingredients, including juice from tomatoes. Simmer 2 hours or cook all day in crock pot.

Ginnie Andersen, St. Paul, Mn.

CHOP SUEY

1 pkg. noodles, boiled
2 lb. hamburger, brown
  in butter
3 large onions, cut up
  fine and browned with
  hamburger

1/2 lb. pork sausage,
  browned
1 large stalk celery, cut up
  and cooked with meat
1 can chicken soup
1 can tomato soup

Add all together and cook slowly. More soup may be added.

Helen M. Gludt, Bottineau, N. D.

OVEN CHOW MEIN

1 lb. ground beef,
  browned in oil
1 c. rice, uncooked
1 c. onions
1 c. celery

1 can chicken rice soup and
  1 can water
1 can mushroom soup and 1
  can water
2 Tbsp. soy sauce

Combine all ingredients and bake in moderate oven 1 hour.

Betty Michon, Detroit Lakes, Mn.

CARAWAY DUMPLINGS
(From Austria)

Sift together into mixing bowl:

1 1/2 c. flour
1 Tbsp. sugar
2 tsp. baking powder

1/2 tsp. salt
1/4 tsp. dry mustard
1/2 tsp. caraway seed

Combine:
1 egg, slightly beaten
2/3 c. milk

2 Tbsp. shortening, melted

Add to dry ingredients all at once. Stir until moistened. Drop by spoonfuls into casserole or Dutch oven.
Adeline Hortsch, St. Cloud, Mn.

FAHEY'S NOODLES
(Super)

1 small pkg. egg noodles
1/2 - 3/4 c. butter

1 c. finely crushed soda
  crackers

Cook noodles. Drain, rinse and set aside. Melt butter; add crumbs. Brown lightly. Add noodles and toss until all coated with cracker mixture. Heat thoroughly and
serve. This may sound like an odd dish, but, it's delicious!
(and addicting).
Colleen Knaus, Grand Forks, N. D.

POTATO DUMPLINGS

8 medium sized potatoes
  put through grinder, or
  can be grated with middle
  holes on grater
1 egg, beaten
1 handful oatmeal

Dash of salt
Less than 1/2 tsp. baking
  powder
Enough flour to thicken until
  you can take in your hand
  and don't stick

Roll into balls about 4 inches across. Put 1 dumpling
in a kettle of boiling, salted water to see that it doesn't fall
apart. If it does, add more flour. Very good with a ham
bone added to the water. Boil 1 hour. Serve with butter
and syrup.
Aster Paulsrud, Willmar, Mn.

POLISH DUMPLINGS
(Kluski Lane)

2 eggs, beaten
1/4 tsp. salt

1 Tbsp. water
1/3 c. all-purpose flour

1. Combine all ingredients and stir until smooth.
2. Hold spoonfuls of batter about 12 inches from boiling
soup (preferably homemade chicken soup with lots of
broth); pour slowly from end of spoon. Let boil about 2 to
3 minutes, or until egg drops float. Approximately 4

servings.

Variation: Prepare above recipe, pour almost continuously from a cup or spoon into boiling soup to form a long "string". Break apart after cooking. Yummy!!!!!
Pat Bruchert, Minneapolis, Mn.

POLISH RAW POTATO DUMPLINGS
(Kartoflane Kluski)

2 c. raw potatoes	1 1/2 c. flour
1 tsp. salt	1/2 c. bread crumbs
2 eggs, beaten	

Grate potatoes fine and drain off brown liquid. (Use a blender if you wish.) Add the beaten eggs, salt, crumbs and flour to make a stiff dough. Drop into boiling salted water from wet spoon. Dumplings should be about 1 1/2 inches long and 1/2 inch in diameter when cooked. They are done as soon as they float to top. Top or mix dumplings with buttered, sauteed onions.
Gloria A. Kurkowski, St. Paul, Mn.

KARTOFLANE KLUSKI
(car-toe-FLA-neh KLU-ski)
(Raw Potato Dumplings)

2 c. grated raw potatoes	1 tsp. salt
2 eggs, beaten	1 1/2 c. flour (approx.)

1. Rinse potatoes and drain well. 2. Combine potatoes with eggs, salt and flour - enough flour to make the dough stiff. 3. Using a wet teaspoon, drop into boiling, salted water. 4. Cook dumplings till they float to the top. (Dumplings should be 1 1/2 x 1/2 inch.) Makes about 4 servings. Delicious with any pork!
Patty Ginter, St. Cloud, Mn.

NOODLE KUEGGEL
(Russian)

1 large pkg. dry egg noodles	1 Tbsp. oil
	1 tsp. salt
5 eggs	1/4 tsp. pepper

Cook noodles, following package directions. Rinse and set aside. Beat eggs until frothy. Add oil, salt and pepper to eggs and stir to mix. Combine eggs and noodles. Turn into a greased 9x9 inch pan or casserole dish. Bake at 350° until golden brown on top, *about 1 hour.

*Serve in place of potatoes. This recipe is plain and can be varied by adding your favorite seasoning.

Deborah Wiss, Minneapolis, Mn.

GERMAN SPAETZLE

1 c. flour
1 egg
1/2 tsp. salt

1/2 c. milk
6 c. water with 1 tsp. salt

Mix flour, egg and salt. Pour in milk gradually, stirring until smooth and thin, like pancake batter. Bring salted water to a boil. Drop small bits of batter from a teaspoon and boil rapidly for 8 - 10 minutes. Drain, rinse with hot water, drain. Makes 2 cups.

Mary Jo Olson, Detroit Lakes, Mn.

ANCHOVY STUFFED EGGS

6 hard-cooked eggs
1/3 c. mayonnaise
1 1/2 Tbsp. anchovy
   paste

Dash of Tabasco sauce
1 Tbsp. chopped green onions
1/8 tsp. pepper
Chopped ripe olives

Cut eggs into halves lengthwise. Press yolks through a sieve. Blend with mayonnaise, anchovy paste, hot sauce, onion and pepper; mix well   Fill egg whites. Top each with chopped ripe olives. Chill.

SAVORY SWISS EGGS

1 c. American cheese,
   grated
2 Tbsp. butter
1/2 c. cream

1/4 tsp. salt
1 tsp. prepared mustard
6 eggs, slightly beaten

Spread cheese over bottom of shallow, well buttered baking dish. Dot with butter. Combine cream, salt and mustard. Pour half of this mixture over cheese. Pour eggs into baking dish. Cover with remaining cream mixture. Bake in a moderate oven (350°) for 25 to 30 minutes. Serve at once. Serves 6.

SHIRRED EGGS IN TOMATOES

Cut a thin slice from the stem end of each tomato, scoop out the pulp and slip 1 egg and sprinkled bread crumbs into each tomato desired. Bake until tomato is tender and the egg is the desired firmness. Serve shirred eggs and tomatoes on a large platter surrounded with lamb chops; small pork sausages or curls of fried bacon may also be added.

SCRAMBLED SUPREMELY

1 medium onion	2 Tbsp. salad oil
2 medium tomatoes or 1/2 can	1/2 tsp. salt Dash of pepper
1/2 green pepper	2 Tbsp. butter
1/2 lb. mushrooms or 1 can	7 eggs (and milk)

Chop onion, green pepper, tomatoes and slice mushrooms. Fry onions till golden, then toss in green pepper, tomatoes and mushrooms. Add salt and pepper and cook over low heat 10 minutes or till tender. In separate skillet, scramble eggs; then either add the above mixture or serve side by side. May be used as a breakfast or brunch dish. Serves 4.

BAKED LUDEFISK

Cut up ludefisk and drain well. Lay in pan. Cover with tin foil tightly. Bake in 425° oven for 20 - 30 minutes.
Joyce Haugen, Fargo, N. D.

BAKED NORTHERN

6 or 8 lb. fresh Northern pike	1/2 c. chopped celery
	1/2 c. chopped onion
1/2 c. butter	1/2 c. chopped fresh tomato
3 c. bread crumbs	1 tsp. curry powder

Place cleaned fish with head left on and salted inside and out on large baking pan. Melt butter in saucepan and add bread crumbs, celery, onion, tomato, curry powder and about 1 cup hot water. Dressing should be just wet enough to stick together, not soggy. Stuff fish and tie with string. Score fish in 3 places and fill, scoring with slices of butter. Bake in 400° oven until the meat of the fish flakes easily (about 45 minutes).

BAKED TORSK

2 (16 oz.) pkg. frozen
   cod fillets, thawed
1/2 tsp. salt
1/4 tsp. pepper
1 large tomato, peeled
   and chopped

2 large green onions,
   chopped, including tops
1/4 c. butter, melted
1 Tbsp. lemon juice
2 Tbsp. parsley, chopped
1 Tbsp. dry sherry

Grease a shallow 1 1/2 quart baking dish. Arrange fish in dish and sprinkle with salt and pepper. Arrange tomato and onions on top of fish. In small mixing bowl, combine sherry, butter and lemon juice. Pour over fish. Lake, uncovered, at 350° for 25 to 30 minutes or until fish is lightly browned and easily flaked. Sprinkle with parsley. Spoon sauce over fish. Serves 3 - 4.
                 Carolyn Brudevold, Fargo, N. D.

CHINESE SEAFOOD

1 (6 1/2 oz.) can crabmeat
1 (4 1/2 oz.) can shrimp
1/2 c. green pepper,
   chopped
1 c. celery, cut fine
1 small can water chestnuts,
   sliced thin

2 Tbsp. parsley, chopped
   fine
1/4 c. onion, minced
1/2 tsp. salt
1 Tbsp. Worcestershire sauce
1 c. mayonnaise
1/4 c. toasted bread crumbs
Paprika

Combine all ingredients except bread crumbs and paprika and place in casserole. Sprinkle bread crumbs over the top, decorate with paprika. Place in preheated 400° oven for 15 minutes only. Serves 6.

CLAM CHOWDER

2 cans minced clams with
   liquid
1 medium onion, diced
3 stalks celery
4 slices bacon, diced

3 carrots
3 potatoes
Salt and pepper
Milk or half & half
Butter

Fry bacon until done; add celery and onion; fry until clear. Add clams and simmer until half the liquid is gone. In the meantime, boil carrots and potatoes separately until done. Then mix and mash lightly, leaving lumps. Mix into clam mixture and add milk or half & half, depending upon how rich you like it. Heat to boiling point. Add lump of butter and serve. Serves 4 to 6.

COTTAGE CHEESE SALMON LOAF

Cheese Layer:

1/2 Tbsp. gelatin
2 Tbsp. cold milk
1/4 c. hot milk

3 c. cottage cheese
1/4 tsp. salt

Salmon Layer:

2 c. red salmon, flaked
1 c. salad dressing
1/2 c. celery, chopped

1 Tbsp. lemon juice
1/2 Tbsp. gelatin
2 Tbsp. cold water

For cheese layer, soak gelatin in cold milk and dissolve in hot milk. Combine with remaining ingredients. Chill until mixture begins to thicken. Pour into mold. Refrigerate until firm. Combine salmon, salad dressing, celery and lemon juice. Soak gelatin in cold water for 5 minutes, then dissolve over hot water. Add to salmon mixture. Cool; pour over cheese layer. To serve, unmold; add watercress, tomato slices. Serves 10.

CRAB FU YUNG

1 c. crabmeat or 1 c.
   rinsed, canned shrimp
1 c. bean sprouts
1/2 c. shredded onion

1/2 c. finely sliced celery
3 Tbsp. oil
6 eggs
1 Tbsp. soy sauce

1 Tbsp. cornstarch   Dash of pepper
1 tsp. salt   Sauce

Put seafood and bean sprouts in large bowl. If using canned sprouts, rinse and drain first. To cut onions in shreds, cut into halves from top to bottom. Put cut side down, on cutting board and finely slice with the grain of the onion, or from top to bottom. Saute onion and celery in oil until limp, about 5 minutes and add to the seafood. Beat eggs, add soy sauce, cornstarch, salt and pepper. Pour over seafood and vegetables and mix thoroughly. Put 1 tablespoonful of mixture on greased griddle or skillet and brown. Turn and brown other side. Keep hot until all are cooked. Pour sauce over top.

Sauce: Cook until thick -

1/2 c. water   1 Tbsp. soy sauce
2 tsp. sherry   2 tsp. cornstarch

Serves 4.

DIFFERENT FRIED FISH

2 lb. dressed fish   1 c. prepared biscuit mix
1 egg   3 Tbsp. catsup
2 Tbsp. water   1/2 c. shortening or salad oil

Dip fish first in beaten egg with water, then in biscuit mix blended with catsup. Fry slowly in heated shortening until golden brown on both sides. Serve with lemon and parsley. Serves 6.

FISH CAKES

2 doz. herring   4 heaping Tbsp. salt
1 medium potato, more if   Pepper
  desired   2 tsp. nutmeg
1 medium onion, more if   4 eggs
  desired   Milk, near 2 qt.

Grind fish, potatoes and onions together. Mix in rest with salt, slowly added (the more salt added, the thicker it gets). Beat, beat, beat with an electric mixer. Fry in shortening. Batter can only be kept in refrigerator a day or two. After fish cakes are fried they can be frozen.

222   Karen Rupert, St. Cloud, Mn.

FIESTA FILLETS

2 lb. fillets, fresh or
  frozen
1/4 c. chopped onion
1/4 c. chopped green
  pepper
3 Tbsp. butter, melted
2 Tbsp. flour

2 c. canned tomatoes
1/2 tsp. sugar
1 tsp. salt
Dash of pepper
1 whole bay leaf
1 whole clove

Thaw frozen fillets. Cut fillets into serving size portions, and arrange in a single layer in a well greased baking pan. Cook onion and green pepper in the melted butter until tender. Blend in flour. Add tomatoes, sugar, salt, pepper, bay leaf and clove. Cook until thick, stirring constantly. Remove bay leaf and clove. Cover fish with the sauce. Bake in a moderate oven (350°) for 25 to 30 minutes or until fish flakes easily when tested with a fork. Makes 6 servings.

FILLETS BAKED WITH SOUR CREAM

1 1/2 lb. fresh or
  frozen fish fillets,
  thawed
3/4 c. commercial sour
  cream
2 Tbsp. grated Parmesan
  cheese

1/4 tsp. dried tarragon leaves
1/2 tsp. salt
1 Tbsp. fine dry bread
  crumbs
1 Tbsp. butter
Lemon wedges
1 tsp. paprika

Heat oven to 350°. Arrange fish fillets on ovenproof platter or broiler pan. Mix sour cream, Parmesan cheese, paprika, tarragon and salt; spread over fish. Sprinkle with bread crumbs and dot with butter. Bake 15 to 20 minutes or until fish flakes easily. Serve with lemon. Serves 4.

FISH PATTIES

1 lb. soft fish
Rosemary leaves
4 eggs, separated
1 tsp. parsley

4 Tbsp. flour
1 clove garlic (or garlic
  powder)
Salt and pepper

Boil fish with rosemary leaves 5 - 7 minutes. Mash well with fork. Separate 4 eggs. Beat egg yolks until thick. Beat egg whites until fluffy. In egg yolks, mix parsley, flour, garlic, salt and pepper. Add fish to yolks and stir. Fold in egg whites, drop by spoonfuls into hot oil for 3 - 4 minutes.

Nancy Kowalke, Nevis, Mn.

JUICY SHRIMP SKILLET

1 can frozen cream of
   shrimp soup
3/4 c. hot water
2/3 c. quick cooking rice
1/2 c. diced pepper (green)
1/2 tsp. curry powder
   (optional)

1/2 tsp. salt
1/2 tsp. pepper
8 oz. frozen clean shrimp
1/2 c. diced ripe olives
1/2 c. slivered, toasted
   almonds

Slowly bring soup and water to a boil and cook till soup has thawed. Add rice, green pepper, shrimp and seasonings. Cover and simmer 10 minutes or till rice and shrimp are done. Just before serving, add ripe olives and sprinkle with almonds. (4 servings)

PERCH PARMIGIANA

6 perch fillets
1/2 c. flour
2 eggs, well beaten
1 tsp. salt
1/4 tsp. pepper
1 c. fine bread crumbs
1/2 c. grated Parmesan cheese

1/2 c. butter
1 (15 oz.) can tomato sauce
1/2 tsp. crushed basil
1/2 tsp. crushed oregano
6 (1 oz.) slices Mozzarella
   cheese

Coat fillets with flour. Combine eggs, salt and pepper. Mix bread crumbs and Parmesan cheese together. Dip fillets into eggs, then coat well with bread crumb mixture. In a frying pan, melt butter and saute fillets slowly until golden brown on each side. Arrange in shallow 2 quart baking dish and cover with tomato sauce. Sprinkle with basil and oregano. Top each fillet with a slice of Mozzarella cheese. Bake 15 to 20 minutes at 350°.

POOR MAN'S LOBSTER

3 qt. water
Scant 3/4 c. sugar

1 tsp. salt
Torsk

Cut torsk into 3 pieces. Boil gently for 15 minutes. Pour off water, replace lid and steam dry. Broil approximately 5 minutes. Serve with lots of butter.

Colette Moger, St. Cloud, Mn.

RIBBON SALMON BAKE

2 (1 lb.) cans salmon, drained, boned and flaked
2 cans condensed cream of potato soup
1 small onion, grated

1/2 c. coarse, soft bread crumbs (1 slice)
1 c. (8 oz.) ctn. dairy sour cream
2 Tbsp. cut chives

Combine salmon, soup, onion and bread crumbs in a medium size bowl; toss lightly to mix. Spoon into a greased baking pan, 9x9x2 inches. Spoon sour cream in rows over salmon mixture; sprinkle with chives. Bake in a moderate oven (375°) for 25 minutes, or until bubbly hot. Mark into serving size blocks; lift out with a pancake turner. Makes 6 to 8 servings.

SALMON BALL

1 (15 oz.) can red salmon
1 (8 oz.) pkg. cream cheese
1 Tbsp. grated onion

1 Tbsp. lemon juice
2 tsp. horseradish
1/4 tsp. salt
1/8 tsp. liquid smoke

Remove bones and skin from salmon and drain. Combine all ingredients and refrigerate 1 hour or overnight. Shape into ball or log. Have ready: One cup chopped nuts (pecans or walnuts) to which 1/4 cup parsley (chopped fine) has been added. Roll salmon ball in nut mixture. Refrigerate.

Diane Schmitz, St. Cloud, Mn.

SALMON LOAF

1 can salmon	2 Tbsp. grated onion
1 1/2 c. bread crumbs	1 egg
1/2 c. milk	1 tsp. salt
2 Tbsp. butter	1/4 tsp. pepper

Drain salmon and break. Add remaining ingredients and mix well. Mold into loaf and bake at 350° till brown.
Kathy Bischof, St. Cloud, Mn.

SALMON LOAF

2 c. about (1 lb. can) drained salmon	1 Tbsp. instant minced onion or 1/4 c. chopped onion
2 c. (1 1/2 slices) soft bread crumbs or cracker crumbs	1/2 c. cream of celery, mushroom or chicken soup or use liquid and water
1/8 tsp. pepper	2 eggs

Heat oven to 375°. In large mixing bowl, combine all ingredients. Shape into a loaf. Bake 40 - 45 minutes. Transfer loaf to a platter. Prepare celery dill sauce by combining:

3/4 c. condensed cream of celery, mushroom or chicken soup	1/4 tsp. dried dill weed, or 2/3 Tbsp. chopped, drained dill pickle
2 Tbsp. salad dressing or mayonnaise	

Combine all ingredients in saucepan.
Marie Miller, St. Paul, Mn.

SCALLOPED OYSTERS

1 can oysters	3/4 c. milk
1 1/2 c. cracker crumbs	Pepper
2 Tbsp. oleo	1 tsp. Worcestershire sauce

Combine all together. Bake 1/2 hour - 30 minutes at 350°.
Karen Rupert, St. Cloud, Mn.

226

SEAFOOD THERMIDOR

1 (4 oz.) can sliced
  mushrooms
1 Tbsp. butter
2 c. cooked seafood (1 c.
  lobster and 1 c. shrimp
  or any desired
  combination)

1 can frozen condensed
  cream of shrimp soup
2 Tbsp. cream
1/4 tsp. mustard
Dash of Tabasco sauce
Grated cheese

Brown mushrooms lightly in butter. Add seafood. Heat soup with cream and seasonings. Combine seafood and soup mixture. Spoon into casserole or individual baking dishes. Sprinkle cheese over top and bake in preheated oven at 375° for 20 - 25 minutes.

SHRIMP FRIED RICE

1/4 c. butter
2 c. cooked or 2 cans
  cleaned shrimp
1 1/4 tsp. salt
1/2 tsp. pepper
2 eggs, beaten

5 c. cooked rice
3 Tbsp. soy sauce
3 green onions, chopped
1/4 c. sliced mushrooms
1/4 c. water chestnuts
1 c. bean sprouts

Melt butter in fry pan, add shrimp and seasonings; saute until lightly browned. Add beaten eggs and stir until well mixed and add rice; saute till golden. Add rest of ingredients and heat thoroughly. Serve at once.
Mary Perron, Owatonna, Mn.

SHRIMPALAYA

1/2 c. minced onion
1/2 c. chopped green
  pepper
3 Tbsp. butter
1 c. wild rice, washed
2 c. boiling water
3 beef bouillon cubes

1 bay leaf
2 c. cubed, cooked ham
2 c. cooked shrimp
1 can frozen cream of shrimp
  soup
1/2 c. milk
Buttered crumbs or croutons

Saute onion and green pepper in butter. Add rice, water, bouillon cubes and bay leaf. Bring to a boil. Cover, reduce heat till rice is tender. Remove bay leaf. Toss rice with ham and shrimp in 2 quart casserole. Combine soup and milk and heat slowly, stirring frequently. Bring just to a boil and pour over rice mixture. Top with buttered crumbs or croutons or with caraway-rye bread crumbs. Bake in a 350° oven for 20 to 30 minutes or till hot and bubbly. Garnish with additional cooked shrimp if desired. Serves 8 to 10.

SHRIMP AND PEA PODS

2 Tbsp. cornstarch
3 Tbsp. sugar
1 c. chicken broth
2/3 c. pineapple juice
1/4 c. vinegar

2 Tbsp. soy sauce
1 Tbsp. butter
1 pkg. frozen pea pods,
  thawed
2 c. shrimp, drained
2 - 2 1/2 c. hot cooked rice

In saucepan, blend the cornstarch and sugar; stir in chicken broth. Add pineapple juice, vinegar, soy sauce and butter. Cook and stir till mixture comes to boiling point. Cover and simmer 5 minutes. Add pea pods and shrimp; heat through. Serve with hot rice. (4 - 5 servings)
Dee Olson, St. Paul, Mn.

STUFFED SHELLS NEOPOLITAN

1 (10 3/4 oz.) can condensed
  cream of celery soup
1/2 tsp. lemon juice
1/4 tsp. oregano leaves,
  crushed
1 (10 oz.) pkg. frozen
  chopped broccoli, cooked
  and well drained

1/2 c. tomatoes, canned,
  drained and chopped
1 (about 7 oz.) can tuna,
  drained and flaked
12 jumbo shells macaroni,
  cooked and drained
1/2 c. grated milk Cheddar
  cheese

Combine soup, lemon juice, oregano, broccoli, tomatoes and tuna. Stuff about 1/4 cup mixture into each shell. In 1 1/2 quart shallow baking dish (10x6x2 inches), arrange stuffed shells. Bake at 400° for 20 minutes or until hot. Sprinkle with cheese, bake 5 minutes more until cheese is melted. Garnish with parsley if desired. Makes 4 servings.
Diane Schmitz, St. Cloud, Mn.

SUSIE'S FISH SUPREME

2 lb. fish fillets
1 1/2 c. sour cream
1/2 c. mayonnaise
2 Tbsp. chopped chives

1/2 lem'n lime, squeezed
Salt and pepper to taste
1 small can mushrooms

Place fillets in an oiled baking dish. Mix all ingredients together. Spread mixture over fish. Bake at 375° for 30 minutes. Serves 4.

Kathy Bishof, St. Cloud, Mn.

TANGY TUNA MOUSSE SQUARES

2 env. unflavored gelatin
1/2 c. cold water
1 c. mayonnaise
2 (6 1/2 oz. or 7 oz.)
cans tuna, flaked
1/2 c. diced celery
1/4 c. chopped, stuffed
green olives

1 Tbsp. finely chopped onion
2 Tbsp. lemon juice
1 1/2 tsp. horseradish
1/4 tsp. salt
1/4 tsp. paprika
1 c. heavy cream,
whipped

Soften gelatin in cold water; dissolve over boiling water. Stir into mayonnaise. Add remaining ingredients except cream. Mix well. Fold in whipped cream. Pour into 10 x 6 x 1 1/2 inch pan. Chill till firm. Cut into squares and serve on greens. Makes 8 to 10 servings.

TROUT BARBECUE

6 trout, 3/4 to 1 lb. each
Salt and pepper
Flour
Olive oil

1/2 c. dry wine (white)
1/3 c. barbecue sauce
Juice of 1 lemon
Oregano

Season fish with salt and pepper. Coat thinly with flour. Fry in oil until half done, about 10 minutes. Place in a baking pan. Mix wine diluted with 2 tablespoons water, barbecue sauce and lemon juice. Baste fish before placing in oven at 375° and baste twice while baking. Fish will be done in about 30 minutes. Sprinkle with oregano and serve hot.

1748-81

TUNA BISCUIT ROLL

1 c. tuna	1 c. Velveeta cheese, cubed
1/4 c. onion, chopped	1/4 tsp. pepper
1 c. drained peas	

Mix and let set while mixing dough:

2 c. flour	1/3 c. oil
3 tsp. baking powder	2/3 c. milk
1 tsp. salt	

Roll out dough into large rectangular shape. Put tuna mixture in middle, slit sides of dough and bring together on top of mixture. Bake at 425° for 20 - 25 minutes.

Sue Hick, Detroit Lakes, Mn.

TUNABURGERS

1 (6 1/2 oz.) can tuna,	1/4 c. onion, chopped fine
drained and flaked	1 egg, hard-boiled, chopped
1/4 c. green pepper,	1/2 pkg. (4 oz.) grated
chopped fine	Cheddar cheese

Mix together. Moisten with salad dressing, put into hamburger buns, wrap in foil and bake in 325° oven for 35 minutes.

Gerri Ruprecht, St. Cloud, Mn.

TUNABURGERS

1 egg	2 tsp. instant minced onion
1 (6 1/2 to 7 oz.) can tuna,	1/8 tsp. salt
drained and flaked	Freshly ground pepper to
1/2 c. uncooked rolled oats	taste
1/3 c. grated carrot	2 Tbsp. oil
1/4 c. mayonnaise	4 thin slices Swiss cheese

In mixing bowl, beat egg well. Add tuna, oats, carrot, mayonnaise, onion, salt and pepper; mix well. Shape mixture into 4 flat patties. Brown in oil in large skillet until golden brown on both sides (takes about 8 minutes). Place slice of cheese on cooked side of each patty to melt while bottom side cooks. Serve on toasted buns or English muffins; add lettuce and tomato, if desired. Makes 4 servings.

230   Kathy Bischof, St. Cloud, Mn.

TUNA CHEESE BAKE

3/4 c. chopped onion
1/2 c. chopped green pepper
1/4 c. butter, melted
1/2 tsp. salt
1 can condensed cream of
  celery soup
1/2 c. milk

2 egg yolks, slightly beaten
2 (7 oz.) cans chunk tuna,
  drained
1 c. shredded American
  cheese
1 Tbsp. lemon juice
3 c. soft bread crumbs
2 egg whites, stiffly beaten

Cook onion and pepper in butter until soft. Stir in salt, soup and milk. Cook, stirring constantly until mixture boils. Stir some of the hot mixture into egg yolks; return to pan, cook 1 minute. Add tuna, cheese, lemon juice and crumbs. Mix lightly, being careful to leave tuna in chunks. Fold in egg whites. Spoon into greased 8 x 8 x 1 1/2 inch baking dish. Bake in moderate oven (350°) for 45 minutes. Makes 6 servings.

TUNA FLYING SAUCERS

1 (7 oz.) can tuna,
  drained and flaked
1/2 c. grated carrot
1 c. diced cheese
1/8 tsp. pepper

2 (8 oz.) pkg. refrigerated
  buttermilk biscuits
1 tsp. onion flakes
1 tsp. Worcestershire sauce

Preheat oven to 400°. In a bowl blend all ingredients except biscuits. Set aside. Separate biscuits and roll out to 20 (5 inch) circles. Top 10 circles with 3 tablespoonfuls each of the tuna mixture, cover with remaining circles. Press edges together with a fork. Place on greased cookie sheet and bake 12 minutes or until puffy and golden.
Kathy Bischof, St. Cloud, Mn.

TUNA SUPREME

2 c. white rice, uncooked
1 c. wild rice, uncooked
2 onions, chopped
4 stalks celery, chopped
1 small can mushrooms,
  drained

2 cans tuna
1 can cream of mushroom
  soup
1 can cream of celery soup
1 can milk (soup can)
Bread crumbs

Cook rices separately in boiling, salted water. Drain and combine them. Saute in butter the onions, celery and mushrooms. Butter a baking dish and add a layer of mixed rice, then a layer of tuna which has been combined with sauteed mixture. Next, pour on a layer of the soups, combined with the milk. Repeat with the layers a second time, ending with soup. Place buttered crumbs on top and bake 30 minutes in a moderately hot oven (375°). Serves about 10.

VINHA DALHOS
(Portuguese Fish)

Dissolve in as small amount of water as possible:

1 tsp. pepper   1 tsp. allspice

Add 5 - 6 whole cloves, 1 bay leaf and a couple of crushed cloves of garlic (according to your taste). Add enough dry wine to cover fish - marinate for several hours (overnight is better). Barbeque over open coals, brushing with melted margarine to which garlic salt has been added. You may also dip fish in crumbs and fry in deep fat. It can also be used for large fish that are to be baked or possibly stuffed. Also good for pork chops.
Marj VanGorp, Alexandria, Mn.

FAR EASTERN FRANKFURTERS

Cut 1 pound of frankfurters diagonally into 1 1/4 inch slices. Cook frankfurters with 1/4 finely chopped onion in 2 tablespoons butter or margarine until lightly browned. Add 1/2 green pepper, cut into julienne-style, 1/4 cup raisins and 1 cup water. Cook slowly 5 minutes. Combine: 1/4 cup brown sugar and 2 tablespoons cornstarch; add an additional 1/4 cup water and mix well. Add to frankfurter mixture and cook, stirring occasionally until clear and thickened. Add 1/4 cup vinegar and 1 (9 ounce) package Italian green beans which have cooked according to package directions and then drained well. Continue to cook briefly until ingredients have heated through and flavors are blended, from 3 to 5 minutes. Serve at once, so green beans do not lose their tempting color, surrounded by 1 (3 ounce) can Chinese noodles. This recipe gives 4 servings.
Karen Karnowski, St. Cloud, Mn.

LOLLIPOP FRANKS

1 c. enriched flour	2 Tbsp. shortening
2 Tbsp. sugar	1 slightly beaten egg
1 1/2 tsp. baking powder	3/4 c. milk
1 tsp. salt	1 lb. (8 to 10) frankfurters
2/3 c. corn meal	

Sift together flour, sugar, baking powder and salt. Stir in corn meal. Cut in shortening; combine egg and milk; add to corn meal mixture, stirring well. Insert wooden skewer into end of each frank. Spread frankfurters evenly with batter. Fry in deep hot fat (375°) for 4 to 5 minutes.

CHINESE FRIED RICE

Fry 1/2 cup finely diced, cooked ham, chicken or pork lightly in 2 tablespoons hot oil. Add:

3 finely sliced fresh mushrooms	1 finely chopped green onion
1 qt. cold cooked rice	2 Tbsp. soy sauce

Fry over low heat 10 minutes. Add 1 well beaten egg, cook and stir 5 minutes more. If color isn't dark enough, add a little more soy sauce. Makes 6 - 8 servings.

Kathy Neels, St. Cloud, Mn.

RICE AND CHEESE DISH
(Serves 6)

1 c. cooked instant rice	3 slightly beaten eggs
1/2 lb. Velveeta cheese	1 1/2 c. scalded milk (add
1/2 c. butter	butter to it to melt)
1 c. bread crumbs	Salt, pepper and a little onion

Put into casserole. Stir a few times while baking for 45 minutes at 350°. Do not cover.

Mary Paul, Minneapolis, Mn.

RICE PILAF

1/4 lb. butter
1 small can mushrooms
2 c. rice, uncooked
3/4 chopped green onion
1 tsp. salt

1 tsp. oregano, crushed
2 cans beef bouillon or 3
  beef bouillon cubes in
  2 c. water

Melt butter in a large skillet, add rice and brown it, stirring occasionally. Add all other ingredients and bring to a boil. Pour into a greased 2 quart covered casserole and bake till done at 350° 45 minutes - 1 hour. Serves 8.
Dee Olson, St. Paul, Mn.

HUNGARIAN GOULASH WITH SAUERKRAUT

Hungarian Goulash:

3 lb. boneless beef chuck
1 lb. onions
1/4 c. salad oil
1 Tbsp. paprika

1 1/2 tsp. salt
1/8 tsp. pepper
1 (10 1/2 oz.) can condensed
  beef broth, undiluted

Sauerkraut:

2 (14 oz.) cans sauerkraut
1 large potato
3 Tbsp. butter or margarine
1/2 c. chopped onion
1 tsp. caraway seed

2 Tbsp. light brown sugar
Boiling water
3 Tbsp. flour
1 c. sour cream

1. Wipe beef with damp paper towels. With sharp knife, cut into 1 1/2 inch cubes. Peel and slice onions (there should be 3 cups). In 6 quart Dutch oven, heat oil over high heat. Add beef cubes in a single layer (do not overcrowd) and saute over medium heat. 2. Continue cooking, turning to brown on all sides. Using tongs, remove beef to a bowl as it browns. Continue browning rest of beef. This will take 20 to 30 minutes in all. Add onion to drippings; cook, stirring until tender and golden - about 10 minutes. 3. Return beef to Dutch oven. Add paprika, salt and pepper, stirring until well combined. Stir in 3/4 cup beef broth. Bring to boiling; reduce heat and simmer, covered, 2 hours or until the beef cubes are fork-tender. While beef cubes cook, prepare sauerkraut. 4. In colander, drain sauerkraut well. Pare potato; grate enough potato to

234

measure 3/4 cup. In hot butter in large skillet, saute chopped onion until golden - about 3 minutes. Add sauerkraut, potato, caraway seed, brown sugar and 2 cups boiling water. 5. Bring to boiling; reduce heat; simmer, uncovered stirring occasionally, 20 minutes or until most of the liquid has evaporated. Meanwhile, in small bowl combine flour and remaining broth; stir until smooth. Gradually add to beef mixture, stirring constantly. 6. Simmer, uncovered, stirring occasionally, 15 minutes longer. Just before serving, slowly stir 1/2 cup hot gravy into sour cream in small bowl. Add slowly to beef mixture; stir to blend. Heat, but do not boil. Serve goulash with sauerkraut. Makes 8 servings.

GERMAN GOULASH

1 1/2 lb. hamburger,
  browned with onions
1/2 bag wide noodles,
  cooked

1 can cream of chicken soup
1 can cream of celery soup
1 (#2) can sauerkraut or
  less

Rinse soup cans with 1 can water. Layer together and season. Bake at 350° until heated through.
Lydia Skaret, Austin, Mn.

CARNIVAL HAM A LA KING

1 (10 oz.) pkg. frozen
  mixed vegetables
1/2 c. chopped onion
1 (4 oz.) can mushroom
  pieces and stems,
  drained
2 Tbsp. butter or margarine

1 (11 oz.) can Cheddar cheese
  soup
1 (10 1/4 oz.) can cream of
  celery soup
1/2 c. milk
1 1/2 c. diced, cooked
  ham

Cook frozen vegetables according to package directions; drain. Meanwhile, saute onion and mushrooms in butter 3 - 5 minutes in large saucepan. Stir in soups and milk until smooth; season to taste. Add cooked vegetables and ham. Heat through, stirring occasionally. Add more milk if desired. Serve over rice, buttered noodles or baking powder biscuits. Makes 6 servings.
Kathy Bischof, St. Cloud, Mn.

HAM (CURED PORK) HASH

3 Tbsp. fat or oil
4 medium potatoes, finely
   chopped
2 medium carrots, finely
   chopped or shredded

1/2 small onion, finely
   chopped
About 1 1/2 c. finely chopped
   cooked, cured pork (left
   from baked picnic shoulder)
Salt as desired

Heat fat in a large fry pan. Add potatoes and cook over low to medium heat until browned on bottom. Turn potatoes. Cover with carrots and onion, then with pork. Cook about 8 minutes longer until potatoes are browned on bottom and are tender. Sprinkle with salt if needed. Makes about 4 cups - 4 servings.

Kathy Bischof, St. Cloud, Mn.

HAM LOAF

1/2 lb. smoked ground
   ham
1 1/2 lb. ground pork
1 lb. ground beef

1 c. rolled oats
1 tsp. salt
1/2 tsp. pepper
1 c. milk

Bake in 375° oven for 1 1/2 to 2 hours.

Marge Johnson, Minneapolis, Mn.

SAUERKRAUT HAM BALLS

2 Tbsp. butter
1/2 c. chopped onion
1 c. ground leftover
   ham
4 c. chopped well drained
   sauerkraut

1/3 c. flour
1/4 tsp. salt
1/3 c. stock (chicken or
   beef bouillon)
Soda cracker crumbs as
   much as needed

For Egg Wash:

1/4 c. flour
3 Tbsp. milk

3 beaten eggs

Saute onions in butter for 5 minutes. Add ham and sauerkraut. Cook 5 minutes, stirring. Sprinkle on flour while stirring. Add bouillon stock and cook until thick. Add salt and stir up. Chill thoroughly, overnight. When chilled, shape into balls (size of a walnut).

For Egg Wash: Beat eggs, add milk and flour, stir until smooth. Dip balls in egg wash and roll in cracker crumbs. Deep fry until golden brown. (About 4 dozen.) These can be frozen and warmed up in oven at 350° to 400° for 15 - 20 minutes.

Karen Rupert, St. Cloud, Mn.

SHERRIED HAM IN CREAM

12 thin slices baked or
  boiled ham (about
  1 1/2 lb. meat)

1 c. dry sherry
1 1/2 c. heavy cream
1 1/2 c. shredded Edam or
  Gouda cheese

Marinate ham in sherry in refrigerator for about 5 hours or overnight. Remove ham from sherry. Roll. Arrange rolls in a single layer in greased shallow baking dish, placing loose ends down. Pour cream over ham. Sprinkle cheese evenly over top. Bake in moderate oven (350°) for 30 minutes. Makes 6 servings.

SWEDISH HAM BALLS

1 lb. ground ham
1 1/2 lb. pork sausage
2 c. bread crumbs

2 beaten eggs
1 c. milk

Mix ingredients together and form into small balls about the size of a walnut (about 36 balls). Place them in a flat baking pan and cover them with a mixture made from the following:

1/2 c. water
1/2 c. vinegar

1/4 c. brown sugar
1 tsp. dry mustard

Bake in a moderate oven (350°) for 1 1/2 hours. Turn meat once and serve hot.

BRAN-BURGER BISCUIT HOT DISH

1 1/2 lb. ground beef
1 c. chopped celery
1/3 c. chopped onion
1/2 c. chopped green
  pepper
1 clove garlic, minced

1 (6 oz.) can tomato paste
3/4 c. water
1 tsp. salt
1 tsp. paprika
1 (16 oz.) can pork & beans
1 (15 oz.) can garbanzo beans

Saute beef, celery, onions, green pepper and garlic until vegetables are limp. Drain off fat, add water, tomato paste, salt, paprika and beans. Put into 12x8 inch or round baking dish. Top with baking powder biscuits and bake at 425° for 25 to 30 minutes. Serves 6 to 8. Check oven to prevent biscuits from burning.

Midge Daulton, St. Paul, Mn.

BROCCOLI HOT DISH

2 c. cooked rice
1 pkg. frozen chopped
  broccoli
1/2 c. chopped celery
1/4 c. chopped onion

1 can water chestnuts, sliced
1 can cream of celery soup
1/2 c. milk
1 (8 oz.) jar Cheez Whiz
1/4 c. butter or margarine

Saute chopped celery and onions in the butter. Then in baking dish combine all ingredients, using only 1/3 of Cheez Whiz. Pour remaining Cheez Whiz across top. Bake uncovered for approximately 40 minutes in 350° oven.

Jacquie Amacher, Willmar, Mn.

BROCCOLI HOT DISH

1 can cream style corn
1 pkg. chicken flavor
  Stove Top dressing
1 beaten egg
1/2 stick margarine, melted

1/2 c. water
1 pkg. chopped broccoli,
  precooked and drained
A little shredded Cheddar
  cheese

Mix in baking dish and bake at 350° for approximately 45 minutes.

Marlys Stoll, Austin, Mn.

BROCCOLI HOT DISH

8 oz. Cheez Whiz
1 can cream of mushroom
　soup
1/2 c. chopped onion
1/2 c. chopped celery,
　parboiled
1 1/2 c. Minute Rice, not
　cooked

1 small can mushrooms and
　juice
1 can water chestnuts
1 box frozen broccoli,
　cooked
1 stick margarine, melted
　(optional)

Put into 2 quart casserole. Bake 40 minutes at 350°.
Sue Hick, Detroit Lakes, Mn.

BROCCOLI HOT DISH

2 sticks butter
2 pkg. frozen broccoli
1/2 onion
2 1/4 c. cooked Minute Rice

1 can mushroom soup
1 c. shredded Cheddar cheese
2 c. milk
1 c. water

Saute butter, broccoli and onion. Add rice, mushroom soup, cheese, milk and water. Bake in 9x13 inch pan at 350° for 25 minutes.
Avis Paulsen, Mn.

BROCCOLI-CHEESE HOT DISH

1 (8 oz.) pkg. frozen
　broccoli
1 (8 oz.) pkg. frozen carrots

1 (8 oz.) pkg. frozen
　Brussels sprouts

Cook vegetables according to directions on package (carrots should be cooked in a saucepan separately). Drain well. Place broccoli and Brussels sprouts in flat glass pan (9x12 inches) or a casserole and place carrots on top. Make the following cheese sauce and pour over the vegetables. Bake, uncovered, for 1/2 hour in preheated oven at 350°.

Cheese Sauce:

1/4 c. melted butter
3 Tbsp. flour
1 c. milk

2 c. diced processed cheese
　(Velveeta)

Melt butter in a small saucepan; add flour and stir until smooth. Add milk and cheese. Stir occasionally as the sauce thickens.

Note: Cheese bubbles as it cooks and browns. So be sure the baking pan is large enough. Serves 6 - 8.

Jean Taylor, Lake Agassie Council,
Grand Forks, N. D.

CHICKEN-ASPARAGUS HOT DISH

1 pkg. Nabisco Triscuits,
    crushed
2 (15 oz.) cans asparagus
4 chicken breasts, cooked
    and cut
2 cans button mushrooms
2 cans cream of chicken soup
1/2 c. mayonnaise
1 small jar chopped pimento

Crush Triscuits and put 1/2 of them into the bottom of a 9x13 inch baking dish. Add the chicken, then the asparagus. Combine the soup, mushrooms, pimento and mayonnaise and pour over the asparagus layer. Top with remaining 1/2 of crumbs and bake in 350° oven for 45 minutes.

Bettie Mallon, Minneapolis, Mn.

CHINESE SHRIMP HOT DISH

3 c. sliced celery, on slant
1/2 c. water
2 Tbsp. butter or margarine
3/4 c. chopped green pepper
1 (5 oz.) can water
    chestnuts, sliced
Salt and pepper to taste
2 (3 oz.) cans chow mein
    noodles
1 c. chopped onions
1 c. sliced mushrooms
1 can cashew nuts (small)
2 (4 1/2 oz.) cans shrimp
1 can cream of mushroom or
    celery soup
1 (4 oz.) can pimentos, cut
    up

Combine celery, onion and water in saucepan. Simmer, covered, until onion is soft. Drain. Lightly brown mushrooms and combine with celery and onion. Alternate ingredients in casserole. Bake 30 minutes at 350°. Serves 8.

Johanna Singewald, St. Paul, Mn.

CHOW MEIN HOT DISH

1 1/2 lb. lean ground
  beef
1/2 c. celery, diced
1/2 c. green pepper,
  diced
1/2 onion, chopped
3/4 c. uncooked rice
  (Uncle Ben's converted)

1 Tbsp. soy sauce
1 can mushroom soup
1 can chicken rice soup
2 soup cans water
Salt and pepper to taste
1 (8 oz.) pkg. chow mein
  noodles

Brown hamburger, celery, green pepper and onion. Add other ingredients except chow mein noodles and bake in 325° oven for 45 minutes. Add noodles and finish baking 45 minutes more. May be frozen. Can use chicken gumbo soup in place of chicken rice soup.

Gerri Ruprecht, St. Cloud, Mn.

CHOW MEIN RICE HOT DISH

Let 1 cup of uncooked rice stand in 4 cups of boiling water. Add 2 teaspoons of chicken bouillon. Mix 1 pound chow mein meat and 1 pound ground beef together. Brown. Add 2 large onions, chopped, and 1/2 stalk chopped celery. Fry together. Add:

6 Tbsp. soy sauce
1 can cream of chicken soup

1 can cream of mushroom
  soup

Add this to rice. Bake all for 1 1/2 hours at 350°. For last few minutes, cover with chow mein noodles and cashew nuts. One can of mushrooms and water chestnuts may be added.

Mary Paul, Minneapolis, Mn.

CORNED BEEF HOT DISH

1 (12 oz.) can corned
  beef, broken into small
  pieces
1 (8 oz.) pkg. egg noodles,
  cooked and drained
  well

1 can cream of chicken soup
1 c. milk
1/2 c. chopped onions
1/4 lb. Velveeta cheese, cut
  into small pieces
1/2 tsp. Accent

Mix together. Put into casserole, cover with layer of crushed potato chips. Bake at 350° for 40 minutes.

1748-81   Gerri Ruprecht, St. Cloud, Mn.   241

CABBAGE HOT DISH

1 lb. hamburger, browned
1 onion, chopped
1 tsp. salt
1/4 tsp. pepper

3 c. shredded cabbage (1 small head)
1 can tomato soup or stewed tomatoes

Place cabbage in casserole, top with hamburger, onion and seasonings. Pour soup over and bake 1 hour at 350°.

Karen Rupert, St. Cloud, Mn.

CHICKEN HOT DISH

3 c. diced chicken
2 hard-boiled eggs, chopped
1 can mushrooms
3/4 c. diced celery

1/2 c. slivered almonds
1 Tbsp. chopped onion
1 can cream of chicken soup
3/4 c. Hellmann's mayonnaise
Chow mein noodles

Stir soup into mayonnaise. Toss with other 6 ingredients. Sprinkle chow mein noodles on top. Bake 30 minutes in 350° oven.

Elsie Ekblad

CHICKEN HOT DISH

1 (3 to 3 1/2 lb.) chicken or 6 to 8 breasts
1 c. broth (saved from chicken)
1 can cream of mushroom soup
2 cans mushrooms
1 lb. sharp Cheddar cheese or use 1/2 Monterey Jack

1/2 c. instant onion (or real jobbies)
1 can cream of chicken soup
2 cans green chili salsa
1 pt. sour cream
1 doz. corn or flour tortillas

Boil chicken until tender. Remove skin and bone chicken, cut into pieces. Combine onions, soups, broth, salsa, mushrooms and cheese (save some cheese for top). Cut tortillas into strips. Layer soup, chicken and flour tortillas twice. Sprinkle cheese on top. Refrigerate 24 hours or freeze until ready to use. Bake 1 hour at 350°. Serves 10 generously.

Ron Ness, St. Cloud, Mn.

RAW MACARONI CHICKEN HOT DISH

2 c. diced, cooked chicken
1 jar pimento
1 c. diced celery
1 (7 1/2 oz.) box elbow
    macaroni (raw)

1/3 lb. Velveeta cheese
1 can cream of mushroom soup
1 can cream of chicken soup
2 c. chicken broth
1 can mushrooms

Mix all ingredients together in casserole, refrigerate overnight. Bake about 1 hour, covered, then sprinkle with crushed potato chips and bake 1/2 hour, uncovered, in 350° oven.

Doris Lehman, Detroit Lakes, Mn.

CHOW MEIN HOT DISH

1 1/2 lb. hamburger
1 c. celery
1/2 onion
2 Tbsp. soy sauce

1 can cream of mushroom soup
1 can chicken rice soup
1 can Veg-All, juice and all
1 1/4 c. chow mein noodles

Brown hamburger, celery and onion. Add soy sauce, soups, Veg-All and 1 cup chow mein noodles. Sprinkle the 1/4 cup chow mein noodles on top. Bake uncovered 1 1/2 hours at 350°.

Avis Paulsen, Verndale, Mn.

CHOW MEIN HAMBURGER HOT DISH

1 lb. ground beef
2 Tbsp. oil or shortening
2 medium onions, cut up
1 c. celery, cut up
1 can mushrooms
1 can cream of chicken soup

1 1/2 c. warm water
1/2 c. uncooked rice
1/4 c. soy sauce
1/4 tsp. pepper
1 can crisp Chinese noodles

Brown meat in hot oil until crumbly, add chopped onion, chopped celery and soup. Rinse out can with warm water, add to mixture. Stir in uncooked rice, soy sauce and pepper. Put into casserole, bake at 350° for 30 minutes. Cover with Chinese noodles and bake 15 minutes more.

Kathy Bischof, St. Cloud, Mn.

CHOW MEIN HOT DISH - MOCK CHOP SUEY

1 lb. hamburger, browned
1 c. celery, chopped in
  with meat
1 onion, chopped in with
  meat

2 c. Minute Rice
2 cans bean sprouts, drained
1 can mushrooms
2 cans cream of mushroom
  soup
1/4 c. soy sauce

Stir up all together and bake 1 hour at 350°.
Karen Rupert, St. Cloud, Mn.

CHOW MEIN HOT DISH

Boil and drain 3 cups chopped celery. Add to browned hamburger and diced onions. Add:

1 can tomato soup
1 can cream of mushroom
  soup

3 Tbsp. soy sauce
2 c. chow mein noodles

Sprinkle more noodles on top. Bake at 350° for 1 hour.
Ginnie Andersen, St. Paul, Mn.

CORNED BEEF HOT DISH

1 (8 oz.) pkg. cooked
  noodles
1 (12 oz.) can corned
  beef
1/4 lb. diced cheese

1 (10 1/2 oz.) can cream of
  chicken soup
1 c. milk
1/2 c. finely chopped onion
3/4 c. buttered crumbs for
  top

Bake in greased 2 quart casserole 45 minutes to 1 hour at 350°. Serves at least 6 - 8.
Mrs. Don Bredenberg, Bemidji, Mn.

CORNED BEEF HOT DISH

1/2 pkg. noodles
1 (12 oz.) can corned beef
1 can cream of chicken
  soup

1 small pkg. American cheese
Onion to taste (cubed or
  shredded)
Salt and pepper
1/2 can condensed milk

Mix together and bake at 350° for 1 hour.
244   Lenora Buck, Fargo, N. D.

COUNTRY PIE

1/2 c. tomato sauce	1/4 c. green pepper
1/2 c. bread crumbs	1 1/2 tsp. salt
1 lb. ground beef	1/2 tsp. pepper
1/4 c. chopped onion	1/8 tsp. oregano

Combine above ingredients in a bowl and mix with a fork. Pat into a pie plate.

Filling:

1 1/3 c. Minute Rice	1 c. water
1 1/2 c. tomato sauce	1 c. Cheddar cheese, save
1/2 tsp. salt	1/2 c. for top

Spoon into shell, cover with foil and bake 25 minutes at 350°, then uncover and top with remaining cheese and bake for another 15 minutes.

Mike & Vonnie Bakke, Willmar, Mn.

CRAB AND SHRIMP HOT DISH

1/2 - 1 medium green pepper, chopped	1/8 tsp. pepper
1 medium onion, chopped	1 tsp. sweet basil
1 c. celery, chopped	1 c. salad dressing (do not substitute)
1 pkg. frozen crabmeat	1 c. cooked rice
1 can shrimp (or fresh shrimp, cooked and cut up)	1 can cream of mushroom soup
	1 (3 oz.) can fried noodles
1/2 tsp. salt	1/4 c. slivered almonds

Mix all together. Crush a few potato chips on top - bake about 45 - 50 minutes at 350°.

Alice Ann Hanson, Grand Forks, N. D.

CREOLE JUMBO HOT DISH

1 lb. ground pork, veal or beef	1 can chicken soup
2 large onions, diced	1 can mushroom soup
2 or 2 1/2 c. celery, diced	2 c. water
	3 Tbsp. soy sauce
1 c. rice, uncooked	1/2 can water chestnuts
	1 can bean sprouts
	Salt and pepper

Brown meat, onions and celery well. Then add rest of ingredients and bake 1 1/2 hours. Add 1 can bean sprouts and bake 1/2 hour.

Diane Schmitz, St. Cloud, Mn.

DELISH HOT DISH

1 lb. ground beef (raw)	1 pkg. Lipton onion soup mix
3 c. tater tots	1 can mushroom soup

Put 1/2 hamburger in bottom of casserole, sprinkle with 1/3 soup mix - add tater tots - remaining hamburger and rest of soup mix. Pour mushroom soup and 1/3 cup water over top. Bake, covered at 350° for 1 hour.

Darlene Lee

FAR EAST - CELERY HOT DISH

4 c. celery, cut into 1 inch diagonal slices	1/4 c. diced pimiento (optional)
1 (5 oz.) can water chestnuts	1/2 c. soft bread crumbs
1 can cream of chicken soup	1/4 c. toasted slivered almonds
	1 Tbsp. melted butter

Cook celery until crisp-tender, about 6 to 8 minutes. Drain. Mix celery, soup, pimientos and thinly sliced chestnuts in a 1 quart casserole. Toss bread crumbs with almonds and melted butter. Sprinkle over casserole. Bake at 350° for 35 minutes.

Mildred Sjastrom, St. Peter, Mn.

FAVORITE MINNESOTA HOT DISH

Layer peeled, cut potatoes, carrots, celery and chopped onions to fill casserole. Crumble in 1 1/2 pounds hamburger (raw). Pour 1 can cream of mushroom soup, 1 can tomato soup, mixed, over top. Cover. Bake at 350° for 45 minutes to 1 hour.

Kathaleen Bischof, St. Cloud, Mn.

FRIED NOODLE HOT DISH

1 lb. hamburger
1 onion, chopped
1/2 c. celery, chopped
1 pkg. chow mein noodles

1 can tomato soup
1 can water
1/4 green pepper, chopped
1 pt. stewed tomatoes, if
    desired

Brown hamburger. Add onion, celery and green pepper. Simmer just until vegetables are slightly tender. Add noodles, soup and water. Put into baking dish and top with bread crumbs. Bake 1 hour at 350°.

Karen Rupert, St. Cloud, Mn.

"4H" HOT DISH
(Serves 6)

1 lb. hamburger
2 c. potatoes, cut up
1 c. celery, diced

2 c. carrots
1/2 c. onions

Put in layers, season lightly.

1 can tomato soup
1 can cream of mushroom soup

1/4 c. water, rinse cans

Pour over above, cover. Bake at 350° for 2 hours, depending on how large carrots are sliced.

Betty Carlson

GROUND BEEF HOT DISH

1 lb. lean ground beef
1 c. raw rice
1 pkg. Lipton dry soup
    mix

1 can cream of mushroom
    soup
1 can water

Crumble meat into casserole (raw). I brown mine a little. Sprinkle rice and then soup blended with soup mix over top. Cover, bake 1 hour at 350°.

Blanch Weidencamp, St. Paul, Mn.

HAMBURGER HOT DISH

1 lb. ground beef
1 medium onion, chopped

1 stalk celery, chopped

Brown above ingredients. Mix in saucepan and heat:

1 can cream of mushroom
  soup
1 can cream of chicken soup

1 can hot water
3 Tbsp. soy sauce
3/4 c. rice

Pour over meat and bake 45 minutes at 350°.
Sue Hick, Detroit Lakes, Mn.

HEARTY BEEF 'N CHEESE CRESCENT PIE

1 1/4 lb. ground beef
1/3 c. chopped onion or
  4 tsp. instant minced
  onion
1/4 c. chopped green pepper
1 (8 oz.) can (1 c.) tomato
  sauce with mushrooms
1 (8 oz.) can (1 c.) cut green
  beans, drained
Paprika

1/4 tsp. cumin seed, if
  desired
1/4 tsp. garlic salt
1/4 to 1/2 tsp. salt
1 (8 oz.) can Pillsbury
  refrigerated quick crescent
  dinner rolls
1 egg, slightly beaten
2 c. (8 oz.) shredded
  Monterey Jack or Cheddar
  cheese

Preheat oven to 375°. In large fry pan, brown ground beef, onion and green pepper; drain fat. Stir in tomato sauce, beans, cumin seed, garlic salt and salt; simmer while preparing crust. Separate crescent dough into 8 triangles. Place triangles in ungreased 9 inch pie pan; press over bottom and up sides to form crust. Combine egg and 1 cup cheese; spread over crust. Spoon hot meat mixture into crust. Sprinkle with remaining cheese and paprika. Bake 20 to 25 minutes. For easier serving, let stand 5 minutes before cutting into wedges. (Refrigerate leftovers.) (5 to 6 servings)

HOT DISH

1 pkg. Creamettes, cooked	1 tsp. salt
1 can Spam, ground	1 can mushroom soup
1 tsp. onion, scraped	1/4 c. milk
1 green pepper, chopped	1/4 lb. strong cheese
1/8 tsp. pepper	

Cook Creamettes, drain. Cool in cold water. To Spam, add onion, green pepper, salt and pepper. Heat soup, milk, and cheese. Add all together. Place in buttered baking dish. Sprinkle with buttered bread crumbs, then chow mein noodles before baking 3/4 hour at 350°.

Lillian Herrick, St. Paul, Mn.

HOT DISH

Brown 1 pound ground beef. Add 1 cup chopped onion and 1 cup chopped celery and brown. Add 2 cups cooked rice and 1/4 cup soy sauce, 1 can mushroom soup, 1 can chicken rice soup. Do not add seasoning, as soy sauce is sufficient.

Helen M. Gludt, Bottineau, N. D.

HOT DISH

Brown 3 pounds hamburger. Drain excess fat and add:

2 medium onions, chopped	1 1/2 c. chopped green
2 c. chopped celery	pepper
	2 cloves garlic, diced

Add:

3 cans tomato soup and	3/4 Tbsp. soy sauce
1 can water	Salt and pepper
1 can bean sprouts	Chili powder and oregano
2 cans mushrooms	(optional)
2 1/2 Tbsp. dark molasses	12 oz. pkg. medium wide
	noodles, cooked

Bake 1 1/2 hours at 350°.

Madaline Danich, St. Paul, Mn.

ITALIAN HOT DISH
(2 large dishes)

1/2 box mostaccioli (do
not cook)
2 lb. hamburger
1/2 lb. Italian sausage
1 small onion
1 large can tomatoes
1 small can tomato sauce

1/2 tsp. oregano
1/2 garlic, minced or 1/2 tsp.
garlic powder
2 cans tomato soup
Salt and pepper
1/2 tsp. sweet basil
2 c. grated Mozzarella cheese

Brown hamburger and sausage, onion and garlic. Add tomatoes, 1 can tomato sauce. Mix other ingredients. Bake at 375° for 1/2 hour, then add Mozzarella cheese. Bake another 1/2 hour. If it becomes too dry, add a little water.

Evelyn Sullivan, St. Paul, Mn.

MEXICAN HOT DISH

2 lb. hamburger
1 medium onion, chopped
2 pkg. taco seasoning
mix
2 c. water

1 small can tomato paste
12 - 16 oz. shredded
Cheddar cheese
1 (8 oz.) bag taco chips,
crushed

Brown hamburger and onions, drain. Add the seasoning mix, water and paste. Simmer uncovered for 10 minutes. Place meat mixture in 9x13 inch pan. Cover with cheese and top with taco chips. Bake at 350° for 25 - 30 minutes.

Avis Paulsen, Verndale, Mn.

MEXICAN ZUCCHINI HOT DISH

3 c. sliced, unpeeled
zucchini

1 c. chopped onions

Saute in 2 tablespoons oil until tender. Add:

1 box frozen whole
kernel corn
1 c. seasoned croutons

1 c. shredded hot pepper
cheese
1/4 c. milk
1/4 tsp. cumin

Mix together and cook on low for 10 minutes. Place in baking dish. Put sliced tomatoes on top. Bake at 325° for 30 minutes.

Vicky Bruggeman, Minneapolis, Mn.

MYSTERY HOT DISH

2 lb. ground beef
1 box seasoned croutons
1 c. cut up celery
1 onion, diced
1/4 c. butter

1/2 c. water
1 can cream of celery
  soup
1 can cream of chicken
  soup

Line bottom of 9x13 inch pan with raw hamburger. Place croutons over meat. Heat other ingredients together and pour over top. Bake at 325° for 1 1/4 hours. Let set 15 minutes. Cut into squares and serve.

Avis Paulsen, Verndale, Mn.

PIONEER HOT DISH

2 qt. grated potatoes
3 medium onions, diced
1/4 c. flour

3 eggs
1 1/2 tsp. baking powder
1 lb. diced bacon

Bake in 9x13 inch pan at 325° for 1 3/4 hours. Leftovers can be sliced and fried.

Darlene Lee

PIZZA HOT DISH

6 oz. long spaghetti
1/3 c. melted butter or oleo
15 oz. tomato sauce
8 oz. Swiss cheese, grated
1 lb. Mozzarella cheese,
  grated

8 oz. pepperoni (just
  use about 4 oz.)
1 lb. ground beef
1 medium onion
1 small can mushrooms

Brown onion and hamburger and 1/2 of butter. The other 1/2 of butter, pour into a 9x13 inch pan or in large bowl. Cook spaghetti, put over butter. Layer rest (making 2 layers of the rest of the ingredients). Bake at 400° for 25 minutes or till bubbles.

Barb Torkelson, Windom, Mn.

PIZZA HOT DISH

1 1/2 lb. hamburger
1 small onion, chopped

Brown and drain.

Dash of pepper
1 tsp. oregano
1/2 tsp. garlic salt

2 (10 oz.) cans pizza sauce
1 (8 oz.) can tomato sauce

Add to above and simmer 15 minutes, then add (1/2 of this mixture):

1 c. milk
1 c. Mozzarella cheese

1 c. sliced pepperoni

Cook and drain 6 to 8 ounces wide noodles, add all this, stir and put into greased casserole. Add last 1/2 of cheese and pepperoni to top.

Claren Kane, Sauk Centre, Mn.

RICE HOT DISH

Brown:
2 lb. hamburger
Onion, chopped

Add:
2 c. rice (raw)
9 c. boiling water
1 can celery soup

1 can mushroom soup
1 to 2 pkg. frozen mixed
   vegetables

Bake 2 hours at 350°.

Kathy Neels, St. Cloud, Mn.

RICE HOT DISH

1 lb. beef, cubed
1 large onion
Stalk of celery

Brown in pan, add:

1/2 c. uncooked rice
1 can chicken soup
1 can mushroom soup

3 c. boiling water
1 Tbsp. soy sauce

252

Bake 2 hours in 325° oven. Add 1 can of peas (optional) and 1 can of mushrooms after 1 hour of cooking.
Bonnie Steffens, St. Cloud, Mn.

RICE HOT DISH

1 3/4 c. Minute Rice	1 lb. hamburger, browned
1 can whole kernel corn	and seasoned
1 can cream of mushroom	1 onion, chopped in with
soup	hamburger
1 can tomato soup	

Combine all together. Bake 1/2 hour or till done at 375°.
Karen Rupert, St. Cloud, Mn.

ROUND STEAK HOT DISH
(6 servings)

1 1/2 lb. round steak,	1 can chicken and rice soup
cubed	1 can cream of mushroom
1 large onion, diced	soup
1/2 c. celery, diced	1 soup can of water or a
1/2 c. instant rice	little less

Brown steak, onion and celery in small amount of fat. Pour into 2 quart casserole. Add rice, soups and water. Blend ingredients. Bake at 350° for 1 1/2 hours.
Arlene Gnoinsky, Fargo, N. D.

SAUERKRAUT HOT DISH

Melt 1/4 cup butter (or margarine) with 1 small chopped onion in it.

1/3 c. sugar	1 qt. sauerkraut
2 Tbsp. caraway seed	

Place in baking dish, bake 1/2 hour at 350°. Good with fowl.
Darlene Lee

SEAFOOD HOT DISH

2 cans shrimp or crabmeat   1 small jar pimento
   or 1 of each   1 tsp. salt
6 c. soft bread cubes   2/3 c. melted butter
6 eggs, well beaten   1 1/2 c. grated cheese
2 Tbsp. chopped onion   2 c. milk

Scald milk, pour over bread cubes; add all ingredients (except eggs). Fold in well beaten eggs.

Sauce:

1 can cream of mushroom   1 c. sour cream
   or cream of celery soup   Pimento for color if desired
1/4 c. milk

Heat ingredients. Pour over individual servings or serve in separate bowl.

Signe Linde, St. Paul, Mn.

SOUP HOT DISH

1 can cream of celery   1 can beef soup
   soup   1 (6 or 8 oz.) pkg. chow
1 can chicken gumbo   mein noodles
   soup   1 lb. hamburger
1 can mushroom soup   1 large onion

Brown hamburger and onion. Add to rest of ingredients. Add enough water so it isn't real thick. Bake at 350° about 1 hour.

Deb Nordby, Fargo, N. D.

STEAK HOT DISH

Cut steak into small chunks and brown with onions. Add:

1 can mixed vegetables   1 can cream of chicken soup
Diced potatoes

Mix all together. Bake 1 hour at 300°.

Edith Weber, Fargo, N. D.

TACO HOT DISH

1 lb. hamburger, fry, season, add onions

2 1/2 c. Bisquick + 3/4 c. water

Spread Bisquick in 13x9 inch pan. Add on:

1 c. chopped tomatoes

1 c. chopped green pepper

Mix together:
1 c. sour cream
2/3 c. salad dressing
1 c. shredded Cheddar cheese

1 c. shredded Mozzarella cheese
1 Tbsp. chopped onion

Put hamburger on top of tomato and green pepper. Spread cream mixture on hamburger. Crush some taco chips to sprinkle on top. Sprinkle on Parmesan cheese. Bake 25 minutes at 350°.

Rachel Bakken, Rochester, Mn.

TASTY HOT DISH

1 lb. hamburger, brown and drain (salt and pepper to taste)
1 medium onion

1 can red kidney beans
1 can tomato soup
2 soup cans diced potatoes

Lay strips of bacon across the top to cover. Bake at 350° for at least an hour or till potatoes are done.

Irene Palokangos, Detroit Lakes, Mn.

TATER TOT HOT DISH

1 pkg. frozen tater tots
1 pkg. peas and carrots
1 c. mushroom soup
1 small can evaporated milk

1/2 c. grated cheese
1 tsp. minced onion
Salt and pepper

Mix all ingredients together and bake at 350° for 45 minutes. Cooked chicken, turkey or tuna may be added. Onion rings may be placed on top before baking.

Harriett Maselie, Minneapolis, Mn.

THREE BEAN HOT DISH

1 1/2 lb. hamburger	1 c. catsup
Onion to taste	1/2 c. brown sugar
1 can pork & beans	2 Tbsp. Worcestershire sauce
1 can lima beans	1/4 c. vinegar
1 can kidney beans	2 Tbsp. lemon juice

Brown hamburger with onion, add the pork and beans. Rinse the lima and kidney beans and add. Combine the catsup, sugar, Worcestershire sauce, vinegar and lemon juice. Add to the mixture. Place in a casserole and bake 45 minutes to an hour.

Fern Groskreutz, Litchfield, Mn.

TRAILER AND CAMPERS PORK CHOW MEIN

Brown strips of pork. Stir in 1 1/2 cans beef or chicken bouillon and 1/2 cup soy sauce. Cook pork until done. Mix 2 tablespoons cornstarch with a little water and add, stir until thickened. Place meat and sauce in a jar or container. Combine:

2 large stalks celery, sliced	1 can bean sprouts, drained
6 green onions, cut up	1/2 head of Romaine lettuce or Chinese cabbage, cut up
1 can water chestnuts, drained and sliced	Parsley
	Sliced raw or sauteed mushrooms

Toss the greens and mushrooms together and place in plastic bag. To serve, heat the meat and sauce, add greens and toss and heat for a couple of minutes. The whole is served over fried noodles, which you can buy in cans.

Marion Baihly

TUNA OR CHICKEN HOT DISH

Have ready 12 slices of bread - both sides buttered (remove crusts). Place 6 slices on bottom of cookie sheet. Add layer of tuna or chicken (other meat may be used). Add chopped celery if desired. Place 6 slices on top. Beat 4 eggs, add 3 1/2 cups milk, salt and pepper. Pour over bread, let stand for a few hours or overnight. Bake 1 hour at 350°. Top with mushroom soup diluted 1/3 - heat.

Marie Doty, Austin, Mn.

TUNA HOT DISH

1 can cream of mushroom　　1 1/2 cans milk
　soup

Heat with cubed cheese till cheese melts.　In 9x13 inch baking dish (greased):

1/2 pkg. cooked noodles　　1 c. drained tuna
1 c. whole kernel corn

Garnish with crushed potato chips and shredded cheese. Bake 1 hour at 300°.

Kathy Neels, St. Cloud, Mn.

WILD RICE HOT DISH

1 1/2 lb. hamburger
1 chopped onion
1 can cream of mushroom
　soup
1 can chicken rice soup
1 soup can water
1 Tbsp. soy sauce

1 small can mushrooms with
　juice
1/2 c. white rice
1/4 c. wild rice, soaked in
　water 2 hours
1 c. chopped celery
Salt and pepper to taste

Brown hamburger and onion; add the remaining ingredients.　Put into buttered baking dish.　Bake 1 1/2 hours at 350°.

Donna Meyer, Detroit Lakes, Mn.

WILD RICE, PORK AND VEAL HOT DISH

2 lb. cubed pork, lean
1 lb. cubed veal
1 c. wild rice, soaked
　overnight
2 cans cream of mushroom
　soup

1 can chicken rice soup
1 small can mushrooms,
　drained
1 c. slivered almonds
2 c. chopped celery
1/2 green pepper, chopped

Brown meat and season to taste.　Add rest of ingredients.　Put into large buttered casserole and bake, covered, 2 1/2 hours at 325°.

Ginnie Andersen, St. Paul, Mn.

ZUCCHINI HOT DISH

In a large casserole, layer sliced zucchini, sliced onions, sliced green pepper and sliced tomato. Salt and pepper to taste. Cover with sliced cheese (Velveeta, American, etc.). Dot liberally with butter and top with seasoned croutons. Bake at 350° for 45 minutes, covered, and 15 minutes, uncovered. The amount can be adjusted for the number of people to be served by adding extra layers or making slices thicker.

Pat Langfitt, Fargo, N. D.

LIVER, ONIONS AND MUSHROOMS IN WINE SAUCE

2 lb. margarine
1 large onion, chopped
1/2 lb. fresh mushrooms, sliced
1/4 tsp. dried oregano
Salt and pepper
1 c. dry white wine
1 lb. calves liver
3 Tbsp. margarine

Saute onions and mushrooms in 2 tablespoons margaarine, add wine and seasonings and cook until the wine is reduced to half. In separate skillet, saute liver with remaining margarine - 2 minutes on one side and 1 minute on the other. Add onion mixture and simmer 1 minute.

Carolyn Brudevold, Fargo, N. D.

LIVER AND GRAVY

Fry 4 - 6 slices of bacon till crisp. Remove from pan, set aside. Dredge 1 pound of thinly sliced liver in flour. Brown liver in hot bacon grease on both sides; remove from pan. Add rest of flour in pan, stir in 2 cups of boiling water with 2 beef bouillon cubes dissolved. Add 1 teaspoon Worcestershire sauce and 1 tablespoon vinegar. Stir till gravy consistency. Place bacon and liver with gravy and serve.

Sue Hick, Detroit Lakes, Mn.

BAKED LASAGNE

1 lb. Italian sausage, bulk pork sausage or ground beef
1 clove garlic, minced
1 Tbsp. parsley flakes
1 Tbsp. basil
1 1/2 tsp salt
1 (1 lb.) can (2 c.) tomatoes
2 (6 oz.) cans (1 1/2 c.) tomato paste

10 oz. lasagne or wide noodles
3 c. cream style cottage cheese
2 beaten eggs
2 tsp. salt
1/2 tsp. pepper
2 Tbsp. parsley flakes
1/2 c. grated Parmesan cheese
1 lb. Mozzarella cheese, sliced thin

Brown meat slowly; spoon off excess fat. Add next 6 ingredients. Simmer, uncovered, 30 minutes to blend flavors, stirring occasionally. Cook noodles in boiling water till tender; drain, rinse in cold water. Meanwhile, combine cottage cheese with eggs, seasonings and Parmesan cheese. Place half the noodles in 13x9x2 inch baking dish; spread half the cottage cheese mixture over; add half the Mozzarella cheese and half the meat sauce. Repeat layers. Bake at 375° for 30 minutes. Garnish with triangles of Mozzarella cheese. Let stand 10 to 15 minutes before cutting into squares. Filling will set slightly. Makes 12 servings.

BEST LASAGNA IN THE WORLD
(Or Empty Pan Lasagna)

1 1/2 lb. ground beef
1 Tbsp. dehydrated onion
2 tsp. salt
1 Tbsp. sugar
1 tsp. chili powder
1 tsp. garlic salt

1 can tomato sauce
1 small can tomato paste
1 small can mushrooms
3 1/2 c. water
3/4 lb. Mozzarella cheese, grated
3/4 lb. lasagna noodles

Brown ground beef with onion and seasonings. Add tomato sauce, paste and water. Bring to boil and simmer 10 minutes. Mixture must be thin. In lasagna pan or 13x9 inch pan, ladle sauce, then uncooked noodles, then cheese. Continue making layers of sauce, uncooked noodles and cheese until pan is filled. Bake at 325° for 1 hour and 20 minutes.

Judith Volkers, Rogers, Mn.

LASAGNE

1 lb. ground beef
2 Tbsp. salad oil
2 cloves garlic, crushed
1 (8 oz.) can tomato sauce
1 (#2) can tomatoes
1 1/2 tsp. salt
9x13 inch pan

1/4 tsp. pepper
1/4 tsp. salt
1/2 tsp. oregano
8 oz. broad noodles
1/2 lb. Mozzarella cheese
3/4 lb. cottage cheese
1/2 c. grated Parmesan
  cheese

Brown ground beef in oil. Add garlic, tomatoes and seasonings. Simmer for 15 to 20 minutes. Cook noodles in boiling water for 15 minutes in 1 1/2 teaspoons salt. Alternate layers of noodles, meat sauce and cheeses, ending with Parmesan cheese. Bake at 375° for 15 to 20 minutes.

Lois Thelen, Detroit Lakes, Mn.

LASAGNE
(Easy)

1/2 pkg. lasagne noodles
  (1 lb. pkg.)
1 jar Ragu spaghetti sauce
1 can tomato soup
12 oz. cottage cheese

2 eggs
2 tsp. parsley flakes
1 lb. ground beef
1/4 lb. Mozzarella cheese

Cook noodles. While cooking, brown ground beef and Ragu sauce and tomato soup. Let simmer. Mix in bowl cottage cheese, eggs, parsley and Mozzarella cheese. Put into 9x12 inch pan in layers. Bottom layer: Beef-Ragu mix; next noodles; third cottage cheese mix; fourth noodles; and on top balance of beef-Ragu mixture. Bake at 350° for 35 minutes. Remove and let stand 10 minutes.

Mrs. Ronald Schwartz, Owatonna, Mn.

LASAGNA

1 lb. ground beef
1/2 lb. pork sausage
1 clove garlic, minced
3/4 c. chopped onion
1 (15 oz.) can tomato sauce
1 lb. can tomatoes
2 Tbsp. chopped parsley

2 tsp. sugar
1 tsp. salt
1/4 tsp. each marjoram,
  thyme, oregano, basil
1 1/2 c. cubed Mozzarella
  cheese
1 1/2 lb. Ricotta cheese

| 1 c. grated Parmesan | 8 oz. pkg. lasagna noodles, |
| cheese | cooked |

Brown ground beef, pork sausage, garlic and onion in a large saucepan. Drain off all fat. Add tomato sauce, tomatoes, parsley, sugar, salt and spices. Simmer uncovered, for 1 hour or until sauce is the consistency of spaghetti sauce. Heat oven to 350°. Pour 1/2 cup sauce into baking pan and alternate with layers of noodles, grated cheese, Mozzarella cheese, spoonfuls of Ricotta cheese, tomato sauce until all ingredients are used. Top layer should be sauce and grated cheese. Bake at 350° for 1 hour.
Jane Bohline, Minneapolis, Mn.

LASAGNA

8 oz. Creamette lasagna	1/4 tsp. garlic powder
1 lb. ground beef	1/4 tsp. pepper
1 medium onion, chopped	2 (15 oz.) cans tomato sauce
1 tsp. Italian seasoning	1 can Campbell's Cheddar
1 tsp. salt	cheese
	1 pkg. pizza cheese

Brown ground beef and onion. Drain. Stir in seasonings and tomato sauce. Simmer slowly for 20 minutes. Prepare noodles according to package directions. Arrange 1 layer of noodles in parallel strips in bottom of greased 9x13 inch pan. Top with 1/3 meat mixture and 1/2 can cheese. Repeat layers, ending with meat. Top with slices of pizza cheese. Bake at 350° for 30 minutes.
Kathy Neels, St. Cloud, Mn.

LASAGNE

Sauce:

1 lb. hamburger	1 tsp. sugar
1 medium onion, chopped	1 Tbsp. butter
1 large can tomato puree	1 tsp. oregano
1 can tomato paste	1 clove garlic, crushed
1 c. water	1/2 tsp. anise seed
1 tsp. sweet basil	Salt and pepper to taste

Have ready:
| 1 pkg. lasagne | 8 oz. shredded Mozzarella |
| 1 small ctn. cottage cheese | cheese |

1748-81

Brown hamburger and onion, drain off fat. Combine
with other ingredients for sauce. Simmer approximately 2
hours. Make lasagne according to package directions.
In 9x13 inch pan, spread sauce in bottom of pan. Layer
noodles, top with cottage cheese, sauce, Mozzarella cheese.
Alternate layers. Bake at 325° for 1 hour. Wait 20 minutes
before serving.

Sue Dierkhising, St. Cloud, Mn.

LASAGNA

Brown:

2 lb. hamburger	4 garlic cloves (or powder equal to that)

Skim off excess fat. Add:

2 (15 oz.) cans tomato sauce	2 tsp. sugar
2 (6 oz.) cans tomato paste	1/2 tsp. pepper
3 tsp. salt	1/4 tsp. oregano
	1/4 c. water

Cover and simmer 30 minutes. Cook 1 pound lasagna
noodles. Drain and rinse well. Fill 9x13 inch pan with
alternate layers of noodles, meat and Mozzarella cheese.
Bake at 375° for 20 minutes.

Joyce Haugen, Fargo, N. D.

ZUCCHINI LASAGNA

2 Tbsp. vegetable oil	1/2 tsp. crushed sweet basil
2 cloves garlic, minced	1/4 tsp. crushed thyme
1/2 c. chopped onion	1 1/2 tsp. salt
1/2 lb. lean ground beef	Black pepper to taste
1 (16 oz.) can tomatoes	1/2 lb. Mozzarella cheese
1 (6 oz.) can tomato paste	1/2 lb. Ricotta or cottage cheese
1 (4 oz.) can sliced mushrooms, drained	1/2 c. grated Parmesan cheese
3/4 c. dry red wine	Zucchini
1 2/3 tsp. crushed oregano	

Saute garlic and onion in oil until onion is golden and
tender, but not brown. Add meat; cook until brown,
stirring frequently. Add tomatoes, tomato paste, mushrooms,

wine and spices. Simmer sauce 1 1/2 hours. Grease a large shallow casserole. Cut zucchini lengthwise into strips 1/4 inch thick. Place half of zucchini strips into casserole. Top with half of Mozzarella cheese and Ricotta cheese (crumble into chunks). Top cheese with half of meat sauce. Repeat layers. Sprinkle with Parmesan cheese. Bake at 350° for 45 to 60 minutes. Serves 4 to 6.

FETTUCCINE ALFREDO
(Italian)

This famous pasta dish - a modern legend - is known only by its Italian name. Alfredo DiLelio opened his restaurant on Via della Scrofa in Rome in 1914 and made the dish so famous that his restaurant became a gathering place for notables and talented people from all over the world.

1 lb. fettuccini (can
  buy frozen cooked less
  than shade of al dente)

1/4 lb. sweet butter, cut
  into 1/4 inch slices
3/4 c. grated Parmesan cheese
3 Tbsp. heavy cream

Have ready a large heated serving and mixing bowl and heated individual bowls - very, very hot. Cook fettuccini just under al dente (the hot bowls will finish the cooking), tasting for texture frequently. Drain and place in the large hot bowl. Immediately add the butter and cheese and toss and toss until the noodles are thoroughly coated. Add cream and toss again. This is a good chance to use a chafing dish on medium heat if you have one big enough. These amounts should be enough for 6 servings, but don't count on it for more than 4 people.

How to cook pasta: It must never be overcooked. The Italian description of proper firmness is al dente, which means "to the tooth". It must never be mushy and gooey. Don't trust exactly to the directions on the package, nor to beginners luck, you will have to test and taste.

For 1 pound of pasta, enough for 4 portions, cook in 6 quarts of boiling water. Bring water to full rolling boil and add 2 tablespoons of salt. Add 1 tablespoon of olive oil. Put pasta in as soon as the water comes to a boil. If you allow the water to boil too long, the salt gives the pasta an unpleasant odor. Add pasta gently and gradually so the water does not stop boiling. Stir with a wooden fork - never a spoon!

Carolyn Smith, Fargo, N. D.

MANICOTTI

Sauce:

2 (6 oz.) cans tomato
   paste
3 c. water
1 chopped onion

2 minced garlic cloves
1 tsp. oregano
Salt and pepper

Simmer 1 hour. While simmering, make -

Meat Filling:

2 lb. ground beef
1/2 c. celery, chopped
   fine

1 clove garlic, minced
1/2 c. chopped onion
1/4 c. green pepper,
   chopped fine

Brown and then add:
1/2 lb. Mozzarella cheese,
   grated

1 egg, beaten with 1/2 c.
   milk

Cool.   Cook manicotti shells in 4 quarts of boiling, salted water with 1 tablespoon of oil for 10 minutes. Drain and rinse in cold water. Handle carefully. Stuff with meat filling. Lay filled shells in a row in a glass cake dish. Slice into thin slices Mozzarella cheese and completely cover shells. Pour tomato sauce over and bake 25 to 35 minutes in 350° oven. Before serving, sprinkle with parsley leaves and Parmesan cheese. Makes 1 package of 14 shells.

Bev Barglof, Detroit Lakes, Mn.

RIGATONI WITH ITALIAN SAUSAGE

1 lb. Italian sausage,
   cut into 1 inch pieces
1 medium onion, peeled
   and chopped
1 green pepper, seeded
   and chopped
1 clove garlic, peeled
   and chopped finely
2 (6 oz.) cans tomato paste
1 (16 oz.) can tomatoes with
   juice
1 c. water

Pinch of crushed red pepper
1 tsp. dried oregano leaves
1 tsp. dried sweet basil
   leaves
1 tsp. salt
1/8 tsp. black pepper
1 bay leaf
2 Tbsp. salt
1 lb. Rigatoni
4 to 6 qt. boiling water
Grated Parmesan cheese

Cook sausage pieces in large saucepan over moderate heat, until brown, stirring occasionally. Remove sausage and set aside. Add onions, green pepper and garlic to saucepan. Cook until tender, stirring occasionally. Add tomato paste, tomatoes, water, red pepper, oregano, basil, 1 teaspoon salt, pepper, bay leaf and sausage. Simmer 2 hours, stirring occasionally. About 20 minutes before serving, add the 2 tablespoons salt to boiling water and add the rigatoni. Cook until just tender; drain. Serve sauce over rigatoni and garnish with Parmesan cheese. Serves 4 to 6.

Ralph Kulhanek, St. Paul, Mn.

SPAGHETTI

1/2 lb. spaghetti	1 large can tomatoes
1 medium can mushrooms	1 1/4 tsp. salt
1 onion, chopped	1/2 can grated Parmesan
1 green pepper, chopped	cheese
1 clove garlic, minced	1/2 can stuffed olives, sliced
5 Tbsp. oil	2 tsp. Worcestershire sauce
1 1/2 lb. ground beef	1 can condensed tomato soup

Saute onion, pepper and garlic in oil. Add beef, cook 20 minutes. Add tomatoes, olives, salt and cheese. Add tomatoes, olives, salt and cheese. Add Worcestershire sauce, mushrooms and tomato soup. Mix well with cooked spaghetti. Put into covered dish and prepare at least 2 days in refrigerator. Cover with Parmesan cheese and bake 1 hour at 350°. (This is delicious and very good to make ahead for weekend company.)

Laurie Sauvageau, Bismarck, N. D.

EASY SPAGHETTI AND MEAT BALLS

1 lb. ground beef	1 tsp. salt
1 small onion, chopped	1/4 tsp. pepper

Mix. Make balls. Brown. Drain off grease.

1 (15 oz.) can tomato sauce	1/2 - 1 tsp. basil
1 tsp. Worcestershire sauce	1/2 tsp. oregano
	1/2 c. water

Mix. Add to above and simmer 20 minutes. Serve with

spaghetti. Sprinkle with Parmesan cheese.

Variations: 1. Skip water for thicker sauce and use meat balls as appetizers.

2. Crumble beef and brown with onions. Add sauce mixture and use as meat sauce.

3. Use meat sauce for mixture in lasagna - layer noodles, sauce, Mozzarella cheese and cottage cheese. Bake at 375° for 30 - 35 minutes. Can sprinkle with Parmesan cheese.

Rita Klassen, St. Cloud, Mn.

IRISH - ITALIAN SPAGHETTI

1 onion, chopped	Dash of red pepper
2 Tbsp. salad or olive oil	1 (10 1/2 or 11 oz.) can
1 lb. ground beef	condensed cream of
1 tsp. salt	mushroom soup
1/2 tsp. chili powder	1 (10 1/2 oz.) can condensed
1/2 tsp. Tabasco sauce	tomato soup
1/4 tsp. black pepper	1 (8 oz.) pkg. long spaghetti
	1/2 c. grated Parmesan cheese

Cook onion in hot oil till golden, add meat and seasonings; brown lightly. Cover; simmer 10 minutes. Add soups, cover and simmer 45 minutes. Cook spaghetti in boiling, salted water until tender. Drain and rinse with hot water. Arrange on hot platter. Pour sauce over spaghetti. Sprinkle with cheese. Makes 4 to 6 servings.

Eileen Rekowski, St. Cloud, Mn.

ITALIAN SPAGHETTI AND MEAT BALLS

Sauce:

2 (#2 1/2) cans (7 c.) tomatoes	1/2 tsp. basil leaves
1/4 c. instant minced onions	1/2 tsp. garlic powder
1/4 c. salad oil	1 tsp. sugar
1/2 tsp. ground black pepper	2 Tbsp. salt
	1 bay leaf
	1 (6 oz.) can tomato paste

Combine all except tomato paste and simmer, covered, 2 hours. Add paste, simmer 1 hour, uncovered. Add meat balls 20 minutes before 1 hour is up. Serve over spaghetti. Sprinkle with Parmesan cheese.

266

Meat Balls:

1 lb. lean ground beef	1/4 tsp. ground black pepper
1 c. soft bread crumbs	1/8 tsp. garlic powder
1 Tbsp. dried parsley flakes	1 tsp. salt
	1 egg, beaten
1 Tbsp. grated Parmesan cheese	2 Tbsp. olive oil

Combine first 8 ingredients. Shape into 1 inch balls. Brown on all sides in hot olive oil. Add to spaghetti sauce. Yield: 12 (1 inch) balls. Freeze leftover sauce.

Don Billadeau, St. Cloud, Mn.

ITALIAN SPAGHETTI AND MEAT BALLS

Chop fine:

1 clove garlic	2 average onions

Add:

1 large or 2 small cans tomato paste	1 1/2 lb. lean beef spareribs, bones and all
1/2 tsp. oregano	2 oz. pepperoni, cut up fine
Salt and pepper	2 Tbsp. sugar
2 large cans whole tomatoes, put in blender	

Cook and simmer 2 1/2 hours. After cooking time, re-move meat from spareribs and cut up and put back into sauce. Add prepared meat balls.

Meat Balls:

1 lb. lean ground beef	1 tsp. parsley
4 slices old bread, wet, squeeze out and mash	1 tsp. salt
	1/4 tsp. pepper
1 clove garlic, chopped fine	1 egg
	1 tsp. oregano
	1/2 c. Parmesan cheese

Make into small to average sized meat balls. Brown and turn until fully cooked. This makes a large amount, but can be kept or frozen for additional use. Add to sauce 1 hour before done.

Recipe from Minneapolis

1748-81   267

MARY'S ITALIAN SPAGHETTI

1/2 c. onion slices
2 Tbsp. olive or salad oil
1 lb. ground beef
2 cloves garlic, minced
2 (1 lb.) cans (4 c.)
  tomatoes
2 (8 oz.) cans (2 c.)
  seasoned tomato sauce
1 c. water

1 (3 oz.) can broiled, sliced
  mushrooms
1/4 c. chopped parsley
1 1/2 tsp. oregano or sage
1 tsp. salt
1/2 tsp. monosodium
  glutamate
1/4 tsp. thyme
1 bay leaf
3 slices crisp bacon,
  crumbled

Have ready:
Long spaghetti, cooked

Grated Parmesan or Romano
  cheese

Cook onion in hot oil till golden. Add meat and garlic; brown lightly. Add remaining ingredients; simmer, uncovered, 2 to 2 1/2 hours or till thick. Remove bay leaf. Serve sauce on hot cooked spaghetti. Pass bowl of grated Parmesan or Romano cheese for folks to help themselves. Makes 6 servings.
Mary Kozel, Grand Forks, N. D.

SHERRY'S GERMAN SPAGHETTI

2 Tbsp. Crisco
1 (3 lb.) chuck roast
1 large can whole tomatoes,
  chopped
1 small can whole tomatoes,
  chopped

1 large can tomato paste
1/2 c. water
2 cloves garlic, crushed
1/8 tsp. red pepper
Salt and pepper to
  taste

Brown roast on both sides in Crisco in roaster. Add rest of ingredients. Mix well. Bake at 325° F. until roast is thoroughly cooked, stirring occasionally. Remove roast to platter, cut into serving pieces. Mix sauce with cooked spaghetti. Serve both for meal. Best spaghetti ever!
Sherry Schneider, Grand Forks, N. D.

SPAGHETTI BRAVISSIMO

1 env. Lipton onion soup
   mix
1 (8 oz.) pkg. spaghetti
1 1/2 qt. boiling water
1 lb. ground beef

1 (8 oz.) can tomato sauce
1 (7 oz.) can tomato paste
1 Tbsp. parsley flakes
1 tsp. oregano
1/2 tsp. sweet basil

In large saucepan, combine Lipton onion soup mix and spaghetti with water; cook 20 minutes or until spaghetti is tender; do not drain. In large skillet, brown meat; stir in tomato sauce, paste, parsley, oregano and basil. Add to spaghetti and heat through. Serves 4.
      Robin Knutson, Willmar, Mn.

FOUCAULT'S SPAGHETTI SAUCE SUPREME

1 1/2 lb. very lean
   ground pork
1 lb. very lean hamburger
1 large onion, chopped
1 green pepper, chopped
   (less if desired)
2 (6 oz.) cans tomato paste
2 (6 oz.) cans water
1 large can tomatoes
1 large can tomato puree
1 can mushrooms
Dab of vermouth

1 Tbsp. salt
1 Tbsp. brown sugar
1 tsp. red peppers
1 Tbsp. basil
1/2 tsp. rosemary leaves
1 tsp. Italian seasonings
2 Tbsp. parsley flakes
2 heaping Tbsp. oregano
1 tsp. minced garlic or 2
   whole cloves
2 bay leaves
30 anise seed

Saute in olive oil, one at a time: Onions, meat, tomatoes, tomato paste, tomato puree, mushrooms. Simmer 6 - 8 hours (slow cooker works great), stirring about every 45 minutes. If desired, boil some Italian sausages and cut into chunks and add the last hour.
      Karen Rupert, St. Cloud, Mn.

ITALIAN MEAT SAUCE

1 lb. ground beef
1 c. chopped onion

2 cloves garlic, minced

Brown above lightly in skillet and drain. Add 2 cups water and remaining ingredients:

2 cans tomatoes (large)

1 Tbsp. brown sugar

1 1/2 tsp. ground oregano   1 bay leaf
1 tsp. salt

Simmer, uncovered, 3 hours or until thickened. Remove bay leaf, serve over hot cooked spaghetti with Parmesan cheese and hot pepper seeds.

S. V. Heinen, Wadena, Mn.

ITALIAN SPAGHETTI SAUCE

Brown 1/4 cup butter and 1/2 cup Mazola oil. Grind or mince 4 large onions and 4 cloves garlic. Brown in butter. Add 1 1/4 pounds pork sausage to onions and brown. Cut up 2 large cans mushrooms (drained - use juice later). Add mushrooms to above. Strain 2 large cans tomatoes (just use juice).

1 small can tomato paste
1 small can tomato sauce
1/2 tsp. black pepper
1 Tbsp. white pepper
1/2 tsp. allspice

2 small handfuls salt
4 bay leaves
1 medium size can tomato
 juice

Add all of the above to sauce. Cook 2 hours then add mushroom juice. Cook 1 1/2 hours longer. Put into sterilized jars and seal. Store in refrigerator and use as wanted. (I usually use more meat and mix ground beef with pork sausage.) Makes about 3 quarts.

Katie Bromen, Sauk Centre, Mn.

MARY'S ITALIAN (POLISH) SPAGHETTI SAUCE

1 lb. ground beef
3 onions, cut fine
3 cloves garlic, whole
Green pepper, chopped
5 sticks celery, chopped
2 cans tomato soup
1 can water
2 small cans tomato paste

1 Tbsp. salt
1 tsp. pepper
1/2 tsp. red pepper
1 tsp. sugar
3 bay leaves
2 Tbsp. Worcestershire
 sauce
1 Tbsp. soy sauce

Put hamburger, onion, green pepper in pan and start frying slowly. Then add celery and rest of ingredients. Hamburger will be fairly brown before you put soup and paste in. Let simmer 3 hours and stir often. Serve over long cooked spaghetti.

270   Mary Harlander, St. Cloud, Mn.

SPAGHETTI SAUCE

1 1/2 lb. veal and ground
  beef
1 (46 oz.) can tomato juice
3 cans (3 lb.) tomatoes
2 c. celery, chopped
1/2 c. green pepper,
  chopped
1 whole fresh garlic

1/2 c. onion, chopped
1 Tbsp. salt
1 tsp. curry powder
1 Tbsp. chili powder
1/4 tsp. cayenne pepper
1/2 tsp. oregano
Paprika to color and any
  other spice you like
Mushrooms, as many as you
  like

Brown meat and onion, add celery, pepper, garlic and the rest of the ingredients and let simmer a couple of hours.
Lydia Skaret, Austin, Mn.

SPAGHETTI SAUCE
(5 people)

1 can tomato paste
  (medium)
1 can tomato sauce
  (large)
4 bay leaves
Oregano (easy)
1 can mushrooms,
  drained

Parsley (small amount)
Salt, pepper
2 Tbsp. sugar
1 onion (medium)
1 clove garlic
1/2 small green pepper

Chop onion, green pepper, garlic - baste slightly in frying pan with small amount of meat ball mixture. Add to sauce. Add small amount of water to thin. Simmer all day.

Meat Balls for Spaghetti:

1 1/2 lb. ground lean
  beef
Salt, pepper
Oregano
Pimento and paprika

2 eggs
Dash of A.1. Sauce
1 clove garlic
1 small onion
1/2 green pepper

Chop real fine garlic, onion, green pepper. Brown in frying pan and add to meat - blend all ingredients well. Add enough cracker meal to make mixture stick. Roll in flour and brown. Add to sauce. Stir sauce occasionally so meat balls do not stick to bottom.
Lu Boyer, Grand Forks, N. D.

SPAGHETTI SAUCE

Brown:

2 lb. ground beef
1 large onion, chopped

1/2 c. celery
1 small can mushrooms

Add:

2 large cans tomato sauce
  (27 oz.)
1 (16 oz.) can whole
  tomatoes
1 (12 oz.) can tomato paste
2 gloves garlic

1/2 bay leaf
2 tsp. chili powder
1 tsp. salt
1/2 tsp. pepper
1 Tbsp. Italian seasoning

Simmer approximately 2 hours till thick.
Sue Hick, Detroit Lakes, Mn.

COLD BEEF LOAF

2 lb. ground beef
1 c. water
1/8 tsp. garlic salt or
  powder
1/2 tsp. mustard seed

2 1/2 Tbsp. Morton's Tender-
  Quick salt
1/4 tsp. pepper
1/4 tsp. onion salt

Mix these ingredients all together real well. Form into
1 or 2 rolls and wrap in foil. Place in refrigerator for 24
hours. Remove foil. (Don't let the icky color fool you.)
Bake meat loaf for 1 hour at 350°. Serve cold. It slices
like salami or other cold cuts. It also can be frozen.
Marion Round, Faribault, Mn.

DUTCH MEAT LOAF

1 1/2 lb. ground beef
1 c. bread crumbs or
  oatmeal
1 onion

1/2 (8 oz.) can tomato sauce
1 egg, beaten
1 1/2 tsp. salt
1/4 tsp. pepper

Mix all ingredients and form into loaf. Place in shallow
pan. Bake in 350° oven. Combine the following:

1/2 can tomato soup

1 c. water

2 Tbsp. mustard 2 Tbsp. brown sugar
2 Tbsp. vinegar

Pour over meat loaf. Bake 1 1/4 hours. Serve over noodles.

Diane Schmitz, St. Cloud, Mn.

HERB AND TOMATO MEAT LOAF

1 1/2 lb. ground beef
2 (8 oz.) cans tomato sauce
1 c. finely chopped celery
1 c. packaged crushed
   herb stuffing mix
1/4 c. grated Parmesan cheese
1 1/2 tsp. oregano
1 tsp. garlic powder
1/2 tsp. basil
2 Tbsp. butter or margarine

In large bowl, blend ground beef with 1 can tomato sauce, the celery, stuffing mix, grated cheese, oregano, garlic powder and basil. Divide mixture in half; mold each portion into loaf shape and place loaves side by side in lightly greased shallow baking pan. Pour remaining can of tomato sauce over both; dot loaves with butter or margarine. Bake at 350° F. for 45 - 60 minutes, basting from time to time with pan drippings. Serves 4 - 6.

Jane Bohline, Minneapolis, Mn.

LAZY DAY MEAT LOAF

4 lb. ground turkey
2 c. soft bread pieces
2 eggs
2 c. beer
1 env. spaghetti sauce mix
3 Tbsp. chopped onion

Combine in order given- pack into Bundt pan. Bake at 350° for 1 1/4 hours. Let stand 10 minutes before un-molding.

Darlene Lee

MEAT LOAF

1 1/2 lb. hamburger
1/4 c. lemon juice
1/2 c. water
1 egg, slightly beaten
4 slices toast, finely
   diced
1/4 c. chopped onion
2 tsp. seasoned salt
1/2 c. catsup
1/3 c. brown sugar
1 tsp. mustard
1/4 tsp. cloves
1/4 tsp. allspice

1748-81

Mix hamburger, lemon juice, water, egg, toast, onion and salt; press in the bottom of a 9x5 inch loaf pan. Blend the rest of the ingredients and pour over the top. Bake at 350° for 30 minutes.

Kathy Bischof, St. Cloud, Mn.

MEAT LOAF

2 lb. hamburger	1/2 Tbsp. poultry seasoning
1/3 c. onions	1 Tbsp. MGS
1/3 c. carrots	1 Tbsp. salt
1/3 c. celery	1/2 Tbsp. pepper
2 Tbsp. soy sauce	1 c. herbal seasoned croutons
1 Tbsp. Worcestershire sauce	3 eggs

Mix together hamburger, soy sauce, Worcestershire sauce, salt, pepper, MSG, poultry seasoning. Set aside. Beat with fork 2 eggs. Add crushed croutons and mix together until mushy. In separate bowl, add chopped vegetables and cook in microwave on high for 2 minutes. Add vegetables and crouton mixture to hamburger.

Gail Olson, Detroit Lakes, Mn.

NORDIC MEAT LOAF

2 lb. ground beef	1 tsp. salt
1 c. chopped, cooked beets	1/8 tsp. pepper
2 eggs, slightly beaten	2 1/2 c. shredded Nokkelost cheese
3/4 c. rye bread crumbs	1 (16 oz.) can stewed tomatoes
1/4 c. chopped onion	
2 Tbsp. chopped capers	2 tsp. cornstarch
2 Tbsp. chopped parsley	1 Tbsp. chopped capers

In a large bowl combine ground beef, chopped cooked beets, eggs, rye bread crumbs, chopped onions, capers, salt and pepper. Blend well. Spread out to 14x10 inch rectangle on waxed paper. Spread 2 cups cheese over all. Roll up in jelly roll fashion from narrow end, using waxed paper to help roll. Transfer to shallow baking pan. Pinch edges under to seal. Bake at 350° for 1 hour, 10 minutes. Meanwhile, in saucepan, combine stewed tomatoes and cornstarch. Cook, stirring until thickened and smooth. Add parsley and capers, reduce heat and simmer 5 minutes, stirring occasionally. Remove from heat. Remove meat loaf from oven, top with remaining 1/2 cup shredded Nokkelost cheese. Bake 5 minutes or until cheese melts. Serves 8 to 10.

Don Billadeau, St. Cloud, Mn.

BETTY CORTRIGHT'S REUBEN MEAT LOAF

1 1/2 lb. ground beef
1 1/2 c. rye bread crumbs
1 1/2 tsp. salt
1/2 c. onion, chopped

1 egg
1 (14 oz.) can or jar of
   sauerkraut, rinsed and
   drained
1 c. Swiss cheese, shredded

Combine meat, crumbs, salt, onion and egg in a large bowl. Place one-half of mixture in a loaf pan and cover with kraut and cheese. Place rest of meat mixture over all. Bake at 350° for 45 minutes. The recipe makes 8 servings.

I was a "runner-up" in a Meat Loaf contest (Minneapolis Star) with this recipe.

Betty Cortright, Minneapolis, Mn.

CASSEROLE MEAT BALLS

1 lb. hamburger
1 egg
3 slices bread, soaked
   in milk

1 onion, diced
Salt and pepper

Beat with electric mixer until fluffy. Form balls and stuff in desired amount of cheese. Brown in skillet. Place in casserole dish. Top with cream of mushroom soup and shredded cheese. Bake at 350° for 40 minutes.

Marilyn Pommier, Willmar, Mn.

HEARTY SWEET AND SOUR MEAT BALLS

1 lb. ground beef
1 egg
1/2 tsp. salt
1/4 tsp. pepper
1 small onion, chopped
1 c. Heartland Natural
   cereal (plain variety)

2 Tbsp. butter
1/4 c. soy sauce
1/2 c. peach preserves
1/2 c. water
Hot rice

Mix together well ground beef, egg, salt, pepper, onion and cereal. With wet hands, shape into small meat balls. Melt butter in 10 inch skillet. Add soy sauce and meat balls. Brown all over. Pour off fat, saving 1 tablespoon of soy sauce drippings. Combine drippings, peach preserves and water. Pour over meat balls. Simmer, covered, for 20 - 25 minutes. Serve hot over rice. Makes 4 servings.

Margaret Zeglin, St. Paul, Mn.

HUNGARIAN VEAL BALLS

1 lb. ground veal	1 clove garlic, crushed
1 egg	Kitchen Bouquet
1/2 c. bread crumbs	Poppy seed
1 tsp. salt	

Mix thoroughly and form into small balls (about 10). Brown all sides in hot fat, adding Kitchen Bouquet. When brown, remove from skillet and make gravy as follows:

3 Tbsp. flour in pan drippings	1 1/2 soup cans milk
1 can cream of mushroom soup	1 (8 oz.) ctn. sour cream

Stir until mixture boils. Add Kitchen Bouquet, enough to make a rich brown texture. Return meat balls and simmer 30 minutes. Add 1 (4 ounce) can mushrooms and heat through. Serve over broad flat noodles sprinkled generously with poppy seed. Only changes to this recipe are ground beef rather than veal, a heartier flavor and skipping the sour cream in the gravy (less calories). I use the soup and 2 cans buttermilk instead. A bit of Carnation milk, rather than the egg in the meat balls makes them a nice smooth texture.

Mrs. Richard Smach, St. Cloud, Mn.

COCKTAIL MEAT BALLS

1 lb. ground beef	1 tsp. onion salt
1 lb. ground pork, ground with beef	1 tsp. garlic salt
4 slices bread, cubed	1 tsp. salt
1/2 c. milk, soak bread in milk	2 (5 oz.) cans water chestnuts, diced fine

276

2 Tbsp. soy sauce   1 tsp. Accent
6 drops Tabasco sauce

Mix all together and form into small balls. Brown in oil or under broiler. Add 1/2 cup water, cover and cook over low heat 20 minutes.

Evelyn Walls, St. Paul, Mn.

COCKTAIL MEAT BALLS

Soak 2 cups cubed fresh bread (3 slices) in 1/2 cup milk. Squeeze milk out.

1 lb. ground beef
1/2 tsp. onion salt
1 tsp. garlic salt
1 Tbsp. soy sauce

1/2 tsp. Tabasco sauce
5 oz. can water chestnuts
cut fine

Mix all together. Make cocktail size meat balls and fry in shortening.

Betty Ladd, St. Paul, Mn.

MEAT BALLS

1 lb. hamburger
2 Tbsp. onion, chopped
1/2 c. dry bread crumbs
1 egg
2/3 c. milk

1 tsp. salt
1/4 tsp. nutmeg
1/8 tsp. pepper
1 Tbsp. brown sugar
1/8 tsp. allspice

Form into good sized balls, roll in flour, brown, simmer. Can put potatoes and carrots in same skillet.

Mrs. E. F. Braun, Owatonna, Mn.

PARISIAN MEAT BALLS

1 1/2 lb. ground round
  steak
4 oz. (1/4 lb.) Roquefort
  cheese, cubed

3 to 4 Tbsp. butter or
  margarine
Salt and pepper
1/2 c. burgundy wine

Season beef with salt and pepper. Flatten rounded tablespoonfuls of meat mixture. Place cube of cheese in center of each, shape into balls. Brown beef balls quickly in butter or margarine; add wine; simmer 3 minutes. Serve hot on wooden picks. This makes about 2 dozen meat balls.

MEAT BALLS

2 lb. lean hamburger	1/2 tsp. pepper
1 c. crushed corn flakes	1/2 tsp. garlic salt
Parsley	1/3 c. ketchup
2 eggs	2 Tbsp. onion soup mix
2 Tbsp. soy sauce	

Mix all ingredients together and roll into small balls. Put raw balls in deep baking dish.

Sauce:

1 can jellied cranberries	2 Tbsp. brown sugar
1 (12 oz.) bottle ketchup	1 Tbsp. lemon juice

Mix and cook until smooth. Pour over raw meat balls and bake at 350° for about 45 minutes. Meat balls may be made larger and used as main dish.
Rosie Schudar, Fargo, N. D.

MEAT BALLS AND GRAVY

4 slices bread, soaked in   1 egg
   3/4 c. milk

Beat with beater till mushy. Add 1 teaspoon baking powder and 3 teaspoons onion soup mix. Mix together and make into meat balls. Roll in flour and brown. Pour off grease. Put into casserole. Mix 2 cans cream of celery soup with 1 3/4 cups water and pour over and bake 45 minutes to 1 hour.
Carol Schjeldahl, Mayville, N. D.

MEAT BALLS IN POTATO CUPS

2 c. seasoned, mashed potatoes	1 stalk celery, finely chopped
1 egg	2/3 lb. ground beef
1/2 small onion, finely chopped	1/2 c. uncooked, quick rolled oats
	1/3 c. reconstituted nonfat dry milk

278

1/2 tsp. salt   Bouillon gravy
Pepper, as desired

Mix potatoes and egg. Make 8 mounds on large greased baking pan. Mix rest of ingredients, except gravy. Shape into 8 meat balls. Press a meat ball part way into center of each potato mound. Bake at 350° about 40 minutes until meat and potatoes are browned. Serve with Bouillon Gravy. Makes 4 servings.

Bouillon Gravy:

1 Tbsp. margarine   1 beef bouillon cube
2 Tbsp. flour   Salt and pepper
1 c. water

Melt fat in fry pan. Remove from heat. Stir in flour. Stir in water and add crumbled bouillon cube and seasonings. Cook and stir until smooth and thickened. Makes about 3/4 cup.

Kathy Bischof, St. Cloud, Mn.

POTATOES AND MEAT BALLS

Peel and slice potatoes in bowl. Take hamburger and make into balls or small patties. Put the hamburger balls - rice and onion on top of sliced potatoes. Salt and pepper. Then pour cream of mushroom soup over the potatoes and hamburger. If you want it more juicy, add some milk. Put into oven and bake till done. Not too hot an oven. Don't make meat balls too big, so meat and potatoes get cooked at the same time.

Shirley Pelzel, St. Paul, Mn.

RUSSIAN MEAT BALLS

1/2 lb. ground beef   1 tsp. finely minced onion
2 Tbsp. dried bread   Dash of pepper
   crumbs, fine, soaked   Pinch of cloves and nutmeg
   in 6 Tbsp. cream   1 Tbsp. butter
1/2 tsp. salt

Take ground beef and put into bowl with bread crumb-cream mixture. Add salt, onion, pepper, cloves and nutmeg. Add butter and mix thoroughly with hands. Shape into little balls. Brown on all sides in hot fat. Remove from pan and make sauce by blending 1 tablespoon fat and 1 tablespoon flour. Add 1 teaspoon meat paste or a bouillon cube dissolved in 3/4 cup boiling water. Stir over low heat until smooth and thick. Add 1/3 cup sour cream. Put meat balls back into pan and simmer in sauce for 8 minutes.

Kathy Bischof, St. Cloud, Mn.

SWEDISH MEAT BALLS

2 lb. ground beef	1 1/2 tsp. salt
1 lb. ground pork	1/2 tsp. pepper
2 beaten eggs	1/2 tsp. cloves
1 c. mashed potatoes	1/2 tsp. allspice
1 c. dry bread crumbs	1/2 tsp. ginger
1 c. milk	1/2 tsp. nutmeg
1 tsp. brown sugar	

Mix together ground beef and pork until well blended. Then add eggs mashed potatoes and dry bread crumbs which have been soaked in the milk. Combine brown sugar and spices and mix with meat mixture. Form into small balls and roll in flour and fry until brown. Add small amount of water and simmer.

Clara O. Johnson, Chanhassen, Mn.

SWEDISH MEAT BALLS

1 1/2 lb. ground beef	1/4 tsp. nutmeg
3/4 c. milk	1 1/2 tsp. salt
1 1/2 c. bread crumbs	Dash of pepper
(remove crusts)	Small onion
1 egg	

Pour milk over bread crumbs, mash well. Cook diced onion in butter. Mix all ingredients, shape into small balls - dip in flour and brown in fat. Add 1 can beef consomme and cook at 350° until liquid is absorbed or until meat is tender. Can be cooked in electric fry pan or in oven. Makes about 26 meat balls.

Helen Evenson, Litchfield, Mn.

SWEET AND SOUR MEAT BALLS

1 lb. lean hamburger or
  ground venison
1/2 lb. ground pork
1/2 tsp. salt
1/4 tsp. garlic powder

1/4 tsp. pepper
1 tsp. mustard
1 (12 oz.) jar Del Monte
  chili sauce (not spicy)
1 (10 oz.) jar grape jelly

Combine meats, salt, garlic powder, pepper and mustard in large bowl and knead with hands until well mixed. Cook chili sauce and jelly together in large skillet over medium heat until jelly melts. Shape meat balls into balls about the size of walnuts, add to sauce a few at a time, carefully stirring to cover meat with sauce. Continue cooking for 30 minutes. Recipe improves when refrigerated for a few days or frozen for a few weeks and reheated.
Gary Meyer, St. Cloud, Mn.

SWEDISH MEAT BALLS

1 lb. ground beef
1/2 lb. ground pork or
  pork sausage
1 medium sized onion,
  chopped

1 or 2 slices bread torn into
  small pieces and soaked in
  enough milk or cream to be
  quite moist
1/2 tsp. sage
Salt and pepper to taste

Mix all ingredients well and shape into meat balls. Brown in heavy skillet - no shortening needed. Drain excess fat. Add 1 can cream of mushroom soup and 1 can milk. Stir until smooth - simmer until meat balls are cooked through, 15 - 20 minutes, depending on size of meat balls.
Lois Sandberg, St. Cloud, Mn.

SWEDISH MEAT BALLS

1 lb. lean ground beef
1/2 lb. lean ground pork
1 c. milk
2 eggs

Salt and pepper to taste
3 crushed rusks
1 small onion, diced

Mix well together and make into small balls and brown. Place in casserole and bake at 350° for 1 1/2 hours.
Borgruy Pinney, Anoka, Mn.

SWEDISH MEAT BALLS

1 1/2 lb. ground beef	1/4 tsp. nutmeg
3/4 c. milk	1 1/2 tsp. salt
1 1/2 c. bread crumbs	Dash of pepper
(remove crusts)	Small onion
1 egg	

Pour milk over bread crumbs, mash well. Cook diced onion in butter. Mix all ingredients, shape into small balls - dip in flour and brown in fat. Add 1 can beef consomme and cook at 350° until liquid is absorbed or until meat is tender. Can be cooked in electric fry pan or in oven. Makes about 26 meat balls.

Helen Evenson, Litchfield, Mn.

SWEDISH MEAT BALLS

3/4 lb. ground beef	1/2 tsp. pepper
1/2 lb. ground lean	1/8 to 1/4 tsp. allspice
pork	1 medium onion, chopped
1/2 c. dry bread crumbs	2 eggs
2 tsp. salt	1/2 c. cream or top milk

Mix all ingredients together. Form into small balls. Fry in butter until brown. Add water and simmer. Serve with brown gravy made from drippings.

Mrs. Robert G. Pearson, Fargo, N. D.

TINY SWEDISH MEAT BALLS

1 c. fine, dried bread	3 eggs, slightly beaten
crumbs	2 tsp. salt
1 c. milk	1/2 tsp. pepper
1/4 c. chopped onion	1/2 tsp. allspice
3 Tbsp. oil	1 tsp. nutmeg
1 lb. beef, ground fine	1 c. water
1 lb. pork, ground fine	

Soak bread crumbs in milk 15 minutes. Cook onion in 2 tablespoons oil in skillet until onion is transparent (about 3 minutes). Combine soaked bread crumbs, onion, meat, slightly beaten eggs and seasonings; mix well but do not knead. Shape into balls. Put remaining fat in skillet and brown balls. Add 1/3 cup water, cover and simmer until tender (about 1 hour). Turn occasionally and add remaining water gradually, when necessary. Serve on toothpicks. Yield: At least 2 dozen.

Clara O. Johnson, Chanhassen, Mn.

SWEET AND SOUR MEAT BALLS

3 eggs, beaten
3 c. bread crumbs (or
   4 1/2 slices bread,
   cubed)
1/2 c. chopped onion

1/4 tsp. pepper
3/4 c. milk
2 tsp. salt
3 lb. ground beef

Mix all together and shape into 6 dozen meat balls. Place on cooky sheet or other low pan, i.e. broiler pan with a pan below to catch drippings. Cool and freeze after baking until browned. Use 24 meat balls with 1 recipe sauce.

Sauce:

1 (13 1/4 oz.) can
   pineapple tidbits
1/2 c. brown sugar
1 c. water
1/3 c. vinegar

1 beef bouillon cube
1 Tbsp. soy sauce
1 green pepper, cut into
   small strips
1 (3 oz.) can water
   chestnuts, drained, sliced

Drain pineapple and reserve syrup. Mix sugar and cornstarch and blend in reserved syrup, water, vinegar, bouillon cube and soy sauce. Cook until thick and bubbly. Stir in frozen meat balls, pineapple, green pepper and water chestnuts. Cover and heat thoroughly - about 30 minutes. Stir often. Serve with wild rice.

Ruth Rehschuh, Minneapolis, Mn.

SWEET AND SOUR MEAT BALLS

2 lb. ground beef
2 eggs
1 Tbsp. grated ginger
   root
4 Tbsp. Kikkoman soy
   sauce
1 (8 oz.) can finely
   chopped water chestnuts

1 medium onion, chopped fine
1 Tbsp. oil
12 Townhouse crackers,
   crumbled
1 tsp. salt
2 Tbsp. ketchup

Mix all ingredients well and form into small balls. When ready to cook, fry on medium high heat. When ready to serve, heat La Choy Sweet and Sour Sauce thoroughly. Add meat balls to sauce, allow to simmer. Green pepper and pineapple chunks can be added if desired. Meat balls can be made ahead of time and kept frozen until you need them.

Yuriko Hinton, Fargo, N. D.

PIEROGI
(pi-eh-ROE-GUI)

2 c. flour	1/2 tsp. salt
2 eggs	1/3 c. water

Mound flour on a bread board and make a well in the center. Drop eggs and salt into well - add water; working from center out. Mix flour into liquid into center with one hand and keep flour mounded with the other hand. Knead until dough is firm and well mixed. Cover dough with a warm bowl and let rest 10 minutes. Divide dough into halves. On floured surface, using half of dough at a time, roll dough as thin as possible. Cut out 3 inch rounds with large biscuit cutter. Place a small spoonful of filling* a little to one side on each round of dough. Moisten edge with water, fold over and press edges together firmly (be sure they're well sealed to prevent filling from leaking out). Drop Pierogi into boiling, salted water - cook gently 3 to 5 minutes, or until Pierogi floats. Lift out of water with perforated spoon.

Note: The dough will have a tendency to dry. A dry dough will not seal completely. Work with half the dough at a time, rolling out a large circle of dough and placing small mounds of filling far enough apart to allow for cutting. Then cut and seal firmly. Never put too many Pierogi in cooking water. The uncooked will stick together and the cooked will get lumpy and tough.

*Fillings:

Cottage Cheese Filling -

1 1/2 c. cream style cottage cheese, drained	1 Tbsp. butter
1 beaten egg	1 1/2 tsp. sugar
	1/2 tsp. salt

Combine thoroughly.

Sausage Filling:

10 oz. skinned and
    chopped Polish sausage
1/4 c. dry bread crumbs

1/2 c. grated cheese or
    chopped mushrooms
1 egg

Combine thoroughly.

Mushroom Filling:

1 1/2 c. chopped mushrooms
1/2 c. chopped onion

2 Tbsp. butter

Saute in butter till onion is tender and add:

1/4 tsp. salt
1/8 tsp. pepper

2 egg yolks

Sauerkraut Filling:

1/3 c. chopped onion,
    cooked in butter till
    tender

1 1/2 c. finely chopped
    sauerkraut
2 Tbsp. sour cream

Cooked Fruit Filling:

2 c. cherries (pitted),
    apples or blueberries
3/4 c. water
1/3 c. sugar

1/2 tsp. cinnamon
1 tsp. lemon juice
2 to 4 Tbsp. dry bread
    crumbs

Combine fruit, water and sugar in a saucepan, bring
to a boil, cook and stir till water is almost gone. Mash
fruit - add cinnamon and lemon juice. Cook and stir over
low heat till fruit mixture is thick. Stir in bread crumbs.

Prune Filling:

2 c. prunes
1 Tbsp. lemon juice

1 Tbsp. brown sugar

Cover prunes with water. Bring to a boil. Remove
from heat and let stand 20 minutes. Remove pits, add lemon
juice and sugar. Cook till liquid is almost gone.
            Patty Ginter, St. Cloud, Mn.

DEEP DISH PIZZA

1 lb. ground beef	1 (16 oz.) can tomatoes
1/4 c. chopped onion	1 pkg. Kraft cheese pizza
1/4 c. chopped pepper	2 (6 oz.) pkg. Mozzarella cheese

Brown meat, drain, add onion and pepper. Cook until tender. Stir in tomatoes, pizza sauce and herb spice mix. Simmer 15 minutes. Prepare pizza dough as directed. Grease hands and pan. Put dough into 13x9 inch pan half way up sides. Cover with half of cheese and half of meat sauce. Repeat with remaining cheese and meat sauce. Sprinkle with grated Parmesan cheese. Bake at 425° for 20 - 25 minutes.

Sue Hick, Detroit Lakes, Mn.

JOE'S TACO PIZZA

Meat:

1 to 1 1/4 lb. lean ground beef, browned	1 pkg. taco seasoning

Add taco seasoning per instructions on the package.

Sauce:

1 (15 oz.) can tomato sauce	1 pkg. taco seasoning
	1 (6 oz.) can tomato paste

The following spices are approximations and may be varied slightly to taste:

1 tsp. onion powder	1 Tbsp. paprika
1 tsp. minced onions	1 Tbsp. oregano
1 tsp. garlic powder	1/2 to 1 tsp. cumin

For extra hot pizza, add 1/2 teaspoon cayenne pepper. Stir and simmer all of the above for about 15 minutes.

Crust:

1 1/4 c. water	1/4 c. sugar
2 1/2 Tbsp. vegetable oil	3/4 c. corn meal
1 tsp. salt	1 pkg. dry yeast
	Flour*

*Enough so that the dough does not stick to your fingers when kneading it (knead only for about 5 minutes), or about 3 cups flour.

After mixing and kneading, let dough set for about 10 minutes. Spread dough on well greased 15 inch pizza pan (or equivalent), building a ridge of dough around the outside. Add the meat to the sauce, mix well, then spread the meat-sauce mixture evenly on crust. Put in preheated 450° oven for 5 minutes. Take out, spread 3/4 pound grated Cheddar cheese on top. Replace in oven and cook until crust is brown. After cooking, top the pizza with generous amounts of chopped lettuce, pieces of tomatoes and crushed Doritos or tortilla shells and serve.

Karen Rupert, St. Cloud, Mn.

HOT SAUCE

2 cans tomato special
1 can tomato sauce
1 small minced onion
1/2 tsp. garlic salt
1 tsp. cumin
1 tsp. cayenne (red) pepper
2 drops Tabasco sauce

Barb Hocking

PIZZA DOUGH

1 pkg. dry yeast
1 c. warm water
3 1/4 c. flour
1/2 tsp. salt

Mix yeast and water, let stand for 5 minutes. Add flour and salt, mix well. You may add up to 1/4 cup of warm water to mix flour. Place hot, wet dish towel over bowl and place in oven on warm. Let rise 25 - 30 minutes. Grease pan and hands and spread dough on large cookie sheet. Add sauce and meats. Bake at 450° for 45 minutes. Add cheese last 10 minutes.

Connie Vivier, Fargo, N. D.

PIZZA NOODLE BAKE

4 c. uncooked egg noodles
1 1/2 lb. ground beef
1/4 c. chopped onion
2 (15 oz.) cans tomato
  sauce
2 c. water
1 1/2 tsp. salt
1/2 tsp. garlic powder
1 tsp. oregano
4 slices Mozzarella cheese

1748-81

Brown ground beef and onion. Add garlic powder, salt, oregano, tomato sauce and water. Pour some sauce mix in bottom of 13x9x2 inch pan. Spread uncooked noodles on top and pour on remaining sauce. Bake at 350° for 1 hour. The last 10 minutes, top with cheese.

Sherry Petersen, St. Cloud, Mn.

MINI-PIZZAS

8 oz. pkg. refrigerator
  biscuits
6 oz. can tomato paste
1 Tbsp. water
1 tsp. oregano

1 small onion (if desired),
  finely chopped
1 c. shredded or finely
  chopped cheese

Roll out or pat biscuits into 4 inch circles on a greased baking pan. Mix tomato paste, water and oregano. Cover biscuits with mixture. Sprinkle with onion (if used) and cheese. Bake at 425° about 8 - 9 minutes until lightly browned. Quickly loosen pizzas from pan.

Kathy Bischof, St. Cloud, Mn.

PIZZA

Crust:

1 yeast cake
1/4 c. lukewarm water
1 Tbsp. sugar
3 c. flour

1 c. Bisquick
3 Tbsp. olive oil
1/2 tsp. salt
1 1/2 c. warm water

Sauce:

2 Tbsp. olive oil
1 small can tomato sauce
1 small can tomato paste
1/2 can water
1/2 tsp. salt

1/4 tsp. pepper
1/4 tsp. garlic powder
1 tsp. oregano
1/2 tsp. parsley flakes

Crust: Mix and let stand until it has risen to double the size, about 1 1/2 hours at room temperature.

Sauce: Combine everything and simmer 1/2 hour. Roll out crust and put into round pizza pans. Add sauce, then whatever meat you like. Top with lots of Mozzarella cheese. Bake in hot oven until cheese melts.

Avis Paulsen, Verndale, Mn.

288

APPLE GLAZED ROAST

Accompany with roasted potatoes and a light, fruity Camay Beaujolais, Gamay Beaujolais or dry Sauvignon Blanc.

1 (12 oz.) jar apple jelly (1 c.)
4 tsp. Dijon style mustard
3 Tbsp. lemon juice, divided
Watercress sprigs for garnish

1 boned and tied pork loin rib end roast (2 1/2 lb.), at room temperature
Salt and freshly ground pepper
1 Tbsp. brandy

In small saucepan melt jelly over low heat. Stir in mustard and 1 teaspoon lemon juice; set aside. Rub roast generously with salt and pepper. Place on rack in shallow roasting pan lined with foil. Roast in preheated 350° oven for 45 minutes. Brush lightly with jelly mixture and continue roasting, brushing with jelly once more, 30 - 45 minutes or until meat thermometer inserted in thickest part of roast registers 165°. Let stand in warm place 10 minutes. Scrape any browned (not burned) drippings (see note) from roasting pan into remaining jelly. Add remaining 2 teaspoons lemon juice and the brandy; heat through. Season generously with salt and pepper. Slice roast thin. Garnish with watercress. Pass sauce as condiment. Makes 6 servings.
Note: You can make the sauce without the drippings, in which case it's best to serve a dry Sauvignon Blanc wine.
Larry Clark, Anoka, Mn.

CREOLE PORK CHOPS

4 center cut loin chops
Salt and pepper to taste
1 c. uncooked rice
2 green peppers, chopped

2 medium onions, chopped
3 c. boiling water
1/4 c. catsup

Season chops with salt and pepper and place in large skillet. Cover with rice, green peppers and onion, salt and pepper again. Combine boiling water and catsup and pour over chops and bring to a boil. Lower heat. Cover and simmer for 1 hour or maybe more, till rice and chops are tender. Serves 4.

LUXEMBOURG PORK CHOPS AND SAUERKRAUT

1/2 lb. bacon
1 (1 lb. 13 oz.) can
  sauerkraut
1 (15 oz.) jar applesauce
1 Tbsp. brown sugar
1/2 tsp. dry mustard
1/4 c. dry white wine
Dash of pepper
1/4 tsp. paprika
6 pork chops

Cut bacon into pieces and saute until crisp; drain and add to sauerkraut along with applesauce, brown sugar, mustard, wine and pepper. Turn into shallow baking dish. Sprinkle with paprika. Saute the chops in bacon drippings until golden brown. Place on top of the sauerkraut. Cover and bake in 350° oven for about 1 hour.
Marion Baihly

MUSTARD GLAZED PORK ROAST

1 (4 to 5 lb.) pork
  loin roast
1 tsp. salt
1/4 tsp. pepper
1/4 c. light brown sugar,
  packed
1 Tbsp. mustard
1 tsp. water
Parsley sprigs

Heat oven to 325°. Sprinkle pork with salt and pepper and place on a rack in roasting pan, with fat side up. Roast about 2 hours, or until meat is tender. Mix brown sugar, mustard and water. Brush pork with about 1/2 of sugar mixture. Roast 15 minutes. Brush with remaining sugar mixture and roast 15 minutes longer. Put roast on a serving platter and garnish with parsley. May freeze leftover.
Marie Miller, St. Paul, Mn.

PARMESAN BREADED PORK CHOPS

4 pork chops, 3/4 inch
  thick
1 egg, beaten
1 tsp. salt
1/4 tsp. pepper
1/3 c. grated Parmesan cheese
1/3 c. dry bread crumbs
2 Tbsp. all-purpose oil

Heat oven to 350°. Dip pork chops in combined egg and seasoning and then in combined cheese and bread crumbs. Heat oil in skillet, brown each chop on both sides. Bake at 350° for 35 minutes, turning chops occasionally. (4 servings)
290   Diane Schmitz, St. Cloud, Mn.

PARTY PORK CHOPS

8 thick sliced pork chops,
    about 3/4 inch
8 onion slices, 1/4 inch
    thick
8 lemon slices, 1/4 inch
    thick

2/3 c. brown sugar
1 1/4 tsp. salt
1/4 tsp. pepper
3 Tbsp. fresh lemon juice
2/3 c. chili sauce

Place chops in single layer in 9x13 inch pan. Place 1 onion slice topped with 1 lemon slice on center of each chop. Blend remaining ingredients and pour over chops. Cover tightly. Bake at 350° for 1 1/2 hours or until chops are tender.

Carolyn Brudevold, Fargo, N. D.

PORK HAWAIIAN

1 egg
2 Tbsp. water
1/4 c. flour
1/4 tsp. salt
2 c. cubed, cooked
    pork
3 Tbsp. cornstarch
1 can mushrooms

1 (13 1/2 oz.) can pineapple
    tidbits, drained (reserve
    juice)
2 Tbsp. vinegar
2 Tbsp. soy sauce
1 medium green pepper
1 (5 oz.) can water chestnuts,
    drained and sliced

Beat egg in medium bowl. Add water, flour and salt and beat until smooth. Stir in meat and mix until coated. Melt shortening in medium skillet and brown meat mixture. Remove and keep warm. Blend cornstarch, pineapple syrup and vinegar and soy sauce in saucepan. Cook over medium heat until mixture thickens and boils. Boil 1 minute. Stir in pineapple, green pepper, water chestnuts and mushrooms. Cook until peppers are tender. Stir in meat and heat through.

Rose Ecklund, Fargo, N. D.

PORK CHOPS - RICE

Pork chops
Minute Rice
1 medium can quartered
    tomatoes

1 medium onion
Season to taste

Brown pork chops in fry pan - heap with precooked Minute Rice. Add tomatoes on top. Add quartered and sliced onion on top of that. Add about half of the fluid from the tomatoes to the bottom of the pan. Bake at 325° for about an hour or more and baste when onions and rice get too crispy.

Thomas E. Broman, Pine City, Mn.

ROAST PORK - DUMPLINGS AND SAUERKRAUT
(Veprova-Knebliky-Zeli)

Have ready, one 6 to 8 pound pork loin roast. Brown in hot grease. Salt and pepper to taste. Sprinkle with 1 to 3 tablespoons caraway seed and roast in 350° oven, closed lid, for 30 minutes per pound.

Sauerkraut:

1 (32 oz.) jar sauerkraut
1 medium onion, chopped
2 Tbsp. oil

3 Tbsp. sugar
1 medium potato, grated raw
3 Tbsp. caraway seed

Brown onion in oil and simmer with sauerkraut, caraway seed and sugar, for 1 hour. Just before serving, add grated raw potato and heat through.

Dumplings:

3 c. flour
4 1/2 tsp. baking powder
1 egg beaten with enough
  milk added to make 1 1/4 c.

1 tsp. salt
6 Tbsp. cooking oil

Combine all ingredients and knead till thoroughly mixed. Roll with hands into long cylinder about 3 inches in diameter. Cut into 8 large dumplings and place in boiling, salted water. Cover and cook 15 minutes. Remove with slotted spoon.

Gravy: Use pan drippings from roast and add sufficient water to make about 3 cups. Thicken, just barely, with cornstarch and add Kitchen Bouquet for rich brown color.

To serve: Each item separately on plate with gravy ladled over all.

Mrs. Richard Smach, St. Cloud, Mn.

BARBECUED PORK ON BUNS

1 c. diced, leftover cooked
   pork
1/2 c. catsup
2 Tbsp. brown sugar

1 Tbsp. vinegar
2 tsp. Worcestershire
   sauce
4 hamburger buns

Combine all ingredients except buns. Heat together until hot and thick and serve on toasted, split buns.
Pearl Paulsrud, Willmar, Mn.

BARBECUED RIBS

4 lb. ribs

1/2 c. chopped onion

Mix together with:
2 garlic cloves
1 1/2 c. catsup
2 Tbsp. vinegar
1/2 tsp. salt

1 tsp. mustard
1/2 tsp. pepper
2 Tbsp. steak sauce
1 c. honey

Simmer ribs in enough water to cover with 2 teaspoons salt for 1/2 hour. Drain. Place in roaster, pour sauce over and bake at 400° for about 1 hour.
Joan Dondreau, Grand Forks, N. D.

BAR-B-Q RIBS

Mix:
2 Tbsp. vinegar
2 Tbsp. Worcestershire
   sauce
1 Tbsp. Heinz 57 sauce
1 Tbsp. salt
1 Tbsp. paprika

1 Tbsp. chili powder
1/2 Tbsp. pepper
2/3 c. sugar
3/4 c. ketchup
1 onion, minced

Double recipe for more than 12 ribs. Bake ribs with salt, pepper and onion for 1 1/2 - 2 hours at 325°. Drain fat, add sauce, bake 1/2 hour at 350°.
Marge Luckscheror, Fargo, N. D.

OVEN BARBEQUED RIBS

3 - 4 lb. spareribs or
loin back ribs, cut
into pieces

1 lemon, thinly sliced
1 large onion, thinly sliced

Sauce:

1 c. catsup (Heinz)
2 - 3 Tbsp. brown sugar
1/4 c. Worcestershire
sauce
1 tsp. chili powder

1 c. water
1 tsp. salt
1 dash liquid smoke
2 dashes Tabasco sauce

Salt ribs - place in shallow roasting pan, meat side up.
Roast at 450° for 30 minutes. Drain fat. Top each piece of
meat with unpeeled lemon and onion.
To make sauce: Combine sauce ingredients; bring to
boil. Pour over ribs, lower temperature to 350°; bake until
well done, about 1 1/2 hours. Baste ribs with sauce every
10 minutes. Add water if sauce gets too thick. (4 servings)
Lajla Hood, South Haven, Mn.

PORK LOIN WITH CHERRY ALMOND SAUCE

6 lb. pork loin
1 (12 oz.) jar cherry
preserves
1/2 c. light corn syrup
1/4 c. red wine vinegar
1/4 tsp. salt

1/4 tsp. ground cloves
1/4 tsp. cinnamon
1/8 tsp. black pepper
1/4 c. slivered, blanched
almonds
1/4 tsp. nutmeg

Roast meat on rack at 325°, about 3 hours. Meanwhile,
combine preserves, syrup, vinegar and spices. Bring to a
boil, boil 1 minute. Add almonds. Baste roast with sauce
several times during last 1/2 hour of roasting time. Serve
remaining sauce with meat. (8 servings)
Mary Vander Laun, Andover, Mn.

WILD RICE AND PORK CHOPS

4 pork chops, 3/4 inch
thick
1 (#2) can tomatoes

1 c. uncooked wild rice
1 onion

Cook rice - brown chops on one side after trimming off fat (I brown that too in little bits and add), pour water in skillet and loosen brown. Put chops in roaster, brown side up. Place rice and onion on top and season. Add tomatoes and water from skillet to equal 1 inch moisture in bottom of pan. Bake at 350° for 30 minutes - lower to 325° for 1 1/2 hours. Baste and season (only need to baste about 4 times). Cover if it looks dry, or add more water.

Kayce Waterbury, St. Paul, Mn.

BARBECUE

2 lb. ground beef	2 tsp. sugar
1 onion	2 tsp. mustard
1 can tomato soup	1 Tbsp. catsup
1 tsp. chili powder	1 tsp. salt
1 Tbsp. vinegar	Pepper

Simmer on low heat for 30 minutes.

Sue Peterson, Grand Forks, N. D.

BARBECUE BEEF
(On Buns)

4 lb. roast	1 tsp. salt
2 Tbsp. vinegar	2 Tbsp. Worcestershire
1 regular size bottle	sauce
ketchup	1 tsp. chili powder
4 c. chopped celery	2 c. water
3 sliced onions	

Place all ingredients in a roaster and bake in a slow oven (300° - 325°) for about 5 hours. As the meat cooks, break apart with fork. Water may be added if mixture becomes dry. Spoon onto buns. Makes 15 - 20 servings.

Mrs. Jerve, St. Cloud, Mn.

BARBECUE HAMBURGERS

Brown 2 pounds ground beef and 2 medium onions, chopped. Add:

1 tsp. paprika	1/2 tsp. pepper
2 tsp. salt	1/2 tsp. chili powder

1748-81

3/4 c. catsup
3/4 c. water

2 Tbsp. vinegar
2 Tbsp. Worcestershire sauce

Simmer about 1 hour. Add water or tomato juice if necessary.

Sue Hick, Detroit Lakes, Mn.

BARBECUED HAMBURGERS

3 lb. hamburger
1/4 c. lemon juice
1/4 c. vinegar
1 qt. catsup

1/2 c. brown sugar
1/2 c. onion, cut fine
1/2 c. celery, cut fine
Salt and pepper

Cook hamburger in skillet, then add rest of ingredients and simmer for 1 hour. Serve hot on hamburger buns.

Edythe Stubbelfeld, St. Paul, Mn.

CRABBIES

6 English muffins, sliced,
  each slice cut into 4
  pieces
1 jar Olde English cheese
  spread
1/4 lb. butter
1 1/2 tsp. mayonnaise

1/2 tsp. seasoned salt
1 can crabmeat, drained
1 clove garlic, chopped
2 tsp. Worcestershire sauce
1 tsp. lemon juice
Dash of Tabasco sauce

Cut English muffins. Combine remaining ingredients except crabmeat and blend with electric mixer. Stir in crabmeat. Spread mixture on pieces of English muffin, place on cookie sheet and put under broiler 3 to 4 minutes until lightly brown. Serve hot. Makes 48 pieces. Can be frozen.

St. Paul, Mn.

CLUB SANDWICH

Toast slices
Butter
Mayonnaise
Sliced turkey

Crisp bacon strips
Tomato slices
Lettuce

Spread a slice of toast with butter and mayonnaise. Add a layer of thinly sliced turkey. Top with another slice of buttered toast, strips of crisp bacon, slices of tomato and a lettuce leaf. Cover with a dab of mayonnaise and a third slice of toast. Skewer together with toothpicks and cut into quarters.

Mrs. E. F. Braun, Owatonna, Ks.

CORNED BEEF SUPPER SANDWICH

2 Tbsp. butter or margarine
3 tsp. prepared mustard
1 large onion, sliced
2/3 c. mayonnaise
1 round loaf (16 oz. -
   7 inch diameter) unsliced
   French, Italian or rye bread

1 (12 oz.) can corned beef,
   chilled, then cut into 10
   slices
4 slices American cheese,
   halved

Preheat oven to 400° F. In skillet, melt butter; stir in 1 teaspoon mustard. Add onion and cook until onion is tender. Meanwhile, mix remaining mustard with mayonnaise. Cut 9 slices in bread, slicing almost, but not completely through, to form 10 pieces. To fill sandwich, spread first slice, then every other with mustard-mayonnaise. In same slices, tuck in corned beef, cheese and onions. Wrap sandwich in foil; bake 20 minutes or until heated through. To serve, completely cut through the unfilled slices. Serve with any remaining mustard-mayonnaise. Yield: 5 sandwiches.

Kathy Bischof, St. Cloud, Mn.

CRESCENT TREAT

Have ready, 2 packages crescent rolls. Unfold rolls of 1 package and place in bottom of pan. Brown 1 1/2 pounds hamburger. Drain fat, add:

1 pkg. Sloppy Joe mix
1 (15 oz.) can tomato sauce

1 tsp. oregano

Mix together and put on top of rolls. Sprinkle on top:

2 c. shredded Cheddar
   cheese

2 c. Mozzarella cheese

Put other package of rolls on top. Bake at 325° for 30 minutes.

Kathy Bischof, St. Cloud, Mn.

EASY BARBEQUE FOR BUNS

Saute 1 pound of hamburger with 1 medium onion, chopped. Add 1 can of chicken gumbo soup and enough catsup for color. Season to taste. Cook well and serve on buns.

Marilyn Helgeson, Fargo, N. D.

EGG SALAD SANDWICH SUPREME

6 hard-cooked eggs, chopped
1 c. (4 oz.) shredded Cheddar cheese
1/4 c. chopped celery

3 Tbsp. stuffed green olive slices
Mayonnaise
Salt and pepper
12 white bread slices
Lettuce

Kathy Bischof, St. Cloud, Mn.

HAWAIIAN DELIGHT

2 c. Hellmann's old fashioned mayonnaise
1 heaping tsp. Beau Monde spice

1 chopped onion
1 pkg. chopped spinach, thawed and wrung out
1 loaf round Kings Hawaiian bread

Mix filling a day ahead. Refrigerate. Hollow out center of bread, put crumbs around outside of loaf- fill with filling. Tear off bread and dip in filling. Also makes a good chip dip.

Kathaleen Bischof, St. Cloud, Mn.

HOT CHICKEN SANDWICH

1 1/2 c. cooked leftover chicken or breasts
2 Tbsp. grated onion juice
2 Tbsp. chopped pimento

1 can cream of mushroom soup
1 c. Franco-American chicken gravy
16 slices bread, cut off crusts

Spread the 16 slices of bread with the gravy. Mix rest of ingredients together and spread on 8 of the slices (mostly in center), cover the remaining 8 slices to make

8 sandwiches. Wrap in foil individually and freeze. When ready to use, beat 1 egg, add 1 tablespoon milk or cream and dip sandwiches in mixture, then coat with crushed potato chips. Place on an unbuttered tin and bake 1 hour at 300°. Serve with fruit mold salad. Excellent for unexpected guests.

Myrtle Solomon, Fargo, N. D.

HOT SPAM (OR HAM) SANDWICHES

1 can Spam (or ham), sliced
1/2 lb. Velveeta (or cheese of your choice)

1 small can mushrooms
1 small onion

Grind together and wrap buns in aluminum foil. Bake 20 to 25 minutes at 350°. Yield: 4 buns.

Bev Barglof, Detroit Lakes, Mn.

HUNGARIAN SANDWICH SPREAD

8 oz. cream cheese
2 sticks butter or margarine
1 Tbsp. mustard

1/2 tsp. caraway seed
1/2 tsp. salt
1 tsp. paprika

Combine all ingredients thoroughly. Good on party rye bread and on snack crackers. Store in refrigerator. Optional: Chopped onions or scallions.

Karen Rupert, St. Cloud, Mn.

INDIAN TACOS

Have ready, 1 loaf frozen Rhodes bread dough. Take loaf out of freezer and place in refrigerator the evening before to thaw (24 hours). Knead dough and roll out on greased surface about 1/4 inch thick (the thinner the better). Cut into 12 squares and pinch all edges. Deep fry till golden brown on both sides. Drain on paper towels. Top with seasoned taco filling, lettuce, tomatoes, cheese and taco sauce.

Connie Vivier, Fargo, N. D.

ITALIAN BEEF SANDWICHES

1 (6 lb.) round or rump   3 large onions
  roast   1 tsp. salt

Place beef in roaster half filled with water, add salt and onions, cover, roast in a 500° oven for about 1/2 hour. Then reduce heat to 325° and continue roasting until tender (about 3 hours). When done, remove from oven, let stand overnight. The next day, remove the fat and slice beef very thin, strain liquid and add:

1/2 tsp. garlic salt   1/2 tsp. salt
1/2 tsp. oregano   1 tsp. Accent
1/4 tsp. basil   1/2 green pepper, sliced
1/2 tsp. Italian seasoning

Bring all to boiling point, place sliced beef and liquid in flat pan, place in oven at 350° for 30 minutes. May be stirred a couple of times to combine well. Serve on hard rolls (warmed). May serve with sandwiches, imported mild pepperoncini peppers.
       Martie Athur, Detroit Lakes, Mn.

KORONIS BARBEQUES

1 1/2 lb. hamburger   1 can cream of chicken soup
1 chopped onion   2 Tbsp. prepared mustard

Slowly cook hamburger and onion until cooked through. Add soup and mustard. Simmer 30 to 45 minutes. Spoon onto hamburger buns.
       Kathaleen Bischof, St. Cloud, Mn.

PIZZA BUNS

1 can Spam, grated   1 can tomato paste
4 oz. Mozzarella or Cheddar   1/2 tsp. oregano
  cheese, grated   1/2 tsp. garlic

Mix together and spread on top 1/2 of bun. Put under broiler. Watch carefully as doesn't take long to heat. Very good.
       Mavis E. Dilts, Valley City, N. D.

PIZZA BURGERS

1 1/2 lb. hamburger	1 tsp. salt
1 can tomato paste	1 tsp. oregano
1 can puree	1/3 tsp. pepper
1/2 c. catsup	1/2 tsp. garlic
10 Tbsp. onions	1 tsp. sugar

Brown hamburger, add the rest of the ingredients. Heat thoroughly. Put on buns, cover with shredded cheese. Place in 350° oven until cheese melts.

Avis Paulsen, Verndale, Mn.

PIZZA BURGERS

Brown:

1 lb. ground beef	1 onion

In separate dish:

1 1/4 c. American cheese, grated	1 tsp. oregano
3/4 c. Mozzarella cheese, grated	1 can Spam, grated
	1 1/2 tsp. salt
	1 regular size jar Ragu sauce

Mix all together and put on open hamburger buns. Bake at 375° for 10 to 15 minutes.

Marion Round, Faribault, Mn.

PIZZA BURGERS

1 lb. hamburger, brown with onion, salt, pepper and drain off grease, cool	1 (10 1/2 oz.) can Chef-Boy-Ar-Dee pizza sauce
1 can Spam, ground up	1/2 lb. grated Mozzarella cheese
	1/2 lb. grated Cheddar cheese

Mix above ingredients together. Spread on English muffin halves and broil until browned, or cheese melts. Keeps well for about a week in refrigerator.

Lu Boyer, Grand Forks, N. D.

SANDWICHES

1 stick soft butter	1 tsp. poppy seed
1 tsp. dry mustard	1 tsp. grated onion

Mix.

12 slices ham	12 slices Swiss cheese

Wrap and heat at 325° for 15 minutes.
Shirley Peterson, Willmar, Mn.

SLOPPY JOES

2 1/2 lb. hamburger	1 can tomato soup
1 onion, cut up	1/4 c. catsup
Salt and pepper	2 Tbsp. Worcestershire sauce
1 (8 oz.) can tomato sauce	3 c. chopped celery

Brown meat until done and simmer the celery and onion in butter. Add all the other ingredients to the meat and the celery and onion. Let simmer for 1 hour.
Mary Paul, Minneapolis, Mn.

SLOPPY JOE'S

2 1/2 lb. hamburger, browned	4 Tbsp. brown sugar
1 lb. chopped onions	4 Tbsp. prepared mustard
2 green peppers, chopped	2 Tbsp. vinegar
1 1/2 c. ketchup	2 tsp. salt
	1/4 tsp. pepper

After hamburger has browned, add all other ingredients and leave on high until onions and green peppers look cooked. Stir occasionally so it won't burn. Lower heat to simmer for 1/2 hour. Can be put into crock pot to simmer until ready to serve.
Patty Dolan, Minneapolis, Mn.

SLOPPY JOES

1/2 c. celery
3 lb. hamburger
1/2 c. catsup
Salt and pepper to taste

1 onion (medium)
Worcestershire sauce (about
    1 tsp. or less)

Mix all together, brown and simmer.
Marion Round, Faribault, Mn.

SLOPPY JOES

Brown:
1 small onion, chopped
1 lb. ground beef

Salt and pepper to taste

Add:
1 can chicken gumbo soup
1 c. catsup

1 tsp. mustard

Cook until desired consistency (about 1/2 hour to 1 hour).
Linda Johnson, Anoka, Mn.

SLOPPY OTTOS

Brown 1 pound hamburger with onion, salt and pepper. *Add drained sauerkraut to taste (about 40% sauerkraut to 60% hamburger is good). Heat through. Add 1/2 pint of sour cream (right before serving), heat for a minute. Serve on dark buns.
    *Bagged sauerkraut is better than canned.
Kayce Waterbury, St. Paul, Mn.

SPAM BUNS

Put through grinder:
1 can Spam
1/4 lb. American cheese

2 - 3 hard-boiled eggs
1 small onion

Moisten with mayonnaise - spread on buns (open face) and broil till golden on top.
Kayce Waterbury, St. Paul, Mn.

TURKEYBURGER

Grind turkey, heat in greased skillet. Sprinkle with Lawry's seasoned salt. Add 1 can celery soup. Let simmer until mostly dry. Serve on hot buns (hamburger).

Marie Doty, Austin, Mn.

DEER SAUSAGE

12 lb. venison
12 lb. pork butts
3/8 c. pepper
2 tsp. garlic salt
8 qt. water (no more than 8%)

7/8 c. preservative salt
3/4 c. pickling salt
1 1/2 boxes mustard seed (2 1/4 oz. size)
1 tsp. marjoram

Grind up your venison and pork butts, combine all ingredients (the water is just to make it slide through the casings easier). Stuff into casings and tie with string. Hang up to dry out, overnight, then smoke.

Karen Rupert, St. Cloud, Mn.

DON'S SUMMER SAUSAGE
(Freezes well)

6 lb. "cheap" hamburger
2 1/2 tsp. freshly ground pepper
2 1/2 tsp. mustard seed
2 1/2 tsp. garlic salt

6 tsp. Morton's Tender-Quick salt
1 - 2 tsp. hickory smoked salt (to taste)
Optional: 3 fresh garlic toes ground (if like garlichy)

Mix well. Refrigerate 24 hours. Mix again, refrigerate 24 hours. Makes 3 short or 2 long rolls. Place on broiler pan. Bake at 140° - 150° for 8 hours. Meat drains as it bakes and forms own casing. If oven heat not hot enough, can turn up to 175°.

Don Billadeau, St. Cloud, Mn.

HEAD CHEESE

3 - 4 lb. pork   Onion
3 - 4 lb. beef   Salt and pepper
1 chicken

    Boil each meat with onion in its own pot. Cool. Take off all the fat. Save juices. Grind and mix meats all together. Add some of the juices. Put into a large lasagna pan, cover with waxed paper and cheesecloth or dish towel. Set something really heavy on top and set in refrigerator. Next day, cut into hunks and wrap in foil and freeze.

Karen Rupert, St. Cloud, Mn.

JAMBALAYA

1 1/2 lb. sausage or   2 Tbsp. parsley, chopped
  cubed beef or chicken   2 cloves garlic, minced
3 Tbsp. bacon drippings,   2 c. rice
  if beef is used   3/4 tsp. red pepper
Salt and pepper for beef   2 tsp. salt
3 Tbsp. flour   1 bunch green onions, chopped
2 medium onions, chopped   2 1/2 c. water

    Brown meat in bacon drippings, remove and add flour. Use a heavy black pot and brown flour to a dark roux (paste). Add onions, parsley and garlic. Cook until soft, add water and rice, salt and pepper and browned meat. When comes to a boil, lower heat to lowest point and cook 1 hour, covered tightly. When rice is done, remove lid and cook a few minutes until rice dries a little. Serves 6 - 8.

POTATO SAUSAGES

4 lb. hamburger   Pepper
7 lb. potatoes, ground   4 Tbsp. (rounded) sausage
  up   seasoning
1 onion, chopped   1 tsp. salt

    Combine all ingredients very thoroughly, stuff into casings, freeze individually. When you want to serve, thaw one out and boil for about 1/2 hour.

Karen Rupert, St. Cloud, Mn.

SALOMI

2 lb. hamburger
1/2 tsp. liquid smoke
1/4 tsp. garlic salt
1 Tbsp. whole mustard
  seed

1/8 tsp. pepper
1/2 tsp. onion salt
2 Tbsp. Morton's Tender-
  Quick salt
1 c. water

Mix and make into 2 rolls and put into foil (shiny side out). Refrigerate 24 hours. Poke holes with fork all over roll. Bake at 325° for 1 1/2 hours.

Mrs. Robert L. Benson, Stillwater

SAUSAGE

2 lb. hamburger
2 tsp. water
2 tsp. liquid smoke
1/8 tsp. pepper

1/4 tsp. garlic powder
1/2 tsp. onion powder
1 tsp. mustard seed
3 Tbsp. Tender-Quick

Mix all ingredients. Divide into sections, roll into tube like sections and wrap in foil (shiny side to meat). Place in refrigerator for 24 hours or more. Poke holes in bottom of foil and bake on broiler pan for 1 1/4 to 1 1/2 hours at 325°. The longer you bake, the firmer it gets.

Georgia Berg, Fargo, N. D.

SAUSAGE ROLL

2 lb. hamburger
3 Tbsp. Tender-Quick
  curing salt
2 tsp. liquid smoke

1/2 tsp. mustard seed
1/8 tsp. pepper
1 c. water
1/2 tsp. garlic powder

Mix together. Make 2 rolls, wrap in tin foil and set for 24 hours in refrigerator. Poke 3 holes in each end of package and put on jelly roll pan. Bake in oven at 350° for 1 hour and 15 minutes.

Thelma Olson, St. Cloud, Mn.

306

SUMMER SAUSAGE

3 lb. ground beef
2 Tbsp. liquid smoke
1/4 tsp. garlic powder
1 Tbsp. mustard seed

1/2 tsp. pepper
1/2 tsp. onion powder
3 Tbsp. Tender-Quick salt
1 c. water

Mix all together. Roll into 3 rolls. Wrap each into tin foil, shiny side outside. Refrigerate 24 hours. Punch holes in bottom of foil rolls. Place in broiler pan and bake 1 1/2 hours at 325°.

Helen M. Gludt, Bottineau, N. D.

SUMMER SAUSAGE

2 lb. hamburger
2 Tbsp. Morton's Tender-
    Quick salt
2 tsp. liquid smoke
1 tsp. garlic powder

1 tsp. onion powder
1/8 tsp. pepper
1 tsp. mustard seed
1 tsp. mustard powder
1 c. water

Mix all together. Roll 2 rolls into foil. Chill 24 hours. Punch holes in bottom of foil. Place on a rack over pan. Bake 1 1/2 hours at 325°. Cool. Wrap in clean foil.

Nancy Kowalke, Nevis, Mn.

GRANDMA'S SUMMER SAUSAGE

2 or 3 lb. cheap hamburger
1/2 tsp. pepper
1/2 tsp. garlic salt
1/3 tsp. onion salt
1 Tbsp. liquid smoke

2 Tbsp. Tender-Quick
    salt (cheaper if bought
    from a meat locker)
1/2 tsp. mustard seed
1 c. cold water

Mix and shape into long strips on tin foil. Twist ends. Refrigerate 24 hours. Bake at 350° for 1 hour and 10 minutes. Serves many!

Wendy Janzen, Windom, Mn.

PORTUGUESE GREEN BEANS WITH SAUSAGE

2 lb. green beans
1 chopped onion
1 tsp. paprika
1 tsp. powdered cloves

1 lb. pork sausage
1 tsp. parsley
1/2 c. water
1 tsp. salt

Cook beans until tender, then put to one side; brown slowly in skillet the onion, paprika, cloves, parsley; then add water and let mixture come to a boil; add sausage and beans. Let cook until sausage is done, then add salt. Serve hot.

Marge VanGorp, Alexandria, Mn.

SAUERKRAUT PUDDING

1 pt. sauerkraut
1/2 lb. pork sausages
2 Tbsp. bread crumbs
2 oz. golden syrup

4 oz. cooked prunes
Small meat balls
2 oz. butter

Fry meat balls in butter. Cut each sausage into 3 pieces. Combine remaining ingredients (except crumbs) with sauerkraut in greased baking dish. Sprinkle with bread crumbs and bake for 1 hour. Serve with toast.

CAMPERS STEW

1 lb. hamburger
1 can sliced carrots
1 medium onion, diced
2 stalks celery
1 can vegetarian vegetable
   soup

1 can tomato soup
1 c. Minute Rice
1 c. water
Salt and pepper to taste

(Can make over open fire in coffee cans or Dutch oven on stove.) Brown meat, then add other ingredients and cook till ingredients are tender.

Nancy Sachs, St. Cloud, Mn.

FIVE HOUR STEW

2 lb. meat (round steak
  or stewing meat)
6 potatoes
6 carrots
1 c. water
3 Tbsp. tapioca

4 onions
1 Tbsp. sugar
1/2 c. celery, chopped
1 can tomatoes
Salt and pepper

Bake at 325° for 5 hours. Do not uncover until done.
Avis Paulsen, Verndale, Mn.

MEXICAN HAMBURGER STEW
(Serves 10)

2 1/2 lb. ground beef
1 medium onion, chopped
2 tsp. salt
1 tsp. chili powder
1/4 tsp. pepper

Dash of garlic salt
1 can tomato soup
1 can vegetable-beef soup
1 (15 oz.) red kidney
  beans, drained

1. Brown hamburger - push to one side. Saute onion until soft; season with salt, chili powder, pepper and garlic salt. 2. Combine soups and kidney beans. Bring to boil - lower heat and simmer 10 minutes. Stir in ground meat. 3. Simmer several minutes to blend flavors. Serve over corn chips with a green salad.
Darlene Matson, St. Cloud, Mn.

MULLIGAN STEW

3 lb. stewing beef,
  cut into cubes
Handful of seasoned
  flour
Oil
2 bay leaves
Water to cover

Any vegetables except
  turnips
1 onion, chopped
Pinch of thyme
Whole allspice
1 Tbsp. parsley

Roll meat in flour and shake off excess. Heat oil and brown meat. Using a Dutch oven, cover with water and simmer for at least 2 hours or until meat is tender. Add any or all of these vegetables, fresh carrots, peas, tomatoes, potatoes, small onions and cook till vegetables are done.
Karen Rupert, St. Cloud, Mn.

OVEN BEEF STEW

1 lb. beef stew meat,
  cubed
1 c. red wine
1 can beef consomme
1/2 tsp. salt

Dash of pepper
1 medium onion, sliced
1/4 c. fine dry bread
  crumbs
1/4 c. flour

Mix in casserole. No need to brown meat. Blend crumbs and flour and blend into mixture. Cover and bake at 300° for 3 hours. Serve over hot noodles. I usually double this.

Marge Johnson, Minneapolis, Mn.

SOUTH OF BORDER BEEF STEW

8 lb. boneless beef chuck,
  cut into 1 inch cubes
1 c. flour
2 Tbsp. salt
1/2 tsp. pepper
1/2 c. lard

4 cloves garlic, minced
4 (#2) cans tomatoes
1 tsp. chili powder
1/2 tsp. Tabasco sauce
4 small green peppers, diced
1 c. ripe olives, sliced
1 Tbsp. Worcestershire sauce

Roll beef cubes in flour combined with salt and pepper. Brown on all sides in hot lard in heavy skillet. Add minced garlic, tomatoes, chili powder, Worcestershire sauce and Tabasco sauce to meat. Cover and simmer for 2 1/2 hours until meat is tender. Add the green peppers and olives for the last 1/2 hour of cooking. Serve over noodles. Serves 24.

STEW
(Out of the Garden)

Zucchini
Tomatoes

Onions
Potatoes

Add:
Celery
Cauliflower

Carrots

I can it in the fall and all I have to do is cook beef or whatever meat you wish to use and your vegetables are all ready.

Mary R. Jones (nearly 83), Spirit Lake, Ia.

SWEET AND SOUR BEEF STEW
(Delicious)

2 or 3 lb. lean beef
  chuck
1/4 c. flour

1 tsp. salt
Dash of pepper

Cut into 1 inch cubes. Mix in bag and shake off excess. Brown well in 2 tablespoons salad oil. Drain off excess fat and add 1/2 cup catsup, 1/4 cup firmly packed brown sugar, 1/4 cup red wine vinegar and 1 teaspoon salt, 1 tablespoon Worcestershire sauce, 1 large onion (chopped), 1 cup water. Add to meat - cover pan, reduce heat and simmer gently for 1 hour and 15 minutes. Add about 6 big carrots (cut into chunks) and cook 60 minutes or until done. Serve inside or over a ring of cooked wide parslied noodles. (This is enough sauce for 3 pounds beef.)

Marty Eger, St. Paul, Mn.

WALDORF ASTORIA BEEF STEW

3 lb. pot roast, cut into
  stew sized pieces or
  you can buy cut up stew
  meat
2 large onions, cut into
  chunks

3 c. carrots, bite sized
1 c. celery, bite sized
Potatoes, quartered or
  halved according to number
  of people served

Sprinkle over the top of above ingredients:

3 Tbsp. tapioca
1 Tbsp. sugar

1 Tbsp. salt
Pepper to taste

Add:
1 can tomato soup

1 can water

Put everything together in 1 large pan or roaster. Bake at 250° for 5 hours with cover on!!! Do not open or stir until done. Do not brown meat first. Enjoy!!!

Margo Schmidt, Minneapolis, Mn.

THE COUNT OF MONTE CRISTO

2 slices white egg bread
  (3x6 inches)
1 oz. Mozzarella cheese
1 oz. sliced turkey breast

3/4 oz. sliced hard salami
  (4 to 5 slices)
1 oz. Old English cheese
Egg batter (mix equal parts
  of egg and whole cream)

Place the following in order given on 1 slice of bread:
2 slices of Mozzarella cheese, 2 slices turkey breast, 4 slices
hard salami, 2 slices Old English cheese and top with slice
of bread. Dip in prepared egg batter mix and heat on grill
until golden brown and cheese melts. Place in holding cover
or plate and serve.
Note: Serve with French fries or fruit cocktail. May
be garnished with pickles, endive or your choice.
Ralph Kulhanek, St. Paul, Mn.

DAYTON'S HOT TURKEY SALAD
(Doubled)

4 c. cooked, diced turkey
  (or chicken)
4 c. diced celery
1 c. toasted slivered
  almonds
2 tsp. diced onion

4 Tbsp. lemon juice
1 c. grated Cheddar cheese
2 c. mayonnaise
1 tsp. salt
2 c. crushed potato chips

Mix all ingredients except potato chips together and
place in baking dish. Top with crushed potato chips and
place in preheated oven at 400° for 15 minutes. Makes 12
servings - serve with fruit cups or salad and roll.
Betty Carlson

FILETTO DI TACCHINO CON FORMAGGIO
(Italian - Turkey Rolls)

1 whole raw turkey breast
1/4 c. flour
2 tsp. salt
1/4 tsp. white pepper
6 thin slices Prosciutto
1/4 c. chicken broth

6 thin slices Mozzarella or
  Swiss cheese
6 cooked asparagus tips
6 Tbsp. butter
1/2 c. Marsala or sweet
  sherry or brandy

Have the turkey breast cut in half through the breast

bone. Remove the skin and bones. Cut each breast half into 3 thin fillets. Pound each as thin as possible. Dip the fillets in a mixture of flour, salt and pepper. Place a slice of ham on each, then a slice of cheese and an asparagus. Roll up carefully and tie with thread or fasten with toothpicks. Melt 4 tablespoons butter in a skillet. Saute the rolls over very low heat until tender and browned. Transfer to a heated serving dish- to the skillet, add the wine, broth and remaining butter. Bring to boil, scraping the pan of browned particles. Pour over the rolls. Serves 6.

Chicken breasts may be prepared in the same manner.
Carolyn Smith, Fargo, N. D.

TURKEY DELUXE

4 c. diced turkey
1 c. chicken stock
2 cans mushroom soup
1 (8 oz.) pkg. Creamettes
  or noodles, cooked as
  directed

1 c. diced celery
1 onion
1 small green pepper or
  pimento

Bake at 350° for 40 minutes and sprinkle Velveeta cheese over the top and bake a few minutes more to melt the cheese. If it looks too dry after the soup is over the top, add a little hot water.
Kathryn Otto, Harvey, N. D.

TURKEY STRATA

4 slices white bread
2 c. finely chopped
  turkey
1/2 c. chopped celery
1/2 c. chopped onion
1/2 c. salad dressing

2 eggs
1 1/2 c. milk
1 (15 oz.) can cream of
  mushroom soup
1/2 c. grated cheese

Trim crusts off bread and cube. Put half of the cubes in the bottom of an 8 inch square pan. Combine turkey, celery, onion and salad dressing; spoon over top of cubed bread in pan. Arrange leftover cubed bread on top. Beat together egg and milk. Pour over mixture in pan and chill 1 hour. Pour mushroom soup on top and sprinkle with grated cheese. Bake 1 hour at 325°.
Kathy Bischof, St. Cloud, Mn.

TURKEY STROGANOFF

3 c. cooked turkey, cut
  into strips
1 (10 3/4 oz.) can
  condensed cream of
  chicken soup
1 (4 oz.) can mushroom
  stems and pieces,
  drained

1/4 c. (small jar) chopped
  pimiento, drained
1 Tbsp. instant minced onion
1 Tbsp. all-purpose flour
1/2 Tbsp. prepared mustard
1 tsp. salt
1/4 tsp. garlic powder
1/3 tsp. pepper
1 c. sour cream

In 10 inch skillet place all ingredients except sour cream; stir to combine. Cook, uncovered, over medium heat, stirring occasionally, until mixture comes to a boil, about 5 minutes. Stir in sour cream; heat through. Serve over toasted English muffins or in pastry shells.

WELSH RAREBIT

1 lb. Cheddar cheese
1/4 c. beer
1 tsp. mustard

A pinch of pepper
8 slices buttered toast

Brown slightly under grill.
      Carolyn Smith, Fargo, N. D.

BREAD
ROLLS
PASTRY

COOKING SUGGESTIONS

To toast coconut for cakes, put in pie pan and place in moderate oven. Stir often from edges, to brown evenly.

* * * * *

Flour should be sifted once before measuring. Fill the cup without packing.

* * * * *

Do not grease the sides of cake pans, grease only the bottoms.

* * * * *

When beating egg whites do not tap beater on bowl of egg whites. The jarring of beater will cause the whites to lose a great deal of their fluffiness. The beater should be tapped on the hand to clear off the whites.

* * * * *

Rub the bottom of the soup cup with a sliced whole garlic to accent the flavor of Navy Bean Soup.

* * * * *

Eggs should be at least three days old before using in cakes.

* * * * *

```
SLOW OVEN . . . . . . . . 250 to 325 degrees
MODERATE OVEN. . . . 350 to 375 degrees
HOT OVEN . . . . . . . . . 400 to 450 degrees
VERY HOT OVEN . . . . 450 to 500 degrees
```

* * * * *

When making cake icing or candy consisting of milk or cream and sugar, add one teaspoon of ordinary table syrup for each cup of sugar used. Boil in the usual way. Your finished product will be much smoother and not so apt to become sugary.

PRESERVED CHILDREN

Take 1 large field, half a dozen children, 2 or 3 small dogs, a pinch of brook and some pebbles. Mix the children and dogs well together; put them on the field, stirring constantly. Pour the brook over the pebbles; sprinkle the field with flowers; spread over all a deep blue sky and bake in the sun. When brown, set away to cool in the bathtub.

ALMOND BREAD

1/2 c. butter	2 tsp. brown sugar
2 c. sugar	1 tsp. salt
4 eggs	1 tsp. almond extract
2 2/3 c. flour	Blanched almonds to sprinkle
1 c. milk	on top before baking

Combine and pour into a buttered and sugared loaf pan. Sprinkle on almonds. Bake at 350° for 1 hour or till done.

Glaze:

8 Tbsp. powdered sugar	1 tsp. almond extract
1 Tbsp. cream	

Stir up and brush over loaf when cooled.
Karen Rupert, St. Cloud, Mn.

SWEDISH APRICOT NUT BREAD

1 c. dried apricots	1/2 - 1 c. brandy

Soak apricots in brandy at least 3 hours, drain and cut each apricot into 6 pieces. Reserve 1/4 cup brandy.

1 c. sugar	2 c. flour
2 Tbsp. softened butter	2 1/2 tsp. baking powder
1 egg, slightly beaten	1/2 tsp. baking soda
Grated rind of 1 lemon	1/2 tsp. salt
1/2 c. orange juice	3/4 c. chopped nuts

Cream sugar and butter till fluffy. Add egg and lemon rind and beat till smooth. Add 1/4 cup brandy and orange juice. Sift dry ingredients together and resift into batter gradually, stirring well. Fold in nuts and apricots. Butter an 8 inch pan and line with brown paper and butter again. Let stand 20 minutes before baking. Bake at 350° for 1 hour. Turn out of pan while hot and peel off paper. Let cool on rack. Mellow for 24 hours before cutting.
Karen Karnowski, St. Cloud, Mn.

BACON CHEESE BREAD

3 3/4 c. biscuit mix
3/4 c. shredded American
  cheese
1 egg

6 slices bacon, cooked crisp
  and broken
1 1/2 c. buttermilk

Mix biscuit mix, cheese and bacon. Beat egg into buttermilk and combine with biscuit mixture. Stir just until blended. Pour into a loaf pan, greased and floured. Bake at 350° for 1 hour. Serve hot. If there is leftovers, toast the slices and serve them hot.

BANANA BREAD

Cream:
1 c. shortening (1/2 butter
  and 1/2 shortening)

2 c. sugar

Add:
6 ripe mashed bananas
4 well beaten eggs
2 1/2 c. cake flour

1 tsp. salt
2 tsp. soda
1 c. walnuts

Blend dry and wet ingredients. Do not overmix. Makes 2 loaves. Bake 45 to 50 minutes at 350°. Check for doneness. It takes 55 to 60 minutes for me.
Recipe from Minneapolis

*BANANA BREAD

1 c. shortening
1 c. sugar
2 eggs, beaten
2 c. flour
1 tsp. soda (level)

3 crushed bananas
1/2 c. chopped walnuts
1 tsp. vanilla
1/2 tsp. salt

Cream sugar and shortening, add eggs, mix well, add soda, salt, and flour. Mix well. Fold in bananas, walnuts, vanilla. Place in greased 9x5 inch loaf pan. Bake at 350° for about 70 minutes or until toothpick does not stick.
*Even I can do these!
From an old W. E. Co. Inst.
Maynard L. Smith, Melrose, Mn.

BANANA BREAD

2/3 c. sugar
1/3 c. shortening
2 eggs
2 tsp. baking powder

1/2 tsp. soda
1/2 tsp. salt
1 3/4 c. flour
1 c. mashed bananas
Walnuts (optional)

Bake at 350° for approximately 30 minutes.
Marlys Stoll, Austin, Mn.

WORLD'S BEST BANANA BREAD

1 c. sugar
1/2 c. shortening
2 eggs
1 1/4 c. mashed bananas

1 1/4 c. flour
1/2 tsp. salt
1 tsp. soda
1/2 c. chopped nuts

Cream sugar and shortening. Add eggs and bananas. Mix well. Stir in flour and nuts, salt and soda until blended thoroughly. Bake 1 hour in 9x5 inch greased and floured loaf pan at 350°. Cool in pan 10 - 15 minutes, then invert on wire rack to cool.
L. Richards

BANANA BREAD

1/2 c. oleo
1 c. sugar
2 eggs
3 very ripe bananas,
    mashed
3 Tbsp. buttermilk
    (add 1 tsp. soda in it)

2 c. flour, sift
1 tsp. baking powder
Pinch of salt
3 or 4 tsp. vanilla
1/2 c. nuts

Mix oleo and sugar, add eggs. Add bananas alternately with the buttermilk and soda mixture and the flour, baking powder and salt. Add vanilla and nuts. Bake at 350° in greased loaf pan for 1 hour or longer.
Bettie Mallon, Minneapolis, Mn.

BANANA BREAD

5 large ripe bananas
4 eggs, well beaten
1 c. shortening
2 c. sugar
4 c. flour

2 tsp. soda
1 tsp. salt
1 Tbsp. lemon juice
1 c. chopped nuts

Beat eggs and bananas well and set aside. Cream together shortening, sugar till light and fluffy. Add bananas and eggs, mix well. Add dry ingredients, mix well, add nuts. Pour into 2 loaf pans or 4 small pans. Bake at 350° for 40 - 45 minutes.

Florence Peine, St. Paul, Mn.

BANANA NUT BREAD

1 c. sugar
2 eggs
2 c. flour
1/2 tsp. soda
1/2 tsp. vanilla
1/2 tsp. salt

1/2 c. oil
3 bananas
1 tsp. baking powder
3 Tbsp. milk
1/2 c. nuts, chopped

Beat sugar and oil. Add eggs and bananas, beat well. Add liquid ingredients to the flour mixture and beat well. Add milk and vanilla and nuts. Mix well. Bake 45 - 60 minutes in 350° oven. Use 9x5x3 inch loaf pan.

Marie Miller, St. Paul, Mn.

BANANA NUT BREAD

1/4 c. shortening
1/2 c. sugar
1 well beaten egg
1 c. bran
2 Tbsp. water
1 1/2 c. mashed bananas

1 1/2 c. flour
1/2 tsp. salt
2 tsp. baking powder
1/2 tsp. baking soda
1 tsp. vanilla
1/2 c. chopped nuts

Cream shortening and sugar, add egg, then bran; mix thoroughly. Combine water and mashed bananas. Add alternately with sifted dry ingredients. Mix thoroughly. Add vanilla and nuts. Bake in greased 5x9 inch loaf pan in moderate oven (350°) for 1 hour. (Any kind of bran can be used successfully.)

Winnie Johnson, St. Paul, Mn.

BEER BREAD

3 c. self-rising flour   12 oz. can lukewarm beer
3 Tbsp. sugar

    Mix, pour into greased loaf pan, let stand 15 minutes and then bake at 450° for 45 minutes.
                 Paula Rogers, Detroit Lakes, Mn.

BEER BREAD

3 c. self-rising flour   1/3 c. honey or sugar
1 (12 oz.) can beer

    Mix together, put into loaf pan. Bake at 350°.
               Norma Lee, Wadena, Mn.

CARAWAY RYE
(Bohemian Style)

    Peel and cut into pieces one small potato; cook until well done. In 1 1/2 quart pan, put 1 cup hot water; add shortening size of egg; let melt. Add 2 tablespoons salt, potato and liquid put through strainer; add enough water to fill pan inch from top. Liquid should be warm. Add 2 packages dry yeast dissolved in 1/2 cup warm water. In mixing bowl, mix 4 cups rye flour and 4 cups white flour. Form well in center and add 2 tablespoons caraway seed, then yeast mixture; beat well. Add flour to make stiff dough (3 cups). Put on floured board and knead well. Place in greased bowl, turning to grease top. Cover; let rise in warm place until doubled, about 2 hours. Turn out on board and cut into 4 loaves. Form each loaf and place on floured cooky sheet, cover, let rise 1 hour. Pick each loaf lightly with fork after forming loaves. Preheat oven to 350°. Lighty pick with fork again and lightly brush top with water before putting in oven to prevent cracking. Bake 1 hour. Slide off pan on cooling rack and grease top.

CHOCOLATE BANANA LOAF

1 1/2 c. sugar
1/2 c. butter
1/2 c. sour milk or
   buttermilk
3/4 tsp. baking soda

2 mashed bananas
2 eggs
1/2 tsp. vanilla
2 c. flour
2 sq. chocolate and nuts if
   desired

Put eggs in before bananas - be sure to mix well.
Bake in loaf pan at 350° for 1 hour.
                    Alice Ann Hanson, Grand Forks, N. D.

BLUEBERRY BANANA BREAD

2 c. sifted flour
2 tsp. baking powder
1/2 tsp. salt

1/2 c. margarine
3/4 c. sugar
2 eggs

   Mix well.   Add:
1 c. ripe bananas, mashed   1 c. blueberries

Fold blueberries in last. Bake at 350° for 1 1/4 hours.
Cool before slicing.
                    Mary Paul, Minneapolis, Mn.

BUTTER BRICKLE BREAD

1 pkg. butter brickle
   cake mix
1 pkg. instant vanilla
   pudding

4 eggs
1 c. water
1/2 c. oil
1/4 c. poppy seed

   Combine first 5 ingredients and mix well. Fold in
poppy seed. Pour into 2 large loaf pans or 6 small loaf
pans and bake at 325° for 45 minutes. Cut and spread
slices (can be made into sandwiches) with following spread:

1 stick softened margarine   1 (3 oz.) pkg. Philadelphia
2 - 3 Tbsp. powdered sugar   cream cheese

   This can also be made in a Bundt pan and use the
spread as a frosting.
                    Mavis Ann Hjulberg, St. Paul, Mn.

CINNAMONY APPLE ROLL

1 1/2 c. sugar	1 Tbsp. butter
2 c. water	1/4 c. cinnamon candies
2 c. finely chopped apples	

Put sugar and water in cake pan. Heat over low heat till dissolved.

Biscuit Dough: Sift together -

2 c. flour	4 tsp. baking powder
1 tsp. salt	

Cut in 6 tablespoons shortening. Stir in 3/4 cup milk, till well blended. Roll out 1/3 inch thick. Roll in oblong roll. Put on apples with a few dabs of butter and a slight sprinkling of sugar and cinnamon. Roll in oblong roll. Cut into 12 equal slices. Place in pan of boiling syrup. Bake 25 minutes (450° oven). Serve warm with syrup from baking pan.

Elynor S. Storkamp, St. Cloud, Mn.

HOT CHEESE CORN BREAD

1 c. yellow corn meal	1 1/2 c. shredded sharp
1 c. sifted all-purpose	American cheese
flour	1 egg
1/4 c. sugar	1 c. milk
1/2 tsp. salt	1/4 c. soft shortening
4 tsp. baking powder	

Heat oven to 375° (moderately hot). Sift together corn meal, flour, sugar, salt and baking powder. Add cheese. Add egg, milk and shortening. Beat with a rotary beater until smooth, about 1 minute. Do not overbeat. Pour into a greased 8 inch square pan. Bake 30 minutes. Cut into squares; serve hot. Serves 8.

COWBOY BREAD

2 1/2 c. flour	1 1/2 tsp. cinnamon
1 1/2 c. brown sugar	2/3 c. butter or shortening

Mix these ingredients to fine crumbs with electric

beater. Measure 1/4 cup for topping and set aside. Add
following ingredients to remaining crumbs:

1 c. buttermilk	2 eggs
1/2 tsp. salt	2 tsp. baking powder
1/2 tsp. soda	

Beat well, pour into pan and sprinkle topping over top.
Bake 20 minutes at 375° or until done.

Myrtle Solomon, Fargo, N. D.

DATE-COCOA BREAD

Pour 1 cup boiling water over 1 cup dates. Add 1 teaspoon soda. Cool while mixing:

3/4 c. sugar	2 Tbsp. cocoa (very rounded)
2 Tbsp. butter	Salt
1 egg	Vanilla
1 1/2 c. flour	1/3 c. walnuts

Pour date mixture over flour, etc. Bake slowly at 350°
about 40 - 45 minutes. Spray cans or pans with Pam.
Makes approximately 4 cans or 2 small loaves. Let set 10
minutes before taking out of pans.

Kathy Neels, St. Cloud, Mn.

DILLY CASSEROLE BREAD

1 pkg. active dry yeast	1 Tbsp. butter
1/4 c. warm water	2 tsp. dill seed
1 c. creamed cottage	1 tsp. salt
cheese, heated to	1/4 tsp. soda
lukewarm	1 egg
2 Tbsp. sugar	2 1/4 to 2 1/2 c. all-purpose
1 Tbsp. instant minced onion	flour

Soften yeast in warm water. In mixing bowl, combine
cottage cheese, sugar, onion, butter, dill seed, salt, soda,
egg and yeast. Gradually add flour to form a stiff dough,
beating well after each addition. Cover; let rise in warm
place until doubled, 50 to 60 minutes. Stir down dough with
a spoon. Place in well greased 8 inch round (1 1/2 or 2
quart) casserole. Let rise again in warm place until doubled
about 30 to 40 minutes. Bake at 350° for 40 to 50 minutes,

until golden brown. Brush with soft butter and sprinkle with coarse salt.

Cecilia, Leverson, Fargo, N. D.

ENGLISH MUFFIN BREAD

2 pkg. yeast
6 c. unsifted flour
1 Tbsp. sugar
2 tsp. salt

2 c. milk
1/4 tsp. baking soda
1/2 c. water
Corn meal

Combine 3 cups flour, yeast, sugar, salt, soda. Heat liquids to 120° - 130° F. Add to dry mixture, beat well. Stir in rest of flour to make stiff batter. Spoon into 2 (8 1/2 x 4 1/2 inch) pans that have been greased and sprinkled with corn meal. Sprinkle tops with corn meal. Cover; let rise in warm place 45 minutes. Bake at 400° for 25 minutes. Remove from pans.

Mrs. Clayone Carlson (Roy), Fargo, N. D.

GEIGOL BREAD
(Chicken Bread)

2 1/2 lb. chicken
1/2 c. chopped onion
1 tsp. salt
1/2 tsp. pepper

1/2 c. half & half or 1 small
  can condensed milk
1 pkg. hot roll mix or your
  own dough

Cut chicken into serving pieces. Prepare roll mix; let rise once. Divide dough in 2 parts, about 2/3 and 1/3. Roll out larger portion and place in a greased 9x12 inch cake pan, keeping dough well up on sides of pan. Arrange chicken pieces in either a horizontal or vertical position (so it can be cut into squares). Sprinkle with salt and pepper. Add the onions, pour cream over all. Roll out smaller portion of dough. Wet edge of dough on sides of pan. Place top crust on meat and pinch to seal. With scissors, cut small "V" across top. Let rise until light. Bake at 375° for 20 minutes, then bake for 40 minutes at 350° or until crust sounds hollow when tapped with knife handle. Serve while it is hot. Can be rewarmed; refrigerate leftovers immediately.

Kathy Bischof, St. Cloud, Mn.

MAMA'S GINGERBREAD
(Recipe over 100 years old)

1 c. sugar
1/2 c. molasses
1/4 c. shortening (can
　use oil)
1/2 tsp. ginger
1 tsp. cinnamon

1 tsp. cloves
1 tsp. soda, dissolved in
　1 tsp. hot water
2 1/2 c. flour
3 eggs, well beaten

Stir all together, add to above ingredients, and mix well. Add flour to other ingredients. Add eggs, the last before baking. Mixture will be thin. Bake at 350° or until cake springs back, about 45 minutes.
Ruth Braun, Owatonna, Mn.

HOBO BREAD

1 1/2 c. raisins
1 c. hot water
1 c. sugar
3 Tbsp. oil
1 egg

2 tsp. soda
2 c. flour
1/2 c. nuts
Pinch of salt

Boil raisins in water, blned sugar and oil. Add egg and salt, add raisin mixture to flour mixture; add nuts. Bake at 325° for 1 hour in 3 (No. 3) cans which have been greased and floured. Fill 1/2 full. Remove from cans before cool.
Helen M. Gludt, Bottineau, N. D.

IRISH SODA BREAD

3 c. sifted flour
2/3 c. sugar
1 Tbsp. baking powder
1 tsp. soda
1 tsp. salt

1 c. raisins or currants
2 eggs
1 1/2 c. buttermilk
2 Tbsp. salad oil

Sift dry ingredients into a large bowl; add raisins and stir gently. In another bowl, blend eggs, buttermilk and oil. Add liquid to dry ingredients all at once and stir by hand only until moist. Turn into greased loaf pan and bake approximately 1 hour, or until center tests done, at 350°. Cool in pan. Be sure bread is completely cooled before slicing. This bread can be baked in a round 1 quart casserole, if desired.

Ione "Corrigan" Brown, Past President,
St. Cloud Council

IRISH SODA BREAD

4 c. unsifted flour	1 c. currants or raisins
1 tsp. salt	1 or 2 tsp. caraway seed
3 tsp. baking powder	4 Tbsp. butter or margarine
1 tsp. soda	1 egg, slightly beaten
1/4 c. sugar	1 3/4 c. buttermilk (or 1 1/2 c. milk and 1/4 c. vinegar)

Combine and sift all dry ingredients in a large bowl. Add shortening and cut in with pastry blender or 2 knives, until crumbly as with pastry. Mix egg with milk, add to dry ingredients and stir till blended. Turn out onto floured board and knead till smooth for 2 or 3 minutes. Divide dough in half and shape each half into round loaf. Place each loaf in a greased 8 inch cake or pie tin. Press dough to sides of pan to make a uniform circle. With floured knife, cut crosses on top of loaves, cut 1 inch deep in the middle. Bake in a preheated 375° oven for 35 to 40 minutes.

Claren Kane, Sauk Centre, Mn.

LEMON BREAD

1/2 c. shortening	1 1/2 c. flour
1 c. sugar	1 tsp. baking powder
2 eggs	1/2 c. milk
1/2 tsp. salt	Grated rind of 1 lemon

Cream shortening and sugar. Add well beaten eggs. Mix in flour, salt and baking powder. Put rind into milk and add to first mixture. Bake in a greased loaf tin for 45 minutes in 350° oven. Remove from oven and pour over while hot, juice of 1 lemon mixed with 1/2 cup sugar.

Bettie Mallon, Minneapolis, Mn.

LEMON BREAD

1/2 c. shortening
1 c. sugar
2 eggs, beaten
1 2/3 c. flour
1 tsp. baking powder
1/2 tsp. salt

1/4 c. milk
1/2 c. nuts, chopped
Grated peel of 1 lemon
 about 1/4 c.
1/2 tsp. lemon juice

Cream shortening with sugar, add eggs. Add flour with baking powder and salt sifted together. Alternate flour and milk, mix in nuts, lemon peel and juice. Pour into greased pan, (5x9 inch loaf pan). Bake at 350° for 1 hour.

Topping:

1/2 c. sugar

Juice of 1 lemon

Mix sugar, lemon juice; spoon over loaf as soon as it comes from oven.
Lillian Herrick, St. Paul, Mn.

OLD FASHIONED JOHNNY CAKE

1/2 c. sugar
1/4 c. butter
1/4 c. vegetable shortening
2 eggs, beaten
1 c. flour

1 c. corn meal
1 tsp. soda
1 tsp. baking powder
1 c. buttermilk

Bake in shallow pan, 8x8 inches or 9x9 inches. Bake at 350° for 45 minutes.
Mrs. E. F. Braun, Owatonna, Mn.

KAMISH
(Jewish Bread)

3 eggs, beaten slightly
 for 1 minute
1 1/4 c. granulated
 sugar
1 c. cooking oil

2 tsp. baking powder
1 rounded tsp. cinnamon
1/4 tsp. salt
4 1/2 c. flour

Beat eggs and add sugar, salt and oil. Beat 1 minute. Add baking powder and cinnamon. Mix well. Add flour a

little at a time. Mold into 2 rolls on a greased cookie sheet.
Bake at 350° for 55 to 60 minutes. Remove from oven and
slice while hot.

Helen Kruse, Fargo, N. D.

LEMON BREAD

1/2 c. vegetable oil	1/2 c. milk
1 c. sugar	1 1/2 c. flour
1 grated rind of lemon	1 tsp. baking powder
2 eggs	1/4 tsp. salt

Combine all ingredients well. Grease and flour loaf
pan. Bake at 350° for 50 minutes or till browned (top will
crack).

Glaze: Combine 1/4 cup sugar and juice of 1 lemon.
Brush over loaf while still warm.

Karen Rupert, St. Cloud, Mn.

NUT ROLL

1 lb. Brazil nuts	1 lb. dates, sliced lengthwise
1 lb. walnuts (whole)	1 small bottle maraschino
1 1/2 c. flour	cherries
1 tsp. salt	1 tsp. baking powder
	1 1/2 c. sugar

Sift flour, salt, baking powder and sugar over dates,
nuts and half the cherries. Beat 4 eggs and stir into mixture. Add remaining cherries and juice. Bake in 2 loaf
pans lined with waxed paper for 1 hour at 325°.

Stan and Phylis Patyk, Sauk Centre, Mn.

NUT BREAD

Blend together:

1 c. sugar	2 c. graham flour
1 c. brown sugar	

Sift together:

1 c. flour	1 tsp. salt
1 tsp. baking powder	

Add alternately to blended ingredients (2 cups sour milk or buttermilk with 1 teaspoon soda dissolved in it) and dry sifted ingredients. Add 1 cup chopped walnuts and 1 1/2 - 2 cups raisins. Use well greased and floured 6x9 inch pan. Bake at 350° for 1 hour.

Sue Hick, Detroit Lakes, Mn.

OATMEAL BREAD

1 c. quick oatmeal	1 tsp. salt
2 c. boiling water	7/8 c. brown sugar
over oatmeal	1 yeast cake (pkg.) in 1/4
5 Tbsp. shortening	c. warm water

Let first 5 ingredients stand until lukewarm after being mixed together. Then add yeast, 2 tablespoons molasses and approximately 4 1/2 cups flour. More molasses and raisins may be added if desired. Let rise. Mix down once and form into 2 loaves. Bake at 350° for approximately 35 - 45 minutes.

Lu Boyer, Grand Forks, N. D.

ORANGE CRANBERRY BREAD

2 c. sifted all-purpose	2 Tbsp. butter or margarine
flour	1/2 c. orange juice
1/4 tsp. salt	2 Tbsp. hot water
1 1/2 tsp. baking powder	3/4 c. chopped nuts
1/2 tsp. soda	1 c. cranberries, coarsely
1 c. sugar	cut
1 egg, slightly beaten	Grated rind of 1 orange

Sift dry ingredients together. Melt butter or margarine. Add egg, butter, orange juice and water to dry ingredients and mix only until dry ingredients are moistened. Fold in nuts, cranberries and orange rind. Pour batter into a greased 9x5 inch loaf pan, allow to stand 20 minutes. Bake in 350° oven for about 1 hour. Makes 1 loaf. (Allow bread to stand 24 hours before cutting. Flavor and cutting improves with standing.)

Karen Rupert, St. Cloud, Mn.

ORANGE NUT BREAD

Blend together:

2 Tbsp. butter   1 c. honey

Add:

1 beaten egg   1 Tbsp. grated orange rind

Mix well. Sift together:

2 3/4 c. flour   1/2 tsp. soda
2 1/2 tsp. baking powder   1/2 tsp. salt

Add alternately with 3/4 cup orange juice. Add 3/4 cup chopped nuts. Bake in loaf pan for 1 hour and 10 minutes at 325° F.

Marge Zig Carlson

POPPY SEED BREAD

1 pkg. lemon cake mix   1 c. water
1 pkg. lemon pudding   1/2 c. salad oil
  (instant)   2 Tbsp. poppy seed
4 eggs

Mix in order given and bake in greased pans (2 loaves or 6 small pans) at 350° for 45 - 50 minutes or 30 - 35 minutes.

Variation: Drizzle with glaze if desired.

Sue Peterson

POPPY SEED BREAD

1 c. margarine   1 tsp. almond extract
1 1/2 c. sugar   1 tsp. soda
4 eggs   1 tsp. baking powder
1 c. buttermilk   1/2 tsp. salt
2 1/2 c. flour   1/2 c. sugar
2 oz. pkg. poppy seed   1 tsp. cinnamon

Mix the 1/2 cup sugar and 1 teaspoon cinnamon and set aside. Soak poppy seeds in buttermilk and almond extract. Cream margarine and sugar, add egg yolk. Add dry ingredients alternately with buttermilk. Beat egg whites and fold into mixture. Put half of batter into each of 2 loaf pans. Sprinkle with the cinnamon-sugar mixture. Add

1748-81   329

remaining batter and sprinkle remaining sugar on top. Bake for 1 hour at 350°.

Bettie Mallon

PEANUT BUTTER BREAD

Shortening	1 3/4 c. milk
1/2 c. creamy peanut butter	2 1/4 c. flour
1 tsp. vanilla	4 tsp. baking powder
3/4 c. sugar	1/2 tsp. salt

Preheat oven to 350°. Grease 9x5x3 inch loaf pan with shortening. Place sugar, peanut butter and vanilla in large mixer bowl. Beat with electric mixer until fluffy. Blend milk into peanut butter mixture gradually. In medium sized mixing bowl, stir together flour, baking powder and salt. At low speed blend 1/3 of flour mixture at a time into the peanut butter mixture, beating smooth after each addition. Spread batter into greased pan and bake 45 - 50 minutes.

Stephanie Foster, St. Cloud, Mn.

PRUNE NUT BREAD

1 c. oil	2 tsp. soda in 1 c.
2 c. sugar	buttermilk
3 eggs, slighty beaten	1/2 tsp. salt
1 Jr. size jar prune	1/2 tsp. cinnamon
and tapioca baby food	1 tsp. vanilla
2 1/2 c. + 1 Tbsp. unsifted	1 c. chopped nuts
flour	

Mix in order given. Add dry ingredients alternately with milk and soda. Pour into 2 well greased and floured bread pans. I use smaller pans and make more loaves. Fill small pans about half full. Bake 1/2 hour at 350°. Reduce to 325° and bake 1/2 hour more.

Irene McDonald, Owatonna, Mn.

PUMPKIN BREAD

Boil 1/2 cup raisins, drain and let cool, but save the raisin juice for the 1/2 cup of liquid you will need.

1 1/2 c. sugar	1/2 tsp. salt

2 eggs
1 c. pumpkin
1/2 c. Wesson oil
1/2 c. water
1 tsp. soda
1/2 tsp. baking powder

1/2 tsp. each of ground
   cloves, cinnamon and
   nutmeg
1 2/3 c. flour
1/2 c. nuts
1/2 c. raisins

Mix in order given. Bake in ungreased loaf pan at 350° for 1 hour or longer.

Bettie Mallon

RHUBARB BREAD

Stir together in this order:

1 1/2 c. brown sugar
2/3 c. salad oil
1 egg
1 c. sour milk

1 tsp. each salt, soda,
   vanilla
2 1/2 c. flour
1 1/2 c. diced fresh rhubarb
1/2 c. chopped nuts

Pour into 2 greased loaf pans. Sprinkle over batter a mixture of:

1/2 c. sugar   1 Tbsp. butter

Bake at 325° about 60 minutes. Don't overbake.

Gerri Ruprecht, St. Cloud, Mn.

RHUBARB BREAD

1 1/2 c. brown sugar
2/3 c. salad oil
1 egg
1 c. buttermilk
1 tsp. salt

1 tsp. soda
1 tsp. vanilla
2 1/2 c. flour
1 1/2 c. rubarb
1/2 c. nuts

Mix all ingredients together. Put into 2 greased 9x5 inch tins. Sprinkle over batter:

1/2 c. sugar   1 Tbsp. butter
1 tsp. cinnamon

Bake at 325° for 1 hour, do not overbake.

R. Arnold, Sauk Centre, Mn.; Karen Rupert, St. Cloud, Mn.; Elynn S. Storkamp, St. Cloud, Mn.

1748-81

SWEDISH CHRISTMAS BREAD

1 c. flour   1 Tbsp. cold water
1/2 c. butter

Mix flour and butter until crumbly. Add cold water and mix. Pat onto ungreased cookie sheet in 3 long strips, 3 inches wide.

1 c. water   3 eggs
1/2 c. butter   1/2 tsp. almond extract
1 c. flour

Put water into saucepan with butter and heat to boiling point. As you take from heat, add flour and stir until smooth. Stir in eggs, one at a time and beat well after each egg. Add almond extract and beat again. Spread on top of first mixture. Bake 55 - 60 minutes at 360°. Frost with powdered sugar-butter frosting. Trim with green and red candied cherries and slivered almonds.
Lois Sandberg, St. Cloud, Mn.

THREE FLOUR BREAD

2 pkg. dry yeast   2 c. milk
1 c. all-purpose flour   1/2 c. brown sugar
1 1/2 c. whole wheat flour   3 Tbsp. shortening
1/2 c. rye flour   2 Tbsp. white sugar
1 Tbsp. salt   2 1/4 - 2 1/2 c. white flour

Combine yeast with 3 first flours. Heat together milk, brown sugar, shortening, white sugar and salt, stirring until lukewarm. Add to dry mixture. Stir in additional flour if needed. Knead 8 - 10 minutes. Let rise to double in size. Bake at 375° for 40 minutes. Makes 2 loaves.
Lillian Herrick, St. Paul, Mn.

WHOLE-WHEAT BROWN BREAD

2 c. whole wheat flour   1 tsp. baking powder
1/2 c. white flour   1 tsp. soda
1 tsp. salt   1 1/2 c. sour milk or
1/4 c. oil   buttermilk
1/4 c. molasses   1/4 c. honey

332

Grease a loaf pan. Combine all ingredients till moist, put into pan. Bake 40 - 50 minutes at 350°.
Karen Rupert, St. Cloud, Mn.

YULEKAGE
(Christmas Bread)

1/4 c. shortening	1/2 c. lukewarm water
1/2 c. sugar	3 cardamon seeds, crushed
1 egg, well beaten	1/2 c. mixed fruit peels
1 tsp. salt	1 c. white raisins
1 pt. whole milk, scalded	8 candied cherries
2 cakes yeast	About 7 c. flour

Dissolve yeast in lukewarm water. While milk is hot, add sugar, shortening, salt and egg. Let mixture become lukewarm. Add yeast and cardamon seed. Add 1/2 of the flour, mix well. Add fruit peel and rest of flour. Knead dough well. Let dough rise, punch down and let rise again. Shape into 3 round loaves on cookie sheet. When double in size, bake at 350° for 1 hour. After baking, mix a little sugar and hot water and wipe over loaves with clean cloth. Decorate with quartered cherries.
Elynor Pederson, Minneapolis, Mn.

ZUCCHINI BREAD

Stir together:

2 c. zucchini, peeled, seeds out and grated	1 c. raisins
2 c. sugar	1 c. walnuts

Beat:

3 eggs	3 tsp. vanilla

Add 1 cup oil. Fold into above mixture:

3 c. flour	3 tsp. cinnamon
1 tsp. salt	1/4 tsp. baking powder
1 tsp. soda	

Makes 2 loaves. Bake for 1 hour at 325°.
Kathy Neels, St. Cloud, Mn.; Arlene Jewell, Bismarck, N. D.: Evelyn Fellows, Austin, Mn.

ZUCCHINI BREAD

3 eggs
2 c. grated zucchini
  (raw)
1 tsp. salt
3 tsp. vanilla
3 c. flour

3 tsp. cinnamon
1/2 to 1 c. nuts
1 c. oil
2 c. sugar
1/4 tsp. baking powder
1 tsp. soda

Beat eggs, add oil, sugar, zucchini and vanilla. Mix lightly. Add flour and dry ingredients. Mix until blended. Bake at 325° for 1 hour. Makes 2 loaves.

Winnie Johnson, St. Paul, Mn.

ZUCCHINI NUT BREAD

3 eggs
1 c. cooking oil
2 c. sugar
2 c. grated or ground
  zucchini
2 tsp. vanilla

3 c. flour
1 tsp. soda
1/4 tsp. baking powder
1 tsp. salt
3 tsp. cinnamon
1/2 c. nuts

Beat eggs till light and foamy. Add oil, sugar, zucchini and vanilla. Mix lightly. Combine dry ingredients and add to oil mixture. Stir just to blend. Bake in 2 greased and floured loaf pans at 325° for 1 hour or until done. Remove from pans at once and cool on racks.

Sandra Aarestad, Fargo, N. D.

ZUCCHINI-PINEAPPLE BREAD

3 eggs
1 c. vegetable oil
2 c. sugar
2 tsp. vanilla
2 c. shredded, unpeeled
  zucchini, drained
1 (8 1/4 oz.) can crushed
  pineapple, well drained

2 tsp. baking soda
1 1/2 tsp. cinnamon
1 tsp. salt
3/4 tsp. nutmeg
1/4 tsp. baking powder
1 c. chopped dates
1 c. chopped nuts
3 c. all-purpose flour

Beat together eggs, oil, sugar and vanilla until thick. Stir in remaining ingredients; mix well. Pour into 2 greased and floured 9x5x3 inch loaf pans. Bake in preheated 350° oven about 1 hour or until wooden pick inserted in center comes out clean. Cool on wire racks for 10 minutes; then remove from pans. Cool completely before slicing.

Mrs. Kurt (Lucille) Jensen, Fargo, N. D.

ZUCCHINI WHEAT GERM BREAD

1 1/4 c. wheat germ
3 c. flour
3 tsp. baking powder
1 tsp. salt
2 tsp. cinnamon
2 eggs

1 3/4 c. sugar
2 tsp. vanilla
2/3 c. oil
3 c. grated zucchini
1 c. nuts

Mix together wheat germ, flour, baking powder, salt, cinnamon and nuts. Beat eggs until light and fluffy. Beat in sugar, vanilla and oil. Stir in zucchini. Gradually stir in dry ingredients. Put into greased loaf pans. Bake at 350° for 1 hour or until pick comes out clean, 8x4 inch pans.

Mrs. Clayone Carlson (Roy), Fargo, N. D.

BEER BISCUITS

4 c. Bisquick
3 Tbsp. granulated sugar

1 (12 fl. oz.) can beer

Bake in well greased hot muffin tins in a preheated 375° oven. Bake 20 minutes or until browned. Servings: 18 medium.

Diane Schmitz, St. Cloud, Mn.

BUTTERMILK BISCUITS

2 c. flour
1/2 tsp. salt
3 tsp. baking powder

1/4 tsp. soda
1/4 tsp. cream of tartar

Mix together and sift. Cut in 1/3 cup shortening. Add 1 cup buttermilk. Handle as little as possible. Roll out on lightly floured board, cut into shape. Grease a baking sheet with butter and bake in 475° oven 12 - 15 minutes.

Dee Olson, St. Paul, Mn.

HOMEMADE BISCUIT MIX

8 c. flour
1 c. dry milk
2 tsp. salt

4 Tbsp. baking powder
1 1/2 c. vegetable shortening

Sift dry ingredients together 3 times. Cut in shortening with pastry blender until it looks like Bisquick. Use as you would the commercial mix.

Dee Olson, St. Paul, Mn.

BUN RECIPE

1 c. milk
1 tsp. salt
2 pkg. dry yeast
7 c. sifted all-purpose
   flour

3 eggs, beaten
1/2 c. sugar
6 Tbsp. shortening
1 c. warm water

Combine milk, sugar, salt and shortening in top of double boiler. Scald and cool to lukewarm. Dissolve yeast in cup of warm water and let stand 5 minutes. Add 2 cups flour to milk mixture and stir in yeast mixture. Beat eggs into batter, blend thoroughly. Add 5 cups flour or less if possible, knead till elastic. Put into greased bowl and cover to rise until double in size. Make into buns and let rise again and bake for 12 minutes at 400°. Brush with butter after baking.

Mike and Vonnie Bakke, Willmar, Mn.

BUNS

2 c. warm potato water
2 c. milk, scalded
1/2 c. butter or lard
1 Tbsp. salt

3/4 c. sugar
3 eggs, beaten
2 pkg. yeast in 1/2 c. warm
   water

Add flour enough to make soft dough (about 12 cups). Let rise once - punch down. Let rise again - punch down - let rest 10 minutes. Make buns - let rise to double in size. Bake at 350° for 15 - 17 minutes.

Darlene Lee

HAMBURGER BUNS

1 c. lukewarm water
1 Tbsp. sugar

1 yeast cake (dry or ??)

Combine above, let stand till yeast is dissolved well.
Then add:

1 c. milk, scalded and
   cooled

3 c. flour

Beat well, then add:

1 egg
1 c. flour

3 Tbsp. sugar
2 tsp. salt

Beat well and add 6 to 7 tablespoons shortening, add
1 or 2 more cups flour while beating, or kneading until no
longer sticky. Let stand and rise until double in size.
Form into balls of desired size. Place on cookie sheets, let
rise till double size again, then bake at 375° for about 20
minutes or until brown.

JACKIE'S BUNS

3/4 c. milk
1 tsp. salt
1/2 c. warm water
1 egg, beaten

1/4 c. sugar
1/4 c. butter
2 pkg. yeast
3 1/2 c. flour

Dissolve yeast in warm water, scald milk. Stir in sugar, salt and butter to the milk. Cool to lukewarm and add
yeast to milk mixture. Add beaten egg. Start with 2 cups
flour, beat till smooth, stir in remaining flour. Butter bowl
and cover, let rise till doubled, punch down. Makes about
1 dozen buns. Let rise in pan some before baking at 400°
for 15 minutes.
Karen Rupert, St. Cloud, Mn.

MOM'S SWEET ROLL DOUGH

1/2 c. warm water
2 pkg. dry yeast
1 1/2 c. lukewarm water
1/2 c. sugar
2 tsp. salt

2 eggs
1/4 c. or less soft
   shortening
5 to 6 c. flour
Few raisins (optional)

Sprinkle yeast into warm water. Set aside. In a large bowl, combine the rest of the ingredients. Add yeast. Mix all well and knead about 10 minutes until a soft dough is formed. Put into greased bowl and let rise until doubled in size. Knead again and let rise 1 hour or so. Shape into rolls and let rise again. Brush with beaten egg and sprinkle with poppy seed. Bake at 400° for about 20 minutes until a nice golden brown. Yum, Yum Good!

Mary Kozel, Grand Forks, N. D.

RANCH STYLE BISCUITS

6 c. flour
4 tsp. baking powder
1/3 tsp. soda
2 tsp. salt
1/2 c. sugar

1/2 c. cooking oil
2 c. buttermilk
2 pkg. dry yeast in 1/2 c.
   warm water

Sift all dry ingredients in bowl, add liquids and mix well. Knead slightly on floured board. Keep in refrigerator covered with foil. These do not have to rise. Pinch off the amount you want to use. Flatten on floured board and cut with cutter. Bake on greased pan at 350° - 375° till light brown (dough will keep as long as a week to 10 days in refrigerator).

Karen Rupert, St. Cloud, Mn.

GRANDMA ECKERT'S BISMARKS

1 pt. warm water
1 c. white syrup
1/4 c. white sugar
1 cake of yeast
2 Tbsp. vanilla

2 eggs
1/2 c. shortening
1 tsp. salt
Choice of jelly

Mix all ingredients. Don't make dough too stiff. Let rise real high. Roll out. Let rise again. Cut into oblong shapes or circles. Drop into hot grease. When golden brown, take out. Take a spoon of jelly and put in the side of each one.

Carol Wentland, Minneapolis, Mn.

KRAUT BRUSCHKE
(German - Beef Kraut Buns)

1 lb. ground beef
1/2 c. sliced onion
3 Tbsp. shortening
1 small can sauerkraut

1 tsp. salt
1/2 tsp. pepper
Bread dough

Brown beef and onions in shortening. Add sauerkraut, heat; then let cool. Roll out circles of dough. Put 2 table-spoonfuls of meat mixture on half. Fold over other half and seal. Place on cookie sheet. Bake at 350° till browned, 30 minutes or less. Eat hot.

Mrs. Clarence Schmitz, Wadena, Mn.

OVERNIGHT BUNS

4 c. boiling water
2 c. sugar

1 c. lard
2 tsp. salt

Pour boiling water over the other 3 ingredients. Mix 1 package yeast (dry Fleischmann's) in 1/2 cup warm water. Add to cooled mixture. Add 4 well beaten eggs and 14 cups flour. Start at 4:00 to cool mixture. At 5:00 add other in-gredients and then mix down every hour until 10:00. Put into greased tins. Make about the size of an egg. Bake until brown.

C. Landwehr, Minneapolis, Mn.

GOLDEN RAISIN BUNS

1 c. water
1/2 c. butter or oleo
1 tsp. sugar
1/2 c. golden raisins

1/2 tsp. salt
1 c. flour
4 eggs

Bring to boil water, oleo, sugar and salt. Add flour all at once. Then over low heat, beat 1 minute until mixture leaves side of pan. Add 1 egg at a time, beat thoroughly. Stir in raisins. Drop by tablespoonfuls onto greased cooky sheet, about 2 inches apart. Bake at 350° for 25 to 30 min-utes until golden brown. Remove and cool slightly. While warm, frost with Lemon Frosting.

Lemon Frosting: Melt 1 tablespoon butter or oleo. Stir in

1 1/2 tablespoons heavy cream. Remove from heat and stir
in 1 cup powdered sugar and 1/2 teaspoon each lemon and
vanilla extract. Beat until smooth.

Marty Eger, St. Paul, Mn.

TACO BUNS

Brown 2 pounds ground beef with onion. Add:

4 oz. shredded Mozzarella cheese	1/4 tsp. garlic salt
	1/4 tsp. oregano
4 oz. shredded sharp cheese	2 cans tomato soup

Keep refrigerated. Put on open face buns and heat
until bubbly.

Carol Watnemo, St. Paul, Mn.

DOUGHNUTS THAT NEVER FAIL

Recipe goes back to 1915. The ginger prevents fat
from soaking in.

1 c. sugar	Pinch of ginger
2 eggs	2 c. flour
1 c. milk	3 tsp. baking powder
Nutmeg to taste	1 tsp. salt

Beat eggs well. Add sugar, milk, nutmeg, ginger,
flour, baking powder and salt. Add more flour to make
dough easy to handle (almost 3 cups in all). Roll out 1/2
inch thick. Fry in hot fat.

Ruth Brown, Owatonna, Mn.

BAKED DOUGHNUTS

1 c. mashed potatoes	1/2 c. sugar
1 cake yeast	1 tsp. salt
1/4 c. warm potato water	2 eggs, well beaten
1 c. milk, scalded	4 1/2 c. flour
3/4 c. shortening	

Add shortening, sugar and salt to scalded milk. Cool
to lukewarm. Add mashed potatoes and yeast that has been

340

dissolved in potato water. Blend in beaten eggs. Work flour in gradually. Cover and let rise until light. Place on floured board and knead. Roll dough 1/2 inch thick. Cut with doughnut cutter with large hole. Place on buttered cookie sheets and let rise until light. Bake in 425° oven until delicately browned. Brush with butter on all sides. While warm, roll in granulated sugar.

Kathy Bischof, St. Cloud, Mn.

FLUFFY POTATO DOUGHNUTS

3 eggs
1 1/3 c. sugar
1/2 tsp. vanilla
1 c. mashed potatoes,
  cooled
2 Tbsp. melted shortening
  or salad oil

4 c. sifted flour
6 tsp. baking powder
Nutmeg
1 tsp. salt
1/2 c. milk

Beat eggs, sugar and vanilla till light. Add potatoes and shortening. Sift dry ingredients, add alternately with milk and potato mixture, beat well. Chill 3 hours. Roll out half of the dough at a time (keep rest refrigerated). Roll onto floured surface to 3/8 inch thick. Cut with doughnut cutter. Fry in Wesson oil.

Mrs. E. F. Braun, Owatonna, Mn.

ALMOND PUFF

Cut 1/2 cup butter into 1 cup flour. Sprinkle with 2 tablespoons water and mix with fork. Round into ball and divide in half. On ungreased baking sheet, pat each half into 12x3 inch strips, about 3 inches apart. In a saucepan, put 1/2 cup butter and 1 cup water. Bring to a rolling boil. Remove from heat and stir in 1 cup flour and 1 teaspoon extract. Stir vigorously over low heat till mixture forms a ball - 1 minute. Remove from heat and beat in 3 eggs at one time, till smooth. Spread on strips, covering completely. Bake at 350° for 60 minutes or until top is crisp and brown. Cool and frost with glaze and sprinkle with nuts.

Glaze:

1 1/2 c. confectioners sugar
2 Tbsp. soft butter

1 to 1 1/2 tsp. almond extract
1 to 2 Tbsp. warm water

Darlene Cherry, St. Paul, Mn.

BRAN FLOUR POPOVERS

1 1/8 c. milk	3 eggs
1/3 c. bran flour	1/2 tsp. salt
2/3 c. white flour	1 tsp. oil

Sift flours together and blend with milk with mixer. Beat eggs in a bowl and add salt and oil; combine with the flour and milk. Put into well greased, preheated popover irons and bake at 400° for 10 minutes, then 350° for 10 - 15 minutes; then 300° for 10 minutes. (Can replace bran flour with oatmeal flour or rye, or whole wheat or corn meal.)

Karen Rupert, St. Cloud, Mn.

DANISH PUFF

1 c. flour	1/2 c. butter
1/2 c. butter	1 c. hot water
2 Tbsp. water	1 tsp. almond extract
1 c. flour	3 eggs

From first 3 ingredients, cut butter into flour, sprinkle in water and mix well with fork. Divide dough in half and pat into 2 equal 12x3 inch strips. Place on cookie sheet. Form next 5 ingredients, mix butter and water and bring to a boil. Remove from heat and add almond extract. Add flour all at once and beat quickly. When smooth, add eggs, one at a time and beat well after each addition. Spread 1/2 of the filling on each strip. Bake 1 hour at 350°. Frost with powdered sugar frosting and sprinkle with chopped nuts. Melts in your mouth!

L. Richards

POPOVERS OF GOLD

Popovers:

1 c. flour	1 tsp. melted butter or
1/4 tsp. salt	margarine
7/8 c. milk	2 eggs

Sift together flour and salt; gradually add milk. Add butter or margarine. Beat eggs well; add. Beat batter 2 minutes with rotary beater. Fill hot greased popover pans or custard cups 2/3 full. Bake in hot oven (450°) for 15

minutes; reduce to 350°; bake 20 minutes. Makes 6.
While they bake, scramble eggs:

6 eggs   1/3 c. milk
3/4 tsp. salt   6 slices bacon, diced
Few grains of pepper

Fry bacon crisp in heavy fry pan. Pour off all but 2 tablespoons of bacon drippings. Beat eggs slightly; add salt and pepper. Add milk. Mix well. Cook in bacon and drippings left in pan, stirring gently to loosen from bottom and side. Split hot popovers and fill.

LEFSE

8 c. mashed potatoes   1/4 c. whipping cream
   (Russets)   1 tsp. salt
1 c. butter (may use   1 tsp. sugar
   1/2 Crisco)

Mash potatoes while warm with cream, salt and sugar. Chill until cold. To 4 cups of potato mixture, knead in 1 cup flour. Take dough size of a large egg, roll very thin on floured board, adding a little more flour if necessary. Bake on both sides and cool between 2 towels to hold steam so lefse doesn't get too dry.
Mike and Vonnie Bakke, Willmar, Mn.

LEFSA

7 c. riced potatoes   1/2 c. melted Crisco (not oil)
3 tsp. salt   1/2 c. good cream
3 tsp. sugar   2 c. flour

Combine all ingredients and chill, roll thin and fry on very hot lefsa grill.
Karen Rupert, St. Cloud, Mn.

LEFSE

Cook white potatoes in jackets. For 3 cups of riced (packed) potatoes, add while potatoes are hot:

1/2 c. melted butter   1 tsp. salt
1 Tbsp. sugar

Cool thoroughly, then add 1 1/2 cups flour. Roll into a long roll and chill. When ready to bake, cut off desired amount and roll thin with floured rolling pin. Use floured lefse stick to handle. Bake on lefse grill. Makes 10 lefse.

Lajla Hood, South Haven, Mn.

SALEM LUTHERAN CHURCH LEFSE

4 c. mashed potatoes
1 tsp salt
1/2 c. cream

1 1/2 c. sifted flour
2 Tbsp. sugar
2 Tbsp. butter, melted

Blend all together. Divide into 8 or 10 parts and roll each part very thin. Place on griddle at low heat. Brown slightly on both sides.

Gladys Schimschock, Annandale, Mn.

LEFSE
(Norwegian)

1 lb. instant potatoes
6 1/2 c. boiling water
2 sticks margarine
1 c. cream or Carnation milk

1 Tbsp. sugar
1 Tbsp. salt
3 c. flour

Stir together the first 6 ingredients. Cool well. Add flour and mix well. Take small portions of dough and roll out very thin into circles, using enough flour on board to prevent sticking. Bake on very hot griddle until brown, turning once. Will be crisp. Place on towel and cover with another towel so steam will soften them. Best eaten same day. May be frozen. (30 large)

Mrs. Jerve, St. Cloud, Mn.

LEFSE

Do not use a mixer.

3 c. milk
3 c. water
1/2 lb. margarine

1/4 c. sugar
Sprinkle of salt

Add 1 package of instant potatoes (24 serving size), 1 pint of half & half. Cool. Mix 3 cups of potato mixture and 1 cup flour. Make small balls. Keep in refrigerator, add a little flour to roll. Bake on grill about 425°.

Irma Holmstrom, Bismarck, N. D.

LEFSE

1 c. milk	Pinch of salt
2 Tbsp. shortening	2 - 3 c. flour

Scald milk, add shortening and salt. Cool. Add 2 - 3 cups flour. Knead like bread dough. Divide into 10 small pieces. Roll and bake just slightly on cookie sheet on top of stove.

Topping:

1 egg, beaten	1/3 c. cornstarch
1/3 c. sugar	1 c. + 3 Tbsp. flour
Pinch of salt	2/3 c. cream

Spread on with knife, then use krina. Bake at 350° about 10 minutes.

Kathy Bischof, St. Cloud, Mn.

BRAN MUFFINS

2 c. 100% bran cereal	2 c. boiling water

Let stand awhile. Add:

4 eggs	1 c. shortening
3 c. sugar	

Sift and add:

5 c. flour	1 tsp. salt
5 tsp. soda	

Add 1 quart buttermilk. Add bran mixture. Stir in 4 cups bran flakes. Put into 5 quart ice cream pail. This will store 4 - 6 weeks in refrigerator. Take out what you want, place in muffin tins. Bake for 20 minutes at 375°.

Deb Nordby, Fargo, N. D.

CRANBERRY MUFFINS

1 c. chopped cranberries   1/2 c. sugar

Mix together and set aside.

2 c. flour	1 egg, slightly beaten
1/4 tsp. salt	3/4 c. sour milk or buttermilk
3/4 tsp. soda	1/4 c. melted shortening or
1/4 c. sugar	oleo

Sift dry ingredients; add egg, oleo, milk. Mix until moistened, only. Fold in cranberries. Bake 20 minutes at 400°. Makes 1 dozen.
Karen Rupert, St. Cloud, Mn.

CRANBERRY MUFFINS AND GLAZE

1 1/2 Tbsp. butter,	1/2 c. sugar
melted	1/4 c. evaporated milk
1/4 c. water	

Mix above ingredients, then add:

1 c. flour	1/2 tsp. salt
1 Tbsp. soda	1 c. whole cranberries

Bake in greased muffin tin 18 - 20 minutes at 350°.

Glaze:

1/4 c. margarine	1 c. sugar
1/2 c. evaporated milk	1 tsp. vanilla

Boil and stir approximately 5 minutes, then heat to serve.
Phyllis Merkel, Minneapolis, Mn.

HAWAIIAN BANANA MUFFINS

2 c. sugar	2 1/4 c. cake flour
1/2 c. shortening	2 1/2 tsp. baking soda
2 Tbsp. salad oil	2 1/2 tsp. baking powder
2 c. bananas	3/4 tsp. salt
3 large eggs	3/4 tsp. vanilla

1 1/2 tsp. lemon juice   1 c. buttermilk

Cream sugar, shortening and salad oil well. Add bananas and cream well. Add eggs and mix well. Combine dry ingredients and add to mixing bowl along with vanilla and lemon juice. Mix at slow speed until ingredients are incorporated. Add buttermilk gradually until smooth. Scrape bowl and mix at medium speed for 3 minutes. Put batter into greased or paper lined muffin pans and bake at 380°. Makes approximately 2 dozen. If not using paper liners, grease pans generously. Other fruits such as pineapple, peach or apricot may be used, but if so, reduce sugar to 1 1/2 cups.

Ione Brown, Past President,
St. Cloud Council

ICEBOX MUFFINS

3 c. white sugar
1 heaping c. Crisco
5 tsp. soda
1 tsp. salt
2 c. boiling water
4 c. Kellogg's All-Bran
(breakfast food)

2 c. Nabisco 100% bran
(breakfast food)
1 qt. buttermilk
5 c. flour
4 eggs, beaten
Raisins (optional)

1. Pour hot water over the Kellogg's All-Bran, let cool. 2. Cream shortening and sugar, add eggs, buttermilk and Nabisco 100% bran. 3. Sift flour, soda and salt together; add all at once with Kellogg's Bran. Fold in only until all dry ingredients are moistened. Add raisins. Bake in greased muffin tins as needed, 15 or 20 minutes at 400°.
Note: This batter will keep in refrigerator 6 - 7 weeks. Recipe makes about 1 gallon. One pint is about 12 muffins. I store mine in Miracle Whip jars or any wide mouthed jar.
Mrs. E. F. Braun, Owatonna, Mn.

MAGIC MUFFINS

Mix together:
1 beaten egg
4 Tbsp. liquid shortening
3/4 c. milk
3/4 c. Malt-O-Meal

1 1/4 c. flour
1/2 c. sugar
1 Tbsp. baking powder
1/2 tsp. salt

Stir until flour is moistened. Fill greased muffin cups 3/4 full. Bake 20 minutes at 400°. Makes 12 muffins.

Lois Sandberg, St. Cloud, Mn.

PRUNE MUFFINS

9 eggs	2 c. milk
2 c. prune juice	1 small pkg. nuts, chopped
2 c. prune pulp (more	6 c. flour (I use 8 c.)
if desired)	3 heaping tsp. soda, mixed
6 c. sugar	with flour
	1 lb. melted margarine

Beat eggs, add rest of ingredients in order listed. Bake 20 - 25 minutes at 350°. The batter may be kept in the refrigerator 3 months, and bake any amount of muffins as desired. I usually make half a recipe. Makes 3 1/2 dozen. I use 5 eggs and 4 1/2 cups flour.

Helen M. Gludt, Bottineau, N. D.

RAISIN BRAN MUFFINS

5 c. flour	5 tsp. soda
3 c. sugar	2 tsp. salt
1 c. salad oil	1 (15 oz.) box raisin bran
3 eggs	cereal
	1 qt. buttermilk

Mix in 5 quart ice cream pail. Bake for 20 minutes at 350°. (Keeps for a month in covered container in refrigerator. Bake some now and some later.) Makes about 4 dozen.

Lorine Kelly, Minneapolis, Mn.

RHUBARB MUFFINS

2 1/2 c. brown sugar,	1 egg
packed	2 tsp. vanilla
1/2 c. salad oil	1 c. buttermilk

Put the mixture into a bowl and stir in 1 1/2 cups cut fresh rhubarb. Sift together:

2 1/2 c. flour	1 tsp. baking powder
1 tsp. soda	1 tsp. salt

348

May add nuts if desired, to first mixture. Fill muffin cups 2/3 full (24 muffins). Bake at 375° for 15 - 25 minutes.

Topping (before baking):

1 Tbsp. margarine, melted   1 tsp. cinnamon
1/2 c. white sugar

Marlene Barton, Grand Forks, N. D.

6 WEEK BRAN MUFFINS

3 c. sugar   4 eggs, beaten
5 c. flour   1 qt. buttermilk
1 tsp. salt   1 c. oil
5 tsp. soda

Combine dry ingredients. Add eggs, oil and buttermilk. Stir until moistened. Fill muffin cups 2/3 full. Bake at 350° for 20 - 25 minutes or until brown. Batter keeps in refrigerator 6 weeks. Makes 5 dozen.
Arlene Freichels, Sauk Centre, Mn.

SIX WEEK MUFFINS

Mix together in very large bowl:

1 (15 oz.) box raisin bran   5 tsp. soda
3 c. sugar   2 tsp. salt
5 c. flour   4 tsp. cinnamon

Add:
4 eggs, beaten   1 c. melted shortening or
1 qt. buttermilk   oil

Mix well and store in refrigerator in covered container. Batter will keep for 6 weeks in refrigerator. To bake, fill muffin cups 1/2 to 2/3 full and bake in 400° oven for 15 - 20 minutes.
Erlene Gallion, St. Cloud, Mn.

SPICY APPLE MUFFINS

2 c. peeled, chopped apples
1/2 c. sugar
3 1/2 c. + 4 Tbsp. flour
1/2 c. sugar
8 tsp. baking powder

1 tsp. salt
1 tsp. cinnamon
2 c. milk
1/2 c. melted shortening or
   oil
2 eggs

Mix apples with first 1/2 cup sugar, set aside. Combine flour, 1/2 cup sugar, baking powder, salt and cinnamon. Combine milk, oil and eggs, beat slightly, add apples. Add liquid ingredients to blended dry ingredients. Stir until all are moist. Fill muffin cups (greased) 2/3 full. Bake at 400° for 20 - 25 minutes.
    Mary Perron, Owatonna, Mn.

WHOLE-WHEAT OATMEAL MUFFINS

1 c. sour milk
1 c. oatmeal
1 1/4 c. whole wheat flour
1/4 tsp. salt
4 tsp. baking powder

1/3 c. honey
2 eggs, beaten
1/3 c. shortening or
   vegetable oil
1/2 c. chopped walnuts

Soak oatmeal in sour milk for 1 hour; add eggs and beat well. Add honey and mix. Add cooled shortening. Add flour sifted with salt and baking powder. Bake in greased muffin pans (or use cupcake papers) in hot oven (400° F.) for 15 to 20 minutes. Yield: 1 1/2 dozen.
    Carmen Moe, Minneapolis, Mn.

ZUCCHINI WHEAT GERM MUFFINS

2 c. flour
1 c. shredded zucchini
3/4 c. wheat germ
1/2 c. brown sugar

1 Tbsp. baking powder
3/4 c. milk
1/4 c. oil
1 egg, beaten

In a large bowl, mix the first 5 ingredients. In a small bowl, mix remaining ingredients. Stir liquid into dry ingredients just until blended. Spoon into 12 greased muffin cups. Bake at 375° for 20 - 25 minutes. Makes 12.
    Dee Olson, St. Paul, Mn.

ZUCCHINI AND WHEAT GERM MUFFINS

In a large bowl, mix together:

2 c. flour
1 c. shredded zucchini
3/4 c. wheat germ
1/2 c. packed brown sugar

1 Tbsp. baking powder
3/4 c. milk
1/4 c. oil
1 slightly beaten egg

Spoon into 12 greased muffin cups. Bake at 375° for 25 minutes.

Yuriko Hinton, Fargo, N. D.

BUTTERSCOTCH RING

Grease and flour a Bundt pan and put 2 dozen frozen rolls into pan. Sprinkle 1/2 package butterscotch pudding over rolls.   Melt and pour over rolls:

1/2 c. butter
1/2 c. brown sugar

1 tsp. cinnamon

Let rise overnight or until double. Bake at 350° for 25 minutes.

*Bread dough can be shaped into balls.

Paula Rogers, Detroit Lakes, Mn.

CARAMEL ROLLS

2 loaves frozen white
   bread dough
1/2 c. margarine
1 tsp. cinnamon

3/4 c. brown sugar
1 (6 oz.) pkg. butterscotch
   pudding mix (regular, not
   instant)
2 Tbsp. milk

Thaw bread dough, but do not let it rise. Break off pieces and roll into walnut sized balls. Put half of the dough balls into the bottom of a well greased Bundt pan. Melt margarine, add the rest of the ingredients and mix well. Pour half of the caramel mixture over the dough and place a second layer of dough balls on the top, then add other half of caramel mixture. Let rolls rise, then bake at 350° for 30 minutes. Flip out of the pan immediately.

Phyllis Kerr, St. Cloud, Mn.

CARAMEL ROLLS IN A BUNDT PAN

Thaw 2 loaves of frozen bread dough in refrigerator overnight. Cut up into 1 1/2 inch cubes. Butter Bundt pan real well. Mix 1/2 cup melted butter, 1/2 cup brown sugar and cinnamon to taste. Dip each dough cube in mix and put layer of cubes in Bundt pan. Sprinkle dry butterscotch pudding on each layer and some nuts or raisins, layer until all gone. Let rise about 30 minutes or until even with pan. Bake in 350° oven for about 30 minutes.

Jane Bohline, Minneapolis, Mn.

CARAMEL PECAN ROLLS
(One bowl method)

5 1/2 - 6 1/2 c. Robin Hood all-purpose flour	1 Tbsp. salt
2 pkg. active dry yeast	1/4 c. softened margarine
2 Tbsp. sugar	2 1/4 c. hot tap water
	Cooking oil

Spoon flour into measuring cup and level off. Pour onto waxed paper. Combine 2 cups flour, undissolved yeast, sugar and salt in large bowl. Stir well to blend. Add margarine. Add hot tap water. Beat with electric mixer at medium speed for 2 minutes. Scrape bowl occasionally. Add 1 cup more flour. Beat with electric mixer at high speed for 1 minute or until thick and elastic. Gradually stir in just enough of remaining flour with wooden spoon to make a soft dough which leaves sides of bowl. Turn out onto floured board. Knead 5 - 10 minutes or until dough is smooth and elastic. Cover with plastic wrap, then a towel. Prepare pans while dough rests on board.

1 c. firmly packed brown sugar	1 c. chopped pecans
1/2 c. melted butter	1/2 c. granulated sugar
3 Tbsp. water	1 tsp. cinnamon
	1/4 c. softened butter

Combine brown sugar, 1/2 cup butter and water. Spread evenly in 2 lightly greased 8 inch round pans and 1 lightly greased 9x13 inch pan or 2 lightly greased 9x13 inch pans. Sprinkle pecans on brown sugar mixture. Combine granulated sugar and cinnamon. Punch down dough at end of 20 minutes rest. Divide in half. Roll each portion into a 10x16 inch rectangle on very lightly buttered board.

Spread evenly with half the remaining butter. Sprinkle with half the sugar mixture. Roll up tightly, beginning with 16 inch side. Seal lengthwise edge. Cut into 16 (1 inch) pieces. Place cut side down in prepared pans. Cover, as basic recipe directs. Refrigerate 2 to 24 hours. Let stand 10 minutes while preheating oven. Bake at 425° for 20 - 25 minutes or until done. Invert pans onto waxed paper covered racks. Let stand 5 minutes. Remove pans. Yield: 32 rolls.

Note: For richer rolls, use Cool Rise Sweet Dough I or II and bake at 375° for 20 - 25 minutes or until done.

Becky Meyers, Windom, Mn.

CARAMEL SWEET ROLLS

Night before, grease Bundt pan. If large pan, use 2 packages Rhodes frozen rolls and place around pan. Over that, sprinkle 1 package of butterscotch pudding (not instant). Melt 1/2 stick of oleo or butter with 1/2 cup brown sugar and 1 teaspoon cinnamon. Pour over rolls and let stand overnight. Bake 35 to 45 minutes at 350°.

Recipe from Minneapolis, Mn.

FROZEN BREAD CARAMEL ROLLS

2 loaves frozen bread
1/2 c. butter or margarine
1 c. brown sugar
2 Tbsp. milk

1 large or 2 small pkg. vanilla pudding mix (not instant)
Cinnamon to taste

Thaw bread dough, but do not permit to rise. Break 1 loaf into small pieces in bottom of greased 9x13 inch pan. Melt butter, then add brown sugar, pudding mix, milk and cinnamon. Mix all together, then pour over broken bread. Break the second loaf on top; let rise 2 1/2 to 3 hours. Bake 30 minutes at 350°.

Thelma Olson, St. Cloud, Mn.

FROZEN BREAD CARAMEL ROLLS

2 loaves frozen bread
1/2 c. butter
1 c. brown sugar

1 large or 2 small pkg. vanilla pudding mix (not instant)
2 Tbsp. milk
Cinnamon to taste

Thaw bread, do not allow to rise. Break 1 loaf up in bottom of greased 9x13 inch pan. Melt butter, then add brown sugar, pudding mix, milk and cinnamon. Mix together then pour over broken bread. Break second loaf on top and let rise for 2 1/2 hours. Bake for 30 minutes at 350°. Remove from oven, let set a few minutes and turn upside down on cookie sheet.

Doris Schmidt, Willmar, Mn.

COTTAGE CHEESE PASTRY

1 lb. butter or margarine   1 lb. sifted flour (4 c.)
1 lb. creamed cottage cheese

Mix with pastry blender to form dough. Add more flour if necessary. Chill overnight. Roll out and cut into crescent shapes or squares. Use Wilderness pie filling (cherry or blueberry). Solo almond filling is very good. May use -

Nut Filling: Have ready 2 cups ground nuts. Mix 2 unbeaten egg whites and nuts. Add:

1 c. sugar   1 tsp. vanilla
Juice of 1 lemon

Place on ungreased cookie sheet. Bake at 400° for 12 minutes until lightly browned. Pastry dough keeps well for 1 week.

Emmy Thielmann

OATMEAL ROLLS

Mix:
1 c. quick oatmeal   2 c. boiling water

Add:
1 tsp. salt   1/3 c. shortening (solid)
1/2 c. molasses

Let cool, then add:
2 eggs   2 pkg. dry yeast dissolved
5 1/2 - 6 c. flour   in 1/2 c. warm water

This is a stir recipe, no kneading, too soft to knead.

354

Let rise once, then form into rolls (have to keep greasing hands to form rolls). Let rise again and bake at 375° about 20 minutes.

Karen Rupert, St. Cloud, Mn.

OUT OF THIS WORLD ROLLS

2 pkg. active dry yeast	1/2 c. sugar
1/4 c. warm water	1 c. warm water
3 eggs, well beaten	4 1/2 c. flour
1/2 c. shortening	2 tsp. salt

Soften yeast in the 1/4 cup warm water. Combine eggs, shortening, sugar, the softened yeast, 1 cup warm water, salt and 2 1/2 cups flour. Beat until smooth. Add remaining flour to make a soft dough. Cover and allow to rise until double. Punch down and place the dough, covered, in the refrigerator overnight. Three hours before baking, remove the dough from the refrigerator. Divide dough in half, roll each half into a rectangle, 1/2 inch thick. Spread with butter. Roll up jelly roll style and cut into 1 inch slices. Place in greased muffin tins, cut side down. Cover and allow to rise 3 hours. Bake at 400° for 12 to 15 minutes. Makes about 3 dozen rolls.

Marge Johnson, Minneapolis, Mn.

MADELINE'S BROWNIES

3/4 c. sifted flour	1/2 c. soft shortening
1 c. sugar	2 eggs
5 Tbsp. cocoa	1 tsp. vanilla
1/2 tsp. salt	1/2 c. chopped nuts

Place all ingredients except nuts in bowl and beat with mixer for 3 minutes. Add nuts and bake in a 6 or 8 inch square pan at 350° for 30 minutes. Don't overbake.

Marge Pye, St. Paul, Mn.

DOUBLE DECKER BROWNIES

1/2 c. shortening	1 c. coconut
1 c. sugar	1 c. flour
2 eggs, well beaten	1/4 tsp. salt
1 tsp. vanilla	1 sq. melted chocolate
	1/2 c. chopped nuts

1748-81

Cream together shortening, sugar, eggs and vanilla. Add sifted dry ingredients. Divide dough into 2 parts. To one part, add melted chocolate and nuts. To second part, add coconut. Spread chocolate mixture into 9x12 inch greased pan, then drop white mixture on top in spoonfuls and spread to cover chocolate mixture. Bake 25 minutes at 350°. Cool. Frost.

Frosting:

1/2 c. white sugar
4 Tbsp. margarine

1/2 c. brown sugar
4 Tbsp. milk

Mix, bring to a good boil. Remove from heat and add 1/2 cup chocolate chips. Let melt. Beat until smooth. Spread on bars. Cut small, they're rich.
Evelyn Walls, St. Paul, Mn.

PIE CRUST

Mix together:
3 c. flour
1 c. shortening

1 tsp. salt

Beat together and add to above ingredients:

1/3 c. cold water
2 Tbsp. vinegar

1 egg

Mix well and roll for pies.
Bev Bartz, St. Paul, Mn.

PIE CRUST

Can be stored in refrigerator until needed.

7 c. flour
4 tsp. salt

2 c. lard

2 crust:

1 crust:

2 c. of mix
4 to 6 Tbsp. ice cold
  water

8 inch - 1 to 1 1/4 c. mix
9 inch - 1 to 1 1/2 c. mix
2 to 4 Tbsp. cold water

Joan Buttweiler, St. Cloud, Mn.

FOOLPROOF PIE CRUST

4 c. flour
1 3/4 c. shortening
1 Tbsp. sugar
2 tsp. salt

1 Tbsp. vinegar
1/2 c. water
1 egg

With a fork, mix together first 4 ingredients. In a separate dish, beat remaining ingredients together with a fork. Combine the two mixtures, stirring with a fork until all ingredients are moistened. Then with hands, mold dough into 5 equal sized balls. Chill 15 minutes before rolling into desired shapes. Dough can be flattened between waxed paper and frozen to use later.

Dee Olson, St. Paul, Mn.

ALMOND CRUSH PINEAPPLE PIE

Pastry for 2 crust, 8 inch
    pie
2 Tbsp. sugar
3 Tbsp. cornstarch
1/4 tsp. salt
1 (20 1/2 oz.) can
    crushed pineapple

2 Tbsp. butter or margarine
1 Tbsp. lime juice
1 Tbsp. sugar
1 1/2 tsp. butter or margarine
1/4 c. light corn syrup
1 tsp. water
3/4 c. sliced, unblanched
    almonds

Line pie pan with pastry. Mix 2 tablespoons sugar, cornstarch and salt in saucepan, then stir in undrained pineapple. Bring mixture to boil over medium heat, stirring constantly. Boil until clear and thickened, 1 to 2 minutes. Stir in the 2 tablespoons butter or margarine and lime juice. Turn into pastry shell; cover with top crust. Seal and flute edges. Bake at 425° for 20 minutes, or until pastry begins to brown. Meanwhile, combine the 1 tablespoon sugar, 1 1/2 teaspoons butter or margarine, corn syrup and water in small saucepan. Cook over low heat until sugar is dissolved and mixture boils. Remove pie from oven. Sprinkle sliced almonds over top crust. Spoon hot glaze evenly over nuts. Return pie to oven; bake about 8 minutes longer, or until topping is bubbly and lightly browned. Cool completely before cutting.

APPLE PIE IN BAG

Unbaked 9 inch pie shell
2 1/2 lb. cooking apples
  (3 or 4 large)
1 c. granulated sugar
1/2 c. + 2 Tbsp. all-
  purpose flour

1/2 tsp. nutmeg or cinnamon
2 Tbsp. lemon juice
1/2 c. very soft butter or
  margarine
Large brown paper bag

About 1 1/2 hours before serving pie: Prepare favorite
pastry or packaged pie crust mix. Then make pie shell,
having fluted or rolled edges. Start heating oven to 400°.
Wash, pare, then quarter apples; cut each quarter into 4
pieces, making 7 cups good sized chunks. In large bowl,
toss apple chunks with a mixture of 1/2 cup granulated sugar, 2 tablespoons flour and the nutmeg or cinnamon, until
each apple chunk is completely coated. Fill pie shell with
apple chunks, piling them high in the center of the pie;
then sprinkle them with lemon juice. Thoroughly mix 1/2
cup each of sugar and flour and the butter, into a soft
paste; spread over top of piled apple chunks. Place pie in
paper bag, closing open end. Set on rack in center of oven
and bake about 1 hour or until pie is done and nicely
browned. Then remove pie from oven and let cool 5 to 10
minutes before carefully removing it from the paper bag.
Then, while still warm, cut pie into wedges and serve as
is with favorite cheese, or topped with ice cream.

APRICOT PUREE PIE

2 c. apricot puree (or
  sieved apricots)
Juice of 1 lemon
1 tsp. grated lemon rind
3/4 c. sugar

1/2 c. commercial sour cream
1 env. unflavored gelatin
2 Tbsp. cold water
1/2 c. boiling water
Pastry for a single crust
  9 inch pie

Combine the apricot puree, lemon juice, lemon peel,
sugar and sour cream. Soften gelatin in 2 tablespoons cold
water; stir in boiling water to dissolve. Blend dissolved
gelatin with apricot mixture and set aside to prepare and
bake the crust (about 40 minutes). Then beat the mixture
with a rotary beater for about 3 minutes or until smooth and
light. Pour into the baked shell and refrigerate at least 2
hours before serving.

BESSIE PYE'S PIE CRUST

1 1/2 c. flour
1/2 tsp. salt

1/2 c. lard (1/4 lb.)
4 Tbsp. milk

Put flour, salt and lard in bowl. Mix with fingers until of coarse texture (size of peas). Add milk and mix into ball. Cut in half and roll out on floured board until size of pan. For apple pie, cut up 6 apples (they shrink). Add cinnamon, sugar, and dot with butter. Bake 10 minutes at 450° for 40 to 50 minutes at 350°.

Marge Pye, St. Paul, Mn.

BRANDY ALEXANDER PIE

1 1/2 c. chocolate
  wafers, crushed
1/4 c. butter or margarine,
  melted
32 large or 3 c.
  miniature marshmallows

1/2 c. milk
1 1/2 c. chilled whipping
  cream
1/4 c. dark creme de cacao
3 Tbsp. brandy

Heat oven to 350°. Mix crumbs and butter in 9 inch pan. Press firmly and evenly against bottom and sides of pan. Bake 10 minutes. Cool. Melt marshmallows with milk over low heat, stirring constantly. Chill until thickened. In chilled bowl, beat cream until stiff. Stir marshmallow mixture to blend. Gradually add creme de cacao and brandy. Fold into whipped cream. Pour into baked crust. Chill 4 hours.

Myrne Daml, Anoka, Mn.

CHOCOLATE CHIP PIE

20 marshmallows
1/3 c. milk
1/2 pt. whipping cream

1 (4 oz.) Hershey's chocolate
  bar
Graham cracker crust

Make graham cracker crust and put into pie plate or 8 or 9 inch square pan. Melt marshmallows with milk in double boiler. Let cool. Fold in whipped cream and grated chocolate bar (saving some to sprinkle on top). Spread in pan and refrigerate.

Jean Carlson

CRAZY BERRY BLUE PIE

1 (9 inch) crumb crust
1/4 c. cold water
1 env. unflavored gelatin
1 c. sweetened condensed
  milk

1/3 c. lemon juice
1 c. (1/2 pt.) sour cream
2 1/2 c. (1 lb. 5 oz. can)
  blueberry pie filling

Put water and gelatin in small saucepan. Place over direct heat and stir until dissolved or mixture is clear. In medium size bowl, combine condensed milk and lemon juice. Stir in gelatin mixture. Fold in sour cream. Mix 1 1/4 cups of pie filling. Turn into crust. Refrigerate 2 - 3 hours. Then garnish pie top with remaining chilled pie filling.
    Kathy Neels, St. Cloud, Mn.

CUSTARD PIE WITH COCONUT

4 eggs
1/2 c. sugar

1 stick soft margarine

Mix together in blender. Add:

1/2 c. flour
2 c. milk

1 tsp. vanilla

Mix in blender, add 1 cup coconut. Pour into unbaked pie shell. Bake 1 hour at 350° or until knife in center comes clean.
    Evelyn Walls, St. Paul, Mn.

FRENCH SILK PIE

1 baked and cooled
  8 inch pie shell
1/2 c. butter
3/4 c. sugar

1 sq. baking chocolate,
  melted
2 eggs
1 tsp. vanilla

Cream butter and sugar. Blend in chocolate and vanilla. Add eggs, one at a time and beat each one 5 minutes. Pour in pie shell and chill 4 hours or overnight. Serve with whipped cream and a stemmed cherry.
    Ione Brown, Past President,
    St. Cloud Council

FUDGE NUT PIE

1/3 c. butter or margarine
3 oz. unsweetened
  chocolate
2 c. sugar
4 eggs, well beaten

1/4 tsp. salt
1 tsp. vanilla
2/3 c. coarsely chopped nuts
1 unbaked 9 inch pie shell

    Melt butter and chocolate in heavy saucepan over low heat. Remove from heat and stir in remaining ingredients. Pour into the pie shell and bake in 350° oven for 45 minutes. Cool before cutting. Serve with ice cream. Very, very rich cut into small pieces.
        Dee Olson, St. Paul, Mn.

FRUIT COBBLER PIE

1 c. sugar
1 c. flour
1/2 tsp. salt
2 tsp baking powder
1 c. milk

1/2 c. melted butter
1 pt. fresh peaches,
  sweetened without stirring
  or 1 (#303) can drained
  boysenberries

    Mix dry ingredients, add milk, melt butter in an 8x8 inch pan. Pour dough into pan. Place fruit over dough. Bake at 375° for 45 minutes. Serve warm.
        Mike and Vonnie Bakke, Willmar, Mn.

KEY LIME PIE

1 tsp. grated lime
1/3 c. lime juice
1 drop green food
  coloring

1 (15 oz.) can Eagle Brand
  condensed milk
2 egg yolks

    Add juice, food coloring to condensed milk. Stir in egg yolks. Top with meringue. Bake 12 to 15 minutes at 350°. Cool 2 to 3 hours.
    P.S. I have used Cool Whip and then just set in refrigerator. Very good too.
        Mavis E. Dilts, Valley City, N. D.

LEMON FILLING

Combine:

2 slightly beaten eggs	4 tsp. grated lemon rind
1 (15 oz.) can sweetened condensed milk	1/4 c. lemon juice
	1/4 tsp. salt

Stir until mixture thickens.

LEMON SPONGE PIE

3 Tbsp. butter or margarine, softened	Dash of salt
1 1/4 c. sugar	1 1/4 c. milk
4 eggs, separated	Grated peel of 2 lemons
3 Tbsp. flour	1/3 c. lemon juice
	1 unbaked 9 inch pie shell

In large bowl cream together butter and sugar until fluffy. Beat in egg yolks, flour, salt, milk, lemon peel and juice. In small bowl with clean beaters, beat egg whites until stiff, but not dry. Fold into milk mixture. Pour into pie shell. Bake in preheated 375° oven for 15 minutes. Reduce heat to 300° and bake 45 mintues or longer until top is golden brown and pick inserted in center comes out clean. Cool on rack.

Jane Bohline, Minneapolis, Mn.

MARGARITA PIE

1 c. finely crushed pretzels	2 Tbsp. lime juice
3 Tbsp. sugar	2 Tbsp. tequila
1/4 c. butter, melted	1 Tbsp. Triple Sec
1 qt. vanilla ice cream	1 tsp. grated lime rind

In small bowl combine pretzel crumbs, sugar and butter. Press into bottom and sides of 9 inch pie pan. Refrigerate. Allow ice cream to soften slightly. Fold in lime juice, rind, tequila and Triple Sec. Spoon into chilled crust and place in freezer 3 to 4 hours. Makes 6 to 8 servings.

Elynor Pederson, Minneapolis, Mn.

MASTERPIECE MINCEMEAT

1 lb. ground lean beef,
   cooked and drained
1 lb. ground suet
6 c. pared, chopped
   apples
2 lb. raisins
1 lb. currants

1 lb. mixed candied fruit
1/2 c. vinegar
2 c. apple cider
2 c. sugar
1 tsp. salt, cinnamon, cloves
1/2 tsp. ginger
1/2 tsp. nutmeg

Combine all ingredients and simmer for 20 minutes.
Seal in jars and process for 10 minutes at 10 pounds pressure
or place in containers and freeze. Makes 12 pints.

MERINGUE

3 egg whites
1/2 tsp. baking powder

6 Tbsp. sugar or 1/2 c.

Combine and beat. Add sugar gradually while beating.
Bake at 400° until lightly browned.
Phyllis Brossart, Rugby, N. D.

NEVER-FAIL PIE MERINGUE

1 Tbsp. cornstarch
6 Tbsp. sugar
1/2 c. water

3 egg whites
Few grains of salt

Mix cornstarch, sugar, water and salt and cook thick
and clear. Cool slightly. Beat egg whites until frothy.
Continue beating while slowly pouring cooked mixture over
and continue beating 5 minutes. Cover cooled filling pie
shell with meringue, sealing edges to crust. Bake at 450°
for 5 - 7 minutes until golden.
Bev Bartz, St. Paul, Mn.

MILLION DOLLAR PIE

1 can Eagle Brand
   sweetened milk
1 large can pineapple,
   crushed, drained

1/3 c. lemon juice
1 c. chopped pecans
1 large ctn. Cool Whip

Mix all ingredients together, pour into 9 inch baked pie
shell, let set in refrigerator for about 4 hours.
Gloria Bergson, Fargo, N. D.

MOCK APPLE PIE

Pastry for 2 crust pie
1 1/2 c. sugar
1 1/2 tsp. cream of
   tartar

2 Tbsp. lemon juice
2 c. water
3/4 tsp. cinnamon

Mix. Boil 5 minutes. Cool Crush 14 - 16 soda
crackers, place in unbaked shell. Pour cooled mixture over.
Cover with top crust and bake at 450° for 10 minutes; 350°
for 20 minutes. (One pie)
Darlene Lee

ORANGE-BANANA CREAM PIE

1 baked pie shell
1 can Mandarin oranges,
   drained

1 or 2 bananas
1 pkg. instant banana cream
   pudding

Follow directions on pudding package, using 1 1/3 cups
cold milk. Arrange oranges and sliced bananas in bottom of
crust. Pour pudding over. Top with whipped cream and
coconut. Chill several hours.
Signe Linde, St. Paul, Mn.

ORANGE PETAL PIE

1 c. rolled oats, uncooked
1/2 c. firmly packed
   brown sugar

1/2 c. flaked or shredded
   coconut
1/3 c. melted butter or
   margarine

Toast oats in shallow pan in 350° oven for 10 minutes.
Combine with remaining ingredients. Press onto bottom and
sides of 9 inch pie plate. Chill while preparing orange
filling.

Filling:

3 oz. pkg. orange flavored
   gelatin

1 c. hot water

364

1/2 c. orange juice   1 c. whipping cream,
                                      whipped

Dissolve gelatin in water. Stir in juice. Chill until mixture begins to set; beat vigorously with rotary beater until fluffy. Fold in cream. Pour into chilled crust. Refrigerate several hours or until set. Decorate with orange sections to resemble flower petals.

PECAN CRUNCH PIE

3 eggs   1 c. pecans, chopped
1/2 tsp. baking powder   1 tsp. vanilla
1 c. sugar   1/2 pt. whipping cream
11 graham crackers

Beat eggs and baking powder. Add sugar very slowly. Beat until very stiff. Crush graham crackers, fold them and the pecans into egg mixture. Add vanilla. Spread in heavily buttered pie pan and bake 30 minutes at 350°. Chill 4 hours and top with whipped cream. Serves 6.
                Irene Blantz, Windom, Mn.

PECAN PIE

1 c. Karo syrup   1 Tbsp. margarine
3 eggs, slightly beaten   1 tsp. vanilla
1/8 tsp. salt   1 c. sugar

Mix above. Add 1 cup pecans, chopped or halves. Pour into 1 (9 inch) pie shell. Bake 15 minutes at 400°; 30 to 35 minutes at 350°. Outer edges of filling should be set, center slighty soft.
                Joan Buttweiler, St. Cloud, Mn.

PECAN PUMPKIN PIE

1/2 c. chopped pecans   1/2 tsp salt
1/4 c. brown sugar   1/2 tsp. nutmeg
1/4 c. melted butter   1 2/3 c. evaporated milk
2 eggs   1 tsp. cinnamon
3/4 c. brown sugar   1/2 tsp. ginger
1 3/4 c. pumpkin   1 (9 inch) unbaked crust

Combine pecans, 1/4 cup brown sugar and melted butter in small bowl. (Heat mixture and reserve this.) Beat eggs slightly in large bowl, add 3/4 cup brown sugar, pumpkin, salt and spices; mix well. Stir in evaporated milk. Pour into pastry shell. Bake in hot oven (425°) for 15 minutes. Reduce heat to 350° for 20 minutes. Arrange hot mixture around edge and in center of pie for topping; bake an additional 10 minutes.

Mrs. E. F. Braun, Owatonna, Mn.

MAGIC PUMPKIN PIE

1 unbaked 8 inch pie
   shell
2 c. pumpkin
1 (15 oz.) can Eagle
   Brand sweetened
   condensed milk

1 egg
1/2 tsp. salt
1/2 tsp. nutmeg
1/2 tsp. ginger
3/4 tsp. cinnamon

In large size mixing bowl, blend together all ingredients, add 1 teaspoon vanilla. Turn mixture into pie shell. Bake 15 minutes at 425°; then 375° until sharp bladed knife inserted near center comes out clean, 40 - 45 minutes. Cool, refrigerate at least 1 hour.

Joan Buttweiler, St. Cloud, Mn.

PUNCH PIE DELIGHT

2 env. unflavored gelatin
1 c. sugar
1 (6 oz.) can frozen
   grape concentrated,
   thawed
1 (15 oz.) can blueberries

2 Tbsp. lemon juice
1 egg white
1 c. dairy sour cream
2 (8 inch) graham cracker
   crumb crusts
1/2 c. flaked coconut

Combine gelatin, sugar, undiluted grape juice, 3/4 cup blueberry juice and lemon juice in saucepan. Heat till gelatin dissolves. Beat egg white till stiff. Slowly dribble in hot syrup while beating, till egg white becomes light and fluffy, about 10 - 15 minutes. Chill till slightly set. Lightly fold in blueberries and sour cream. Pile filling into crumb crusts. Garnish pie with flaked coconut. Makes 2 (8 inch) pies.

REFRIGERATOR PIE

1 1/3 c. crushed corn
  flakes
3 Tbsp. confectioners sugar

1/4 c. butter, melted over
  hot water
1/2 tsp. vanilla

Mix well. Line 9 inch pie tin. Chill 1 hour. Add 1 cup fresh fruit or berries. Cover with filling of 3 stiffly beaten egg whites and 9 tablespoons sugar. Top with whipped cream and garnish
Darlene Lee

CREAMED RHUBARB PIE

2 c. rhubarb, cut up
3 Tbsp. butter
1 c. milk

2 Tbsp. flour
2 egg yolks
1 c. sugar

Cook mixture till done and put into baked pie shell. Cover with beaten egg whites.
Martie Athey, Detroit Lakes, Mn.

RHUBARB CUSTARD PIE

2 large eggs
1 Tbsp. milk
3 Tbsp. flour
3 c. pink rhubarb

1 1/2 c. sugar
1/2 tsp. nutmeg
3/4 Tbsp. butter

Beat eggs and milk. Stir in flour, sugar and nutmeg together and pour over rhubarb. Dot with butter - put crust on top and bake until nicely browned at 350° for about 1 hour.
Edith Weber, Fargo, N. D.

RHUBARB PIE

3 slightly beaten eggs

3 Tbsp. milk, added to eggs

Mix and stir in:
2 c. sugar
1/2 c. flour

3/4 tsp. nutmeg
4 c. diced rhubarb

Cover with crust. Bake in 400° oven until knife inserted is clean.
1748-81   Joan Buttweiler, St. Cloud, Mn.

RHUBARB PIE

4 c. rhubarb, cut up	2 Tbsp. flour
1 c. sugar	2 Tbsp. butter

Mix first 3 ingredients together and spread evenly into a 9 inch pan. Dot with butter.

1 c. sugar	1/4 tsp. salt
1 c. flour	1 egg
1 tsp. baking powder	

Sift dry ingredients together. Stir in egg. Sprinkle mixture over rhubarb so crumbs fall into rhubarb. Bake at 350° for 40 minutes.

Stan and Phylis Patyk, Sauk Centre, Mn.

SODA CRACKER PIE

3 egg whites, beaten stiff	16 soda crackers, crushed
1/4 tsp. cream of tartar	1 c. walnuts, cut up
1 c. sugar	1 tsp. vanilla

Grease 9x13 inch pan and bake 30 to 40 minutes at 325°. Cut into serving pieces, top with sweetened fresh or frozen strawberries. Top with whipped cream.

Recipe from Minneapolis, Mn.

SOUR CREAM PIE

1 c. raisins, washed in hot water and set aside	3 eggs (save 2 whites for top of pie)
1/2 c. brown sugar	2 Tbsp. flour
1/2 c. white sugar	1/2 tsp. cinnamon
1 c. sour cream	1/2 tsp. nutmeg

Add raisins, boil this mixture until thick, then pour into baked pie shell after it is cooled. Top with meringue made with the 2 egg whites and bake till meringue is brown.

Kathryn Otto, Harvey, N. D.

SOUR CREAM -RAISIN PIE

Beat 2 egg yolks. Add 1/2 cup sugar sifted with:

1 Tbsp. flour	A pinch of salt
1 tsp. cinnamon	

Add:

1 c. thick sour cream	3/4 c. raisins

Mix everything and cook until thick. Pour into baked pie crust and top with meringue.

Phyliss Brossart, Rugby, N. D.

SOUR CREAM RAISIN PIE

Pastry for 2 (8 inch) pie crusts	1 c. white sugar
1 c. dairy sour cream	1 tsp. vanilla
1 egg	1 c. raisins

Blend sugar and egg, add sour cream and vanilla. Mix well by hand. Add raisins and pour mixture into pastry lined pie plate. Dot with specks of butter and top with second crust. Brush top with slightly beaten egg white or little milk. Sprinkle on sugar. Bake in 425° oven for about 30 minutes. Do not overbake, bake only until crust is nicely browned. The filling will be creamy and raisins juicy. It's a rich pie.

Marty Eger, St. Paul, Mn.

SOUR CREAM RAISIN PIE

Cook for 5 minutes:

1 1/2 c. raisins	1 1/2 c. water

Mix in separate bowl:

3/4 c. sugar	1/2 tsp.salt
2 1/2 Tbsp. flour	

Mix in another bowl:

3 egg yolks, slightly beaten	1/2 c. milk

Mix egg mixture into sugar mixture and pour into raisin

mixture and cook till thick. Take off fire and cool slightly, then add 1/2 cup cultured sour cream, 1/2 teaspoon cinnamon. Pour into baked crust and top with meringue. Beat 3 egg whites, then add 1/4 cup sugar and beat till fluffy. Pour on pie and bake till light brown.

Margie Stullz, Big Lake, Mn.

SHORTCUT CHEESE PIE

1 (6 oz.) pkg. semi-sweet chocolate pieces
1 (3 oz.) pkg. cream cheese, softened
1/4 c. light brown sugar

1 (2 oz.) pkg. dessert topping mix
9 inch chilled graham cracker crust

Melt chocolate over hot (not boiling) water. Remove from heat. Stir in cheese till it is blended. Stir in sugar. Prepare topping mix as directed on package; blend 1/2 cup of topping into chocolate mixture. Fold in remaining topping. Spread filling in crust. Chill overnight. Yield: 8 servings.

Chocolate Graham Crust: Mix thoroughly -

1 1/2 c. graham cracker crumbs
1/4 c. brown sugar
1/8 tsp. nutmeg

1/3 c. melted butter
1 oz. sq. unsweetened chocolate, melted

Press into 9 inch pie pan. Chill till firm.

STRAWBERRY SERENADE PIE

Pastry:

1 c. + 2 Tbsp. flour
1/2 tsp. salt

1/3 c. corn oil
2 Tbsp. cold water

Cheese layer:

1/2 c. sifted powdered sugar
1/2 tsp. almond extract
1/2 tsp. vanilla

1 (3 oz.) pkg. cream cheese
1 c. whipping cream, whipped

Glazed Strawberry Filling:

1 qt. fresh strawberries	1 Tbsp. cornstarch
1/4 c. granulated sugar	3 drops red food coloring
1 tsp. lemon juice	1 tsp. butter
7/8 c. water	

For pastry, sift together flour and salt; blend in corn oil thoroughly with fork. Sprinkle all of water over mixture; mix well. Press dough firmly into ball. (If too dry, add 1 more tablespoon corn oil.) Flatten ball slightly; immediately roll into 12 inch circle between 2 pieces of waxed paper. Peel off top paper; place pastry in 9 inch pie pan, paper side up. Peel off paper; fit pastry loosely into pan. Trim 1/2 inch beyond pan edge. Fold under, flute, prick well. Bake 12 to 15 minutes in 450° oven. Remove from oven. Cool.

Cheese layer: Add sugar and flavorings to cream cheese and beat until smooth and fluffy. Fold in whipped cream. Spread evenly over bottom of baked pie shell. Chill thoroughly.

Glazed Strawberry Filling: Wash and hull strawberries; cut strawberries into halves. Add sugar and mix; let stand and drain thoroughly. Combine lemon juice and strawberry liquid and add enough water to make 1 cup liquid. Blend small amount of the liquid with cornstarch in saucepan. Gradually add remaining liquid. Cook over medium heat 3 to 5 minutes, or until thick and clear. Remove from heat. Add food coloring and butter. Cool. Arrange drained strawberries over chilled cheese layer. Spoon glaze over strawberries. Chill until served.

SKILLET PEACH PIE

Make biscuit dough to line an 8 inch skillet. Top dough with 6 fresh peaches, peeled and sliced. Mix:

1/2 c. sugar	1/4 tsp. cinnamon
1/2 tsp. salt	1 1/2 Tbsp. soft butter

Sprinkle over peaches, fold biscuit dough toward center leaving a hole in the center. Bake at 425° for 25 minutes. Serves 6.

Dee Olson, St. Paul, Mn.

STRAWBERRY PIE

Graham Cracker Crust:

1 pkg. graham crackers,   1/3 c. sugar
  crushed   1/4 c. melted butter

Cream Cheese Filling: Beat well -

1 (8 oz.) pkg. Philadelphia   1/2 c. sugar
  cream cheese   2 eggs, beat one at a time

Pour into crust. Bake 20 minutes at 325°. Prepare 1 package of strawberry Junket (follow directions on package). Cool. Add 1 quart fresh whole strawberries. Pour onto filling. Cool 4 hours or overnight!
Yvonne Weiss, Fargo, N. D.

GLORIA'S SURPRISE BEAUTY PIE

Crust:

2 c. vanilla wafers,   1/2 c. butter, melted
  crushed   6 Tbsp. powdered sugar

Soften 1 (8 ounce) package cream cheese. Add 1 cup sugar, vanilla. Fold in 1 pint cream, whipped and 2 cups miniature marshmallows. Use 9x13 inch pan. Use fresh strawberries, cut on top of cream mixture, then spread topping.

Topping:

1 box Junket dessert   1 box frozen strawberries
  (strawberry)

Follow directions on box. When cooled, spread on top of above mixture.
Gloria Smith, Windom, Mn.

CAKES

COOKIES

DESSERTS

HANDY CHART OF KITCHEN MATH
(Size of Pans and Baking Dishes)

Cooking need never become a crisis, when you use our handy charts. Need a 4 or 6-cup baking dish? Will your fancy mold be the right size for the recipe? See below for the answers.

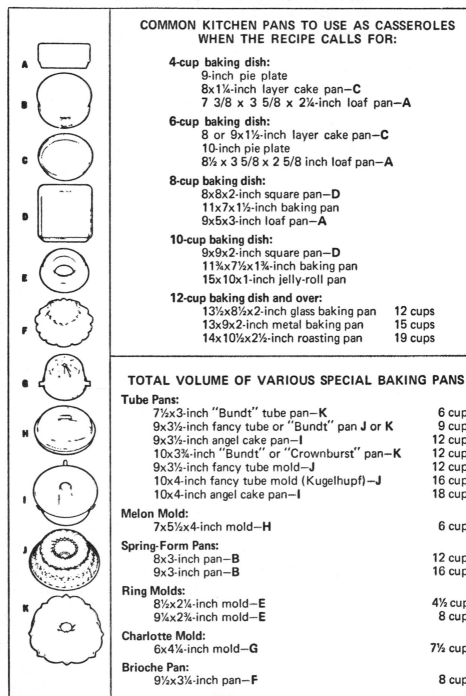

COMMON KITCHEN PANS TO USE AS CASSEROLES WHEN THE RECIPE CALLS FOR:

4-cup baking dish:
9-inch pie plate
8x1¼-inch layer cake pan—**C**
7 3/8 x 3 5/8 x 2¼-inch loaf pan—**A**

6-cup baking dish:
8 or 9x1½-inch layer cake pan—**C**
10-inch pie plate
8½ x 3 5/8 x 2 5/8 inch loaf pan—**A**

8-cup baking dish:
8x8x2-inch square pan—**D**
11x7x1½-inch baking pan
9x5x3-inch loaf pan—**A**

10-cup baking dish:
9x9x2-inch square pan—**D**
11¾x7½x1¾-inch baking pan
15x10x1-inch jelly-roll pan

12-cup baking dish and over:
13½x8½x2-inch glass baking pan   12 cups
13x9x2-inch metal baking pan   15 cups
14x10½x2½-inch roasting pan   19 cups

TOTAL VOLUME OF VARIOUS SPECIAL BAKING PANS

Tube Pans:
7½x3-inch "Bundt" tube pan—**K**   6 cups
9x3½-inch fancy tube or "Bundt" pan **J** or **K**   9 cups
9x3½-inch angel cake pan—**I**   12 cups
10x3¾-inch "Bundt" or "Crownburst" pan—**K**   12 cups
9x3½-inch fancy tube mold—**J**   12 cups
10x4-inch fancy tube mold (Kugelhupf)—**J**   16 cups
10x4-inch angel cake pan—**I**   18 cups

Melon Mold:
7x5½x4-inch mold—**H**   6 cups

Spring-Form Pans:
8x3-inch pan—**B**   12 cups
9x3-inch pan—**B**   16 cups

Ring Molds:
8½x2¼-inch mold—**E**   4½ cups
9¼x2¾-inch mold—**E**   8 cups

Charlotte Mold:
6x4¼-inch mold—**G**   7½ cups

Brioche Pan:
9½x3¼-inch pan—**F**   8 cups

ALMOST-FROM-SCRATCH RUM CAKE

1 pkg. white or yellow
  cake mix
4 eggs
3/4 c. milk

3/4 c. melted butter and
  Wesson oil (half each)
1 tsp. vanilla
1 small pkg. instant vanilla
  pudding mix

For Rum Syrup:

1 c. sugar
1/2 c. butter

1/4 c. water
1/4 c. light rum

Combine cake mix, eggs, milk, butter with oil, vanilla and pudding mix in large mixer bowl. Beat 4 minutes with electric mixer. Pour into greased and floured 12 cup Bundt pan or angel food pan. Bake at 350° for 1 hour or until done. Cool in pan 5 minutes. Meanwhile, cook sugar, butter and water together until sugar is dissolved. Add rum. Remove cake from pan and prick top with fork. Return cake to pan and pour hot rum syrup over it. Leave in pan about 15 minutes. Serve as is, or with whipped cream. Serves 12.

ANGEL FOOD DELIGHT

Tear up 1 large angel food cake into a 9x13 inch pan. Mix 1 package lime jello following directions on box. Add to jello - a small can of crushed pineapple and a small jar of maraschino cherries, sliced up. Pour this mixture over the cake and refrigerate until set. Cut into squares and top with whipped cream and a whole cherry before serving.
              Anonymous (Corky) Selegeby,
              Minneapolis, Mn.

APPLE-E-SPICE CAKE

2 Tbsp. sugar
1/2 tsp. cinnamon
2 c. (1 lb. 4 oz. can)
  pie sliced apples,
  drained (reserve juice)

1 pkg. Pillsbury yellow cake
  mix
1 c. liquid (see following)
3 eggs
1 tsp. cinnamon

Grease 10 inch Bundt or tube pan and sprinkle with mixture of 2 tablespoons sugar and 1/2 teaspoon cinnamon. Drain apple slices; add enough water to the liquid to make 1 cup. In large bowl, blend dry cake mix, 1 cup liquid, 3 eggs and 1 teaspoon cinnamon until moistened; beat as directed on package. By hand, stir in drained apple slices. Pour into prepared pan. Bake at 350° for 35 - 45 minutes. Cool upright in pan for 15 minutes; remove from pan. Cool. Glaze with powdered sugar glaze.

Jane Bohline, Minneapolis, Mn.

APPLESAUCE CAKE

1/3 c. shortening	1 tsp. soda
3/4 c. sugar	1/2 tsp. cinnamon
1/2 tsp. salt	1/2 tsp. cloves
1 egg	2 c. chopped nuts (optional)
1 c. + 1 Tbsp. applesauce	1 c. chopped dates
1 1/2 c. flour	

Spread in 9x13 inch greased cake pan. Bake in 350° oven for 1/2 hour. Cool.

Easy Penuche Icing (for Applesauce Cake): Melt 1/2 cup butter (or margarine) on low heat. Add 1 cup brown sugar. Bring to a boil. Boil for 1 minute. Add 1/4 cup milk. Bring to boil again, boil for 2 minutes. Remove from heat. Cool. Beat in 1 3/4 cups powdered sugar. Frost cake. If too thick, add a small amount of milk.

Mrs. Luella (Lu) Boyer, Grand Forks, N. D.

BAKELESS CAKE

2 c. sugar	1 c. chopped nuts
1 lb. butter	1 large can pineapple
3 egg whites	2 lb. vanilla wafers

Cream butter and sugar together. Add nuts and pineapple. Mix well and fold in the whites. Line the bottom of a pan with the wafers. Spread a thin layer of the mixture over them and cover with a layer of wafers, etc., until all is used. Press down well. Keep in cold place for at least 12 hours before serving. Serve with whipped cream.

Kathy Bischof, St. Cloud, Mn.

BANANA SPLIT CAKE

Layer 1:

1 1/2 c. flour	2 Tbsp. sugar
1/2 c. butter	1/2 c. walnuts

Mix and press into 9x13 inch pan. Bake 15 minutes in 350° oven. Cool.

Layer 2:

2 sticks butter	2 eggs
2 c. powdered sugar	1 tsp. vanilla

Beat until firm. Spread over crust.

Layer 3: 3 large bananas, sliced, which have been dipped in pineapple juice.

Layer 4: 2 (No. 2) cans crushed pineapple, well drained. Spread over bananas.

Layer 5: 1 large container Cool Whip, cover entire cake.

Layer 6: Sprinkle with chopped nuts and halved maraschino cherries. Chill well.

Leone Laschinger, Minneapolis, Mn.

BANANA SPLIT CAKE

1 1/2 c. margarine	5 sliced bananas
2 c. crushed graham cracker crumbs (28)	1 can crushed pineapple, drained
2 c. powdered sugar	1 (16 oz.) ctn. Cool Whip
2 eggs	1 c. walnuts or maraschino cherries

Mix crushed crumbs and 1/2 cup of margarine. Pat mixture into the bottom of a 9x13 inch pan. Beat together eggs, 1 cup of margarine and powdered sugar. Spread light mixture over crust. Cover with sliced bananas, then layer on pineapple. Top with Cool Whip; sprinkle on walnuts or cherries. Refrigerate overnight.

Kathy Bischof, St. Cloud, Mn.

BANANA SPLIT CAKE
(Refrigerate)

Mix together:

2 c. crushed graham crackers

1 stick melted margarine

Line 9x13 inch pan with crackers. Whip for 10 minutes:

2 c. powdered sugar
2 sticks margarine

2 eggs

Spread on top of graham cracker crust. On top of cream mixture:

3 large bananas, sliced

1 large can crushed pineapple, drained

Spread 1 large carton Cool Whip on top of fruit. Top with quartered cherries and chopped nuts.

Rachel Bakken, Rochester, Mn.

BOHEMIAN COFFEE CAKE

Cream well:

1 c. margarine
1 3/4 c. sugar

4 eggs

Add:

1 tsp. vanilla
1/2 tsp. salt

2 tsp. baking powder
3 c. flour

Mix well. Spread batter on greased cookie sheet. Save 1 cup of batter. Put 1 can of cherry or blueberry pie filling on top of batter. Spoon remaining 1 cup of batter on fruit. Bake 30 - 35 minutes at 350°. Frost with powdered sugar icing - almond flavoring. Drizzle on cool cake.

Rachel Bakken, Rochester, Mn.

BOILED RAISIN CAKE

Kathy Pierce, Minneapolis, Mn., in the Data Center brought us this delicious cake in April. It was such a hit, that everyone was asking for the recipe. Now we would like to share it with all of you:

Cake:

1 lb. raisins	1 tsp. nutmeg
1/2 c. shortening	1/2 tsp. ginger
1 1/2 c. sugar	2 tsp. cinnamon
2 eggs	1 1/2 tsp. soda
2 c. flour	1/2 tsp. salt
1 c. juice from cooked raisins	

Rinse raisins and cover with water. Cook for 20 minutes. Drain and save 1 cup of liquid. Cream shortening and sugar until fluffy. Add eggs, spices and soda, mix well. Add flour and liquid, alternating half and half. Fold in raisins and 1 cup chopped nuts (if desired). Grease and sugar 9x13 inch pan. Bake at 350° for approximately 1 hour.

Note: The secret to this cake is boiling the raisins. Don't try and take any shortcuts.

Frosting:

Powdered sugar	Butter flavored maple syrup
Vanilla	(regular maple syrup can
Butter	be used)

Mix well until light and fluffy.
Kathy Pierce, Minneapolis, Mn.

BUTTER SPONGE CAKE

4 eggs	2 Tbsp. melted butter in 1 c.
2 c. sugar	boiled milk
Salt	2 c. flour
2 tsp. vanilla	2 tsp. baking powder

Beat eggs until light and add sugar, salt, flavoring. Beat in butter and milk. Sift flour and baking powder. Beat egg mixture in quickly. Bake at 350° for 1 hour or till done.

Karen Rupert, St. Cloud, Mn.

1748-81

CARROT CAKE

2 c. sugar
1 1/2 c. oil
4 eggs
2 c. flour
1 tsp. cinnamon

1 tsp. soda
1 tsp. salt
1 c. nuts
2 1/2 c. grated carrots
1 Tbsp. vanilla

Mix and bake at 325° for 45 minutes.   Frost with:

8 oz. Philadelphia
  cream cheese
1 stick margarine

1 lb. powdered sugar (2 1/2
  c.)
1 tsp. vanilla

Mrs. Florence Brainard, Valley City, N. D.

CARROT CAKE

2 c. white sugar
4 eggs
1 1/4 c. Mazola oil
2 c. flour

1/2 tsp. salt
2 tsp. soda (slight)
3 tsp. cinnamon
3 c. ground carrots

Beat eggs, add sugar, oil, flour and dry ingredients, carrots last.

Frosting:

1 small (3 oz.) pkg.
  Philadelphia cream cheese
2 Tbsp. melted butter

1 3/4 c. powdered sugar
2 tsp. vanilla

Mix and spread on cool cake.
Lenna Adderman, Fargo, N. D.

CARROT CAKE

2 c. sugar
2 1/3 c. flour
2 tsp. cinnamon
1 tsp. salt
2 tsp. soda

1/2 tsp. baking powder
1 c. oil
4 eggs
3 small jars carrot baby
  food

Beat all together until well mixed, put into 9x13 inch pan. Bake at 350° for 40 - 50 minutes, or bake in 2 pans

378

for 35 - 40 minutes to get bars.

Frosting:

1 3/4 c. powdered sugar
1/4 c. margarine or butter
1 (3 oz.) pkg. cream cheese
1/4 tsp. vanilla
1/2 c. walnuts or almonds

Irene Palokangas, Detroit Lakes, Mn.

CARROT CAKE

2 1/2 c. flour
1 1/2 tsp. cinnamon
1/3 tsp. salt
1 c. sugar
1 c. crushed pineapple,
  well drained
2 tsp. vanilla
1/2 c. coconut
1/2 tsp. baking soda
2 tsp. baking powder
3 eggs
1/2 c. oil
2 1/2 c. carrots, grated
1/2 c. chopped pecans

Sift together flour, baking soda, cinnamon, baking powder, salt and set aside. Beat eggs until light and fluffy. Add sugar, oil, pineapple and vanilla. Beat until well blended. Beat in 1/3 of the flour mixture at a time until blended. Stir in carrots, coconut and pecans. Bake in greased 9x13 inch pan at 350° for 40 - 45 minutes. Test to see if done. Can bake in a greased-floured Bundt pan. Put a glaze on the top of cake or frost with cream cheese frosting.

Marie Miller, St. Paul, Mn.

CHERRY GLAZED POUND CAKE

1 lb. margarine, softened
3 c. sugar
12 eggs, separated
4 c. flour, sifted twice

Cream together margarine and sugar. Beat egg yolks until thick and lemon colored. Beat egg whites until stiff and stand in peaks. Alternately add egg yolks, egg whites and flour to margarine-sugar mixture. Beat until light and smooth. Pour into a well greased and floured 10 inch tube pan. Bake in 325° oven approximately 1 1/2 hours or until golden brown. Allow to cool in pan for 30 minutes before removing.

Honey-Cherry Glaze Sauce: Combine 1 pound 5 ounce

1748-81

379

can instant cherry fruit filling with 1 tablespoon lemon juice and 2 tablespoons honey. Simmer over low heat for 5 minutes. Serve over pound cake.
Corky Selgeby

CHOCOLATE CAKE
(Very Moist)

2 c. flour
2 c. sugar
1/2 c. cocoa
1 tsp. salt
1 tsp. baking powder
1/2 c. hot water dissolved
    with 3 tsp. soda

1/2 c. oleo or butter
2 c. buttermilk or sour
    milk (vinegar and sweet
    milk)
2 tsp. vanilla
2 eggs

Sift flour, sugar, cocoa, salt and baking powder. Add water and soda mixture. Melt oleo or butter. Add the milk, vanilla and eggs. Beat till smooth. Bake in 9x13 inch pan at 375° for 35 - 40 minutes.
Margie Stultz, Big Lake, Mn.

CHOCOLATE CARROT CAKE

2 c. flour
3 Tbsp. cocoa
2 c. sugar

2 tsp. baking soda
2 tsp. cinnamon
1 tsp. salt

Add:
4 beaten eggs
1 1/2 c. Wesson oil

3 c. shredded carrots

Grease and flour Bundt (or angel food) pan. Bake at 350° for 1 hour.

Topping:

3 oz. pkg. cream cheese
1/2 stick (1/4 c.) margarine

1 c. powdered sugar
1 tsp. vanilla

Beat till smooth.
Kayce Waterbury, St. Paul, Mn.

380

CHOCOLATE CHIP-DATE-NUT CAKE

1 c. dates, cut up
1 c. hot water
1 tsp. soda
1 c. white sugar
1 c. shortening (or
   1/3 c. oil)
1 3/4 c. flour

2 eggs
1 Tbsp. cocoa
1/4 tsp. vanilla
1 bag chocolate chips
1/2 c. chopped walnuts
Salt

Combine first 3 ingredients and let stand. Mix sugar, shortening, flour, eggs, cocoa, salt, vanilla and nuts. Mix both mixtures together. Put into a 9x13 inch pan. Sprinkle 1/2 cup nuts and 1/2 cup chips on top of cake and bake at 350° for 40 minutes.

Karen Rupert, St. Cloud, Mn.

CHOCOLATE ECLAIR CAKE

Filling:

3 c. milk
2 pkg. vanilla instant pudding

1 (8 oz.) ctn. Cool Whip

Beat milk and pudding till thick. Add Cool Whip and beat till blended.

Frosting:

2 Tbsp. butter
2 pkg. Choco-Bake or
   chocolate, melted
1 Tbsp. light corn syrup

3 Tbsp. milk
1 Tbsp. vanilla
1 1/2 c. powdered sugar

Line a 9x13 inch pan with graham crackers. Spread with 1/2 of pudding mixture, another layer of graham crackers. Add rest of pudding mixture, top with crackers. Frost. Chill for 24 hours.

Emmy Thielmann

CHOCOLATE OATMEAL CAKE

In large bowl pour 1 3/4 cups boiling water over 1 cup uncooked oatmeal. Let stand 10 minutes. Add:

1 c. brown sugar	1 tsp. vanilla
1 c. white sugar	1 stick margarine

Stir until margarine melts. Beat in 2 eggs. Sift together and add:

1 3/4 c. flour	1/2 tsp. salt
1 tsp soda	2 Tbsp. cocoa

Add above to oatmeal mixture and add 3/4 cup chocolate chips. Pour into greased and floured 9x13 inch pan. Sprinkle top with 1 cup chocolate chips and 1/2 cup nuts. Bake at 350° for 40 minutes.

CHOCOLATE SAUERKRAUT CAKE

2 1/4 c. flour	1 1/4 tsp. vanilla
1 tsp. baking soda	1/4 tsp. salt
1 tsp. baking powder	1/2 c. cocoa
1 1/2 c. sugar	1 c. water
2/3 c. shortening	1/2 c. kraut, drained and
3 eggs	chopped

Sift together flour, soda and baking powder. Set aside. Cream sugar and shortening. Add eggs. Mix well. Then add vanilla, salt and cocoa. Mix well, alternately add flour mixture and water, add kraut. Bake in greased and floured pan, 2 (8 inch) square pans or 1 (13x9 inch) pan, at 375° for 35 minutes.

Mary Lempe, St. Cloud, Mn.

CHOCOLATE ZUCCHINI CAKE

1 c. brown sugar	2 1/2 c. flour
1/2 c. white sugar	1/2 tsp. allspice
1/2 c. margarine	1/2 tsp. cinnamon
1/2 c. oil	1/2 tsp. salt
3 eggs	4 Tbsp. cocoa
2 tsp. vanilla	2 c. peeled and grated
1/2 c. buttermilk or sour	zucchini
milk	

| 1/2 c. chocolate chips | 2 tsp. baking soda |

Mix all together. Add chocolate chips last. Bake in 9x13 inch pan at 350° for 45 minutes. Ice with chocolate frosting.

Shirley Erickson, Fargo, N. D.

CHOCOLATE ZUCCHINI CAKE

1/2 c. margarine	4 Tbsp. cocoa
1/2 c. oil	1 tsp. soda
1 3/4 c. sugar	1/2 tsp. baking powder
2 eggs	1/2 tsp. cinnamon
1 tsp. vanilla	1/2 tsp. salt
1/2 c. sour milk	2 c. zucchini
2 1/2 c. flour	

Cream shortening and sugar. Add eggs and vanilla, beat. Sift dry ingredients together and add all with sour milk. Mix in zucchini. Spread in 9x13 inch pan. Top with a topping of 1/2 cup chocolate chips, 1/2 cup brown sugar and 1/2 cup nuts. Bake at 325° for 40 - 45 minutes.

Mary Paul, Minneapolis, Mn.

CHOCOLATE ZUCCHINI CAKE

1 c. brown sugar	1/2 tsp. allspice
1/2 c. white sugar	1/2 tsp. cinnamon
1/2 c. butter	1/2 tsp. salt
1/2 c. oil	2 tsp. baking soda
3 eggs	4 Tbsp. cocoa
1 tsp. vanilla	2 c. grated zucchini
1/2 c. buttermilk	1/2 to 1 c. chocolate chips
2 1/2 c. flour	

Cream sugar, butter and oil together in large bowl. Add eggs, vanilla, buttermilk, mix well. Measure dry ingredients into sifter, sift into bowl. Mix well, then add zucchini, grating it into bowl. Stir until well blended. Pour into greased, floured 9x13 inch pan. Sprinkle chocolate chips on top and bake at 325° for 45 minutes. Instead of using chocolate chips, the cake can also be frosted.

Carol Chisholm, St. Cloud, Mn.

CHOCOLATE ZUCCHINI CAKE

2 1/2 c. flour
1/2 c. cocoa
2 1/2 tsp. baking powder

1 1/2 tsp. soda
1 tsp. salt
1 tsp. cinnamon

Combine:
3/4 c. soft margarine
2 c. sugar

3 eggs, add one at a time,
beat well after each

Add:
2 tsp. vanilla
2 tsp. grated orange peel
2 c. shredded zucchini

1/2 c. milk
1 c. walnuts

Pour into greased Bundt pan. Glaze with powdered sugar frosting. Bake at 350° for 1 hour.

Faye Matson, Bismarck, N. D.

"COKE" CAKE

2 c. flour
2 c. sugar
1 tsp. salt
3 Tbsp. cocoa
2 sticks (1 c.) margarine

1 tsp. vanilla
1 1/2 c. miniature
marshmallows
1/2 c. buttermilk
1 tsp. soda
1 c. Coke

Combine flour and sugar, heat margarine, cocoa and Coke to boiling point. Add marshmallows. Pour over flour and sugar mixture. Stir well. Add buttermilk, eggs, soda and vanilla. Beat well - this will be thin. Put into greased and floured pan (9x13 inch) and bake at 325° for 30 - 35 minutes.

Icing:

1/2 c. margarine
About 3 1/2 c. powdered
sugar

3 Tbsp. cocoa
6 Tbsp. Coke
1 c. pecans

Combine margarine, Coke and cocoa, bring to a boil. Add powdered sugar and nuts - frost cake.

Sue Peterson, Grand Forks, N. D.

COCA-COLA CAKE

1 c. margarine, softened	1 tsp. soda
1 3/4 c. sugar	3 Tbsp. cocoa
2 eggs	1/2 c. buttermilk
2 c. flour	1 c. Coca-Cola
1/4 tsp. salt	1 c. miniature marshmallows

Cream shortening and sugar. Add eggs. Sift dry ingredients and add to sugar mixture with buttermilk. Add Cola and fold in marshmallows. Bake at 350° for 30 to 35 minutes. Make a frosting of the following.

Frosting:

1/2 c. margarine	1 box powdered sugar
3 Tbsp. cocoa	1 tsp. vanilla
1/3 c. Coca-Cola	3/4 c. chopped nuts

Bettie Mallon, Minneapolis, Mn.

COCOA-COLA CAKE

1 c. margarine	2 eggs
2 c. flour	1/2 c. buttermilk
1 3/4 c. sugar	1 c. cocoa
3 Tbsp. cocoa	1 1/2 c. small marshmallows
1 tsp. soda	1 tsp. vanilla

Preheat oven to 350°. Combine all ingredients except Cola and marshmallows in large bowl, mix 1 minute at medium speed. Add Cola, blend well. Fold in marshmallows. Pour batter into greased 9x13 inch pan. Bake 40 - 45 minutes. Cool 30 minutes.

Cola Icing:

1/2 c. margarine	1/3 c. Cola
3 Tbsp. cocoa	3 1/2 c. powdered sugar

Beat until smooth.

Florence Peine, St. Paul, Mn.

CRANBERRY CAKE

1 c. sugar	3 tsp. baking powder
2 c. flour	1 c. milk
1/2 tsp. salt	2 c. raw cranberries
2 Tbsp. butter	

Mix ingredients and bake for 30 minutes at 400°.

Sauce:

1 c. butter	1/2 c. half & half
1 c. sugar	

Simmer slow until thick. Serve warm sauce on each piece of cake.

Elaine Geelan, Minneapolis, Mn.

CRAZY CAKE
(American)

Sift into ungreased 9x13 inch pan:

3 c. flour	1/2 c. cocoa
2 c. sugar	1 tsp. salt
2 tsp. soda	

Make 3 holes with spoon. In first hole add 3/4 cup of salad oil, second hole 2 teaspoons of vinegar; third hole 1 teaspoon of vanilla. Pour in 2 cups of water and mix. Bake at 350° for 35 - 40 minutes. This will also make about 20 cupcakes.

Gertie Helm, Bismarck Council
Bismarck, N. D.

CRAZY CHOCOLATE CAKE

3 c. flour	1 tsp. salt
2 c. sugar	2/3 c. oil
1/3 c. cocoa	3 tsp. vinegar
2 tsp. soda	1 tsp. vanilla
2 c. cold water	

Mix gently by hand right in a 9x13 inch cake pan. Bake at 350° for 1/2 hour or till done.

Karen Rupert, St. Cloud, Mn.

CRAZY CHOCOLATE CAKE

3 c. flour
2 tsp. soda
1 tsp. salt
1/3 c. cocoa
2 c. sugar

2 tsp. vinegar
1 tsp. vanilla
3/4 c. salad oil
2 c. warm water

Sift dry ingredients into large pan, 9 x 13 x 2 1/2 inches, which has been well greased. Make 3 holes in mixture with spoon. In one hole, put vanilla; in another vinegar and in the third, pour the salad oil. Pour 2 cups warm water over entire mixture and blend gently, but thoroughly with fork. Do not beat. Bake for 30 minutes in 350° oven.

Marge Johnson, Minneapolis, Mn.

CREME DE MENTHE CAKE

To a white cake mix, add 2 tablespoons creme de menthe. Bake as directed on box. When cool, poke holes in cake with a straw. Pour 1 can of Hershey's syrup over cake. Frost with 1 medium carton of Cool Whip to which 2 tablespoons creme de menthe has been added. Be sure to use green creme de menthe.

Mary Perron, Rochester Council

DANISH CHRISTMAS CAKE

1 yellow cake mix
1 can vanilla pudding
1 pkg. macaroons

Whipping cream
Currant jelly

Bake cake in layer pans, cut each layer in half horizontally. Crush macaroons and add to pudding. Fill first layer with 1/2 pudding mix, second with currant jelly; third with rest of pudding mix. Frost with whipped cream.

Mrs. Ronald Schwartz, Owatonna, Mn.

DARK FRUIT CAKE

1 c. white sugar
1 c. shortening
1 c. sour milk
3/4 c. white corn syrup
2 tsp. soda
3/4 tsp. salt
1 tsp. cinnamon

1 c. brown sugar
1 egg
3 sq. chocolate, melted
4 c. flour
1/2 tsp. allspice
1/2 tsp. cloves

Add dates, raisins, nuts and *candied fruit as desired. Combine all ingredients and pour into 2 loaf pans. Bake at 325° for about 1 hour.

*Maraschino cherries can be used instead of candied fruit.

Gemma Pierson

DEVILS FOOD

1 c. boiling water
3 Tbsp. cocoa
2/3 c. margarine (scant)
2 c. sugar
2 c. flour

1 1/2 tsp. soda
1/2 c. sour milk
2 eggs
Vanilla

Pour water on margarine and cocoa. Cool. Add sugar, flour, soda, milk and eggs. Mix well (mixer can be used). Add vanilla. Use greased 9x13 inch pan. Bake 40 minutes in 350° oven.

Emily Hoeft, Paynesville

EGGLESS COLD WATER CHOCOLATE CAKE

Sift together 3 times:
3 c. regular flour
2 c. sugar, or less
1/3 c. cocoa

1 tsp. soda (rounded)
1 tsp. salt

Mix with fork:
3/4 c. vegetable oil
2 Tbsp. vinegar

1 1/2 tsp. vanilla
2 c. cold water

Bake in ungreased pan at 350° for 30 - 35 minutes. Can be mixed in pan that you bake in (9x13 inches).

Madeline Frese, Colorado Springs, Co.

EASY SHORT CAKE

Mix together:

2 c. flour	1 tsp. salt
1/2 c. sugar	1 Tbsp. baking powder

Add:

1/3 c. melted butter	2/3 c. milk

Bake at 450° for 12 minutes.
Sue Hick, Detroit Lakes, Mn.

FRESH APPLE CAKE

2 c. white sugar	2 eggs
1 tsp. cinnamon	1 1/2 c. Crisco oil
1 tsp. vanilla	1 tsp. salt
1 c. nuts	1 tsp. soda
3 c. apples, cut fine	2 c. flour

Beat eggs, add sugar, oil and vanilla. Stir well. Add all other ingredients. Add apples and nuts. Mix together lightly. Bake at 350° for 1 hour and 5 minutes in 9x13 inch pan. Mix:

1/4 tsp. cinnamon	1/4 c. white sugar

Sprinkle on top before baking.
Erlene Gallion, St. Cloud, Mn.

FRESH PEACH CAKE

Bake and cool one white cake.

1 pkg. vanilla pudding	1 c. sour cream
1 c. milk	

Cook together and cool. Place sliced peaches on top of cake. Then put pudding mix over peaches. Spread 1 large container of Cool Whip over pudding and sprinkle chopped nuts on the top.
Joanne Kunz, Jamestown, N. D.

FROZEN RHUBARB CAKE

1 1/2 c. sugar
1 c. sour milk
1/2 c. shortening
1 egg
1/4 tsp. salt

1/2 tsp. nutmeg
1 tsp. vanilla
1 tsp. soda
2 c. flour
2 c. frozen rhubarb, diced

Topping:

1/4 c. sugar

2 tsp. cinnamon

Cream together sugar and shortening. Add egg and beat. Mix in milk, vanilla and dry ingredients, add drained rhubarb. Pour into pan and sprinkle with topping. Bake in 9x13 inch pan at 350° for 35 minutes. To make sour milk, I mix 1 cup milk and 1 tablespoon vinegar or lemon juice.
Faye Matson, Bismarck, N. D.

FRUIT CAKE

2 c. sugar
1 c. butter
1 c. milk
5 eggs
3 c. flour
2 tsp. baking powder
1/2 tsp. cinnamon, cloves,
    mace, salt

1/2 c. dark raisins
1 lb. walnuts
1 lb. Brazil nuts
1/2 lb. fruit mix
Cherries (1/2 lb. red, 1/2 lb.
    green)
Pineapple
1/2 c. white raisins
Vanilla

Combine all ingredients. Pour into 3 bread tins. Bake 1 1/2 hours or till done, at 300°. When cooled, wrap in dishtowels soaked in brandy or wine. Wrap that up in aluminum foil, then put in a plastic bag in refrigerator.
Karen Rupert, St. Cloud, Mn.

FRUIT-COCKTAIL CAKE

2 1/4 c. flour
2 tsp. soda
1 tsp. salt
1 c. firmly packed brown
    sugar
1/2 c. chocolate chips

2 eggs
1/4 c. soft oleo
1 lb. can fruit cocktail,
    undrained
1/2 c. chopped walnuts

390

Combine all ingredients except chocolate chips and nuts. Blend 2 minutes. Add fruit-cocktail and then stir that in. Sprinkle chips and nuts on top after it's in a 9x13 inch pan. Bake 35 - 40 minutes at 350°. (Can serve with whipped cream on top, if desired.)

Karen Rupert, St. Cloud, Mn.

GELATIN EASTER EGGS IN CAKE NEST

Break some egg shells so carefully that just the tips of the shells are broken when the eggs are removed. Dry the shells; pour fruit gelatin of different colors into them. Set the filled egg shells upright in custard or muffin cups and chill until gelatin is firm. Then break away egg shells and put the bright colored "eggs" in a "nest" of hollowed out angel food, sponge or chiffon cake. Cover with butter icing and green tinted coconut.

GERMAN APPLE BUNDT CAKE

2 c. sugar
1/4 c. orange juice
1 c. oil
2 1/2 tsp. vanilla
4 eggs
3 c. flour
3 tsp. baking powder

1/2 tsp. salt
1 c. chopped nuts or 1 c. raisins
2 c. apples, peeled, cored and diced
1 tsp. cinnamon
1 Tbsp. sugar

Beat together sugar, orange juice, oil, vanilla and eggs with an electric mixer at high speed. Sift together dry ingredients, then blend into first mixture. Fold in nuts. Place 1/3 of the batter into a greased Bundt pan. Sprinkle with half of a mixture of the apples, sugar and cinnamon. Pour on another 1/3 of the batter. Sprinkle on the rest of the filling and top with last 1/3 of the batter. Bake at 350° for 55 - 60 minutes. Cool pan 10 minutes upside down, then remove from pan. Sprinkle with powdered sugar.

Kathy Bischof, St. Cloud, Mn.

GERMAN RAW APPLE CAKE

4 c. chopped raw apples   1 c. chopped walnuts

Combine in large bowl.

2 c. flour   2 tsp. cinnamon
2 c. sugar   1 tsp. salt
2 tsp. soda

Sift together over apples and nuts.

2 eggs   2 tsp. vanilla
1/2 c. oil

Mix and add to apple mix. Blend well. Spread in 9x12 inch greased pan and bake at 375° for 45 minutes.

Pearl Fellman, Brainerd, Mn.

GERMAN SUMMER CAKE

Pour 1 1/2 cups boiling water over 1 teaspoon soda and 1 cup dates, cut up. Cool. Cream:

3/4 c. shortening   2 eggs
1 c. sugar

Mix well and add:
1 1/2 c. flour   3/4 tsp. soda

Mix all ingredients and put into 10x13 inch pan.

Topping:

1/2 c. brown sugar   1/2 c. nuts
1 pkg. chocolate chips

Bake at 350° for 35 minutes or longer.

Mrs. W. A. (Pearl) Gross, Fargo, N. D.

HEATH BAR CAKE OR DESSERT
(Serves 10 - 12)

2 c. brown sugar	1 tsp. soda
2 c. sifted flour	1 tsp. salt
1/2 c. butter	1 tsp. vanilla
1 beaten egg	1/2 c. chopped pecans
1 c. milk	6 Heath bars

Mix first 3 ingredients, setting aside 1 cup of mix. Add rest of ingredients and beat well. Pour into greased 9x13 inch pan. To the 1 cup of mix, add 6 crushed Heath bars and 1/2 cup chopped pecans. Sprinkle on top of cake and bake at 350° for 35 minutes. May be served with ice cream or whipped topping.

Carla Kangas, Detroit Lakes, Mn.

HARVEY WALLBANGER CAKE

1 pkg. Duncan Hines white or yellow cake mix	4 eggs
	1/4 c. water
1 (4 oz.) pkg. instant vanilla pudding	1/4 c. vodka
	1/4 c. orange juice
1/2 c. Crisco oil	1/4 c. Galliano

Blend all ingredients in large bowl. Beat at medium speed for 2 minutes. Bake in greased and floured 10 inch tube pan or Bundt pan, at 350° for 45 - 55 minutes, until center springs back when touched lightly. Poke holes in warm cake with fork and pour the following frosting over:

2 tsp. vodka	2 tsp. Galliano
2 tsp. orange juice	

Add powdered sugar to desired consistency (about 1 cup). Pour on cake, then sprinkle powdered sugar on cake.

Bettie Mallon, Minneapolis, Mn.

KRUM KAKE

4 eggs, separated	2 c. flour
1 1/4 c. sugar	1/2 tsp. cardamon or vanilla
1/2 c. melted butter	(flavoring)
1 c. cream, whipped	

Use 4 bowls. Whip egg whites stiff. Whip cream. Whip egg yolks until lemon colored. Add butter to sugar (cream) in larger bowl. Add yolks. Alternate flour and cream, fold in egg whites. Place teaspoonful in Krum Kake iron, press. Makes 95 - 100. Roll while warm on cone.

Alvera Solvie, Glenwood, Mn.

KRUM KAKE

1/2 c. cream (whipping)	2 1/2 c. flour
1/2 c. butter	1/2 tsp. salt
1 1/2 c. sugar	1 tsp. vanilla
4 eggs, beaten	

Drop 1 teaspoonful of batter onto Krum Kake iron and bake on both sides until golden brown. Roll into cone shape immediately.

Mrs. Robert G. Pearson, Fargo, N. D.

LEMON SUPREME CAKE

1 pkg. lemon cake mix	3/4 c. Mazola oil
4 eggs	3/4 c. water
1 pkg. lemon jello	

Topping:

1/2 c. lemon juice	2 c. powdered sugar

Mix and pour over cake after making holes with fork while cake is hot.

Karen Karnowski, St. Cloud, Mn.

LIGHT OLD FASHIONED FRUIT CAKE

Sift together into large bowl:

4 c. sifted flour	1 1/2 tsp. cinnamon
1/2 tsp. baking powder	1 tsp. nutmeg
1 1/2 tsp. salt	

Add:

1 lb. whole pecans	3/4 lb. (1 3/4 c.) whole can-
3/4 lb. (1 3/4 c.) chopped,	died cherries (red, green)
candied pineapple	1 lb. golden raisins

394

Mix until all fruit and nuts are well coated with dry ingredients (set aside). Cream 1 cup butter, gradually add 2 1/4 cups sugar, creaming until light and fluffy. Add:

6 unbeaten eggs, beating well after each

3 Tbsp. (1 oz. bottle) brandy flavoring

Add to fruit mixture, mix well. Pour into 10 inch tube pan or 2 (9x5x3 inch) pans or 4 (1 pound) coffee cans lined with aluminum foil, filling pans 2/3 full. Bake in slow oven (275°) for 2 3/4 to 3 hours. One-half hour before cake is done, brush top with honey or light corn syrup. If desired, decorate cake with fruit and nuts, return to oven to finish baking. Cool cake completely - wrap with cloth that has been soaked in brandy (good brandy); then wrap in aluminum foil and store in cool place for a week.

Mary Patyk, Sauk Centre, Mn.

MAGIC CARAMEL CAKE

Caramelize 1 can sweetened condensed milk by cooking in hot water 3 hours.

10 graham crackers
1/4 tsp. salt
1 c. chopped nuts

1 c. sugar
3 eggs

Beat sugar, eggs and salt together. Add nuts and crushed graham crackers. Bake in 9 inch pan 20 to 30 minutes at 325°. Cool and spread the can of caramel over top. Serve with whipped cream.

Marge Johnson, Minneapolis, Mn.

MANDARIN ORANGE CAKE

Beat 2 eggs. Add:
2 c. flour
2 c. sugar
2 tsp. soda

1 tsp. salt
2 (8 oz.) cans Mandarin oranges, drained

Mix thoroughly and pour into greased pan. Bake 30 - 35 minutes at 350°. While warm, frost with following:

3/4 c. brown sugar
3 Tbsp. milk

2 Tbsp. butter

Bring to a boil in small saucepan; pour over warm cake.

MEXICAN WEDDING CAKE

Blend:

2 c. flour	2 tsp. baking soda
2 c. sugar	

Stir in:

1 c chopped nuts	2 beaten eggs
1/3 c. Crisco oil	

Mix well. Add:

1 (20 oz.) can crushed pineapple, including juice	1/3 c. chopped cherries

Add coconut and raisins (about 1/3 cup of each). Mix. Bake in 9x13 inch pan for 35 to 40 minutes.

Frosting:

8 oz. cream cheese	1 tsp. vanilla
1 stick oleo	2 c. powdered sugar

Mix well. Use all frosting.
Madaline Danich, St. Paul, Mn.

NEVER FAIL SPONGE CAKE

1 1/4 c. flour	1/4 tsp. salt
1 tsp. baking powder (level)	

Sift above ingredients together 3 times.

5 egg whites	1/2 c. cold water
5 egg yolks	1 tsp. vanilla
1 1/2 c. sugar	

Beat egg yolks until lemon colored and add 3/4 cup of sugar gradually. Beat well. Beat egg whites stiff and fold in 3/4 cup of sugar. Add flour mixture alternately to the egg yolks with cold water and vanilla. When well blended, fold in the egg whites. Bake in an angel food tin for 40 minutes in a 375° oven. When cake is baked, turn pan upside down and let cool. The bigger the eggs, the bigger the cake.
Erma P. Swanson, Minneapolis, Mn.

NORWEGIAN DUMP CAKE

1 large (15 1/2 oz.) can
  crushed pineapple
1 large (15 1/2 oz.) can
  cherry pie filling
1 box dry white or yellow
  cake mix
1 c. finely chopped walnuts
2 sticks butter, cut fine

Do not mix all together! Place in 13x9 inch cake pan in layers as listed. Bake at 350° F. for 35 minutes.
Dena Stoddard

HEATH BAR CAKE

1 pkg. white cake mix
1 pkg. (small) instant
  chocolate pudding
2 c. water
2 eggs or 1 egg and 2 egg
  whites

Mix per cake directions. Bake at 350° F. Cool.

Frosting:

1 c. powdered sugar
2 egg yolks
1/4 c. butter

Mix together; add:
1 c. whipped cream
1 tsp. vanilla

Spread on cake. Sprinkle 3 (20¢) crushed Heath bars over top. Refrigerate.
Marge Roman, Minneapolis, Mn.

NUT CAKE

1 1/2 c. sugar
1 1/2 c. butter or oleo
3 eggs (whites beaten
  and added last)
1 c. milk
1 c. nuts
1 tsp. vanilla
1 1/2 tsp. baking powder
Salt to taste
2 1/2 c. flour

I bake in tube pan. Bake at about 350°. Sort of heavy cake, it is winter one for me.
Mrs. James R. McQuaid, Anoka, Mn.

OATMEAL CAKE

1 1/4 c. water	1 1/3 c. flour
1 c. quick oatmeal	1 tsp. soda
1 stick margarine	1/2 tsp. cinnamon
2 eggs	3/4 tsp. salt
1 c. brown sugar	1 tsp. vanilla
1 c. white sugar	

Pour the boiling water over oatmeal and stir. Add margarine, eggs and sugar, then sifted ingredients. Bake in medium sized pan at 350° for 45 minutes. When done, while still hot, spread icing on and broil until light brown.

Icing:

6 tsp. margarine	1 c. chopped pecans
1/2 c. brown sugar	1 c. chopped coconut
1/4 c. evaporated milk	

Marilyn Johnson, Albert Lea, Mn.

OATMEAL CAKE

1 1/2 c. boiling water	1 1/2 c. flour
1 c. quick cooking oats	1 tsp. soda
1/2 c. butter	1 tsp. cinnamon
1 c. brown sugar	1 tsp. nutmeg
1 c. granulated sugar	1 tsp. salt
2 eggs	

Pour boiling water over the oats and let stand. Cream butter and sugars. Add eggs and stir in cooled oatmeal, flour, soda, cinnamon, nutmeg and salt. Place in greased 9x13 inch pan. Bake at 350° for 30 to 35 minutes. Cool and spread with broiled icing.

Margaret Fruetel, Mn.

OATMEAL CAKE

Pour 1 1/4 cups boiling water over 1 cup quick cooking oatmeal and 15 dates, cut up; let stand 20 minutes, then add:

1/2 c. shortening	1 c. white sugar

1 c. brown sugar	1 tsp. vanilla
2 eggs	1 1/2 c. flour
1 tsp. cinnamon	1 tsp. soda
1 tsp. nutmeg	1/4 tsp. salt

Bake in large cake pan 30 minutes at 350° F. Spread topping over cake while warm and brown under broiler about 2 minutes:

3 Tbsp. butter	1 c. nuts
2/3 c. brown sugar	4 tsp. cream
1 c. coconut	

Stan and Phylis Patyk, Sauk Centre, Mn.

ORANGE CAKE

1 c. sugar	1 tsp. soda
1/2 c. shortening	1 tsp. vanilla
2 eggs	1 c. raisins
3/4 c. sour milk	1 orange peeling
2 c. flour	

Cream sugar, eggs and shortening. Dissolve soda in sour milk, add alternately with flour to sugar mixture. Grind raisins and orange peel together and add. Bake for approximately 35 minutes at 350°, or till tests done. Frost with 1/3 cup soft butter, beat in 1 1/2 cups powdered sugar. Add 3 - 4 tablespoons orange juice, 1 1/2 teaspoons vanilla.
Sue Hick, Detroit Lakes, Mn.

PEACHES AND CREAM CHEESECAKE

Grease bottom and sides of 1 (9 inch) pie pan. Combine in bowl:

3/4 c. flour	1 pkg. dry vanilla pudding
1 tsp. baking powder	mix (not instant)
1/2 tsp. salt	3 Tbsp. butter
1 egg	1/2 c. milk

Beat 2 minutes at medium speed. Pour into the pie plate. Drain 1 can sliced peaches (reserve juice) and place slices on the batter in pie plate. Combine in small bowl, 1 (8 ounce) package cream cheese, 1/2 cup sugar and 3 tablespoons peach juice. Beat 2 minutes at medium speed. Spoon over the peaches to within 1 inch of edge of batter. Combine 1 tablespoon sugar and 1 teaspoon cinnamon and sprinkle over cheese mixture. Bake at 350° for 30 minutes. Cool before serving.

Dee Olson, St. Paul, Mn.

PEAR CAKE

1 1/2 c. vegetable oil	1 tsp. cinnamon
2 c. sugar	1 tsp. vanilla
3 eggs	2 c. chopped pears, large
3 c. sifted flour	can well drained
3/4 tsp. salt	1 c. chopped pecans
1 tsp. baking soda	(optional)

Beat oil, sugar and eggs together. Sift flour, salt, soda and cinnamon together. Add the egg mixture. Add vanilla. Fold in nuts and pears. Put into 10 inch greased and floured Bundt pan. Batter is thick. Bake at 325° for 1 hour and 20 minutes. Cool cake 20 minutes before removing from pan. When cake is cool, sprinkle powdered sugar over top and put a glaze made from pear juice and powdered sugar.

Glaze:

1 c. powdered sugar	1/2 tsp. vanilla
2 - 3 Tbsp. liquid	

Use a thin glaze that spreads quickly.

Mary Paul, Minneapolis, Mn.

PINEAPPLE DREAM CAKE

1 yellow cake mix	1 large can crushed pineapple
1 small box vanilla	1/2 to 3/4 c. chopped nuts
pudding (cooked)	1 large container Cool Whip
1 large pkg. cream cheese	

Bake cake according to directions on box. While still warm (just out of oven), poke holes in cake and spread pineapple, juice and all, over cake evenly. Blend cream cheese with pudding while pudding is still warm. Spread over cake and pineapple. Top with Cool Whip and garnish with nuts. Keep refrigerated until serving.

400 Rose Ecklund, Fargo, N. D.

PINEAPPLE REFRIGERATOR CAKE

1 box white cake mix (I prefer sour cream white)
1 large (11 to 16 oz.) can crushed pineapple
1 large box French vanilla pudding (instant or cooked)
1 medium ctn. Cool Whip or whipping cream
Chopped walnuts or pecans
8 oz. cream cheese, softened

Bake cake as directed in 13x9 inch pan. Cool. Drain pineapple well. Make pudding while cake is baking and set aside to cool, or if instant, to warm. (Cold pudding makes cream cheese lumpy.) Mix pudding and cream cheese together. Spread mixture on cooled cake. Spoon on and spread the pineapple over pudding mixture. (Press down into pudding.) Frost with whipped cream and garnish with chopped nuts. Refrigerate.

Jeanne Segebarth, Minneapolis, Mn.

PLAIN CAKE FROM AN 1850 COOKBOOK

My aunt made this for family get-togethers at our farm. It was requested by the nieces and nephews, as they thought Aunt Celia always beat a lot of love in her cake. I never make it, but that I think of her.

Take the butter left from breakfast, 2 or 3 eggs, a handful of sugar, as much milk as you think you will need, and enough flour to make a thick batter. If milk is sweet, add 2 teaspoons baking powder to flour. If milk is sour, add 1 teaspoon soda. Roll up tissue paper in loose ball and put in oven. When it browns in 10 minutes, the oven is ready. Put in cake and bake till done. (Mrs. Walter Gabbow)

Sent in by Ruth Braun, Owatonna, Mn.

POKE AND POUR CAKE

9x13 inch pan
1 (18 1/2 oz.) pkg. white cake mix
1 (3 oz.) pkg. cherry, raspberry or strawberry gelatin

Prepare cake mix as directed on package. Pour into greased and floured 9x13 inch pan. Bake as directed on package. Cool 15 minutes. Meanwhile, prepare gelatin as

1748-81

directed on package. With tines of fork, poke holes to bottom of cake at 1/2 inch intervals. Gently pour gelatin evenly over cake. Refrigerate 3 to 4 hours before serving. Serve with whipped cream. Store in refrigerator.

Arlene Byrne, Rochester, Mn.

POPCORN CAKE

Have ready, 14 cups popped popcorn. Cook till all mixed together:

1 stick margarine	1 tsp. vanilla
1/2 c. oil	1/2 tsp. salt
1 (10 1/2 oz.) pkg. marshmallows	

Mix into popped corn and add 1/2 cup gumdrops (any color) and put into greased 9x13 inch pan. Cool real well for Halloween or Christmas treats.

Margie Stultz, Big Lake, Mn.

POPCORN CAKE

8 qt. popcorn	2 pkg. spiced gumdrops
1/2 c. butter or oleo	2 pkg. Spanish peanuts
2 pkg. miniature marshmallows	

Melt oleo and marshmallows together, add all other ingredients and stir up. Press into buttered cake pan and buttered angel food cake pan.

Karen Rupert, St. Cloud, Mn.

POPCORN CAKE

1 (10 oz.) can yellow huskless popcorn	1 (24 oz.) pkg. miniature marshmallows
1/2 lb. butter or margarine	1 lb. can salted cocktail nuts (optional)
1 (10 oz.) pkg. small gumdrops	

Pop the corn according to directions, dissolve the marshmallows in melted butter. Combine popcorn, gumdrops and nuts. Add the marshmallow mixture. Mix well and press into buttered pan.

402   Joan Dondoneau, Grand Forks, N. D.

POPCORN CAKE

4 qt. popped popcorn	1 lb. spiced gumdrops
1 lb. Spanish peanuts,	1 bag large marshmallows
without skins	1/2 lb. butter or margarine

Mix popcorn, peanuts and gumdrops in large bowl. Melt marshmallows and butter. Pour over mixture in bowl and mix thoroughly. Butter an angel food cake pan. Put in mixture and press firmly. Refrigerate overnight. Remove from pan and let set out about 15 - 20 minutes before cutting with a very sharp knife or electric knife.

Sharon Christian

POPCORN CAKE

9 qt. popped corn	1 lb. marshmallows
1 lb. small gumdrops,	1/2 c. Mazola oil
take out black ones	1/2 c. butter
1/2 lb. salted peanuts	

Melt in top of double boiler or over low heat, the marshmallows, Mazola oil and butter. Pour melted marshmallow mixture over warm popcorn. Stir quickly with wooden spoon and pack firmly and quickly into 2 well buttered tube pans. Refrigerate for 1/2 hour before removing from pan. (Cut gumdrops into smaller pieces for more color.)

Jean Carlson

POPPY SEED CAKE

1 pkg. white or yellow	4 eggs
cake mix	1 pkg. vanilla or lemon
1 c. water	instant pudding mix
1/2 c. oil	4 Tbsp. poppy seed

Mix together dry cake mix and pudding mixed with poppy seed. Add water and shortening. Add one egg at a time, beating after each addition. Pour batter into a well greased Bundt pan. Bake at 350° for 45 minutes. Allow cake to cool in pan 15 minutes. Before removing, drizzle with glaze made of powdered sugar, lemon juice and butter.

Helen M. Gludt, Bottineau, N. D.

POPPY SEED CAKE

3/4 c. butter (shortening   2 tsp. baking powder
   or margarine)   4 egg whites, beaten
1 1/2 c. sugar   1 tsp. vanilla
2 c. sifted flour

First soak 1/2 cup poppy seed in 1 cup milk overnight or 2 - 4 hours. Cream butter and sugar. Add dry ingredients with soaked poppy seed-milk mixture. Fold in beaten egg whites and put into greased 9x13 inch pan or 2 layer pans. Bake at 350° for 25 - 30 minutes.
    Mary Harlander, St. Cloud, Mn.

POPPY SEED CAKE

Soak for 1/2 hour:
1 c. milk   1/2 c. poppy seed

Cream:
3/4 c. butter or margarine   1 1/2 c. sugar

Add soaked poppy seed.

2 c. flour   1 tsp. vanilla
2 tsp. baking powder

Add to above mixture. Fold in 4 beaten egg whites. Bake in 9x13 inch pan at 350° for 30 minutes.

Frosting:

1 c. sugar   1/3 c. milk
1/4 c. butter or margarine

Boil for 1 minute and 15 seconds. Cool and add 1 teaspoon vanilla. Beat and spread on cooled cake.
    Jo Nell Murack, Fargo, N. D.

POPPY SEED BUNDT CAKE

Combine in bowl:
1 pkg. white cake mix   1 c. warm water
4 eggs   1 pkg. instant cocoanut
1/8 c. poppy seed   pudding mix (dry)
1/2 c. cooking oil

404

Beat 4 minutes. Pour into Bundt pan or 2 loaf pans and bake at 325° - 350° for 40 - 50 minutes.
Marge Johnson, Minneapolis, Mn.

POPPY SEED TORTE CAKE
(Old Polish Recipe)

Cake:

3/4 c. poppy seed   3/4 c. milk

Soak poppy seed and milk overnight.

3/4 c. butter or margarine   1 1/2 c. sugar

Cream butter and sugar. Mix with milk and poppy seed.

2 c. flour   1/4 tsp. salt
2 tsp. baking powder   4 stiffly beaten egg whites

Sift dry ingredients and add. Fold in beaten egg whites and bake in waxed paper lined round cake pans at 350° for 30 - 40 minutes. Cool cake 10 minutes, remove from pan.

Filling:

1/2 c. sugar   1 1/2 c. milk
1 Tbsp. cornstarch   4 egg yolks, well beaten

Put into double boiler after it starts cooking, add sugar and cornstarch. Cool. Add 1 teaspoon vanilla and 1/2 cup chopped walnuts. Cool filling and spread between layers of cake.
Mary Lempe, St. Cloud, Mn.

RED CAKE

1/2 c. oleo   2 c. flour
1 1/2 c. sugar   1 tsp. soda
1 heaping tsp. cocoa   1 tsp. vinegar
1 c. buttermilk   1/2 tsp. salt
1 tsp. vanilla   2 eggs, well beaten
2 oz. red food coloring

Sift flour, salt and cocoa 3 times. Cream sugar and oleo. Add eggs. Add alternately flour mixture and buttermilk. Add red food coloring and vanilla. Fold in soda and vinegar, mixed together. Bake at 350° for 40 minutes in greased and floured pan.

Icing: Cook until thick 1/4 cup flour and 1 cup milk. Do not cool. Cream until fluffy, 1/2 cup oleo and 1 cup sugar. Mix together and add 1 cup coconut. It will be rather warm. Slightly cool and frost.

Mary Ann Hanson, Detroit Lakes, Mn.

RHUBARB BUNDT CAKE

Cream:

1/2 c. shortening	1/2 c. brown sugar
1 c. white sugar	1 egg

Add dry ingredients alternately with buttermilk:

2 1/2 c. sifted flour	1 tsp. soda
1 tsp. salt	1 c. buttermilk

Add:

2 c. cut rhubarb	1 tsp. vanilla
1/2 c. chopped nuts	

Put 1/2 of topping (1/2 cup sugar and 1 teaspoon cinnamon) in bottom of greased Bundt cake pan. Add cake dough and put other 1/2 of topping on top. Bake 45 - 50 minutes at 350°.

Lois Sandberg, St. Cloud, Mn.

RAW APPLE CAKE

1 c. white sugar	1/2 c. cold coffee
1/2 c. butter	1 1/2 c. flour
1 egg	1 tsp. soda
1/2 tsp. cinnamon	1/2 c. chopped nuts
1/4 tsp. cloves	1 1/2 c. chopped apples
1/4 tsp. nutmeg	

Blend ingredients and bake in 9x9 inch pan for 45 minutes at 350°.

Darlene Schlottman, St. Cloud, Mn.

RHUBARB CAKE

1 1/2 c. brown sugar	2 c. rhubarb
1/2 c. shortening	2 c. flour
1 c. sour milk	1/2 tsp. vanilla
2 eggs	Pinch of salt
1 tsp. soda	

Mix shortening and brown sugar. Add eggs and vanilla. Stir in milk, flour, soda and salt. Add rhubarb last. Mix well. Pour into 9x13 inch pan and top with 1/4 cup sugar mixed with 1 teaspoon cinnamon. Bake at 350° for 40 - 45 minutes.

Georgia Berg, Fargo, N. D.

RHUBARB CAKE

2 c. sugar	2 eggs
2/3 c. shortening	3 c. flour
2 tsp. cinnamon	1 c. cold coffee
1/2 tsp. cloves	1 c. raisins or dates
1/2 tsp. nutmeg	1 c. nuts
1/2 tsp. salt	2 Tbsp. white and brown
2 tsp. soda	sugar
	2 c. rhubarb

Mix and add 1 cup raisins or dates, 2 cups of finely cut rhubarb and 1 cup nuts. Bake at 350° to 375° approximately 1 hour (O.K. to test in 35 minutes). Mix 2 tablespoons of white and brown sugar. Spread over top and put in oven again till done. It is very rich. Powdered sugar frosting or whipped cream is good, too.

Harriett Haggard, Anoka, Mn.

RHUBARB CAKE

1 egg	2 c. flour
1 1/2 c. brown sugar, packed	1 tsp. soda
	1/2 tsp. salt
1/2 c. shortening	1 1/2 c. raw rhubarb, cut
1 tsp. vanilla	fine, add to batter
1 c. sour milk	

Topping:

1/2 c. brown sugar, packed   1 tsp. cinnamon
Chopped nuts (as many as you like)
1748-81   Betty Michon, Detroit Lakes, Mn.

RHUBARB CAKE

1/2 c. shortening	1/2 tsp. soda
1 1/2 c. sugar (white, brown or half and half)	1/2 tsp. baking powder
	Pinch of salt
	2 c. flour
1 egg	1 tsp. vanilla
1 c. buttermilk	2 c. rhubarb, cut small, or peaches or apples

Topping:

1/2 c. sugar   Cinnamon

Karen Rupert, St. Cloud, Mn.

RHUBARB CAKE

Cut 5 cups of raw rhubarb into bite sized pieces and spread in a greased 9x13 inch cake pan. Over the rhubarb, sprinkle 1 cup of sugar and 1 small package of dry strawberry jello. Over this spread 3 cups of miniature marshmallows. Take 1 large package of white cake mix and prepare it according to package directions. Pour over rhubarb mixture. Bake 1 hour at 350°. Serve with whipped cream.
Marilyn Helgeson, Fargo, N. D.

RHUBARB CAKE

1 1/2 c. brown sugar	1 tsp. soda
1/2 c. shortening	1/2 tsp. salt
1 c. sour milk	2 c. sifted flour
1 egg	1 1/2 c. raw rhubarb, cut

Cream shortening and sugar; add milk and egg. Sift dry ingredients; add to mixture. Stir in rhubarb. Pour into greased and floured 9x13 inch pan. Top with 1/4 cup sugar and 1 teaspoon cinnamon mixture. Bake at 350° for 30 minutes. Top with whipped cream when serving.
Mary Jo Conneran, Fargo, N. D.

RHUBARB CAKE

1/2 c. white sugar
1 c. brown sugar
1/2 c. shortening
1 egg
1 c. sour milk

2 c. sifted flour
1 tsp. soda
1 tsp. vanilla
1 1/2 c. cut up rhubarb

Mix ingredients as listed, except rhubarb. Put part of dough in 9x13 inch pan. Mix rhubarb with rest of dough and spread over dough in pan. Mix 1/3 cup white sugar and 1 teaspoon cinnamon and sprinkle over batter. Bake in 350° oven for 40 to 50 minutes.

Madaline Danich, St. Paul, Mn.

RHUBARB CAKE

1/2 c. shortening
1 1/2 c. brown sugar
1 c. buttermilk
1 egg

1 tsp. baking soda
1/2 tsp. salt
2 c. flour
2 c. chopped rhubarb

Topping:

1/2 c. white sugar
1 tsp. cinnamon

1 Tbsp. butter

Mix together and put on top of the cake in an 8x8 inch or 7x11 inch pan. Bake at 350° for 1 hour.

Jane Bohline, Minneapolis, Mn.

RHUBARB CAKE

Cream:
1 1/2 c. brown sugar
1 egg

1/2 c. shortening

Sift:
2 c. flour
1/2 tsp. salt

1 tsp. soda

Add alternately to creamed mixture with 1 cup buttermilk or sour milk and 1 teaspoon vanilla. Add 1 1/2 cups chopped rhubarb. Bake in 13x9 inch pan 30 minutes at 350°.

Topping: Add 1/2 cup white sugar, 1/2 teaspoon cinnamon over top before baking.

1748-81

RHUBARB UPSIDE DOWN CAKE

Make a white cake, put into a 9x13 inch pan. Mix together:

3 c. rhubarb   1 Tbsp. cinnamon
1 1/3 c. sugar

Sprinkle over cake batter. Pour 1/2 pint whipping cream over rhubarb. Bake at 350° for 50 minutes. Let stand 15 minutes, tip out onto a cake plate.
Karen Rupert, St. Cloud, Mn.

UPSIDE DOWN RHUBARB CAKE

Melt in baking pan (9x13 inches):

2 Tbsp. butter   3/4 c. sugar
2 c. cut rhubarb

Mix batter while above is melting - over medium heat. Beat 2 eggs hard for 4 minutes. Add 1 cup sugar, 1/3 at a time. Add 2 tablespoons butter melted in 1/2 cup hot milk alternately with:

1 c. sifted flour   1 tsp. baking powder
1/4 tsp. salt   1/2 tsp. vanilla

Pour over hot rhubarb. Bake 30 minutes in 350° oven. Top with sweetened whipped cream.
Lois Sandberg, St. Cloud, Mn.

SHEET CAKE

Sift together:
2 c. sugar   2 c. sifted flour

Boil in pan and pour over flour and sugar:

4 Tbsp. cocoa   1 c. water
1/2 c. Crisco oil   1 stick oleo or butter

Add this to above:
2 beaten eggs   1 tsp. soda
1/2 c. buttermilk

410

Beat all together a moderate amount of time. Grease pan and bake in 350° oven for about 35 minutes.

Icing: Boil together in pan -

1 stick oleo or butter	1 box powdered sugar
4 Tbsp. cocoa	1 tsp. vanilla
6 Tbsp. buttermilk	1 c. nuts

Ice the cake while it is still hot.
Ione Wahl, Minneapolis, Mn.

SIS BONNIE'S KANSAS CAKE

Put in pan:

1 c. cold water	1/2 c. shortening
1 stick margarine	3 - 4 Tbsp. cocoa

Bring to boil. Put into large bowl:

2 c. flour	2 c. sugar

Add chocolate mixture. Add:

2 eggs	1/2 c. butter
Dash of salt	1/2 c. milk
1 tsp. soda	1 tsp. vanilla

Bake at 350° in deep cookie sheet pan, about 35 minutes.

Frosting:

1 stick margarine, melted	2 - 3 Tbsp. milk, heated
3 - 4 Tbsp. cocoa	

Add powdered sugar and vanilla.
Kathy Bischof, St. Cloud, Mn.

SPICE CAKE

2 c. sugar	2 tsp. cinnamon
2 c. raisins	2 c. water
1 tsp. cloves	1 c. margarine
1 tsp. salt	

Mix ingredients in large saucepan. Cook to boiling, simmer 5 minutes. Remove from heat and let cool till crust forms on top. Add:

4 c. flour   2 tsp. soda

Mix well. Bake in 9x13 inch pan, greased, at 300° until firm. To keep cake moist, put a saucepan of water in the oven while baking, or wet rags tied around the pan.
Kathy Neels, St. Cloud, Mn.

STRAWBERRY ANGEL CAKE

1 pkg. strawberry jello   1 pkg. frozen strawberries
1/2 c. boiling water   1 c. whipping cream
Dash of salt   Small angel food cake

   Custard:

2 eggs, beaten   4 Tbsp. lemon juice or
4 Tbsp. sugar   vinegar
                                 1 Tbsp. butter

Mix eggs, sugar, lemon juice and beat together and cook about 5 minutes. When cold, add to whipped cream.
Mix gelatin in boiling water. Add frozen berries and salt. Let set until slightly thick, then fold into whipped cream and custard mixture. Break cake into bite sized pieces, scatter in bottom of an 8x11 inch cake pan. Alternate with cake and whipped cream mixture. Refrigerate. This can be put into 9x13 inch pan - it just makes a thinner dessert.
Harriett Haggard, Anoka, Mn.

STRAWBERRY CAKE

1 pkg. white cake mix   1/2 c. strawberries
   (I used Duncan Hines)   1/2 c. oil
1 (3 oz.) pkg. strawberry   1/2 c. water
   jello   4 eggs

Mix well and bake at 350° for 30 minutes.

Dressing:

1 pkg. Dream Whip, whipped   1/2 c. strawberries (I use
                                 juice from berries)
412   Mary R. Jones, Spirit Lake, Ia.

STRAWBERRY WHAT'S IT CAKE

8 oz. miniature marshmallows
1 pkg. white or yellow cake
  mix

4 c. strawberries
1 (3 oz.) pkg. strawberry
  gelatin

Cover the bottom of a greased 9x13 inch cake pan with marshmallows. Prepare cake mix according to directions on box and pour over marshmallows. Crush strawberries and mix with dry gelatin, then spoon over batter. Bake at 350° for 45 - 55 minutes.

Kathy Neels, St. Cloud, Mn.

STREUSEL COFFEE CAKE

Cream:
1/2 c. butter
1 tsp. vanilla

1 c. sugar

Add 4 eggs. Sift together:

1 tsp. baking powder
1 tsp. soda

1/4 tsp. salt

Add sifted dry ingredients and 1 cup buttermilk to creamed mixture. Mix well.

Streusel Filling:

2 c. brown sugar
6 Tbsp. flour
6 Tbsp. melted butter

2 tsp. cinnamon
3/4 c. chopped nuts

In greased pan, put 1/3 of streusel filling. Add 1/2 of batter, then 1/3 of streusel filling. Spread remaining batter and 1/3 of streusel filling on top. Bake in 9x13 inch pan at 350° for 45 minutes.

Lorraine Pauls, Fargo, N. D.

TEXAS SHEET CAKE
(Bars)

Boil:
1 c. water
2 sticks oleo

5 Tbsp. cocoa

Need not cool. Beat 2 eggs, add:

2 c. sugar
1/2 c. buttermilk
1/2 tsp. soda
1/4 tsp. salt

1/2 tsp. cinnamon
1 tsp. vanilla
2 c. flour

Combine with above and bake in greased and floured jelly roll pan. Cool. Batter is quite thin. Bake at 350° for 25 to 30 minutes or longer.

Frosting for Texas Sheet Cake:

6 Tbsp. oleo
1/3 c. milk

1 c. sugar

Bring to a boil, boil 1 minute (or longer). Remove from heat, add 1/2 cup chocolate chips and 1 teaspoon vanilla. Beat and spread on cake.

Cecilia Leverson, Fargo, N. D.

THANKSGIVING FRUIT CAKE

1 c. butter
1 c. brown sugar
1 c. molasses
4 eggs
Nutmeg
1/2 lb. currants

1/2 lb. raisins
1/4 lb. citron
1 tsp. each cassia (bought in
    drug store), allspice,
    cloves
1 tsp. baking soda
4 c. flour

Cream butter and sugar. Add other ingredients. Mix well. Bake at 325°.

Ruth Brown, Owatonna, Mn.

TOM SMITH'S CAKE

Make one lemon cake. Cool! Punch holes with fork all over top. Make 1 package lemon jello (using only 1 cup of boiling water). Mix with 1 cup 7-Up. Pour mixture evenly over cake. Refrigerate! Make 1 package instant lemon pudding mix with whipped topping of some sort (use about 1 to 1 1/2 cups whip). Frost! Eat all leftover stuff while you refrigerate completed cake.

TUTTI FRUTTI BUNDT CAKE
(Microwave or Conventional Oven)

2 c. sugar
1 c. cooking oil
4 eggs
1 (8 oz.) can crushed
   pineapple, undrained
2 c. sliced bananas (2 - 3
   medium)
1 tsp. almond extract

2 tsp. grated orange peel
2 c. unsifted all-purpose flour
1 c. whole wheat flour
1 tsp. salt
1 tsp. baking powder
1/2 tsp. soda
1 c. chopped dates

Glaze:

1 Tbsp. oleo
1 1/2 c. unsifted powdered
   sugar

2 1/2 to 3 Tbsp. orange juice
1/4 tsp. almond extract

Blend together sugar and oil in large mixing bowl. Beat in eggs, blend in pineapple, bananas, extract and orange peel. Add flours, salt, baking powder and soda. Blend with electric mixer at low speed until well mixed. Stir in dates Grease a Bundt cake pan. Pour batter into pan, spreading evenly. Microwave (medium - 50%), uncovered, 18 minutes, rotating dish once. Then, microwave on high 9 to 10 minutes or until no longer doughy. Let stand 15 minutes. Invert onto serving plate. Cool completely. Glaze. (All-purpose flour can be substituted for whole wheat flour.) For conventional oven: Bake at 350° for 1 hour to 75 minutes or until done.

Karen Rupert, St. Cloud, Mn.

VIRGINIA'S DATE CAKE

1 c. dates, chopped
1 tsp. soda
1 1/2 c. hot water
1 egg
3/4 c. shortening
1 c. sugar

2 c. flour
1/2 tsp. soda
1/2 tsp. salt
1/2 c. sugar
1 (6 oz.) pkg. chocolate chips
1/2 c. nuts

Add 1 teaspoon soda to chopped dates. Pour boiling water over dates and soda and let cool. Meanwhile, cream shortening and sugar. Add egg and mix well. Add date mixture. Sift flour, salt and 1/2 teaspoon soda. Combine with other mixture and mix well. Pour into greased 9x13

1748-81

inch pan. Mix chocolate chips, nuts and sugar. Spread evenly over batter and bake at 350° for 35 - 40 minutes.

WATERGATE CAKE

1 box white cake mix
1 box pistachio pudding
1 c. Wesson oil

1 c. ginger ale
3 eggs
1/2 c. chopped nuts

Mix together. Bake at 350° till done in 9x13 inch pan.

Frosting:

1 large (13 oz.) ctn. Cool
Whip (may also use 1 pkg.
Dream Whip)

1 box pistachio pudding
1 c. milk

Beat and put on cake. May add green food coloring.
Deb Nordby, Fargo, N. D.

WEDDING CAKE

This is an old time recipe, taken from "Good Old Days". From Fannie Farmers niece, Mrs. Genevieve Morley, born 1876, died 1970.

Cream together:
2 c. butter

4 c. sugar

Add 8 eggs and 4 egg yolks, lightly beaten. Add 2 cups milk alternately with 8 cups flour (sifted 3 times with 12 teaspoons baking powder). Add 4 cups currants, floured. Bake at 350°.
Ruth Brown

YELLOW BUTTER CAKE

Bake yellow butter cake in 9x13 inch pan and cool. Slice into 1/4 inch strips, narrow way.

Frosting:

2 sq. or 1 c. unsalted
butter

3 1/2 c. powdered sugar
4 eggs

Cream butter; add and beat in powdered sugar. Add eggs, one at a time and beat 5 minutes after each egg. Add 1/2 teaspoon vanilla. Put the cake on bottom of pan, then layer of frosting, etc. Should end up with 3 layers. Refrigerate.

Sue Peterson, Grand Forks, N. D.

ZUCCHINI CAKE

2 c. flour	1 c. raisins
2 c. sugar	1 c. nuts
2 tsp. soda	4 eggs
2 1/2 tsp. cinnamon	3 c. grated raw zucchini
1 tsp. salt	1 1/2 c. Wesson oil

Mix all ingredients and pour into a 9x13 inch pan. Bake in a moderate oven for 45 minutes.

Frosting:

1 (8 oz.) pkg. cream cheese	2 c. powdered sugar
	1 tsp. vanilla
1 stick or 1/2 c. margarine	1 c. chopped pecans

Cream cheese and margarine, add sugar, vanilla. Spread on cake. Sprinkle nuts on top. Half of recipe is enough unless you want a thick frosting.

Fern Groskreutz, Service Representative
Litchfield, Mn.

BLUEBERRY-PEACH COFFEE CAKE

1 pkg. Duncan Hines wild blueberry muffin mix	1/4 c. sugar
	1/4 c. flour
	1/2 tsp. cinnamon
1 (1 lb.) can sliced peaches	2 Tbsp. (1/4 stick) butter or margarine

Preheat oven to 400°. Wash blueberries and drain peaches. Spread fruit on paper towels and set aside. In a small bowl, combine sugar, flour and cinnamon. Cut in butter and set aside. Mix muffin batter as directed on the label, except do not fold in the blueberries. Spread batter in a greased 8 inch square pan. Top with drained blueberries and peach slices. Sprinkle cinnamon mixture over the fruit. Bake at 400° for 25 minutes, until golden brown.

1748-81

417

BUTTERSCOTCH COFFEE CAKE

1 pkg. yellow cake mix	3/4 c. oil
1 pkg. instant butterscotch pudding mix	3/4 c. water
	4 eggs

Mix all and turn into 9x13 inch cake pan. Sprinkle before baking with topping and cut through batter.

Topping:

1/2 c. sugar	1 tsp. cinnamon
1/2 c. chopped nuts	1 tsp. cocoa

Bake at 350° for 35 - 40 minutes.
Shirley Way, Minneapolis, Mn.

COFFEE CAKE

Cream:

1/2 c. shortening	1 tsp. vanilla
3/4 c. sugar	3 eggs, adding one at a time

Beat well. Blend in:

2 c. sifted flour	1 tsp. baking soda
1 tsp. baking powder	1/2 pt. commercial sour cream

Topping: Mix well -

6 Tbsp. butter	2 tsp. cinnamon
1 c. brown sugar	1 c. chopped nuts

Grease tube type pan and line with waxed paper. Pour half of batter into pan, alternating with topping, ending with topping on top. Bake at 350° for 1 hour.

COFFEE CAKE

3/4 c. sugar	1 1/2 c. flour
1/4 c. soft shortening	2 tsp. baking powder
1 egg	1/2 tsp. salt
1/2 c. milk	

Cream sugar, shortening and egg; mix well. Add milk alternately with flour, baking powder and salt, sifted together.

Topping: Mix 1 1/2 teaspoons cinnamon with 1/2 cup brown sugar on top. Bake at 325° for 25 - 35 minutes. I use pie tins.

Lillian Herrick, St. Paul, Mn.

KUCHEN
(German Coffee Cake)

Crust: Dissolve 1 package yeast in 1/4 cup warm water. Combine:

1 c. scalded milk	1 tsp. salt
3 Tbsp. shortening	1 well beaten egg
3 Tbsp. sugar	

Add:
Yeast mixture	3 1/2 c. flour

Let rise for a short time after pressing into pie tins (greased).

Filling:

3 - 4 eggs, beaten	2 c. sugar
4 heaping Tbsp. flour	1 qt. sour cream

Cook over low heat until mixture comes to a boil. Pour into prepared dough, pressed into pie tins (greased). Add any of the following if desired - apples, fresh peaches, rhubarb, raisins, prunes, dry cottage cheese. Sprinkle with cinnamon and sugar. Bake at 350° for 1/2 hour.

Mrs. Lu Boyer, Grand Forks, N. D.

GRANDMOTHER'S COFFEE CAKE

4 c. flour	3 eggs (1 egg white retained
1 c. milk, scalded and	for next morning)
cooled	1/2 lb. lard (1 c.)
3 Tbsp. sugar	1 env. yeast in warm water
	Salt

Mix with a wooden spoon and put into a covered, greased bowl overnight. Refrigerate. Next morning, divide

in half. Roll each quite thin into a rectangle. Spread with a
a little egg white, partially beaten. Any kind of filling can
be used. This person used prunes or dates. Sprinkle
with a little brown sugar and cinnamon and turn 1/3 over,
then put other 1/3 on top. Put a few slits in it. Let rise
till light and bake at 350° for 25 minutes.

Ruth Braun, Owatonna, Mn.

KUCHEN
(German)

2 c. warm milk	2 eggs
1/2 c. sugar	1/2 c. shortening, melted
1 or 2 pkg. yeast	5 c. flour
1 tsp. salt	

Dissolve yeast in warm milk and add rest of the ingredients and mix well. Let rise until double in bulk, about 30
to 40 minutes. Roll out small portions on a floured board
a size to fit pie tins, with dough part way up on the sides.
Makes about 10. Fill with the following.

Filling:

2 1/2 c. cream or evaporated milk	1 pkg. regular vanilla pudding
1 c. sugar	4 eggs, beaten
3 Tbsp. flour	3 Tbsp. cottage cheese

Mix all together. Put fruit on crust and pour filling
over this. Do not fill to top of crust. Sprinkle a mixture of
cinnamon and sugar over and bake at 350° about 30 minutes. Fruit can be prunes, raisins, canned peaches, apples,
rhubarb or apricots.

Helen Kruse, Fargo, N. D.

KUCHEN

1 c. sugar	1 c. milk
2 eggs	2 tsp. baking powder
1 c. cream	1 tsp. vanilla

Add enough flour to make soft dough. Using large
tablespoonful of dough, roll out in circle to fit in bottom of
pie pan. Top with thick cream, sugar and cinnamon.

Bake at 375°. (If using store cream, add an egg or two to thicken cream.) Makes about 12.

Phyllis Brossart, Rugby, N. D.

COFFEE CAKE

3/4 c. sugar	1 1/2 c. flour
1/4 c. salad oil	2 tsp. baking powder
1 egg	1/2 tsp. salt
1/2 c. milk	

Mix and pour half of this batter into an 8x8 inch pan. Top with a mixture of:

1/2 c. brown sugar	1/2 c. chopped nuts
2 Tbsp. flour	2 Tbsp. melted butter
2 tsp. cinnamon	

Then pour the other half of the mixture over the topping. Bake for 30 minutes at 350°.

Elsa Ditty, St. Cloud, Mn.

PINEAPPLE ORANGE COFFEE CAKE

2 1/4 c. flour	1/2 tsp soda
1/2 c. sugar	1/2 tsp. salt
1 1/2 tsp. baking powder	2/3 c. butter

Blend in large bowl till crumbly. Stir in 2/3 cup orange juice and 2 eggs till well blended. Pour into greased 9x13 inch pan, greased only on the bottom. Combine 1 cup crushed pineapple, undrained, and 1/2 cup orange marmalade (or apricot or peach preserves). Spoon over batter. In small bowl, combine till crumbly:

1/3 c. flour	1/3 c. sugar
1/2 tsp. cinnamon	3 Tbsp. softened butter

Sprinkle topping over pineapple. Bake at 375° for 25 - 35 minutes. Serve warm.

Kathy Neels, St. Cloud, Mn.

CHERRY COFFEE CAKE

1 c. white sugar
1/2 c. brown sugar
1/2 c. oil
4 eggs

2 c. flour
1 tsp. baking powder
1 tsp. vanilla

Mix 2 sugars until well blended - add remainder of ingredients. Spread 1/2 of dough in bottom of pan. Add pie filling, then remaining dough. Sprinkle top with cinnamon and sugar mixture. Bake in 9x13 inch pan at 325° for 45 - 50 minutes.

Carol Edwards, Anoka, Mn.

COFFEE CAKE

1 box white cake mix
1 box instant vanilla
  pudding
1 c. sour cream

4 eggs
1 tsp. vanilla
2/3 c. oil

Mix together and beat 4 minutes.

1/2 c. sugar
1/2 c. nuts

1 tsp. cinnamon

Mix sugar, nuts and cinnamon. Grease Bundt pan or angel food pan. Alternate cake mixture with sugar and cinnamon. Bake 50 - 60 minutes at 350°. Stays moist several days.

Gina Michels, Willmar, Mn.

CHERRY COFFEE CAKE

2 1/4 sticks margarine
1 1/2 c. sugar
2 c. flour

1 can cherry or blueberry
  pie mix
4 eggs, separated
1 tsp. vanilla or lemon extract

Beat egg whites (stiff) and set aside. Cream margarine, sugar and egg yolks. Add flour and vanilla or lemon extract. Beat this well. Add stiffly beaten egg whites. Grease or spray a 9x13 inch pan. Pour in dough - except 1 cup. Spread pie filling over top. Drop extra dough by small spoonfuls over pie mix. Bake at 350° for approximately

30 minutes. Sprinkle with powdered sugar, or drizzle with frosting.

Claren Kane, Sauk Centre, Mn.

COFFEE CAKE

1 c. honey and nut flakes, crushed to make 1/2 c.
2 Tbsp. brown sugar
2 Tbsp. melted butter
1/4 tsp. cinnamon

Mix together. This is topping.

1 1/4 c. flour
1 1/2 tsp. baking powder
1/2 tsp. salt
1 tsp. cinnamon
1/2 c. shortening

1 c. corn flakes, crushed to make 1/2 c.
1/2 c. brown sugar
1 egg
3/4 c. milk

Stir together dry ingredients. In large bowl, beat shortening and sugar, add egg, beat well. Add corn flakes and milk. Add flour mixture, stirring slowly only until combined. Spread in greased 8x8 inch pan. Sprinkle with topping, pressing into batter. Bake at 375° for about 25 minutes. Cool 5 minutes, cut into squares.

Helen M. Gludt, Bottineau, N. D.

BLACK BOTTOM CUPCAKES

Filling:

1 (8 oz.) pkg. cream cheese
1 beaten egg
Dash of salt
1 c. milk chocolate chips

Beat until fluffy, then add chips.

Batter:

1 1/2 c. flour
1/2 c. cocoa
1 c. water
1 tsp. soda

1 c. sugar
1/2 c. oil
1 Tbsp. vinegar

Fill cups 1/2 full of batter and spoon cream cheese mixture on center top. Bake 20 minutes at 350°.

Lynn Mehelich, Sauk Centre, Mn.

1748-81

CHEESE CAKE CUPCAKES
(Here come the calories)

Cream together:

3 (8 oz.) pkg. cream cheese   1 c. sugar

Beat in 5 eggs, one at a time. Add 1 1/2 teaspoons vanilla. Pour into cupcake papers in muffin tins, 3/4 full. Bake at 300° for 40 minutes. Don't brown - just let rise. Cool - a hole will form on top. Spoon topping into hole and put 1/2 teaspoonful of jelly on top. Return to oven for 5 minutes.

Topping:

1 c. sour cream   1/4 tsp. vanilla
1/2 c. sugar

Keep in refrigerator. These will freeze very well for later use.

Joyce Joransen, Minneapolis, Mn.

FILLED   CUPCAKES

1 pkg. chocolate cake mix   1 c. sugar
1 (5 oz.) pkg. cream cheese   1/8 tsp. salt
1 egg   1 pkg. chocolate chips

Make up cake according to directions on package. Fill cupcake liners 2/3 full. Combine cream cheese, egg, sugar and salt in saucepan until well mixed. Fold in chips. Drop 1 tablespoonful of filling on top of batter. Mix as for cupcake directions on mix.

Marge Johnson, Minneapolis, Mn.

MINCEMEAT   CUPCAKES

1/3 c. shortening   1/2 tsp. soda
1 c. brown sugar   1/2 tsp. salt
2 eggs   1/2 c. sour milk
1 tsp. cinnamon   1/2 c. mincemeat
1/2 tsp. cloves   1/2 c. nuts, chopped
1 3/4 c. flour

Cream shortening, sugar and eggs together until

creamy. Add sifted flour, cloves, cinnamon alternately with sour milk. Add mincemeat and nuts. Bake at 375° for 25 minutes.

Frosting:

2 Tbsp. shortening
2 c. powdered sugar

2 Tbsp. milk, warmed
1/2 tsp. vanilla

Lillian Herrick, St. Paul, Mn.

PEANUT BUTTER CUPCAKES

1/3 c. shortening
1/2 tsp. salt
1 tsp. vanilla
1 c. brown sugar
1/2 c. peanut butter

2 eggs, well beaten
1/2 c. brown sugar
2 c. sifted flour
2 1/2 tsp. baking powder
3/4 c. milk

Combine shortening, salt, vanilla; add 1 cup brown sugar, cream well. Add peanut butter, mix well. Beat eggs, add 1/2 cup brown sugar. Add to creamed mixture. Add flour, baking powder with milk. Bake at 350° for 25 - 30 minutes.

Peanut Butter Icing:

1 1/3 c. chunky peanut
   butter

3 c. sifted powdered sugar
1/4 - 1/3 c. milk

Stir together until creamy.
                Lillian Herrick, St. Paul, Mn.

SELF-FILLED CUPCAKES

Make up 1 package chocolate cake mix (pudding mix cakes do not work), as directed. Fill muffin tins with paper liners, 2/3 full.

Filling:

8 oz. cream cheese,
   softened
1/3 c. sugar

1 egg
Dash of salt

Cream together preceding ingredients. Stir in 1 cup chocolate chips. Drop by teaspoonfuls onto top of mixture in each cupcake. Bake at 350° for 20 minutes. Makes 27 - 30 cupcakes.

Lu Boyer, Grand Forks, N. D.

SELF-FILLED CUPCAKES

1 pkg. chocolate cake mix	Dash of salt
1 (8 oz.) pkg. cream cheese	1 egg
1/3 c. sugar	1 pkg. chocolate chips

Mix cake according to directions on package. Line muffin tins with paper cups and fill 2/3 full. Beat cream cheese with sugar. Beat in egg and salt. Stir in chocolate pieces. Drop filling by rounded teaspoonfuls into each cupcake. Bake according to directions on cake package. Makes about 30 cupcakes.

Jane Bohline, Minneapolis, Mn.

BOILED MILK FROSTING

1 1/4 c. white sugar	Pinch of cream of tartar, or
1/2 c. milk	1 Tbsp. white corn
1 tsp. butter	syrup
1/2 tsp. vanilla	

Melt butter in pan, add sugar, cream of tartar and milk. Stir until mixture reaches the boiling point. Boil without stirring, until mixture forms a soft ball when dropped into cold water. Cool. When lukewarm, add vanilla and beat until right consistency to spread. Makes an excellent icing for Spice and Chocolate Cakes.

Helen-May Johnson, Chanhassen, Mn.

BROILED ICING FOR OATMEAL CAKE

1/4 c. brown sugar	6 tsp. butter
1/2 c. granulated sugar	1/4 c. light cream
1 c. coconut	1/4 tsp. vanilla
1 c. chopped nuts	

Put all ingredients into double boiler and cook until blended. Frost cake. Place frosted cake under oven broiler until frosting starts to turn brown and bubbly. Cool.

Margaret Fruetel, Minneapolis, Mn.

CARAMEL FROSTING

1 c. brown sugar
1 egg

1/4 c. cream or Carnation milk

Mix well and cook 2 - 3 minutes, stirring constantly.
Mary Harlander, St. Cloud, Mn.

CARAMEL CREME FROSTING

1/2 c. brown sugar
1/4 c. sour cream

1 1/2 c. powdered sugar

Melt and heat brown sugar and sour cream, but do not boil. When sugar is well dissolved, remove from heat, add powdered sugar, vanilla and dash of salt. Excellent way to use sour cream on hand. Good on bars, cakes, cookies, rolls, etc.

CHOCOLATE FROSTING

1 c. sugar
1/4 c. milk
1/4 c. butter or margarine

1 sq. chocolate or 1/4 c. cocoa
Vanilla

Cook over medium heat. Boil 2 minutes. Cold water for 2 minutes - beat.
Gina Michels, Willmar, Mn.

CHOCOLATE FROSTING

1/4 c. melted Crisco
   (or butter or shortening)
1/2 c. cocoa
1/4 tsp. salt

1/2 c. milk
1 1/2 tsp. vanilla
3 1/2 c. confectioners sugar, sift if lumpy

Combine Crisco, cocoa and salt; then milk and vanilla. Mix in sugar in 3 parts.
Carol Arndt, Windom, Mn.

DRESSING FOR ANGEL FOOD CAKE

1/2 c. sugar
4 egg yolks, beaten
3/4 c. pineapple juice

16 marshmallows, cut
1 c. cream, whipped

Cook in double boiler until marshmallows are melted. Cool. Add 1 cup cream, whipped. Store in refrigerator. Spoon onto cut angel food. May also be used for fruit salad.
Ruth Smith, St. Paul, Mn.

EASY COOKED CHOCOLATE FROSTING

1 c. sugar
1/3 c. cocoa
1/3 c. shortening

1/3 c. milk
1 tsp. vanilla

Mix except for vanilla. Boil 3 minutes. Add vanilla and beat to spreading consistency.
Kathaleen Bischof

FUDGE FROSTING

1 c. sugar
1/4 c. milk

4 Tbsp. butter
2 Tbsp. cocoa

Boil 1 minute, stirring constantly. Cool. Put on cake.
Mary Harlander, St. Cloud, Mn.

MAPLE FROSTING

About 1 c. powdered sugar
About 1 stick margarine
Slurp of milk

Maple flavoring
Walnuts

Kathy Neels, St. Cloud, Mn.

NEVER FAIL FROSTING

1 egg white
1 c. sugar
3/4 tsp. vanilla

1/4 tsp. salt
1/4 tsp. cream of tartar
1/3 c. boiling water

428

Combine all in a bowl. Place this bowl into a slightly larger bowl of boiling water. Beat about 6 minutes until stiff enough to spread. Makes a lot.

Ruth Braun, Owatonna, Mn.

NEVER FAIL CARAMEL ICING

4 Tbsp. butter
6 Tbsp. cream or
   evaporated milk
3/4 c. brown sugar

1 3/4 c. powdered sugar
   (about)*
1/2 tsp. vanilla

Melt butter in a saucepan. Add brown sugar and melt again. Add cream and allow to boil vigorously 1 minute. Remove from heat. Immediately start adding the powdered sugar, beating until smooth. When slightly cooled, add vanilla. *Continue adding the powdered sugar until consistency to spread. The amount of sugar you use depends on how you fill cup. I like this icing on Chocolate Cake.

Helen-May Johnson, Chanhassen, Mn.

NEVER-FAIL CHOCOLATE FUDGE FROSTING

1 3/4 c. white sugar
2/3 c. cream or small
   can Carnation milk
2 Tbsp. butter

1/4 lb. marshmallows
3/4 pkg. chocolate chips
Pinch of salt
1 tsp. vanilla

Boil sugar, cream, butter and salt 5 minutes. Remove from heat and add cut up marshmallows and chocolate chips. Stir until both are well dissolved. Frosting stays creamy.

Note: To get a different flavor, try using the mint flavored chocolate chips. Yummy.

Helen-May Johnson, Chanhassen, Mn.

ORANGE SAUCE FOR ANGEL FOOD CAKE

1 (7 oz.) can frozen
   orange juice
3 Tbsp. cornstarch
2 Tbsp. butter
3/4 c. sugar

Juice of 1 lemon
2 fresh oranges, sectioned
   and cut into halves
1 (#2) can sliced peaches,
   drained

Combine cornstarch and sugar. Dilute orange juice

1748-81

to 2 cups. Add cornstarch mixture to juice. Add butter
and lemon juice. Cook until thick. Cool. Add oranges and
peaches. May be chilled or served at room temperature.
Serve on angel food cake slices.

Carolyn Brudevold, Fargo, N. D.

QUICK EGG WHITE FROSTING

2 egg whites	1/4 c. sugar
3/4 c. light corn syrup	1 1/2 tsp. vanilla (or other
Dash of salt	flavoring)

Heat syrup to boil, beat egg whites and salt till foamy
on high speed (about 1/2 minute). Add sugar slowly, beat
till stiff (about 1 minute). Slowly add hot syrup, then add
vanilla, beat for 5 minutes or till becomes thick enough to
spread. Frosts 2 layers or angel food cake.

Marion Round, Faribault, Mn.

QUICK JELLO FROSTING

Whip 1 package Lucky Whip per directions. Add 1
package jello, beat until mixed. Good on angel food or white
layer cake.

Darlene Lee

QUICK CARAMEL FROSTING

3 Tbsp. brown sugar	4 Tbsp. hot black coffee
2 Tbsp. butter	

Stir until sugar melts. Add:

2 c. powdered sugar	1 tsp. vanilla

Beat well. If too stiff, add tiny bit of milk or cream.

Darlene Lee

SEA FOAM FLUFFY FROSTING

Mix in top of double boiler:

2 unbeaten egg whites	Dash of salt
1 1/2 c. packed brown sugar	1/3 c. water

Beat over boiling water (with egg beater or high speed of electric mixer) 7 minutes, or until frosting will stand in stiff peaks. Remove from water, add 1 teaspoon vanilla and beat 1 minute. Frosts a 9x13 inch pan (good on spice cake).
Karen Rupert, St. Cloud, Mn.

SILK AND GOLD FROSTING

2 Tbsp. Spry or Crisco	1 tsp. orange rind
1 Tbsp. butter	1/4 tsp. salt

Cream together, add 1 egg yolk and beat well. Add 2 cups powdered sugar with 1 teaspoon lemon juice, 2 teaspoons orange rind. Beat until light and creamy!
Bev Larson, Bismarck Council

WHITE FROSTING

Cook until thick:

3/4 c. milk	3 Tbsp. flour

Remove from heat and add 1 1/2 teaspoons vanilla. Cool. Beat until creamy:

6 Tbsp. shortening	3/4 c. white sugar
6 Tbsp. butter	

Add to cooled mixture. Beat and spread.
Darlene Lee

ALMOND COOKIES

1 c. brown sugar	1/2 c. oatmeal
1/2 c. shortening	1/2 tsp. soda
1 egg	1/2 tsp. baking powder
1 c. flour	1/2 tsp. salt

1 tsp. almond extract   1 (7 oz.) can flaked coconut

Mix in order given. Place on ungreased cooky sheet.
Bake 10 - 12 minutes at 375°.

Mrs. Lillian Herrick, St. Paul, Mn.

ANGEL COOKIES

1/2 c. butter	1 tsp. vanilla
1/2 c. shortening	2 c. flour
1/2 c. white sugar	1 tsp. soda
1/2 c. brown sugar	1 tsp. cream of tartar
1/2 c. nuts	1/2 tsp. salt
1 egg	1 (6 oz.) pkg. butterscotch chips

Form into balls and tip half ball into water, then into
sugar. Bake to a golden brown.

Lillian Herrick, St. Paul, Mn.

ANGEL COOKIES

1/2 c. white sugar	1 egg
1/2 c. brown sugar	1 tsp. vanilla
1 c. shortening	2 c. flour
1 tsp. soda	1 tsp. cream of tartar

Mix in order given. Shape into walnut sized balls.
Dip in water, then into sugar. Bake.

Darlene Lee

ANGEL CRISPS COOKIES

1/2 c. white sugar	2 c. flour
1/2 c. brown sugar	1/2 tsp. salt
1 c. shortening	1 tsp. soda
1 egg	1 tsp. cream of tartar
1 tsp. vanilla	

Cream sugars and shortening. Add egg, vanilla and
dry ingredients which have been sifted together. Form
into balls and dip top half in water, then in white sugar.
Press down in center. Bake at 400° for 5 minutes.

Karen Rupert, St. Cloud, Mn.

ANIMAL COOKIES

1 lb. margarine	2 1/2 tsp. baking soda
3 3/4 c. sugar	2 Tbsp. vanilla
10 Tbsp. milk	8 or 9 c. flour (enough to
5 eggs	make a stiff dough to roll)

Cream margarine and sugar; add eggs, milk and vanilla; blend thoroughly. Add baking soda to flour and add to first mixture a little at a time, blending after each addition. Roll on floured board and cut into desired shapes. Bake in 350° oven for 7 to 10 minutes. Makes 20 dozen cookies.

APPLE MACAROONS

Preheat oven to 375°.

4 or 5 medium apples, peeled and sliced very thin	1/2 tsp. cinnamon
	1/2 c. coconut
	1/2 c. nuts (optional)
1/2 c. sugar	

Slice apples thinly into 9x9 inch pan. Sprinkle sugar and cinnamon on top. Sprinkle coconut and nuts over above mixture.

Topping:

1/4 c. vegetable shortening	3/4 c. flour
1/4 c. butter or margarine	1/4 tsp. salt
1/2 c. sugar	1/2 tsp. vanilla
1 egg	

Mix melted butter and shortening, sugar and egg in small bowl. Add the remaining ingredients, mix and pour over mixture in pan. Bake 35 minutes until golden brown. Good with whipped topping or ice cream.

Helen Ryan, Scandia Mn.

APPLESAUCE COOKIES

1 1/4 c. sifted flour	1 1/2 c. oats
1 tsp. baking powder	1 c. applesauce
1/2 tsp. baking soda	1 egg
1/4 c. milk	1 c. sugar

1 tsp. cinnamon
1/2 tsp. nutmeg
1/2 tsp. salt

1/2 c. shortening
1 c. chocolate chips

Sift flour, baking powder and baking soda. In a small bowl, put milk and oats; mix in applesauce. Add egg, sugar, spices, salt and shortening. Pour over dry ingredients and mix. Add chocolate chips. Drop on greased cookie sheet. Bake at 375° for 15 minutes. Yield: 5 dozen.
Joan Billadeau, St. Cloud, Mn.

BANANA COOKIES

1 c. soft shortening
  (half margarine)
1 c. sugar
2 eggs
3 c. flour
1 c. ripe bananas, mashed

1/2 tsp. salt
1/2 c. buttermilk
1 1/2 tsp. soda (in buttermilk)
1 tsp. vanilla
1 c. chopped walnuts

Cream shortening and sugar. Add the eggs and mix well. Next, add the salt and vanilla. Alternate the flour and buttermilk, mixing well after each addition. Fold in the mashed bananas and walnuts. Chill 1 hour. Drop by teaspoonfuls onto greased cookie sheet. Bake for 10 minutes and 350°. When cool, frost with the following:

2 c. powdered sugar
1/4 c. margarine

1 tsp. vanilla and enough
  milk to make a spreading
  consistency

Jean Taylor, Grand Forks, N. D.

BLUEBERRY OATMEAL COOKIES

1 pkg. Duncan Hines
  wild blueberry muffin
  mix
3/4 c. quick cooking oats

1/4 c. brown sugar
1/3 c. cooking oil
1 Tbsp. milk
1 egg

Preheat oven to 375°. Wash blueberries; drain on paper towels. In a medium bowl, combine all but blueberries; mix well. Drop from a teaspoon onto an ungreased cookie sheet. Make a deep depression in the center of each cookie and fill with 7 - 8 well drained blueberries. Push

434

dough from sides to cover berries and pat down. Bake at 375° for 8 - 10 minutes until light brown.

BRANDY SNAPS

3/4 c. molasses
1/2 c. sugar
1 tsp. ginger
1 1/2 c. whipping cream
3 Tbsp. brandy

3/4 c. butter or margarine
1 c. flour
2 tsp. brandy
1/2 c. powdered sugar

Heat oven to 350°. 1. Mix molasses, butter and sugar in top of double boiler. Heat over simmering water - stir constantly until sugar dissolves and mixture is smooth; remove from heat. Mix flour, ginger, beat into molasses mixture gradually. Beat in 2 teaspoons brandy till smooth. 2. Drop batter by teaspoonfuls onto well greased cookie sheet - about 6 teaspoons only. Bake 6 minutes until cookies are in 3 - 4 inch rounds. Coat wooden spoon handle with butter. 3. Allow cookies to cool slightly. Loosen from sheet with metal spatula. Working quickly, wrap each cookie around handle of wooden spoon to form cylinder - if cookies cool too quickly, return to oven to warm up. Cool on wire rack. 4. One hour before serving, whip cream, beat in sugar until stiff. Fold in 3 tablespoons brandy. Pipe through cookie cylinder, refrigerate until served.
Note: Cylinder cookies can be made up 2 days in advance, store in airtight container at room temperature.
Mary Lempe, St. Cloud, Mn.

GRANNY RIEDER'S BROWN COOKIES

1 c. lard or shortening
1 c. sugar
3 eggs
1 tsp. salt
1 c. sour milk

5 tsp. soda
1 c. molasses
1 tsp. ginger
2 tsp. cinnamon

Use own judgement in adding flour, about 6 cups. Roll cookies and cut into any shape for holiday's. Bake at 350° for about 10 minutes or so. Cool and frost. The less flour used to roll, the more tender the cookie.
Joan Buttweiler, St. Cloud, Mn.

BUTTER BRICKLE COOKIES

Cream:

1 c. white sugar   1 1/4 c. shortening
1 c. brown sugar

Sift together:

4 c. flour   1 tsp. cream of tartar
1 tsp. soda   1/2 tsp. salt

Add:

2 eggs   1 tsp. vanilla

Beat well. Crush in 4 packages Butterfinger candy bars, so they are in large chunks. Add to dough. Shape into rolls 2 inches in diameter and wrap each in waxed paper or foil. Chill until firm. Cut chilled rolls into 1/2 inch slices. Bake at 350° for about 10 minutes or until lightly browned. Makes about 12 dozen cookies.

Marge Carlson, Sauk Centre, Mn.

CARDAMON DATE DROPS

2 c. sifted flour   1/4 c. shortening
1/2 tsp. baking soda   1 c. firmly packed brown
Seeds from 10 cardamon   sugar
   seeds crushed fine (roll   2 eggs
   with rolling pin between   1 Tbsp. milk
   waxed paper)   1 pkg. dates, chopped
1/8 tsp. salt   1/2 c. chopped nuts
1/2 c. margarine

Measure flour, soda and salt into sifter. Cream margarine and shortening with sugar until fluffy. Beat in eggs and milk. Sift in dry ingredients, a third at a time, blending to make soft dough. Stir in dates, nuts and cardamon seeds. Drop by teaspoonfuls onto ungreased cooky sheet. Bake 15 minutes at 350°.

CARAMEL CHIP COOKIES

1/2 c. peanut butter   1 pkg. caramel chips (2 c.)

Melt in double boiler. Then add 6 cups of Kellogg's Special K breakfast food and mix well. Drop by teaspoonfuls onto waxed paper.

Mrs. W. E. Gollehon, Fargo, N. D.

UNBAKED CARAMEL COOKIES

2 c. sugar
2/3 c. evaporated milk
   (small can)
3/4 c. margarine

1 (3 3/4 oz.) pkg. instant
   butterscotch pudding
2 3/4 c. quick oats
1 c. coconut

In large saucepan, cook sugar, margarine and milk until it reaches a rolling boil. Stir to avoid scorching. Remove from heat. Stir in remaining ingredients. Cool for 15 minutes. Drop by teaspoonfuls onto waxed paper. Makes 4 to 5 dozen.

Helen Schmidt, Fargo, N. D.

CEREAL CUTOUTS

2 1/2 pkg. semi-sweet
   chocolate pieces
   (2 1/2 c.)

2/3 c. white corn syrup
1 (5 1/2 oz.) pkg. crisp
   rice cereal

Melt chocolate in 3 quart saucepan over hot, not boiling water. Stir in corn syrup thoroughly. Pour in rice cereal; mix until all kernels are coated. Spread in jelly roll or roasting pan; cut with animal or fancy cooky cutter or form into balls.

CHEESE-DATE FOLDOVERS

1/2 c. margarine
1 c. grated sharp
   American cheese
   (approx. 1/4 lb.)

1 1/3 c. flour
1/4 tsp. salt
2 Tbsp. water

Cream margarine and cheese until light. Sift dry ingredients, blend into cheese mixture. Add water and mix. Chill 4 to 5 hours.

Filling:

1 c. chopped dates
1/2 c. brown sugar

1/4 c. water

Combine and cook over medium heat. Stir occasionally and cook until consistency of jam. Cool. Roll dough to 1/8 inch thickness on well floured surface. Cut with 2 3/4 inch

CHEWY BAR COOKIE

2/3 c. margarine
4 c. quick oatmeal
1 c. brown sugar

2 tsp. vanilla
1/2 c. corn syrup

Melt margarine, add rest of ingredients. Bake in greased 9x13 inch pan at 350° for 12 minutes. Cool.

Frosting (Chewy Bar Cookie): Melt 1 cup chocolate chips, add 1 cup peanut butter. Beat together by hand and spread over cooled dough. Put in refrigerator to set.
Vivian McMonigle, Detroit Lakes, Mn.

CHIPPER COOKIES

1 c. brown sugar
1 c. white sugar
1 c. shortening
2 eggs, beaten
1 tsp. vanilla

1 c. flour
1 tsp. soda
1 tsp. salt
4 c. rolled oats
1 c. coconut

Mix in order given. Shape into balls. Bake at 375° for 15 minutes. (5 dozen)
Darlene Lee

CHOCOLATE CHIP COOKIES

3/4 c. white sugar
3/4 c. brown sugar
1 c. shortening
2 eggs
2 c. oatmeal

1 c. chocolate chips
1 c. chopped walnuts
1 tsp. soda
1 tsp. salt
1 1/2 c. flour

Add 1 or 2 tablespoons water to moisten while mixing. Drop on cookie sheet with teaspoon. Bake 10 or 12 minutes at 350°.

CHOCOLATE CHIP COOKIES

1/2 c. shortening	2 eggs
1/2 c. butter or margarine	1 tsp. vanilla
1 c. white sugar	1/2 tsp. water
1 c. brown sugar, packed	

Combine and mix well. Add:

2 1/3 c. flour	1 (12 oz.) bag chocolate chips
1 tsp. soda	

Drop by teaspoonfuls onto greased cookie sheet. Bake at 375° until golden brown.

Gretchen Marquart, Fargo, N. D.

CHOCOLATE CHIP COOKIES

1 c. oleo	1 tsp. soda
3/4 c. brown sugar	1/4 c. hot water
3/4 c. white sugar	1/2 tsp. salt
2 eggs	1/2 c. nuts, chopped
1 tsp. vanilla	1 c. chocolate chips
1/4 c. real lemon juice	3 c. flour

Mix, drop by teaspoonfuls. Bake 17 minutes at 350°.

Karen Rupert, St. Cloud, Mn.

CHOCOLATE CHIP COOKIES
(With Oatmeal)

1 c. shortening	1 pkg. chocolate chips
3/4 c. white sugar	3/4 c. brown sugar
2 c. oatmeal	1 1/2 c. flour
1 tsp. soda in 1 1/2 tsp.	2 little eggs
warm water	Salt

Cream shortening and sugars, add eggs and beat. Add soda dissolved in water. Gradually add flour and oatmeal together with chocolate chips. Drop from spoon and bake 15 minutes at 350°. (You can roll into balls.)

Ellen Tilton, Windom, Mn.

HELEN PETERSON'S CHOCOLATE CHIP COOKIES

1/2 c. butter
2 c. brown sugar
2 eggs
1 tsp. vanilla

1/2 tsp. salt
Scant tsp. soda
1 tsp. cream of tartar
1 pkg. chocolate chips

Blend together in mixer bowl. Slowly add 3 1/2 cups (scant) flour. Bake one cookie before all flour is added to test. Add more flour as needed. Careful - too much flour will produce tough cookies. Bake at 350° for 10 - 12 minutes.

Helen Peterson, St. Paul, Mn.

CHOCOLATE MACAROONS

1/2 c. salad oil
4 sq. melted chocolate
2 c. sugar
4 eggs

2 tsp. baking powder
2 c. sifted flour
Pinch of salt

Form into balls and roll in powdered sugar before you bake at 350° F. for 10 minutes.

Lenna Alderman, Fargo, N. D.

CINNAMON ALMOND STICKS
(Jewish)

2 eggs
1 c. sugar
3/4 c. oil
2 tsp. vanilla

1/2 c. slivered almonds
1 1/2 tsp. baking powder
2 1/2 c. flour

Mix in order given. Refrigerate several hours or overnight, after forming into 4 rolls on large cookie sheet. Bake at 375° for 25 minutes. Remove from oven; cut into pieces 1/2 inch thick, using sharp, narrow bladed knife. Place on sides on cookie sheet. Sprinkle with cinnamon-sugar. Return to a 200° oven to toast for 1/2 hour or more.

Hint: I run blade of knife under rolls before slicing. I also invert slices on sheet for last part of toasting, sprinkling cinnamon-sugar on this side also.

Lu Boyer, Grand Forks, N. D.

COCONUT COOKIES

1 c. white sugar	1 tsp. soda
1 c. brown sugar	1/2 tsp. baking powder
1 c. shortening	2 2/3 c. flour
2 eggs	2 c. coconut
1/4 tsp. salt	Nuts and vanilla

Cream sugars and shortening, add eggs, coconut and beat well. Add dry ingredients, vanilla and nuts. Form into balls on an ungreased cookie sheet. Bake 15 - 20 minutes at 350°. (7 1/2 to 8 dozen)

Karen Rupert, St. Cloud, Mn.

COCONUT CREAM COOKIES
(Kokosdrommar)

2/3 c. sugar	1 c. flaked coconut
1 c. butter	2 c. all-purpose flour
(not oleo)	1/2 tsp. ammonium carbonate*
1 Tbsp. vanilla sugar*	

Preheat oven to 300° F. Cream sugar and butter until light and fluffy. Add the vanilla sugar, coconut and flour mixed with the ammonium carbonate. Work the dough smooth. Shape into small balls and place on the cookie sheet. Makes 5 dozen.

*Sugar and carbonate can be bought at Maid of Scandinavia stores.

(These cookies just melt in your mouth.)

Helen-May Johnson, Chanhassen, Mn.

COWBOY COOKIES

1 c. shortening	1 tsp. soda
1 c. white sugar	1/2 tsp. baking powder
1 c. brown sugar	1/2 tsp. salt
2 eggs, unbeaten	2 c. oatmeal
1 tsp. vanilla	1 small pkg. chocolate chips
2 c. flour	1/2 c. nuts
1 tsp. cream of tartar	

Cream shortening and sugar together. Add eggs and vanilla. Mix well. Add cream of tartar, flour, soda, baking powder and salt. Mix well. Add oatmeal, chocolate chips

1748-81

and nuts. Form into small balls (do not flatten, so they turn out round). Bake at 350° for 10 - 15 minutes.

Avis Paulsen, Verndale, Mn.

CRACKER JACK COOKIES

1 c. shortening	1 tsp. soda
1 c. white sugar	1 tsp. salt
1 c. brown sugar	1 tsp. vanilla
2 eggs	2 c. oatmeal (quick)
1 1/2 c. flour	1 c. coconut
1 tsp. baking powder	2 c. Rice Krispies

Cream shortening, sugar. Add eggs and vanilla. (Beat.) Sift flour, baking powder, salt and soda, add to above. Add oatmeal, coconut, Rice Krispies. Roll into small balls. No need to flatten. Bake 10 minutes at 375° or until lightly browned.

Johanna Singewald, St. Paul, Mn.

HONEY COOKIES

1 c. honey	1 c. sugar
1 c. butter	1 c. water
1 tsp. salt	

Bring the above mixture to a boil. Remove from heat and cool. Beat in:

2 eggs	2 tsp. nutmeg
2 tsp. soda	Anise (either anise powder (1/2 tsp.) or anise extract

Add 5 to 6 cups flour; mix well. Let stand overnight in refrigerator. Roll, not too thin. Cut in desired shapes and bake at 350°. Dough will be soft so keep in refrigerator and roll small amount at a time. Frost and decorate.

Frosting:

1 egg white, beaten stiff	1 c. powdered sugar
	Vanilla

Elizabeth Klug, Dickinson, N.D.

CREAM CHEESE COOKIES

1 c. sugar
1 c. shortening or butter
1 (3 oz.) pkg. cream
  cheese
1 egg

2 1/4 c. flour
Salt
1 tsp. vanilla
1 tsp. almond or lemon
  extract

Cream sugar and shortening and cheese. Add egg and beat. Sift flour in and salt. Mix and add vanilla, lemon or almond. Roll into balls and press with sugared fork. Bake 8 - 10 minutes at 350° to 375°. (Burns real easy, this is a light colored cookie.)

Karen Rupert, St. Cloud, Mn.

CRUNCHY JUMBLE COOKIES

1 1/4 c. flour
1/2 tsp. soda
1/4 tsp. salt
1/2 c. butter
1 c. sugar

1 tsp. vanilla
1 egg
2 c. Rice Krispies
1 c. (6 oz.) chocolate chips
1 c. raisins

Cream sugar and butter, add eggs and vanilla. Add dry ingredients and mix until combined. Add cereal, chocolate chips and raisins. Bake about 12 minutes at 350° or until lightly browned. Remove immediately from baking sheets.

Kathy Neels, St. Cloud, Mn.

CRY BABIES

1 c. shortening
1 c. sugar
1 c. molasses
2 eggs
4 c. flour

1 tsp. salt
1 tsp. ginger
2 tsp. soda
1 c. buttermilk
Icing

Beat together in mixer bowl shortening, sugar, molasses and eggs. Sift flour, salt, ginger and soda together and add about a third at a time alternately with thirds of the buttermilk. Mix well and drop cookies from teaspoon onto lightly greased baking sheets. Bake at 375° for 10 to 12 minutes. Remove from cooky sheets to cooling racks and frost cookies while warm by spooning a little icing over the top of each and letting it run down the sides of the cooky.

Icing: Mix in small bowl -

2 c. confectioners sugar   1 tsp. lemon extract
1/4 c. milk

Makes 8 dozen small cookies.

CRY BABY COOKIES

1/2 c. + 1 Tbsp. shortening   Salt
1/2 c. + 1 Tbsp. sugar   3/4 tsp. soda
1/2 c. molasses   1 c. coconut
1 egg, well beaten   1 c. raisins
2 1/4 c. flour   1/2 c. nuts
1/2 Tbsp. baking powder   1/2 c. milk
   (this is correct)

Mix in order given. Bake in 350° oven. Makes around 5 dozen.
Emily Hoeft, Paynesville, Mn.

CZECH VOSKVARKI CUKLOVINKEY
(Crackling Cookies)

2 c. finely ground   2 tsp. baking powder
   voshvarki (cracklings)   2 tsp. cinnamon
2 c. brown sugar   2 tsp. ginger
1/2 c. milk   1/2 tsp. salt
2 eggs   1 tsp. vanilla
1 tsp. baking soda   4 c. flour

Combine cracklings with eggs, beaten one at a time.
Add milk. Add all dry ingredients. Drop by teaspoonfuls
into greased cookie sheet. Bake 10 to 15 minutes at 350°.
Mrs. Cecilia Bulera, St. Paul, Mn.

THUMBPRINT COCONUT COOKIES

3 c. flaked coconut   1/2 c. butter, melted
2 c. powdered sugar   and slightly cooled

Mix well. Form into balls. Make indentation in middle,

carefully, so as not to crack cookies. Refrigerate to harden. Add 1 teaspoon butter to 3 bags of Choco-Bake. Put a small amount in indentation.

Kathy Neels, St. Cloud, Mn.

DATE DROP COOKIES

1 (8 oz.) pkg. dates, cut up	1/2 c. hot water
	1 tsp. soda

Let stand until cool.

2/3 c. butter	1 tsp. each cloves, cinnamon
1 c. sugar	1/2 c. chopped nuts
2 eggs	Salt
2 1/4 c. flour	

Cream butter and sugar, add eggs, beat. Mix. Sift spices with flour. Mix alternately with date mixture. Drop by teaspoonfuls onto cookie sheet. Bake at 350° for about 12 minutes.

Signe Linda, St. Paul, Mn.

GRANNY RIEDER'S DATE FILLED COOKIES

1 lb. dates, cut up	1/4 tsp. salt
1/2 c. sugar	2/3 c. water
1 Tbsp. flour	

Cook until mixed.

1 c. white sugar	1 tsp. soda
1/2 c. shortening	2 eggs
4 Tbsp. sour cream	1/2 tsp. salt
1 tsp. vanilla	2 Tbsp. baking powder

Add own judgement in flour, about 5 cups until dough is easy to roll. Cut into rounds, about 2 1/2 inches. Use one for bottom and put filling in center, then put on top round and pinch with fork around edges to seal. Bake until light gold on edges at 350°. This batter also makes good cut out cookies for holidays. The less flour used to roll, the more tender the cookie.

Grandma's recipes are from her mothers in the 1800's.

Joan Buttweiler, St. Cloud, Mn.

DUSTY MILLER COOKIES

3/4 c. shortening
1 c. sugar
1 egg, beaten
1/4 c. molasses
2 c. sifted flour

2 1/2 tsp. soda
1 tsp. ginger
1 tsp. cinnamon
Confectioners sugar

Cream shortening and sugar. Add egg and molasses. Sift flour, soda and spices together. Stir into creamed mixture, chill. Form into ball size of a walnut and roll in powdered sugar. Place 2 inches apart on greased cookie sheet. Bake at 400° for 10 minutes.

Diane Schmitz, St. Cloud, Mn.

FRENCH COOKIES

1 c. chopped dates
1 c. chopped walnuts
1 c. powdered sugar

1 c. creamy peanut butter
2 Tbsp. soft butter
2 c. chocolate chips

Mix first 5 ingredients together well. Roll into small balls. Melt chocolate chips and roll balls in melted chocolate. Place on waxed paper. Keep someplace cool until completely set. Yield: 75.

Diane Schmitz, St. Cloud, Mn.

FORGOTTEN KISSES

Heat oven to 400°.

2 egg whites
Pinch of salt
1/2 tsp. cream of tartar

3/4 c. sugar
3 1/2 tsp. vanilla

Beat egg whites till frothy, add pinch of salt, cream of tartar. While beating slowly, add the sugar and vanilla. Beat very stiff, now use your imagination. Add 2 teaspoons green food coloring and package of mint chocolate chips, or 2 teaspoons red coloring and 1 cup shredded coconut or your combination. Drop by teaspoonfuls onto ungreased cooky sheets. Put into oven, turn off heat and leave in oven overnight.

Marian Balsley, Minneapolis, Mn.

446

FORGOTTEN MERINGUE

Set oven at 375°. Take 2 egg whites and pinch of salt. Beat until it stands in peaks. Beat in gradually 3/4 cup white sugar, 1 teaspoon vanilla and coloring if desired. Mix in 1 cup chocolate chips or dates, or anything one cares to. Drop by teaspoonfuls onto greased cooky sheet. Put into oven and turn off the oven. Leave them in overnight.

FRUIT COOKIES

1 1/2 c. brown sugar
1/2 c. butter
3 c. flour
4 eggs, beaten
1 Tbsp. milk
2 1/2 tsp. soda
1 tsp. allspice
1/2 c. whiskey

5 or 6 c. chopped pecans (I think 5 is enough)
1 lb. candied cherries, cut up
1/2 lb. pineapple (candied), cut up, or you can buy them already cut
1 box raisins (about 4x5 inch size box)

Soak fruit and nuts in whiskey overnight. Cream butter and sugar, eggs, milk and add flour, soda and allspice. Then add fruit and nuts mixture and drop by teaspoonfuls onto greased cookie sheet. Bake 30 minutes in 275° oven.
Alice Ann Hanson, Grand Forks, N. D.

FUNNY FACE COOKIES

1/3 c. raisins
3 c. flour
2 tsp. cream of tartar
1 tsp. soda
1/2 tsp. salt

1 c. lard
2 eggs
1 c. sugar
1 tsp. vanilla

Put flour, soda, cream of tartar and salt into sifter and sift into large bowl. Add lard and mix. Beat eggs in small bowl. Add sugar and vanilla and add to flour. Shape into balls. Place on cooky sheet and flatten with glass. Decorate with raisins. Bake 8 to 10 minutes.

GINGER COOKIES

3/4 c. shortening, melted	2 1/2 tsp. soda
1 c. sugar	1 tsp. ginger
1 egg	1 tsp. cinnamon
4 Tbsp. molasses	Salt (good pinch)
2 c. flour	

Let the soda work to frothy stage in the molasses. Roll into balls, then in sugar. Bake at 375° until they crack.

Mike and Vonnie Bakke, Willmar, Mn.

GINGER COOKIES

1 c. sugar	2 1/2 tsp. soda
3/4 c. shortening	1 tsp. ginger (scant)
1 egg	1/2 tsp. cloves
4 Tbsp. molasses	1/2 tsp. cinnamon
2 c. flour	1/4 tsp. salt

Cream shortening and sugar. Add other ingredients, mix well. Roll into balls and sugar. Bake at 375° for 10 minutes.

Kathy Neels, St. Cloud, Mn.

GINGERSNAPS OR PEPPERKAKAR

1 c. butter	1 tsp. cardamon
1 1/2 c. sugar	2 tsp. soda
1 egg, beaten	1 tsp. cinnamon
2 Tbsp. dark syrup	1 tsp. ginger
3 1/4 c. flour	1 tsp. cloves

Cream butter and sugar; add beaten egg and syrup. Sift flour with ingredients. Add to first mixture. Mix well. Put dough into refrigerator overnight. Roll thin and cut into desired shapes. Bake in 375° oven for 10 - 12 minutes. Yield: 60 cookies.

Borgny Pinney, Anoka, Mn.

THE VERY BEST GINGERSNAPS

3/4 c. Crisco
1 c. sugar
1 egg
1/4 c. light molasses
2 c. sifted flour

2 tsp. soda
1/4 tsp. salt
1 tsp. each cinnamon, ginger,
cloves

Roll into balls about walnut size. Roll in sugar. Place on cookie sheet 2 inches apart. Bake at 375° F. for 12 minutes.

Frieda Steeves, Fargo, N. D.

GLAZED FRESH APPLE COOKIES

1/2 c. shortening
1 1/3 c. brown sugar
1 egg
2 c. sifted all-purpose
flour
1 tsp. soda
1/2 tsp. salt
1 tsp. cinnamon

1 tsp. ground cloves
1/2 tsp. nutmeg
1 c. nuts
1 c. finely chopped,
unpeeled apple
1 c. chopped raisins
1/4 c. apple juice or milk

Cream shortening, brown sugar and egg. Add 1/2 of the dry ingredients, chopped nuts, apple, raisins and mix. Blend in apple juice or milk. Add remaining flour mixture, mixing well. Drop by teaspoonfuls onto greased sheet. Bake at 400° for 10 - 12 minutes. Spread with vanilla glaze while cookies are hot.

Vanilla Glaze:

1 1/2 c. sifted powdered
sugar
2 1/2 Tbsp. apple juice
or light cream

1/8 tsp. salt
1/4 tsp. vanilla
1 Tbsp. butter

Blend all ingredients well.

Diane Schmitz, St. Cloud, Mn.

GOOD COOKIES

1 c. shortening
1 c. white sugar

2 c. oatmeal
2 c. chopped dates

Heat all together over medium heat in heavy saucepan, until dissolved. Remove from heat and let cool. Add:

2 eggs, beaten
2 c. flour
1/2 tsp. salt

1 tsp. baking soda
1 tsp. cinnamon

Mix together with cooked mixture and form into balls the size of walnut. Flatten with fork dipped into cold water. Sprinkle with sugar. Bake at 350° for 12 to 15 minutes. Yield: 6 dozen.

Helen Kruse, Fargo, N. D.

GROUND RAISIN COOKIES
(Swedish)

1 c. shortening
  (1/2 butter)
3/4 c. white sugar
3/4 c. brown sugar
1 egg, slightly beaten
3 c. flour

1 tsp. baking soda
1 1/2 Tbsp. hot water
1 c. ground raisins
1 tsp. cinnamon
1/2 tsp. nutmeg

Rinse raisins in water, they'll be easier to grind. Mix everything together, roll into walnut sized balls, flatten with glass dipped first in water and then into sugar. Bake at 350° F. for 12 to 15 minutes. Yield: 80 - 100 cookies.

Helen-May Johnson, Chanhassen, Mn.

HAWAIIAN DROP COOKIES

Cream thoroughly:
1 1/4 c. sugar
1/2 Tbsp. vanilla

2/3 c. shortening
1/2 tsp. almond

Blend in 1 egg, till mixture is fluffy. Sift together:

2 c. flour
2 tsp. baking powder

1/2 tsp. salt

Add dry ingredients and 3/4 cup well drained Santa Fe brand crushed pineapple to above mixture. Mix well. Drop on ungreased cookie sheet. Bake slowly at 325° for 20 minutes. Cookies are better stored for 24 hours. Makes about 4 dozen.

Kathy Bischof, St. Cloud, Mn.

HONEY AND NUT CHERRY COOKIES

1 3/4 c. flour
1/2 tsp. soda
1/2 tsp. salt
3/4 c. margarine, softened
1 c. sugar
1/2 c. firmly packed
  brown sugar

1 egg
1 tsp. vanilla
2 c. Kellogg's honey and
  nut corn flakes cereal
1/3 c. finely chopped
  cherries

1. Stir together flour, soda and salt. Set aside. 2. In large mixing bowl, beat margarine, sugars until light and fluffy. Add eggs and vanilla. Beat well, add flour mixture, mixing until well combined. Stir in cereal and cherries. Drop by level tablespoonfuls onto greased baking sheets. 3. Bake in oven at 350° F. about 12 to 14 minutes or until golden brown. Cool slightly before removing from baking sheets. Place on wire racks. About 4 dozen.

Helen M. Gludt, Bottineau, N. D.

ITALIAN HOLIDAY COOKIES

1 c. butter
1/3 c. sugar
1 egg yolk
1/4 tsp. vanilla extract
Preserves of your choice

1 1/2 c. sifted all-purpose
  flour
1/2 tsp. salt
1 egg white, slightly beaten
1 c. flaked coconut

Cream together butter and sugar until light and fluffy. Stir in egg yolk and vanilla. Sift together flour and salt, blend into creamed mixture. Chill dough at least 1 hour. Shape into ball about 1 inch in diameter. Dip balls into egg white and roll in coconut. Place a greased baking sheet. Press top of each ball with thumb slightly to form an indentation. Bake 20 to 25 minutes at 300° F. Cool and fill indentation with preserves. Makes 3 1/2 dozen.

Gloria Bergson, Fargo, N. D.

JELLY BALLS

1 c. butter   1/2 tsp. cream of tartar
3/4 c. sugar

   Beat until light and fluffy. Now add:

2 egg yolks   2 c. flour

   Roll into small balls, dip ball into slightly beaten egg white, then dip into chopped walnuts and make a dent into the ball, place cookie on a greased cookie sheet and put a tiny bit of jelly in the dent. Bake about 15 minutes at 350°.
Kathryn Otto, Harvey, N. D.

JUMBO RAISIN COOKIES

   Boil for 5 minutes:
1 c. water   2 c. raisins

   Cool in water and then drain. Cream:

1/2 c. Spry   1 c. white sugar
1/2 c. butter   1 c. brown sugar

   Add 3 eggs. Fold in:

3 c. flour   1 1/2 tsp. cinnamon
1 tsp. baking powder   1/4 tsp. nutmeg
1 tsp. soda   1/4 tsp. allspice
1 tsp. salt

   Add:
1 tsp. vanilla   1 c. nuts

   Chill dough. Form into balls, dip in sugar. Bake at 350°.
Sharon Brogren, Willmar, Mn.

REFRESHING LEMONADE COOKIES

1 c. butter or margarine   1 tsp. baking soda
Sugar   1 can frozen lemonade
2 eggs   concentrate, thawed
3 c. flour

452

Preheat oven to 400°. In mixing bowl cream together butter and 1 cup sugar. Add eggs, one at a time, beating well after each addition. Combine flour and baking soda. Stir dry ingredients into egg mixture alternately with 1/2 cup of the lemonade concentrate. Drop by teaspoonfuls 2 inches apart onto ungreased baking sheets. Bake 8 minutes or until edges of cookies are lightly browned. Remove and brush lightly with remaining lemonade and sprinkle with sugar. Cool on wire rack. Makes about 7 dozen cookies.

Sharon Christian

M & M PARTY COOKIES

1 c. shortening	2 1/4 c. sifted flour
1 c. brown sugar	1 tsp. soda
1/2 c. granulated sugar	1 tsp. salt
2 tsp. vanilla	1 1/2 c. M & M's (plain)
2 eggs	candy

Blend shortening and sugars. Beat in vanilla and eggs. Sift remaining dry ingredients together. Add to the sugar and egg mixture. Mix well. Stir in 1/2 cup M & M candy. Save remaining candy for decorating. Drop from teaspoon onto an ungreased cookie sheet. Bake at 375° for 10 - 12 minutes. Makes about 6 dozen 2 1/2 inch cookies.

Diane Schmitz, St. Cloud, Mn.

GRANDMOTHER BRINKERHOFF'S MOLASSES COOKIES
(German)

5 1/2 c. flour (or less)	2 tsp. baking powder
3 tsp. soda	1 tsp. salt
3/4 tsp. ginger	1 tsp. cinnamon
1 c. shortening	1 c. sugar
1 egg, beaten	1/2 tsp. vanilla
1 c. dark molasses	1/2 c. strong coffee

Mix all together. Roll 1/4 inch thick. Cut with 2 inch round cookie cutter. Bake on greased sheet at 375° or 400°. 8 to 10 minutes.

Lemon Frosting:

2 3/4 c. powdered sugar	1/2 tsp. salt

1 egg   1 tsp. vanilla
1 Tbsp. corn syrup   2 Tbsp. lemon juice
1/2 c. shortening   1 Tbsp. lemon peel

Mix sugar, salt and egg. Blend in syrup. Blend in the rest and add sugar and water for consistency. Spread on cookies.

Elynor S. Storkamp, St. Cloud, Mn.

MONSTER COOKIE

8 tsp. baking soda   2 tsp. vanilla
4 c. white sugar   2 Tbsp. corn syrup
1 doz. eggs   2 lb. M & M's
2 lb. brown sugar   1 lb. chocolate chips
3 lb. peanut butter   1 lb. butter
18 c. oatmeal

Bake at 350° for 6 - 8 minutes. Make cookies any size you want, does not matter.

Debbie Neubauer, Pat Christiansen, Minneapolis, Mn.

NO-BAKE COOKIES

1 (3 oz.) pkg. cream   1/4 tsp. vanilla
    cheese   1 c. coconut
2 1/2 c. sifted powdered   Pinch of salt
    sugar

Cream cheese. Add other ingredients. Form into shape of walnuts. Roll in coconut if you wish. Can be colored coconut.

Kathy Bischof, St. Cloud, Mn.

DENA STODDARD'S NO BAKE COOKIES
(For a quick treat)

2 (6 oz.) pkg. butterscotch   2/3 c. chunky peanut butter
    chips   5 c. uncrushed corn flakes
1 (6 oz.) pkg. chocolate
    chips

Melt chips in top of double boiler, add peanut butter

and stir until well blended. Pour over corn flakes and mix.
Drop by teaspoonfuls onto waxed paper. Let set until cool.
                    Harriet Maselie

NORWEGIAN HOLIDAY COOKIES

2 egg yolks, hard- cooked	1 c. sifted flour
	1/2 c. butter
1/4 c. sugar	1/4 tsp. almond extract

Cream butter. Rub egg yolks through a strainer. Add
to creamed butter. Add sugar and 1/2 the flour. Knead
well. Add remainder of flour and extract. When kneaded
well, cut off into small pieces and shape into small cakes.
Roll in colored sugar. Place on ungreased cookie sheet and
bake at 375° for 15 minutes.
                    Kathy Bischof, St. Cloud, Mn.

NUTRITIOUS COOKIES

1 c. margarine	1 tsp. cloves
1 c. brown sugar	1 tsp. allspice
1 c. white sugar	1 1/2 c. flour
2 eggs	1/2 c. wheat germ
1 tsp. soda	3 c. rolled oats
1 tsp. salt	2 c. raisins
1 tsp. cinnamon	1/2 c. nuts

Cream margarine and sugars and add eggs. Sift dry ingredients and add with wheat germ, oats and raisins. Drop
on greased cookie sheets and bake at 350° for 12 minutes.
Dough can be formed into refrigerator cookie rolls and sliced
as needed. Bake them 8 to 10 minutes. Makes 5 dozen.
                    Adeline Hortsch, St. Cloud, Mn.

BANANA OATMEAL COOKIES

Cream:
3/4 c. shortening	1 c. sugar

Add:
1 c. mashed bananas	1 1/2 c. flour
1 3/4 c. oatmeal	1/2 tsp. soda
1/2 c. chopped nuts	1/4 tsp. salt
1 egg	

1748-81   455

1/4 tsp. nutmeg   1/8 tsp. cinnamon

Drop by teaspoonfuls onto greased cookie sheet. Bake at 350° for 10 minutes.

Renee Ulberg, Bismarck, N. D.

CHOCOLATE OATMEAL BONBON'S

1 c. shortening
1 c. sugar
1 egg
2 sq. chocolate
1/2 tsp. salt

1 1/2 tsp. vanilla
3/4 c. flour
1 tsp. baking powder
1 1/4 c. oatmeal

Stir up all ingredients. Chill, roll into balls. Bake at 350° for 10 - 12 minutes or till done. Frost with Chocolate Icing.

Chocolate Icing: Mix -

1 c. sifted confectioners
   sugar
1/4 c. cream

1 sq. unsweetened
   chocolate, melted
1 tsp. vanilla

Karen Rupert, St. Cloud, Mn.

CHOCOLATE OATMEAL COOKIES

1/2 c. shortening   1 egg
1 c. sugar

Cream the above. Blend in:

1 (1 oz.) sq. chocolate   2 Tbsp. water
1 tsp. vanilla

Add:
1 c. flour   1/2 tsp. soda
1 c. oatmeal

Mix all together. Form into 1 inch balls. Flatten with glass dipped in sugar. Bake at 350° for 10 - 12 minutes on greased cookie sheet.

Mrs. William Meyer, St. Paul, Mn.

456

OATMEAL COOKIES
(Blue Ribbon - South Dakota State Fair - 1938)

Cream:
1 c. sugar	1 c. shortening
1 c. brown sugar	

Add:
2 eggs	1/2 tsp. salt
1 c. ground raisins	

Dissolve 1 teaspoon soda in 1/4 cup hot water, add. Add 2 cups rolled oats. Add 3 cups sifted flour. Add:

1 tsp. vanilla	1/2 c. walnut meats

Roll into small balls. Flatten with glass dipped in sugar. Bake at 350° for 10 - 12 minutes.

Eva Lyn Dody, Minneapolis, Mn.

FAMOUS OATMEAL COOKIES

3/4 c. shortening, soft	1/4 c. water
1 c. firmly packed	1 tsp. vanilla
brown sugar	1 c. sifted flour
1/2 c. granulated sugar	1 tsp. salt
1 egg	1/2 tsp. soda
	3 c. oatmeal, uncooked

Beat shortening, sugar, egg, water and vanilla together. Sift flour, salt, soda and add to the creamed mixture. Blend well. Stir in oatmeal. For variety, add chopped nuts, raisins, chocolate chips or coconut as you wish. Drop by teaspoonfuls onto greased cookie sheets. Bake in 350° oven for 12 - 15 minutes. Makes 5 dozen.

Mrs. W. E. Gollehon, Fargo, N. D.

OATMEAL CRISPIES

1 c. shortening	1 tsp. salt
1 c. brown sugar	1 tsp. soda
1 c. white sugar	3 c. quick cooking
2 well beaten eggs	oatmeal
1 tsp. vanilla	1/2 c. chopped nuts
1 1/2 c. flour	

Thoroughly cream shortening and sugars, vanilla and eggs. Mix well. Add sifted dry ingredients. Add oatmeal and nuts. Mix well. Shape into 2 rolls, wrap in waxed paper. Chill thoroughly or overnight. Slice 1/4 inch thick. Bake on ungreased cookie sheet in moderate oven (350°) for 10 minutes. Makes 5 dozen.

Mary Lempe, St. Cloud, Mn.

OATMEAL RAISIN COOKIES

Boil 10 minutes:

1 c. shortening	1 c. water
1 1/4 c. sugar	1 1/2 c. raisins
1/2 tsp. cinnamon	1/2 tsp. nutmeg

Cool till shortening is thickening. Add:

2 eggs, slightly beaten	1 tsp. salt
2 c. flour	1 tsp. vanilla
1 tsp. soda	1/2 c. nuts
2 c. oatmeal	

Refrigerate overnight. Bake at 375°.

Kathy Neels, St. Cloud, Mn.

SEEDED RAISIN OATMEAL COOKIES (1879)

Mix with hands:

3 c. flour	3 c. oatmeal
2 c. brown sugar	1 lb. lard

Add:

1 lb. seeded raisins, ground	1 c. buttermilk
1 tsp. soda	1/4 tsp. salt

Mix well, adding more flour to handle easily. Chill. Roll and bake at 350° - 375° for 10 minutes.

Ruth Braun, Owatonna, Mn.

SOFT OATMEAL COOKIES

Cover 1 cup raisins with water and boil until water is almost gone. Add 1 cup Crisco. Cool and add:

1 c. sugar	1 tsp. nutmeg
2 eggs	1 c. chopped nuts
1 tsp. cinnamon	Pinch of salt
1 tsp. soda	

Mix well and add:

2 c. oatmeal	2 c. flour

Drop by teaspoonfuls onto lightly greased cookie sheet. Bake at 350° for 10 minutes.

Renee Ulberg, Bismarck, N. D.

THIN OATMEAL COOKIES

1 c. margarine	1/2 c. brown sugar
1/2 c. white sugar	1/2 tsp. salt
1/2 tsp. soda in 1/4 c.	1 c. flour
hot water	1 tsp. vanilla
3 c. rolled oats	

Cream margarine, white sugar, brown sugar and salt. Add rest of ingredients, mix well. Let stand for 10 minutes. Drop onto cookie sheet by teaspoonfuls and flatten very thin with fork dipped in hot water. Bake at 350° for about 8 minutes. Remove from pan PDQ. Count to 15 , then take from pan.

Kathy Neels, St. Cloud, Mn.

PEANUT BLOSSOMS

Sift together:

1 3/4 c. flour	1/2 tsp. salt
1 tsp. soda	

Cream:

1/2 c. shortening	1/2 c. peanut butter

Add:

1 unbeaten egg	1 tsp. vanilla
2 Tbsp. milk	

Beat well. Blend in the dry ingredients, mix thoroughly. Shape into balls and roll in sugar. Place on ungreased cooky sheet. Bake at 375° for 8 minutes, remove and press chocolate candy kiss on top, pressing down so cooky cracks around edge. Return to oven 2 to 3 minutes.

PEANUT BLOSSOMS
(Cookies)

1 3/4 c. regular flour	1/2 c. shortening
1 tsp. soda	1/2 c. peanut butter
1/2 tsp. salt	1 egg
1/2 c. sugar	2 Tbsp. milk
1/2 c. firmly packed	1 tsp. vanilla
brown sugar	48 milk chocolate candy
	kisses

Combine all ingredients except candy in large mixer bowl. Mix on lowest speed of mixer until dough forms. Shape dough into balls, using a rounded teaspoonful for each. Roll balls in sugar; place on ungreased cookie sheets. Bake at 375° for 10 to 12 minutes. Top each cookie immediately with a candy kiss; press down firmly so cookie cracks around edge.

Phyllis Curran, Red River Valley Council

PEANUT BUTTER COOKIES

1 c. butter	2 eggs
1 c. brown sugar	3 c. flour
1 c. white sugar	1/2 tsp. soda
1 c. chunky peanut butter	1/2 tsp. salt

Make these big - about golf ball size - flatten with glass bottom dipped in sugar and bake at 350° for 10 - 12 minutes.

Helen Peterson, St. Paul, Mn.

PERSIMMON COOKIES

Mix together:

3/4 c. sugar	1/2 c. shortening
1/4 c. brown sugar	1 egg

Add 1 cup persimmon pulp and mix. Add:

2 c. flour	1/2 tsp. cinnamon
1 tsp. soda	1 c. raisins or nuts
1/2 tsp. salt	

Drop by spoonfuls and bake at 350° for 10 minutes.
Evelyn Fellows, Austin, Mn.

QUICK COOKIES

1 c. brown sugar	2 Tbsp. hot water
1 c. shortening	2 c. flour
1/2 tsp. soda	1/4 c. peanut butter

Cream the brown sugar and shortening. Dissolve the soda in the hot water and add to the creamed mixture. Add the flour and peanut butter. Roll into balls and flatten with palm of hand or fork. Bake for 15 minutes at 350°. Cool before removing from pan.

QUICKIE PEANUT BUTTER COOKIES

1 c. peanut butter (plain or chunky)	1 tsp. baking soda
1 c. sugar	1 egg

Mix all ingredients together with a fork. Roll into walnut sized balls and press lightly down with a fork. Bake at 350° for 8 to 10 minutes. Makes 3 to 4 dozen cookies.
Carol Ann Hanson, Minneapolis, Mn.

RAISIN COOKIES

1 c. seedless raisins	1 c. butter or margarine

Grind raisins and cream with shortening. Add:

1 1/2 c. white sugar	1 tsp. baking soda
2 beaten eggs	2 c. quick oatmeal
2 c. flour	1 c. nuts, if desired

Roll into balls. Butter the bottom of a glass, dip in sugar and press cookie. Bake in 350° oven.
Mrs. Robert L. Benson, Stillwater

RAISIN BAR COOKIES

1 c. raisins, cooked and drained
2/3 c. liquid from raisins
2/3 c. shortening
1 egg
1 c. brown sugar
1 c. white sugar
1 tsp. vanilla
3 1/2 c. flour
1 tsp. baking powder
1 tsp. soda
1 tsp. salt
1 tsp. cinnamon
1/2 c. nutmeats

Mix as for other cookies and spread in large pan, 11 1/2 x 17 1/2 inches. Bake at 350° - 370° till done. Have powdered sugar frosting ready and spread over while warm.
Marion Gugat, Sauk Centre, Mn.

RANGER COOKIES

1 c. shortening
1 c. white sugar
1 c. brown sugar
3 eggs
1 tsp. vanilla
2 c. flour
1/2 tsp. salt
1 tsp. soda
1 tsp. baking powder
2 c. oatmeal
2 c. corn flakes
1 c. coconut

Mix in order given. Drop on greased cookie sheets. Bake 12 - 15 minutes at 350°.
Arlene Freichels, Sauk Centre, Mn.

ROCKY NUT COOKIES

4 egg whites, beaten stiff
2 c. sugar
1 c. cocoanut
1 c. walnuts
4 c. corn flakes
Vanilla

Bake in slow oven until brown. Bake on parchment paper. Remove fast.
Mrs. James R. McQuaid, Anoka, Mn.

ROCKY ROAD COOKIES

1 (6 oz.) pkg. chocolate chips
1/2 c. margarine
2 eggs
1 c. sugar
1 1/2 c. flour
1/2 tsp. baking powder
1/4 tsp. salt

1/2 tsp. vanilla   3/4 c. chopped nuts

Heat oven to 400°. Melt 1/2 package chocolate chips and margarine over low heat; cool. Sift flour, baking powder and salt together; add remaining chocolate bits and nuts to flour mixture; set aside. Beat eggs, add sugar and vanilla; add to melted chocolate mixture. Combine wet and dry mixtures and blend well. Drop by teaspoonfuls 2 inches apart on greased baking sheet. Bake 8 minutes or until almost no imprint remains when touched with finger. Makes 2 dozen cookies.

Liz Tuft, St. Paul, Mn.

ROLLED MOLASSES COOKIES

1 1/4 c. shortening	1 tsp. allspice
1 c. sugar	1 tsp. ginger
6 c. flour	1 tsp. cinnamon
2 tsp. soda	1 c. dark molasses
1 tsp. salt	1 c. cold coffee

Cream shortening and sugar. Mix coffee and molasses alternately with dry ingredients. Roll on floured board 1/4 inch thick. Cut into desired shape. Bake on greased pan at 350° for 12 minutes. Frost with powdered sugar icing.

Lu Boyer, Grand Forks, N. D.

ROLLED WHITE COOKIES
(Excellent for holiday cutouts)

1 c. butter	1/2 tsp. sugar
1 c. sugar	1 tsp. cinnamon
2 eggs, beaten	1/4 tsp. nutmeg
4 Tbsp. thin cream	1 tsp. lemon extract
3 c. flour	

Cream butter and sugar. Add beaten eggs and mix thoroughly. Add cream, vanilla and dry ingredients. Cool dough before rolling out. Cut with cookie cutters dipped in flour. Thicker dough gives better taste. Bake at 350° for 5 - 6 minutes. Decorate when cool.

Robin Knutson, Willmar, Mn.

SALTED PEANUT COOKIES

2 c. brown sugar,
  packed
1 c. melted shortening
2 eggs, beaten
1 tsp. vanilla
2 c. oatmeal

2 c. flour
1 tsp. baking powder
1 tsp. soda
1 c. salted peanuts
1 c. corn flakes

Melt shortening, add sugar and cream well. Add beaten eggs and vanilla, mix well. Add flour mixed with baking powder and soda, mix. Add oatmeal, peanuts and corn flakes, mix well. Refrigerate approximately 2 hours. Roll in small balls, flatten and press with fork dipped in sugar. Bake at 375° for 11 minutes.

Mavis Ann Hjulberg, St. Paul, Mn.

SALTED PEANUT COOKIES

Cream together:
1 c. brown sugar
1 c. white sugar

1 c. shortening

Add:
2 eggs, one at a time
1 c. crushed corn flakes
1 c. salted peanuts
1 tsp. baking powder

2 c. flour
1 c. oatmeal
1 tsp. soda

Cream sugars and shortening. Add eggs and dry ingredients. Mix well. Roll into balls, press down with fork and sprinkle with sugar. Bake at 350° till lightly browned.

Kathy Neels, St. Cloud, Mn.

SESAME COOKIES

1 c. margarine
2 c. brown sugar
2 eggs
2 tsp. vanilla
1 1/2 c. flour
1 tsp. soda

3 c. rolled oats
1/2 c. nuts
2 Tbsp. roasted sesame
  seeds (bake at 350° about
  5 minutes, let cool and
  add last)

Spoon onto cookie sheet and bake at 350° for 8 - 10 minutes. Makes 4 dozen.

Linda Graf, Fargo, N. D.

SCOTCH SHORTBREAD

1/2 lb. butter   2 c. sifted flour
1/2 c. powdered sugar

Mix butter till creamy. Add flour gradually, then add sugar. Work into a small ball. Press into pan and prick all over the top with a fork. Pinch around the edges. Bake 30 minutes at 350°.
Marj VanGorp, Alexandria, Mn.

SUGAR COOKIES

1/2 c. powdered sugar	1/2 tsp. vanilla
1/2 c. white sugar	2 c. + 2 heaping Tbsp. flour
1/2 c. margarine	1/2 tsp. salt
1/2 c. vegetable oil	1/2 tsp. soda
1 egg	1/2 tsp. cream of tartar

Roll into balls and flatten with a glass. Roll in sugar. Bake at 375° for 10 minutes. This is 1/2 recipe (makes 60).
Ruth Braun, Owatonna, Mn.

MOM'S SUGAR COOKIES

1 c. powdered sugar	4 1/2 c. flour
1 c. butter	1 tsp. soda
1 c. Wesson oil	1 tsp. cream of tartar
1 c. white sugar	1/2 tsp. salt
2 eggs	1 tsp. vanilla

Chill dough, roll into balls, flatten with glass dipped in sugar. Bake at 350°. Don't brown to much.
Kathy Neels, St. Cloud, Mn.

SOUR CREAM SUGAR COOKIES

2 c. sugar	Pinch of salt
1 c. butter	1 tsp. soda (in cream)
3 eggs	1 tsp. vanilla
1 c. sour cream	Flour to roll

Roll, cut, sprinkle sugar on top and bake at 375° F.
Linnea Pajari, Detroit Lakes, Mn.

SPRITS COOKIES

Cream 1/2 pound butter (not oleo).

2/3 c. sugar
Yolks of 3 eggs
2 1/2 c. flour

4 grated bitter almonds, or
almond extract

Mix. Bake in moderate oven. Makes 60 Sprits.
Mrs. James R. McQuaid, Anoka, Mn.

SUGAR COOKIES

1 c. shortening
1 egg
1/2 tsp. soda
1 tsp. vanilla

1 c. sugar
2 c. flour
1/2 tsp. cream of tartar

Cream shortening and sugar. Add egg and dry ingredients and vanilla. Mix well, roll into balls, roll in sugar. Place on greased sheet and press with fork. Bake at 350° until lightly browned.
Arlene Byrne, Rochester, Mn.

SUGAR COOKIES

3 c. flour
1/2 tsp. baking powder

1/2 tsp. baking soda
1 c. margarine

Mix this all together like pie crust.

2 eggs
1 c. sugar

1 tsp. vanilla

Beat these together well. Add to the above. Mix and roll out thin. Use a little flour as you roll out cookies.
Mrs. William G. Speare, Rugby, N. D.

SUGAR COOKIES

1 c. margarine
1 c. Crisco
1 c. powdered sugar
1 c. white sugar

2 eggs
4 c. flour
1 tsp. cream of tartar
1 tsp. soda

1/2 tsp. salt   2 tsp. vanilla

Chill. Roll into balls. Flatten ball with a fork. Sprinkle a little sugar on top.

Norma Haugland, Fargo, N. D.

GRANDMA'S NEVER FAIL SUGAR COOKIES

1 c. lard (or shortening)   1/4 tsp. nutmeg
3 c. flour   1 tsp. soda
Pinch of salt   2 tsp. baking powder

Mix like pie crust until crumbly.

1 c. sugar   1/4 c. milk
2 eggs   1 tsp. vanilla

Beat together in another bowl. Mix together, roll out on floured board or make into balls and flatten with sugared glass. Can add more flour if necessary to ease rolling out. Bake at 375° for 8 - 10 minutes.

Rita Klassen, St. Cloud, Mn.

SUGAR COOKIES
(Very good)

Cream:
3/4 c. oil   1 c. sugar
1 c. oleo or butter   1 c. powdered sugar

Add:
2 eggs   1 tsp. vanilla (could add 1
                                       tsp. lemon juice or 1 tsp.
                                       almond flavoring)
Sift and add:
4 c. + 4 Tbsp. flour   1 tsp. cream of tartar
1 tsp. salt   1 tsp. soda

Make a ball and flatten with glass dipped in sugar. Bake for 8 - 10 minutes at 350°.

Margie Stultz, Big Lake, Mn.

SUGAR COOKIES

3 1/2 c. sifted flour   1 1/2 c. sugar
2 1/2 tsp. baking powder   2 eggs
1/2 tsp. salt   3 tsp. vanilla
1 c. soft butter   Butter
                              Sugar

Preheat oven to 400°. Sift flour, baking powder and salt together. Cream together butter and sugar. Add eggs and vanilla, beating until light and fluffy. Gradually add sifted dry ingredients. Form dough into balls 1 inch in diameter and place about 2 inches apart on greased baking sheet. Butter bottom of large, flat water tumbler, dip into sugar and then press balls of dough down until they are about 1/8 inch thick. Bake 10 to 12 minutes, until edges are golden. If a soft cookie is desired, the dough may be dropped by rounded teaspoonfuls onto cookie sheets The dough may also be chilled and rolled out to cut with cookie cutters.

Blanche Weidencamp, St. Paul, Mn.

SOUR CREAM DROPS

1/2 c. butter   1 tsp. soda
1 1/2 c. brown sugar   1/2 tsp. baking powder
2 eggs, well beaten   1/2 tsp. salt
1 c. thick sour cream   1/2 tsp. vanilla
2 1/2 c. sifted flour   1 c. chopped nuts

Chill dough for a short time. Drop by teaspoonfuls onto cookie sheet. Bake for 10 minutes at 400° F. Frost with frosting when cooled.

Frosting: Melt 6 tablespoons butter in a frying pan until browned. Add -

1 1/2 c. powdered sugar   1/2 tsp. vanilla
4 Tbsp. hot water

Frosting will be thin at first, but will thicken as it stands a while. Makes about 11 dozen cookies.

Marie VanHorn, St. Paul, Mn.

468

SUNFLOWER SEED COOKIES

2/3 c. white sugar
2/3 c. brown sugar
1/2 c. shortening
1/2 c. butter
2 eggs
1 tsp. hot water

1 tsp. vanilla
1 tsp. soda
1 tsp. salt
1 1/2 c. flour
2 c. oatmeal
1 1/2 c. sunflower seed

Cream shortenings, add sugars gradually. Add eggs, mix after each addition. Add hot water and vanilla. Add dry ingredients. Mix. Drop by teaspoonfuls onto greased cookie sheet, bake at 350° for 10 - 12 minutes.

Sue Hick, Detroit Lakes, Mn.

SUNFLOWER SEED COOKIES

2 c. sugar
3 c. flour
1 tsp. soda
1 tsp. baking powder
1 c. butter

1 c. shortening
1 tsp. vanilla
1 c. coconut
1 c. roasted sunflower nuts

Sift dry ingredients together. Cut in butter and shortening. Add vanilla and coconut. Last, add the nuts. Shape into 2 inch diameter rolls and refrigerate till chilled to slice well. Slice and bake at 350° for 10 minutes.

Jane Bohline, Minneapolis, Mn.

TURTLES

Melt:
12 oz. chocolate chips

12 oz. butterscotch chips

Add:
White peanuts

Shoestring potatoes

Drop onto waxed paper and chill. Easy and so good!

Gina Michels, Willmar, Mn.

1748-81

UNIQUE DATE COOKIES

1 c. white sugar	1 c. brown sugar
1 c. shortening	3 eggs
4 c. flour	1 tsp. salt
1 tsp. soda	1 tsp. vanilla

Roll out and spread with boiled mixture of 1 pound dates, chopped nuts, 1/2 cup sugar, 1/2 cup water, cooled. Roll up and refrigerate, slice and bake at 350° for 10 - 12 minutes.

Karen Rupert, St. Cloud, Mn.

WALNUT SANDIES

1 c. butter	1 1/4 c. flour
1/2 c. sugar	3/4 c. walnuts, chopped
1 1/2 c. oatmeal	

Cream butter and sugar. Add all other ingredients. Roll into balls and flatten on cookie sheet. Bake at 350° for 15 minutes.

Mary Jo Olson, Detroit Lakes, Mn.

ALMOND BARS

1/2 c. slivered almonds	1 c. coconut

Toast in oven till brown. Melt:

1/2 c. butter	40 marshmallows

To 4 cups corn flakes, add almond and coconut mixture. Pour butter and marshmallow mix over and mix as Rice Krispies bars. Flatten in an 8x11 inch pan. Melt large Hershey's bar and spread on top. Chill and cut into squares.

Narda Mae Veile, Fargo, N. D.

470

ANGEL FOOD BARS

1 pkg. One-Step angel food 1 (22 oz.) can lemon pie filling
   cake mix (as is) 1 c. coconut

    Mix all together and put on a lightly greased jelly roll pan. Bake 20 - 25 minutes at 350°. Cut into bars and glaze or frost.

               Phyl Mathe, St. Paul, Mn.

APPLE BARS

1 c. sugar 1/2 tsp. soda
1/2 c. butter 1/2 tsp. cinnamon
1 egg, beaten 2 c. raw apples, cut fine
1 1/2 c. flour

    Cream sugar, butter and egg. Add dry ingredients and stir in apples. Spread into greased 8x10 inch pan. Sprinkle with mixture of:

1/2 c. brown sugar 1/2 c. chopped walnuts
1/2 tsp. cinnamon

    Bake at 350° for 30 minutes.
           Kathy Bischof, St. Cloud, Mn.

APPLE BARS

1 yellow cake mix 1/2 c. butter
1/2 c. coconut

    Combine and pat into 9x13 inch ungreased pan and up on the sides.

1 can apple pie mix 1/2 c. sugar
   or applesauce 1 tsp. cinnamon

    Spread apple pie mix on top. Sprinkle sugar and cinnamon over apples.

1 egg 1 c. sour cream

    Blend egg and sour cream and spoon on top. Bake 25 - 35 minutes at 350°. Serve warm or cold. Refrigerate leftover.
        Gina Michels, Willmar, Mn.

APPLE SLICE BARS

2 1/2 c. flour   1 heaping Tbsp. sugar
1 tsp. salt   1 c. shortening

Mix above as pie crust, then combine 2 egg yolks with milk to make 2/3 cup. Mix and roll out half to fit cookie sheet. Sprinkle with lightly crushed corn flake crumbs, then peel and slice 8 - 10 apples. Over apples, put 1 cup sugar mixed with 1 scant teaspoon cinnamon. Then roll out rest of crust and put over mixture. Take 2 egg whites, beat till stiff and spread over top crust. Bake 1 hour at 350°. Then take 1 cup powdered sugar and mix with enough milk to drizzle over top while still warm.
Kathy Neels, St. Cloud, Mn.

APPLESAUCE BARS

1 c. sugar   1/2 tsp. cinnamon
3/4 c. shorteing   1 c. chopped nuts
1 egg   1 c. chopped dates or raisins
2 c. applesauce   1/4 tsp. salt
2 c. flour   1 tsp. vanilla
2 Tbsp. soda

Cream shortening and sugar, add egg, slightly beaten. Put dates or raisins in applesauce. Add to shortening. Sift dry ingredients and add to mixture, add vanilla. Bake at 350° for 25 minutes in a jelly roll pan, 11x16 inches. Powdered sugar icing may be spread on if desired.
Helen M. Gludt, Bottineau, N. D.

BARS

1 can crushed pineapple   2 eggs
1 1/2 c. sugar   Salt
2 c. flour   1 c. chopped nuts
2 tsp. soda

Mix and bake in 9x12 inch pan for 30 - 35 minutes at 350°. Cool and frost with 1 stick of margarine, 3 - 4 ounces cream cheese and 2 cups powdered sugar.
Shirley Peterson, Willmar, Mn.

BROWNIES

1 stick butter or margarine
1 c. sugar
1 tsp. vanilla
4 eggs

1 can Hershey's syrup
1 c. + 2 Tbsp. flour
1/2 tsp. baking powder

Mix and bake in 11x15 inch pan at 350° for 30 minutes. Frost while bars are warm.

Marge Johnson, Minneapolis, Mn.

BROWNIES

Melt together over hot water:

2 sq. unsweetened
chocolate

1/3 c. shortening

Beat in:
1 c. sugar

2 eggs

Sift together and stir in:

3/4 c. flour
1/2 tsp. baking powder

1/2 tsp. salt

Mix in 1/2 cup nuts. Spread in well greased 8 inch square pan. Bake at 350° for 30 - 35 minutes, till top has dull crust. A slight imprint will be left when top is touched lightly with finger. Cool slightly. Cut into 16 (2 inch) squares.

Edie Lymburner, Park Rapids, Mn.

BROWNIE DROPS

1/2 c. shortening
2 (1 oz.) sq. chocolate
1 c. brown sugar
1/2 c. buttermilk or
sour cream
1 egg

1 tsp. vanilla
1 1/2 c. sifted flour
1/2 tsp. baking powder
1/2 tsp. soda
1/4 tsp. salt
1 (6 oz.) pkg. chocolate chips

Melt together shortening, 1 1/2 squares chocolate (reserve 1/2 square for frosting). Add sugar, butter, milk, egg and vanilla. Blend well. Sift together dry ingredients

1748-81

and add to chocolate mixture. Bake in 375° oven for 10 - 12 minutes. Frost when warm.

Frosting: Melt together -

1/2 sq. chocolate	2 Tbsp. butter

Blend in:

1 c. sifted powdered sugar	1/2 tsp. vanilla
1 Tbsp. hot water	

Diane Schmitz, St. Cloud, Mn.

CHOCOLATE SUNDAY BROWNIES

Beat together:

1/4 lb. butter or margarine	4 eggs, 2 at a time
1 c. sugar	

Add:

1 tsp. vanilla.	1 c. + 1 Tbsp. flour
1 can chocolate syrup	1/2 c. nutmeats

Put into 11x15 inch pan. Bake at 350° for 30 minutes.

Frosting:

6 Tbsp. margarine	1 1/2 c. sugar
6 Tbsp. milk	Chocolate chips

Bring to a boil and beat for 30 seconds. Remove from heat and add 1 package chocolate chips.

Nancy Kowalke, Nevis, Mn.

CHOCOLATE SYRUP BROWNIES

1/2 c. butter	1 lb. chocolate syrup
1 c. sugar	1 c. + 1 Tbsp. flour
1 tsp. vanilla	1/2 c. nuts
4 eggs	1/2 tsp. baking powder

Bake 30 minutes in 350° oven in 10x15 inch pan.

Frosting:

1 c. sugar	1/4 c. butter
	1/4 c. milk

Bring to full boil and add 1/2 cup chocolate chips. Cool and beat. Add 1 teaspoon vanilla.

Lucille Jansen, Sauk Centre, Mn.

HERSHEY BROWNIES

4 eggs, beaten
1 c. flour
1 c. sugar

1 c. Hershey's chocolate syrup
1/2 c. Crisco oil
1/2 c. nuts

Mix all together. Bake at 350° for 20 minutes.

Mary Jane Schmitz, Wadena, Mn.

MOIST BROWNIES

1/2 c. margarine
1 c. sugar
4 eggs

1 (1 lb.) can Hershey's
  syrup
1 c. + 1 Tbsp. flour
1/2 c. chopped nuts

Mix ingredients together well. Pour into a greased and floured jelly roll pan. Bake at 350° for 20 - 25 minutes. Frost while warm.

Frosting:

6 Tbsp. margarine
6 Tbsp. milk

1 1/2 c. sugar

Boil 45 seconds. Add 1/2 cup chocolate chips and beat until smooth. Spread hot frosting on warm brownies.

Pat Langfitt, Fargo, N. D.

BUTTER CHEWS

3/4 c. butter
3 Tbsp. sugar

1 1/2 c. flour

Blend thoroughly, spread in greased pan and bake at 375° for 15 minutes or until light brown.

3 egg yolks, beaten
2 1/4 c. brown sugar
1 c. chopped nuts

3/4 c. coconut
3 egg whites, beaten

1748-81

Blend sugar and egg yolk. Stir in nuts and coconut. Fold in egg whites. Spread over baked crust and return to oven for 25 - 30 minutes. Cut into small squares.

Diane Schmitz, St. Cloud, Mn.

BUTTERSCOTCH BARS

1/4 c. butter or margarine

2 (6 oz.) pkg. butterscotch chips

Melt in pan and stir in 1 cup peanut butter (chunk style). Add:

1/2 c. coconut

1 pkg. miniature marshmallows

Press into 9x13 inch pan and sprinkle 1/2 cup coconut on top.

Sharon Brogren, Willmar, Mn.

BUTTERSCOTCH BARS

Beat 2 eggs. Add:

1 c. white sugar

3/4 c. oleomargarine

Boil slowly for 2 minutes and let cool. Add:

2 1/2 c. graham cracker crumbs
1/2 c. cocoanut

1/2 c. nutmeats
2 c. miniature marshmallows

Press this into 9x13 inch pan. Top with package of butterscotch chips, melted with 3 tablespoons peanut butter. No baking.

Marilyn Helgeson, Fargo, N. D.

CALIFORNIA BARS

15 graham crackers, crushed
1 c. chocolate chips

1 c. coconut
1 can sweetened condensed milk

Mix crushed graham crackers, chocolate chips, coconut and add condensed milk. Spread into a greased pan; bake for 20 minutes at 375°. Remove from oven, cool and cut into desired size squares.

Marge Carlson, Sauk Centre, Mn.

CARAMEL BARS

32 light caramels   5 Tbsp. cream

Melt together in double boiler.

1 1/4 c. flour   1/4 tsp. salt
3/4 c. brown sugar   3/4 c. oleo or butter
1/2 tsp. soda

Pack 3/4 of mixture into 7x11 inch pan and bake for 10 minutes at 350°. Pour 1 (6 ounce) package chocolate chips over this and add caramels. Put rest of crumbs on top and bake another 10 minutes.

Bonnie Sarby

CARAMEL BARS

32 light caramels   5 Tbsp. half & half or
                             condensed milk

Melt together.

1 c. flour   1/2 tsp. soda
1 c. oatmeal   1/4 tsp. salt
3/4 c. brown sugar   3/4 c. melted butter

Put half of batter into cake pan. Bake 10 minutes. Sprinkle 6 ounces of chocolate chips and 1/2 cup chopped pecans over batter in pan. Spread caramel over that, cover with remaining crumbs. Bake at 325° for 15 minutes. Cut while warm.

Irene Callahan, Austin, Mn.

CARAMEL BARS

Mix and put into 9x13 inch pan and bake 10 minutes at 350°:

1 c. flour   1/2 c. powdered sugar
1/2 c. butter   1 Tbsp. evaporated milk

Melt in double boiler and spread on crust:

1 bag caramels   1/2 c. butter
1/4 c. evaporated milk 1 c. powdered sugar

Then melt:

1 (6 oz.) pkg. chocolate chips

2 Tbsp. evaporated milk
Vanilla

Spread over caramels and refrigerate.
Linda Seidel, Audubon, Mn.

CARAMEL LAYER BARS

1 (14 oz.) pkg. light caramels
1/3 c. evaporated milk
1 German chocolate cake mix

3/4 c. butter, melted
1/3 c. evaporated milk
1 c. chopped nuts
1 (6 oz.) pkg. chocolate chips

Preheat oven to 350°. Grease and flour 13x9 inch pan. Combine first 2 ingredients. Cook over low heat. Stir constantly until caramels melt; keep warm. Combine other ingredients except chocolate chips. Stir by hand until dough holds together. Press 1/2 of dough into pan, reserve the rest for top. Bake for 6 minutes. Sprinkle with chocolate chips and spread caramel mixture over chips. Add the rest of dough. Bake for 15 - 20 minutes. Cool completely.
Donna Meyer, Detroit Lakes, Mn.

CARAMEL LAYER SQUARES

14 oz. light caramels (about 50 caramels)
1/3 c. evaporated milk
1 pkg. Pillsbury German chocolate cake mix

3/4 c. butter or margarine, melted
1/3 c. evaporated milk
1 c. chopped nuts
1 c. (6 oz. pkg.) chocolate chips

Preheat oven to 325°. Grease and flour a 9x13 inch pan. In saucepan combine caramels and 1/3 cup evaporated milk. Cook over low heat, stirring constantly until caramels are melted. Keep warm. In a large bowl, combine remaining ingredients except chocolate chips. Stir, by hand, until dough holds together. Press 1/2 of dough into prepared pan, reserving remaining dough for topping. Bake for 6 minutes. Remove from oven, sprinkle chocolate chips over baked crust; spread caramel mixture over chips and spread reserved cake topping over caramel mixture. Return to oven and bake an additional 15 to 25 minutes. Cool completely. Makes about 3 to 4 dozen bars.
478

CARAMEL MORSEL BARS

49 (14 oz. bag) Kraft caramels
3 Tbsp. water
5 c. crisp rice cereal or toasted oat cereal

1 c. peanuts
1 (6 oz.) pkg. (1 c.) Nestle semi-sweet real chocolate morsels
1 (6 oz.) pkg. (1 c.) Nestle butterscotch flavored morsels

Melt caramels with water in saucepan over low heat. Stir frequently until sauce is smooth. Pour over cereal and nuts; toss until well coated. With greased fingers, press mixture into greased 13x9 inch baking pan. Sprinkle morsels on top; place in 200° F. oven for 5 minutes or until morsels soften. Spread softened morsels until blended to form a frosting. Cool; cut into bars.

Barb Torkelson, Windom, Mn.

CARROT BARS

Cream:
2 c. sugar
1 c. salad oil

4 eggs

Add:
2 c. flour
1 tsp. salt

2 tsp. soda
1 1/2 tsp. cinnamon

Then add 2 jars Junior size carrot baby food. Batter will be thin. Pour into a greased 9x13 inch pan and bake 30 minutes at 350°.

Frosting: Blend with electric mixer -

8 oz. cream cheese
1/2 stick margarine

2 tsp. vanilla
2 c. powdered sugar

Faye Matson, Bismarck, N. D.

CARROT BARS

4 eggs
2 c. sugar
3/4 c. salad oil
2 c. flour
2 tsp. soda

1 tsp. salt
2 tsp. cinnamon
1 1/2 c. cooked carrots or
use 3 small or 2 Junior
size baby food jars of
carrots

Beat eggs well, add sugar, salad oil, flour, soda, salt, cinnamon and carrots. Mix well. Put batter into two 9x13 inch pans, greased and floured. Bake at 350° for 30 minutes.

Frosting: Combine -

4 Tbsp. soft margarine
2 (3 oz.) pkg. cream
cheese

1/2 tsp. vanilla
1 lb. powdered sugar

Spread on bars.
Ardis Peterson, Rochester, Mn.

CHERRY CHIP BARS

Crust:

2 c. flour
1 c. oleo

6 Tbsp. powdered sugar

Mix and pat into bottom of 9x13 inch pan. Bake 15 minutes at 350°. Beat:

4 eggs
1 3/4 c. sugar
1 tsp. baking powder

2 tsp. vanilla
1/2 tsp. salt
3 Tbsp. flour

Mix together. Stir in:
3/4 c. coconut
1 (6 oz.) pkg. cherry chips

3/4 c. crushed pineapple

Add to crust and bake 20 minutes or until set, at 350°.
Edythe Stubbelfeld, St. Paul, Mn.

CHERRY SLICE BARS

1 c. butter or margarine
1 3/4 c. sugar
4 eggs
1 tsp. vanilla or almond
  extract

3 c. flour
1/2 tsp. salt
1 can cherry pie filling

Cream butter and sugar. Add eggs and extract. Beat well. Add flour and salt. Mix until smooth. In an 11x17 inch greased pan, spread all but 1 1/4 cups batter. Spread pie filling over this to half inch from edge. Add remaining batter by spoonfuls over the filling. Bake at 350° for about 40 minutes. When cool, sprinkle with powdered sugar or drizzle with thin powdered sugar frosting.

Nancy Kowalke, Nevis, Mn.

CHERRY WALNUT BARS

2 1/2 c. unsifted flour
1/2 c. sugar
1 c. softened butter
2 eggs
1 c. packed brown sugar
1/2 tsp. salt
1/2 tsp. baking powder

1/2 tsp. vanilla
1 (10 oz.) jar maraschino
  cherries, reserve juice
1/2 c. chopped walnuts
1 Tbsp. soft butter
1/2 c. coconut

Mix together thoroughly the flour, 1/2 cup sugar and butter. Press into 9x13 inch pan. Bake at 350° for 20 minutes. Combine eggs, brown sugar, salt and baking powder and vanilla. Drain cherries (reserving juice) and chop. Stir cherries and walnuts into egg mixture. Place on top of baked crust. Return to oven and bake for 25 minutes. Remove and cool. Make a frosting of 1 tablespoon butter and powdered sugar, using enough cherry juice to get consistency you want. Spread or drizzle topping over bars. Sprinkle with coconut.

Bev Bartz, St. Paul, Mn.

CHEWIES

2 eggs
5 Tbsp. flour
1 tsp. vanilla
2 Tbsp. butter

1 c. brown sugar
1/4 tsp. soda
1/2 c. nuts

1748-81

481

Melt butter in 9x9 inch pan. Beat eggs slightly. Mix
dry ingredients, stir into eggs. Add nuts and vanilla.
Pour into pan (do not stir). Bake at 350° for 20 minutes.
When cool, cut into squares and roll in powdered sugar.
Darlene Lee

CHIP BARS

1 stick margarine
1 c. graham crackers
 (14 crackers)

1 (6 oz.) pkg. chocolate
 chips
1 c. chopped walnuts
1 can sweetened condensed
 milk

Melt margarine in 9x13 inch pan in oven while it is preheating. Add other ingredients in order in layers. Bake at
350° for 20 - 25 minutes. Cool and cut small. Remove from
pan as soon as cool
Mary Bauer, Minneapolis, Mn.

CHRISTMAS BARS

Crust:

1 1/4 sticks margarine
1/3 c. brown sugar

1 1/2 c. flour

Mix together. Pat into a 9x13 inch baking pan. Bake
15 minutes at 325°. Cool well. Dissolve 2 envelopes Knox
gelatine in 1/2 cup cold water - place these 2 ingredients
in large mixing bowl. In a saucepan, place:

2 c. white sugar

1/2 c. water

Boil 2 minutes. Pour this syrup mixture over gelatine
and beat at high speed until very stiff. Add:

1/2 c. chopped, well
 drained cherries

1/2 c. chopped walnuts

Pour over the cooled crust. Sprinkle with cocoanut.
Cool well and slice into bars (do not bake the second part).
Freezes well.
Jean Taylor, Grand Forks, N. D.

CHOCOLATE BUTTERSCOTCH BARS

Melt 1/3 cup butter. Add:

1/2 c. sugar   2 Tbsp. milk

Bring to boil. Remove from heat and stir in:

1 (6 oz.) pkg. chocolate   1 tsp. vanilla
  chips

Stir until smooth and cooled. Beat in one at a time, 2 eggs. Add dry ingredients.

3/4 c. flour   1/4 tsp. soda
1/2 tsp. salt

Stir in 1/2 cup nuts. Bake in 9x13 inch pan at 350° for 25 minutes. Do not overbake. Cover top with miniature marshmallows immediately (2 cups). Melt 1/2 of a 6 ounce package of chocolate chips and 1/2 package butterscotch chips and 1 tablespoon butter. Pour over marshmallows. Chill. Takes awhile to harden. Cut into bars.

CHOCOLATE CHERRY BARS

1 can cherry pie filling   1 fudge cake mix
2 eggs   1 tsp. almond extract

Beat until well mixed. Bake in 9x13 inch pan 25 - 30 minutes at 350°.

Frosting:

1 c. sugar   5 Tbsp. butter
1/3 c. milk   1 c. chocolate chips

Combine and boil 1 minute. Stir in 1 cup chocolate chips. Beat until smooth
                Gina Michels, Willmar, Mn.

CHOCOLATE CHERRY BARS

1 chocolate cake mix,
  regular or fudge
2 eggs

1 can cherry pie filling
1 tsp. almond extract

Mix by hand, put into greased 10x15 inch pan. Bake at 350° for 25 minutes.

Frosting:

1 c. brown sugar
3 Tbsp. margarine

3 Tbsp. milk

Bring to boil, remove from heat and add 1/2 cup chocolate chips. Stir until chips are melted and until of spreading consistency.
Kathy Bischof, St. Cloud, Mn.

CHOCOLATE CHERRY BARS

1 pkg. devils food cake
  mix
1 (21 oz.) can cherry
  pie filling

1 tsp. almond extract
2 eggs

Mix all ingredients - beat 2 minutes. (Frost while warm.)

Frosting for Chocolate Cherry Bars:

1 c. sugar
5 Tbsp. butter

1/3 c. milk
6 oz. semi-sweet chocolate
  chips

Combine sugar, butter, milk - boil 1 minute, stirring constantly. Remove from heat - stir in chips until smooth.
Darlene Lee

CHOCOLATE CHIPS BARS

1/2 c. oleo
1/3 c. white sugar
1/3 c. packed brown
  sugar
1 egg

1 c. flour
1 tsp. vanilla
1/2 tsp. soda
1/2 tsp. salt

484

| 1/2 c. chopped nuts | 1/2 c. chocolate chips |
| | (miniature size work well) |

Soften oleo with sugars. Add remaining ingredients, blend well. Spread in a greased 9x13 inch pan. Bake at 375° for 15 - 20 minutes or until light golden brown.

Karen Rupert, St. Cloud, Mn.

CHOCOLATE DELUXE BARS

2 c. sugar	1/2 c. sour milk
2 c. flour	2 eggs, slightly beaten
1 c. oleo	1 tsp. soda
1 c. water	1 tsp. vanilla
1/4 c. cocoa	

**Read through instructions before starting!!

Sift flour and sugar into large bowl. Combine in a saucepan, oleo, water and cocoa, bring to boiling point. Pour over flour and sugar while hot. Mix well. Add sour milk, egg, soda, vanilla, mix well. Grease and flour a large jelly roll pan (17x11 inches) and bake at 350° for 20 - 25 minutes. Don't overbake. (This is a thin batter.)

Frosting:

| 1/2 c. oleo | 6 Tbsp. milk |
| 1/4 c. cocoa | Chopped walnuts |

Combine in pan and bring just to the boiling point (medium heat and keep stirring). Pour this over about 1 pound powdered sugar (I use less), stir up well. Add 1 teaspoon vanilla and stir in, frost cooled brownies.

Karen Rupert, St. Cloud, Mn.

CHOCOLATE--CARAMEL BARS

Melt in double boiler, low heat:

| 1 (14 oz.) bag caramels | 1/3 c. evaporated milk |

Melt 3/4 cup oleo, add in:

| 1 chocolate cake mix | 1/3 c. evaporated milk |
| 1 c. chopped walnuts | |

Take half of this cake mixture and pat into the bottom of a 9x13 inch pan, bake for 6 minutes at 350°. Sprinkle cake mixture with bag of chocolate chips, cover with the melted caramel. Put the rest of the cake mixture on and bake for 15 - 18 minutes. Cool bars, cut, then put in refrigerator 30 minutes to set the caramel.

Karen Rupert, St. Cloud, Mn.

CHOCOLATE--PEANUT BUTTER BARS

1 3/4 c. flour	1/2 tsp. salt
1/2 c. sugar	2/3 c. oleo
1/2 c. brown sugar	1 tsp. vanilla
1/2 tsp. soda	1 egg

Combine ingredients in bowl. Beat 3 minutes at medium speed. Pat into a greased 9x13 inch pan.

1/3 c. peanut butter	2 Tbsp. honey

Stir up together and spread over base you have in pan.

1 c. miniature marshmallows	6 oz. pkg. chocolate chips

Sprinkle marshmallows and chocolate chips on top of everything. Bake 20 - 25 minutes until golden brown, at 375°.

Glaze:

1 oz. sq. unsweetened chocolate	1 Tbsp. corn syrup
2 Tbsp. water	1 c. powdered sugar

Combine first 3 ingredients in saucepan. Stir over low heat until chocolate melts. Blend in sugar until smooth. Drizzle over bars.

Karen Rupert, St. Cloud, Mn.

CHOCOLATE REVEL BARS

1 c. butter	2 c. brown sugar

Cream. Add:

2 eggs	2 tsp. vanilla

Add:

2 1/2 c. flour   1 tsp. soda

Add:

1 tsp. salt   3 c. oatmeal

Filling:

12 oz. chocolate chips   1 c. nuts (optional)
15 oz. sweetened condensed   1/2 tsp. salt
  milk   2 tsp. vanilla
2 Tbsp. butter

Spread 2/3 of crumb mixture. Spread filling over crumb mixture and use remaining crumb mixture to spread on top. Bake at 350° for 25 - 30 minutes.
Diane Schmitz, St. Cloud, Mn.

COCONUT BARS

2 c. graham cracker   1/2 c. butter
  crumbs   1/4 c. sugar

Put into bottom of oblong cake pan and bake at 325° for 15 minutes. Combine:

1 can sweetened condensed   1 (7 oz.) pkg. coconut
  milk

Spread on first mixture and put into oven for 10 minutes more. Melt 1 (6 ounce) package chocolate chips or milk Hershey's bars on top. Cool and cut.
Diane Schmitz, St. Cloud, Mn.

CONGO SQUARES

2/3 c. butter   1/2 tsp. salt
2 1/4 c. brown sugar,   3 eggs
  firmly packed (1 lb.)   1 c. chopped nuts
2 1/2 c. sifted flour   1 c. chocolate chips
2 1/2 tsp. baking powder

Melt butter in saucepan. Stir in brown sugar. Remove from heat and let cool 10 minutes. Stir flour, baking powder and salt - one at a time beaten eggs into sugar mixture.

Then add nuts and chocolate chips, beating well. Spread into a greased pan. Bake at 350° for 25 - 30 minutes.
Diane Schmitz, St. Cloud, Mn.

CRANBERRY PECAN BARS

Crust:

1/2 c. butter, softened
2 tsp. vanilla
2 Tbsp. sugar

1/2 tsp. salt
1 c. flour
1/2 c. finely chopped pecans

Topping:

1 c. chopped cranberries
1/2 c. flaked coconut
1/2 c. finely chopped
   pecans
2 Tbsp. flour

Grated rind of 1 orange
2 c. sugar
3 egg yolks
1/3 c. cream

To make crust, mix butter and vanilla with sugar, salt and flour, mixing until crumbly. Stir in chopped pecans and press mixture into a very thin layer in a 9x13 inch pan. Bake at 350° about 10 minutes or until lightly browned. Meanwhile, mix together the chopped cranberries, coconut, pecans, flour, orange rind, sugar, egg yolks and pour over crust. Bake 25 - 30 minutes or until lightly browned.
Karen Rupert, St. Cloud, Mn.

CREAM PUFF BARS

1 c. flour
1/2 c. butter

2 Tbsp. water

Mix like pie dough and pat on bottom of jelly roll pan.

1 c. water
1/2 c. butter
1 c. flour

3 eggs
1/2 tsp. almond extract

Heat water and butter to boiling point. Remove and add flour. Stir until smooth. Add eggs, one at a time, beating well after each. Add extract and spread over first mixture. Frost with 1 cup powdered sugar, 1 teaspoon

488

butter, 1/2 teaspoon almond extract and a little milk **or** cream. Bake at 350° for 55 minutes.

Bev Bartz, St. Paul, Mn.

CRUNCHY FUDGE SANDWICH

1 (6 oz.) pkg. (1 c.)
  butterscotch morsels
1/2 c. peanut butter
4 c. Kellogg's Rice
  Krispies cereal
1 Tbsp. water

1 (6 oz.) pkg. (1 c.) semi-
  sweet chocolate morsels
1/2 c. sifted confectioners
  sugar
2 Tbsp. butter **or** margarine

Melt butterscotch with peanut butter in heavy saucepan over very low heat, stirring constantly until well blended. Take off heat. Add Rice Krispies cereal, stirring until well coated with butterscotch mixture. Press half of cereal mixture into buttered 8x8x2 inch pan. Chill in refrigerator while preparing fudge mixture. Set remaining cereal mixture aside. Combine chocolate, sugar, butter and water. Stir over hot water until chocolate melts and mixture is well blended. Spread over chilled cereal mixture. Spread remaining cereal mixture evenly over top. Press gently. Chill. Remove from refrigerator for about 10 minutes before cutting into squares. Yield: 25 (1 1/2 inch) squares.

Diane Schmitz, St. Cloud, Mn.

DATE AND ORANGE BARS

1/2 lb. dates
1/2 c. sugar

2 Tbsp. flour
1 c. water

Mix together, cook until thick and cool.

3/4 c. butter
1 c. brown sugar
2 eggs
1 tsp. soda in 2 Tbsp.
  water
1 3/4 c. flour

1 tsp. vanilla
1/2 c. nuts
1 (15 oz.) pkg. orange slices,
  cut into thirds lengthwise
Pinch of salt

Cream shortening and sugar. Beat in eggs, add soda, vanilla, flour, salt and chopped nuts. Spread half of mixture into greased 9x12 inch pan, cover with orange slices and top with remaining batter. Bake at 350° for 40 minutes.

Lucille Jansen, R. Arnold, Sauk Centre, Mn.

DIAGONAL BARS

2 c. sifted all-purpose
   flour
1/2 tsp. baking powder
2/3 c. sugar

3/4 c. butter, softened
1 egg
2 tsp. vanilla extract
Jam or jelly (apricot or
   raspberry)

Sift flour, baking powder and salt in mixing bowl. Blend in butter, egg and vanilla to form dough. Divide into 4 parts. Shape each into a roll 13 inches long and 3/4 inch thick. Place 2 rolls on each cookie sheet, about 4 inches apart. Make depression 1/4 to 1/3 inch deep in each roll down the center. Fill depression with jam or jelly. Bake for 15 to 20 minutes at 350° F. or until golden brown. While still warm, dripple your favorite powdered sugar icing down center over jelly, and cut diagonally. (4 dozen bars)

Gloria Bergson, Fargo, N. D.

DOUBLE CARAMEL BARS

9x9 inch pan:

9x13 inch pan:

Melt in double boiler:

32 caramels
5 Tbsp. Pet milk

64 caramels
10 Tbsp. Pet milk (small can)

Have ready:

1 c. flour
1 c. quick oatmeal
3/4 c. brown sugar
1/2 tsp. soda
1/4 tsp. salt
3/4 c. butter, melted

2 c. flour
2 c. quick oatmeal
1 1/2 c. brown sugar
1 tsp. soda
1/2 tsp. salt
1 1/2 c. butter, melted

Have ready:

1/2 c. chocolate pieces
1/2 c. nuts

1 c. chocolate pieces
1 c. nuts

Combine in large bowl till crumbly. Put 1/2 of crumbs in pan and bake 10 minutes at 350°. Remove from oven and sprinkle chocolate chips over top. Cover with caramel mixture and nuts. Sprinkle rest of crumbs on top and bake 12 - 15 minutes at 350°. Cut while warm. Fantastic!

490   Marge Johnson, Minneapolis, Mn.

DOUBLE CHOCOLATE CRUMBLE BARS

Bottom Layer:

1/2 c. margarine   3/4 c. sugar

Cream. Add:
2 eggs   2 Tbsp. cocoa
1 tsp. vanilla   1/4 tsp. baking powder
3/4 c. flour   1/4 tsp. salt
1/2 c. chopped nuts

Beat all ingredients well and spread on greased 9x13 inch cake pan. Bake at 350° for 15 - 20 minutes. Remove from oven, spread 2 cups miniature marshmallows over top and bake 3 minutes. Cool thoroughly. In saucepan, melt:

1 c. chocolate chips   1 c. peanut butter

When melted, add 1 1/2 cups Rice Krispies. Spread over top. Chill and cut.
Phyllis Curran, Red River Valley Council

EASY BAR RECIPE

Butter jelly roll pan. Cover bottom of pan with whole graham crackers. Cook 1 cup butter and 1 cup brown sugar for a minute (do not use margarine). Spread on top of crackers. Sprinkle slivered almonds on top. Bake 8 to 10 minutes at 350°.   Cut when warm.
Norma Haugland, Fargo, N. D.

ENERGY BARS

2 c. quick or old   1/4 c. honey
  fashioned oats, uncooked   3 Tbsp. butter or
3 c. miniature marshmallows   margarine
1/2 c. chunk-style peanut   1 c. raisins
  butter

1. Toast oats in shallow baking pan in preheated 350° F. oven, about 15 minutes or until golden brown. Line a 9 inch square baking pan with aluminum foil; grease. 2. Melt marshmallows with peanut butter, honey and butter in medium-sized saucepan, or double boiler, over low heat,

stirring constantly; remove from heat. 3. Stir in toasted oats and raisins. Place in prepared pan, spreading evenly. Chill until firm. To serve, remove foil and cut into squares.

Carmen Moe, R.N., Minneapolis, Mn.

EXPENSIVE CALORIE BAR

1/2 c. margarine
1/2 c. butter
1/2 c. cornstarch

1/2 c. sugar
2 c. flour

Cream all together. Mixture will be somewhat crumbly. Spread in 15x10 inch pan and bake at 350° for 20 minutes.

Second layer:

4 eggs
1/2 tsp. baking powder
1 1/2 c. coconut
1 1/2 c. chopped nuts

4 Tbsp. flour
2 c. brown sugar
2 tsp. vanilla

Mix all together and spread over baked crust. Bake 25 minutes at 350°. Cool. Frost with the following:

1/2 c. margarine at room
  temperature
3 c. powdered sugar

8 oz. cream cheese at room
  temperature
1 tsp. vanilla

Cream all together and frost bars. Refrigerate. Cut bars small - very rich, but delicious!

Mrs. William Meyer, St. Paul, Mn.

FROSTED MALLOW BARS

1/3 c. butter
1 sq. unsweetened
  chocolate
2 eggs
1 c. chopped nuts
1 tsp. vanilla

16 marshmallows, cut into
  halves
1/2 tsp. baking powder
1 c. sugar
3/4 c. flour
1/2 tsp. salt

Melt butter and chocolate. Remove from heat. Add sugar and mix. Add flour, salt and baking powder, blending well. Add eggs and beat. Mix in chopped nuts and vanilla. Pour into 11x7 inch greased pan. Bake at 350° for 35 minutes. Top with marshmallow halves and return to oven 2 - 3 minutes. Spread and frost.

Diane Schmitz, St. Cloud, Mn.

FUDGE BARS

1 pkg. Pillsbury fudge
   cake mix
2 eggs, beaten

1 (#2) can Wilderness cherries
1 tsp. almond extract

Stir these 4 ingredients by hand. Grease and flour 16x11 inch cookie sheet. Bake at 350° for 25 - 30 minutes.

Frosting:

1/2 c. sugar
2 1/2 Tbsp. butter

3 Tbsp. milk

Boil 1 minute, stirring constantly. Add 1/2 package chocolate chips.

Elsie Ekblad

FUDGE LAYER BAR

12 oz. chocolate chips
2 Tbsp. butter

1 can Borden's sweetened
   condensed milk

Melt in double boiler.

1 c. shortening
2 c. brown sugar
2 eggs
1 tsp. soda

1 tsp. vanilla
2 1/2 c. flour
1 1/2 c. oatmeal (quick oats)

Put 2/3 into greased 9x13 inch pan, cover with chocolate mixture. Mix 4 tablespoons water with the rest and put it on top. Bake 25 - 30 minutes at 350°.

Pat Anderson, Minneapolis, Mn.

FUDGE-FULL PEANUT-BUTTER BARS

1 pkg. yellow cake mix
1 c. peanut butter

1/2 c. oleo, melted
2 eggs

Filling:

1 c. (6 oz. pkg.) semi-
   sweet chocolate chips
1 (14 oz.) can sweetened
   condensed milk

2 Tbsp. oleo
1 pkg. coconut pecan or
   coconut almond frosting
   mix

Read through all directions first, before starting.
Combine cake mix, peanut butter, oleo and eggs by hand. Stir until dough holds together. Press 2/3 of dough into bottom of an ungreased 9x13 inch pan. Reserve remaining dough for topping.
Prepare filling: Combine chocolate chips, sweetened condensed milk and oleo. Melt over low heat, stirring constantly until smooth. Remove from heat, stir in frosting mix. Spread filling over dough in pan. Crumble reserved dough over filling. Bake at 350° for 20 - 25 minutes until light golden brown. Cool completely, cut into about 36 bars.

Karen Rupert, St. Cloud, Mn.

FUDGE SQUARES

1 can sweetened
   condensed milk

1 (6 oz.) pkg. chocolate chips
2 Tbsp. butter

Melt together over low heat. Remove from heat and add 1 teaspoon vanilla. Set aside. Cream:

1/2 c. butter
1 c. brown sugar

1 egg

Add:
1 1/4 c. flour
1/2 tsp. soda

1 1/2 c. oatmeal
1/4 tsp. salt

Mix together well. Put 2/3 mixture into 9x12 inch pan. Pour into chocolate mixture to which 1/2 cup nuts has been added. Bake 25 minutes at 350°. Cut while warm.

Rosie Schudar, Fargo, N. D.

GERMAN HONEY BARS

1 1/3 c. honey or molasses	1/4 c. chopped candied orange
3/4 c. sugar	or lemon peel
3 Tbsp. butter	1/4 tsp. ginger
2 c. flour	1/2 tsp. cardamon
1 tsp. baking powder	1/2 tsp. cinnamon
1/4 c. blanched almonds	1/8 tsp. cloves
1/4 c. citron	1 1/2 to 2 c. more flour

Heat slightly in a saucepan, honey and sugar. Add butter, stirring constantly until melted. Sift together 2 cups of flour and baking powder and add. Stir in almonds, citron, peel and spices. Add enough of the rest of the flour to make a sticky, soft dough. Pat out into a 1/4 inch thickness onto 4 greased 8x8 inch pans or 2 (13x9 inch) pans. Bake at 350° about 25 minutes. Watch carefully, as they easily become too hard and are never a very dark brown. Frost or glaze with a lemon powdered sugar icing.
Kathy Bishof, St. Cloud, Mn.

GRAHAM CRACKER BARS

1/2 c. butter	1 c. graham cracker crumbs
1 c. coconut	1/2 c. milk
1 c. brown sugar	Salt

Boil 10 minutes. Pour over whole crackers in pan. Cover with another layer of whole crackers - press lightly. Cover with powdered sugar frosting.
Darlene Lee

GUSSIE NUT GOODIE BARS
(Tongue-Tickling Recipe)

2 c. (12 oz. pkg.)	1 c. peanut butter
chocolate chips	1 (10 oz.) pkg. miniature
2 c. (12 oz. pkg.)	marshmallows
butterscotch chips	1 lb. salted Spanish peanuts

Melt chocolate, butterscotch chips and peanut butter in top of double boiler. Cool. Stir in remaining ingredients. Spread in 1 buttered 9x13 inch pan for thick bars, or 2 buttered 9x13 inch pans for thin ones. Cool before cutting. Yield: 35 bars/pan.
From Minneapolis, Mn.

1748-81

HONEY ALMOND SQUARES

Bake one Duncan Hines Pudding recipe white cake mix as directed on package, in 13x9x2 inch pan. Cool, then cream 1 (8 ounce) package cream cheese (room temperature) and gradually add 1/4 cup honey. Beat until smooth. Spread cream cheese mixture on cake. Sprinkle with sliced almonds. Store in refrigerator.

Mike and Vonnie Bakke, Willmar, Mn.

LEMON BARS

1 pkg. one-step angel
   food cake mix

1 can Wilderness lemon
   instant pie filling

Mix the two ingredients together. Put on greased jelly roll pan and bake at 350° for 15 to 20 minutes or until done (check with toothpick or by touch - the time and temperature depends on your oven). Frost with a powdered sugar, Philadelphia cream cheese frosting or with plain powdered sugar sprinkled over the top.

LEMON BARS

2 c. flour
1 c. butter (no oleo)

1 c. powdered sugar

Mix and pat into 9x13 inch pan. Bake at 350° for 20 minutes. Combine:

4 eggs, well beaten
1 3/4 c. sugar
1 lemon (juice of)

1 tsp. baking powder
2 Tbsp. flour
1 c. flaked coconut

Mix well and pour over crust and bake another 15 to 20 minutes.

Recipe from Minneapolis, Mn.

LEMON BARS

2 c. flour
1/2 c. powdered sugar

1/2 c. butter
1/2 c. lard

Mix together and pat into 9x13 inch pan. Bake 10

minutes in 350° oven - cool slightly.

Filling:

4 eggs, beaten	4 Tbsp. lemon juice, plus
2 c. sugar	grated rind of 1 lemon
4 Tbsp. flour	

Mix together and pour over crust. Bake 25 minutes at 350° until lightly browned. Dust with powdered sugar on thin frosting while still warm.

Diane Schmitz, St. Cloud, Mn.

LEMON BARS

1 c. flour	1/4 c. powdered sugar
1/2 c. butter or margarine	

Mix and pat into 9x13 inch pan (ungreased). Bake 15 minutes at 350°.

2 c. sugar	6 Tbsp. lemon juice
4 eggs	1 tsp. baking powder
4 Tbsp. flour	

Beat and pour over first layer. Bake 25 minutes at 350°. Cool. Frost with:

1 1/2 c. powdered sugar	1 tsp. vanilla
1 Tbsp. soft butter or margarine	2 Tbsp. lemon juice

Gretchen Marquart, Fargo, N. D.

LEMON CHEESE BARS

1 Duncan Hines Pudding recipe yellow cake mix	1/3 c. sugar 1 tsp. lemon juice 2 eggs
1 (8 oz.) pkg. cream cheese, softened	1/3 c. oil

Mix dry cake mix, 1 egg and 1/3 cup oil until crumbly. Reserve 1 cup. Pat remainder of mixture lightly into an ungreased 9x13 inch pan. Bake 15 minutes at 350°. Beat

cheese, sugar, lemon juice and 1 egg until light and smooth. Spread over baked layer. Sprinkle with reserved crumb mixture. Bake 15 minutes longer. Cool. Cut into squares.
Marie Miller, St. Paul, Mn.

MAGIC COOKIE BARS
(Makes 24 bars)

1/2 c. oleo	1 (6 oz.) pkg. semi-sweet
1 1/2 c. graham cracker	chocolate chips
crumbs	1 (3 1/2 oz.) pkg. flaked
1 (14 oz.) can sweetened	coconut
condensed milk*	1 c. nuts

Melt butter in 13x9 inch pan. Sprinkle crumbs over butter. Pour milk over crumbs and top evenly with rest of ingredients. Press down gently. Bake at 350° for 25 minutes. Cool and cut.
*How to make sweetened condensed milk:

3/4 c. sugar	1 c. + 2 tsp. powdered milk
1/2 c. hot water	

Mix and leave set 5 minutes.
Sue Loehrer, St. Cloud, Mn.

MANDARIN ORANGE BARS

2 c. flour	2 eggs
2 c. sugar	2 (11 oz.) cans Mandarin
2 tsp. soda	oranges
1 tsp. salt	Juice from 1 can oranges

Mix ingredients. Pour into greased and floured bar pan. Bake at 350° for 25 - 30 minutes. Frost when cool with a cream cheese frosting.
Pat Langfitt, Fargo, N. D.

MARSHMALLOW BARS

Prepare crust of:

3/4 c. margarine	1 1/2 c. flour
1/3 c. brown sugar	

498

Press into 9x13 inch pan and bake at 350° for 15 minutes. Cool. Dissolve in large mixing bowl 2 envelopes of Knox gelatine, in 1/2 cup cold water. Boil for 1 minute -

2 c. white sugar   1/2 c. water

Pour over gelatine and beat until very thick (like divinity). Takes from 15 to 20 minutes. Add 1/2 cup drained, chopped maraschino cherries, 1/2 cup chopped walnuts, dash of salt and 1 teaspoon vanilla. Pour over the cooked crust and sprinkle coconut over the top. When cool, cut into bars.

Helen Kruse, Fargo, N. D.

MARSHMALLOW BROWNIES

Grease bottom and sides of 9 inch square pan.

1/2 c. butterscotch chips   1/4 c. margarine

Melt in 3 quart heavy saucepan over medium heat, stirring constantly. Remove from heat, cool to lukewarm.

3/4 c. flour   1/2 tsp. vanilla
1 tsp. baking powder   1/4 tsp. salt
1/3 c. packed brown   1 egg
  sugar

Add to butterscotch mixture and mix well.

1 c. marshmallows   1 c. chocolate chips

Fold into butterscotch batter just until combined, about 5 strokes. Spread in prepared pan. Bake at 350° for 20 minutes to 25 minutes. Do not overbake. Center will be jiggly, but becomes firm upon cooking.

Dena Stoddard, Minneapolis, Mn.

MATRIMONY BARS

Date Mixture: Boil until soft and well done - cool -

1 medium pkg. dates,   1 c. sugar
  cut fine   1/2 c. water

Mix into crumbly mess:

1 3/4 c. quick oatmeal	1 tsp. soda
1 3/4 c. flour	1 c. shortening
1 c. brown sugar	

Put 1/2 in pan. Pour in dates. Top with other 1/2. Bake in 350° oven for 30 minutes.

Marge Johnson, Minneapolis, Mn.

MISSISSIPPI MUD BARS

4 eggs	1 1/2 c. unsifted flour
1 c. margarine, softened	1/4 c. cocoa
2 c. sugar	1 c. chopped nuts
1 tsp. vanilla	1 (7 oz.) jar marshmallow
Dash of salt	creme

In large mixing bowl, medium speed, beat eggs, margarine, sugar and vanilla until light and fluffy. Add flour, salt and cocoa. Beat until well blended. Fold in nuts. Spread evenly in greased 9x13 inch pan, bake 40 to 45 minutes at 350°. Immediately place dollops of marshmallow creme on top and spread until smooth. Let cool at least 1 hour before frosting.

Frosting:

1/3 c. margarine	1/3 c. milk
1/2 c. cocoa	1 tsp. vanilla
2 1/2 c. powdered sugar	

Melt margarine, stir in cocoa. Cook for 1 minute. Add remaining ingredients, mix until smooth. Spread on top of marshmallow. Cut into 1 inch squares. Freezes well. These are very rich.

Evelyn Walls, St. Paul, Mn.

MOIST SPICE BARS

1 c. sugar	1 c. shortening
1 1/2 c. water	1 c. raisins
1/2 tsp. cinnamon	1/2 tsp. cloves

Cook above ingredients for 10 minutes. Cool. Add: 2 cups flour, 1 teaspoon soda and 1 egg, beaten. Bake in

9x13 inch pan at 350° for 45 minutes. When cool, frost with powdered sugar or powdered sugar frosting.

Kathy Neels, St. Cloud, Mn.

MONKEY BARS

4 tubes buttermilk
  biscuits
3/4 c. white sugar

1 tsp. cinnamon
1/2 c. nuts

Cut each of biscuits into fourths. Shake in sugar and cinnamon. Place each piece in a greased Bundt or tube pan. Sprinkle nuts on top. Bring to boil:

1 c. brown sugar
3/4 c. butter

1 1/2 tsp. cinnamon
1 Tbsp. milk or cream

Pour over pan and bake at 350° for 30 minutes or longer. Let stand 5 minutes and then turn pan upside down on waxed paper. (These are like caramel rolls.)

Edith Weber

NAVINO BARS

2 c. finely crushed
  graham crackers

1 c. fine coconut
1/2 c. nuts, chopped

Combine and pat into the bottom of a 9x13 inch pan.

1/2 c. butter or oleo
1 tsp. vanilla
1/4 c. sugar

3 Tbsp. cocoa
1 egg

Cook in a double boiler till custard like. Pour all but 2 tablespoonfuls on top of your crust.

3/8 c. butter or oleo
3 Tbsp. milk

2 Tbsp. custard you saved
2 c. powdered sugar

Stir up and let stand 5 minutes.

4 sq. semi-sweet chocolate

1 Tbsp. butter or oleo

Melt together; spread on top.

Karen Rupert, St. Cloud, Mn.

NO-BAKE PEANUT BUTTER BARS

2 c. crushed graham   1 c. peanut butter
  crackers   1 c. melted margarine
2 c. powdered sugar

    Melt margarine, add ingredients. Press into 9x13 inch
pan. Frost with melted Hershey's bars. Refrigerate.
         Gina Michels, Willmar, Mn.

NUT BARS

1 1/2 c. flour   1/2 c. soft butter
3/4 c. sugar   1/4 tsp. salt

    Mix until crumbly and pat down into a 9x13 inch pan.
Bake 10 minutes at 350°. Melt following in a double boiler
(water not boiling):

1 (6 oz.) pkg. butterscotch   Dash of salt
  chips   2 Tbsp. butter
1/2 c. light corn syrup   1 Tbsp. water

    Stir until smooth. Remove from stove and add 1
(12 ounce) can mixed nuts. Spread quickly and evenly
over baked layer. Bake another 10 minutes at 350°.
         Madaline Danich, St. Paul, Mn.

NUT GOODIE BARS

    Melt together in a double boiler:

1 (12 oz.) pkg chocolate   2 c. peanut butter (smooth
  chips   or chunky)
1 (12 oz.) pkg. butterscotch
  chips

    Put half of the above mixture into a buttered 12x16
inch pan and put in the refrigerator or freezer.

    Filling:

1 c. butter   1/4 c. regular vanilla
1/2 c. Carnation evaporated   pudding (dry)
  milk

502

Mix together and boil 1 minute. Add 1 teaspoon maple flavoring. Add 2 pounds confectioners sugar. Spread on top of refrigerated mixture and put into refrigerator again. Add 1 pound peanuts to remaining chocolate mixture and spread over filling. Keep refrigerated. Cut into small squares.

Dorothy Savig, Minneapolis Council

OATMEAL BARS

1 1/4 c. boiling water	2 eggs
1 c. oatmeal	1 tsp. vanilla
1/2 c. butter	1 1/2 c. flour
1 c. white sugar	1/2 tsp. salt
1 c. brown sugar	1 tsp. soda

Pour water over oatmeal and set aside. Cream butter and sugar. Add other ingredients. Mix and add oatmeal mixture. Bake at 350° for 30 minutes or less. Use a 15x10 inch pan.

Frosting:

1 1/2 c. butter or margarine	6 Tbsp. cream
1 1/2 c. brown sugar	1 tsp. vanilla

Bring to full boil and boil 2 minutes. Cool. Beat. Spread on bars. Tastes like penuche candy.

Bev Bartz, St. Paul, Mn.

OATMEAL BARS

1 c. quick cooking oatmeal	1 1/4 c. boiling water

Pour water over oatmeal, let stand in a bowl for 20 minutes.

1/2 c. shortening	1 c. white sugar
1 c. brown sugar	

Cream together. Add 2 eggs and 1 teaspoon vanilla. Mix well.

1 1/2 c. flour	1/2 tsp. salt
1 tsp. soda	

1748-81

Add to creamed mixture. Add oatmeal last. Pour into a greased 9x13 inch pan. Bake for 25 minutes at 350°. When bars are cooled, frost with the following:

1/2 c. butter or margarine	6 Tbsp. Carnation milk
1 1/2 c. brown sugar	1 tsp. vanilla

Mix together in a saucepan, boil 2 minutes. Add 1/2 cup chopped walnuts. Beat until frosting starts to thicken. Spread over bars.

Jean Taylor, Grand Forks, N. D.

OATMEAL CARAMEL BARS

1 (14 oz.) pkg. caramels	1 tsp. soda
1/2 c. evaporated milk	1/2 tsp. salt
or light cream	1 c. melted butter
2 c. flour	1 (6 oz.) pkg. chocolate
2 c. quick rolled oats	chips
1 1/2 c. brown sugar	1 c. chopped pecans

Melt caramels in evaporated milk in heavy saucepan. Cool slightly, combine remaining ingredients except chocolate chips and pecans, in large bowl. Press 1/2 of crumbs into bottom of greased 9x13 inch pan, bake at 350° for 10 minutes. Remove from oven. Sprinkle with chocolate chips and pecans. Spread on caramel ingredients and rest of crumbs. Bake 15 - 20 minutes more. Chill 1 - 2 hours.

Karen Rupert, St. Cloud, Mn.

ONE STEP BARS

1/2 c. butter or margarine	1 c. walnuts, chopped
1 1/2 c. graham crackers,	1 c. coconut
crushed	1 (14 oz.) can condensed
1 c. chocolate chips	milk

Melt butter. Mix with graham cracker crumbs right in the 9x13 inch pan. Flatten evenly. Pour condensed milk over crumbs. Sprinkle chocolate chips, coconut and nuts over this. (Amounts of coconut, nuts and chips can vary according to taste.) Bake for 25 minutes at 300°. Put into refrigerator to firm before cutting into squares.

Linda Johnson, Anoka, Mn.

PEANUT BROWNIES

1/4 c. creamy peanut
  butter
1/4 c. butter
3 sq. unsweetened
  chocolate
3 eggs
2 c. sugar

1/2 c. peanut halves
1 tsp. vanilla
1 c. sifted flour
1/2 tsp. baking powder
1/4 tsp. salt
1 c. peanuts, coarsely
  chopped
1 oz. sweet cooking chocolate

Melt and blend butter, peanut butter and unsweetened chocolate in top of double boiler over boiling water. Cool to lukewarm. Beat eggs until thick and fluffy. Add sugar gradually, beating well. Beat in cooled chocolate mixture and vanilla. Stir in flour, baking powder and salt sifted together. Fold in chopped peanuts. Turn batter into greased 9x13 inch pan. Spread evenly. Bake in moderately hot oven (275°) for 30 minutes or until wooden pick comes out clean. Cool and cut into bars. Makes 30 brownies.
  Peanut People. Touch a dot of melted sweet cooking chocolate (or chocolate decorator icing) to flat sides of peanut halves, one at a time, arranging 6 on each brownie to form peanut men. If desired, border top edge of brownies with creamy white decorator icing.

PEANUT BUSTER BARS

1 lb. Hydrox cookies,
  crushed
1/3 c. melted butter
1/2 gal. vanilla ice
  cream
1 1/2 c. Spanish peanuts

2 c. powdered sugar
1 1/2 c. evaporated milk
2/3 c. chocolate chips
1/2 c. butter
1 tsp. vanilla

Mix crushed cookies and butter together and pat into the bottom of a 9x13 inch pan. Cut vanilla ice cream into slices and layer over the crushed cookie mixture. Press peanuts on top of ice cream and keep in freezer. Combine powdered sugar, milk, chocolate chips and 1/2 cup butter in saucepan and bring to boil. Boil 8 minutes, stirring constantly. Add vanilla and mix. When cool, pour over ice cream and freeze. Cut into squares and serve.

PEANUT BUTTER BARS

1 2/3 c. graham crackers,
  crushed
1/2 lb. softened margarine

1 lb. box powdered sugar
1 c. peanut butter

Mix together with hands, pat onto cookie sheet.

Frosting: Melt 2 cups chocolate chips and spread on top.

Renee Ulberg, Bismarck, N. D.

PEANUT BUTTER CUP BARS

2 c. crushed graham
  cracker crumbs
2 c. powdered sugar

1 c. melted butter
1 c. peanut butter (creamy
  is best)

Mix above ingredients together and put into a 9x13 inch pan.

Topping: Melt 1 (12 ounce) package milk chocolate chips and add 2 tablespoons peanut butter, mix well and pour over graham cracker mixture and refrigerate.

Mary Sommers, Minneapolis, Mn.

PECAN PIE SURPRISE BARS

1 pkg. yellow cake mix
1/2 c. oleo

1 egg
1 c. chopped pecans

Filling:

2/3 c. reserved cake mix
1/2 c. packed brown sugar
1 1/2 c. dark corn syrup

1 tsp. vanilla
3 eggs

Grease bottom and sides of 9x13 inch pan. Reserve 2/3 cup dry cake mix for filling. In large bowl, combine remaining dry cake mix, oleo and 1 egg. Mix until crumbly. Press into prepared pan, bake at 350° for 15 - 20 minutes until light golden brown. Meanwhile, prepare filling by combining all ingredients, beat at medium speed 1 - 2 minutes. Pour filling over partially baked crust; sprinkle with pecans. Return to oven; bake 30 - 35 minutes until filling is set. Cool, cut into 36 bars.

Karen Rupert, St. Cloud, Mn.

PUMPKIN BARS

4 beaten eggs
1 c. salad oil
2 c. sugar
1 c. pumpkin
1/2 tsp. salt

2 tsp. cinnamon
1 tsp. soda
1 tsp. baking powder
2 c. flour

Mix ingredients well. Pour into a greased and floured bar pan. Bake at 350° for 25 - 30 minutes. Frost while warm.

Frosting:

3 oz. cream cheese
3/4 lb. powdered sugar
6 Tbsp. margarine or butter

1/2 c. milk
1/2 tsp. vanilla

Mix well. Spread on warm bars. Freezes well!
Pat Langfitt, Fargo, N. D.

PUMPKIN SQUARES

1 pkg. yellow cake mix
  (save 1 c. dry mix)

1/2 c. butter or margarine,
  melted
1 egg

Mix above together, put into greased and floured 9x13 inch pan.

Filling:

1 lb. 14 oz. can pumpkin
  pie mix

2 eggs, slightly beaten
2/3 c. milk

Mix all together.

Topping:

1 c. dry cake mix
1/4 c. sugar
1 tsp. cinnamon

1/4 c. butter, melted
1/2 c. nuts

Mix until crumbly, spread on top of cake. Sprinkle with topping. Bake 45 - 50 minutes at 350°.
Lydia Skaret, Austin, Mn.

RHUBARB BARS

Prepare and bake a graham cracker crust in a 9x13 inch pan. Reserve 1/2 cup crumbs for topping.

4 c. rhubarb (fresh or frozen)
2 c. sugar

1 pkg. strawberry or raspberry jello
2 c. miniature marshmallows
1 c. whipped cream

Boil rhubarb and sugar until done. Remove from heat and add package of jello. Let mixture stand until warm. Stir in marshmallows until they begin to melt. Fold in whipped cream. Pour over crust, then sprinkle crumbs or flaked coconut on top. Chill until firm.
Kathy Bischof, St. Cloud, Mn.

RHUBARB BARS

3 c. fresh rhubarb
2 Tbsp. cornstarch

1 1/2 c. sugar
1/4 c. water

Cook until thick. Remove from fire and add 1 teaspoon vanilla, cool.

Crust:

1 1/2 c. flour
1 c. brown sugar
1 c. shortening

1 1/2 c. oatmeal
1/4 tsp. baking soda
1/2 c. nuts, chopped

Mix. Pat 3/4 of above mixture into bottom of 9x13 inch pan. Pour cooled rhubarb mixture over crust mixture. Sprinkle rest of crust mixture over top. Bake 30 minutes at 375°.
Grayce Funke, Minneapolis, Mn.

RHUBARB BARS

Crust:

2 1/2 c. flour
1 c. shortening

3 Tbsp. sugar
1/2 tsp. salt

Combine. Beat 2 egg yolks, add milk to egg yolks to

make 2/3 cup. Add milk/egg mixture to dry ingredients to make crust.

Filling:

2 c. crushed corn flakes	2 Tbsp. flour or 1 Tbsp.
3 Tbsp. sugar	cornstarch

Mix:

5 c. rhubarb, cut up	2 Tbsp. flour or 1 Tbsp.
2 c. sugar	cornstarch
1/2 tsp. cinnamon	2 Tbsp. butter

Divide crust into 2 portions. Let bottom crust come up the sides of a 9x13 inch cake pan. Sprinkle corn flake mixture over bottom crust. Top with rhubarb mixture. Pat on top crust and seal edges. Bake at 425° for 25 - 30 minutes. Frost with powdered sugar icing when cool.

Lu Boyer, Grand Forks, N. D.

RHUBARB BARS

3 - 4 c. chopped rhubarb	2 Tbsp. cornstarch stirred
1 1/2 c. sugar (or less)	into 1/4 c. water
1 tsp. vanilla	

Mix all together and cook till thick. Cool slightly. For crust and topping, mix together:

1 1/2 c. quick oatmeal	1 c. brown sugar
1 1/2 c. flour	1/2 tsp. soda
2 sticks oleo	

Pat 3/4 of crust into bottom of 9x13 inch pan. Pour filling over crust. To remainder of crust add cocoanut or nuts or both. Place over filling and bake at 350° for 30 to 40 minutes. Cocoanut browns easily so top of bars may be covered with aluminum foil the last 10 - 15 minutes of baking.

Helen DelZoppo, St. Cloud, Mn.

RHUBARB BARS

2 c. flour	1 c. butter
10 Tbsp. powdered sugar	

Mix together and press into large pan (I use 9x13 inch) and bake 15 to 20 minutes at 325°. Cool above.

4 beaten eggs	1/2 c. flour
3 c. sugar	4 c. finely cut rhubarb

Spread this over cooled crust and bake for 40 minutes at 350°.

Alice Ann Hanson, Grand Forks, N. D.

RHUBARB BARS

1 c. flour	1 tsp. baking powder
1/4 tsp. salt	1/4 c. margarine

Cut butter into dry ingredients as for pie crust and mix. Add 1 beaten egg and 1 tablespoon milk. Mix and press into 9x9 inch pan. Cover with 2 cups rhubarb, cut fine. Sprinkle over this 1/2 package strawberry jello. Make crumb topping of following and put on top.

1/4 c. margarine	1/2 c. flour
1 c. sugar	

Bake at 375° for 45 minutes. Cool and cut into bars.

Helen Kruse, Fargo, N. D.

RHUBARB CRUNCH BARS

1 c. flour, sifted	2 eggs
5 Tbsp. powdered sugar	2 c. rhubarb, cut
1/2 c. butter	

Sift together:

1 1/2 c. sugar	3/4 tsp. baking powder
1/4 c. flour	Dash of salt

Mix flour, powdered sugar and butter. Pat into ungreased pan. Bake 15 minutes at 350°. Beat eggs till fluffy; and gradually add dry ingredients. Add rhubarb - pour over crust. Bake for 35 minutes. The egg mixture comes to top and forms a crust.

Karen Ruter, Minneapolis, Mn.

RHUBARB DREAM BARS

1 c. flour	1/2 c. butter
5 Tbsp. baking powder	

Mix together and press into 9 inch square pan. Bake at 350° for 15 minutes.

2 eggs	1/4 c. flour
1 1/2 c. sugar	3/4 tsp. salt
2 c. rhubarb, cut	

Beat eggs, beat in sugar; mix in flour, salt and rhubarb. Spread over crust and bake 35 minutes at 375°.

Karen Rupert, St. Cloud, Mn.

SALTED NUT BARS

1 1/2 c. flour	1/2 c. brown sugar
1/4 c. white sugar	1/2 c. butter
1/4 tsp. salt	

Cream butter and sugars. Add flour and salt, mix and press into a jelly roll pan. Bake at 350° for 10 minutes.

1 (6 oz.) pkg. butterscotch chips	Dash of salt
	1/2 c. white sugar
2 Tbsp. butter	1 Tbsp. water

Melt in double boiler. Pour 1 can of mixed nuts or plain peanuts over the baked layer. Pour melted syrup over nuts. Return to oven for 10 minutes longer. Cut while warm.

Georgia Berg, Fargo, N. D.

SCOTCH BARS

1/2 c. butter	1 egg yolk
1/4 c. granulated sugar	1/2 c. sifted flour
1/4 c. brown sugar, packed	1/2 c. rolled oats
	1 (6 oz.) pkg. chocolate chips
1/2 tsp. vanilla	1/2 c. chopped nuts

Cream butter, both sugars and vanilla thoroughly. Add egg yolk and beat until light and fluffy. Stir in flour and rolled oats. Blend well. Spread in greased 7x11 inch pan. Bake in 350° oven 20 - 25 minutes. Remove from oven and allow to cool. Melt chocolate chips over hot water and stir until smooth. Spread melted chocolate over baked bars and sprinkle with nuts.

Diane Schmitz, St. Cloud, Mn.

7 LAYER BARS

Place 1/2 cup melted butter in 9x13 inch pan. Melt in oven, then add:

1 c. graham cracker crumbs	1 c. flaked coconut
1 (6 oz.) pkg. chocolate chips	1 (5 oz.) can sweetened condensed milk
1 (6 oz.) pkg. butterscotch chips	1 c. chopped nuts

Bake 30 minutes in 350° oven. Cut while warm.
Mary Klaers, Willmar, Mn.

SPECIAL K BARS

1/2 c. Karo light syrup	2/3 c. creamy peanut butter
1/2 c. sugar	3 c. Special K cereal

Bring to a boil syrup and sugar. Remove from heat and add peanut butter. Pour the hot mixture over Special K cereal. Stir together and spread in a buttered 9x13 inch pan. Frost with 4 ounces of Hershey's chocolate, melted.
Kathy Neels, St. Cloud, Mn.

SPECIAL K BARS

6 c. Special K cereal
1 c. light corn syrup
1 c. sugar
2 tsp. vanilla

1 c. peanut butter
1 c. (6 oz.) chocolate chips
1 c. (6 oz.) butterscotch
  chips

Put cereal into a large bowl. Cook sugar and syrup until mixture boils. Take off fire. Stir in peanut butter and vanilla and mix well. Pour over cereal and mix well. Press into a 9x13 inch buttered pan, cool to harden. Melt chocolate and butterscotch chips together and spread over bars. Cool. Do not cool in refrigerator too long before cutting or they are too hard to cut.

Karen Rupert, St. Cloud, Mn.

SPRINKLE BARS

1 stick butter or margarine
1 c. graham cracker
  crumbs (12 sq.)
1 c. coconut

1 small pkg. butterscotch
  chips
1 small pkg. chocolate chips
1 can Eagle Brand sweetened
  milk
1 1/2 c. chopped nuts

Melt butter. Pour into 9x13 inch pan. Sprinkle graham cracker crumbs over butter. Sprinkle on coconut, butterscotch chips, chocolate chips. Sprinkle on Eagle Brand milk. Sprinkle on nuts. Bake at 350° for 30 minutes. Cut into squares.

Diane Schmitz, St. Cloud, Mn.

SPRINKLE BARS

Melt 1 stick oleo in bottom of 9x13 inch pan. Sprinkle 1 cup crushed (12 squares) graham crackers on top of melted oleo. Sprinkle on top:

1 c. coconut
1 pkg. chocolate chips
1 pkg. butterscotch chips

1 (15 oz.) can Eagle Brand
  milk
1 1/2 c. chopped nuts

Bake at 350° for 30 minutes and cut into bars.

C. Landwehr, Minneapolis, Mn.

3 TIER BARS

Tier 1:

1/2 c. butter	4 Tbsp. cocoa (unsweetened)
1 egg, unbeaten	1 tsp. vanilla
5 Tbsp. sugar	

Cook this over hot water until it forms a thin custard. Add 2 cups crushed graham crackers, 1 cup coconut and 1/2 cup nuts. Put into 9x9 inch buttered pan and spread with the following filling.

Tier 2:

4 Tbsp. butter	2 c. powdered sugar
3 Tbsp. milk	Green food coloring
2 Tbsp. dry vanilla pudding mix	Peppermint flavoring

Cream butter, milk and remaining ingredients. Spread over the crumb mixture and set in refrigerator until firm.

Tier 3:   Frost with -

2 Tbsp. powdered sugar	1 pkg. chocolate chips,
3 Tbsp. milk	melted

Cut into squares and serve.
Sue Hick, Detroit Lakes, Mn.

TOFFEE SQUARES

1 c. margarine	2 c. flour
1 c. packed brown sugar	1 c. chocolate chips
1 tsp. vanilla	1 c. nuts (optional)

Cream butter, brown sugar and vanilla. Add flour and 1/2 cup chocolate chips and 3/4 cup nuts. Press into bottom of greased 15x10 inch pan. Bake at 350° for 20 minutes. Immediately sprinkle with 1/2 cup chocolate chips. When soft, spread to frost. Sprinkle with 1/4 nuts. Cut into squares while warm.
Ginnie Andersen, St. Paul, Mn.

TOFFEE SQUARES

1 c. butter
1 c. brown sugar
1 egg yolk, well beaten
2 c. flour

1 tsp. vanilla
6 oz. chocolate chips or
   Hershey's bars
1/2 c. chopped nuts

Cream butter and sugar, add yolk, flour, vanilla. Pat onto cookie sheet. Bake at 350° for 20 minutes. Melt chocolate, spread while hot. Sprinkle with nuts.
Darlene Lee

YELLOW CAKE BARS

4 eggs, well beaten
2 c. white sugar
2 c. flour

2 tsp. baking powder
1/4 tsp. salt

Add 2/3 cups boiling water. Beat until well mixed. Put into large jelly roll pan. Bake at 350° for 25 - 30 minutes. Frost when cool with powdered sugar frosting and sprinkle heavily with crushed Planters salted peanuts.
Carol Koosman, Minneapolis, Mn.

YUMMY BARS

1 (18 1/2 oz.) pkg.
  German chocolate cake
  mix
3/4 c. melted butter
1/3 c. evaporated milk
  (small can equals 2/3
  c.)

1 (6 oz.) pkg. chocolate chips
1 c. chopped nuts
50 caramels (1 bag) (Krafts
  is best)
1/3 c. evaporated milk

Mix together dry cake mix, melted butter and 1/3 cup of evaporated milk. Spread 1/2 the batter on a lightly greased 9x13 inch pan. Bake at 350° for 6 minutes. (When I spread this on the bottom of the pan, I push it down with my fingers - it's easier that way.) Sprinkle the baked portion with chocolate chips and nuts. Melt caramels with remaining 1/3 cup milk and drizzle over chips and nuts. Pat the remaining cake mixture on top and bake another 20 minutes at 350°. (The first thing I do, is put the caramels and milk in double boiler and melt. They are ready when you need them.)
Dorothy Savig, Minneapolis Council

YUMMY SUMMER BARS

Crust:

1 1/2 c. flour   3/4 c. butter

Cut together and add 3/4 cup chopped nuts. Pat into 9x13 inch pan. Bake 20 minutes at 350°. Cool.

1 (8 oz.) pkg. Philadelphia   1 c. powdered sugar
    cream cheese, softened

Fold in 1 cup (9 ounces) Cool Whip. Spread over crust. Prepare 1 regular Royal instant butter pecan or coconut and 1 instant butterscotch pudding by beating into 3 cups milk. Spread over cheese layer. Put Cool Whip over top. Sprinkle with toasted coconut. Refrigerate - freezes well.
Shirley Pelzel, St. Paul, Mn.

YUM YUM BARS

Bring to boil:
1 c. white syrup   1 c. brown sugar

Add 1 cup peanut butter and stir until melted. Add:

8 c. corn flakes   1 c. peanuts

Press into buttered jelly roll pan.

Frosting (Yum Yum Bars): Melt 1/2 cup peanut butter and 1 (6 ounce) package chocolate chips. Spread over top.
Doris Schmidt, Willmar, Mn.

ZUCCHINI BARS

3 eggs, beaten	1/2 tsp. baking powder
1 c. oil	1 tsp. salt
2 c. white sugar	1 Tbsp. cinnamon
2 c. ground zucchini	1/2 tsp. nutmeg
1 tsp. vanilla	1/2 tsp. cloves
3 c. flour	1/2 tsp. allspice
1 tsp. soda	1/2 c. crushed walnuts

Mix first 5 ingredients, add remainder and mix well.

Bake 45 minutes in jelly roll pan at 325°.

Frosting for above:

1/3 stick margarine	1/2 lb. powdered sugar
4 oz. cream cheese	1 tsp. vanilla

Whip all together and spread on cooled bars. May sprinkle with crushed walnuts.

Arlene Jewell

ANGEL FOOD CAKE DESSERT

1 angel food cake	1/2 pt. whipping cream
1 c. boiling water	1 pkg. frozen strawberries
1 pkg. strawberry jello	

Dissolve jello in boiling water. Add strawberries, chill until firm. Whip cream and add strawberry mixture. Cut cake into 3 layers, spread strawberry mixture between layers and chill. This can be made a day in advance. Serve plain or with whipped cream. Also can be put back into angel food pan until ready to serve.

Irma Holstrom, Bismarck, N. D.

APPLE CHOP BAKE

2 tart apples, cored	1 (18 oz.) can dry pack sweet
1/4 c. butter	potatoes
1/3 c. brown sugar	4 loin pork chops (1 inch
1/4 tsp. cinnamon	thick)
Dash of mace	2 Tbsp. oil
1 tsp. salt	1/4 tsp. pepper

Slice unpeeled apples crosswise 1/4 to 1/2 inch rings. Melt butter in ovenproof 2 quart skillet. Add brown sugar, cook, stirring constantly over medium heat until consistency of caramel sauce. Add apples, sprinkle with cinnamon and mace. Simmer 8 - 10 minutes, turning once. Arrange sweet potatoes over apples. Brown pork chops with salt and pepper. Arrange chops on top of sweet potatoes. Bake in a 325° oven until chops are tender (30 to 45 minutes).

C. Landwehr, Minneapolis, Mn.

APPLE CRISP

5 c. sliced, pared tart
  apples
1 c. brown sugar
3/4 c. quick cooking rolled
  oats

3/4 c. enriched flour
1 1/2 tsp. cinnamon
1/2 c. butter

Arrange apples in buttered 9 inch pie plate. Combine brown sugar, flour, oats and cinnamon; cut in butter until crumbly. Press mixture over apples. Bake at 350° for 45 - 50 minutes or until top is browned. Serve with ice cream or top with whipped cream.

Mary Ann Hanson, Detroit Lakes, Mn.

APPLE DELITE

1/4 c. butter
1 c. sugar
1 egg, beaten
1 c. sifted flour
1 tsp. soda
1/4 tsp. cinnamon

1/2 tsp. nutmeg
1 tsp. vanilla
1/4 tsp. salt
1/2 c. nuts, chopped
2 1/4 c. diced apples

Cream butter and sugar together. Add egg and vanilla. Stir in flour, soda, cinnamon, nutmeg and salt. Fold in apples and nuts. Batter will be stiff. Bake in an 8x8 inch pan at 350° for 1 hour in greased pan. Can also use 11x9 inch pan, bake 45 minutes. Serve with Orange Sauce and whipped cream.

Orange Sauce:

1/2 c. brown sugar
1/2 c. white sugar
1/2 c. orange juice

1 egg, beaten
1/4 c. butter

Cook together until thick. Cool.

Marty Eger, St. Paul, Mn.

APPLE GOODIES

3 c. chopped apples	1 Tbsp. cinnamon
1 c. sugar	

Mix together and put into greased baking dish. Mix and sprinkle over above:

1/3 c. oatmeal	1/4 tsp. baking powder
2/3 c. flour	1/4 tsp. soda
2/3 c. brown sugar	1/4 tsp. salt
	1/3 c. slightly melted butter

Bake in 350° oven for 45 minutes. Serve with whipped cream.

Marge Johnson, Minneapolis, Mn.

APPLE GOODIES

3 c. sliced apples, peeled	1 Tbsp. flour
	Salt
1 c. white sugar	1 tsp. cinnamon

Mix all together and place in a long pan. Crumb together:

3/4 c. oatmeal	1/4 tsp. baking powder
3/4 c. flour	1/2 c. melted butter
1/4 tsp. soda	(margarine)
	3/4 c. brown sugar

Pour this over the apple mixture and bake 40 minutes.

Ellen Tilton, Windom, Mn.

JABŁUSZKA W CIESCIE
(yab-WOO-ska vuh chee-EH-see)
(Apples in Blankets)

1 lb. apples, pared and cored	1/3 c. sour cream
	1 1/4 c. flour
2 eggs	1/4 c. buttermilk
1/3 c. sugar	Fat for deep frying, heated to 365°
Dash of salt	
Powdered sugar	Nutmeg or cinnamon

1. Slice apples crosswise to make rings 3/8 inch thick.
2. Beat eggs with sugar until thick and foamy. Add salt.
Beat in small amount of flour alternately with sour cream and
buttermilk. Beat till batter is well mixed. 3. Coat apple
slices with batter. Fry in hot fat till golden. 4. Drain -
sprinkle with powdered sugar - add a dash of nutmeg or
cinnamon, if desired.

Patty Ginter, St. Cloud, Mn.

APPLE PASTRY

For pastry: Cut 1 1/2 cups Crisco into 3 cups flour.
Sprinkle with 5 - 6 tablespoons milk or water. Stir until it
forms a ball. Roll out half of dough to fit a jelly roll pan.
Cover the bottom pastry layer with thinly sliced apples.
Sprinkle with cinnamon and sugar (about 1 cup sugar mixed
with 2 teaspoons cinnamon). Dot with butter. Roll out remaining pastry for top crust. Seal edges of pastry together,
prick top crust with a fork and brush with milk. Bake at
425° for 30 minutes. When it cools, drizzle with powdered
sugar icing.

Variation: Use tart cherries instead of apples. Combine 1/4 cup flour with about 1 cup of sugar. Sprinkle over
cherries. Sprinkle with almond extract and dot with butter.
Continue as above.

Gail Holm, Minneapolis, Mn.

APRICOT DELIGHT

2 c. (1 lb. 1 oz.) can
  apricot halves
8 to 10 cooked prunes
1 (3 oz.) pkg. orange
  flavored gelatin

3/4 c. boiling water
1 c. undiluted evaporated
  milk
2 Tbsp. lemon juice
1/4 c. chopped nuts

Drain the prunes and apricots thoroughly. Cut into
pieces. Place gelatin in mixing bowl. Add boiling water.
Stir until dissolved. Chill until syrupy. Chill evaporated
milk in refrigerator tray until soft ice crystals form around
edges of tray (15 to 20 minutes). Whip until stiff (about
2 minutes). Add lemon juice. Whip very stiff (2 minutes
longer). Stir apricots, prunes and nuts into chilled gelatin.
Fold whipped evaporated milk into gelatin-fruit mixture.
Spoon into a 2 quart mold. Chill until firm (about 2 hours).
Unmold by dipping into hot water for a few seconds. Serves
8 to 10.

520   Mrs. Corinne Vevea, Anoka, Mn.

APRICOT PEACH DESSERT FRITTERS

3/4 c. all-purpose flour
1/4 c. sifted confectioners
  sugar
2 tsp. baking powder
1/2 tsp. salt
1/8 tsp. nutmeg
1 egg
Confectioners sugar

1 Tbsp. salad oil
1/3 c. canned apricot nectar
1 Tbsp. lemon juice
1/2 c. chopped dried apricot
  halves
1/3 c. chopped pecans
Salad oil or shortening for
  deep frying

Sift flour with 1/4 cup sugar, baking powder, salt and nutmeg. In a large bowl with a rotary beater, beat egg with 1 tablespoon salad oil, apricot nectar and lemon juice until well combined. Using a wooden spoon, gradually stir flour mixture into egg mixture. Gently stir in apricots and pecans to mix well. In a deep fryer, slowly heat salad oil (at least 2 inches) to 365° on deep frying thermometer. Into hot fat, drop apricot mixture by spoonfuls, a few at a time; or use a small ice cream scoop. Deep fry fritters, turning once, until golden brown on both sides - about 5 minutes in all. Drain well on paper towel. Sprinkle with confectioners sugar. Serve with brandy sauce. Makes about 12 fritters.

Brandy Sauce:

1/4 c. butter
1/2 c. sugar
1/4 c. light corn syrup

1/3 c. heavy cream
Dash of salt
3 Tbsp. brandy

Melt butter in saucepan over low heat. Stir in sugar, syrup, cream and salt. Bring to boiling, keep stirring, reduce heat and keep stirring 2 minutes longer. Add brandy; simmer 2 minutes. Serve warm with fritters. Makes 1 cup.

BANANA FUDGIES

1 (6 oz.) pkg. semi-
  sweet chocolate pieces
1/2 c. sifted flour
1/2 tsp. baking powder
1/4 tsp. salt

2 eggs
1/2 c. sugar
1 c. mashed bananas (about
  3 medium sized)
1 tsp. vanilla
1 c. chopped walnuts

Melt chocolate in top of a small double boiler over

simmering water; remove from heat. Sift flour, baking powder and salt onto waxed paper. Beat eggs well in a medium sized bowl; beat in sugar gradually; stir in melted chocolate and mashed bananas. Sift in dry ingredients, blending well. Stir in vanilla and walnuts. Pour into a greased baking pan, 8x8x2 inches. Bake in moderate oven, 350° for 40 minutes or until firm on top. Cool completely in pan, then cut into about 2 inch squares. Makes 16 bars.

BANANA SPLIT DESSERT

Mix:

1 stick margarine	2 c. crushed vanilla wafers

Spread on the bottom of a 13x9 inch cake pan. Mix and beat 15 minutes on high speed:

2 eggs	2 c. powdered sugar
2 sticks margarine	

Spread over crust. Slice and layer 3 or 4 bananas over filling. Spread 1 (No. 2) can crushed and drained pineapple over bananas. Mix 2 packages of Dream Whip according to directions and spread over pineapple. Top with chopped nuts and cherries. Refrigerate several hours before serving.

Sharon Christian

BAKLAVA
(Greek)

Have ready 1 pound filo (can be purchased frozen).

Filling:

3 c. or more chopped nuts (walnuts, pecans, almonds, pistachios or any combination desired)	1/2 tsp. cinnamon
	1 lemon, grated rind only
	1/2 lb. melted sweet butter or clarified salted butter
1/4 c. sugar	Whole cloves

Topping:

3 c. sugar	1/8 tsp. cream of
2 c. water	tartar

Juice of 1 lemon   2 tsp. brandy flavoring or
                                    1/4 c. honey

Bring filo to room temperature. Mix ingredients for filling in a bowl and set aside. Melt butter and clarify. Keep
it in pan to reheat if it cools and doesn't flow easy. Use
pastry brush to oil generously the bottom and sides of a
large rectangular baking pan. Cut filo an inch larger than
your pan. Use scissors. Place sheet of filo in pan and
sprinkle lightly with warm butter. Place another sheet of
filo on top of the first sheet, and sprinkle lightly with butter again. Continue until you have spread 6 or more sheets.
Spread half of the filling, including the corners - cover with
6 or more sheets of filo, sprinkling with butter in between.
Add remaining filling. Cover with remaining sheets, oiling
each one. Roll edges and tuck inside of pan. Do not trim.
Oil the top with remaining butter. Before baking, cut
through the top layers only, into diamond shapes. Make
vertical cuts, 1 inch apart. Turn pan (horizontally) and
make cuts at an angle, 1 inch apart. Stick a whole clove in
the center of each diamond. Besides adding flavor, it helps
keep the layers together. Bake at 350° for 1 hour. Check
it during the last 20 minutes to see if it is browning evenly.
Begin boiling the syrup 20 minutes before taking baklava
out of the oven. Pour hot syrup over hot baklava immediately after removing it from oven. Use ladle or large spoon
to distribute syrup evenly over it all. Set aside to cool at
room temperature, not in the refrigerator!! Keep in pan
overnight or at least 4 hours before cutting and serving.
                    Carolyn Smith, Fargo, N. D.

FATTIGMAND
(Norwegian - Bakkelse)

5 egg yolks   5 Tbsp. thick sweet cream
2 egg whites   2 c. flour
5 Tbsp. sugar   1/4 tsp. salt
1/2 tsp. ground cardamon

Beat egg yolks and whites until light. Add sugar,
beat again till sugar is dissolved. Add cream, continue
beating - add seasoning and enough flour to make soft dough
(stiff enough to roll out - if dough is cold, can be rolled
thinner and cakes lighter). Roll on floured board. Cut into
diamond shape - fry in deep fat (350°) until light brown.
Drain on absorbent paper, sprinkle with powdered sugar.
Store in tight container when cool.

1748-81   Alvera Solvie, Glenwood, Mn.   523

BLUEBERRY SLUMP

To 2 pints blueberries, add 1 inch of water in fry pan and cook. Sweeten to taste. When bubbling, add Bisquick dumplings. Cook with cover on for 10 minutes and off for 10 minutes. Serve in bowl. First dumpling, then spoon on berries. Add chunk of butter and top with cream.

Marge Johnson, Minneapolis, Mn.

BONBON DESSERT

Cover bottom of 9x13 inch pan with vanilla wafers. Cream:

2/3 c. butter	2 c. powdered sugar

Add:

3 beaten egg yolks, add	1 tsp. vanilla
	1/2 c. nuts
2 sq. melted chocolate	3 stiffly beaten egg whites, fold in

Pour over vanilla wafers. Put 1 quart bonbon ice cream on top and freeze.

Marge Johnson, Minneapolis, Mn.

NORWEGIAN FRIED BOWTIES

3 eggs	2 3/4 c. flour
1/4 c. sugar	Salad oil for frying
1/4 c. milk	Confectioners sugar
1/2 tsp. salt	

In medium bowl with wooden spoon, mix eggs, sugar, milk, salt and 1 cup flour until well blended. Stir in remaining flour. Wrap dough in plastic wrap and refrigerate 2 hours or until easy to handle. On lightly floured surface, with lightly floured rolling pin, roll dough into 4 x 1/2 inch rectangles. Cut 1 inch lengthwise slit in center and gently pull to make bowtie. In 12 inch skillet over medium heat, heat 3/4 inch oil to 350°. Gently drop several bowties at a time and fry 1 1/2 minutes or till golden brown. Drain bowties on paper towel and cool. Store in tightly covered container. Just before serving, sprinkle with powdered sugar. Will keep 1 week or freeze longer. Makes 7 dozen.

524　　　　　Robin Knutson, Willmar, Mn.

FRUIT BROCHETTES

Strawberries
Wedges of pineapple
Peach, pear and
  banana wedges

1 small can Mandarin
  oranges
2 inch squares Cheddar
  cheese

Batter:

1 c. sifted flour
1/2 tsp. salt
1 tsp. baking powder

1/4 c. corn oil
1 egg, beaten
1 c. milk

Mix all together well. Alternate fruit and cheese on skewers. Dust lightly with flour. Dip into batter, drain, fry in deep fat. Fry brochettes golden brown, turning and browning on all sides. Drain and serve hot, dusted with powdered sugar.

BIG BATCH BROWNIES

2 c. sugar
1 1/2 c. flour
1 tsp. baking powder
3/4 c. cocoa
1 c. chopped nuts

1 1/3 c. Crisco
4 eggs
1 Tbsp. white syrup
1 tsp. vanilla

Mix all at once and put into cake pan. Bake about 30 minutes at 350°. Don't overbake.
Norma Lee, Wadena, Mn.

BUTTER BRICKLE DESSERT

12 graham crackers,
  crushed

12 soda crackers, crushed
1 stick margarine, melted

Put into 9x13 inch pan and chill.

2 pkg. instant vanilla
  pudding

2 c. milk
1 qt. butter brickle ice cream

Blend. Pour over crust and refrigerate. Prepare 1 package Dream Whip and spread on top. Sprinkle with 3 crushed Heath bars.
Dorothy Erickson, Fargo, N. D.

BUTTERSCOTCH DESSERT

First layer:

1 c. flour   1/2 c. butter
1/2 c. crushed nuts

Mix and pat into 9x13 inch pan. Bake 10 - 15 minutes at 350°. Cool.

Second layer:

1 (8 oz.) pkg. cream   1 c. powdered sugar
  cheese   1 c. Cool Whip

Mix and put on cooled crust.

Third layer:

2 pkg. butterscotch pudding   3 c. milk

Mix pudding with milk, boil until thick. Cool. Put onto rest of dessert. Put rest of Cool Whip (1 cup) on top. Sprinkle with chopped nuts.

Mary Jo Olson, Detroit Lakes, Mn.

CHEESECAKES

2 (8 oz.) pkg. cream   3/4 c. sugar
  cheese   Pinch of salt
1 tsp. lemon juice   Vanilla wafers
1 tsp. vanilla   1 can cherry pie filing
2 eggs   Cupcake baking cups

Mix cream cheese, lemon juice, vanilla, eggs, sugar and salt with electric mixer until smooth. Line muffin tins with baking cups. Place 1 vanilla wafer in each cup and fill 3/4 full with cheese mixture. Bake 20 minutes in a 350° oven. Cool 1 hour and refrigerate or freeze. Before serving, top each with cherry pie filling. Makes 15 - 17 cakes.

E. McFarlane, Minneapolis, Mn.

CHEESE CAKE

Dissolve 1 package lemon jello in 1 cup boiling water. Add 3 tablespoons lemon juice, cool. Cream together 1 (8 ounce) package Philadelphia cream cheese with 1 cup sugar and 1 teaspoon vanilla. Add gelatin and mix well. Whip 1 large can Pet milk which has been chilled overnight. Fold into gelatin mixture.

Crush 1 pound graham crackers; add 1 cup margarine and 1/2 cup sugar and mix well. Line a 9x13 inch pan with part of the crumbs. Then add filling. Sprinkle with remainder of crumbs over top. Place in refrigerator to keep cool.

Note: Don't mix the cheese with the mixer; fold in until well mixed.

Barb Torkelson, Windom, Mn.

CHEESECAKE

Crust:

1 c. flour	1/2 c. butter
1/4 c. sugar	1 slightly beaten egg yolk
1 tsp. grated lemon peel	1/4 tsp. vanilla

Combine flour, sugar and lemon peel. Cut in butter till mixture is crumbly. Add egg yolk and vanilla. Blend thoroughly. Pat 1/3 of dough on bottom of 9 inch spring form pan (sides removed). Bake at 400° about 6 minutes or till brown. Cool.

Cheese Filling:

5 (8 oz.) pkg. cream cheese	3 Tbsp. flour
1/4 tsp. vanilla	1/4 tsp. salt
3/4 tsp. grated lemon peel	5 eggs (1 c.)
1 3/4 c. sugar	2 egg yolks
	1/4 c. heavy cream

Soften cream cheese; beat till fluffy. Add vanilla and peel. Add sugar, flour and salt; gradually blend into cheese. Add eggs and yolks, one at a time, beating well after each. Gently stir in cream. Turn into crust lined pan. Bake in very hot oven (500°) for 5 to 8 minutes, or till top edge of crust is golden. Reduce oven to 200°; bake 1 hour longer. Remove from heat; cool in pan about 3 hours. Remove sides of pan. Glaze (optional).

Glaze:

2 to 3 c. fresh strawberries	1 1/2 Tbsp. cornstarch
1 c. water	1/2 to 3/4 c. sugar

Crush 1 cup of strawberries; add the water and cook 2 minutes; sieve. Mix cornstarch with sugar (amount depends on sweetness of berries). Stir into hot berry mix. Bring to boil, stirring constantly. Cook and stir till thick and clear. (Add a few drops red food coloring, if needed.) Cool at room temperature. Place remaining strawberries atop cooled cheese cake; circle with halved pineapple rings. Pour glaze over strawberries; chill about 2 hours. Very good.

Voreen Topel

CHERRY DESSERT

2 cans pie filling mix (cherry or blueberry)	1 pkg. yellow or white cake mix (dry)
	3/4 c. melted butter

Put pie filling in bottom of pan, sprinkle cake mix over top. Drizzle butter over top. Bake at 350° for 45 minutes.

Sue Hick, Detroit Lakes, Mn.

CHERRY DESSERT

4 c. miniature marshmallows	1 1/2 c. graham cracker crumbs
1 c. heavy cream (whipped)	
1 can cherry pie filling	1/3 c. butter
	3 Tbsp. sugar

Combine graham cracker crumbs, butter and sugar in bowl. Spread half of crumb mixture in cake pan. Put marshmallows in whipped cream. Mix well. Spread cherry pie filling over crumbs, then spread cream and marshmallows over cherry filling. Sprinkle remaining crumbs on top. Chill 3 - 4 hours before using.

Nancy Kowalke, Nevis, Mn.

CHERRY OR BLUEBERRY DESSERT

1 c. sugar
5 eggs
1 c. vegetable oil
2 c. flour

1 tsp. baking powder
1 large can cherry or
   blueberry pie filling

Mix first 5 ingredients. If dough is too stiff, add 1/4 cup milk. Pour 3/4 into 9x13 inch cake pan. Put can of pie filling on top of dough. Sprinkle with remaining dough. Sprinkle cinnamon-sugar over this and bake at 350° for 30 minutes.

June Neal, Sauk Centre, Mn.

CHOCOLATE ANGEL FOOD DESSERT

Melt 12 ounces chocolate chips in double boiler. Add 4 tablespoons water and 2 tablespoons sugar. Also add 4 beaten egg yolks. Beat thoroughly and cool; then fold in beaten egg whites and 1 pint of stiffly whipped cream. Butter a 9x13 inch pan and tear angel food cake into it. Put layer of cake, 1/2 chocolate, then layer of cake and rest of chocolate. Sprinkle nuts on top. Cover with waxed paper and store in refrigerator 24 hours.

Marge Johnson, Minneapolis, Mn.

CHOCOLATE DREAMS

In a 9x9 inch square pan, layer the following items:

1 c. flour
1 c. margarine

1 c. chopped walnuts or
   pecans

Melt the margarine and add the other ingredients. Press mixture into bottom of pan to form crust. Bake at 350° for 20 minutes or until light brown. Set aside to cool.

1 c. powdered sugar
8 oz. softened cream cheese

1 small pkg. Cool Whip

Whip together and spread on cooled crust.

1 small pkg. vanilla
   instant pudding

1 small pkg. chocolate instant
   pudding
2 c. milk

Blend together till thickened and spread on top of Cool Whip mixture. For finishing touches, add whipped cream and chocolate shavings if desired. Chill before serving.
Nancy Fechtner, Fargo, N. D.

CINNAMON SLEDGES

1 c. margarine or butter	2 c. flour
1/2 c. brown sugar	1 Tbsp. cinnamon
1/2 c. white sugar	1/8 tsp. salt
1 egg	1 1/2 c. chopped pecans

Preheat oven to 300°. Cream together margarine, sugars, egg yolk until fluffy. Mix flour, cinnamon and salt to creamed mixture and beat until blended. Spread into jelly roll pan. Beat egg white until fluffy and spread on top of batter. Sprinkle with nuts and press lightly into batter. Bake 35 - 40 minutes. Makes 3 dozen.
Dee Flandrick

FRESH PEACH COBBLER

Peel and pit 3 to 6 peaches (depending on size). Cut into halves and put into 9 inch baking dish. Combine:

1 c. sugar	1 tsp. cinnamon

Sprinkle over peaches. Cream:

1/2 c. butter	1/2 c. sugar

Add:

1 egg yolk	1/4 tsp. salt
1/4 c. milk	1/2 tsp. vanilla

Set this mixture aside. Crush 16 graham crackers into fine crumbs. Add 1 teaspoon baking powder to the crumbs. Add crumbs to the batter. Beat 1 egg white and fold in. Pour batter over peaches. Bake at 375° for 25 minutes. Serve warm or cold with whipped cream or ice cream.
Lorine Kelly, Minneapolis, Mn.

COCONUT CRUNCH

2 c. flour
1/3 lb. butter
1/2 c. brown sugar

2 c. Angel Flake coconut
1 large (13 oz.) ctn. Cool Whip

Mix together and brown on cookie sheet at 350°. Cook together 3 packages vanilla pudding mix and cool. Put 2/3 of mixture into 13x9 inch pan. Place pudding, then Cool Whip and rest of crumbs on top. Chill.

Marion Round, Faribault, Mn.

CRANBERRY DESSERT
(Serves 4 - 6)

1 1/2 Tbsp. butter
1/2 c. sugar
1/4 c. water
1/4 c. Carnation evaporated milk

1 c. flour
1/2 tsp. salt
1 tsp. soda
1 c. raw cranberries

Bake at 350° for 25 minutes in an 8x8 inch greased pan. Can double recipe and use 9x13 inch pan.

Sauce Recipe:

1/4 lb. butter
1 c. sugar

1/2 c. Carnation milk
1 tsp. vanilla

Bring to boil. Serve warm.

Betty Carlson

DATE BALLS

1/2 c. butter
3/4 c. white sugar
1/2 lb. dates, chopped
1 beaten egg
1 Tbsp. milk

1/2 tsp. salt
1 tsp. vanilla
1/2 c. chopped nuts
2 c. Rice Krispies
Coconut

Cook butter, sugar and dates till boiling. Mix egg, vanilla, milk and salt. Add to mixture and cook 2 minutes. Cool, add nuts and cereal. Roll into balls and roll in coconut.

Sue Hick, Detroit Lakes, Mn.

DATE TORTE

4 egg whites
Pinch of cream of tartar
1 c. sugar

1 c. dates
1 c. nuts, cut up

Beat egg whites and cream of tartar until stiff. Add sugar gradually, beating while you add. Add nuts and dates. Put into greased 9 inch pie tin. Bake 1 hour at 300°. Do not open oven during baking time. Serve with whipped cream or ice cream. Serves 6.

Del Hadersbeck, St. Cloud, Mn.

DANISH DESSERT

Crust:

20 graham crackers,
    crushed

1/4 c. melted margarine or
    butter
1/4 c. sugar

Mix together. Put into pan, 9x13 inches, and bake 7 minutes at 350°. Cool.

1 box lemon jello

1 c. boiling water

Chill till syrupy, then whip. Cool well 1 can Carnation milk, then whip. Beat together:

1 (8 oz.) pkg. cream
    cheese

1 c. sugar
1 tsp. vanilla

Combine all mixtures together and pour over crust and chill. Cook:

1 box Junket

1 c. cold water

It will get real thick, then add 1 box or package of frozen berries (raspberries or strawberries), stir till thawed. Spread on top of the creamed cheese filling and refrigerate again till set. Could be made the day before and set in the refrigerator all night.

Margie Stultz, Big Lake, Mn.

DREAMY ORANGE DELIGHT

1 (6 oz.) pkg. orange
  gelatin
2 (3 1/2 oz.) pkg.
  vanilla pudding
4 1/2 c. hot water

1 (12 oz.) ctn. frozen
  whipped topping
2 (11 oz.) cans Mandarin
  oranges, drained

Combine gelatin, pudding and water. Boil until mixture is clear. Chill overnight. Before serving, fold in whipped topping and oranges. This makes a large salad, and is especially attractive served in a clear glass bowl.

Liz Tuft, St. Paul, Mn.

FINGER JELLO

2 c. water
1 c. sugar

2 large pkg. jello

Bring water to boil, add jello and sugar, boil 1 minute, stirring occasionally.

1 1/2 c. cold water

5 pkg. unflavored gelatin

In a bowl, add water and gelatin and stir. Put jello mixture into gelatin, add 1 cup cold water, stir and pour into 9x13 inch pan and store in refrigerator. Cut into squares.

Helen Martin, Fargo, N. D.

FINSKA KAKOR
(For the holiday jar)

3/4 c. soft butter
1/4 c. sugar
1 tsp. almond flavoring
2 c. sifted flour

1 egg white, slightly beaten
1 Tbsp. sugar
1/3 c. finely chopped,
  blanched almonds

Mix together butter, sugar and flavoring. Stir in flour and mix thoroughly with hands. Chill dough. Roll out 1/4 inch thick. Cut into strips 2 1/2 inches long and 3/4 inch wide. Brush tops lightly with egg white. Mix 1 tablespoon sugar and almonds. Sprinkle over tops of cookies. Transfer strips to ungreased baking sheet. Bake at 350° for about 17 to 20 minutes.

FOAM RINGLETS

1/2 lb. butter	1/4 small yeast cake
1/2 pt. whipping cream	dissolved in the cream
2 c. flour or more	

Whip butter until light and creamy; add cream which contains the yeast. Continue whipping, adding gradually approximately 2 cups of the flour or more, so that the dough can be handled easily with the hands. Let rise until light. Then cut bits of dough and form into long rope, shape into ringlets or pretzels. Place on baking pans (cooky sheets work nicely) without additional rising. Bake in 350° oven for 30 minutes.

BANANA FRITTERS SUPREME

Cut ripe bananas into halves lengthwise, then cross-wise. Soak for 1 hour in lemon juice and sugar to taste. Thin recipe for Delicate Fritter Batter slightly with milk, dip in each section of banana and fry in hot fat. Drain and serve with melted currant jelly.

Delicate Fritter Batter:

1 1/2 level tsp. baking powder	1/4 level tsp. salt
1 level c. (4 oz.) flour	1 egg, separated
2 level Tbsp. cornstarch	1/4 c. milk
4 level Tbsp. sugar	1 Tbsp. olive oil

Mix flour, baking powder, cornstarch, salt and sugar; sift 3 times. Beat yolk and white of egg separately; add beaten yolk and milk alternately to flour mixture; then add olive oil and beat until smooth. Finally, fold in stiffly beaten egg white. Drop by spoonfuls into plenty of hot, but not smoking, fat. Fry golden brown, turn; drain out with a skimmer and lay on absorbent paper. Trim and dust with powdered sugar and serve at once. Use this batter for plain fritters and sweet and fruit fritters of all kinds. In using vegetables and shell fish, etc., omit sugar. Sufficient for 10 large fritters.

HOT FRUIT COMPOTE

1 pkg. pitted prunes
  (3/4 lb.)
1 pkg. dried apricots
  (1/2 lb.)
1 tall can pineapple
  chunks and juice

1 can Mandarin oranges and
  juice
1 can cherry pie mix
1/2 c. cooking sherry

Put fruit and juice in order given - with cherries and sherry on top. Do not wash pitted prunes. Bake in 350° oven for 1 hour in 8x8 inch or 9x9 inch pan. Do not grease pan.

HOMEMADE ICE CREAM

1 qt. whipping cream
1 qt. + 3 c. whole milk
12 egg yolks

3 c. sugar
2 tsp. salt
4 Tbsp. vanilla

Scald milk and cream in a large pan. In a large bowl, beat egg yolks and salt together. Add about 3 cups of the hot milk to the egg yolks, beating constantly, then pour into the pan of hot milk. Add sugar and stir over medium heat till mixture coats spoon or just starts to boil. Add vanilla. Cool, then pour into an ice cream freezer and freeze.
                Dee Olson, St. Paul, Mn.

FROSTY LEMON COOLER

1 c. crushed cocoanut
  bar cookies (about 17
  to 18)

3 Tbsp. melted butter

Combine, save about 2 tablespoons for topping. Press into 9x9x2 inch pans.   Combine:

2 egg yolks
1 tsp. grated lemon peel

1/3 c. lemon juice
Dash of salt

Add 2/3 cup sugar, set aside. Beat until stiff:

2 egg whites
2/3 c. nonfat dry milk

2/3 c. water

Add yolk mixture at low speed. Pour over cookie mixture. Sprinkle with remaining crumbs. Freeze.

Mrs. E. F. Braun, Owatonna, Mn.

FROZEN CHEESE CAKE

1 c. sugar	1/2 pt. whipping cream
3 eggs, separated	8 oz. pkg. cream cheese
Pinch of salt	1 tsp. vanilla

Cream sugar and cheese. Beat egg yolks and salt with a fork and add to cheese mixture. Beat till creamy. Beat egg whites stiff and fold in mixture. Fold in whipping cream and vanilla. Pour over graham cracker crust. Sprinkle a few crumbs over top. Freeze.

Lorraine Solberg, St. Cloud, Mn.

FRUIT SOUP - SCANDINAVIAN

6 oz. dried apricots	3 1/2 oz. dried prunes
3 oz. dried apple	2 1/2 oz. large raisins
3 oz. dried peaches	2 qt. water

Soak the above 2 hours. Add:

1 c. sugar	1/2 lemon, sliced
3 to 6 Tbsp. pearl tapioca	3 sticks cinnamon, broken

Pour into crock pot and cook on low until fruit is tender. Fifteen minutes before soup is done, add 1 cup red wine. Turn off heat - when partially cool, add package or 2 of frozen raspberries.

Marion Baihly

SCANDINAVIAN FRUIT SOUP
(Søt Suppe)

6 1/2 c. water	1 c. Minute Tapioca
1 c. raisins	1 stick cinnamon
1 c. prunes (any other dried fruit can also be used)	Juice of 1 lemon

Boil until fruit is tender. Add 1 cup grape juice.

Fresh strawberries can also be stirred in. Serve hot or cold.

Joyce Haugen, Fargo, N. D.

FRUKTSOPPA
(Fruitsoup)

1/2 lb. prunes	Red coloring
1 c. whole dried apricots	1 large cinnamon stick
1/2 c. dried peaches, cut	1 tsp. vinegar
1/2 c. dried pears, cut	Pinch of salt
3/4 c. raisins	11 c. water or fruit juice
1 orange, cut into	1 c. sugar
quarters	6 Tbsp. cornstarch in cold
1/2 lemon, cut in half	water

Slowly cook prunes, water or juices, sugar, lemon, orange, cinnamon stick, vinegar and salt about 10 minutes. Then add other dried fruits and cook until tender (about 30 minutes). Add cornstarch and let come to a boil. Remove from heat. Add red coloring. Remove orange and lemon rind.

Clara O. Johnson, Chanhassen, Mn.

GIFTA - CHRISTMAS DESSERT
(Scandinavian)

2 or 3 (1 lb.) cans	2 Tbsp. butter, melted
whole cranberry sauce	2 c. whipping cream
1/4 c. sugar	1/4 c. confectioners sugar
2 c. cracker crumbs	1 tsp. vanilla
(saltines)	

Mix sugar with cranberries in a bowl. Combine melted butter and cracker crumbs in another bowl. Whip cream and add confectioners sugar and vanilla. Using a glass bowl, put in layers of crumbs, cranberries and whipped cream. Repeat layers and refrigerate for 2 - 3 hours before serving. Should be eaten the same day it is prepared.

Borgny Pinney, Anoka, Mn.

GLORIFIED RICE

Cook 1 cup rice in a small amount of water to which you add 1 teaspoon salt. Blanch and add to 1 package lemon or orange jello. In jello, add 1/2 cup sugar - use pineapple juice in place of cold water. Add 1 can sliced pineapple. Can also use Mandarin oranges. When ready to serve, whip 1/2 pint cream and fold into rice-jello mixture.

Helen Evenson, Litchfield, Mn.

GRANDMA'S RHUBARB BUTTER CRUNCH

3 c. rhubarb	3 Tbsp. flour
1 c. sugar	

Mix, place in 6x10 inch baking dish.

1 c. brown sugar	1/2 c. butter and 1/2 c.
1 c. rolled oats	margarine
	1 1/2 c. flour

Mix, sprinkle over rhubarb. Bake at 375° for 40 minutes.

HARVEST TORTE

4 c. diced tart apples, unpeeled	1 Tbsp. melted butter
1 c. sugar	1 tsp. vanilla
1/2 c. sifted flour	1/2 c. coarsely chopped walnuts
1/2 tsp. baking powder	1/2 c. pitted dates, cut up
1 egg	

Combine all ingredients. Stir until thoroughly mixed. Do not beat. Turn into greased 8x8x2 inch pan. Bake in a hot oven (400°) for about 40 minutes or until apples are done. (Test with a fork.) Cut into squares and serve (hot or cold) with whipped cream, cream or vanilla ice cream. Makes 6 to 9 servings.

HAWAIIAN DELIGHT

1 pkg. Jiffy cake mix
1 pkg. Jell-O instant
    pudding mix (vanilla
    or pineapple)

1 (8 oz.) pkg. cream cheese,
    softened
1 (20 oz.) can crushed
    pineapple, well drained
1 large ctn. Cool Whip

1. Prepare cake mix as directed. Bake in 9x13 inch pan and cool. 2. Prepare pudding and blend in softened cream cheese until well blended. 3. Then spread mixture on cooled cake. 4. Spread pineapple over pudding mixture. 5. Top with Cool Whip, chill 2 hours or overnight.

        Doris Lehmann, Detroit Lakes, Mn.

HOT FRUIT COMPOTE

1 (30 oz.) can peach
    halves
1 (16 oz.) can pear
    halves
1 (16 oz.) can apricot
    halves

1 (18 oz.) can dark sweet
    cherries
1/4 c. brown sugar
1/4 tsp. cinnamon
1/4 tsp. nutmeg
1/3 c. rum (or red wine)

Drain fruit. Arrange in layers in shallow 2 quart bake and serve container. Mix sugar and spices and sprinkle over fruit. Pour on rum. Bake, uncovered, at 325° F. for 1 hour or more. Serve hot with main course. Good with ham, turkey or chicken.

        Dee Fletcher, Pelican Rapids, Mn.

ICE CREAM CLOWN

Scoop round ball of ice cream on plate for "face". Press raisins or bits of chocolate into face for eyes and nose and slice of maraschino cherry for mouth. Use inverted ice cream cone for hat. Make clown's ruff and frills on hat from whipped cream.

ICE CREAM CRUNCH

1/2 c. brown sugar
2 c. flour
1 c. margarine

1/2 c. oatmeal
1/2 c. chopped nuts

Mix and press onto a cookie sheet. Bake at 400° for 15 minutes, then crumble. Spread half on bottom of 9x13 inch pan with 1/2 gallon softened vanilla ice cream. Crumble with other half of mixture. Drizzle 3/4 jar butterscotch topping over all. Freeze until serving.

Ginnie Andersen, St. Paul, Mn.

KOLACHY

1 c. butter (room
    temperature)
1 (8 oz.) pkg. cream
    cheese (room
    temperature)

1/4 tsp. vanilla extract
2 1/4 c. all-purpose flour
1/2 tsp. salt
Thick jam or canned fruit
    filling, such as apricot or
    prune

1. Cream butter and cream cheese till fluffy. Beat in vanilla extract. 2. Combine flour and salt, add in fourths to butter mixture, blending well. Chill dough until easy to handle. 3. Roll dough to 3/8 inch thickness on floured surface. Cut out 2 inch circles, place on ungreased baking sheets. 4. Make a "thumbprint" about 1/4 inch deep in each cookie. Fill with jam. 5. Bake at 350° F. for 10 to 15 minutes or until delicately browned on edges. Approximately 3 1/2 dozen.

Pat Bruchert, Minneapolis, Mn.

ICE CREAM KOLACKY
(Czech)

4 c. flour
2 Tbsp. sugar

1 lb. butter
1 pt. vanilla ice cream

Sift flour. Measure, blend with sugar. Cut in butter until mixture resembles fine corn meal. Add softened ice cream and blend well. Wrap in foil or heavy waxed paper and chill overnight. Roll out 1/4 inch thick, cut into squares, fill with a teaspoonful of desired filling - cottage cheese, prune, poppy seed or different cooked fruit. Pinch

corners together and bake at 350° for 20 to 25 minutes.
These can also be frozen after baking.

Clara Lisko, Bismarck Council

DANISH KRINGLE

Soak 1 package yeast in 1/4 cup lukewarm water. Scald
1/2 cup milk, cool. Add 1 egg yolk and combine with yeast.
Add this to flour mixture. Combine like pie crust:

2 c. flour	1/2 tsp. salt
2 Tbsp. sugar	1/2 c. butter

Refrigerate for 2 - 48 hours. Roll out. On middle
1/3 area of dough, brush with egg white - then with filling.
Fold over; pinch edges together - also ends of dough. Let
rise for 1/2 hour. Bake at 350° for 20 minutes. Frost with
powdered sugar frosting.

Frosting:

1 c. chopped pecans	1 c. brown sugar
1/2 c. butter	

Spread on first mixture. Bake 50 to 60 minutes at 350°.
Cool. Frost with:

1 c. sifted powdered sugar	1 Tbsp. butter
	1/2 tsp. almond extract

Add cream to spread. Sprinkle slivered almonds on top.

Mrs. Robert G. Pearson, Fargo, N. D.

NEVER FAIL DANISH KRINGLE

1 cake yeast	1 tsp. salt
1/2 c. lukewarm water	3 eggs, separated
4 c. flour	1 c. lukewarm milk
1 c. lard	Brown sugar and dates or
3 Tbsp. sugar	raisins and nuts

Dissolve yeast in water. Mix in a bowl the flour, lard,
sugar and salt as for pie crust. Beat egg yolks in bowl and
add milk. Add the yeast and egg-milk mix to flour mix and
beat well. Cover and set in refrigerator overnight. In

morning, divide dough into 4 parts. Roll each piece into thin strip about 9 inches wide and as long as it will roll. Spread each with egg white, beaten stiff. Sprinkle brown sugar on this and cut up dates, chopped apples, raisins or nuts. Fold dough, one edge over 1/3 of width. Fold other side over width of dough. Shape like ring or pretzel on greased cookie sheet. Be sure edges are sealed well. Let rise for 2 hours. Bake 30 minutes in 350° oven. Ice with powdered sugar icing while warm. Flavor the icing with almond extract.

Helen Kruse, Fargo, N. D.

KRINGLES
(Norwegian - Kring-lah)

1 c. sugar	1 tsp. soda
1/2 c. shortening (lard	1/2 tsp. salt
is best)	4 1/2 c. flour (about)
2 eggs	1 - 2 tsp. nutmeg
2 c. buttermilk	

Cream sugar and shortening. Beat in eggs. Stir in buttermilk. Mix soda, salt and nutmeg in about 2 cups flour. Mix into first mixture, adding more flour till dough is somewhat firm, but still sticky. Lightly flour a bread board and put a small pile of flour in left corner. Take about a tablespoonful of dough. Drop it into the pile and coat it with flour. Roll into pencil shape on board and put on cookie sheet and make kringle shape (similar to pretzel, except ends are side by side rather than crossed). Bake at 375° for 15 minutes. Best second day. Can spread with butter.

Mrs. Clarence Schmitz, Wadena, Mn.

SWEDISH KRINGLE

Mix like pie crust:

1/2 c. oleo or butter	1 Tbsp. water
1 c. flour	

Pat out on cookie sheet in 2 long narrow strips. Cook to boiling:

1 c. water	1/2 c. margarine

542

Then add 1 cup flour, stir till leaves sides of pan. Remove from heat, add 3 eggs, one at a time. Beat after each. Add 1/2 teaspoon almond. Spread this mixture on top of the unbaked crust. Bake 50 - 55 minutes in 350° oven. Cool slightly. Frost with:

1 c. powdered sugar   Enough milk to spread
1 Tbsp. butter   frosting easily on strips
1/2 tsp. almond flavoring

Margie Stultz, Big Lake, Mn.

KRUMB KAKE

2 eggs   1 1/2 c. flour
1 c. sugar   1 tsp. vanilla
1 c. cream

Beat eggs, add sugar and mix. Add cream, flour and vanilla. Put 1 tablespoonful of batter on hot iron. Bake on both sides, shape on roller. Makes 36.
Darlene Lee

LADYFINGER DESSERT

2 1/2 doz. ladyfingers   2 1/2 Tbsp. powdered sugar
3 eggs, separated   2 1/2 Tbsp. hot water
2 bars sweet chocolate   Vanilla

Dissolve chocolate in hot water. Add sugar, then egg yolks, one at a time. Beat thoroughly after each addition. Beat egg whites and add to chocolate mixture. Arrange ladyfingers in angel food tin - pour chocolate mixture over them. Refrigerate and serve with whipped cream. Angel food pieces can be substituted for ladyfingers.
Ruth White

LAZY DAY PEACH DESSERT

1 qt. peach sauce, or   1/2 c. butter, softened
   1 (29 oz.) can   1 c. nuts, chopped (optional)
1 pkg. butterbrickle   1 c. coconut (optional)
   cake mix

Pour 1 quart peach sauce, juice and all, into 9x13 inch greased cake pan. Mix dry cake mix with the 1/2 cup butter; add the nuts or coconut if desired. Sprinkle over the sauce. Bake at 350° about 45 minutes. Serve with whipped cream.

Donna Meyer, Detroit Lakes, Mn.

FROSTY LEMON COOLER

1 c. crushed cocoanut bar cookies (about 17 - 18)	3 Tbsp. melted butter

Combine. Save about 2 tablespoons for topping. Press into 9x9x2 inch pan. Combine:

2 egg yolks	1/3 c. lemon juice
1 tsp. grated lemon peel	Dash of salt

Add 2/3 cup sugar. Set aside. Beat until stiff:

2 egg whites	2/3 c. water
2/3 c. nonfat dry milk	

Add yolk mixture at low speed. Pour over cookie mixture. Sprinkle with remaining crumbs. Freeze.

Mrs. E. F. Braun, Owatonna, Mn.

FROZEN LEMON DESSERT

Bake and cool one angel food cake.

3 lemons (juice)	1 can Eagle Brand milk
1 pt. whipping cream	2 Tbsp. sugar

Beat Eagle Brand milk 20 minutes. Add lemon juice and sugar. Whip cream until stiff. Cut cake into slices and alternate layers of cake and filling mixture. End top layer with cream mixture. Use a 9x13 inch pan. Keep in freezer.

Recipe from Minneapolis, Mn.

LEMON DESSERT

1/2 c. flour   1/4 c. finely chopped nuts
1/2 stick melted butter

Mix together with fork like pie crust and pat lightly into 9x9 inch pan or 8x11 inch pan and bake at 350° for 15 minutes - cool. (I doubled this whole recipe to serve 11 people, so I used a regular cake pan.)

1/2 c. powdered sugar   1 (3 oz.) pkg. cream cheese

Mix together until smooth and fluffy (beat with mixer). Fold in 1/2 container of Cool Whip (small size). Spread 1/2 of this over cooled part. Blend package of lemon instant pudding with 1 1/2 cups milk. Mix until smooth. When it begins to thicken, spread over second part. Refrigerate - spread Cool Whip over top when it is set.
Betty Ladd, St. Paul, Mn.

LIME DESSERT

1 pkg. lime jello   1 c. hot water

Mix and cool. Add 1 cup cream, whipped. Separate 3 eggs. Beat whites and add 1/3 cup sugar and 1/2 teaspoon vanilla. Fold into jello (green coloring may be added). Line a 9x13 inch pan with crushed chocolate Hydrox cookies - a small package. Pour into jello mixture and save a few crumbs for the top. Serve with whipped cream.
Mrs. W. E. Gollehon, Fargo, N. D.

LEMON DESSERT

Butter 9x13 inch pan. Mix together and press into pan:

2 1/2 c. vanilla wafers,   1/2 c. butter
   crushed

Have ready:
6 egg yolks, well beaten   1 (12 oz.) can frozen lemonade
1 can Eagle Brand milk   1 (8 oz.) ctn. Cool Whip

Add milk and lemonade to egg yolks and beat well. Fold

in Cool Whip, pour over crumb mixture and refrigerate while whipping 6 egg whites, adding 3/4 cup sugar. Spread over lemon mixture. Put under broiler long enough to brown. Put into freezer. Will keep up to 2 weeks, covered.

Lydia Skaret, Austin, Mn.

MISSISSIPPI MUD

4 eggs
1 c. margarine, softened
2 c. sugar
1 tsp. vanilla
1 1/2 c. unsifted flour

1/4 c. unsweetened cocoa
Dash of salt
1 c. chopped pecans
1 (7 oz.) jar marshmallow
   creme (1 1/4 c.)

Frosting:

1/3 c. margarine
1/2 c. unsweetened cocoa
1/3 c. milk

1 tsp. vanilla
2 1/2 c. powdered sugar

Preheat oven to 350°. Grease a 13x9 inch baking pan. In a large bowl with electric mixer at medium speed, beat eggs, margarine, sugar and vanilla until light and fluffy. Add flour, cocoa and salt. Beat just until well blended. Fold in pecans. Spread batter evenly in pan. Bake 40 to 45 minutes. Immediately place dollops of marshmallow creme on cake; spread until smooth. Let cool for at least 1 hour before frosting.

Ralph Kulhanek, St. Paul, Mn.

NORTH POLE PEARS

Make a meringue of:
3 egg whites
1/2 c. sugar

1/4 tsp. cream of tartar

Pare and halve 4 pears; place them in baking dish, put a scoop of ice cream in each half and cover with meringue. Bake in a 450° oven for 4 or 5 minutes. Serves 8.

GREAT GRANDMOTHER'S RAISIN SPICE LOAF

1 c. sugar	1 egg, beaten
Shortening size of	1 c. raisins
an egg	3/4 c. raisin water

Cook together 2 minutes. Start with 1 cup water - cool slightly. Sift together:

1 3/4 c. flour	1/2 tsp. cloves
1 tsp. cinnamon	1 tsp. soda

Cream sugar and shortening, add egg. Add dry ingredients alternately with raisin water. Add raisins. Bake in greased and floured loaf pan (350°) for 50 minutes to 1 hour.

Shirley Way, Minneapolis, Mn.

GOLDEN RAISIN TEA LOAF

1 c. strong tea	2 tsp. allspice
1/2 c. golden raisins	1 tsp. soda
1 1/4 c. flour	1/2 tsp. salt
1/2 c. sugar	1/4 c. shortening

Make tea. Wash raisins and add to hot tea. Sift flour, measure and sift together with sugar, allspice, soda and salt. Cut in shortening till fine. Add tea and raisins to flour and mix thoroughly. Pour into a greased and floured loaf pan. Bake in 350° oven for 1 hour.

Dee Olson, St. Paul, Mn.

MANDARIN ORANGE CAKE DESSERT

2 c. sugar	1 tsp. soda
2 c. flour	1 tsp. salt
2 eggs	2 tsp. vanilla
2 cans oranges, drained	Nuts

Mix dry ingredients. Add other ingredients. Mix until batter consistency. Pour into 9x13 inch buttered pan. Bake at 350° for 30 - 35 minutes.

Topping:

1 1/2 c. brown sugar	6 Tbsp. milk
6 Tbsp. butter	

Stir together and bring to a boil. Pour over the dessert while still warm.

Evelyn Fellows, Austin, Mn.

MARSHMALLOW DELIGHT

1 pkg. marshmallows   1 c. milk

Melt together and cool.

1 c. crushed pineapple,   1/2 pt. whipping cream,
    drained   whipped

Fold together and put into graham cracker crust. Top with some crushed graham crackers. Refrigerate.

Bonnie Steffens, St. Cloud, Mn.

PEACHY CHEESECAKE
(No Bake)

Crust:

1 1/2 c. graham cracker   1/2 c. butter or margarine,
    crumbs   melted
1/3 c. sugar

Mix together and press into 9 inch cheesecake pan. Save some crumbs for decoration on top.

Cheesecake:

2 (8 oz.) pkg. cream   1 (4 1/2 oz.) container Cool
    cheese   Whip
1 env. unflavored gelatin   2 Tbsp. lemon juice
1 small can sweetened   1 (33 oz.) can sliced peaches
    condensed milk   in syrup

Drain syrup off peaches - save 4 - 5 peaches for garnish - the rest put into blender. Take 1/2 cup of peach syrup and unflavored gelatin - put in pan; heat on stove until dissolved. Mix into peaches that are blended. Whip cream cheese, then add lemon juice and sweetened condensed milk. Blend, add peach mixture and blend. Fold in whipped cream. Put into pan, then add crumbs and peaches.

Mary Ann Hanson, Detroit Lakes, Mn.

PEACH DELIGHT

Mix together:

24 crushed graham crackers

1/4 c. butter
1/4 c. sugar

Save 1 cup for topping. Take 1/2 cup milk and 24 marshmallows; melt in double boiler - cool. Whip 1 cup cream, add 1 tablespoon sugar and 1 teaspoon vanilla. Mix with marshmallow mixture and add 1 1/2 cups diced peaches. Put crumb mixture into 9x9 inch pan, add filling, top with the cup of topping. Refrigerate.

Mrs. W. A. (Pearl) Gross, Fargo, N. D.

PECAN TARTS

Crust:

1 (3 oz.) pkg. cream cheese
1 stick butter or margarine

1 c. flour
1/4 tsp. salt

Filling:

1 egg
3/4 c. packed brown sugar
Pinch of salt

1 Tbsp. soft butter
1 tsp. vanilla
1/2 c. coarsely chopped pecans

Make a pastry by putting cream cheese and butter into bowl. Cut in flour and salt with pastry blender. Squeeze dough together with fingers, if necessary. Cover and refrigerate. Break up egg with a fork and add remaining filling ingredients. Mix well. Press a small amount of dough into miniature muffin tins, forming a small pie crust. If you use tins that are 2 inches across the top of each, this recipe makes 24. Spoon about a teaspoonful into each tart. Bake at 325° for 25 minutes.

Jane Bohline, Minneapolis, Mn.

PEANUT MARSHMALLOW CHEWS

1 1/2 c. flour
2/3 c. brown sugar
1/2 tsp. baking powder
1 tsp. vanilla

1/2 tsp. salt
1/4 tsp. soda
1/2 c. margarine
2 egg yolks

Mix together, press into 9x13 inch pan. Bake at 350° for 12 - 15 minutes. Sprinkle on 3 cups miniature marshmallows. Put into oven 1 - 2 minutes until puffy. Cool. Prepare topping.

Topping:

2/3 c. white corn syrup
1/4 c. butter

2 tsp. vanilla
1 (12 oz.) pkg. peanut
    butter chips

Heat in double boiler until chips are melted and blended. Add 2 cups crisp rice cereal and 2 cups salted peanuts. Spread on crust. Chill. Makes 2 1/2 dozen yummies.

PECAN TORTS

1/2 c. butter
3 oz. cream cheese

1 c. sifted flour

Cream together butter and cream cheese. Add flour. Press into muffin cups (I use the small muffin pans).

Filling:

3/4 c. brown sugar
1 Tbsp. butter
2/3 c. chopped pecans

1 tsp. vanilla
1 egg
1/8 tsp. salt

Combine ingredients, put into tart shells. Bake 30 minutes at 325°. Let cool a few minutes before taking out of pan.

Irma Holmstrom, Bismarck, N. D.

PINEAPPLE FLUFF

This recipe has become an Easter tradition at our house.

First layer:

1 1/2 c. flour	1/2 c. margarine
2 tsp. sugar	3/4 c. chopped nuts

Mix like pie crust and press into 9x13 inch pan. Bake 15 - 20 minutes until very lightly browned, in 350° oven. Cool thoroughly.

Second layer:

2 sticks butter or margarine	2 c. powdered sugar 1 tsp. vanilla
2 eggs	

Beat ingredients together for <u>15</u> minutes. Pour over crust.

Third layer:

1 pt. whipping cream	1 large can crushed, drained
2 or 3 Tbsp. sugar	pineapple

Whip the cream and when almost stiff, add the sugar and whip a little longer. Fold in the well drained pineapple. Cover second layer with this. Chill overnight.
Rosemary Rotar, Minneapolis, Mn.

PINEAPPLE FRITTERS

1 c. flour	1 egg, beaten
1 tsp. baking powder	1/3 c. milk
1/4 tsp. salt	1 Tbsp. melted fat
2 Tbsp. sugar	1 Tbsp. lemon juice
1/4 tsp. cinnamon	1 c. shredded pineapple,
1/4 tsp. nutmeg	drained

Heat electric deep fat fryer to 350°. Mix and sift dry ingredients into small bowl. Beat egg slightly; add milk. Now stir the liquid mixture into the dry ingredients, beating to a smooth batter. Add the lemon juice and pineapple. Drop by a teaspoon into hot oil, cooking 3 or 4 minutes at a time. Turn when they come to the surface. Fry to delicate brown, which will require about 5 minutes. Lift from oil with basket; allow to drip briefly and drain on an absorbent paper. Dust with powdered sugar. Serve hot with Fritter Sauce.

Fruit Fritter Sauce:

1/2 c. sugar
2 Tbsp. cornstarch
1 1/2 c. water

2 Tbsp. butter
1/2 tsp. vanilla

Combine sugar and cornstarch in saucepan. Add water, stirring, and cook until thick and transparent. Remove from heat; add butter and vanilla. Serve warm, but not hot in plain or fruit fritters.

PRETZEL DESSERT

First layer:

2 1/2 c. pretzels, crushed
3 Tbsp. powdered sugar

3/4 c. butter, melted

Mix together and press into bottom of 9x13 inch pan. Bake 10 minutes at 350°. Cool.

Second layer:

1 (8 oz.) pkg. cream
   cheese

1 egg
1 c. powdered sugar

Beat together and then fold in 1 (8 ounce) carton Cool Whip. Put into refrigerator to cool.

Third layer:

2 c. boiling water

1 large box strawberry jello

Mix these two and add 2 boxes of frozen strawberries. Thicken and spread on top of second layer. Refrigerate.
Peni Lundeen, St. Cloud, Mn.

PUDDIN' STICKS

1/2 env. unflavored
  gelatin
1/2 c. cold water
1/2 c. boiling water

1 c. light cream or evaported
  milk
Milk
1 pkg. instant pudding

Dissolve gelatin in cold water. Add boiling water and stir until clear. Add light cream or evaporated milk and enough milk to make the total mixture 3 1/2 cups. Add pudding; beat 1 minute. Pour into popsicle molds and freeze until firm.

PUMPKIN CHIFFON DESSERT

60 large marshmallows
2 c. pumpkin
1 tsp. cinnamon

1/2 tsp. ginger
1/2 tsp. salt

Melt together over low heat and cool. Fold in 2 containers Cool Whip (1 quart). Spread mixture over graham cracker crust in 9x13 inch pan. Then spread a cup of Cool Whip over top and refrigerate. (Optional: Can sprinkle toasted coconut or nuts on top.)
Kathy Neels, St. Cloud, Mn.

QUICK DESSERT

Use ungreased 8x8 inch pan. Mix 1 small package Jiffy cake mix with 3 tablespoons melted butter. Put apple pie filling in pan and sprinkle the above crumbs on top. Bake in 350° oven for 35 - 40 minutes.
Marge Johnson, Minneapolis, Mn.

RASPBERRY DESSERT

18 graham crackers,
  crushed
1/2 c. powdered sugar
1/4 c. melted butter or
  margarine
1 pkg. raspberry gelatin mix

2 c. raspberries
30 marshmallows (large size)
1 c. whipped cream
1/2 c. chopped nuts
1/2 c. milk

Combine graham cracker crumbs with powdered sugar

and melted margarine. Press firmly into the bottom of a 9x13 inch pan. Dissolve gelatin in 1 cup of boiling water; stir in raspberries. Let gelatin and berries partially set, then spread it on top of crumbs. Melt marshmallows on top of double boiler with milk. Let cool. Add whipped cream to melted marshmallow mixture and spread over berries. Sprinkle with walnuts. Refrigerate overnight.

Kathy Bischof, St. Cloud, Mn.

RASPBERRY DESSERT

Make graham cracker pie crust. Mix:

1/2 c. butter	1 1/2 c. powdered sugar

Cream well. Beat 2 eggs and spread on crust. Whip 1 cup cream.

1 pkg. thawed frozen raspberries	2 Tbsp. raspberry juice

Place whipped cream and raspberries on top of butter and powdered sugar. Sprinkle rest of graham cracker crumbs on top. Refrigerate.

Mrs. W. A. Carlson

RØMMEGRØT

1 qt. cream	1 c. flour
4 c. milk	A pinch of salt

Let cream warm up gradually and let it bubble slowly for 20 minutes - stirring occasionally. Add cup of flour, sprinkle it in. Stir until it forms a ball - keep on stirring until butter begins separating from the ball - pour it off as it accumulates. Save butter. When 1/2 to 3/4 cup of butter has been poured off, start adding the milk until all has been added. Add a pinch of salt. Put into bowl and serve with cinnamon and sugar and a little of the butter sprinkled on top. The result is a smooth pudding. (12 - 14 servings)

Pearl Paulsrud, Willmar, Mn.

554

RHUBARB CRISP

3 c. cut up rhubarb	1/3 c. white flour
1/2 c. coconut	1/4 c. wheat germ
1/4 c. white sugar	1/8 tsp. salt
1/4 c. brown sugar	2 Tbsp. soft margarine

Place rhubarb in greased glass baking dish. Sprinkle coconut on top. Mix remaining ingredients until crumbly. Place on top of rhubarb and coconut. Bake 30 minutes at 350°. Serve warm or cold. Top with whipped cream, if desired.

Evelyn Walls, St. Paul, Mn.

RHUBARB CRISP

Mix:

1 1/2 c. brown sugar	2/3 c. butter
1 c. flour	4 c. rhubarb

Place rhubarb in bottom of greased pan. Mix other 3 ingredients together and put over rhubarb. Bake at 350° for 45 minutes.

Sue Hick, Detroit Lakes, Mn.

RHUBARB CRUNCH

5 c. cut up rhubarb	1 egg
2 c. sugar	1 regular pkg. yellow cake mix
4 Tbsp. flour	1 1/2 sticks margarine

Mix rhubarb, sugar, flour and egg. Spread over bottom of 9x13 inch pan. Sprinkle dry cake mix over top. Crumble margarine over top of entire mixture. Bake 40 minutes at 350°.

Kris Olson, Minneapolis, Mn.

RHUBARB DESSERT

Crust:

1 c. flour	1/2 c. margarine
2 Tbsp. sugar	Pinch of salt

1748-81

Filling:

4 c. diced rhubarb	3/4 c. milk
4 egg yolks, beaten	4 Tbsp. flour
1 1/2 c. sugar	

Mix crust, pat into 9x13 inch pan. Bake 10 minutes at 325°. Mix filling and pour over crust and bake 45 minutes at 325°. Make a meringue of 4 egg whites, 1/2 teaspoon cream of tartar and 8 tablespoons sugar. Beat egg whites and cream of tartar till frothy., gradually beat in sugar a little at a time, beating till stiff and glossy. Bake at 400° for 8 - 10 minutes.

Mike and Vonnie Bakke, Willmar, Mn.

RHUBARB DESSERT

Crust:

2 Tbsp. sugar	1 c. flour
1/2 c. butter or margarine	1/4 tsp. salt

Press into greased 9x9 inch pan. Bake 22 minutes.

Filling:

3 Tbsp. flour	3 egg yolks
3 c. cut rhubarb	1/2 c. whipping cream
1 1/2 c. sugar	

Cook until thick, in heavy kettle. Stir to prevent sticking. Spread filling on baked crust. Cover with meringue.

Norma Haugland, Fargo, N. D.

RHUBARB DREAM DESSERT

1 c. flour	1/4 c. flour
5 Tbsp. powdered sugar	3/4 tsp. salt
1/2 c. butter	2 c. rhubarb, finely diced
1 1/2 c. sugar	2 eggs, beaten

Combine 1 cup flour, powdered sugar and butter. Press into 9x9 inch ungreased pan. Bake at 350° for 15

556

minutes. Meanwhile, combine sugar, flour and salt. Add beaten eggs. Fold in rhubarb. Pour over baked crust and bake at 350° for 35 minutes. May be served with whipped cream if desired.

Liz Tuft, St. Paul, Mn.

RHUBARB KUCHEN A LA MODE

1 c. flour
1 Tbsp. sugar
1 1/2 tsp. baking powder
1/8 tsp. salt
2 Tbsp. butter or
  margarine
1 egg
2 Tbsp. milk

1 (3 oz.) pkg. strawberry
  jello
1/3 c. sugar
3 Tbsp. flour
5 c. rhubarb
2/3 c. sugar
1/3 c. flour
3 Tbsp. butter
Vanilla ice cream

Combine the 1 cup flour, 1 tablespoon sugar, baking powder and salt. Cut in 2 tablespoons butter till mixture resembles coarse crumbs. Beat egg with milk, add to flour mixture. Stir till dry ingredients are moistened. Pat dough evenly on bottom and 1 inch up sides of 9x9 inch pan. Combine the jello, 1/3 cup sugar and 3 tablespoons flour. Add to rhubarb and mix well. Turn into crust lined pan. Combine the remaining 2/3 cup sugar and 1/3 cup flour, cut in the remaining butter till crumbly. Sprinkle evenly over rhubarb filling. Bake in 375° oven for 45 minutes or till rhubarb is tender and topping is lightly browned. Cool completely, cut into squares and top each with vanilla ice cream. Makes 8 servings.

Gerri Ruprecht, St. Cloud, Mn.

RHUBARB TORTE

1 c. sifted flour
1/2 c. butter

5 Tbsp. powdered sugar

Cream and flake as pie crust. Press into 9x12 inch cake pan and bake 12 minutes at 350°.

3 eggs, well beaten
1 1/2 c. sugar
Pinch of salt
1 tsp. vanilla

1/2 c. nuts
1/4 c. flour
3/4 tsp. baking powder

Pour over 3 cups raw cut up rhubarb which has been placed over first baked mixture. Bake 30 minutes at 350°. Cool and serve with whipped cream or ice cream.

Arlene Gnoinsky, Fargo, N. D.

RHUBARB TAPIOCA

1 c. sugar	2 c. diced rhubarb
1 c. water	1/4 tsp. salt
3 Tbsp. instant tapioca	

Cook ingredients together, starting out over low heat, until rhubarb is tender and pudding is thick.

Carol Watnemo, St. Paul, Mn.

RHUBARB TART

Crust:

1 c. shortening	2 c. flour
(solid Crisco)	1/2 c. brown sugar

Mix and pat into bottom of a 9x13 inch pan, bake at 350° for 10 minutes.

Filling:

6 c. rhubarb	1/2 tsp. vanilla
6 egg yolks	1 c. evaporated milk
2 c. sugar	6 Tbsp. flour

Mix and pour over crust. Bake at 350° for 45 minutes.

Meringue:

6 egg whites	1/2 tsp. salt
12 Tbsp. sugar	1/4 tsp. cream of tartar

Beat egg whites with cream of tartar until frothy. Gradually beat in sugar, a little at a time. Continue beating until stiff and glossy. Do not underbeat. Beat until sugar is dissolved. Beat in flavoring, vanilla. Pile meringue onto hot rhubarb tart. Bake 8 to 10 minutes at 400° or until delicately browned. Cool away from drafts.

Karen Rupert, St. Cloud, Mn.

SPICED RHUBARB

1/2 c. shortening
1 c. sugar
1 egg
2 c. sifted flour
1 tsp. baking powder
1/4 tsp. cloves
1/2 tsp. baking soda

1/2 tsp. salt
1/2 tsp. cinnamon
1 c. thin sweetened rhubarb
  sauce
1 c. raisins
1 c. chopped nuts (optional)

Cream shortening, gradually beat in sugar. Add egg, beating until light and fluffy. Sift dry ingredients together. Use 1/2 cup to mix with nuts and raisins. Add dry ingredients alternately with rhubarb sauce to egg mixture. Stir in floured fruit and nut mixture. Drop from teaspoon onto greased baking sheet. Bake in 350° oven until tops spring back under finger tip pressure, about 15 minutes. Makes 3 dozen.

RHUBARB TORTE

1 c. flour
1/2 c. margarine
5 Tbsp. powdered sugar
2 eggs, beaten
1 1/2 c. sugar

1/4 tsp. salt
1/2 c. flour
3/4 tsp. baking powder
2 1/2 c. rhubarb, cutup

Mix first 3 ingredients like pie crust. Pat into 9x13 inch pan. Bake until brown 10 - 12 minutes at 350°. Beat 2 eggs and add sugar. Mix remaining ingredients into egg and sugar mixture. Spread over browned crust. Bake 30 minutes at 325°. Serve with whipped cream. Do not cover.
Lydia Skaret, Austin, Mn.

ROSETTES

3 eggs, slightly beaten
2 tsp. sugar
1/4 tsp. salt

1 c. milk
1 c. flour
1 Tbsp. lemon extract

Add sugar to slightly beaten eggs, then add milk. Add flour, salt and beat until smooth. Add flavoring. Fry till done in 350° oil.
Robin Knutson, Willmar, Mn.

ALMOND SWEDISH RUSK

1 c. sugar
1/2 c. butter
2 eggs
1/2 c. sour cream or
   buttermilk

1 tsp. almond flavoring
1 c. chopped almonds
1 tsp. soda
3 c. flour, sifted
Pinch of salt

Bake in bread pans. Makes 2 loaves. Bake at 300° for 45 minutes. Take out of pan and slice size of toast. Put on cookie sheet and brown in oven on both sides till light and golden brown.

      Blanche Weidencamp, St. Paul, Mn.

SALTED PEANUT CHEWS

Crust:

1 1/2 c. flour
2/3 c. brown sugar
1/2 tsp. baking powder
1/2 tsp. salt

1/4 tsp. soda
1/2 c. oleo, softened
1 tsp. vanilla
2 egg yolks

Bake 15 minutes in 350° oven. Add 3 cups marshmallows, put back into oven till puffy. Cool.

Topping:

2/3 c. corn syrup
1/4 c. oleo
2 tsp. vanilla

1 (12 oz.) pkg. peanut
   butter chips
2 c. Rice Krispies
2 c. Planter's peanuts

Cook syrup, oleo, butter chips until melted, add Rice Krispies, peanuts and vanilla; or microwave 3 minutes. Chill.

      Irma Holmstrom, Bismarck, N. D.

SANDBAKKELS - SAND TARTS

2 c. butter
2 c. sugar
1 egg, beat well before
   adding

4 1/2 c. flour
1 tsp. almond extract

Cream butter and sugar, add well beaten egg and extract. Mix until it becomes a firm dough. Press into sandbakkel pans. Bake in moderate (350°) oven until lightly browned. From my Swedish Cook Book.

Betty Carlson

SHERBET DESSERT

18 crushed macaroons
 (or any other crisp
 cookie)
1 pt. whipping cream
5 Tbsp. sugar

1 c. chopped walnuts
1 tsp. vanilla
3 pt. sherbet - use 3
 different colors

Whip cream and add vanilla. Gently mix in crushed cookies, sugar and walnuts. Put 1/2 of this into 9x13 inch pan and pat down. Spoon the sherbet over this - mixing up the colors. Cover with rest of the cream mixture. Keep in freezer until serving time.

Elsa Ditty, St. Cloud, Mn.

SHRIMP-PINEAPPLE FRITTERS

7 oz. frozen deveined
 uncooked shrimp
1 2/3 c. all-purpose flour
3 tsp. baking powder
1 tsp. salt
1/4 tsp. curry powder

2 eggs
2 Tbsp. salad oil
2 Tbsp. lemon juice
1 (8 3/4 oz.) can crushed
 pineapple
Salad oil or shortening for
 deep frying

Cook shrimp as package label directs, using unsalted water. Drain well. Chop shrimp medium fine. Sift flour with baking powder, salt and curry powder. In a large bowl with rotary beater, beat eggs with 2 tablespoons salad oil, the lemon juice and undrained crushed pineapple until well combined. Using a wooden spoon, stir flour mixture gradually into egg mixture. Gently stir in shrimp to mix well. Heat salad oil for frying. Drop shrimp mixture into hot fat by spoonfuls, a few at a time. Turn once, fry until golden or about 5 minutes. Drain well. Makes 18 fritters. Serve with Curry Sauce.

Curry Sauce:

3 Tbsp. butter

2 Tbsp. finely chopped onion

3 Tbsp. flour	1/8 tsp. ginger
4 tsp. curry powder	1/8 tsp. pepper
1 tsp. sugar	2 c. milk
1 tsp. salt	2 tsp. lemon juice

Melt butter in saucepan. Add the onion, saute until tender. Remove from heat. Stir in flour, curry powder, sugar, salt, ginger and pepper to make a smooth mixture. Gradually stir in milk. Bring to boil over medium heat, stirring. Reduce heat; simmer 1 minute. Stir in lemon juice. Serve warm with shrimp.

SHIRLEY'S CREAM CHEESE CAKE

1 yellow cake mix	1 stick melted butter
2 eggs	

Prepare cake, put into 13x9 inch cake pan. Mix:

1 (8 oz.) pkg. Philadelphia cream cheese	1 lb. powdered sugar
	2 eggs

Spread on top. Bake at 350° for 50 - 55 minutes.
Marge Johnson, Minneapolis, Mn.

STRAWBERRY BAVARIAN

Dissolve 1 (3 ounce) package strawberry jello in 1 cup boiling water. Add 1 (10 ounce) package frozen strawberries, stir until berries separate and jello begins to thicken. Fold in 1 1/2 cups thawed Cool Whip. Spoon into serving bowl and chill till set (about 30 minutes).
Linda Borgman, Sauk Centre, Mn.

STRAWBERRY CHANTILLY

1 (4 serving size) pkg. Jell-O pudding (vanilla)	2 1/4 c. water
	1 env. Dream Whip whipped topping mix*
1 (3 oz.) pkg. strawberry Jell-O	1 c. sliced sweetened strawberries

*Or use 1 (4 1/2 ounce) container Cool Whip, thawed.
Combine pudding mix, gelatin and water in a saucepan.

Cook and stir over medium heat until mixture comes to a full boil and is clear. Chill until slightly thickened. Prepare whipped topping mix as directed on package and thoroughly blend into chilled pudding mixture. Chill until firm - about 3 hours. Spoon into individual dessert dishes. Top with strawberries. Makes 4 cups or 6 - 8 servings.

Kathy Neels, St. Cloud, Mn.

STRAWBERRY CONFECTION

1 can Eagle Brand milk
1 lb. ground coconut
1 pkg. strawberry jello

1 tsp. vanilla
1/4 lb. ground almonds

Add red coloring to milk. Add jello and dissolve. Add other ingredients and chill at least 1 1/2 hours. Shape into strawberries and roll in jello. Make leaves of powdered sugar - colored green.

Kathy Bischof, St. Cloud, Mn.

STRAWBERRY DELIGHT

Topping and Crust:

1/2 c. butter
1/4 c. brown sugar

1 c. flour
1/2 c. chopped nuts

Mix and put into oven and bake at 350° about 15 minutes. Cool. Crumble about 2/3 of topping in glass dish and save other for topping.

Filling:

1 pkg. frozen strawberries
2 egg whites
1 c. sugar

1 Tbsp. lemon juice
1 tsp. vanilla
1/2 pt. whipping cream (can)

Mix first 5 ingredients. Beat 15 - 20 minutes. Fold in whipping cream. Pour into dish and put on topping. Freeze overnight. Can be served with whipped cream.

Mary Klaers, Willmar, Mn.

FRESH STRAWBERRY DESSERT

8x8 inch pan
1/2 c. margarine

2 Tbsp. sugar
1 c. flour

Press into pan, bake at 375° for 12 minutes.

1 c. sugar
1 generous c. water

2 Tbsp. cornstarch

Cook until clear. Add 3 heaping tablespoons of wild strawberry jello. Cool crust and syrup - pour on sliced strawberries - about 1 pint. (Do not use frozen strawberries.)

Madonna Mueller, Jamestown, N. D.

STRAWBERRIES WITH MOCK DEVONSHIRE CREAM
(English)

3 pt. fresh strawberries
1/2 c. whipping cream

Powdered sugar
1 c. dairy sour cream

Arrange berries in glass bowl. Cover, refrigerate. Beat whipping cream and powdered sugar (to taste) in chilled bowl until stiff - fold in sour cream. Serve over strawberries. Sprinkle with brown sugar.

Mary Lempe, St. Cloud, Mn.

STRAWBERRY PRETZEL DESSERT

1 1/2 c. pretzels, crushed
  not too fine
1/2 c. sugar
1/2 c. margarine or butter
1/2 c. sugar
1 (8 oz.) pkg. cream cheese

2 pkg. strawberry jello
2 c. boiling water
2 (10 oz.) pkg. frozen
  strawberries or raspberries
1 large ctn. Cool Whip

Mix pretzels, 1/2 cup sugar and margarine. Pack into greased 9x13 inch cake pan. Bake 6 minutes at 325°. Cool. Cream 1/2 cup sugar and cheese till fluffy. Combine with Cool Whip, mixing thoroughly. Spread over pretzel layer. Dissolve jello in the boiling water. Add the frozen fruit and mix well. Allow to set slightly, then spread on cheese layer. Refrigerate.

Johanna Singewald, St. Paul, Mn.

ICE CREAM AND STRAWBERRY MOLD

1 (3 oz.) pkg. strawberry
   flavored gelatin
1 c. hot water
1 c. cold water

1 pt. strawberrry ice
   cream
1 pt. fresh strawberries

1. Dissolve the gelatin in hot water. Add the cold water. 2. Add ice cream, and when it melts, add the fresh strawberries. 3. Pour into a mold or glass serving bowl and refrigerate for at least 3 hours.

Winnie Johnson, St. Paul, Mn.

SWEDISH TORTE

1/2 c. butter
1/2 c. sugar
4 egg yolks, well beaten
4 Tbsp. milk

1 c. + 1 Tbsp. flour
1 tsp. baking powder
1 tsp. vanilla

Cream butter and sugar together. Add beaten egg yolks, milk, flour, baking powder and vanilla. Mix all ingredients and put into 2 layer cake tins. Make a meringue of:

4 egg whites, beaten stiff   1 c. sugar

Put this meringue on top of the cake batter. Bake in 300° oven around 30 - 35 minutes. Cool. Then put 2 layers together with a spread of whipped cream between. Sprinkle sliced, toasted almonds on top if desired.

Kathy Bischof, St. Cloud, Mn.

SVENSKA TORTA
(Swedish Torte)

1/2 c. sugar
1/2 c. butter
4 egg yolks
5 Tbsp. milk

2 tsp. baking powder
1 c. flour
1/8 tsp. salt

Mix as for cake and spread thin in cake tins.

Meringue:

4 egg whites   1 c. sugar

1748-81

1/2 c. nutmeats   1 tsp. flavoring

Beat egg whites until stiff. Add sugar and flavoring. Spread mixture over cake batter and sprinkle with nutmeats. Bake at 350° F. for 45 minutes. When done, let stand in tins to cool. When ready to serve, spread with whipped cream and enjoy.

(In Scandinavia the Torte is served on a lovely cake plate and cut at the table.)

Helen-May Johnson, Chanhassen, Mn.

SWEET SOUP

10 c. water
1 c. prunes
1 c. raisins
1 c. currants
1 c. sugar (scant)
1 stick cinnamon (2 inch size)
1/2 tsp. salt
1 Tbsp. vinegar

1/2 c. tapioca
1 c. cooked apples
1 can frozen grape juice (6 oz. size)
1 c. water
1 orange (fresh with peeling)
1 (8 oz.) pkg. dried apricots

Cook prunes and water about 10 minutes. Add prunes, currants, apricots, cinnamon and salt. Cook additional 15 minutes. Add tapioca and orange (sliced into rings). Simmer about 5 minutes. Add grape juice, water (1 cup) and vinegar before removing from heat. Add apples (which were cooked previously by themselves so they are not mushy) when soup is removed from heat. Can be eaten hot or cold.

Carol Anderson, Fargo, N. D.

2-TONE DESSERT

Base layer:

1 1/2 c. flour   1/2 c. nuts
3/4 c. butter

Mix, press into greased jelly roll pan, bake at 350° for 10 minutes.

Next layer:

1 (8 oz.) pkg. Philadelphia   1 c. powdered sugar
  cream cheese

566

Beat together until light, fold in 9 ounce carton Cool Whip. Spread on crust and let set.

Third layer:

2 (4 oz.) pkg. instant   2 1/2 c. milk
  pistachio pudding

Mix until thick. Put on layer. Top pudding mix with Cool Whip. Can decorate top with chopped chocolate.
Mary Jo Conneran, Fargo, N. D.

SWEDISH TEA WAFERS

1 c. butter   2 c. flour
1/2 c. whipping cream

Mix like pie crust. Cut into circles about 1 1/2 inches in diameter. Dip circles in granulated sugar and prick with fork. Bake at 350° until lightly browned. (Don't roll too thin.)

Cream Filling:

1/4 c. butter   1 tsp. vanilla (I use 1/2
3/4 c. powdered sugar   tsp. almond extract)
1 egg yolk

Mix together. Place between 2 wafers.
Mrs. Robert G. Pearson, Fargo, N. D.

WALNUT TURTLES

2 c. walnuts   1/2 tsp. vanilla
36 caramels   2/3 c. chocolate chips
3 Tbsp. margarine   1 1/2 tsp. shortening

Cover baking sheets with waxed paper and arrange walnuts (chopped pieces) 1 inch apart. Place caramels in pan over double boiler, heat until caramels are melted completely. Stir occasionally. Remove from heat. Add vanilla and margarine and stir until thoroughly mixed. Drop by teaspoonfuls onto walnuts. Melt chocolate with shortening over hot (not boiling) water and spread over caramels.
Mary Jo Conneran, Fargo, N. D.

YUMMY CHOCOLATE DESSERT

First layer:

1 c. flour
2 Tbsp. sugar

1 stick soft margarine

Press into 9x13 inch pan and bake at 350° for 12 minutes and cool.

Second layer:

8 oz. softened Philadelphia
  cream cheese

2/3 c. powdered sugar
1/2 (9 oz.) ctn. Cool Whip

Spread over first layer.

Third layer:

3 pkg. instant chocolate
  pudding

4 c. milk

Beat together, let stand short time and spread over second layer.

Fourth layer: Spread rest of Cool Whip on top layer and sprinkle with chopped nuts. Refrigerate. Serves 21 - 24. Freezes well.

Kay Buzzell, Marshall, Mn.

BREAD PUDDING

1 1/2 c. dry stale bread
  (broken)
3 c. milk
2 Tbsp. butter or
  margarine, melted

1/2 c. sugar or honey
1/2 tsp. salt
1/2 tsp. cinnamon
1/2 tsp. nutmeg
2 eggs

Soak bread in milk and sugar 15 minutes. Stir in beaten eggs, butter and seasoning. Put into greased baking dish and bake at 350° for 1 hour. One cup raisins may be added.

Sue Hick, Detroit Lakes, Mn.

CAKE CRUMB PUDDING

2 eggs
2 c. milk
2 c. cake crumbs

4 Tbsp. sugar
1 tsp. vanilla

Beat eggs; add milk, cake crumbs, sugar and vanilla. If desired, 1/2 cup chopped nuts, coconut or chocolate chips may be added. Bake in greased casserole in slow oven about 45 minutes. Serve with cream.

CHRISTMAS PLUM PUDDING
(English)

To be in time for Christmas, one should begin making the plum pudding about a month ahead of time. This English specialty needs to age for a couple of days before it is cooked and it needs to age a minimum of 3 weeks afterwards. Because the recipe calls for many ingredients and requires long cooking, it appears to be more difficult than it really is, the result is well worth the effort.

6 slices stale white bread
5 1/2 oz. beef suet
3 1/2 oz. raisins
3 1/2 oz. dried currants
1 3/4 oz. candied citron
   or lemon
1 3/4 oz. candied cherries
1 tart apple (5 1/2 oz.)
2 1/2 oz. chopped almonds
Grated peel of 2 oranges
Grated peel of 1 lemon
10 level Tbsp. flour
   (2 1/2 oz.)

11 Tbsp. level Tbsp. sugar
   (5 1/2 oz.)
1 knife tip ground cinnamon
1 knife tip ground ginger
1 knife tip ground nutmeg
1/2 tsp. salt
3 eggs
Juice of 1 lemon
Juice of 1 orange
1/2 c. brandy
1/2 c. sherry
12 lumps sugar
2 Tbsp. brandy

1. Grate the white bread finely. 2. Remove the skin from fat and grind or grate it finely. 3. Soak the raisins and currants for 5 minutes in hot water. Drain and dry them well. 4. Chop the candied citron and cherries coarsely. 5. Peel the apple and grate it. 6. Put all the above items into a large bowl. 7. Combine the chopped almonds, orange and lemon peel, flour, sugar, spices and salt and fold them into the first mixture. Mix well. 8. Break the eggs into the mixture. Add the lemon and orange juice and work it together well either by hand or by machine. 9. Work the

brandy and sherry into the mixture. 10. Put the doughlike mixture into a stone or pottery crock and allow to rest, refrigerated, for 48 hours. 11. Lightly grease a China pudding mould or a 2 1/2 pint Pyrex bowl. Put the dough in the mould. Cover it with greased waxed or parchment paper. 12. Grease the center of a large dishtowel or piece of cheesecloth. Dust it with flour, stretch it tightly over the top of the mould on top of the waxed paper, and tie the ends securely. Continue around the side of the mould. 13. Put the mould on a trivet in a large pot. 14. Fill the pot with boiling water, enough to reach 3/4 of the way up the side of the mould. 15. Boil the plum pudding for 6 hours. Add boiling water as needed in order to keep a constant water level. 16. Remove the mould from the pot and allow it to cool to room temperature. 17. Remove the cloth and the paper. Unmould the pudding and wrap it in greased aluminum foil. Make sure that the pudding is well covered. 18. Allow it to rest in the refrigerator or other cool place for a minimum of 3 weeks. 19. Before serving it, return the pudding to the mould. Cover it tightly with a lid or aluminum foil, set it in a pan of water and cook it again for 3 hours. (This can be done in the oven. If it is heated on top of the stove, be sure to put the mould on a trivet in the pan of water.) 20. Unmould the pudding on a tray and top it with lumps of sugar. 21. Warm 2 tablespoons of brandy lightly; pour it over the sugar on the pudding and ignite it. Serve the pudding flaming. Plum Pudding may be served with a variety of sweet sauces.

Hot Apricot Brandy Sauce:

1 (10 oz.) jar apricot jam

1/3 c. brandy

Mix the jam and brandy together. Heat them gently, stirring occasionally.

Carolyn Smith, Fargo, N. D.

CRANBERRY STEAM PUDDING

2 c. whole cranberries
1/2 c. light molasses
1 1/2 c. flour

1/2 c. hot water
2 tsp. soda

Place flour in bowl and add cranberries, then molasses. Mix soda and water. Add to mixture. Grease cans (2 juice cans - can use regular size vegetable can). Steam about an hour. Fill pan 2/3 way up can - set can on rings. Cover top of can with foil.

Pudding can be frozen. Can heat pudding in foil in oven. Sauce is what makes the pudding so good!

1/2 c. butter   1 c. sugar
1/2 c. coffee cream

Cook till thick and syrupy - about 15 minutes. Add 2 teaspoons vanilla.

Carolyn Smith, Fargo, N. D.

OLD FASHIONED PUDDING

2 1/2 c. flour   1 c. seedless raisins
1/8 tsp. salt   1 c. chopped walnuts
1/2 tsp. cinnamon   1 Tbsp. dark molasses
1/2 tsp. cloves   1 egg, beaten
1 c. brown sugar   1 tsp. baking soda
1 c. finely chopped suet   1 c. sour milk or buttermilk

Sift flour with salt, cinnamon and cloves. Mix raisins, nuts and brown sugar thoroughly. Combine molasses, egg, baking soda, suet, and milk. Add nut mixture and milk mixture to dry ingredients. Grease and flour a 9x5 inch loaf pan. Cover with 2 sheets of waxed paper tied loosely, but securely. Steam over low heat for 1 1/2 hours. Serve hot.

Hard Sauce:

1/2 c. butter   1 tsp. vanilla
1 1/2 c. powdered sugar   1/2 tsp. lemon extract

Cream butter until soft. Add sugar gradually. Cream until consistency of whipped cream. Add flavorings. Beat. Refrigerate. Serve very cold on hot pudding.

Kathy Bischof, St. Cloud, Mn.

BAKED ORANGE PUDDING

3 egg yolks   1/2 c. evaporated milk
2 Tbsp. sugar   1 Tbsp. lemon peel or 1 Tbsp.
3 Tbsp. flour   orange rind
2 Tbsp. softened butter   1 c. orange juice

3 egg whites   1/2 c. sugar, minus 2 Tbsp.
1/4 tsp. salt

Beat the egg yolks slightly. Add the sugar and stir in the flour and butter, blending well. Gradually add the evaporated milk, lemon or orange rind and orange juice and mix well. Beat the egg whites with the salt until almost stiff. Gradually add the sugar. Blend the two mixtures carefully. Pour into greased custard cups. Bake at 350° for 40 - 60 minutes in a pan of hot water which reaches about half way on the custard cups. Yield: About 8 - 10 custard cups.

OZARK PUDDING

1 egg   1/4 tsp. salt
3/4 c. sugar   1/4 tsp. baking soda
2 Tbsp. flour   1/2 c. chopped nuts
1 1/4 tsp. baking powder   1/2 c. peeled apples, diced

Beat egg with sugar until light. Sift together flour, baking powder, salt and soda. Add to egg and beat well. Stir in nuts and apples and pour into buttered pie tin. Bake in preheated oven at 350° for 20 - 25 minutes. Pudding will rise high and then fall when done. Serve warm or cold with whipped cream.
Marge Johnson, Minneapolis, Mn.

PUDDING

1 pt. pineapple   3 lemons, juice
1 c. old fashioned tapioca   1 c. sugar
   (pearl)

Soak 1 cup tapioca in 2 cups water 4 hours. Add 1 more cup water and cook in double boiler until thick and clear. While hot, add sugar, juice. I just put in bowl and dish out as wanted. Serve with cream.
Mrs. James R. McQuaid, Anoka, Mn.

PINEAPPLE SPONGE

Soak 1 package Knox gelatine in as little water as possible. After it has dissolved, add a boiling syrup made of:

1 c. water   1 c. sugar

Stir well and add 1 can shredded pineapple when it begins to thicken. Stir in 1 pint whipped cream, whipped real thick, turn into mold which will give it a brick shape. Serve in slices like brick ice cream, with or without cream on top.

Mrs. James R. McQuaid, Anoka, Mn.

RAISIN PUDDING

Boil together:

2 c. brown sugar	2 Tbsp. butter
3 c. water	2 tsp. vanilla

Batter:

1 c. brown sugar	2 c. flour
2/3 c. milk	4 tsp. baking powder
1 c. raisins	

Pour over hot syrup which has been poured into regular size cake pan. Bake at 375° for 30 minutes.

Kathy Bischof, St. Cloud, Mn.

RHUBARB PUDDING

4 c. fresh rhubarb	1 c. sugar
Water enough just to cover	1/2 tsp. salt

Bring to boil and boil for 3 minutes till tender. Add 1 small package of strawberry jello, stir till dissolved. Add 3 heaping tablespoons of cornstarch that has been dissolved in cold water. Stir until thick and pour into serving dishes.

Mary Ann Hanson, Detroit Lakes, Mn.

RICE PUDDING

1 1/2 c. cooked rice
  (about 3/4 c. dry)
2 eggs
1/2 c. sugar
2 c. milk

1/2 c. raisins
1 tsp. vanilla
1/2 tsp. nutmeg
1/4 tsp. salt

Beat eggs, add sugar, nutmeg, salt and mix. Add rest of ingredients and pour into buttered baking dish. Bake in a slow oven (325°) about 30 minutes. Serve warm or cold with cream. Store leftover pudding in refrigerator.
Sue Hick, Detroit Lakes, Mn.

SWEDISH PUDDING

1 c. whipping cream
1 env. unflavored gelatin

1 c. sugar

Combine cream, sugar and gelatin and heat until sugar and gelatin are dissolved. Remove from heat and cool until slightly thick. Add 1 cup sour cream and 1/2 teaspoon vanilla. Chill. Serve topped with sweetened raspberries or strawberries. Serves 6.
Gladys Schimschock, Annandale, Mn.

VERONA'S CHOCOLATE PUDDING DESSERT

1 c. flour
1/2 c. margarine

1/2 c. chopped nuts

Mix and pat into 9x13 inch pan, bake 15 minutes at 350°. Cream:

1 (8 oz.) pkg. cream
  cheese

1 c. powdered sugar
1 tsp. vanilla

Blend in 1 cup Cool Whip. Spread over cooked crust. Add 3 cups cold milk to 1 large package instant chocolate pudding. Spread over cheese mixture. Top with 1 cup Cool Whip, then top this with chocolate shavings, nuts or whatever.
Carol Arndt, Windom, Mn.

CANDY
JELLY
PRESERVES

TEMPERATURE TESTS
FOR CANDY MAKING

There are two different methods of determining when candy has been cooked to the proper consistency. One is by using a candy thermometer in order to record degrees, the other is by using the cold water test. The chart below will prove useful in helping to follow candy recipes:

TYPE OF CANDY	DEGREES	COLD WATER
Fondant, Fudge	234 - 238°	Soft Ball
Divinity, Caramels	245 - 248°	Firm Ball
Taffy	265 - 270°	Hard Ball
Butterscotch	275 - 280°	Light Crack
Peanut Brittle	285 - 290°	Hard Crack
Caramelized Sugar	310 - 321°	Caramelized

In using the cold water test, use a fresh cupful of cold water for each test. When testing, remove the candy from the fire and pour about ½ teaspoon of candy into the cold water. Pick the candy up in the fingers and roll into a ball if possible.

In the SOFT BALL TEST the candy will roll into a soft ball which quickly loses its shape when removed from the water.

In the FIRM BALL TEST the candy will roll into a firm but not hard ball. It will flatten out a few minutes after being removed from water.

In the HARD BALL TEST the candy will roll into a hard ball which has lost almost all plasticity and will roll around on a plate on removal from the water.

In the LIGHT CRACK TEST the candy will form brittle threads which will soften on removal from the water.

In the HARD CRACK TEST the candy will form brittle threads in the water which will remain brittle after being removed from the water.

In CARAMELIZING, the sugar first melts then becomes a golden brown. It will form a hard brittle ball in cold water.

O'HENRY BARS

1 c. sugar	1 1/3 c. peanut butter
1 c. Karo syrup	6 c. Rice Krispies

Bring sugar and syrup to boil. Add peanut butter and Rice Krispies. Spread on greased cookie sheet. Frost with 2 cups chocolate chips and 1 cup butterscotch chips melted, in top of double boiler. Chill and cut into squares.

C. Landwehr, Minneapolis, Mn.

ALMOND BRITTLE

3/4 c. melted butter	*1 bag blanched or slivered
1 c. sugar	almonds

Cook 10 - 12 minutes or until almonds start to crack. It should be rather a caramel color. Spread quickly in a 9x13 inch pan and sprinkle with chocolate chips. Spread when soft. Break into pieces when hard.

*I use 1/2 bag almonds.

Karen Rupert, St. Cloud, Mn.

ROGER'S PEANUT BRITTLE

1 c. white corn syrup	2 Tbsp. butter
2 c. white sugar	2 tsp. vanilla
1/2 c. water	2 tsp. soda (baking soda)
1 (12 oz.) pkg. raw	1/2 tsp. salt
Spanish peanuts	

Combine syrup, sugar and water, bring to 230° over medium heat in heavy pan. Add peanuts and continue cooking until mixture reaches 300°. Remove from heat, add butter, vanilla, salt and baking soda. Stir until blended. Pour and spread on large cookie sheet (buttered). When cool, break into pieces. Makes about 1 1/2 pounds.

Roger Farley, Sartell, Mn.

PEANUT BRITTLE

1 1/2 tsp. soda
1 tsp. water
1 tsp. vanilla
1 1/2 c. sugar
1 c. water

1 c. light corn syrup
3 Tbsp. butter or margarine
1 lb. shelled, unroasted
    peanuts (raw)

Butter 2 baking sheets, keep warm. Combine soda, water and vanilla, set aside. Combine sugar, water and syrup in large pan, cook over medium heat, stirring* constantly to 240°. Will burn easily if not watched carefully and stirred. At 300°, remove from heat and add soda mixture and stir in thoroughly. Quickly pour onto cookie sheets and spread to about 1/4 inch thick. Cool and break into pieces.
　*Wooden spoon works best.
            Diane Schmitz, St. Cloud, Mn.

CARAMELS

10x14 inch jelly roll pan
4 c. sugar

1 pt. white syrup
2 pt. whipping cream

Put sugar, syrup, 1 pint cream in heavy kettle and boil to 235°. Add other pint of cream and boil to 245°. Add 1 teaspoon vanilla and pour into pan. Cool and cut into squares and wrap in waxed paper.
            Jo Nell Murack, Fargo, N. D.

HONEY CARAMELS

1 1/2 c. sugar
1 1/2 c honey
1/2 c. light brown sugar
1/2 c. butter

1 c. evaporated milk
1/4 tsp. salt
1 tsp. vanilla

Blend sugar, honey, salt. Boil to soft ball stage. Very slowly add milk; then pieces of butter so boiling does not stop. Cook to hard ball (254°). Remove from heat, add vanilla. Pour into buttered pan. When cool, cut into squares and wrap in waxed paper.
            Darlene Lee

CINNAMON NUTS

1 c. sugar
1 tsp. cinnamon

1/4 tsp. cream of tartar
1/4 c. water

Cook until soft ball stage, stir in 2 cups walnuts or pecans, put on waxed paper and break apart.
Georgine Isakson, Fargo, N. D.

DIVINELY DIFFERENT DIVINITY

No. 1:

3 c. granulated sugar
1/2 c. light corn syrup

2/3 c. water

Boil until it spins a thread 18 inches long.

No. 2:

2 egg whites

1/8 tsp. salt

Beat until frothy. Add 1 package jello (any flavor), and beat until stiff. Add the syrup gradually, beating constantly until thick. Drop by teaspoonfuls onto waxed paper. Top with walnut halves or pecans, if desired.
Kathy Bischof, St. Cloud, Mn.

BOILED FUDGE

Cut up and melt 2 squares semi-sweet chocolate. Add:

1 1/2 c. white sugar (mix
  with chocolate)
7 Tbsp. milk

1/4 tsp. salt
1 Tbsp. white corn syrup
2 Tbsp. shortening
2 Tbsp. butter (or margarine)

Cook on medium heat. Keep stirring until it comes to a rolling boil. Boil about 3 minutes. Add 1 teaspoon vanilla. Cool. Beat with mixer until it thickens and loses gloss. Add walnuts to taste. Spread on greased dinner plate. Put into refrigerator until set. Cut into 1 inch squares. Makes good fudge frosting. Boil for approximately 1 minute.
Lu Boyer, Grand Forks, N. D.

6 MINUTE FUDGE

2/3 c. evaporated milk   2 c. sugar

Bring to boil over low heat. Boil 6 minutes. Remove from heat and add:

1/4 lb. butter   Vanilla
6 oz. pkg. chocolate chips   Nuts

Put into 9 inch pan.
Gina Michels

PEANUT BUTTER FUDGE

2 c. sugar   1 pt. marshmallow cream
2/3 c. milk   (I use a 7 oz. jar)
1 c. chunky peanut butter   1 tsp. vanilla

Combine sugar and milk in pan and cook over medium heat to soft ball stage. Remove from heat. In a warm mixing bowl, combine marshmallow cream, peanut butter and vanilla. Add cooked syrup and mix well. Pour into a greased pan. Cool and cut into squares (8 inch square pan).
Lu Boyer, Grand Forks, N. D.

THACHUS PET FUDGE

5 to 7 large marsh-   10 large marshmallows
  mallows, cut into squares   2/3 c. (5 1/3 oz. can)
6 sq. (6 oz.) semi-sweet   evaporated milk
  chocolate   1 c. chopped walnuts
1/2 c. butter   1 tsp. vanilla
2 c. sugar

Spread quartered marshmallows on tray and freeze till firm. Place chocolate and butter in large mixing bowl; set aside. Combine sugar, 10 large marshmallows and evaporated milk in heavy saucepan. Bring to a boil, stirring constantly; then boil 5 minutes, stirring constantly. Pour over chocolate and butter; stir until mixture is well blended - begins to thicken. Add walnuts, vanilla and frozen quartered marshmallows. Pour into lightly buttered 8 inch square pan. Chill until firm. Cut into squares. Store covered, in a cool place. Makes 2 pounds.
578   Marie Miller, St. Paul, Mn.

VELVEETA CHEESE FUDGE

1 lb. oleo or butter
1 lb. cheese
4 lb. powdered sugar

1 c. cocoa
1 Tbsp. vanilla
6 oz. nuts (or 12 oz.)

Melt butter, cheese till smooth. Mix cocoa and sugar, add cheese mix. Add nuts and vanilla. Mix well. Pour into greased pan. Cool and cut. Makes 6 1/2 pounds.

Mary Jane Schmitz, Wadena, Mn.

WHITE FUDGE

2 1/2 c. granulated sugar
1/2 c. dairy sour cream
1/4 c. milk
2 Tbsp. butter
1 Tbsp. light corn syrup

1/4 tsp. salt
2 tsp. vanilla
1 c. coarsely chopped nuts
1/3 c. quartered candied
  cherries

Combine sugar, sour cream, milk, butter, corn syrup and salt in heavy 2 quart saucepan. Stir over moderate heat until sugar is dissolved and mixture reaches a boil. Boil over moderate heat 9 to 10 minutes to 238° F. (soft ball stage). Remove from heat and allow to stand until lukewarm (110° F.), about 1 hour. Add vanilla and beat until mixture just begins to lose its gloss and hold its shape. (Requires very little beating.) Quickly stir in cherries, walnuts if you like and turn into greased pan. Makes 1 1/2 pounds.

M. R. Jones, Spirit Lake, Ia.

RICE KRISPIE CANDIES

Melt:
2 lb. almond bark

1 c. peanut butter

Add:
3 c. Rice Krispies
2 c. mini marshmallows

2 c. dry roasted nuts

Drop by teaspoonfuls onto waxed paper.

Carol Arndt, Windom, Mn.

GOOF BALLS

Melt in top of double boiler:

1 pkg. Kraft caramels   1 can Borden's Eagle Brand
1/4 c. butter or margarine   milk

Dip marshmallows into caramel mixture until coated. Roll into Rice Krispies cereal until coated. Chill. These can be frozen.

Bernita Engel, Minneapolis, Mn.

MINTS

1 (3 oz.) pkg. Philadelphia   2 1/2 c. powdered sugar
  cream cheese (room
  temperature)

Knead together until smooth (use your hands). Divide into as many colors and/or flavors as you want. Add food coloring very sparingly. Add 1 or 2 teaspoons of flavoring to taste. Pinch off pieces size of marble, roll in granulated sugar, press into molds. Remove (I hit end of mold on table). Let stand on cookie sheet, waxed paper, etc., until dry, for a few hours. These can be frozen. Makes about 125 - 150 pieces.

Flavors I use:

Rum + butter   Orange
Vanilla + almond   Mint or peppermint
Lemon

Thelma Olson, St. Cloud, Mn.

PEANUT BUTTER CUPS

1/2 c. margarine   1 c. peanut butter
2 c. powdered sugar   2 1/2 lb. chocolate almond
  (sift to remove lumps)   bark

Mix the first 3 ingredients. Melt almond bark in 200° oven. Put a drop of chocolate in bottom of small candy wrapper, add about 1 teaspoonful of peanut butter mixture and top with more chocolate.

Georgia Berg, Fargo, N. D.

580

PEANUT BUTTER CUPS

1 bag chocolate Candy Quik	2 c. powdered sugar
1 c. peanut butter	1/4 c. butter

Mix Candy Quik in double boiler. Melt butter separately and mix with peanut butter and sugar. Roll into balls, flatten. Pour Candy Quik in bottom of liner. Add 1 flattened ball and cover with Candy Quik.
Diane Schmitz, St. Cloud, Mn.

PEANUT CANDY

12 oz. butterscotch chips	12 oz. salted peanuts (Virginia)

Melt chips and stir in nuts. Drop on waxed paper and cool. So simple and yet soooo good!!!!!
Eloise Cole, Minneapolis, Mn.

ENGLISH TOFFEE

1 c. white sugar	1 tsp. vanilla
1/2 lb. butter	3 small Hershey's bars (plain)
3 Tbsp. water	3/4 c. chopped nuts

Place first 4 ingredients into saucepan and cook until brown (10 minutes). Stir constantly. Pour into buttered 9x9 inch pan. Place Hershey's bars on top when melted, spread evenly. Sprinkle nuts over top. When cool, break into pieces.
Grayce Funke, Minneapolis, Mn.

ENGLISH TOFFEE
(Similar to Heath Bar)

1 stick butter	3/4 c. chopped nuts
3/4 c. brown sugar, packed	3 - 4 Hershey's bars (or chocolate chips)

Spread chopped nuts over bottom of 8x8 inch square pan. Bring butter and brown sugar to boil over slow heat. Boil 7 minutes, stirring constantly. Pour at once over nuts. Spread quickly. Place chocolate on top and spread. Cool in refrigerator. Break into pieces.
Shirley Way, Minneapolis, Mn.

EASY TOFFEE

3/4 c. chopped walnuts   1/2 c. oleo
3/4 c. brown sugar   1/2 c. chocolate chips

Butter pan (8x8 inches), sprinkle in nuts. Cook sugar and oleo to 290°, stirring often. Spread over chopped nuts, sprinkle on chips. Let stand a minute or so, then spread. Chill thoroughly, then break into pieces.
Roger Farley, Sartell, Mn.

WALNUT TOFFEE

1 1/2 c. chopped walnuts   2 c. sugar
1/2 c. water   1/2 c. light corn syrup
1 c. butter

Combine sugar, water, corn syrup and butter. Heat to boiling, stirring until sugar is dissolved. Cover and cook 5 minutes. Uncover and boil to hard crack stage - 300° Remove from heat, stir in coarsely chopped walnuts and quickly spread into a greased 10x15x1 inch pan. Let stand to cool. Melt 1 package milk chocolate over warm, not hot, water. Spread over cooked toffee and sprinkle with 3/4 cup finely chopped walnuts. Let stand until chocolate is set. Break into pieces. Delicious!!
Harriett Maselie, Minneapolis, Mn.

APRICOT RHUBARB JAM

6 c. rhubarb   6 c. sugar
2/3 c. water   2 pkg. apricot jello
1 can apricot pie filling

Cook rhubarb, cut into small pieces, with water until done. Then add pie filling, sugar and jello. Boil for 5 minutes. This can be made with cherry pie filling, cherry jello or any of the canned pie filling with like jello.
Margaret Miller, St. Cloud, Mn.

582

BEET JELLY

3 c. beet juice
1 pkg. Sure-Jell

1 pkg. Kool-Aid (raspberry, grape, strawberry) or juice of 1 lemon

Bring to boil, add 4 cups sugar (5 cups if you use lemon). Boil until jelly drips from spoon. Put into sterilized jars.

Darlene Lee

BEET RASPBERRY JELLY

3 c. beet juice
1/4 c. lemon juice

1 box Sure-Jell

Boil for 2 minutes. Add:
4 c. sugar

1 (3 oz.) box raspberry jello

Boil 4 or more minutes. I use the drip spoon test. Pour into jars and seal with wax. Makes 6 (1/2 pint) jars.

Recipe from Minneapolis, Mn.

BLUE-BARB JAM

3 c. finely cut rhubarb or 1 (12 to 16 oz.) pkg. frozen rhubarb, thawed

3 c. crushed blueberries
7 c. sugar
1 (6 oz.) bottle liquid fruit pectin

If fresh rhubarb is used, simmer gently until tender. Combine with blueberries in large saucepan; add sugar and mix. Place over high heat; bring to full rolling boil and boil hard for 1 minute, stirring constantly. Remove from heat and add pectin. Stir and skim for 5 minutes. Ladle into hot sterilized glasses. Cover at once with thin layer paraffin. Makes about 9 (1/2 pints).

BREAKFAST MARMALADE

2 oranges
2 lcmons

2 grapefruit

Wash the fruit and slice into paper thin strips, placing

the seeds in a little cheesecloth sack. Measure the fruit and for every cupful, add 2 cups of water. Let stand 24 hours. Remove seeds. Cook until the fruit is tender and let stand until cool. Measure fruit and add an equal amount of sugar. Cook over low heat until thick. Pour into sterile jars at once.

GRAPE JELLY

1 1/2 pt. Welch's grape
   juice
1 box Sure-Jell

3/4 c. water
5 1/4 c. sugar

Bring first 3 ingredients to a boil. Add sugar. Boil 1 minute or until it sheets from spoon. Skim and pour into glasses. Makes about 6 average glasses of jelly.
Mrs. E. F. Braun, Owatonna, Mn.

GRAPE BEET JELLY

Peel and dice 4 large beets, cover with water and bring to a boil. Simmer for about 20 minutes. Drain and save the juice.

4 c. beet juice
1 pkg. Sure-Jell
4 c. sugar

2 pkg. unsweetened grape
   Kool-Aid

Measure juice and put into large kettle. Stir in Sure-Jell and bring to a boil. Add 1 cup sugar at a time and bring to a boil after each cup. After all sugar is added, boil hard for 1 minute. Remove from burner and add grape Kool-Aid. Stir and then put into jars and cover with wax (not quite 3 pints). (If you can beets or make beet pickles, scrub your beets before boiling and seal up that juice for this recipe.)
Karen Rupert, St. Cloud, Mn.

GREEN PEPPER JELLY

6 1/2 c. sugar
3 large green peppers,
   seeded and cut up
1 1/2 c. white vinegar

1 bottle Certo
Green food coloring
2 Tbsp. crushed red pepper

584

Put green pepper and some of the white vinegar into processor and grind. Put green pepper, sugar, red pepper and rest of vinegar into large pan and bring to a rolling boil, skim foam. Add Certo and boil 3 minutes longer. Add green food coloring and put into jars. Spread cream cheese on crackers and garnish with jelly. Delicious!!!

MYSTERY JAM

1 qt. canned tomatoes	2 Tbsp. lemon juice
4 tart cooking apples	1 Tbsp. grated orange rind
2 c. sugar	1/4 tsp. cinnamon

Wash and cut apples, removing stems and blossom ends. Do not peel or core. Stew apples and tomatoes together until apples are tender. Force through a sieve or food mill. Add sugar and lemon juice to pulp. Cook slowly until thick. Remove from heat; stir in orange rind and cinnamon. Pour into sterilized glasses and seal with coat of paraffin.

ORIENTAL PEAR JAM

8 medium sized pears	1 (4 oz.) pkg. crystallized
1 c. crushed pineapple	ginger, diced
4 c. sugar	

Peel and core pears; put through a food chopper. Mix with remaining ingredients. Cook approximately 30 minutes, stirring frequently. Pour into hot sterilized jars; seal. Makes 2 1/2 pints.

PEAR-ORANGE MARMALADE

12 Bartlett pears, diced	2 large oranges, diced, with
1 (#2) can crushed	peel
pineapple	1/2 c. maraschino cherries,
	chopped

Measure and use 3/4 cup sugar to each cup pulp. Let stand overnight. Cook slowly and carefully till thick and clear. Add cherries. Pour into scalded jars - seal with wax.

Shirley Way, Minneapolis, Mn.

RHUBARB MARMALADE

Mix:

9 c. rhubarb   9 c. sugar

Let stand overnight. Add:

3 ground (medium sized)
  oranges, peel 1 orange
  so you use rind from 2
  oranges only

1 (20 oz.) can crushed
  pineapple, drain off a
  little juice
1/2 c. ground walnuts (if
  desired)

Bring to boil and boil hard for approximately 15 to 20 minutes. Seal in sterilized pint jars.

Norma Haugland, Fargo, N. D.

RHUBARB REFRIGERATOR JAM

4 - 5 c. rhubarb, cut up
3 c. sugar

1 (3 oz.) pkg. strawberry
jello

Mix together rhubarb and sugar, let stand 1/2 hour till sugar melts. Cook over medium heat till done. Stir in jello. Cool. Put into jars and refrigerate.

Carla Kangas, Detroit Lakes, Mn.

STRAWBERRY RHUBARB JAM

4 c. strawberries, washed
  and stemmed
1 lb. rhubarb (fresh or
  frozen)

1/4 c. lemon juice
1 (1 3/4 oz.) pkg. powdered
  pectin
5 1/2 c. sugar

Prepare home canning jars and lids according to manufacturer's instructions. Crush strawberries, place in a large (6 to 8 quart) saucepot. Wash rhubarb if fresh, remove and discard leaves. Finely chop rhubarb. Measure 2 cups rhubarb into saucepot with strawberries. Add lemon juice and pectin. Bring to a full boil over high heat. Add sugar, return to a full boil. Boil hard 1 minute, stirring constantly. Remove from heat. Skim foam. Carefully ladle into hot jars, leaving 1/4 inch head space. Adjust caps. Process 10 minutes in boiling water bath canner. This recipe makes about 6 (8 ounce) jars.

Arlene Jewell, Bismarck, N. D.

BEVERAGES
& MISCELLANEOUS

FOOD QUANTITIES
FOR SERVING 25, 50 and 100 PERSONS AT PICNIC

Do you have trouble deciding how much of various foods to take to a picnic? Here are some suggested figures on 25, 50 and 100 servings, taken from "Planning Food For Institutions," a USDA handbook.

FOOD	25 SERVINGS	50 SERVINGS	100 SERVINGS
Sandwiches:			
Bread	50 slices or 3 1-lb. loaves	100 slices or 6 1-lb. loaves	200 slices or 12 1-lb. loaves
Butter	½ pound	¾ to 1 pound	1½ pounds
Mayonnaise	1 cup	2 to 3 cups	4 to 6 cups
Mixed Filling (meat, eggs, fish)	1½ quarts	2½ to 3 quarts	5 to 6 quarts
Mixed Filling (sweet-fruit)	1 quart	1¾ to 2 quarts	2½ to 4 quarts
Lettuce	1½ heads	2½ to 3 heads	5 to 6 heads
Meat, Poultry or Fish:			
Wieners (beef)	6½ pounds	13 pounds	25 pounds
Hamburger	9 pounds	18 pounds	35 pounds
Turkey or chicken	13 pounds	25 to 35 pounds	50 to 75 pounds
Fish, large whole (round)	13 pounds	25 pounds	50 pounds
Fish, fillets or steaks	7½ pounds	15 pounds	30 pounds
Salads, Casseroles:			
Potato Salad	4¼ quarts	2¼ gallons	4½ gallons
Scalloped Potatoes	4½ quarts or 1 12x20" pan	8½ quarts	17 quarts
Spaghetti	1¼ gallons	2½ gallons	5 gallons
Baked Beans	¾ gallon	1¼ gallons	2½ gallons
Jello Salad	¾ gallon	1¼ gallons	2½ gallons
Ice Cream:			
Brick	3¼ quarts	6½ quarts	12½ quarts
Bulk	2¼ quarts	4½ quarts or 1¼ gallons	9 quarts or 2½ gallons
Beverages:			
Coffee	½ pound and 1½ gal. water	1 pound and 3 gal. water	2 pounds and 6 gal. water
Tea	1/12 pound and 1½ gal. water	1/6 pound and 3 gal. water	1/3 pound and 6 gal. water
Lemonade	10 to 15 lemons, 1½ gal. water	20 to 30 lemons, 3 gal. water	40 to 60 lemons, 6 gal. water
Desserts:			
Watermelon	37½ pounds	75 pounds	150 pounds
Cake	1 10x12" sheet cake 1½ 10" layer cakes	1 12x20" sheet cake 3 10" layer cakes	2 12x20" sheet cakes 6 10" layer cakes
Whipping Cream	¾ pint	1½ to 2 pints	3 pints

AMARETTO

2 c. sugar   2 c. water

Bring to boil and simmer 10 minutes. Remove from heat. Add:

2 c. brandy   3 - 4 tsp. almond extract
2 c. vodka

Place in airtight container for a couple of days. Makes 3 pints.
A. T. Isakson, Fargo, N. D.

BLOOMER DROPPERS

1 (6 oz.) can pink   4 peach halves (no syrup)
   lemonade   13 ice cubes
1 (6 oz.) can vodka

Blend all ingredients in blender. Freeze. To serve, add 2 scoops and fill glass with 7-Up. Stir.
Gail Peterson, Frazee, Mn.

CHOCOLATE-CINNAMON SWIZZLE

3/4 c. instant chocolate   1 c. soft chocolate chip mint
   flavored mix   ice cream
1 tsp. cinnamon   1 (7 oz.) bottle soda water,
1 1/2 c. milk   chilled

Combine all ingredients except soda water, in large bowl; stir to mix well or beat with rotary beater until smooth. Then pour 4 tall glasses. Fill each glass with soda. Stir well. Serve at once. (4 servings)

HOT CHOCOLATE MIX
(5 quart ice cream pail full)

1 (8 qt.) box Carnation
instant dry milk
1 c. powdered sugar

1 lb. Nestle's Quik (or a little
more)
8 oz. jar Cremora

Mix together. Put 1/3 cup mix in cup - fill with hot
water.

Darlene Lee

SNOWMOBILERS HOT CHOCOLATE MIX

Mix all this together:
8 qt. Carnation powdered
milk
1 lb. can Nestle's Quik

6 oz. Coffee-mate
3/4 c. powdered sugar

Use 2 tablespoonfuls or 1 coffee scoop full of the mix
in a cup and add hot water. Yield: 56 cups. Can store in
an airtight container.

Mary Ann Hanson, Detroit Lakes, Mn.

SPICED CIDER

1 tsp. allspice
2 (2 inch) sticks cinnamon
12 whole cloves

2 qt. cider
2/3. c. brown sugar,
firmly packed
Nutmeg

Bundle up spices into bag. Put cider in pan and add
sugar. Heat to boiling point. Add spice bag and cook
slowly about 10 minutes or until spicy enough to suit your
taste. Remove spice bag. Serve hot with a sprinkle of
nutmeg.

Kathy Bischof, St. Cloud, Mn.

COFFEE BAVARIAN

1 c. finely crushed
graham crackers
1/4 c. melted butter or
margarine
1 env. unflavored gelatin

1/2 c. cold water
1/2 c. sugar
1 Tbsp. instant coffee
granules
1/4 tsp. salt

1 c. evaporated milk   Chocolate curls if desired
2/3 c. evaporated milk

Mix butter and cracker crumbs. Press into bottom of
an 8 inch pan. Chill. In a saucepan, soften gelatin in water
and add sugar, coffee and salt. Stir over medium heat until
gelatin and sugar dissolve. Remove from heat. Stir in 1
cup of the milk. Chill until firm. Put mixture into large
bowl of mixer. Beat on low speed till broken up, then beat
in 2/3 cup of the milk on high speed until fluffy. Pour
over crumbs and chill until firm. Cut into 9 servings and
decorate with chocolate curls.

Dee Olson, St. Paul, Mn.

IRISH COFFEE

Cream, rich as an Irish   Sugar, sweet as the tongue
  brogue   of a rogue
Coffee, strong as a   Whiskey, smooth as the wit
  friendly hand   of the land

Heat a stemmed whiskey goblet or Irish mug. Pour in
1 jigger of Irish whiskey (the only whiskey with the smooth
taste and full body needed). Add 3 cubes of sugar; fill goblet with strong, black coffee to within 1 inch of brim. Stir
to dissolve sugar. Top off to the brim with whipping
cream; it will float on top. Do not stir after adding the
cream as the true flavor is obtained by drinking the hot
coffee and Irish whiskey through the cream.

This will considerably increase your "balarney"
capacity.

Ione" Corrigan" Brown, Past President
St. Cloud Council

CHOKECHERRY BOUNCE
(Jack Pine Savage)

3 lb. cleaned chokecherries   2 fifths liquor (I use vodka)
3 1/2 c. sugar   1 gal. jug

Put chokecherries into jar, cover with liquor and sugar.
Every day or so, turn upside down to dissolve sugar. Put
back on shelf till Christmas. Don't seal tight until it sets
a couple of weeks. Makes a very fine cherry brandy. Orig-
inal recipe called for pie cherries, but have had just as
good results with chokecherries.

1748-81   Mrs. Clarence Schmitz, Wadena, Mn.   589

CREAM DE MENTHE

1 qt. vodka
1 qt. water
4 c. white Karo syrup

1/2 oz. peppermint extract
Green food coloring

Let stand in bottles 3 weeks before using (add ice cream in blender).
Diane Schmitz, St. Cloud, Mn.

FROZEN FRUIT CUPS

1 (6 oz.) can frozen
  lemonade
1 (6 oz.) can orange
  juice
1 (10 oz.) pkg. frozen
  strawberries

1 (#2) can pineapple tidbits
  and juice
3 - 4 sliced bananas
Scant 2 c. water
Scant 1/2 c. sugar

Combine and stir. Freeze in 5 ounce Dixie cups. Thaw 1 1/2 hours before serving.
Gina Michels, Willmar, Mn.

HOLIDAY EGGNOG
(Very rich!)

9 egg yolks
2 c. sugar
2 qt. softened ice cream

1 c. rum
1 c. brandy
1 c. bourbon or whiskey

Beat egg yolks and sugar well, beat in softened ice cream. Then add rum, brandy and whiskey. Blend well, store covered in freezer. Makes about 4 1/2 quarts.
Roger Farley, Sartell, Mn.

HOT PINEAPPLE EGGNOG

8 eggs
6 1/2 c. pineapple or
  other fruit juice

1 pt. cream
1 c. sugar
1/4 c. chopped orange peel

Separate egg yolks and whites. Beat yolks thoroughly in half the sugar. Beat whites thoroughly in remaining sugar. Bring pineapple juice to a boil. Add cream. Reheat and pour over egg yolk mixture. Fold egg whites into hot mixture. Sprinkle with orange peel. Serves 12.

VODKA ORANGE FIZZIES

1 (6 oz.) can lemonade
1 (6 oz.) can orange juice
1 c. sugar

1 c. water
1 c. vodka
1 c. strong Team

Freeze. Then mix 1/3 to 1/2 cup of this mixture with 7-Up and crushed ice.

Elsa Ditty, St. Cloud, Mn.

FRUIT COOLER

1/2 c. Tang
1/2 c. sugar

3/4 c. cold water

Mix these together. Add:

3 sliced bananas
1 box frozen strawberries
1/2 c. crushed pineapple
    with juice

1 (8 oz.) can fruit cocktail
    with juice

Dish into 4 ounce paper cups and freeze. Makes 11 or 12 servings. To serve, unmold in sherbet dish and spoon 3 tablespoons 7-Up over each serving. Should stand about 15 to 20 minutes to thaw slightly before serving. It should be partially frozen when served.

R. W. Neale, St. Cloud, Mn.

ORANGE JULIUS

6 oz. can frozen orange
    juice
1 c. milk
1 c. water

1/4 c. sugar
1 tsp. vanilla
10 - 12 ice cubes

Combine all ingredients in blender. Cover and blend until smooth, about 30 seconds. Serve immediately. Makes about 4 servings.

Georgia Berg, Fargo, N. D.

KAHLUA

1 (2 oz.) jar instant coffee

4 c. sugar
2 c. boiling water

Stir and let cool about 2 hours. Add:

1 pt. brandy

1 vanilla bean, split lengthwise

Put bean in large bottle and pour kahlua in. Leave sealed for 30 days. Makes 2 fifths.

Marge Johnson, Minneapolis, Mn.

KAHLUA

3/4 c. instant coffee
4 c. water
3 3/4 c. sugar

1/4 c. pure vanilla extract
1 fifth vodka

Boil sugar and water 5 minutes. Add coffee and cool to lukewarm. Add vanilla and vodka - pour in bottle and let set for 2 weeks. After dinner drink served with crushed ice.

Irene Wall, Little Falls, Mn.

HOT BUTTERED LEMONADE

Extract 1/2 cup lemon juice with juicer. Into electric blender place:

1/2 c. sugar
3 c. boiling water

2 Tbsp. butter
1 tsp. lemon peel

Blend to dissolve sugar and add 1/2 cup lemon juice. Pour into mugs and top with lemon slice. Drop a cherry into mug for color. Serves 4.

PLUM BRANDY

1 pt. vodka
1 lb. rock candy

1 c. pitted canned plums, drained or 1 c. pitted overripe fresh plums

Combine ingredients in a large sterile jar with stopper or lid. Let stand in a dark, cool place at least 3 months, turning occasionally, plum brandy gets better the longer it stands.

Myrtle Solomon, Fargo, N. D.

PLUM CORDIAL

Fill 1 quart jar with ripe wild sugar plums, pierce each plum with several holes. Add 1/2 cup sugar per quart. Fill jar with rum, vodka or whiskey. Store about 30 - 60 days. Serve after straining.

Marjory E. Welken, Valley City, N. D.

PUNCH
(Serves large punch bowl)

1 (12 oz.) can frozen orange juice	1 can pineapple juice
1 (12 oz.) can frozen lemonade	1 can Hawaiian Punch

Freeze and stir until slush. Add 2 bottles of ginger ale when ready to serve.

Ginnie Andersen, St. Paul, Mn.

BOSTON CLUB PUNCH

Juice of 9 doz. lemons	3 1/2 qt. good champagne
4 large fresh pineapple, cut into small chunks, or 8 (#2 cans) pineapple chunks	1/2 pt. Curacao
	10 boxes frozen strawberries or fresh strawberries, sliced and sweetened
3 1/2 lb. sugar (7 c.)	6 oranges, cut into thin
3 1/2 qt. white wine	rounds and quartered, rinds left on

Combine lemon juice, pineapple and sugar. Immediately before serving, add remaining ingredients and pour over large chunks of ice. This makes about 11 gallons.

CRANBERRY PUNCH

2 qt. cranberry juice
12 oz. can frozen orange
    juice

12 oz. can frozen lemonade
1 qt. ginger ale

Mix cranberry juice, orange juice, lemonade and water to reconstitute the frozen juices. Chill thoroughly. Add ginger ale just before serving. Makes 50 (4 ounce) servings.

COFFEE PUNCH
(Serves 80 to 100)

1 small jar instant
    coffee (4 oz.)
4 c. boiling water

3 qt. vanilla ice cream
3 qt. chocolate ice cream
12 qt. milk

Mix coffee and boiling water. Cool. When ready to serve, add ice cream and milk.

Gloria Bergson, Fargo, N. D.

FROTHY EGGNOG PUNCH

12 egg whites
12 egg yolks
1 c. sugar
1 qt. rich milk
1 Tbsp. sherry or
    rum flavoring

6 (7 oz.) bottles lemon-lime
    carbonated beverage
    (lime-lemon variety)
1 pt. vanilla or eggnog ice
    cream
Nutmeg

Beat egg whites to soft peaks and set aside. Beat egg yolks; gradually beat in sugar. Slowly add milk and mix until well blended. Add sherry or rum flavoring. Fold yolk mixture into egg whites. Pour mixture into punch bowl. Float scoopfuls of ice cream on top. Slowly pour in chilled lemon-lime carbonated beverage and sprinkle top with nutmeg. Serves 25.

HOT CRANBERRY PUNCH

2 c. boiling water
3 c. sugar
2 c. orange juice
2 c. lemon juice

2 pt. bottles cranberry juice
8 tea bags
2 qt. boiling water

Pour 2 cups boiling water over tea bags and steep for 5 minutes. Dissolve sugar in 2 quarts boiling water. Combine and add the remainder of juices. Serve hot. Serves 30 persons.

HOT FRUIT PUNCH

3 c. unsweetened
  pineapple juice
1 (12 oz.) can apricot
  nectar

3 c. apple juice
1 c. orange juice
6 cinnamon sticks
10 whole cloves

Combine ingredients and heat to boiling. Simmer 15 to 20 minutes. Strain, serve hot.
Kathy Bischof, St. Cloud, Mn.

HOT FRUIT PUNCH

3 pt. canned apple juice
3 inch stick cinnamon
1 tsp. nutmeg
1/2 c. sugar

2 (1 pt. 2 oz.) cans pineapple
  juice
1 (46 oz.) can orange juice
2 medium oranges
30 whole cloves

Simmer apple juice and spices 20 minutes. Add sugar and remaining juices. Stud oranges with cloves and add to punch. Heat, but do not boil. Fill heated punch bowl. Makes about 25 servings.

MAI-TAI PUNCH

2 (12 oz.) cans frozen
  orange juice
2 (12 oz.) cans frozen
  pink lemonade

2 (12 oz.) cans frozen limeade
1 qt. vodka
1 pt. light rum
1 qt. Mai-Tai mix

Add required water to the frozen concentrates. Add liquor and Mai-Tai Mix. Makes enough for 2 punch bowls.
1748-81   Carolyn Brudevold, Fargo, N. D.   595

PARTY PUNCH

2 recipes (including sugar and water) strawberry Kool-Aid
2 (8 oz.) cans frozen orange juice and 3 cans water
2 (8 oz.) cans frozen lemonade and 3 cans water
2 (46 oz.) cans pineapple-grapefruit juice
1 bottle maraschino cherries and juice (optional)
2 large bottles ginger ale

Mix all ingredients (except ginger ale) at least 4 hours before serving. Chill. Add ginger ale. Pour over ice ring. Serves 50.

Kathy Neels, St. Cloud, Mn.

EASY PARTY PUNCH

2 pkg. Kool-Aid (raspberry)
2 c. sugar
2 qt. water
1 (46 oz.) can pineapple juice
1 qt. 7-Up or ginger ale

Mix Kool-Aid, sugar and water. Add pineapple juice. Chill. Pour over ice in punch bowl. Add chilled 7-Up or ginger ale last. Serve at once. Serves 50 (1/2 cups).

Norma Haugland, Fargo, N. D.

QUICK COOLER

1 1/2 Tbsp. instant coffee
3 c. cold milk
1/3 c. chocolate syrup
2 Tbsp. sugar
1 pt. vanilla ice cream

Combine instant coffee, milk, syrup and sugar and beat until blended. Pour into glasses and top with scoop of ice cream. Serves 4.

RASPBERRY FLOAT

3 pkg. raspberry flavored gelatin
4 c. boiling water
1 1/2 c. sugar
4 c. cold water
1/2 c. lime juice
2 1/4 c. orange juice
1 1/4 c. lemon juice
1 qt. bottle ginger ale
2 (10 oz.) pkg. frozen raspberries

Dissolve gelatin in boiling water; add sugar, cold water and juices; chill. When time to serve, pour punch into punch bowl. Add ginger ale and frozen raspberries. Stir until raspberries break apart and are partially thawed. Makes 4 quarts.

RHUBARB BEVERAGE

Cook rhubarb that has been covered with water, until tender. Strain juice. To each 4 cups juice, add 1/2 cup sugar and 1/2 cup pineapple juice. Bring to boil. Seal or chill.

CREME A RHUM

1 1/4 c. sugar
6 egg yolks
1 env. unflavored gelatin
1/8 tsp. salt
1 c. orange juice

1/2 c. white wine
1/4 c. cold water
1/4 c. lemon juice
3 Tbsp. rum
2/3 c. cream, whipped

In a double boiler, combine the sugar, egg yolks, salt, orange and lemon juices, wine and rum. Place over heat and beat continuously with an egg beater until foamy and thickened. Remove from heat and add gelatin which has been softened in the cold water. Cool until it is syrupy. Fold in the whipped cream. Pour into a well oiled quart mold and chill for at least 3 hours. Unmold and serve with whipped cream. Serves 6. This has a light, rather tart taste that is excellent after a heavy meal. Whole fresh strawberries are an attractive garnish. Other fruits may be used, if desired, such as sliced peaches or raspberries.

RUSSIAN TEA

1 c. instant tea
2 c. sugar
1 (3 oz.) pkg. Wyler's
  lemonade mix

1 tsp. cloves
2 tsp. cinnamon
1 (14 oz.) jar Tang*

*Half of a 27 ounce jar is 1 2/3 cups, which is 14 ounces.
Karen Rupert, St. Cloud, Mn.

TEA PUNCH

4 qt. water
3 c. sugar
2 (6 oz.) cans lemon juice
1 qt. apple juice

2 qt. cranberry juice
1 pt. orange juice
1 pt. strong black tea

Mix water and sugar and bring to boil. Combine with rest of ingredients. Mix well. Chill before using. Makes 2 gallons or 40 servings.

CHERRY OR BLUEBERRY PIE SHAKE

1 (#2) can (2 1/2 c.)
  cherry or blueberry pie
  mix

2 pt. vanilla ice cream
1 c. milk
4 tsp. lemon juice

Place pie filling, 3 cups ice cream, milk and lemon juice in mixer bowl. Blend well. Pour into 4 tall glasses (chilled). Top each with a scoop of remaining ice cream. To use blender, divide this recipe for 2 batches.

SLOE GIN FIZZ

1 Tbsp. sloe gin
1 Tbsp. half & half

1 Tbsp. Mr. T's sweet & sour
2 c. crushed ice

Put into blender, blend thoroughly (30 - 45 seconds). Pour into 12 ounce glass. Fill remainder of glass with club soda. Garnish with a cherry. Makes 1.
Connie Vivier, Fargo, N. D.

SLUSH

9 c. water

2 c. sugar

Bring to a boil and boil 20 minutes. Cool. Add:

1 (12 oz.) can frozen
  orange juice

1 (12 oz.) can frozen
  lemonade
2 c. vodka

Mix and put into freezer till ready to use. Will not freeze hard. When ready to use, add 1 quart 7-Up. Stir. Makes 13 cups.

598   Karen Rupert, St. Cloud, Mn.

APRICOT SLUSH

1 qt. apricot juice
1 qt. pineapple juice
1 (12 oz.) can frozen
  lemonade

1 (12 oz.) can frozen orange
  juice
1 pt. apricot brandy
1 c. vodka

Mix in ice cream bucket. Freeze. To serve - spoon 1/2 glass full with Squirt or 7-Up.

Lenora Buck, Fargo, N. D.

BRANDY SLUSH

7 c. water

2 c. sugar

Bring to boil. Add 4 tea bags for 5 minutes, cool. Add:

1 (12 oz.) can frozen
  orange juice

1 (12 oz.) can frozen
  lemonade

Mix together in 5 quart pail. Add 1 quart brandy. Freeze. Serve 1/3 glass slush. Add 7-Up.

LIME SLUSH

9 c. water

1 - 2 c. sugar

Bring to boil and cool. Add:

2 (6 oz.) cans frozen
  orange juice concentrate
2 c. tea (1 tea bag for
  each cup)

2 (6 oz.) cans frozen
  unsweetened lemon
  concentrate
2 1/2 c. vodka

Mix in an expandable container and freeze for at least 24 hours before serving. Beat frozen mixture to slush consistency with electric mixer. Spoon into glasses. Use half slush and half 7-Up or other. Freeze in 5 quart pail.

Sue Hick, Detroit Lakes, Mn.

LIME SLUSH

2 pkg. lemon-lime Kool-Aid   3 c. vodka
1 (48 oz.) can pineapple   2 c. sugar
   juice   2 qt. water

     Take from 2 quarts water - 2 cups water and bring to boil with sugar and Kool-Aid, stir well. Add rest of water, pineapple juice and vodka. Mix well. Freeze in 5 quart pail. Let freeze 1 day, then mix again and refreeze. Fill glass half full and add 7-Up.
                Mike and Vonnie Bakke, Willmar, Mn.

RHUBARB SLUSH

8 c. rhubarb   3 c. sugar
2 qt. water   1/2 c. lemon juice

     Cook till tender - then strain. Add:

1 small pkg. strawberry   2 c. vodka (optional)
   jello

     Freeze in ice cream pail. Scoop into glasses and add 7-Up or strawberry pop.
              Edie Lymburner, Park Rapids, Mn.

VODKA SLUSH

2 c. sugar   8 c. water

     Simmer 15 minutes. Add:

1 large can concentrated   1 large can concentrated
   orange juice   lemonade
                        2 c. vodka

     Mix together. Freeze in 5 quart ice cream pail - put in glass (half full), add 7-Up or club soda.
              A. T. Isakson, Fargo, N. D.

VODKA SLUSH

7 c. water   3 c. sugar

Bring to boil and cool. Boil 2 cups water, add 4 green tea bags and cool. Add:

1 (12 oz.) can frozen   1 (12 oz.) can frozen orange
  lemonade   juice, undiluted
3 c. vodka

Place in 5 quart ice cream pail. Add cooled tea, water and sugar water. Freeze. Dip in and scoop into glasses, add 7-Up and serve.

      Becky Neal, Sauk Centre, Mn.

SPICED TEA TREAT

Place in a saucepan:
6 tea bags   1/4 tsp. allspice
1/4 tsp. cinnamon   Dash of nutmeg

Add 2 1/2 cups boiling water. Cover. Allow to stand for 3 to 5 minutes; strain. Add 3/4 cup sugar. Stir until dissolved; cool. Add:

1/2 c. orange juice   1 c. grapefruit juice
1/3 c. lemonade   1 1/2 c. cold water

Mix well. Chill until ready to serve. Makes about 1 quart.

PEACH OR STRAWBERRY DAIQUIRI

1 small can frozen   3 fresh peaches, or
  lemonade   1 can frozen strawberries
1 Tbsp. Grenadine
  or powdered sugar

Using lemonade can to measure - add 3/4 to 1 can light rum. Begin blending. Add ice to fill blender.

      Mary Erickson, Detroit Lakes, Mn.

STRAWBERRY DAIQUIRIS

1 (6 oz.) can pink
  lemonade

1 pkg. frozen strawberries
1/2 c. white rum

Mix lemonade, strawberries and rum in blender - puree speed. Add ice, still pureeing, till blender full. Freeze and serve frozen.

Margaret G. Russek, Minneapolis, Mn.

STRAWBERRIES CARDINAL

1 1/2 qt. strawberries
1/4 to 1/3 c. sugar
1 (10 oz.) pkg. frozen
  raspberries, thawed

2 Tbsp. sugar
1 Tbsp. orange liqueur
1 tsp. fresh lemon juice

Wash berries, place on paper towels and pat dry. Leave small berries whole, slice the large ones into halves. Place in your prettiest bowl and sprinkle with 1/4 to 1/3 cup sugar. Stir lightly with rubber spatula. Cover and chill. In electric blender, blend the thawed raspberries with their juice at high speed until slightly frothy. Strain to remove seeds. Stir in orange liqueur and lemon juice. Cover and chill. Just before serving, ladle the sauce over the straw-berries. Use just enough to coat them lightly.

Marion Baihly

SUNRISE SPECIAL

1 banana, sliced
1 can frozen orange juice

1 egg
6 ice cubes, crushed

Combine all ingredients in a blender and mix until well blended.

SWEDISH RHUBARB WINE

7 lb. rhubarb

1 lb. raisins

Put into cheesecloth bag.

3 1/2 gal. water

14 lb. sugar

1/2 cake yeast	1/2 c. warm water

Dissolve yeast in water.

1 env. Knox gelatine	*1 lingenberry
1/2 c. cold water	

*If available, otherwise, forget it.

Dissolve gelatine in cold water. Mix all ingredients together in large crock. Put cheesecloth bag of rhubarb and raisins into crock and weigh down with plate or something heavy. Let stand for 2 weeks. Take bag out and let drip for one day. Siphon into gallon jugs. Let stand for 2 weeks and siphon again. Bottle. Wine is ready to drink.

Swede Fellman, Brainerd, Mn.

TOMATO JUICE

Wash and cook tomatoes. Sieve. In each quart jar, put the following:

1 tsp. salt	Short tsp. sugar
1/4 tsp. celery salt	

Place jars in pressure cooker for 5 minutes at 5 pounds pressure.

Mary Ann Hanson, Detroit Lakes, Mn.

WE THREE

3 c. sugar	Grated rind of 1 orange
3 c. water	Grated rind of 1 lemon
Juice of 3 oranges	1 (#2) can crushed pineapple
Juice of 3 lemons	

Boil sugar and water together 5 minutes and cool. Add strained fruit juice, rind and pineapple. Pour into pans and freeze. Requires no stirring while freezing.

Linnea Pajari, Detroit Lakes, Mn.

FIRE VODKA
(Krupnik)

1 1/2 c. honey
2/3 c. water
1 tsp. vanilla extract
1/4 tsp. nutmeg
8 sticks cinnamon

2 whole cloves
3 strips lemon peel, 2
   inches each
1 (4/5 qt.) bottle vodka

1. Combine honey with water, vanilla, spices and lemon peel in large saucepan. Bring to boil. Cover. Simmer 5 minutes. 2. Add vodka, remove from heat. 3. Serve hot or cooled. About 1 quart.
    Pat Bruchert, Minneapolis, Mn.

WASSAIL BOWL

2 qt. apple cider
2 c. sugar
2 tsp. whole allspice
2 tsp. whole cloves

6 cinnamon sticks
1 qt. cranberry juice
1 pt. orange juice
1 1/2 c. lemon juice

Combine cider and sugar in large pan. Tie spices in cheesecloth; add to cider. Cover; simmer 15 minutes. Remove spices; add remaining ingredients; simmer 10 minutes. Garnish with lemon and orange slices; serve hot. Makes about 1 gallon.

WATERMELON TO WATCH THE
HOPKINS RASPBERRY FESTIVAL PARADE BY

Discovered on a long-ago summer afternoon by a band of creative paradewatchers from the University of Minnesota.

1 watermelon

1 qt. (or more) vodka or
   grain alcohol

The day before the parade, cut a bunghole in the watermelon. Drain out some of the water. Pour in as much vodka or alcohol as the watermelon will receive. Replace the plug cut from the watermelon. Place it in the refrigerator or other cool place to chill overnight. Eat it while watching the parade, and you will realize why the Hopkins Raspberry Festival Parade is the greatest parade in the world.

CHILDRENS CRYSTAL GARDEN SOLUTION
(Fun to watch grow)

4 Tbsp. non-iodized salt   4 Tbsp. water
4 Tbsp. liquid bluing   1 Tbsp. ammonia

Spoon over bits of porous material - rock, board, sponge, charcoal, etc. Make sure solution covers bottom of container. Drip a little food coloring (1 or 2 colors) over garden.

Kathy Bischof, St. Cloud, Mn.

CHILDRENS PLAY DOUGH

1 c. salt   1 Tbsp. oil (use less oil in
1 c. water   the summer)
3 c. flour

Mix all ingredients together and store in airtight containers. May use food coloring for different colors.

Kathy Bischof, St. Cloud, Mn.

SWEETENED CONDENSED MILK

2 c. warm water   3/4 c. sugar
1 c. + 2 Tbsp. powdered milk

In double boiler dissolve milk in water, blend and add sugar. Stir till it starts to thicken (17 minutes). Cool. Equals 1 can. Use when cool.

HOMEMADE SWEETENED CONDENSED MILK

3 Tbsp. melted butter or   1 c. instant nonfat milk
   margarine   1/3 c. boiling water
2/3 c. sugar   Pinch of salt

Put into blender and process till smooth. It makes the same amount as the canned, and it can be used in any recipe calling for sweetened condensed milk. Keeps several weeks in refrigerator.

Darlene Lee, St. Cloud, Mn.

COUGH MEDICINE

Equal parts:
Honey   Brandy
Lemon juice (warm)

Georgine Isakson, Fargo, N. D.

FUDGESICLES

1 pkg. chocolate pudding   3 1/2 c. milk
   (not instant)   1/4 c. sugar

Mix well, cook as for pudding (won't thick like a pudding does). Put into Freeze Tups and freeze. Makes 18.

Karen Rupert, St. Cloud, Mn.

GRANOLA

5 c. old fashioned oatmeal   1 c. sunflower nuts
1 c. soya flour   1 c. dry milk
1 c. wheat germ   1 c. Wesson oil
1 c. almonds   1 c. honey
1 c. raisins   2 tsp. cinnamon

Mix and bake 60 minutes - in a covered pan. Stir every 15 minutes.

Esla Ditty, St. Cloud, Mn.

MARGE'S STUFFING

1 1/2 lb. loaf bread   1/4 c. minced onion
1/2 c. butter   2 Tbsp. poultry seasoning
1 Tbsp. salt   2 c. chopped celery (parboil)
1/4 tsp. white pepper

Toss lightly, but do not pack fowl.

Marge Johnson, Minneapolis, Mn.

ICE CUBES

1 pkg. raspberry Kool-Aid   1/2 c. sugar
  (or any flavor)   4 c. pineapple juice

    Put into 2 trays or ring mold. Serve with ginger ale or in any other punch.
                         Sharon Brogren, Willmar, Mn.

POPSICLES

1 pkg. jello   2 c. boiling water
1 pkg. Kool-Aid   2 c. cold water
1/2 c. sugar

    Dissolve jello, Kool-Aid and sugar in the boiling water, then add cold water. Put into Freeze Tups and freeze. Makes 18.
                        Karen Rupert, St. Cloud, Mn.

BAR B. Q. SAUCE

3/4 c. catsup   1/2 tsp. salt
1/2 c. water   1 tsp. paprika
2 Tbsp. vinegar   1 tsp. chili powder
2 Tbsp. Worcestershire   1 tsp. mustard seed
  sauce   1/2 c. brown sugar

    Simmer until thick.
                    Martie Athey, Detroit Lakes, Mn.

BAR B. Q. SAUCE

1/2 c. catsup   1/3 to 1/2 c. brown sugar
1/4 c. water   1 tsp. mustard
1/4 c. chopped onion   1/4 c. oil
1 1/2 Tbsp. Worcestershire   Garlic salt (to taste)
  sauce   Dash of Tabasco sauce

    Mix all and simmer 5 - 10 minutes.
                  Shirley Way, Minneapolis, Mn.

BARBECUE SAUCE

1 qt. catsup
1/4 c. A.1. Sauce
3/4 c. molasses
1/8 c. vinegar
1/4 c. oil

5/8 oz. liquid smoke
1/2 tsp. onion salt
1/4 c. brown sugar
1/2 bottle beer

Eileen Rekowski, St. Cloud, Mn.

BAR B. Q. SAUCE

3/4 c. catsup
1/2 c. water
2 Tbsp. vinegar
2 Tbsp. Worcestershire
sauce

1/2 tsp. salt
1 tsp. paprika
1 tsp. chili powder
1 tsp. mustard seed
1/2 c. brown sugar

Simmer until thick.
Martie Athey, Detroit Lakes, Mn.

BING CHERRY ICE CREAM SAUCE

2 c. pitted, quartered,
fresh sweet cherries
1/2 c. sugar
1/4 c. water

1/4 c. light corn syrup
2 Tbsp. cornstarch
2 Tbsp. cold water
1 Tbsp. lemon juice

Combine cherries, sugar, 1/4 cup water and corn syrup in saucepan. Blend cornstarch with 2 tablespoons water and add to cherry mixture. Cook over low heat, stirring constantly until thickened. Stir in lemon juice. Makes 2 cups. Add 1 tablespoon of rum, if desired.
Johanna Singewald, St. Paul, Mn.

COCKTAIL SAUCE
(For Seafoods and Vegetables)

Combine and chill thoroughly:

1/2 c. chile sauce
1/3 c. catsup

1/3 c. prepared horseradish
1 1/2 tsp. Worcestershire
sauce

Note: For a sharper sauce, add 1/4 teaspoon salt, 2 tablespoons lemon juice, dash of pepper and a few drops of Tabasco sauce.

Ralph Kulhanek, St. Paul, Mn.

CHOCOLATE SAUCE

2 sq. chocolate   2 Tbsp. butter

Melt together over low heat.

1 c. sugar   1 tsp. vanilla
1 small can Carnation milk

Add sugar to chocolate and butter, mix until all is mixed real well. Add Carnation milk, put back on stove and boil 1 minute. Add vanilla. Delicious on ice cream.

Mary Harlander, St. Cloud, Mn.

REGAL CHOCOLATE SAUCE

1/2 c. light corn syrup   3 sq. unsweetened chocolate
1 c. sugar   1 tsp. vanilla
1 c. water   1 c. evaporated milk

Combine syrup, sugar and water. Cook to soft ball stage (236°). Remove from heat. Add chocolate and stir until melted. Add vanilla. Slowly add evaporated milk and mix. Makes 3 1/2 cups.

Marge Johnson, Minneapolis, Mn.

CORDIAL FOR ICE CREAM

Put into 2 quart jar in this order during raspberry season:

1 c. sugar   1 c. raspberries
1 c. gin

Tip up and back every week. Use at Christmas.

HOMEMADE BAR-B-QUE SAUCE

1/2 c. oleo
4 tsp. liquid smoke
1/2 c. vinegar
2 tsp. mustard
1 tsp. pepper

4 Tbsp. Worcestershire sauce
1/2 c. honey
4 Tbsp. brown sugar
2 tsp. salt
1 1/2 c. catsup

Bring all ingredients to a boil. Simmer about 15 minutes. Makes about 1 quart. Will keep in the refrigerator for 3 - 4 weeks.
Jane Bohline, Minneapolis, Mn.

HOT FUDGE SAUCE

1 c. sugar
2 Tbsp. cornstarch

1 c. milk
2 Tbsp. cocoa (more if desired)

Stir together, boil till thick. Take off fire and add 2 tablespoons butter and 1 teaspoon vanilla
Karen Rupert, St. Cloud, Mn.

HOT FUDGE SAUCE

3 sq. chocolate

1/4 lb. butter

Melt and add:
1 c. sugar

1 can Carnation milk

Boil gently until thick. Serve warm. Refrigerate any left over.
Mrs. Ronald Schwartz, Owatonna, Mn.

HOT FUDGE SAUCE

1/2 c. butter
4 sq. unsweetened chocolate
1/2 tsp. salt

3 c. sugar
1 large can Carnation milk
1/2 tsp. vanilla

Melt butter and chocolate and salt in double boiler, add sugar, 1/2 cup at a time, blend after each. Add the milk slowly and mix in well. Add vanilla. Cook over medium heat, 10 - 15 minutes. Makes 3 cups of yummy hot fudge.
Gloria Bergson, Fargo, N. D.

MARINADE SAUCE

1 c. oil
1/2 c. lemon juice
3/4 c. soy sauce
1/4 c. prepared mustard

1/4 c. Worcestershire sauce
1 1/2 tsp. salt
1 tsp. pepper
1 tsp. garlic powder

Mix all together. Keeps for 3 months in the refrigerator. Marinate beef 48 hours in sauce.

Renee Ulberg, Bismarck, N. D.

FRESH MARINARA SAUCE

6 lb. (about 15 medium
   sized) ripe tomatoes
Boiling water
6 cloves garlic, pressed
   or minced
2 large onions, chopped
3 or 4 large carrots,
   finely chopped

1/3 c. oil
2 Tbsp. dried basil leaves or
   1/3 c. finely chopped fresh
   basil leaves
1 Tbsp. dried oreagno leaves
   or 3 Tbsp. finely chopped
   fresh oregano leaves
2 1/2 tsp. salt
3/4 to 1 tsp. pepper

Immerse tomatoes, a few at a time, in boiling water to cover, for about 1 minute. Lift them out with a slotted spoon and plunge into cold water. Peel skin. Coarsely chop tomatoes to get 11 to 12 cups. In a 5 quart or large kettle, cook the garlic, onion and carrots in the oil over medium heat, stirring occasionally until onions are translucent. Add the tomatoes, basil, oregano, salt and pepper. Bring to boil, lower heat and simmer rapidly, uncovered, stirring occasionally until sauce is very thick and reduced by about half, about 1 1/2 hours. Makes 1 1/2 to 2 quarts.

Jane M. Schumacher

RIB SAUCE

Brown 1 chopped onion in 2 tablespoons butter. Add:

1/4 c. vinegar
1/2 c. catsup
1/2 c. brown sugar
3 Tbsp. chili sauce

1 Tbsp. mustard
2 Tbsp. A.1. Sauce
Juice of 1 lemon

Mix together. Good on spareribs, adding to the ribs during the last 1/2 hour of baking.

1748-81   Jean Taylor, Grand Forks, N. D.

SPAGHETTI SAUCE

1 1/2 lb. veal and ground beef
1 (46 oz.) can tomato juice
3 cans (3 lb.) tomatoes
2 c. celery, chopped
1/2 c. green pepper, chopped
1 whole fresh garlic

1/2 c. onion, chopped
1 Tbsp. salt
1 tsp. curry powder
1 Tbsp. chili powder
1/4 tsp. cayenne pepper
1/2 tsp. oregano
Paprika to color and any other spice you like
Mushrooms (as any as you like)

Brown meat and onion, add celery, pepper, garlic and the rest of the ingredients and let simmer a couple of hours.
Lydia Skaret, Austin, Mn.

TERIYAKI SAUCE
(Marinade for steak or chicken)

1 can beef broth
1/2 c. dry red or white wine
1/3 c. soy sauce
1 1/2 tsp. seasoned salt

1/4 c. chopped green onion tops
1 clove garlic, finely minced
3 Tbsp. lime juice
2 Tbsp. brown sugar or honey

Mix all together and pour over meat.
Dee Olson, St. Paul, Mn.

WAIKIKI ROOM RIB SAUCE
(Excellent with boneless pork roast as appetizer)

For years the denizens of the Waikiki Room in the Nicollet Hotel turned coy whenever I asked them for the makeup of the barbecue sauce on their incomparable Cantonese ribs. After some experimenting, however, I came close, and the maitre d'hotel finally tipped me off to the one necessary ingredient I was leaving out.

1/2 c. brown sugar
1/2 c. soy sauce
1/2 c. honey
1 piece fresh ginger about the size of a walnut

1/2 c. catsup
1/4 tsp. pepper
1 clove garlic

Shoosh everything together in an electric blender. Or, else grate the ginger and garlic and mix everything together. Rub spareribs first with Chinese seasoning salt - 6 teaspoons salt, 1 teaspoon Chinese spice powder, 1/2 teaspoon monosodium glutamate, mixed together - and then marinate them in a shallow dish or pan in the sauce above. While barbecuing, baste them frequently with the sauce. During the last 5 or 10 minutes of barbecuing, baste them with honey or sprinkle them with sugar for a glazed finish. Sauce is sufficient for 3 to 5 pounds of spareribs.

For double recipe: 1/4 to 1/2 teaspoon each anise seed, cinnamon, ground cloves, fennel, Schwann pepper. Do not use all, rub meat and discard balance.

Footnote: Try barbecuing or baking pork chops basted with this sauce, and you may never eat pork chops any other way again. Also a good sauce for barbecuing slices of pork rump.

WHITE SAUCE BASE

2 Tbsp. butter or margarine	1/2 tsp. Tabasco pepper
2 Tbsp. flour	sauce
1/4 tsp. salt	1 c. milk

Melt butter or margarine in saucepan over low heat Blend in flour, salt and pepper sauce. Gradually stir in milk. Cook over medium heat, stirring constantly until sauce thickens and comes to a boil. Simmer 1 minute, continuing to stir. This recipe makes about 1 cup.
Arlene Jewell, Bismarck, N. D.

BEER BATTER
(This one's not Polish!)

1 c. flour	1 tsp. baking powder
1/2 tsp. baking soda	1/2 tsp salt

Mix together and add:

2 beaten eggs	3/4 c. beer
1 c. sour cream	

Good with fish, onions, mushrooms and other fresh vegetables!!!
Patty Ginter, St. Cloud, Mn.

** NOTES **

INDEX OF RECIPES

APPETIZERS, PICKLES, RELISHES

Braunschweiger Ball
Braunschweiger Loaf - - - - - - 3

Braunschweiger Spread
Caramel Corn
Caramel Corn
Caramel Popcorn - - - - - - - - 4

Caramel Corn
Baked Caramel Corn
Baked Caramel Popcorn - - - - 5

Microwave Caramel for Popcorn
Old Fashion Caramel Corn
Oven Caramel Corn - - - - - - - 6

Rainbow Gelatin Popcorn Balls
Cheese Puffs
Hot Sausage and Cheese Puffs - 7

Olive Cheese Puffs
Cream Cheese Ball
Crab Ball - - - - - - - - - - - 8

Ham Ball
Hot Crabmeat Appetizer
Don's Wife's Yummy Cheese
   Ball - - - - - - - - - - - - 9

The Best Cheese Ball
Cheese Ball
Cheese Ball - - - - - - - - - 10

Cream Ball
Pineapple Cheese Ball
Snow Ball Cheese Ball
Caramelized Chicken Wings - - 11

36 Chicken Wings
Marinated Chicken Wings
Chopped Beef Spread - - - - - 12

Cocktail Meat Balls
Whipped Hamburger Balls
Fruta de Compota - - - - - - - 13

Authentic Swiss Fondue
Chicken Liver Pate - - - - - - 14

Chicken Liver Pate
Liverwurst Ball
Liver Spread - - - - - - - - - 15

Nuts and Bolts
Olive Liver Pate - - - - - - - 16

Pecan Spread
Pickled Gizzards
Salmon Party Ball - - - - - - 17

Saucy Fruit Cup
German Sauerkraut Balls
Shrimp Pu-Pu Hawaiian - - - - 18

Super, Super Bowl Sunday
   Snack
Woodchuck
Bean Dip - - - - - - - - - - 19

Bean Dip
Cheese Dip
Hot Cream Cheese Dip - - - - 20

Chili Tomato Sauce Dip
Crab Dip
Curry Dip
Hot Chipped Beef Dip - - - - 21

Dill Dip
Rose Nord's Dilly Dip
Hot Dip
Hot Mexican Dip - - - - - - - 22

Hot Mexican Dip
Party Dip
Hot Pecan Dip
Piquant Dip - - - - - - - - - 23

Shelia's Hot Cheese Dip
Shrimp Dip
Shrimp Dip - - - - - - - - - 24

Shrimp Dip
Pom Pom's Shrimp Dip
Raw Vegetable Dip - - - - - - 25

Shrimp Dip
Sourdough Dip
Spinach Dip
Spinach Dip - - - - - - - - - 26

Taco Dip
Ginny's Taco Dip
Taco Dip - - - - - - - - - - 27

Taco Dip
Taco Mexican Dip
Tucson Dip - - - - - - - - - 28

Vegetable Dill Dip
Vegetable Dip
Vegetable Dip
Vegetable Dip - - - - - - - - 29

Webster's Wacky Wombero Dip
Yvonne's "Hot" Cheese Dip
Dilled Pickled Beans
Beet Pickles - - - - - - - - - 30

Pickled Beets
Beet Pickles
Bread and Butter Pickles - - - 31

Bread and Butter Pickles
Bread and Butter Pickles
Bread and Butter Pickles - - - 32

Cucumber Slices
Especially Good Dill Pickles
Dill Pickles - - - - - - - - - 33

Dill Pickles
24 Hour Dill Pickles
Pickled Eggs - - - - - - - 34

Pickled Fish Recipe
Herring (Pickled Fish)
Pickled Fish - - - - - - - - - 35

Pickled Fish
Pickled Northern - - - - - - 36

Kosher Pickles
Kosher Sweet Pickles
Refrigerator Cucumbers - - - 37

Refrigerator Pickles
Refrigerator Pickles
Apple Relish - - - - - - - - - 38

Beet Relish
Carrot Relish
Green Tomato Relish - - - - - 39

Quick Corn Relish
Sherries Relish
Sweet Tomato Relish - - - - - 40

SOUPS, SALADS, VEGETABLES

Borsch
Bouja
Cauliflower Soup - - - - - - - 43

Christmas Eve Oyster Stew
Clam Chowder - - - - - - - - 44

Easy Clam Chowder
Cream of Cauliflower Soup - - 45

Cream of Potato Soup
Czech Cabbage Soup - - - - 46

Diet Cabbage Soup
Easter Soup
Finn Soup - - - - - - - - - 47

German Potato-Bean Soup
Hamburger Soup
Minestrone Soup - - - - - - 48

Ox-Tail Soup
Split Pea Soup
Tomato Soup - - - - - - - - 49

Apple Cheese Salad
Apricot Jello Salad
Apricot Salad - - - - - - - 50

Avocado Shrimp Boat
Bean Salad
3 Bean Salad - - - - - - - - 51

Blueberry Jello Mold
It's the Berries - Blueberry
   Salad
Broccoli and Cauliflower Salad
Butter Pecan's Salad - - - - 52

Cabbage Salad
Cauliflower-Broccoli Salad
Cauliflower-Broccoli Salad - - 53

Cheese Pineapple Salad
It's the Berries - Cherry Salad
Cherry Salad
Chicken Salad - - - - - - - 54

Citrus Salad
Cole Slaw
Favorite Slaw
Hot Slaw - - - - - - - - - - 55

Cranberry Salad
Cranberry Marshmallow Salad
Frozen Cranberry Salad - - - 56

Creamy Fruit Salad
Crisp Macaroni Salad
Christmas Cranberry Salad - - 57

Christmas Ribbon Salad
Cucumber Onion Jello Mold
Dayton's Hot Turkey Salad - - 58

Delicious Salad
Easy Summer Salad
Fluffy Gelatin Salad - - - - 59

Fruit Salad
Fruited Cheese Salad
Fruit Salad - - - - - - - - 60

Frozen Cabbage
Frozen Cranapple Salad
Frozen Fruit Cup - - - - - - 61

Frozen Cherry Salad
Frozen Grape Salad
Green Salad Mold- ~ ~ ~ ~ ~ ~   62

Green Vegetable Salad Mold
Ice Cream Fruit Salad
Layered Delight Salad ~ ~ ~ ~   63

Layered Lettuce Salad
Layered Lettuce Salad ~ ~ ~ ~   64

24-Hour Salad
24 Hour Layer Salad
7 Layer Salad ~ ~ ~ ~ ~ ~ ~ ~   65

Make Ahead Lettuce Salad
Lemon Filling Salad ~ ~ ~ ~ ~   66

Lemon Jello Salad
Macaroni Salad
Hearty Macaroni Salad ~ ~ ~ ~   67

Mandarin Duet Salad
Marinated Vegetable Salad ~ ~   68

Mock Chicken Salad
Molded Chicken Salad (or
    Tuna) - - - ~ ~ ~ ~ ~ ~ ~   69

Mom's Wilted Lettuce
Oriental Salad - - ~ ~ ~ ~ ~   70

Overnight Fruit Salad
Overnight Salad
Overnight Fruit Salad ~ ~ ~ ~   71

Overnight Fruit Salad
Easy Orange Salad
Frozen Pea Salad
Pea Salad ~ - ~ ~ ~ ~ ~ ~ ~   72

Pineapple Glow Salad
Pistachio Salad
Pistachio Salad ~ ~ ~ ~ ~ ~   73

Charlies Cafe Potato Salad
German Potato Salad
Hot German Potato Salad - ~ ~   74

Potato Salad
Potato Salad Western Style - ~   75

Sour Cream Potato Salad
Pretzel Jello Salad
Prune Salad - ~ - ~ ~ ~ ~ ~   76

Purple Passion Salad
Quick Apricot Fruit Salad
Easy Quick Salad ~ ~ ~ ~ ~   77

Quick Fruit Salad
Quick Tomato Aspic Salad
Raspberry Salad- - - - ~ ~ ~   78

Raspberry-Applesauce Mold
Raw Vegetable Salad
Rhubarb Salad - - - ~ ~ ~ ~   79

Seafoam Salad
Seafood Salad
San Francisco Salad
Shrimp Cauliflower Salad - -   80

Shrimp Salad
Shoestring Salad
Spinach Salad with Hot Bacon
    Dressing - - - - ~ ~ - ~   81

Spring Salad
Sunshine Salad
Taco Salad - - ~ ~ ~ ~ ~ ~   82

Taco Salad
Taco Salad
Taco Salad - - - ~ ~ ~ ~ ~   83

Tapioca Jello Salad
Tbula Salad
24 Hour Salad - - - - ~ ~ ~   84

Tuna Fish Salad
Vegetable Salad
Vegetable Salad - - - ~ ~ ~ ~   85

24 Hour Vegetable Salad
Molded Waldorf Salad
Watergate Salad
Watergate Salad - - ~ ~ ~ ~ ~   86

Yum Yum Salad
Anyday Dressing
Banana Cream Dressing - ~ -   87

Cole Slaw Dressing
Cole Slaw Dressing
Cottage Cheese Salad Dressing
French Dressing - - - - ~ ~ ~   88

French Dressing
French Dressing
French Dressing
French Dressing - - - ~ ~ ~ ~   89

Fruit Salad Dressing
Glaze for Ham
Hubble House Dressing
Marinated Vegetables - - ~ ~   90

Mock Sour Cream
Orange Cream Cheese Salad
Papaya Seed Dressing
Potato Salad Dressing - - - ~   91

Dressing for Potato Salad
Lem'n Lime Seafood Dressing
Delicious Salad Dressing
Zippy Salad Dressing - - - - 92

Dressing for Slaw
Thousand Island Dressing - - 93

Thousand Island Dressing
Thousand Island Dressing
Western Dressing
Baked Corn - - - - - - - - - 94

Baked Vegetable Dish
Barbequed Beans
Bar-B-Q Beans in Crock Pot
Bean Bake - - - - - - - - 95

"Beans"
Baked Beans - - - -   - - 96

Baked Beans
Baked Beans
Baked Beans - - - , 97

Baked Beans Supreme
Bean Bake - - - - - - - - 98

Easy Baked Beans
Calico Beans
Calico Beans - - - - - - - - 99

Calico Beans
Campers Beans
Different Calico Beans - - - - 100

Marge Pye's Baked Beans
Old Settlers Beans
Baked Bean and Sausage
    Casserole - - - - - - - - - 101

Beets in Orange Sauce
Harvard Beets
Cheese-Broccoli Side Dish - - 102

Broccoli-Corn
Broccoli Rice
Baked Cabbage Puff - - - - - 103

Cabbage Rolls
Frozen Cabbage
Cabbage Slaw - - - - - - - - 104

Carrots au Gratin
Marinated Carrots - - - - - - 105

Cauliflower and Green Beans
    Curry
Exotic Celery
Corn Souffle - - - - - - - - 106

Corn Stuffing Balls
Baked Corn
Corn Pie (Vegetable) - - - - - 107

Baked Cranberries
Creamy Cukes
Cucumbers
Cucumbers in Sour Cream - - 108

Danish Cucumbers
Domates Yemistes - - - - - - 109

Supreme French Style Green
    Beans
Herb Buttered Green Beans
Tangy Green Beans
Guacamole - - - - - - - - - 110

Stewed Tomato Salad
Marinated Carrots
Marinated Tomatoes - - - - - 111

Marinated Vegetables
Mushroom Dish
Mushrooms with Madeira - - - 112

Polish Wild Mushrooms with
    Onions
Stuffed Mushrooms - - - - - - 113

Onions
Butter Sauteed Onions
Festive Filled Onions - - - - - 114

Onion Pie
Easy au Gratins
Cheese Potatoes - - - - - - - 115

Hash Browns
Hash Brown Potatoes
Deluxe Hash Browns - - - - - 116

Deluxe Hash Browns
Onion and Butter Potatoes
Oooh-la-la Potatoes
Oriental Pick-Up Sticks - - - 117

Baked Hash Brown Potatoes
Vegetables - Czech Potatoes
    and Barley
Party Potatoes - - - - - - - 118

Patio Potatoes
Pizza Potatoes
Roadside Potatoes - - - - - - 119

Scalloped Potatoes
Scalloped Potatoes - - - - - - 120

Sweet Potatoes
Quick Quiche
Curried Rice - - - - - - - - - 121

Green Rice
Italian Rice
Parmesan Rice
Wild Rice Stuffing - - - - - - 122

German Scalloped Sauerkraut
German Sauerkraut - - - - - 123

Fiesta Onions
Stuffed Peppers for Two
Marinated Vegetables - - - - 124

Easy Garden Vegetable Pie
Vegetable Medley - - - - - - 125

Fire and Ice Tomatoes
Scalloped Carrots
Tomato Pie - - - - - - - - 126

Tomatoes Vinaigrette
Skillet Zucchini - - - - - - 127

MAIN DISHES

Menu
Caldo Verde
Alcatra - - - - - - - - - 129

Fruta de Compota
Baked Steak - - - - - - - - 130

Beef Burgundy
Beef Jerky
Beef and Olive Ragout - - - - 131

Beef Oriental
Beef Stroganoff - - - - - - 132

Beef Stroganoff
Chopped Beef Stroganoff
Beef Tostada Pie - - - - - - 133

Enchilada Sauce and Enchiladas
Filet de Boeuf en Croute
  "Excellence" - - - - - - - 134

Best Roast Beef in the
  World - - - - - - - - - 135

Butter Basted Rump Roast
Children's Party Bar-B Cups - 136

Delectable Pot Roast
Deviled Swiss Steak
Dinner on a Bun - - - - - - 137

Fleishkuhle
German Meat and Sauerkraut - 138

Giant Burger
Greek Beef and Noodles
Hamburger Deluxe - - - - - - 139

Hamburger Heaven
Hamburger Stroganoff
Hamburger Stroganoff - - - - 140

Hamburger Noodle Stroganoff
Hamburger Pie
Hard Tack
Hot Corned Beef Barbecue - - - 141

House of Schwarzenberg Pot
  Roast
Impossible Hamburger Pie - - - 142

Italian Beef Roast
Italian Delight - - - - - - - 143

Iva Blehr's Beef in Sherry
Jellied Corned Beef
Kau Kau Beef - - - - - - - 144

Krautwickel
Perfect Standing Rib Roast
Italian Steak - - - - - - - 145

Lamb Paprika Blintzes - - - - 146

Open-Faced Pizzaburger
Pepper Steak
Pepper Steak - - - - - - - 147

Pheasant la Chasseur
Pizza Roll
Roast Bear - - - - - - - - 148

Roast Wild Duck Provencale - - 149

Sauerbraten - - - - - - - 150

Sherried Wild Rice Stuffing
Souper Skillet Pasta
Spanish Rice with Ground
  Beef - - - - - - - - - 151

Super Nachos - - - - - - - 152

Surprise Hamburger
Sweet and Sour Meat - - - - 153

Taco Mix Pie Bake
Shish Kabobs
Teriyaki Shish Kabobs - - - - 154

Teriyaki Steak
Veal in Wine with Mushrooms - - 155

Wild Rice and Steak Dish
Wrapped Roast
Yukamush - - - - - - - - 156

Bacon and Eggs Breakfast
Breakfast Casserole
Breakfast Egg Dish - - - - - - 157

Breakfast Souffle
Eggs and Ham for Brunch
Egg Omelet - - - - - - - - - 158

Egg and Sausage Casserole
Mary Jane's French Toast
French Toast Dolls - - - - - - 159

Granola
Ham and Egg Brunch
Maria's Egg Dish - - - - - - - 160

Best Pancakes You Ever Ate
Bon Appetit Blueberry
    Pancakes - - - - - - - - 161

Fleiskpankaka
Old Fashioned Buckwheat Cakes
Ugnspankaka - - - - - - - - 162

Oven Baked Pancakes
Pancakes
Pancakes
Pletts - - - - - - - - - - - 163

Speedy Potato Pancakes
3 Week Pancakes - - - - - - - 164

Sausage Souffle
Scotch Eggs
Sunday Breakfast Casserole - 165

Cranberry-Nut Waffles
Waffles with Ham Applesauce - 166

Sour Cream Waffles
Corn Fritters
Cabbage Rolls - - - - - - - - 167

Chinese-Style Dinner with
    Cabbage and Rice
Golabki - - - - - - - - - - 168

Kaldomar
Kielbasa Polska and Cabbage - 169

Stuffed Cabbage
Baked Bean and Sausage
    Casserole - - - - - - - - 170

Baked Cabbage Casserole
Beef Stew Casserole
Broccoli Casserole - - - - - 171

Broccoli Casserole
Broccoli Casserole
Broccoli Casserole - - - - - - 172

Broccoli Casserole
Brunch Casserole - - - - - - 173

Cabbage Casserole
Carrot Casserole
Carrot and Onion Casserole - - 174

Casserole Meat Balls
Casserole Potatoes
Celery Casserole - - - - - - - 175

Cheesy Turkey Casserole
Chicken Casserole
Chicken Casserole - - - - - - 176

Chicken Casserole
Chicken Casserole
Chicken or Crabmeat
    Casserole - - - - - - - - - 177

Chicken Curry Casserole
Chinese Seafood Casserole - - 178

Company Casserole
Crabmeat Casserole
Crown Casserole - - - - - - - 179

Double Shrimp Casserole
Egg Casserole
Easy Scalloped Ham
    Casserole - - - - - - - - 180

Enchilada Casserole
Fluffy Potato Casserole - - - - 181

Green Bean Casserole
Ground Beef Casserole
Herb Spinach Casserole - - - - 182

Low Cal Vegetable Casserole
Marge's Vegetable Casserole - 183

Meat Loaf Casserole
Mexican Casserole - - - - - - 184

Oven Croquettes
Party Casserole
Pizza Casserole - - - - - - - 185

Pork Chop Casserole
Pork Chop and Rice Casserole - 186

Potato Casserole
Potato Casserole
Reuben Casserole
Rice-Broccoli Casserole - - - - 187

Rice Casserole
Rice Casserole - - - - - - - - 188

Salmon Casserole
Sauerkraut Casserole
Sauerkraut-Meat Casserole - - 189

Seafood Casserole
Sharon's Hash Brown Casserole
Shipwreck Casserole - - - - - 190

Stuffed Steak Casserole
Summer Squash Casserole
Summer Yellow Squash
    Casserole - - - - - - - - - 191

Super Supper Casserole
Swedish Baked Rice Casserole- 192

Sweet Potato Casserole
Taco Casserole   - - - - - - - 193

Tricky Turkey Casserole
Tuna Casserole
Tuna Cashew Casserole - - - - 194

Vegetable Casserole
Wild Rice Amandine en
    Casserole
Wild Rice Casserole
Wild-Rice-Chicken Casserole - 195

Wild Rice Casserole
World's Fair Casserole - - - - 196

Zucchini Vegetable Casserole
Toasty Cheese Bake
Triple Cheese Bake   - - - - - 197

Baked Chicken Dish
Cheesy Chicken
Chicken Allison
Chicken Baked with
    Barbecue Sauce - - - - - - 198

Chicken Breasts in Sour Cream
Chicken Breasts in Wine
Chicken Canapes - - - - - - 199

Chicken Caneloni
Chicken in the Chips - - - - - 200

Chicken Delight
Chicken Delight
Chicken Divine - - - - - - - 201

Chicken in a Dish
Chicken Gourmet - - - - - - 202

Chicken Kiev
Chicken Kiev - - - - - - - - 203

Chicken Continental
Chicken Loaf
Chicken and Rice - - - - - - 204

Chicken in Sour Cream with
    Dumplings
Chicken on Sunday
Chicken Supreme - - - - - - 205

Chicken and Wild Rice
Chicken and Wild Rice- - - - - 206

Chinese Chicken
Chinese Chicken - - - - - - 207

Chow Mein
Chow Mein
Chicken Chow Mein - - - - - 208

Marty's Pork Chow Mein
Cream Baked Chicken - - - - 209

Deluxe Baked Chicken
Festival Chicken Spaghetti
Fluffy Rice and Chicken- - - - 210

Oven Baked Chicken
Oven Baked Chicken
Luau Chicken with Rice
Pressed Chicken Loaf - - - - - 211

Sweet and Sour Chicken
Sweet 'n Sour Drumsticks - - - 212

Sweet-Sour Chicken Wings
Don's Chili
Chili - - - - - - - - - - - 213

Chili
Cincinnati Chili
Texas Chile - - - - - - - - 214

Chop Suey
Oven Chow Mein
Caraway Dumplings - - - - - 215

Fahey's Noodles
Potato Dumplings
Polish Dumplings - - - - - - 216

Polish Raw Potato Dumplings
Kartoflane Kluski
Noodle Kueggel - - - - - - 217

German Spaetzle
Anchovy Stuffed Eggs
Savory Swiss Eggs - - - - - 218

Shirred Eggs in Tomatoes
Scrambled Supremely
Baked Ludefisk
Baked Northern - - - - - - 219

Baked Torsk
Chinese Seafood - - - - - - 220

Clam Chowder
Cottage Cheese Salmon Loaf
Crab Fu Yung - - - - - - - 221

Different Fried Fish
Fish Cakes - - - - - - - - - 222

Fiesta Fillets
Fillets Baked with Sour Cream
Fish Patties - - - - - - - - 223

Juicy Shrimp Skillet
Perch Parmigiana - - - - - - 224

Poor Man's Lobster
Ribbon Salmon Bake
Salmon Ball - - - - - - - - 225

Salmon Loaf
Salmon Loaf
Scalloped Oysters - - - - - - 226

Seafood Thermidor
Shrimp Fried Rice
Shrimpalaya - - - - - - - - 227

Shrimp and Pea Pods
Stuffed Shells Neopolitan - - - 228

Susie's Fish Supreme
Tangy Tuna Mousse Squares
Trout Barbecue - - - - - - 229

Tuna Biscuit Roll
Tunaburgers
Tunaburgers - - - - - - - - 230

Tuna Cheese Bake
Tuna Flying Saucers
Tuna Supreme - - - - - - - 231

Vinha Dalhos
Far Eastern Frankfurters - - - 232

Lollipop Franks
Chinese Fried Rice
Rice and Cheese Dish - - - - - 233

Rice Pilaf
Hungarian Goulash with
    Sauerkraut - - - - - - - 234

German Goulash
Carnival Ham a la King - - - - 235

Ham (Cured Pork) Hash
Ham Loaf
Sauerkraut Ham Balls - - - - 236

Sherried Ham in Cream
Swedish Ham Balls - - - - - 237

Bran-Burger Biscuit Hot Dish
Broccoli Hot Dish
Broccoli Hot Dish - - - - - - 238

Broccoli Hot Dish
Broccoli Hot Dish
Broccoli-Cheese Hot Dish - - - 239

Chicken-Asparagus Hot Dish
Chinese Shrimp Hot Dish - - - 240

Chow Mein Hot Dish
Chow Mein Rice Hot Dish
Corned Beef Hot Dish - - - - - 241

Cabbage Hot Dish
Chicken Hot Dish
Chicken Hot Dish - - - - - - 242

Raw Macaroni Chicken Hot Dish
Chow Mein Hot Dish
Chow Mein Hamburger
    Hot Dish - - - - - - - - 243

Chow Mein Hot Dish -
    Mock Chop Suey
Chow Mein Hot Dish
Corned Beef Hot Dish
Corned Beef Hot Dish - - - - 244

Country Pie
Crab and Shrimp Hot Dish
Creole Jumbo Hot Dish - - - - 245

Delish Hot Dish
Far East - Celery Hot Dish
Favorite Minnesota Hot Dish - - 246

Fried Noodle Hot Dish
"4H" Hot Dish
Ground Beef Hot Dish - - - - 247

Hamburger Hot Dish
Hearty Beef 'n Cheese
    Crescent Pie - - - - - - - - 248

Hot Dish
Hot Dish
Hot Dish - - - - - - - - - - 249

Italian Hot Dish
Mexican Hot Dish
Mexican Zucchini Hot Dish - - 250

Mystery Hot Dish
Pioneer Hot Dish
Pizza Hot Dish - - - - - - - 251

Pizza Hot Dish
Rice Hot Dish
Rice Hot Dish - - - - - - - - 252

Rice Hot Dish
Round Steak Hot Dish
Sauerkraut Hot Dish - - - - - 253

Seafood Hot Dish
Soup Hot Dish
Steak Hot Dish - - - - - - - - 254

Taco Hot Dish
Tasty Hot Dish
Tater Tot Hot Dish - - - - - - 255

Three Bean Hot Dish
Trailer and Campers Pork
    Chow Mein
Tuna or Chicken Hot Dish - - 256

Tuna Hot Dish
Wild Rice Hot Dish
Wild Rice, Pork and Veal
    Hot Dish - - - - - - - - - 257

Zucchini Hot Dish
Liver, Onions and Mushrooms
    in Wine Sauce
Liver and Gravy - - - - - - - 258

Baked Lasagne
Best Lasagna in the World - - 259

Lasagne
Lasagne
Lasagna - - - - - - - - - - 260

Lasagna
Lasagne - - - - - - - - - - 261

Lasagna
Zucchini Lasagna - - - - - - 262

Fettuccine Alfredo - - - - - - 263

Manicotti
Rigatoni with Italian Sausage - 264

Spaghetti
Easy Spaghetti and Meat
    Balls - - - - - - - - - - 265

Irish - Italian Spaghetti
Italian Spaghetti and Meat
    Balls - - - - - - - - - - 266

Italian Spaghetti and Meat
    Balls - - - - - - - - - - 267

Mary's Italian Spaghetti
Sherry's German Spaghetti - - 268

Spaghetti Bravissimo
Foucault's Spaghetti Sauce
    Supreme
Italian Meat Sauce - - - - - 269
1748-81

Italian Spaghetti Sauce
Mary's Italian (Polish)
    Spaghetti Sauce - - - - - 270

Spaghetti Sauce
Spaghetti Sauce - - - - - - - 271

Spaghetti Sauce
Cold Beef Loaf
Dutch Meat Loaf - - - - - - 272

Herb and Tomato Meat Loaf
Lazy Day Meat Loaf
Meat Loaf - - - - - - - - - 273

Meat Loaf
Nordic Meat Loaf - - - - - - 274

Betty Cortright's Reuben
    Meat Loaf
Casserole Meat Balls
Hearty Sweet and Sour
    Meat Balls - - - - - - - 275

Hungarian Veal Balls
Cocktail Meat Balls - - - - - 276

Cocktail Meat Balls
Meat Balls
Parisian Meat Balls - - - - - 277

Meat Balls
Meat Balls and Gravy
Meat Balls in Potato Cups - - - 278

Potatoes and Meat Balls
Russian Meat Balls - - - - - 279

Swedish Meat Balls
Swedish Meat Balls - - - - - 280

Sweet and Sour Meat Balls
Swedish Meat Balls
Swedish Meat Balls - - - - - 281

Swedish Meat Balls
Swedish Meat Balls
Tiny Swedish Meat Balls - - - 282

Sweet and Sour Meat Balls
Sweet and Sour Meat Balls - - 283

Pierogi - - - - - - - - - - 284

Deep Dish Pizza
Joe's Taco Pizza - - - - - - 286

Hot Sauce
Pizza Dough
Pizza Noodle Bake - - - - - 287

Mini-Pizzas
Pizza - - - - - - - - - - - 288
623

Apple Glazed Roast
Creole Pork Chops - - - - - 289

Luxembourg Pork Chops
  and Sauerkraut
Mustard Glazed Pork Roast
Parmesan Breaded Pork
  Chops - - - - - - - - - - 290

Party Pork Chops
Pork Hawaiian
Pork Chops - Rice - - - - - - 291

Roast Pork - Dumplings and
  Sauerkraut - - - - - - - - 292

Barbecued Pork on Buns
Barbecued Ribs
Bar-B-Q Ribs - - - - - - - - 293

Oven Barbequed Ribs
Pork Loin with Cherry
  Almond Sauce
Wild Rice and Pork Chops - - - 294

Barbecue
Barbecue Beef
Barbecue Hamburger - - - - - 295

Barbecued Hamburgers
Crabbies
Club Sandwich - - - - - - - - 296

Corned Beef Supper Sandwich
Crescent Treat - - - - - - - 297

Easy Barbeque for Buns
Egg Salad Sandwich Supreme
Hawaiian Delight
Hot Chicken Sandwich - - - - 298

Hot Spam (or Ham) Sandwiches
Hungarian Sandwich Spread
Indian Tacos - - - - - - - - 299

Italian Beef Sandwiches
Koronis Barbeques
Pizza Buns - - - - - - - - - 300

Pizza Burgers
Pizza Burgers
Pizza Burgers - - - - - - - - 301

Sandwiches
Sloppy Joes
Sloppy Joes - - - - - - - - - 302

Sloppy Joes
Sloppy Joes
Sloppy Ottos
Spam Buns - - - - - - - - - - 303

Turkeyburger
Deer Sausage
Don's Summer Sausage - - - - 304

Head Cheese
Jambalaya
Potato Sausages - - - - - - - 305

Salomi
Sausage
Sausage Roll - - - - - - - - - 306

Summer Sausage
Summer Sausage
Grandma's Summer Sausage - - 307

Portuguese Green Beans
  with Sausage
Sauerkraut Pudding
Campers Stew - - - - - - - - 308

Five Hour Stew
Mexican Hamburger Stew
Mulligan Stew - - - - - - - - 309

Oven Beef Stew
South of Border Beef Stew
Stew - - - - - - - - - - - - 310

Sweet and Sour Beef Stew
Waldorf Astoria Beef Stew - - 311

The Count of Monte Cristo
Dayton's Hot Turkey Salad
Filetto di Tacchino con
  Formaggio - - - - - - - - - 312

Turkey Deluxe
Turkey Strata - - - - - - - - 313

Turkey Stroganoff
Welsh Rarebit - - - - - - - - 314

BREAD, ROLLS, PASTRY

Almond Bread
Swedish Apricot Nut Bread - - 315

Bacon Cheese Bread
Banana Bread
*Banana Bread - - - - - - - - 316

Banana Bread
World's Best Banana Bread
Banana Bread - - - - - - - - 317

Banana Bread
Banana Nut Bread
Banana Nut Bread - - - - - - 318

Beer Bread
Beer Bread
Caraway Rye - - - - - - - - 319

Chocolate Banana Loaf
Blueberry Banana Bread
Butter Brickle Bread - - - - - 320

Cinnamony Apple Roll
Hot Cheese Corn Bread
Cowboy Bread - - - - - - - - 321

Date-Cocoa Bread
Dilly Casserole Bread - - - - 322

English Muffin Bread
Geigol Bread - - - - - - - - 323

Mama's Gingerbread
Hobo Bread
Irish Soda Bread - - - - - - 324

Irish Soda Bread
Lemon Bread - - - - - - - - - 325

Lemon Bread
Old Fashioned Johnny Cake
Kamish - - - - - - - - - - - 326

Lemon Bread
Nut Roll
Nut Bread - - - - - - - - - - 327

Oatmeal Bread
Orange Cranberry Bread - - - 328

Orange Nut Bread
Poppy Seed Bread
Poppy Seed Bread - - - - - - 329

Peanut Butter Bread
Prune Nut Bread
Pumpkin Bread - - - - - - - 330

Rhubarb Bread
Rhubarb Bread - - - - - - - 331

Swedish Christmas Bread
Three Flour Bread
Whole-Wheat Brown Bread - - 332

Yulekage
Zucchini Bread - - - - - - - 333

Zucchini Bread
Zucchini Nut Bread
Zucchini-Pineapple Bread - - - 334

Zucchini Wheat Germ Bread
Beer Biscuits
Buttermilk Biscuits - - - - - 335

Homemade Biscuit Mix
Bun Recipe
Buns - - - - - - - - - - - - 336

Hamburger Buns
Jackie's Buns
Mom's Sweet Roll Dough - - - - 337

Ranch Style Biscuits
Grandma Eckert's Bismarks - - 338

Kraut Bruschke
Overnight Buns
Golden Raisin Buns - - - - - - 339

Taco Buns
Doughnuts That Never Fail
Baked Doughnuts - - - - - - 340

Fluffy Potato Doughnuts
Almond Puff - - - - - - - - - 341

Bran Flour Popovers
Danish Puff
Popovers of Gold - - - - - - - 342

Lefse
Lefsa
Lefse - - - - - - - - - - - 343

Salem Lutheran Church Lefse
Lefse
Lefse - - - - - - - - - - - - 344

Lefse
Bran Muffins - - - - - - - - 345

Cranberry Muffins
Cranberry Muffins and Glaze
Hawaiian Banana Muffins - - - 346

Icebox Muffins
Magic Muffins - - - - - - - - 347

Prune Muffins
Raisin Bran Muffins
Rhubarb Muffins - - - - - - - 348

6 Week Bran Muffins
Six Week Muffins - - - - - - - 349

Spicy Apple Muffins
Whole-Wheat Oatmeal Muffins
Zucchini Wheat Germ Muffins - 350

Zucchini and Wheat Germ
  Muffins
Butterscotch Ring
Caramel Rolls - - - - - - - - 351

Caramel Rolls in a Bundt Pan
Caramel Pecan Rolls - - - - - 352

Caramel Sweet Rolls
Frozen Bread Caramel Rolls
Frozen Bread Caramel Rolls - - 353

Cottage Cheese Pastry
Oatmeal Rolls - - - - - - - 354

Out of This World Rolls
Madeline's Brownies
Double Decker Brownies - - - 355

Pie Crust
Pie Crust - - - - - - - - - 356

Foolproof Pie Crust
Almond Crush Pineapple Pie - 357

Apple Pie in Bag
Apricot Puree Pie - - - - - 358

Bessie Pye's Pie Crust
Brandy Alexander Pie
Chocolate Chip Pie - - - - - - 359

Crazy Berry Blue Pie
Custard Pie with Coconut
French Silk Pie - - - - - - 360

Fudge Nut Pie
Fruit Cobbler Pie
Key Lime Pie - - - - - - - - 361

Lemon Filling
Lemon Sponge Pie
Margarita Pie - - - - - - - 362

Masterpiece Mincemeat
Meringue
Never-Fail Pie Meringue
Million Dollar Pie - - - - - - 363

Mock Apple Pie
Orange-Banana Cream Pie
Orange Petal Pie - - - - - - 364

Pecan Crunch Pie
Pecan Pie
Pecan Pumpkin Pie - - - - - 365

Magic Pumpkin Pie
Punch Pie Delight - - - - - 366

Refrigerator Pie
Creamed Rhubarb Pie
Rhubarb Custard Pie
Rhubarb Pie - - - - - - - - 367

Rhubarb Pie
Soda Cracker Pie
Sour Cream Pie - - - - - - 368

Sour Cream-Raisin Pie
Sour Cream Raisin Pie
Sour Cream Raisin Pie - - - - 369

Shortcut Cheese Pie
Strawberry Serenade Pie - - - 370

Skillet Peach Pie - - - - - - 371

Strawberry Pie
Gloria's Surprise Beauty Pie - 372

CAKES, COOKIES, DESSERTS

Almost-From-Scratch Rum
    Cake
Angel Food Delight
Apple-E-Spice Cake - - - - - 373

Applesauce Cake
Bakeless Cake - - - - - - - 374

Banana Split Cake
Banana Split Cake - - - - - 375

Banana Split Cake
Bohemian Coffee Cake - - - - 376

Boiled Raisin Cake
Butter Sponge Cake - - - - - 377

Carrot Cake
Carrot Cake
Carrot Cake - - - - - - - - 378

Carrot Cake
Cherry Glazed Pound Cake - - 379

Chocolate Cake
Chocolate Carrot Cake - - - - 380

Chocolate Chip-Date-Nut
    Cake
Chocolate Eclair Cake - - - - 381

Chocolate Oatmeal Cake
Chocolate Sauerkraut Cake
Chocolate Zucchini Cake - - - 382

Chocolate Zucchini Cake
Chocolate Zucchini Cake - - - 383

Chocolate Zucchini Cake
"Coke" Cake - - - - - - - - 384

Coca-Cola Cake
Cocoa-Cola Cake - - - - - - 385

Cranberry Cake
Crazy Cake
Crazy Chocolate Cake - - - - 386

Crazy Chocolate Cake
Creme de Menthe Cake
Danish Christmas Cake - - - - 387

Dark Fruit Cake
Devils Food
Eggless Cold Water
    Chocolate Cake - - - - - - 388

Easy Short Cake
Fresh Apple Cake
Fresh Peach Cake - - - - - - 389

Frozen Rhubarb Cake
Fruit Cake
Fruit-Cocktail Cake - - - - - 390

Gelatin Easter Eggs in Cake
    Nest
German Apple Bundt Cake - - 391

German Raw Apple Cake
German Summer Cake - - - - - 392

Heath Bar Cake or Dessert
Harvey Wallbanger Cake
Krum Kake - - - - - - - - 393

Krum Kake
Lemon Supreme Cake
Light Old Fashioned Fruit
    Cake - - - - - - - - - - 394

Magic Caramel Cake
Mandarin Orange Cake - - - - 395

Mexican Wedding Cake
Never Fail Sponge Cake - - - 396

Norwegian Dump Cake
Heath Bar Cake
Nut Cake - - - - - - - - - 397

Oatmeal Cake
Oatmeal Cake
Oatmeal Cake - - - - - - - - 398

Orange Cake
Peaches and Cream
    Cheesecake - - - - - - - 399

Pear Cake
Pineapple Dream Cake - - - - 400

Pineapple Refrigerator Cake
Plain Cake from an 1850
    Cookbook
Poke and Pour Cake - - - - - 401

Popcorn Cake
Popcorn Cake
Popcorn Cake - - - - - - - - 402

Popcorn Cake
Popcorn Cake
Poppy Seed Cake - - - - - - - 403

Poppy Seed Cake
Poppy Seed Cake
Poppy Seed Bundt Cake - - - - 404

Poppy Seed Torte Cake
Red Cake - - - - - - - - - - - 405

Rhubarb Bundt Cake
Raw Apple Cake - - - - - - - 406

Rhubarb Cake
Rhubarb Cake
Rhubarb Cake - - - - - - - - 407

Rhubarb Cake
Rhubarb Cake
Rhubarb Cake - - - - - - - - 408

Rhubarb Cake
Rhubarb Cake
Rhubarb Cake - - - - - - - - 409

Rhubarb Upside Down Cake
Upside Down Rhubarb Cake
Sheet Cake - - - - - - - - 410

Sis Bonnie's Kansas Cake
Spice Cake - - - - - - - - - 411

Strawberry Angel Cake
Strawberry Cake - - - - - - - 412

Strawberry What's It Cake
Streusel Coffee Cake
Texas Sheet Cake - - - - - - 413

Thanksgiving Fruit Cake
Tom Smith's Cake - - - - - - 414

Tutti Frutti Bundt Cake
Virginia's Date Cake - - - - - 415

Watergate Cake
Wedding Cake
Yellow Butter Cake - - - - - - 416

Zucchini Cake
Blueberry-Peach Coffee Cake - 417

Butterscotch Coffee Cake
Coffee Cake
Coffee Cake - - - - - - - - 418

Kuchen
Grandmother's Coffee Cake - - 419

Kuchen
Kuchen - - - - - - - - - - - 420

1748-81

Coffee Cake
Pineapple Orange Coffee Cake- 421

Cherry Coffee Cake
Coffee Cake
Cherry Coffee Cake ~ ~ ~ ~ ~ 422

Coffee Cake
Black Bottom Cupcakes - - - - 423

Cheese Cake Cupcakes
Filled Cupcakes
Mincemeat Cupcakes ~ - ~ ~ ~ 424

Peanut Butter Cupcakes
Self-Filled Cupcakes - - - - ~ 425

Self-Filled Cupcakes
Boiled Milk Frosting
Broiled Icing for Oatmeal
    Cake - - - - - - - - - - - 426

Caramel Frosting
Caramel Creme Frosting
Chocolate Frosting
Chocolate Frosting - ~ ~ ~ ~ ~ 427

Dressing for Angel Food Cake
Easy Cooked Chocolate
    Frosting
Fudge Frosting
Maple Frosting
Never Fail Frosting ~ ~ ~ ~ ~ 428

Never Fail Caramel Icing
Never-Fail Chocolate Fudge
    Frosting
Orange Sauce for Angel
    Food Cake ~ ~ ~ ~ ~ ~ ~ ~ 429

Quick Egg White Frosting
Quick Jello Frosting
Quick Caramel Frosting ~ ~ ~ 430

Sea Foam Fluffy Frosting
Silk and Gold Frosting
White Frosting
Almond Cookies ~ ~ ~ ~ ~ ~ ~ 431

Angel Cookies
Angel Cookies
Angel Crisps Cookies~ ~ ~ ~ 432

Animal Cookies
Apple Macaroons
Applesauce Cookies ~ ~ ~ ~ ~ 433

Banana Cookies
Blueberry Oatmeal Cookies ~ ~ 434

Brandy Snaps
Granny Rieder's Brown
    Cookies ~ ~ ~ ~ ~ ~ ~ ~ 435

Butter Brickle Cookies
Cardamon Date Drops
Caramel Chip Cookies - ~ - ~ ~ 436

Unbaked Caramel Cookies
Cereal Cutouts
Cheese-Date Foldovers ~ ~ ~ ~ 437

Chewy Bar Cookie
Chipper Cookies
Chocolate Chip Cookies ~ ~ ~ ~ 438

Chocolate Chip Cookies
Chocolate Chip Cookies
Chocolate Chip Cookies ~ ~ ~ ~ 439

Helen Peterson's Chocolate
    Chip Cookies
Chocolate Macaroons
Cinnamon Almond Sticks~ ~ ~ ~ 440

Coconut Cookies
Coconut Cream Cookies
Cowboy Cookies ~ - - ~ ~ ~ 441

Cracker Jack Cookies
Honey Cookies - - - ~ ~ ~ ~ 442

Cream Cheese Cookies
Crunchy Jumble Cookies
Cry Babies - ~ ~ ~ ~ ~ ~ ~ ~ 443

Cry Baby Cookies
Czech Voskvarki Cuklovinkey
Thumbprint Coconut Cookies ~ 444

Date Drop Cookies
Granny Rieder's Date Filled
    Cookies ~ ~ ~ ~ ~ ~ ~ ~ ~ 445

Dusty Miller Cookies
French Cookies
Forgotten Kisses - ~ ~ ~ ~ ~ ~ 446

Forgotten Meringue
Fruit Cookies
Funny Face Cookies~ ~ ~ ~ ~ ~ 447

Ginger Cookies
Ginger Cookies
Gingersnaps or Pepperkakar ~ 448

The Very Best Gingersnaps
Glazed Fresh Apple Cookies ~ ~ 449

Good Cookies
Ground Raisin Cookies
Hawaiian Drop Cookies - ~ - ~ 450

Honey and Nut Cherry Cookies
Italian Holiday Cookies ~ ~ ~ ~ 451

Jelly Balls
Jumbo Raisin Cookies
Refreshing Lemonade
    Cookies - - - - - ^ ^ ^ ^ 452

M & M Party Cookies
Grandmother Brinkerhoff's
    Molasses Cookies - - ^ ^ ^ 453

Monster Cookie
No-Bake Cookies
Dena Stoddard's No Bake
    Cookies - - - ^ ^ ^ - ^ ^ 454

Norwegian Holiday Cookies
Nutritious Cookies
Banana Oatmeal Cookies ^ ^ ^ 455

Chocolate Oatmeal Bonbon's
Chocolate Oatmeal Cookies ^ ^ 456

Oatmeal Cookies
Famous Oatmeal Cookies
Oatmeal Crispies - ^ ^ ^ ^ ^ 457

Oatmeal Raisin Cookies
Seeded Raisin Oatmeal
    Cookies - - ^ ^ ^ ^ ^ ^ ^ 458

Soft Oatmeal Cookies
Thin Oatmeal Cookies
Peanut Blossoms - ^ ^ ^ ^ ^ 459

Peanut Blossoms
Peanut Butter Cookies
Persimmon Cookies - ^ ^ ^ ^ 460

Quick Cookies
Quickie Peanut Butter Cookies
Raisin Cookies - - ^ ^ - - 461

Raisin Bar Cookies
Ranger Cookies
Rocky Nut Cookies
Rocky Road Cookies ^ - - 462

Rolled Molasses Cookies
Rolled White Cookies ^ ^ ^ 463

Salted Peanut Cookies
Salted Peanut Cookies
Sesame Cookies - - ^ ^ ^ ^ 464

Scotch Shortbread
Sugar Cookies
Mom's Sugar Cookies
Sour Cream Sugar Cookies ^ ^ 465

Sprits Cookies
Sugar Cookies
Sugar Cookies
Sugar Cookies - ^ ^ ^ ^ ^ 466

Grandma's Never Fail Sugar
    Cookies
Sugar Cookies- - - - - - - - 467

Sugar Cookies
Sour Cream Drops - - - - - - 468

Sunflower Seed Cookies
Sunflower Seed Cookies
Turtles - - - - - - - - - 469

Unique Date Cookies
Walnut Sandies
Almond Bars - - - - - - - - 470

Angel Food Bars
Apple Bars
Apple Bars - - - - - - - - - 471

Apple Slice Bars
Applesauce Bars
Bars - - - - - - - - - - - 472

Brownies
Brownies
Brownie Drops - - - - - - - 473

Chocolate Sunday Brownies
Chocolate Syrup Brownies - - 474

Hershey Brownies
Moist Brownies
Butter Chews - - - - - - - 475

Butterscotch Bars
Butterscotch Bars
California Bars - - - - - - - 476

Caramel Bars
Caramel Bars
Caramel Bars - - - - - - - 477

Caramel Layer Bars
Caramel Layer Squares - - - - 478

Caramel Morsel Bars
Carrot Bars - ^ - - - - - 479

Carrot Bars
Cherry Chip Bars - - - - - 480

Cherry Slice Bars
Cherry Walnut Bars
Chewies - - - - - - - - - - 481

Chip Bars
Christmas Bars - - - - - - 482

Chocolate Butterscotch Bars
Chocolate Cherry Bars - - - - 483

Chocolate Cherry Bars
Chocolate Cherry Bars
Chocolate Chips Bars - - - - 484

Chocolate Deluxe Bars
Chocolate--Caramel Bars - - - 485

Chocolate--Peanut Butter Bars
Chocolate Revel Bars - - - - 486

Coconut Bars
Congo Squares - - - - - - - 487

Cranberry Pecan Bars
Cream Puff Bars - - - - - - 488

Crunchy Fudge Sandwich
Date and Orange Bars - - - - 489

Diagonal Bars
Double Caramel Bars - - - - 490

Double Chocolate Crumble Bars
Easy Bar Recipe
Energy Bars   - - - - - - - - 491

Expensive Calorie Bar
Frosted Mallow Bars - - - - 492

Fudge Bars
Fudge Layer Bar - - - - - - 493

Fudge-Full Peanut-Butter Bars
Fudge Squares - - - - - - - 494

German Honey Bars
Graham Cracker Bars
Gussie Nut Goodie Bars - - - 495

Honey Almond Squares
Lemon Bars
Lemon Bars
Lemon Bars - - - - - - - - 496

Lemon Bars
Lemon Cheese Bars - - - - - 497

Magic Cookie Bars
Mandarin Orange Bars
Marshmallow Bars - - - - - 498

Marshmallow Brownies
Matrimony Bars - - - - - - 499

Mississippi Mud Bars
Moist Spice Bars   - - - - - 500

Monkey Bars
Navino Bars   - - - - - - - 501

No-Bake Peanut Butter Bars
Nut Bars
Nut Goodie Bars - - - - - - 502

Oatmeal Bars
Oatmeal Bars - - - - - - - 503

Oatmeal Caramel Bars
One Step Bars - - - - - - - 504

Peanut Brownies
Peanut Buster Bars - - - - - 505

Peanut Butter Bars
Peanut Butter Cup Bars
Pecan Pie Surprise Bars - - 506

Pumpkin Bars
Pumpkin Squares - - - - - - 507

Rhubarb Bars
Rhubarb Bars
Rhubarb Bars - - - - - - - 508

Rhubarb Bars - - - - - - - 509

Rhubarb Bars
Rhubarb Bars
Rhubarb Crunch Bars - - - - 510

Rhubarb Dream Bars
Salted Nut Bars - - - - - - 511

Scotch Bars
7 Layer Bars
Special K Bars - - - - - - - 512

Special K Bars
Sprinkle Bars
Sprinkle Bars - - - - - - - 513

3 Tier Bars
Toffee Squares - - - - - - - 514

Toffee Squares
Yellow Cake Bars
Yummy Bars - - - - - - - - 515

Yummy Summer Bars
Yum Yum Bars
Zucchini Bars - - - - - - - 516

Angel Food Cake Dessert
Apple Chop Bake - - - - - - 517

Apple Crisp
Apple Delite - - - - - - - - 518

Apple Goodies
Apple Goodies
Jabluszka W Ciescie - - - - - 519

Apple Pastry
Apricot Delight = = = = = = -520

Apricot Peach Dessert
Fritters
Banana Fudgies = = = = = = -521

Banana Split Dessert
Baklava = = = = = = = = = -522

Fattigmand = = = = = = = = = -523

Blueberry Slump
Bonbon Dessert
Norwegian Fried Bowties = = -524

Fruit Brochettes
Big Batch Brownies
Butter Brickle Dessert = = = -525

Butterscotch Dessert
Cheesecakes = - = = = = = = -526

Cheese Cake
Cheesecake = = = = = = = -527

Cherry Dessert
Cherry Dessert = - = = = = -528

Cherry or Blueberry Dessert
Chocolate Angel Food Dessert
Chocolate Dreams - = = = = -529

Cinnamon Sledges
Fresh Peach Cobbler - = = = -530

Coconut Crunch
Cranberry Dessert
Date Balls - - = = = = = -531

Date Torte
Danish Dessert = = = = = -532

Dreamy Orange Delight
Finger Jello
Finska Kakor = = = = = = -533

Foam Ringlets
Banana Fritters Supreme - - -534

Hot Fruit Compote
Homemade Ice Cream
Frosty Lemon Cooler - = = = -535

Frozen Cheese Cake
Fruit Soup - Scandinavian
Scandinavian Fruit Soup = = -536

Fruktsoppa
Gifta - Christmas Dessert- = -537

Glorified Rice
Grandma's Rhubarb Butter
    Crunch
Harvest Torte = = = = = = = 538

Hawaiian Delight
Hot Fruit Compote
Ice Cream Clown = = = = = = 539

Ice Cream Crunch
Kolachy
Ice Cream Kolacky = = = = = 540

Danish Kringle
Never Fail Danish Kringle = = 541

Kringles
Swedish Kringle = = = = = = 542

Krumb Kake
Ladyfinger Dessert
Lazy Day Peach Dessert - = = 543

Frosty Lemon Cooler
Frozen Lemon Dessert = = = = 544

Lemon Dessert
Lime Dessert
Lemon Dessert = = = = = = = 545

Mississippi Mud
North Pole Pears = = = = = 546

Great Grandmother's Raisin
    Spice Loaf
Golden Raisin Tea Loaf
Mandarin Orange Cake
    Dessert = = = = = = = = 547

Marshmallow Delight
Peachy Cheesecake = = = = = 548

Peach Delight
Pecan Tarts - = = = = = = 549

Peanut Marshmallow Chews
Pecan Torts - = = = = = = 550

Pineapple Fluff
Pineapple Fritters = = = = = 551

Pretzel Dessert - = = = = = 552

Puddin' Sticks
Pumpkin Chiffon Dessert
Quick Dessert
Raspberry Dessert - = = = = 553

Raspberry Dessert
Rømmegrøt - = = = = = = 554

Rhubarb Crisp
Rhubarb Crisp
Rhubarb Crunch
Rhubarb Dessert - - - - - - -555

Rhubarb Dessert
Rhubarb Dream Dessert   -556

Rhubarb Kuchen a la Mode
Rhubarb Torte - - - - - - - -557

Rhubarb Tapioca
Rhubarb Tart - - - - - - - -558

Spiced Rhubarb
Rhubarb Torte
Rosettes   - - - - - - - - -559

Almond Swedish Rusk
Salted Peanut Chews
Sandbakkels - Sand Tarts - -560

Sherbet Dessert
Shrimp-Pineapple Fritters - -561

Shirley's Cream Cheese
    Cake
Strawberry Bavarian
Strawberry Chantilly   - - -562

Strawberry Confection
Strawberry Delight   - - - -563

Fresh Strawberry Dessert
Strawberries with Mock
    Devonshire Cream
Strawberry Pretzel Dessert- -564

Ice Cream and Strawberry Mold
Swedish Torte
Svenska Torta - - - - - - -565

Sweet Soup
2-Tone Dessert   - - - - - -566

Swedish Tea Wafers
Walnut Turtles - - - - - - -567

Yummy Chocolate Dessert
Bread Pudding - - - - - - -568

Cake Crumb Pudding
Christmas Plum Pudding - - -569

Cranberry Steam Pudding - -570

Old Fashioned Pudding
Baked Orange Pudding   - - -571

Ozark Pudding
Pudding - - - - - - - - - -572

Pineapple Sponge
Raisin Pudding
Rhubarb Pudding- - - - - - 573

Rice Pudding
Swedish Pudding
Verona's Chocolate Pudding
    Dessert - - - - - - - - 574

CANDY,   JELLY,   PRESERVES

O'Henry Bars
Almond Brittle
Roger's Peanut Brittle - - - 575

Peanut Brittle
Caramels
Honey Caramels - - - - - - 576

Cinnamon Nuts
Divinely Different Divinity
Boiled Fudge- - - - - - - - 577

6 Minute Fudge
Peanut Butter Fudge
Thachus Pet Fudge- - - - - 578

Velveeta Cheese Fudge
White Fudge
Rice Krispie Candies - - - - 579

Goof Balls
Mints
Peanut Butter Cups - - - - 580

Peanut Butter Cups
Peanut Candy
English Toffee
English Toffee - - - - - - - 581

Easy Toffee
Walnut Toffee
Apricot Rhubarb Jam- - - - 582

Beet Jelly
Beet Raspberry Jelly
Blue-Barb Jam
Breakfast Marmalade - - - - 583

Grape Jelly
Grape Beet Jelly
Green Pepper Jelly- - - - - 584

Mystery Jam
Oriental Pear Jam
Pear-Orange Marmalade- - - 585

Rhubarb Marmalade
Rhubarb Refrigerator Jam
Strawberry Rhubarb Jam - - 586

BEVERAGES AND MISCELLANEOUS

Amaretto
Bloomer Droppers
Chocolate-Cinnamon Swizzle- -587

Hot Chocolate Mix
Snowmobilers Hot Chocolate
    Mix
Spiced Cider
Coffee Bavarian - - - - - - -588

Irish Coffee
Chokecherry Bounce - - - - -589

Cream de Menthe
Frozen Fruit Cups
Holiday Eggnog
Hot Pineapple Eggnog - - - -590

Vodka Orange Fizzies
Fruit Cooler
Orange Julius - - - - - - - -591

Kahlua
Kahlua
Hot Buttered Lemonade
Plum Brandy - - - - - - - -592

Plum Cordial
Punch
Boston Club Punch - - - - -593

Cranberry Punch
Coffee Punch
Frothy Eggnog Punch - - - -594

Hot Cranberry Punch
Hot Fruit Punch
Hot Fruit Punch
Mai-Tai Punch - - - - - - - -595

Party Punch
Easy Party Punch
Quick Cooler
Raspberry Float - - - - - - -596

Rhubarb Beverage
Creme a Rhum
Russian Tea - - - - - - - -597

Tea Punch
Cherry or Blueberry Pie Shake
Sloe Gin Fizz
Slush - - - - - - - - - - -598

Apricot Slush
Brandy Slush
Lime Slush - - - - - - - - - -599

Lime Slush
Rhubarb Slush
Vodka Slush - - - - - - - - 600

Vodka Slush
Spiced Tea Treat
Peach or Strawberry Daiquiri- 601

Strawberry Daiquiris
Strawberries Cardinal
Sunrise Special
Swedish Rhubarb Wine - - - - 602

Tomato Juice
We Three - - - - - - - - - 603

Fire Vodka
Wassail Bowl
Watermelon to Watch the
    Hopkins Raspberry Festival
    Parade By - - - - - - - 604

Childrens Crystal Garden
    Solution
Childrens Play Dough
Sweetened Condensed Milk
Homemade Sweetened
    Condensed Milk - - - - - - 605

Cough Medicine
Fudgesicles
Granola
Marge's Stuffing - - - - - - - 606

Ice Cubes
Popsicles
Bar B. Q. Sauce
Bar B. Q. Sauce - - - - - - 607

Barbecue Sauce
Bar B. Q. Sauce
Bing Cherry Ice Cream
    Sauce
Cocktail Sauce - - - - - - - - 608

Chocolate Sauce
Regal Chocolate Sauce
Cordial for Ice Cream - - - - 609

Homemade Bar-B-Que Sauce
Hot Fudge Sauce
Hot Fudge Sauce
Hot Fudge Sauce - - - - - - 610

Marinade Sauce
Fresh Marinara Sauce
Rib Sauce - - - - - - - - - - 611

Spaghetti Sauce
Teriyaki Sauce
Waikiki Room Rib Sauce- - 612

White Sauce Base
Beer Batter - - - - - - - 613

** NOTES **

** NOTES **

** NOTES **

** NOTES **

** NOTES **

** NOTES **

This Cookbook is a perfect gift for Holidays, Weddings, Anniversaries and Birthdays.

★ ★ ★ ★ ★ ★

★ ★ ★ ★ ★ ★